'"To win the military battle but lose the political war could well become the US fate in Vietnam," observed Bernard Fall in 1962. In *Number One Realist*, Nathaniel Moir gives us a superbly rich biography, combined with an illuminating history of irregular and revolutionary warfare, subjects on which Fall was one of the twentieth century's pioneering authorities. This is much more than a contribution to the history of that long and complex war in Indochina, the end of which Fall did not live to see. It is a profound study of war as a perennial human phenomenon and how best to think and write about it.'

Niall Ferguson, Milbank Family Senior Fellow, Hoover Institution, Stanford, and author of *Kissinger, 1923–1968: The Idealist*

'Moir shines with this timely, relevant appraisal of Bernard Fall, the most perceptive critic of French and American political-military operations in Southeast Asia during the Cold War era. A superb evaluation of Fall and his influential scholarship on revolutionary warfare.'

Gregory A. Daddis, USS Midway Chair in Modern U.S. Military History, San Diego State University

'Original and exceptionally well-researched, this will be popular amongst scholars and readers of the Second World War and the Cold War.'

Craig Whiteside, Associate Professor of National Security Affairs, U.S. Naval War College, and a co-author of *The ISIS Reader*

'Moir's book illuminates the contributions of a very influential figure and fills a major gap in the historiography of the Vietnam War, the history of military thinking on Revolutionary Warfare. Enlightening.'

Sophie Quinn-Judge, author of *Ho Chi Minh* and *The Third Force in the Vietnam War*

'Bernard Fall remains one of our foremost up-close analysts of the long struggle for Vietnam. In this superb study he gets the nuanced and incisive treatment he deserves.'

Fredrik Logevall, Professor of History, Harvard University

NUMBER ONE REALIST

NATHANIEL L. MOIR

Number One Realist

Bernard Fall and Vietnamese Revolutionary Warfare

OXFORD
UNIVERSITY PRESS

Oxford University Press is a department of the
University of Oxford. It furthers the University's objective
of excellence in research, scholarship, and education
by publishing worldwide.

Oxford   New York
Auckland   Cape Town   Dar es Salaam   Hong Kong   Karachi
Kuala Lumpur   Madrid   Melbourne   Mexico City   Nairobi
New Delhi   Shanghai   Taipei   Toronto

With offices in
Argentina   Austria   Brazil   Chile   Czech Republic   France   Greece
Guatemala   Hungary   Italy   Japan   Poland   Portugal   Singapore
South Korea   Switzerland   Thailand   Turkey   Ukraine   Vietnam

Oxford is a registered trade mark of Oxford University Press
in the UK and certain other countries.

Published in the United States of America by
Oxford University Press
198 Madison Avenue, New York, NY 10016

Copyright © Nathaniel L. Moir 2021

All rights reserved. No part of this publication may be reproduced,
stored in a retrieval system, or transmitted, in any form or by any means,
without the prior permission in writing of Oxford University Press,
or as expressly permitted by law, by license, or under terms agreed with
the appropriate reproduction rights organization. Inquiries concerning
reproduction outside the scope of the above should be sent to the
Rights Department, Oxford University Press, at the address above.

You must not circulate this work in any other form
and you must impose this same condition on any acquirer.

Library of Congress Cataloging-in-Publication Data is available
Nathaniel L. Moir.
Number One Realist: Bernard Fall and Vietnamese Revolutionary Warfare.
ISBN: 9780197629888

Printed in the United Kingdom on acid-free paper by
Bell and Bain Ltd, Glasgow

To my family and in memory of John Zdrazil

CONTENTS

Acknowledgments   xi
Prologue   xv

Introduction   1
1. First Impressions of a War   33
2. Germany, 1946–1951   75
3. First Reflections on a War   111
4. Seven Years of War in Indochina   137
5. The Ending is a Beginning   179
6. The Wind and the Water   227
7. An Unassailable Position of Total Weakness   281
8. 1961–1967   317

Epilogue   371
Notes   385
Bibliography   483
Index   501

ACKNOWLEDGMENTS

As Adam Horovitz once explained, "when you've got so much to say, it's called gratitude." In that spirit, I am fortunate to have many people and institutions to thank. Foremost, my thanks to Richard Fogarty at the University at Albany, State University of New York (SUNY). Rick's professionalism, example, humor, and generosity of spirit and time made my work with him a great experience. I could not have had a better mentor, and my thanks to Jack Talbot for introducing me to Rick. I would also like to thank my committee members Ryan Irwin, Michitake Aso, and Brian Nussbaum. Ryan, Mitch, and Brian each helped me in so many ways that made me a better historian and writer.

I was also fortunate to work with great colleagues and professors during my time as an Ernest May Postdoctoral Fellow in History and Policy at the John F. Kennedy School of Government, Harvard University. Thanks to all in my cohort years for their friendship and constructive suggestions on parts of this book. In the years taken to develop my study of Bernard Fall, Fredrik Logevall was generous in many ways and helped me during several years when I was not even his student. Fred's scholarship and his highlighting the importance of Bernard Fall early on added a wonderful dimension to his generosity as a mentor over the years. My sincere thanks to him. At Harvard, I would also like to thank Calder Walton, Susan Lynch, Kate McCabe, Justin Winokur, Raleigh Browne, and others who helped me as a fellow and in my follow-on work at the Kennedy School as an Associate in the Applied History Project.

Several historians provided model scholarship, support, and advice along the way. My thanks to Andrew Preston, Mario Del Pero, Mark Atwood Lawrence, Christopher Capozzola, Niall Ferguson and the Hoover History Working Group, Graham Allison and the Harvard Applied History Project,

ACKNOWLEDGMENTS

and David Lowe and the Deakin University Contemporary Histories Research Group. One of the highlights during my career has been learning from others and the friendships I have gained through SHAFR, the Society of Military History, and the US Commission of Military History. Among my many colleagues gained during a SHAFR Summer Institute, I want to thank Mike Graziano for sharing archival research, and Carla Konta. Carla's constructive comments at an early stage in this project stuck in my mind over the years and demonstrated the enduring value of a kind word.

This book would not have been possible without extensive time spent conducting archival research, and several institutions and organizations provided generous support through grants and fellowships. I want to thank the Smith Richardson Foundation for a World Politics and Statecraft Fellowship, the Lyndon B. Johnson Foundation for a Moody Research Grant, the United States Marine Corps Heritage Foundation, the Dirksen Congressional Center, the United States Army Heritage and Education Center for a General and Mrs. Matthew B. Ridgway Research Grant, the John F. Kennedy Presidential Library for a Marjorie Kovler Research Fellowship, the Eisenhower Foundation for a grant to conduct research at the Dwight D. Eisenhower Presidential Library, the Society of Military History for an ABC-CLIO research grant, the United States Commission of Military History for support to travel and present early research in Beijing, China, the Clements Center at the University of Texas at Austin for the opportunity to attend one of their great summer seminars, and SHAFR for its generosity and invitation to attend a summer seminar. I am especially grateful for these opportunities because of the colleagues and friends I gained through these experiences. At the University at Albany, SUNY, a Joseph E. Persico Fellowship, the Dr. Jagadish Garg Doctoral Award, and grants provided by the Graduate Student Employee Union and the University at Albany History Department provided support during the early stages of my research. Early on, the John F. Kennedy Presidential Library gave me insight into the national treasures that are the Presidential Libraries and Museums. My thanks to the many archivists who helped me along the way, especially those at the JFK Presidential Library during my many research visits. In addition, I wish to thank Paul Rich at *Small Wars & Insurgencies*, Jeff Kaplan at *Terrorism and Political Violence*, and Octavian Manea at *Small Wars Journal* for support and encouragement, and forums in which to develop my scholarship.

C. Hurst & Co. Publishers has been an ideal organization and a pleasure to work with in developing this book. Thanks to Michael Dwyer, Anna Benn for

ACKNOWLEDGMENTS

helpful copy-editing, Cate Bickmore, Sebastian Ballard, Daisy Leitch, and the entire Hurst team for their work and support. Michael A.K.G. Innes deserves a special word of thanks for introducing me to Hurst and Michael Dwyer. Mike has been a great colleague and supporter of this project from an early stage and throughout. Another personal highlight in completing this book has been the opportunity to speak with Dorothy Fall about her husband, Bernard Fall. My thanks to Dorothy for sharing her time and thoughts and also thanks to Patricia, Elisabeth, and Nicole Fall for their support and permission to include family photos of Bernard Fall in this book. Along the way, I have been fortunate to receive insights from Robert Cowley, David Marshall, and Karl Purnell regarding their interactions with Bernard Fall. My many discussions with Rob over the years have been a joy. *Semper Fi*, and thanks to David for hosting me to discuss his career in the Marine Corps and his time spent with Bernard Fall on the Street Without Joy in February 1967. And thanks to Karl for sharing thoughts on journalism and Fall's work. Finally, as to any mistakes of omission or commission made within this book, those are all mine.

I am grateful to have many life-long friends: thanks to each of you! While I was in the final stages in completing this book, my teacher, mentor, and friend John Zdrazil passed away after a battle with cancer. John's influence and guidance helped me in so many ways, and I do not think this book would exist without him: may his memory be a blessing. My greatest thanks go to my family for their support. My mother and father, Mary and Wes Moir, provided encouragement, advice, and help throughout this project. It all began with my Dad pointing out the value of Bernard Fall's writing when I was at the beginning of my road towards attempting to understand war in Southeast Asia. It continued with my Mom and Dad's unending support for me in seeing this book through. Thanks to my brother, Dan, my extended family, and my great family-in-law as well. My wife, Beth, and our sons, Lawson, Liam, and Phoenix, have supported me in every way. They made completing this book a great chapter among the many others we have developed together so far.

In closing, as historian David Bell writes, "Identifying with individuals in the past is central to the writing of good history, and to the experience of reading it."[1] If this is so, I believe I have succeeded as far as the first six words of Bell's statement are concerned. I identify with Bernard Fall as a scholar-soldier and share his belief in the value of developing foreign and domestic policy according to objective facts, and not on what one wishes those facts to be. As to the second half of Bell's statement, whether I have written good history, that is for the reader to judge.

PROLOGUE

On the campus of St. Olaf College, located on a hill in Northfield, Minnesota, Holland Hall's leaded windows offered a view of oak trees and red, yellow, and orange sugar maples in the autumn of 1960. The campus outside of the department of religion and history classrooms, like those found on Carleton College's campus across the Cannon River, exemplified the type of bucolic environment that eventually led Northfield leaders to adopt the town motto, "cows, colleges, and contentment" for signs along routes entering the town. As the professor of a course on comparative religion that autumn, a 46-year-old professor, Dr. Ansgar Sovik, met with one of his students after class to offer some advice. The student knew Sovik was a veteran of World War II, so he sought Sovik's advice about joining the US Navy. While the young man wanted to see the world, he was also aware of ongoing conflict in Southeast Asia and wanted to read more about Indochina and its history. Sovik told the young man, my father, that he should read Bernard Fall's work to learn more about the region.

Sovik possessed ample reason to recognize the relevance of Fall's scholarship on Southeast Asia. The son of Norwegian missionaries, Sovik was born in Hankow, China, on 3 March 1914 and attended grade school at the Kikungshan American school until the mid-1920s.[1] As an elementary student, Sovik recalled seeing a skirmish—an event likely linked to the Northern Expedition between Kuomintang and either Beiyang government troops or a warlord's troops—from his classroom window.[2] Investigating the place where the fight had recently concluded, Sovik saw an 11-year-old friend mistakenly pick up a grenade, only to have it explode in his hand. Years later, and following in his parents' footsteps, Ansgar studied religion and graduated from St. Olaf College in 1934. He conducted subsequent study at Luther Seminary in

St. Paul, Minnesota, and at the menighetsfakultet in Oslo before returning to St. Olaf College in 1938 to teach in the Department of Religion in 1939.[3]

When the United States entered World War II, Sovik volunteered for military service as a Navy chaplain in 1942 and gained a commission in the US Navy as a Lieutenant Junior Grade.[4] After chaplain training school in Norfolk, Virginia, he was assigned to the First Marine Division, sent by train to the West Coast, shipped to New Zealand, and then deployed with the marines to Guadalcanal in early August 1942.[5] Sovik's baptism by fire arrived before he went ashore. On 8 August, Japanese aircraft—including twenty-nine Mitsubishi G4M light bombers and fifteen long-range Mitsubishi A6M2 Model 21 Zeros—flew from Rabaul and attacked US Navy ships during the second day of the Guadalcanal landing.[6] In this attack, a Japanese bomber (known as a "Betty") smashed into the superstructure of the USS *George Elliott*, engulfing the ship in flames. Sovik was among the surviving crew and marines who evacuated to shore with only the clothes on their backs, losing everything else. At least seventeen sailors and marines died in the attack, and after the remaining personnel evacuated the ship, the USS *George Elliott* was scuttled by the USS *Hull*, a destroyer among the Allied ships supporting the Guadalcanal landings.[7]

Thirteen days later, on 21 August, Sovik wrote of his first contact with Japanese forces on the island in what was later called the Battle of the Tenaru.[8] "The 2nd battalion, to which I was attached, was guarding the west flank of our troops, along the Tenaru River, not really a river, but a stream so dry that there was a sand-pit just before it entered the ocean."[9] Describing what the marines nicknamed "Alligator Creek," Sovik added, "About 1 a.m., the Japanese attacked. They ran into a single barbed wire our troops had put up … They had kept charging and shouting. About 700 were killed. We lost 34 men." At the service the next day for the deceased US personnel, Sovik noted, "It was the largest single group I had at a funeral."[10]

After enduring heavy fighting and supporting marines and sailors on Guadalcanal for four months, Sovik left to recuperate in Australia in December 1942.[11] Sovik remained in the South Pacific, witnessed much of the brutal island-hopping campaign, and fulfilled his military commitment in 1944. He dealt with his wartime experience inwardly, through the consolation of religion, and outwardly, as a teacher and human-rights advocate with significant world experience.[12] After World War II, he continued graduate study at Princeton Theological Seminary, earning a Masters of Theology degree in 1946 and then a Doctorate of Theology degree at the Lutheran School of

PROLOGUE

Theology in Chicago.[13] He returned to St. Olaf College to teach religion until retiring in 1979.[14]

Ansgar Sovik and Bernard Fall shared much in common as humanitarians who endured war and as teachers who helped others understand conflict and the societies in which it occurred. Both encountered violence at a young age, and their experiences of World War II and the changing world order after 1945 added to their knowledge. Readers of Fall's scholarship, including Sovik's student at St. Olaf College who joined the US Navy in 1961 and later deployed as an advisor with the Vietnamese brown-water navy, benefitted from Fall's scholarship because it helped them make sense of their own experiences of war. Crucially, Fall's writing and the evidence he produced also helped others discern facts concerning the war, to understand why some policies were misguided, and to see when others manipulated information for political ends. In this way, and among societies that grapple with identifying and agreeing upon facts and standing up for the rights of all people, regardless of race and ethnicity, teachers like Sovik and Fall also defended democracy in crucial ways.

George Orwell observed similar problems with the idea of "truth decay" in times of war and during serious social unrest. In his own experience, Orwell recognized, "The fact is that every war suffers a kind of progressive degradation with every month that it continues, because such things as individual liberty and a truthful press are simply not compatible with military efficiency."[15] The progressive degradation of truth that invariably characterizes war, along with the degradation of the humans prosecuting it and suffering its effects, is as evident today as it was in Orwell's and Fall's time. To the extent he was capable, Fall fought against such degradation in reporting by writing about the facts as he saw them in Southeast Asia. To gain access to facts, Fall believed he had to see them for himself. His effort to understand war began when his family, Austrian Jews from Vienna, emigrated to southern France after the Anschluss of Austria by Germany on 12 March 1938. In France, finding a path that led him to write perceptively about war began with losing his parents to Nazi persecution. Much later, in Vietnam in early 1967, the inner drive he regarded as his "machine" guided him to the Street Without Joy near Hue in South Vietnam.

INTRODUCTION

"L'avenir se dérobe, quand le soldat se tait."
("The future is obscured, when the soldier is silent.")

Jean Lacouture[1]

"Whoever of your correspondents overheard me, overheard me somewhat incompletely. My exact words were that U.S. fire-power had made the Vietnam war 'militarily unlosable.'

Britain achieved a similar situation in Cyprus; France achieved it in Algeria, and the U.S. still holds Guantanamo. The political benefits derived from these three 'unlosabilities' are here for everyone to see.

I have never claimed for myself the place of 'the No. 1 pessimist' about Vietnam—but if a place of 'No. 1 realist' is available, I'll be glad to stake out a claim for it."

Bernard Fall, Howard University
Letter to the Editor
Newsweek, 11 October 1965[2]

"Under heaven nothing is more soft and yielding than water.
Yet for attacking the solid and strong, nothing is better;
It has no equal.
The weak can overcome the strong;
The supple can overcome the stiff.
Under heaven everyone knows this,
Yet no one puts it into practice."

Lao Tsu[3]

NUMBER ONE REALIST

The "Street Without Joy"—Vietnam, February 1967

February 19, 1967. This is Bernard Fall in the Street Without Joy, the old area where the French fought in 1953. I am lying right now in a small stone hut near a big church in a small village with part of the First Battalion, 9th Marine Infantry Regiment and we just walked across something like 12 kilometers of sand dunes and tomorrow morning we're going to push Southeastward where supposedly there is part of a Viet Cong battalion, Viet Cong battalion 800....[4]

The Marine Corps' records echoed Fall's tape-recorded narrative, adding, "the 802nd Battalion was a main force unit that had been reported in this area to collect rice."[5] Fall continued the next day:

I walked behind a fellow ... thought I walked pretty well in his traces. Apparently, I stepped slightly aside and all of a sudden the ground gave way under me and this was one of these punji stake traps that the V.C. sets with very sharp points and if you fall on this you pierce your foot and go to the hospital. I was very lucky because when I felt the ground yield under my feet I threw myself forward so that my whole body weight shifted to my knees and hands and so the gap gave way and nothing happened to me but it ... ah, shakes you up a bit and now we are sitting in a deserted farm destroyed by gunfire.[6]

On his seventh trip to Vietnam, Bernard Fall arrived on 21 December 1966. "Three days after his arrival," according to *Newsweek* correspondent and friend, François Sully, "Fall, who loved to be out with troops, answered a U.S. Marine Corps invitation to spend Christmas at Camp J.J. Carroll on the U.S. frontline facing the 17th Parallel. It was a miserable, rainy Christmas. Fall rode shotgun for the Marine mail truck."[7] In addition to the artillery base at Camp J.J. Carroll, he visited the "Combined Action Company (CAC) 31 over at Marble Mountain."[8] There, he found the Combined Action Platoon, which paired Marine Corps units with Vietnamese Platoons for operations "an interesting concept," explaining, "I saw it while the French were fighting here in Viet-Nam in 1953–54."[9] In early 1967, there was little Fall had not seen in terms of tactics, organization, and operations, and for these reasons, military personnel viewed him as one of the most highly regarded journalists in Vietnam.[10] According to historian Fredrik Logevall, "Many a junior officer who shipped out to Saigon ... carried with him a dog-eared copy of *Street Without Joy*, or *Hell in a Very Small Place*, Fall's searing account of Dien Bien Phu in 1954."[11]

The respect between Fall and military personnel was mutual. As Sully explained, "Fall was full of admiration for the Marines fighting in the mud of Quang Tri Province but appalled by what he saw, stating 'There is too much

INTRODUCTION

artillery and a tragic lack of infantry. We are building miniature Dien Bien Phus everywhere.'"[12] Fall's concerns were prescient, considering combat at Khe Sanh in late 1967 and as the Tet holiday approached in early 1968. American policymakers—especially President Lyndon B. Johnson, who pondered fighting at Khe Sanh over a custom-made sand table in the White House—feared that the battle might become a conclusive defeat for the United States. The significance of France's defeat at Dien Bien Phu in May 1954 was lost on neither Johnson nor Fall, as the latter's study, *Hell in a Very Small Place*, demonstrated.[13]

On 19 February 1967, adverse weather grounded helicopters, so Fall left on a foot patrol with 1/9th Marines in support of Phase I of Operation Chinook II. The operation focused on the littoral terrain along Route 1 in Northwest Thua Thien Province, northwest of the city of Hue. This area of operations was part of I Corps, the northern region of South Vietnam, and 1/9th Marines was responsible for patrolling a section called "Leatherneck Square".[14] The "Square"—marked by points at Con Thien, Cam Lo, Gio Linh, and Dong Ha—contained 40 miles of contested terrain with an eastern border that converged with Route 1, formerly called "*La Rue Sans Joie*" by the French and, in translation, the "Street Without Joy" by the Americans. The unit Fall accompanied in February 1967, the 1/9th Marines, also had a troubled reputation for sustaining the most prolonged period of combat and having the highest Killed in Action (KIA) rate of any marine unit during the Vietnam War.[15]

According to writer Michael Herr:

> Of all the hard-luck outfits in Vietnam, [1/9th Marines] was said to be the most doomed, doomed in its Search-and-Destroy days before Khe Sanh, known for a history of ambush and confusion and for a casualty rate which was the highest of any outfit in the entire war. That was the kind of reputation that takes hold most deeply among the men of the outfit itself, and when you were with them you got a sense of dread that came out of something more terrible than just a collective loss of luck.[16]

David Marshall, a Marine pilot and First Lieutenant attached to 1/9th Marines as the Forward Air Controller (FAC) for the battalion, was with Fall during Operation Chinook II in February 1967. In a letter to Fall's spouse, Dorothy, Marshall wrote, "I traveled with the point rifle company engaged and controlled airstrikes from the ground. I had been in Dr. Fall's company for about 3 days with 'D' Company and then 'C' Company. Unfortunately, most of us were too ignorant to take full advantage of Dr. Fall's insights. He was impossible to dislike."[17]

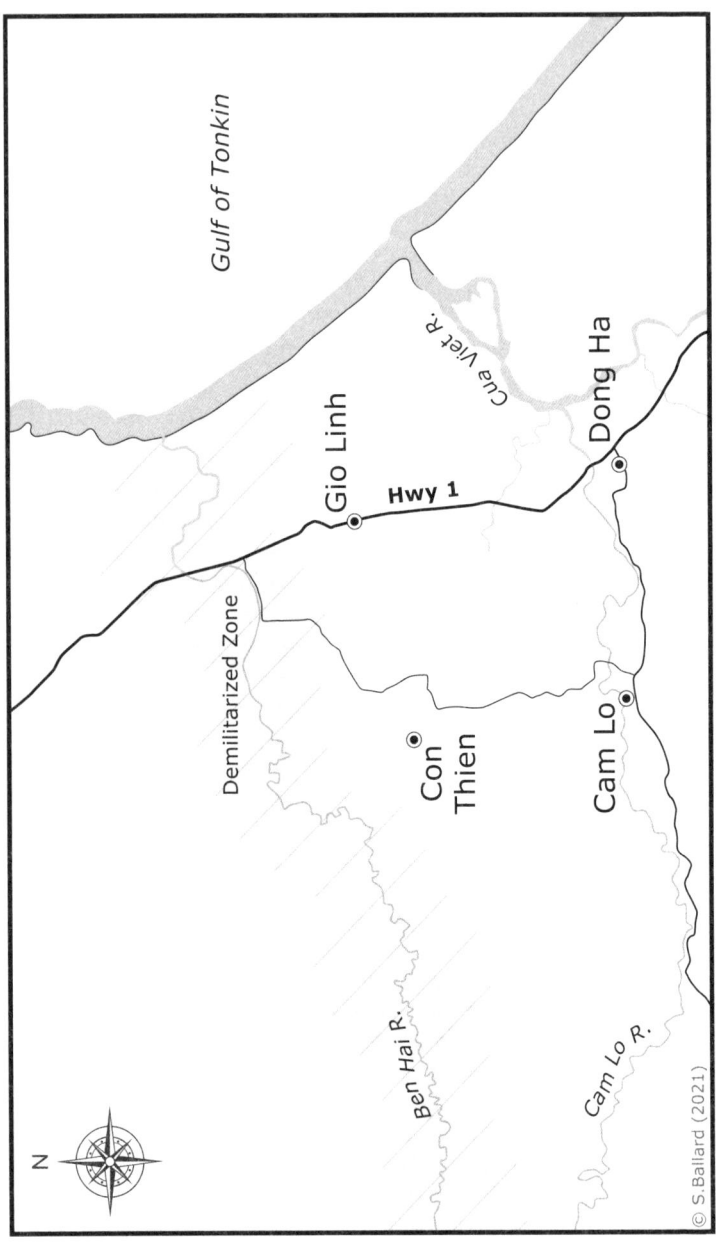

INTRODUCTION

In his letter, Marshall described differences between operations near Con Thien and what the 1/9th Marines would encounter when Operation Chinook II began on 16 February.

> Our battalion had been in heavy combat against the NVA up north near the DMZ—mostly near the firebase of Con Thien. There were no mines or booby traps there and no civilians. It was a completely conventional war. We were then sent down to the Street Without Joy for an operation. There were civilians and Viet Cong there and lots of mines. We started taking many casualties from the mines. Therefore, we had our troops walking in the rice paddies and not on the mined dikes. When we came to a hedgerow, we hacked our way through the thicker thorny parts to further avoid mines in the hedgerow openings.[18]

According to the Marine Corps' records: "February 19, 1967 the Battalion moved to Phong Dien district [Thua Thien Province] YD 527347. From this location the movement continued by tactical march across the sand flats into the A.O. [area of operations]."[19] The chronology continued, "On February 20, 1967, Company 'A' and 'C' commenced a deliberate coordinated search and destroy mission with an axis of advance along the road moving to the southeast. This sweep continued southeast to the river at YD 597398."[20]

The next day, on 21 February, Fall added to his taped transcript:

> Well, we're moving out again on the Street Without Joy—it's the third day now and what you heard before were the noises of the crickets and the frogs next to us where we were sleeping out in the open. It started to drizzle afterwards and now we've got thick-packed fog at 9:00 in the morning—supply chopper couldn't come in but we had enough food for this morning and on we go now ... We have been walking now for two and a half days in a virtual desert. Now we're with Able Company on the road and Able has found a mine. Charlie Company already exploded a mine with a trip wire and apparently one fellow is hurt.[21]

He continued:

> Afternoon of the third day. Still on the street. Now bunker system out there they're going to blow up. The weather is finally cleared and we have an observation plane over our heads, turning around shepherding us. But Charlie Company has fallen very badly behind now there's a big hole in our left flank and there's some people running away from us obviously getting out of the way ... Trying to move across ... we've got to start firing if they move ...
>
> Fall: There's our machine gun firing! They're running!
>
> Voice: Moving off to the left ... running.
>
> Fall: There's our mortar!

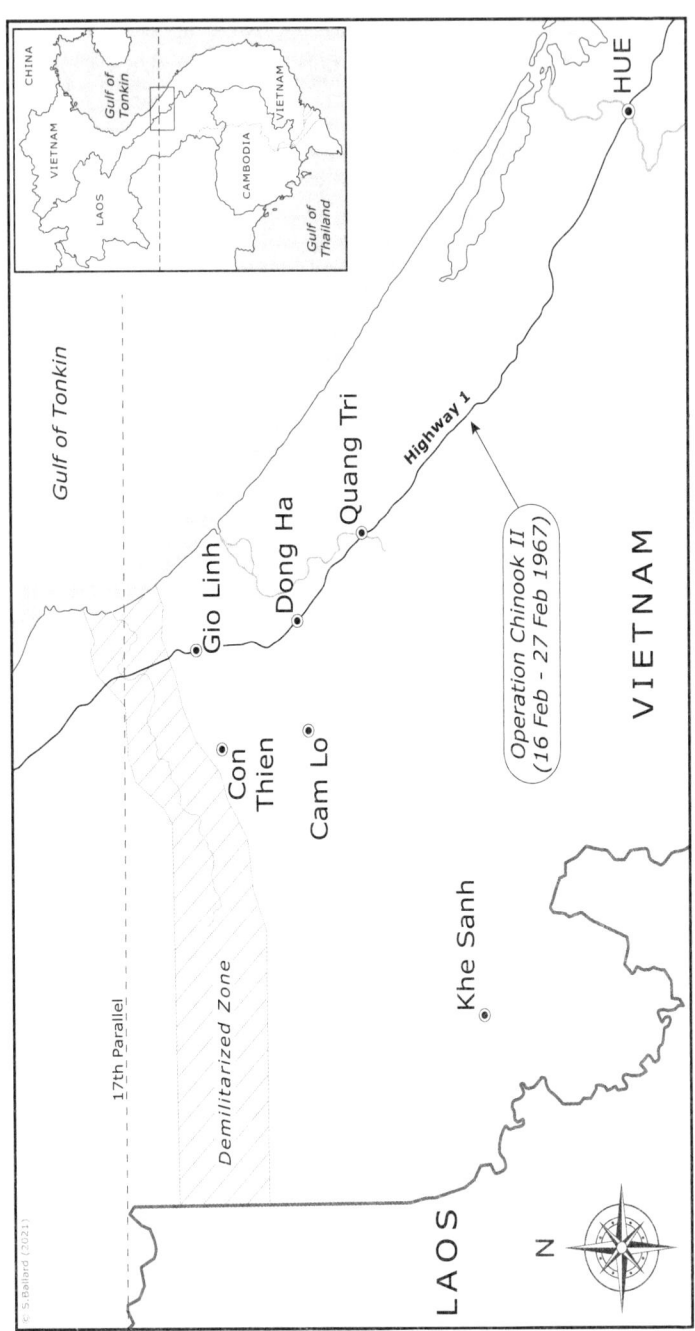

Street Without Joy region, Thua Thien Province, Vietnam

INTRODUCTION

Voice: What are they shooting at? ... See that guy right in the center? You can hardly see—move across—got on a white jacket—see that hat? Set up for about 1,100 meters—open up with a burst of 20 ...

Fall: It's impossible at 1,100 meters to distinguish with ...

["Gunfire" recorded on tape transcript.]

Fall: There's no return fire whatever but the two boys who are with us—they are former Vietcong returned to the government side and are fighting now with the government forces—well, they assured us that Charlie Company is moving right through the area and by tonight we will know whether what we killed were genuine V.C. with weapons or simply people.[22]

In David Marshall's account:

Dr. Fall continued to walk on the dikes despite warnings from many of us. I personally advised him not to do it twice. It was embarrassing to us to tell him this because he knew more about Vietnam than all of us put together. He wished me goodbye and left "C" Company that was moving southeastward on the left side of the Street and moved over to join "A" Company that was moving in the same direction on the right side of the Street. He was walking on a dike along with GySgt (Byron) Highland when they reached the intersection of that dike and the Street.[23]

Fall's tape-recorded transcript continued:

I personally looked through binoculars of the platoon leader from the machine gun platoon and I saw people fleeing to the boats and waving the Vietnamese government flag with three red stripes on a yellow background. Find out more about this later ... This is Bernard Fall on the Street Without Joy ... first in the afternoon about 4:30—shadows are lengthening and we've reached one of our phase lines after the fire fight and it smells bad—meaning it's a little bit suspicious ... Could be now an amb.[24]

"I was about 150 meters away," Marshall recalled, "when I heard a very loud explosion. I saw Dr. Fall's and GySgt Highland's bodies several feet in the air." The Marine Corps' records cited the detonation of an M16 antipersonnel mine at that moment. However, based on his visual confirmation of the blast, Marshall wrote Dorothy Fall: "You were told that it was a 'bouncing betty' mine. It was not. It was either a buried 155 mm artillery shell or a 250 lb. bomb. These 'dud' ordinances were gathered by the V.C. and rigged as large mines."[25] The Marine Corps' report concluded, "The author, along with a Marine ISO representative, was killed instantly. Four other Marines were wounded in this detonation including 2 ISO Marines." The report's last line included the Alpha company commander's assessment of Fall: "As I personally

7

observed him earlier in the afternoon, it was apparent that he was a man who wanted to be up front."[26]

Andrew Rankin Memorial Chapel, Washington, DC—6 March 1967

Bernard Fall's funeral was held at Andrew Rankin Memorial Chapel at Howard University in Washington, DC, on 6 March 1967. Howard University President, Dr. James Nabrit, Jr.; the French Ambassador to the United States, Charles Lucet; United States Army Major General William P. Yarborough; and Senator J. William Fulbright, Chairman of the US Senate Foreign Relations Committee, offered eulogies. Fulbright reflected on 6 March: "Bernard Fall was proud of his independence of thought, as he had every right to be. As an independent scholar, he tried, in his own words, 'to attempt to explain events and to analyze ... not to plead a case, expound a theory or dictate a course of action.'"[27] Fulbright added:

> If the role of the independent scholar is ever to be understood for the beneficial influence it can have in our democracy, it will be because of the work of such brilliant and valiant and dedicated men as Bernard Fall. Those who knew him need no monument to hold him in their memories. His writings will serve as both monument and epitaph.[28]

On 24 February 1967, only three days after Fall's death, Fulbright had provided an even more powerful statement before the US Senate: "Bernard Fall has played a more important part in the Vietnam War than any other writer. He not only wrote history but also participated in its making; he was a historian who looked to the future as well as to the past."[29] As recorded in statements before Congress, from 1 March 1967, eleven members of the US House of Representatives also offered tributes to Fall. Each described the importance of Fall's scholarship and how his work informed their views regarding the ongoing war in Southeast Asia.[30] Henry B. González of Texas, the longest-serving Hispanic member of Congress, offered a prominent statement on 2 March 1967:[31]

> Mr. Speaker, in paying my respects to the memory of Bernard Fall I am paying a tribute to intellectual honesty, moral integrity and scholarship. The remarkable quality about Bernard Fall and his writings on Vietnam and southeast Asia was that he always gave to his listeners and readers practical knowledge about the world ... Bernard Fall assumed the risk of violent death knowingly in order to search for the truth, and he died in that search. For this reason, as well as the great contributions he made to the public dialog over Vietnam, his death is tragic for the Nation and the entire world. Having read much of his work,

INTRODUCTION

including his latest book, "Hell in a Very Small Place," I know that his loss is irreplaceable."[32]

Dozens of newspapers across America and Europe echoed Representative González's thoughts in numerous obituaries honoring Fall.[33] The 2 March 1967 edition of the Paris-based *Le Figaro* stated: "With his death, at forty years old, Bernard Fall was, without a doubt, the greatest world expert on questions related to Indochina."[34] According to *Le Monde*, also published in Paris, "Fall was an intransigent researcher who refused to believe all propaganda."[35] In the United States, the *Nashville Tennessean* circulated a common theme, reporting that: "Bernard B. Fall, journalist-historian widely regarded as knowing more about Vietnam than almost any other Westerner, was killed yesterday ... A tall, amiable man with a zest for life, Fall was a veteran of the Vietnam scene since 1953. He was one of the few Westerners to have interviewed Ho Chi Minh, the Communist leader of the North."[36]

In a more politicized view, the *Harvard Crimson* explained: "Fall was not just another professor who wrote critical books and articles about America's policy in Vietnam. He didn't spend much time organizing petitions to the President. His first-hand reports of the war served as a far more convincing indictment."[37] The *Crimson*'s obituary to Fall, published on 24 February 1967, concluded: "Fall again and again pointed up the inconsistency between words of peace and policies of destruction. He spent more than 20 years of his life observing war in Southeast Asia. The ultimate tragedy is that he might have had cause to continue for another 20 years." The *Crimson*'s statement proved to be tragically prescient: after war between South Vietnam, North Vietnam, and the United States ended in 1975, war between a reunified Vietnam and the Khmer Rouge began in 1975, and Vietnam went to war with China in 1979. These "forever wars" in Southeast Asia did not formally conclude until 1991 with the signing of the Comprehensive Cambodian Peace Agreements.[38] It is almost certain that Fall would have been an outspoken critic of these wars, just as he was of those he observed firsthand.

US soldiers, sailors, airmen, and Marines also acknowledged Fall's scholarship. Former US Senator and Navy pilot John McCain considered Fall's books, *Street Without Joy* and *Hell in a Very Small Place*, along with Neil Sheehan's *A Bright Shining Lie*, among the best analyses of the Vietnam War. McCain commented in 2018, "Fall's two classics on the French Indochina War warned us about the mistakes we should have avoided making in Vietnam," while Sheehan's book about John Paul Vann "shows how we went about making them anyway."[39] Former army ranger and Vietnam veteran,

Secretary of State, and Chairman of the Joints Chiefs of Staff Colin Powell added, "*Street Without Joy* was a textbook for those of us going to Vietnam in the first wave of President Kennedy's advisers."[40] Powell's remark was both figuratively true and literally accurate. *Street Without Joy* was a primary source used in courses at Fort Bragg, North Carolina in the early 1960s for soldiers preparing to deploy to Vietnam.[41]

Another Vietnam veteran, Ronald H. Griffith, recalled: "In 1964 I was placed on orders for Vietnam, where I was to serve all of 1965 as an advisor with the Army of the Republic of Vietnam. In preparation for this assignment, I attended the Army's Special Warfare School at Fort Bragg, North Carolina. During our six weeks of training, one of our guest lecturers was a French gentleman by the name of Bernard Fall who had written a book on the French military's experience in Indochina titled *Street Without Joy*."[42] Griffith noted that he carried a copy of Fall's book with him to Vietnam in 1965. His copy, undoubtedly, included many dog-eared pages.

The reading lists for US Army Special Warfare courses taught at Fort Bragg in 1963 included numerous works by Fall. In "A-700: Problems of Development and Internal Defense" several of his articles were assigned reading. In "3610A/3: Counterinsurgency in Indochina," *Street Without Joy* was the primary text. At the time, US Army Major General William P. Yarborough—widely regarded as the father of modern US Special Forces—served as commandant of the Special Warfare Center and School.[43] Yarborough made it a point to include Fall's scholarship in Special Forces training, and he was the one responsible for inviting Fall to lecture and meet with soldiers at the base in Fayetteville on numerous occasions. In May 1964, according to the base newspaper, *The Paraglide*, Yarborough introduced Fall to Special Forces personnel as "one of few acknowledged experts on Vietnam."[44] In offering eulogies to Fall at Howard University—the institution where Fall had taught as a professor of International Relations since 1957—Yarborough, Senator Fulbright, French Ambassador Charles Lucet, and Howard University President Dr. James Nabrit, Jr. recognized Fall and the value of his scholarship.[45] This book investigates why Fall's scholarship mattered then, and it concludes with why his scholarship remains relevant today.

Bernard Fall—history and relevance

Number One Realist: Bernard Fall and Vietnamese Revolutionary Warfare is a history of Bernard Fall's scholarship, and it investigates how Vietnamese revo-

INTRODUCTION

Political map, Indochina

lutionary warfare developed in Indochina after World War II. It argues that Fall understood Vietnamese revolutionary warfare to be a product of interdependent factors, including political, military, economic, social, and others that were unique to conflict in Indochina. He was uncommon as an insightful analyst of war because of the experience and knowledge he brought to his study and his early recognition of the Viet Minh's approach to warfare, which they used to defeat the French in 1954 during the First Indochina War.

Ultimately, Fall's study of warfare in Vietnam, Laos, and Cambodia after World War II can be distilled to this: America's failure to implement lessons learned from France's experiences in Indochina, and America's failure to develop policies and political solutions to counter Vietnamese revolutionary warfare, narrowed US policy options within the broader strategic concept of containment. This narrowing of feasible political options related to South Vietnamese governance and policies and those made by Americans led to overly militarized approaches after America's full intervention in Vietnam in 1965. Fall quickly came to realize in 1965 that these approaches would not defeat Vietnamese communist-led revolutionary warfare.

In addition, while Fall was an anti-communist, he explained early in 1965 that North Vietnam did not pose a threat to America's role in Asia. Even losing South Vietnam to a potentially new, reunified, and communist-controlled Vietnam would not pose an existential threat to the United States or its regional primacy. Fall made his view on this matter prominent during an interview with Lawrence Spivak on NBC's *Meet the Press* on 31 January 1965. Early in their discussion, Spivak asked Fall: "You don't evidently hold to the domino theory, that is if we lose South Vietnam we may finally have to fight in the Philippines or possibly Hawaii?" To which Fall replied, "As I said before, I don't think we have to lose South Vietnam any more than we have to lose Europe because we lost Czechoslovakia."[46] Although the remark was somewhat cryptic, Fall's point was this: if the domino theory was not invoked when Czechoslovakia was "lost to communism" in 1948, or when China was "lost to communism" in 1949, why should losing Vietnam invoke it?[47] Ultimately, Fall believed the United States had interests in Vietnam but that its interests were neither vital nor worth the cost of its blood and treasure, even at the expense of American credibility in 1965.

Similarly, Fall indicated that eliminating communism in Vietnam was not so important that it necessitated the unleashing of an overmilitarized policy and massive war effort that would destroy Vietnam and its people. His concerns formed a crucial, guiding, and underlying thread that weaves through

INTRODUCTION

and contributes to a larger fabric forming Fall's scholarship. Often, he made his views abundantly clear. In other cases, in contrast, his views were sometimes submerged and entangled, which complicates his scholarship. More transparently, Fall's involvement in World War II and its aftermath were central to developing his later understanding of Vietnamese revolutionary warfare in Indochina. He would have been unable to formulate his conception of revolutionary warfare without this knowledge and his experiences of World War II and those gained at the Nuremberg Trials. Similarly, Fall's experience studying Indochina firsthand during France's occupation of the region in 1953 was critical to his scholarship. Without this almost 10-month-long research trip, he would have had only a small foundation on which to build and cultivate his unique blend of expertise and personal insight into Vietnamese revolutionary warfare.

Through an intellectual biographical framework, this is a history and analysis of the development of Fall's thought on revolutionary warfare, a term he used consistently after 1958 to describe conflict in Indochina. It is a history that seeks to describe and assess how Fall came to recognize processes and approaches, such as guerrilla warfare tactics contributing to revolutionary warfare, which he had first encountered during World War II as a member of the Maquis fighting Nazis and French collaborators in the Alps south of Geneva in Haut-Savoie, France. By building on his experiences and researching Vietnam, Laos, and Cambodia, Fall did not exclude the Cold War's broader geopolitical considerations in his work. However, he focused primarily on Vietnamese leaders, people, organizations, history, and society. More than Americans or the French, Vietnamese across the political spectrum were the agents for change in his analysis in which he was most interested. His focus on Vietnamese, Laotian, and Cambodian agency—rather than an emphasis on Western perspectives—was one of many unique qualities Fall's scholarship demonstrated in the 1950s and 1960s.

Fall wrote when many readers in the West, especially in the United States, were unfamiliar with Vietnam and its history. Moreover, his interest in and understanding of Indochina, its people, and the region's diverse histories grew significantly after his first research trip in 1953. He also integrated an evolving and dynamic set of skills in the social sciences with his World War II military experiences, and he combined these in a way that informed his subsequent analyses of warfare in Vietnam. Timing-wise, he undoubtedly also benefited from growing academic interest in non-Western culture in the post-World War II era. The appearance and growth of academic fields, such as area studies and others, revealed a new dimension of academia at the time. For example, Fall may have been one of the earliest analysts to assimilate and apply ideas and methods from the emerging discipline of operational anthropology in his study of contemporary political problems in Indochina.[48] His scholarship into the agronomics, sociology, linguistics, and ethnic diversity of Indochina did not match that found in the work of Pierre Gourou, Charles Robequain, Paul Mus, and Gerald Hickey, or located in studies created by archeologists specializing in Southeast Asia, such as Philippe Groslier.[49] Yet, Fall endeavored to incorporate and synthesize others' scholarship into his own to form an analysis of warfare in Indochina in the 1950s and early 1960s that provided readers with a great deal to consider. Fall's most unique contribution, however, consisted of his diagnostic analysis of Vietnamese revolutionary warfare. He developed this by integrating his personal experience of war as a researcher at the Nuremberg Trials with his direct observation and careful study of Indochina and its role within international affairs during and after World War II.

People who did not share Fall's interest in understanding Indochina, especially American policymakers unfamiliar with and uninterested in the culture in Southeast Asia, rarely arrived at a similar level of analysis as Fall. The problematic political relationship between Vietnamese and American allies between 1955 and 1961 added strain to effective governance in South Vietnam. These years were critical because problems with US policy toward Vietnam, especially US financial foreign assistance and aid projects between 1955 and 1961, contributed to the undermining of the Republic of Vietnam's economy and political legitimacy in South Vietnam. Poor political choices by South Vietnamese leaders, such as Ngo Dinh Diem's decision to remove Vietnamese villagers' elected officials in 1956 and his subsequent decision to replace them with government appointees, also added significant internal strife that degraded President Diem's administration's legitimacy.

Diem's decisions and rule by diktat, such as the Communist Denunciation campaign and the draconian National Security Law (the 10/59 decree), certainly gutted communist leadership in South Vietnam during the late 1950s. However, these decrees also fueled grievances that aided the National Liberation Front's formation in December 1960. In the most trenchant analysis of revolution in My Tho province that is available to readers today, David Elliott pointed out that, with the arrest of communists left and right in My Tho, critical transitions were also occurring: "What seemed at the time to have been a nearly complete pacification of My Tho province by 1958 looks

INTRODUCTION

in retrospect to have been the point at which the essential groundwork for a revolutionary revival was laid."[50] Accounting for these murky transitions occurring in real time—from 1953 onward, and in both North, Central, and South Vietnam—forms part of the substance of Fall's work.

While Fall did not possess the clarity of time found in Elliott's remarkable analysis of revolution in My Tho province, Fall's scholarship provides many snapshots of revolutionary warfare in development. Fall found plenty of problems in Diem's decisions. Yet Fall did not merely blame only Diem for shortfalls, nor focus solely on the United States for theirs. He knew that the Vietnamese effort to form and employ revolutionary warfare, which re-emerged with the National Liberation Front's formation in late 1960, contributed to an intractable problem for the United States in committing itself to what became the Second Indochina War. Fall argued that it was critical to understand Vietnamese agency and commitment to these processes during the Second Indochina War. The centrality of Vietnamese agency, and protracted Vietnamese commitment to independence—whether construed as nationalist, communist, or a hybrid of both—is central to understanding the value of Fall's scholarship.

This book is not a history of revolutionary warfare or total war. Instead, it investigates how Bernard Fall understood and described Vietnamese revolutionary warfare in Indochina after World War II. It is a history indelibly tied to Bernard Fall, so it may be considered a form of contextual or intellectual biography, but its focus is not exclusively on Fall's life. Instead, its focus centers on the unique circumstances through which Fall came to identify, study, and describe revolutionary warfare in Indochina. Necessarily, this entails recounting Fall's experiences and the formation of his knowledge in detail. These processes are foremost considerations in Chapters 1 through 3 that document the early period of Fall's life that led him to his study of Indochina. As a result, however, assessing these details reveals a synergy and broader contour to what Fall regarded as Vietnamese revolutionary warfare.

In a key respect, Fall serves as a vehicle to describe the form of warfare that the Viet Minh and their successors successfully utilized to defeat two powerful Western nations in the mid- to late-twentieth century. Fall, like anyone, was imperfect, and his analysis was not without flaws. However, his timing, prolific scholarship, and commitment to relate the facts as he saw them, and not as one would wish them to be, distinguish his thought and work. Vietnamese revolutionary warfare is therefore described in this book—as Jeremy Black aptly described how best to approach military history—"in terms of the multiple, political, social and cultural contexts that gave, and give it meaning."[51]

How did Fall define revolutionary warfare? The most concise description he offered is found in his article, "The Theory and Practice of Insurgency and Counterinsurgency," originally published in April 1965.[52] In it, Fall wrote:

> Let me state this definition: RW=G+P, or, "revolutionary warfare equals guerrilla warfare plus political action." This formula for revolutionary warfare is the result of the application of guerrilla methods to the furtherance of an ideology or a political system. This is the *real* difference between partisan warfare, guerrilla warfare, and everything else ... Political action, however, is the difference.

He added:

> The political, administrative, ideological aspect is the primary aspect. Everybody, of course, by definition, will seek a military solution to the insurgency problem, whereas by its very nature, the insurgency problem is military only in a secondary sense, and political, ideological, and administrative in a primary sense. Once we understand this, we will understand more of what is actually going on in Viet-Nam or in some of the other places affected by RW.[53]

In addition to the term's clear Maoist origins, Fall's use of the word "revolutionary" was inspired by French military officers who fought in Indochina. Most prominently, these officers included Colonel Gabriel Bonnet and Colonel Charles Lacheroy. There were other officers, such as Jean Hogard and Roger Trinquier, who also influenced Fall's thinking and provided a basis for his investigation of critical components of revolutionary warfare, such as parallel hierarchies.[54] Many of these officers contributed to the French journal *Revue Militaire D'Information*, which was a critical, even essential, source of information for Fall.[55] Notably, the primary resources he collected after 1953 included almost every issue of this journal published between 1957 and 1963. Researchers examining the subject of revolutionary warfare, the Viet Minh, the National Liberation Front, and almost any other aspect of conflict in Indochina after World War II may benefit from consulting the extensive primary sources available in Fall's collected papers.

Revolutionary warfare and parallel hierarchies, and their interdependence, deserve further description. Parallel hierarchies, discussed in Chapters 5 and 7, were Viet Minh-led social and administrative apparatuses used to form shadow government structures. Parallel hierarchies functioned either through subversion of a competing government institution or through the establishment of an entirely new organization that competed for administrative control over a local population. In one case that Fall cited in the early 1950s, the

INTRODUCTION

Viet Minh gained control over tax revenue in rural areas in North Vietnam by eliminating government tax collectors. This form of administrative control, he believed, was a reliable indicator that a parallel hierarchy used to collect taxes was at work. Not only did such a parallel hierarchy prevent the critical lifeblood of income collection, it indicated an authentic challenge and even replacement of local governance. Critically, this control was not a "military" function. Instead, it was based on civilian administration of a society. Taxation and control over teachers' placement in villages—another example in the domain of education Fall emphasized—were critical functions in determining the broader social control over a local population.

Fall understood that Western military planners and officers often failed to see taxation, tax collectors, and teachers as "targets" or critical nodes in controlling society. Similarly, Fall recognized that the Viet Minh—in contrast to Western planners—saw these social entities and their functions as "political targets" of considerable importance. These social entities did not possess a center of gravity in the same manner as a center of gravity in a military sense: they were difficult to target or control without a clear understanding of the society in which they operated. In Indochina, Fall noticed these processes that focused on social control instead of "military control" in 1953, before using terms like "revolutionary warfare" and "parallel hierarchies" to describe them. However, Fall consistently used these terms after 1957. He based his use of these terms on personal field observations, reflection, discussion with others, and his insights into the Viet Minh gained through his study of Vietnamese journals (in translation) and French journals, such as *Revue Militaire D'Information*.

A central argument in this book is that this broader phenomenon of social vs. military control was not unique to conflict in Indochina. In a critical respect, Fall began to formulate how these processes, especially parallel hierarchies, functioned *before* coming to Southeast Asia. His experiences during and immediately after World War II, both in the Maquis of the French Resistance in Vichy France and as a student of political warfare, were central to his recognition of parallel hierarchies and how they functioned. In other words, Fall understood how social and political control functioned in conflict—as opposed to control through military force alone—and this understanding provided a foundation on which he built his later analysis of Vietnamese revolutionary warfare. In the context of Indochina, the terms "revolutionary warfare" and "parallel hierarchies" helped him better articulate and describe the social and political components of what he regarded as a system of competitive control over a society.

As noted, Fall conveyed Gabriel Bonnet's description of revolutionary warfare as "a quasi-mathematical equation: 'partisan war plus psychological war equals revolutionary warfare.'"[56] In this example, the integration of political rationales—in the form of changing behavior through psychological warfare—makes this formation distinct from partisan warfare (primarily conducted through guerilla warfare, such as ambushes and other tactics) alone. Fall explained his vision of the "partisan" component with a slight variation in 1961, writing: "Revolutionary Warfare occurs when guerrilla methods are used to further an ideology." Later, he modified the partisan/guerrilla component again by adding, "according to Bonnet, Revolutionary Warfare is the application of irregular warfare methods to the propagation of an ideology or political system."[57] It is critical to point out that Fall used partisan, guerilla methods, and irregular warfare methods somewhat interchangeably. What is notable is that he envisioned them as somewhat separate from the "psychological/ideological/political" components needed to formulate the broader construct of revolutionary warfare.

This distinction—between tactical approaches (partisan/guerrilla/irregular warfare methods) and psychological/ideological/political elements—is imperative to note. Most fundamentally, the integration and product of these two factors—the partisan/guerrilla/irregular joining with the psychological/ideological/political—forms revolutionary warfare. As Fall understood it, this integration and product (in an almost mathematical sense) of the two factors also make revolutionary warfare distinct. In an important sense, guerrilla warfare without ideology and political motivation is only about the tactical application of warfare. In a period of conflict and revolution, politics and ideology without tactical application through irregular/partisan/guerrilla warfare tactics is an ivory tower. In a key respect, therefore, the first part of this book is about how Fall's personal experiences during and immediately after World War II contributed to his understanding of this dichotomy and its synthesis. In turn, the second part of this book is about how Fall distinguished between these two factors and their synthesis, and how he recounted this overall process in the broader historical, political, and social environment of Indochina in which revolutionary warfare formed and functioned.

In Indochina, Fall identified the Viet Minh's targeting of government officials as social and political control in practice at the local level. In adopting these practices, the Viet Minh essentially operated within a framework between the defensive and equilibrium stages found in Mao Tse-tung's thought. The Viet Minh did not seek to defeat military forces outright but instead sought to gain administrative control over a local population within the critical social structure of the Vietnamese. Such a grip over the population was a condition that, if met, would later enable weaker forces to achieve a decisive military victory over stronger opponents in conventional military action. The Viet Minh victory over French forces at Dien Bien Phu, as Fall knew, was the expression of processes that occurred over years and that were difficult to trace and measure through quantitative means. In contrast to applying quantitative methods, such as those used in political science, Fall applied historical comparisons and filtered them through his perspicacious judgment and insight. He used history not as a formulaic guide but to help formulate a historical sensibility and understanding of context. These skills enabled him to understand the past's utility in studying the present and the events he lived through. Studying Fall's scholarship, as a result, provides a model from which historians, analysts, military service members, and others may gain an understanding of how history, when contextualized appropriately, may assist in the analysis of current problems.

Fall recognized that authentic and lasting Viet Minh victory began with local-level political and social control. These conditions invariably preceded and often foreshadowed success on the battlefield. Set-piece battles, as the Viet Minh victory at Dien Bien Phu embodied, were only a final stage in an often-drawn-out process that ebbed and flowed. The critical importance of political warfare as a shaping operation and as a condition for military success is central to Fall's concept of revolutionary warfare. In simple terms, this conglomerate of political warfare/revolutionary warfare resulted from the multiplication of tactical and psychological/political/ideological factors, and this is how it differs from partisan or guerrilla warfare. "Partisans" and "guerrilla" fighters, Fall asserted, "are designed to operate in support of a regular force engaged in open warfare."[58] In contrast, "Revolutionary Warfare fighters seek primarily to establish a rival regime via the system of parallel hierarchies." These concepts, along with critical geographical factors provided by sanctuaries with protective terrain and politically safe harbors, constituted warfare employed by the Viet Minh against the French, and by the National Liberation Front and its North Vietnamese allies against the United States.[59] In Fall's words:

> I believe that the whole problem of the meaning of "war" in the new context will have to be re-examined sooner or later, to take into account the facts that parallel hierarchies, revolutionary warfare, and active sanctuaries are here to stay and that our present response of concentrating on the external military symptoms of the problem simply has no bearing on the preponderant politico-socio-economic components.[60]

Today, in the contemporary security environment—where irregular and political warfare will figure prominently in great power competition between China and the United States—Fall's study of revolutionary warfare offers much. These potential lessons are discussed in numerous places in this book, especially in the book's epilogue. In his day, Fall recognized that these "preponderant" social and political components were often challenging to measure or to comprehensively and succinctly describe. Even among the Viet Minh, with the apparent advantages they had in terms of language and other factors, such social and political advantages were not always acted upon with successful outcomes. Fall often described how many Viet Minh military failures originated with the Vietnamese communists' inaccurate readings of social and political conditions. The Viet Minh sometimes overestimated their control and legitimacy, and they could act in ways that backfired: forcing disastrous land reform policies upon Vietnamese farmers in 1953 and 1956 are two examples discussed in this book. The French, Americans, and anti-communist Vietnamese were not the only ones who made political mistakes that alienated Vietnamese individuals and societies. The Viet Minh and their successors made many mistakes, and Fall attempted to balance this knowledge and use it to assess the overall and building escalation of conflict leading to the Second Indochina War in the early 1960s.

Fall's critiques of the Saigon-based Republic of Vietnam's (RVN) policies and American policies certainly loom large in the later chapters of this book. In crucial respects, Fall was one of the earliest critics of US policy, and his critiques began as early as 1956. By 1964, Fall's doubts concerning elements of US policy toward Vietnam were not only embedded into and documented through almost a decade of his reporting and scholarship, but his doubts had also spread to other journalists and military thinkers. However, before 1965, Fall did essentially believe the United States could succeed in Vietnam, and he primarily defined success as a viable two-state solution along similar lines to those existing in Germany and Korea.[61] In 1964, his reasons for believing in the viability of a "two-state" solution centered on the United States' limited involvement that relied upon a robust advisory effort and foreign financial assistance to South Vietnam that had improved significantly after 1961. The increased and improved coordination of foreign assistance—initiated through the US Foreign Assistance Act of 1961 that established USAID—and a capable and limited advisory program indicated a wise and controlled policy approach to support anti-communist efforts in Vietnam.

Despite these efforts, there were still severe problems that had to be solved, to be sure. Many problems, such as those emanating from South Vietnamese

INTRODUCTION

governance, extended beyond America's control. Fall's concern that the RVN could achieve political stability and legitimacy was constant in his writing, certainly as early as 1956. Among a diverse South Vietnamese population, with deeply held contentious politics that preceded the Republic of Vietnam's establishment in 1955, a lack of popular support and a lack of perceived political legitimacy associated with the RVN created insurmountable obstacles. Fall quickly recognized that this problem was one that no American President could overcome. Despite all the President's high-quality advisors and available military forces, as well as access to massive American financial aid, Vietnam's reunification could only be achieved in a lasting manner by the Vietnamese.

Large-scale American intervention, beginning in early 1965, was not a solution to the political problems Fall perceived. These factors are discussed in Chapter 8. They highlight a series of overly militarized approaches that contributed to Fall's change of heart regarding the potential for American success in Vietnam. Some of these factors included political turbulence in South Vietnam after Ngo Dinh Diem's assassination in late 1963; increased capacity of the National Liberation Front; grievances among the Buddhist population in the south; the contentious manipulation of the Gulf of Tonkin Incident to justify increased aggressive actions by the United States; and, finally, the US decision to intervene with conventional military forces in 1965. Among all the factors that contributed to his quickly changing perspective, the decision to initiate virtually unlimited aerial bombardment—initially through Operation Flaming Dart and then through Operation Rolling Thunder in March 1965—consolidated Fall's grave doubts. Soon after Rolling Thunder began, Fall's worst fears centered on the potential enactment of a purely or excessive military solution. More than any other factor, this potential and its realization as 1965 and 1966 unfolded caused him to become an outspoken critic of US policy.

His essay, "This Isn't Munich, It's Spain," published in the December 1965 issue of *Ramparts*, is a central and representative document in this latter period of Fall's scholarship. He recorded his observations on how the over-militarization of foreign policy was destroying the Vietnamese people and degrading American humanity, writing, "There seems to be a predisposition on our side to no longer be able to see the Vietnamese as people against whom crimes can be committed. This is the ultimate impersonalization of war."[62] Fall drew this connection from his experience of systematic violence perpetrated by Nazi Germany against civilians during World War II and as a researcher during the Nuremberg Trials in 1947 and 1948. If the United States were to hold to its moral compass, a value he believed guided the US and its allies' "Crusade in Europe" against fascism, the United States should not allow such systematic violence against Vietnamese civilians to continue in the name of anti-communism. As a result of his frustration and anger over the destruction of Vietnam and its people caused by American policy, he became a key source of information for the anti-war movement. From its earliest stages at the inaugural teach-ins over the weekend of 15–16 May 1965 in Washington, DC, Fall's scholarship provided source material for anti-war platforms, and even among leaders in the US Senate, such as J. William Fulbright.[63] *Number One Realist*, therefore, seeks to show how the origins for Fall's views on this matter grew out of his experience of World War II and as a research analyst during the Nuremberg Trials.

As a result of this knowledge, Fall questioned whether the United States could succeed in Vietnam and do so in a manner that adhered to its professed values promoting life, liberty, and equality. Even though he was an anti-communist and wanted to see the Republic of Vietnam endure as a non-communist country, he quickly recognized the imperative of a political solution that military force could not achieve. As his *Ramparts* article indicated, after 1965 he believed that the war could not be won, short of by Vietnam's complete devastation. In that event, it would embody only a Pyrrhic and ultimately counterproductive victory for the United States. This recognition led him to take an increasingly bitter view, particularly since he did not perceive Vietnam as a critical theater in the Cold War. Obliterating the country was not only immoral; it was strategically unnecessary.

Fall's views on this matter were pronounced by 1965, and they escalated in correlation with an American policy he saw as increasingly destructive through 1965, 1966, and early 1967. Earlier, his concerns focused on guiding US policy to adapt more effectively to the realities of revolutionary warfare in Indochina. This form of political warfare, after all, did not only consist of a communist revolution against French imperialism and the Americanization of a re-emerging war after 1955. It also included a compound of changes against the Confucian ordering of Vietnamese society, amounting to a social revolution in a rapidly changing country as it encountered modernization. The diverse numbers of factors at work changing Vietnam help explain why Fall focused on economic, religious, social, historical, and other cultural-related subjects more than military-focused aspects of conflict. It is also why he was so interested in what the Vietnamese thought, and why he explored the ways they adapted to a rapidly changing world in the decades before and after

INTRODUCTION

World War II. In his writings from 1954 through 1966, the preponderance of discussion he gives to Vietnamese organizations and political views demonstrated this awareness and his interest in Vietnam.

What were the sources and nature of his insight? Fall began writing about Indochina in 1954, but his study of its roots would eventually go back much further than that.[64] The historical background contributing to Fall's thought is crucial because part of what made his work insightful is that he took deeper historical context into account when trying to understand contemporary events. Here a metaphor is useful: Vietnamese anti-colonialism, communism, nationalism, and a sophisticated and multivarious sense of Vietnamese identities, let alone those found in the diverse societies of Laos and Cambodia, formed numerous social fabrics. Revolutionary warfare threaded into and throughout that fabric and was contested by other Vietnamese in its formation. Short of destroying that fabric, however, it was difficult for outsiders to weave themselves into that fabric to change its character, let alone its future.

Fall knew, as a European, that he could not weave his way into Vietnamese society. Still, he could recognize the way war developed and functioned in society through empathy and a historical sensibility generated by his own experience with war. Fall's scholarship demonstrates this knowledge of Vietnamese revolutionary warfare from the outside, but it does so without essentializing Vietnam or a specific sense of Vietnamese identity. Instead, Fall was a humanitarian. If there was an essentialist quality in humans that Fall recognized and made an invariable and unrelenting effort to understand, it was their capacity for good, as much as their capability for evil.

At the very heart of Fall's humanitarianism, the matter of political legitimacy is foremost in his analysis of revolutionary warfare and policy related to this form of political warfare. As described in Chapter 4, Fall's assessment of the Viet Minh's disastrous land reform policies in 1953 and 1956 degraded their legitimacy in the eyes of Vietnamese farmers. Numerous negative political repercussions grew out of these problems. Revolts in 1956 against the Viet Minh in Nghe An Province, the birthplace of Ho Chi Minh, attested to the Viet Minh's struggle to reassert their control. Numerous political problems in the Republic of Vietnam and the excessive number of grievances against the South Vietnamese government revealed serious problems in legitimacy there as well. The critical point Fall appeared to concede was the importance of gaining administrative control of a people as an organization's primary effort. Ideally, this administrative grip entailed gaining legitimacy of political and social control from the perspective of the governed peoples. The critical social value forming political legitimacy is why organizational-administrative power outweighed pure military power alone in importance: authentic legitimacy is ideally given by the governed. It is not something that can be taken by the governing and last for long. In simple terms, this is why dictators turn to coup-proofing, disinformation, martial law, and other means to remain in power.

In the case of the Viet Minh during the First Indochina War, and in cases where the National Liberation Front dominated in the Second Indochina War, these ideas involving legitimacy led Fall to write a signal remark regarding modern political warfare: "When a country is being subverted it is not being outfought; it is being out-administered."[65] He added, "Once we understand this, we will understand more of what is actually going on in Viet-Nam or in some of the other places affected by Revolutionary Warfare."[66] Political legitimacy in "out-administering" a competitor, regardless of their military power, is what mattered most. The problem was that this was not the approach taken by the United States in 1965 and later. In a letter to John Paul Vann on 1 January 1965, Fall explained, "Everybody speaks the platitude that the war will have to be won on the terrain and among the SVN (South Vietnamese) people—and then goes on right back to one more pass with M-113's and napalm."[67] Over-militarized solutions led Fall to believe, at least in the initial years of large-scale war in 1965 and 1966, that the United States failed to employ other means, aside from military power, to force a political settlement.

At its core, military power was irrelevant without political legitimacy. As Fall put it to his friend, the French journalist François Sully, "A U.S. Marine can fly a helicopter better than anyone else, but he simply cannot indoctrinate peasants with an ideology worth fighting for."[68] Indoctrinating such ideology, Fall well knew, could only be achieved through Vietnamese compliance. As much as he loved the US Marine Corps and the Marines' historical legacy, forcing an ideology on Vietnamese peasants was not their job, and solely killing Vietnamese would not accomplish their mission. Fall's goal, as a scholar of war in Southeast Asia, included informing policymakers why they should stop ordering Marines, and other military personnel, from endlessly seeking to achieve the impossible in Vietnam.

Fall's scholarship has lessons for today and is not locked in time as only relevant to an "age of revolutions" during the 1950s and 1960s. In other words, "revolutionary warfare" is not an anachronism or archaic term that describes only wars of decolonization after World War II or conflicts during the Cold War across the Global South. Fall recognized revolutionary warfare

INTRODUCTION

as an approach to conflict in which political legitimacy and achieving legitimate governance that earned popular support were the tactical, operational, and strategic goals in war. RAND Analyst Douglas Pike pointed out that this approach was difficult to defeat because of its political nature: "The Vietnamese Communists conceived, developed, and fielded a dimensional new method for making war ... and most important, that it is a strategy for which there is no known proven counterstrategy."[69] The vast social consequences involved in revolutionary warfare may alarm analysts of war and those responsible for planning for it when ordered to do so. *Number One Realist: Bernard Fall and Vietnamese Revolutionary Warfare* seeks to shed light on how Fall construed revolutionary warfare and the cultural and historical contexts in which it functioned. As a secondary goal, this analysis also seeks to show how reducing overly militarized solutions and increasing diplomatic and political warfare approaches may offer better solutions to blunt or deter adversarial intent and capabilities far more than solely relying upon military forces for these jobs.

Number One Realist is the first book to focus entirely on Bernard Fall's scholarship. It is built, however, on the work of other scholars who have seen value in Fall's writing. Fredrik Logevall, in his 2013 Pulitzer Prize-winning history *Embers of War*, incorporated Fall's perspective on the Americanization of war in 1965. Logevall observed:

> Bernard Fall, over the previous decade, had become America's most respected expert on the First Indochina War, the author of numerous books and articles notable for their informed and dispassionate analysis ... Certainly, this astonishingly prolific writer, had he lived, would have produced more important books and articles on the struggle for Vietnam, works that would have reached a wide audience and added enormously to Americans' collective knowledge.[70]

Logevall concluded his history of the First Indochina War by noting how Fall believed that the United States was following in France's footsteps in Indochina. Ultimately, as both Fall and Logevall explained in their work, there were few lasting political solutions that military force alone could provide.

In another analytical approach incorporating Fall's methodological approach to warfare, Craig Whiteside remarked that the inspiration for his paper "The Islamic State and the Return of Revolutionary Warfare" originated with Fall, "whose writings about the Vietnam wars often reflected an amazement of the subversive nature of revolutionary warfare and its paralyzing effect on government."[71] Whiteside added, "Fall delighted in contrasting public pronouncements of government control by French military or

American political observers who counted secure provinces instead of obscure assassinations or uncollected taxes."[72] In fundamental ways and through numerous books and articles, David Kilcullen also builds on Fall's analysis of revolutionary warfare, but with an updated lexicon that incorporates assessments of social networks and conflict ecosystems. In these complex systems, participants utilize technological advancements, for example, in communication platforms that were previously inaccessible for non-state actors. These characteristics increase their asymmetric capacity to undermine state power in ways that are playing out in profound ways through cyber, information, and other means that do not rely on powerful conventional forces. In many respects, Whiteside and Kilcullen have proven to be key thinkers who advance themes similar to those Fall advocated.

Even in a resurging environment of "great power and strategic competition," it should not be surprising that asymmetric, irregular, and political warfare will be used as a primary approach among not only non-state actors but among "great powers" as well. In Kilcullen's view, social media, massive increases in urbanization and population growth, and the coastal location of many large cities worldwide that are all affected by climate change, add critical dimensions to conflict. Kilcullen's integration of social, political, economic, and environmental relationships echoes an underlying influence found in Fall's thought on revolutionary warfare.[73] On the idea of competitive control as the strategic goal in a given society in conflict, Kilcullen's insights are particularly relevant and build on Fall's work. Kilcullen indicated this in his 2013 book, *Out of the Mountains*, when he noted: "Fall's later writings, give a series of examples of this idea of competitive control—an idea that's not spatial ('insurgent-controlled' or 'contested areas') or structural ('networks' and 'movements') but rather functional."[74] As a more encompassing form of competitive control that is functional, this idea of revolutionary warfare indicates how Fall provides value to contemporary discussions and ways of thinking about conflict today.

* * *

As a work of intellectual biography and history, this is the first book-length study in English to assess Bernard Fall's scholarship. It relies primarily on Fall's papers since so little sustained analysis of Fall's work currently exists in secondary literature. Dorothy Fall wrote a memoir of her husband and their life together, but it does not provide an analytical scholarly assessment of Fall's work. Instead, Dorothy Fall related Fall's life and importance among those who knew him, with an eye to helping others know of his important contribution to the study of war in Vietnam. Fall's scholarship, as Mrs. Fall's work and this book both indicate, was significantly valued during his life by other scholars and journalists. French scholars and Fall's friends, Philippe Devillers and Jean Lacouture, described Fall's contributions to understanding conflict in Indochina and often referenced his work in their writing.[75]

Another French scholar of Indochina, Paul Mus, also contributed a detailed preface for one of Fall's earliest publications.[76] Mus applauded Fall's approach to the study of conflict because Fall focused upon human social networks and their operations. The attention to nuance Fall revealed indicated his interest in advancing a humanitarian perspective and critiquing the underlying politics that instigated and perpetuated civil war in Indochina. In addition to a holistic approach incorporating diverse Vietnamese societies, Mus explained, Fall also "soberly made apparent, the combatants' point of view."[77] The French journalist and Fall's friend, François Sully, wrote a detailed and informative commentary about Fall and his personality as an individual, but Sully's thoughts on Fall remain unpublished.[78] It should be pointed out that Sully intended to write a book about Fall, but Sully died in Indochina in 1971 before completing his planned work.[79] This book, in many respects, seeks to fulfill the goal Sully envisioned.

Other writers and scholars provide well-informed source material and commentary on Fall's relevance and value as a scholar, but those contributions are limited to articles.[80] Their work, in many respects, demonstrates why Fall deserves sustained scholarly analysis that a book-length study provides. As the United States increased its efforts in Southeast Asia, prominent journalists—including Peter Arnett, Walter Cronkite, I.F. Stone, David Halberstam, and others—regarded Fall as an authority and inspiration in their reporting. In Dorothy Fall's account of her husband, Peter Arnett described Fall's influence as pervasive, writing:

> At the time, Fall's books, particularly *Street Without Joy* and *The Two Viet-Nams*, were the only written books freely available. Bernard's works on the French Indochina war were the reference works ... In the press corps he was an immensely popular man and always available to converse and to freely give his opinions and to tell wonderful stories about his own experiences. We'd meet at Bodard's or Givral's (cafes in Saigon). He'd be holding court there. Bernard gave us the moral support to look at the negative aspects of the war at a time when U.S. authorities were insisting we look only at the positive.[81]

David Halberstam reinforced Arnett's point: "The most important thing about Bernard Fall was that he was the man who taught us about that small fierce country's past when we most desperately needed it."[82]

Perhaps the most widely recognized journalist of his time, Walter Cronkite consulted with Bernard Fall for material that informed Cronkite's newscasts on war in Vietnam. Fall provided Cronkite with a unique perspective because Fall met Ho Chi Minh and North Vietnamese Prime Minister Pham Van Dong in 1962. When Cronkite sought more information about Ho Chi Minh and the widespread appeal Ho created among Vietnamese, Fall was the definitive source for such knowledge on the North Vietnamese leader at the time.[83] Among readers with a leftist political orientation, journalist I.F. Stone's *Weekly* also invariably relied upon source material provided by Fall. Stone and Fall met regularly to discuss conflict in Indochina as the United States increased its escalation after 1965.[84] Author Jonathan Schell also pointed to Fall as an influence, adding, "Bernard Fall was the acknowledged authority and writer on the subject [of Indochina]. He was the man to read if they wanted to find out about this country that we were tearing apart."[85] A key outcome of this book, therefore, is to demonstrate why Schell and others were correct in their assessments and to demonstrate how Fall's experiences and scholarship contributed to his place as the foremost scholar on warfare in Indochina in the twentieth century.

* * *

Number One Realist consists of a prologue, introduction, eight chapters, and an epilogue. Chapter 1 examines Fall's life during World War II because his experiences during the war contributed to his understanding of civil conflict. Fall was a Jewish émigré to France from Austria before World War II. During the war, he joined several French Resistance groups before eventually joining the Maquis in Haut-Savoie, and then the Free French Army in later stages of the war. As described in Chapter 1, Fall decided to join the Resistance after his mother's deportation to Auschwitz and after the Gestapo murdered his father in November 1943. Confronted with the possibility he would either be targeted or conscripted for labor, he had few other options. After the war, his experience of war extended to the Nuremberg Trials in 1947 and 1948. There, he worked for the War Crimes Commission, analyzing the Krupp Corporation and its role as a critical producer of Nazi armament using slave labor.

As the subject of Chapter 2, Fall's war experiences and his post-war analyses at Nuremberg compelled him to consider the institutional matrix of Nazi ideology and corporatism that enabled the Third Reich to establish power in 1933 and pursue war throughout Europe. The armaments industry led by

INTRODUCTION

Krupp and other corporations, Fall learned, was a keystone that facilitated Nazi imperialism. In his later analysis of Vietnam, Fall was a committed anticommunist. However, he feared that the military-industrial complex inflicting war in Vietnam reflected a similar integration of industry and militarization to that which had contributed to the destruction of his family and most of Europe. The systematic overreliance on militarized solutions concerned Fall because he believed that Vietnam did not pose a direct national security threat to the United States. He also found it troubling, because domino theory-related rationales for intervention had already been discredited in 1964 by Sherman Kent, Chairman of the Board of National Estimates, a year before large-scale military intervention in 1965.[86] Fall's concern over the moral dimension of war in Vietnam was also pronounced, as noted, after large-scale American intervention in early 1965.

Most critically, Fall was concerned with the way American politicians rationalized intervention. In December 1965, Secretary of State Dean Acheson remarked:

> The end sought by our foreign policy ... is, as I have said, to preserve and foster an environment in which free societies may exist and flourish. Our policies and actions must be decided by whether they contribute to or detract from achievement of this end. They need no other justification or moral or ethical embellishment.[87]

The lack of moral "embellishment" Acheson viewed as unnecessary was remarkable because it demonstrated a dismissal of social and political justice that Fall perceived as principal in guiding what he perceived as the correct and useful course for US foreign policy. A significant factor in Fall's scholarship consists of his waking up to the realization that the United States' claim to exceptionalism was tied up in exempting itself of rules that it applied to other countries. Acheson's remark not only demonstrated a shocking hubris, it also indicated a belief among elite policymakers that the United States could determine its exemption from moral "embellishments" that might otherwise stand in the way of achieving its policy goals.

As Fall understood it, Acheson's statement indicated that US foreign policy and military force deployment was an instrument of sovereignty that did not have to adhere to rules that applied to others. This "rule-making that the United States did not have to follow itself" was a form of not only exceptionalism but positivism too. This was a type of mindset that Fall feared because Acheson's statement sought to justify unlimited warfare in Vietnam without moral or ethical constraints. At its core, this apprehension was rooted in Fall's knowledge of, and experience enduring and surviving, World War II. Fall spoke to this directly:

> I spent 1946–48 at the Nuremberg trials as a young research analyst and in a number of cases I heard the Germans attempt to excuse atrocities as acts committed by troops of their allies. This did not absolve the Germans of their responsibility. (By the way, both Viet-Nam and the United States have signed and ratified the 1949 Geneva Convention on War Victims.) The reality in Viet-Nam is that the international rules of war are not obeyed.[88]

Fall understood this "impersonalization" of war directly from his experience of World War II, throughout which violence, intentionally inflicted upon civilians, was committed as a matter of policy. Chapter 3 describes how Fall decided to study the wars in Indochina after meeting Amry Vandenbosch, a professor at the School of Advanced International Studies (SAIS) at Johns Hopkins University. As a result of his decision and new focus, Fall traveled to Indochina to study the war firsthand in 1953. Chapter 3 documents this nearly ten-month research trip during which Fall gathered extensive materials for his first book, *The Viet-Minh Regime*, his 1955 doctoral dissertation, and articles he published between 1954 and 1956. His first trip to Vietnam formed a foundation for this early tranche of scholarship and contributed the majority of source material for his 1961 book, *Street Without Joy*. This early trip to Vietnam also provided a research baseline to assess subsequent changes in Indochina in later trips.

Chapter 4 focuses on events in Indochina which led to the First Indochina War and the two different Vietnamese governments that formed there after World War II. After the return of France's troops to Indochina in 1946, conflict between the Democratic Republic of Vietnam, led by Ho Chi Minh, and the French-supported Associated State of Vietnam, led by Vietnamese Emperor Bao Dai, set the stage for three decades of war. Chapter 4, therefore, provides background into the history which Fall incorporated so thoroughly in his scholarship.

Chapter 5 examines the Vietnamese communist organization, the Viet Minh. This group was not the only anti-colonial organization to emerge after the World War II, but they dominated other Vietnamese groups and became the most consequential organization during the period of decolonization. Fall's 1954 study, *The Viet-Minh Regime*, focused on Viet Minh history and organization. In this critical work—almost entirely unexamined by previous scholars—Fall showed how the Viet Minh successfully fought the French as well as their Vietnamese competitors, including Vietnamese nationalist groups and others. Chapter 5 also devotes a section to the Viet Minh's internal security apparatus, which helped the organization achieve competitive control over contested societies in North Vietnam after 1946. For example, Fall assessed that the Cong An, Trinh Sat, and Dich Van were essential to the social-political control of the Vietnamese population and especially in fighting the French. These organizations used tactics Fall recognized from his time in the Maquis during World War II, especially related to anti-collaboration measures. Chapter 5 concludes with later developments during the First Indochina War, particularly France's Operation Lorraine, which contributed to the eventual defeat of the French at Dien Bien Phu in April and May 1954.

Chapter 6 focuses on Fall's second trip to Vietnam in 1957. Most critically for his future scholarship, the changes he witnessed resulted in an article for *The Nation* called "Will South Vietnam Be Next?" published in May 1958.[89] In addition to the article, Fall described changes he saw in Vietnam during a speech to the Association of Asian Studies meeting in New York City in April 1958. The speech and article sharply criticized aid developed and implemented to support the Republic of Vietnam by the US State Department-led International Cooperation Administration. This case of outspoken and sincere honesty would have lasting consequences for Fall's career.

Chapter 7 expands upon this series of events by analyzing another critical article Fall published in *Pacific Affairs* in September 1958 called "South Vietnam's Internal Problems." This article demonstrated how Fall's scholarship reflected growing concern as the United States increased its intervention in Vietnam through the late 1950s and into 1960.[90] Chapter 7 assesses how American officials began to privately recognize the validity of Fall's criticisms of the Diem administration and America's policies in Vietnam. In one of the most revealing cases, the American advisor to Ngo Dinh Diem, Wesley Fishel, privately criticized Ngo Dinh Diem while pointing out how Fall gained far more accurate information on South Vietnam than the US government was able to retrieve. Other advisors to Diem, notably American Air Force Brigadier General Edward Lansdale, acknowledged Fall's critiques but denigrated his work because he thought Fall represented the misguided French view that was angry over France's defeat in Indochina. Chapter 7 focuses primarily, however, on Fall's use of the term "revolutionary warfare," a term he used consistently after 1958. He was adamant that revolutionary warfare differed regionally in Vietnam because of diversity in population and environmental factors, but he was also careful to explain how it evolved from the First to the Second Indochina War.

Chapter 8 addresses the period between 1961 and 1966 when, in December that year, Fall left for Vietnam for his last trip to study the National Liberation Front. The chapter addresses Fall's analysis of the Laotian Crisis, his views on the critical importance of reform in the Ngo Dinh Diem administration before Diem's death in late 1963, and especially Fall's influence in the public sphere, among other intellectuals, military personnel, and members of the US Congress and Senate, particularly Senator J. William Fulbright. The latter part of Chapter 8 focuses on Fall's turn to an anti-war position and his role as a public intellectual influencing debate over American intervention in Vietnam after 1965.

The book's epilogue considers the legacy and relevance of Bernard Fall's scholarship in an era of re-emerging great power competition. At a time when disagreement over facts is common, and when facts are manipulated to gain political power rather than put to the service of the common good, it is worthwhile to revisit Fall's scholarship and its value today. In light of growing attention to irregular warfare, or "Gray Zone" conflict as it is often regarded, Fall's views on revolutionary warfare has much to offer those studying conflict and ways to mitigate it. The life Fall lived enabled him to recognize Vietnamese revolutionary warfare in Indochina, and the book's epilogue points to how his scholarship provides numerous lessons that endure today and may continue to endure into the future. Fall's scholarship serves as a reminder of why it is important to recognize and accept facts for what they are, not as we wish or imagine them to be. Bernard Fall's journey in recognizing the facts found in the many faces of warfare began in southern France on 1 September 1939.

1

FIRST IMPRESSIONS OF A WAR

I—Nice, France 1939

The outbreak of war in Europe on 1 September 1939 challenged Bernard Fall's earliest preconceptions of conflict. Later in life, he described this, writing:

> You know, I was just an average young boy, and to me war was ... I'd seen war in the movies, of course, and war, somehow in European movies, always gets depicted as being either at night or in the middle of rain and I'll never forget ... when war broke out ... it was a perfectly sunny Riviera day ... I was waiting for the thunder and the rains to come down and nothing happened. In a way I was quite disappointed that war would start out on this perfectly banal, beautiful day.[1]

In addition to movies on war, themes of poverty found in dramatic movies, such as André Hugon's 1938 film *La Rue Sans Joie*, translated as *Street Without Joy*, provided Fall with additional perspectives related to social and economic unrest during the dark months preceding the breakout of war in 1939.[2]

From his first encounter with it, war did not necessarily involve tanks, battles, and soldiers fighting from one trench to another. It could be something a person did not even initially see occurring around them. Fall's reflections on his experiences as a twelve-year-old boy in Nice, France in September 1939—described in November 1966, three months before his death—are poignant considering the adversity Fall endured after World War II began. He recognized that warfare did not always reveal itself clearly, unlike its portrayal in the films he watched. Instead, from his first experience, Fall undoubtedly noticed that warfare unfolded in ways that seeped into his day-to-day existence: prewar anti-Jewish sentiment and discrimination, the day-to-day struggles his family endured fleeing Vienna after the Anschluss of Austria in March 1938, fears associated with the potential outbreak or war, and disinformation and lies in the media of his day all contributed to a series of bewildering complexities. These factors—more than tanks, battles, and soldiers fighting trench to trench—were the ways war revealed itself to Bernard Fall and his family before and after 1 September 1939.

Unlike others living in Poland in September 1939, Fall was fortunate not to experience the immediate and direct onslaught of German armed forces and the Soviet Red Army converging on his home in the south of France. However, whether he could see it or not, he was at the beginning of a struggle with war, and World War II shaped not only his life but also his views on warfare. The war would provide a framework of reference points for his later analysis of conflict, but he did not impute a historical weight to this experience in a manner that predetermined his later views on warfare in Indochina. Fall lost a great deal in World War II, but he also developed an ability to look forward using his experience in the French Resistance, Maquis, and the French army during France's liberation. He assessed war in nuanced, detailed, and socially focused ways that transcended conceptions of war as only military operations, divorced from the societies in which it was fought. In Fall's earliest experience, war was always among the people, and war was never fought by armies alone.

As a member of the French Resistance after 1943, Fall's efforts against Nazi aggression and his knowledge of Nazi atrocities informed his understanding of warfare in the later stages of World War II. After the war, Fall's military experiences continued to shape his subsequent work as a researcher for the War Crimes Commission at the Nuremberg Trials. This knowledge and his analysis developed at Nuremberg contributed to his capabilities which later, in and after 1953, he applied in assessing revolutionary warfare in Indochina. Fall's encounters with war were those of a civilian forced to fight for survival, who further adapted to become a soldier and, subsequently, who later became a scholar of war as well. These factors provided Fall with insight into war as it affected civilians, and how this civil dimension intersected with formal applications of military power through organized armed forces. Later in his life, this accumulation of experiential factors enabled him to develop a unique and trenchant approach in explaining warfare to those who sought to understand conflict in Southeast Asia during and after World War II. Yet Fall's analysis on the pervasive social nature of revolutionary warfare in Indochina, in many respects, is difficult to understand fully without knowing his early life.

Bernard Fall was born in Vienna, Austria on 19 November 1926 to Anna Seligmann and Leo Fall, a merchant. As a Jewish family, the Falls endured anti-Semitism in Austria that the global economic depression magnified. Discrimination against Jewish communities in Vienna was further exacerbated by lingering frustration with the Versailles Treaty adjudicating World War I. After the Anschluss of Austria by Germany in March 1938, Leo and Anna sent Bernard and his younger sister Lissette to Paris. Bernard stayed with Anna's sister Marcelle and her husband, Auguste Biret, a couple who owned a bookshop near the Champs-Élysées, while Lissette lived with another sister of Anna's.[3] Anna and Leo remained in Austria to provide for Leo's family members, and, after several chaotic months, Anna managed to reunite with Lissette and Bernard in Paris. Leo Fall later reunited with his family in Vichy-controlled Nice after Anna had relocated Bernard and Lissette there from Paris. In Nice, the Fall family moved to the Villa Beauregard, a kibbutz administered by the Nice Refugee Committee, an organization of French Jews supporting Jewish émigrés.[4]

Two years after France's defeat in June 1940, the Third Reich's subjection of Vichy France in 1942 hit families like the Falls hard. Under Nazi jurisdiction, in August the Vichy police raided many residences where Jewish émigrés lived, in order to evict them for deportation, and thus was the fate that befell the Falls.[5] During a raid on the Villa Beauregard, Leo Fall and other men fled, believing the Vichy authorities sought only to detain the male occupants. Instead, Vichy police forces targeted all Villa inhabitants, including Fall's mother and sister. Bernard's sister, Lissette, avoided deportation due to a temporary Vichy regulation that spared children with parental agreement, which Anna provided. Lissette's life was spared, but Anna was detained, sent to Drancy, and then deported to Auschwitz, where she died.[6] Bernard, ill at the time, avoided arrest only because a Vichy officer sympathetically decided to delay arresting him until the sixteen-year-old recuperated. With this break, Henry Frankiel, a French army veteran and family friend, interceded and protected a convalescing Bernard in his home in Nice.[7] Not long after Anna's deportation, Lissette and Bernard reconnected and rented a room on the Avenue Georges Clemenceau while their father remained in hiding and joined the French Resistance.[8] Eventually, Lissette found refuge at the Convent de Clarisse in Cimiez in Nice, while Bernard joined several Zionist resistance

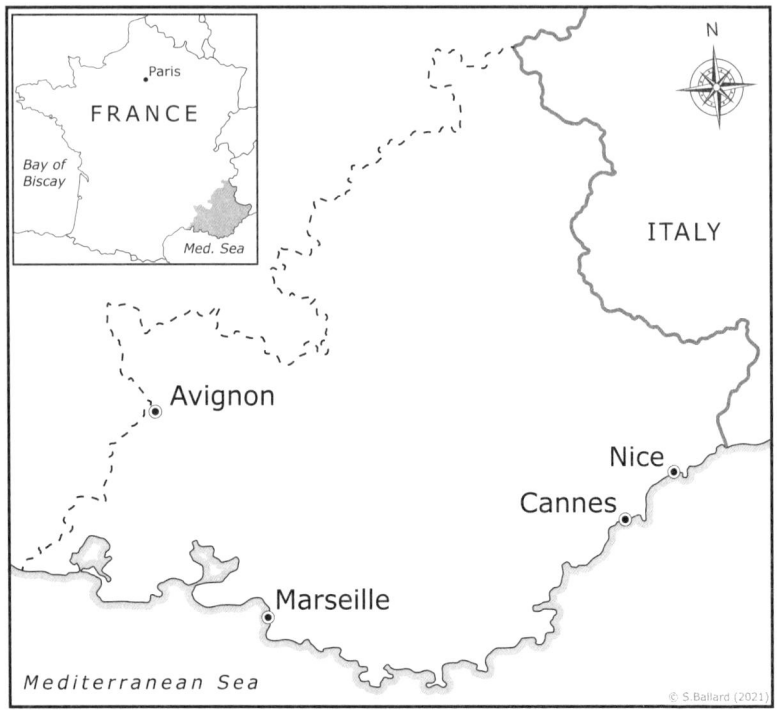

Map of Southern France

groups and, as cover, a paramilitary Vichy youth group called *Les Compagnons de France*. In late 1942, Leo was captured by Vichy authorities and sent to a military barracks known as *Caserne d'Auvare*. Eventually, he was released, only to resume his support for the resistance.[9]

Fall's family was one among tens of thousands targeted in Vichy, France. French Jewish councils' denunciation of foreign Jews, however—an action that led to the breaking of Fall's family and others—added another bitter layer of betrayal.[10] Jewish councils had been created as aid associations across Europe, but they soon faced a socially divisive dilemma. According to Istvan Deák, in many countries, "council members faced the choice between collective death and trying to satisfy the Germans by offering Jewish skills to the war industry." In Amsterdam in 1940, in Deák's judgment, "members of the Jewish Council did not have to fear immediate extermination; there is no excuse for their servile submission to the Germans to whom they gave the name and data of every Jew in the Netherlands."[11] Similar processes were at work in Vichy-controlled France as well, with families like Fall's being denounced as foreigners. As collaborators, some French Jewish councils possibly shared a sense of protected status similar to that of the Dutch councils.

In Timothy Snyder's view, foreigners were obvious targets in France, and "Jews without French citizenship were about ten times more likely to be deported to Auschwitz than were Jews with French citizenship."[12] The Fall family's attempt to assimilate by learning French or through other means was therefore for naught in such circumstances and against such unforgiving odds. The breaking of Fall's family, as Jewish émigrés, was perhaps inevitable in occupied France since, in Snyder's perspective, "the Holocaust was mainly a crime against Jews who, from a French perspective, were foreign."[13] Even though Fall became a naturalized French citizen after the war, as a result of his military service in the French army in late 1944 and 1945, he possibly retained an "outsider" sense of identity as a foreign-born Jew. He did not discuss these matters in his papers, his relative silence regarding his family's denunciation and betrayal by other Jews speaks volumes, and the raid on his family's home at the Villa Beauregard undoubtedly had a lasting and profound effect on him. In many respects, this bitter series of events likely enhanced his acute sense of social complexities involving collaboration, betrayal, political allegiance, and moral and religious compromise.

In his analysis of the political economy of denunciation, Stathis Kalyvas demonstrates a correspondence between retaliation and betrayal. Fear of potential retaliation, Kalyvas emphasizes, serves as one of the central brakes that prevent denunciations: "The supply of denunciations is subject to a fundamental constraint, namely the likelihood of retaliation faced either by the denouncer or by the local committee that vets denunciations."[14] Kalyvas further argues: "This dimension, of course, is standard in organized crime: credible threats of retaliation discourage witnesses from testifying."[15] Since the Fall family, along with other foreigners, had no recourse for retaliation, their vulnerability was magnified among Jewish councils willing to betray them. This period of Fall's life was also significant because it contributed to his comprehension of war as more than just set-piece battles he learned about in books, or by watching movies about them. Since his emigration from Austria in 1938, but especially in 1942 and 1943, Fall's experience of war did not consist of battles and tactical maneuvers. War was about political categorizations and the exploitation of social, ethnic, and religious divisions. Fall did not lose his mother in battle; he lost her because German and Vichy policy directed it and because those whom the Falls trusted, out of motivations related to self-preservation, betrayed them.

In Fall's case, the socio-political components of identity were the critical factors that determined who was targeted in denunciations, who might be expelled to a camp or left unharmed. More than recounting battles or operations, these social factors compelled him to assess a holistic range of human action across his local society to comprehend what was happening as war directly enveloped him in 1942. Fall incorporated such assessments across a wide range of socially based factors in his later scholarship, and these were further investigated with intensity and with a physical and mental capacity for work he later identified as his "machine."[16] This drive and tireless work ethic possibly served as a form of coping mechanism to withstand or persevere through personal anger and pain created by his family's betrayal to Nazi aggression by fellow Jews in France.

After Anna Fall's deportation in 1942, Bernard initially joined a Vichy youth paramilitary organization, *Les Compagnons de France*, to obscure his status as a foreign Jew. At this point, he also changed his given name from the Germanic "Berthold" to the more common Francophonic "Bernard"; after the war, he retained the B for "Berthold" as his middle initial.[17] Fall's spouse, Dorothy Fall, explained that he only joined *Les Compagnons de France* to obscure his participation in several other underground Zionist groups, including *Les Eclaireurs Israélites de France* (EIF), *Armée Juive*, and *Mouvement de la Jeunesse Sioniste*.[18] He later described his joining the *Compagnons* as a front for his association with other groups because it was a "plain boy scout movement in France, but at that time, even the boy scouts were political."[19] Despite being a member of these Zionist groups, according to Dorothy Fall, Bernard did not emphasize Jewish religiosity as a motivating factor for joining them. Still, it is likely that political, social, and religious divisions among the Jewish population in southern France, particularly between recent émigrés to France and French Jews, intensified his comprehension of social distinctions among Jewish communities. In many respects, Fall's willingness to engage with *Les Compagnons* as a protective front was a matter of applying intensified street smarts motivated by survival.[20]

Bernard Fall, sixteen at the time of the raid on their home in France, had lost his mother, and he would soon lose his father as well. In the summer of 1943, Leo Fall was transported to the *Hôpital Pasteur* after developing a hernia. In November 1943, he returned to a clinic after developing peritonitis. While Leo Fall was undergoing treatment on 27 November 1943, the Gestapo raided the clinic and beat and murdered him.[21] In a 1966 interview, Bernard claimed that "we found his body in a ditch with twelve other people ..."[22] At this point, Fall did not return to the cover *Les Compagnons de France* had provided him in 1942. In November 1943, he joined an organization called *Les Eclaireurs Israélites de France*, a Zionist organization forced underground after being outlawed earlier in 1943 by Vichy Commissioner for Jewish Affairs Louis Darquier de Pellepoix.[23] After his father's death, Fall and members of this organization who had found Leo Fall interred him in a cemetery in Cimiez, in northeast Nice, possibly the *Cimetière du Monastère*. Fall commented on this environment of partisan-associated violence, writing, "it's quite incredible for Americans to believe that people could live like that—but we did."[24] After his mother and father's death, Bernard's participation in the French Resistance intensified, and he would eventually join the Maquis in Haute-Savoie and the Free French Army.

As 1943 progressed, especially with his recognition that the Allies would eventually invade France after gaining footholds in North Africa and Sicily, Fall recognized that any alternatives other than resistance were grim. After losing their parents, his sister Lissette found protection in a convent in France, but Fall had few options aside from the Maquis. He could join the Resistance, or he could remain in Nice, where he would almost certainly be conscripted as a laborer and sent to Germany. As a young Jew, Fall would then either endure horrible work conditions at a munition factory in Essen or elsewhere in support of the Third Reich's war effort. The inevitable other option was either deportation, like his mother, or to be murdered as a suspected French Resistance member, like his father.

Fall's decision to join the Maquis was made with urgency because there was a significant increase in the conscription of laborers for deportation to work in Germany after February 1942. Initially, the Nazis' "Service for Obligatory Labor" mandated recruiting individuals born between 1920 and 1922 for labor in Germany. However, these age parameters expanded along with the Nazis' demand for armaments and soon included Fall's 1926 birth-year group.[25] Therefore, it was only a matter of time before he would face conscription, deportation, and forced labor. As a result, he decided to take his chances serving in the Maquis where, despite the fact that he would inevitably face combat, he had a greater chance of survival if the Allies successfully regained France.

Fall described his earlier attempt to join the Maquis on 8 November 1942, two months after his mother's deportation: "I was arrested by Italians with a group that had hijacked *La Penerf*, a French tanker, to join the Americans in North Africa after they had landed. Released (I was under 16 and the Italians were nice guys), I joined again and 'graduated' to the permanent maquis in Savoie."[26] The legitimacy ensuing from the commitment of what Fall regarded as "permanent" Maquis appeared fundamentally important to him.[27] However, the only clarification he offered was in using the term "graduated," by which he indicated that joining the Maquis in Haute-Savoie was a point of no return. This decision was irreversible because, if captured, he would undoubtedly face execution. After his father's death in November 1943, Fall therefore turned to the Maquis full-time, later commenting, "There were no recruiting posters offering me free travel and education while protecting my country; no recruiting sergeant in a shiny uniform had mirrored in front of me the wonderful opportunities that military service held … the Vichy government of Marshal Pétain had driven home the point that the Resistance was in Britain's pay and that Germany was not only invincible—the time was *before* Stalingrad and El-Alamein—but was the wave of the future."[28] The death of Fall's father and mother, the threat of his inevitable conscription for labor in Germany, and his lack of other options framed his decision to join the Maquis. As he wrote, "there were no recruiting posters for the Resistance." None were needed.

In contrast to his conflicting feelings regarding his Jewish identity, Fall recounted his subsequent participation in the secular French Resistance with pride, particularly his service in Haute-Savoie, claiming, "I was finally in a real Maquis."[29] During liberation, this experience and Fall's later participation in *Forces Françaises de l'Intérieur* (FFI) and the French army framed a crucial and defining period for his life. His French underground and army service undoubtedly provided a sense of legitimacy, or authenticity, among other service personnel in military matters. Moreover, participation in the Resistance demonstrated credibility and loyalty to the anti-Nazi cause in France and among Americans before and after V-E Day.[30] Unlike members of Vichy France's military in Indochina during World War II, let alone those in southern France, Fall did not have to carry political baggage filled with accusations of disloyalty to France and the other Allies. Most importantly, he incorporated the knowledge experiences he gained from his experiences and consolidated it into a foundation for subsequent research into social, political, and military interconnections in warfare.

Fall's efforts in the Resistance and among the Maquis in Haute-Savoie were an essential baseline in his professional life. Not surprisingly, he later cited this experience to legitimize his understanding of guerrilla warfare's core tactics, such as the virtues of ambush or falling back before adversaries could inflict superior firepower. Who could better understand guerrilla tactics than one who had been forced to use them against Nazi forces to survive? Fall's experiential learning consisted of a refined ability to identify different social dimensions and identities in conflicts in which civilian and military distinctions were often blurred, such as when the Maquis targeted civilians collaborating with German forces. Irregular forces, of which Fall was a member before joining the FFI and French army, provided him with a different perspective than what he would have otherwise gained through solely formal military service. He eventually gained a formal military assignment in the later stages of liberation, but Fall was never simply an infantryman, a marine, or a soldier. Indeed, he became a soldier. However, before he ever joined a formal military unit he was a German- and French-speaking amalgamation of Austrian émigré, persecuted Jew, and former paramilitary member of several Resistance groups, including one used to obscure his Jewish background. Ultimately, therefore, his military training piled onto a bitter series of experiences rooted in his life as a civilian, when he had initially confronted war and the betrayal of his family.

In a wartime reflection on his service in Haute-Savoie and how collaboration and betrayal factored into conflict, Fall added:

> In the Maquis region the civilians often suffered, for the Germans and the police slew hostages and burned villages to demonstrate that it was unwise to help guerrillas. Betrayal killed more men than actual combat in the years before the great battles. In the south, there were 2000 men (boys really) in the Maquis of the various Resistance organizations + 8000 "independents." For the most part, they lived miserably. From which it is evident that the Maquis had nothing. Nothing except the will to fight.[31]

This statement, written in April 1945, was one of the few documents Fall committed to paper during the war, and it revealed what he had experienced, even as the war entered its closing stages in Europe. Stathis Kalyvas' thoughts on the tangibility of willpower as an essential basis for survival in war add clarity to an immensely fraught process. In Kalyvas' view, "As violence becomes the 'main game in town,' survival becomes increasingly central for civilians. This is particularly true of peasants whose everyday attitude has been described with terms such as 'pragmatism,' 'fatalism,' or 'resilient adaptation.'"[32] Fall's scholarship, when considered in the contexts of conflict in which he matured as an individual and scholar, manifests many of the themes Kalyvas explores because they were problems Fall physically encountered.

Fall's participation in warfare as a guerrilla fighter was not only formative; in giving him an active part to play in the Resistance, it possibly mitigated the pain of losing his parents. According to Dorothy Fall, before his parents' death:

> Bernard was an ardent Zionist in those days, but by the end of the war his attitude would change, and he rejected his Jewish identity. One major reason for this was the willingness of the Jewish committee, the organization of Jewish elders who worked with the Vichy police, to give up the names of the refugee families in the Villa Beauregard to the police ... whatever justifications the Jewish elders might offer, he could never forgive such a betrayal.[33]

Perhaps more than any other, this event heightened Fall's sensitivity to manipulating and exploiting political and social distinctions that intensified war among civilian populations. When the factors of collaboration, betrayal, and denunciation intersected with the organized violence inflicted by powerfully equipped armed forces, violence in civil war was multiplied.

II—The Maquis

Two months before Fall attempted to join Allied forces in North Africa by boarding *La Penerf*, Nazi demands for labor escalated, requiring all French males between eighteen and fifty to register for work by 4 September 1942. These orders were a vast expansion of conscription built upon the "Service for Obligatory Labor" decree earlier in 1942. By February 1943, registered males between twenty-one and twenty-three were forced to register and were often compelled to work in support of the German war effort. An even more significant expansion of compulsory labor occurred in 1944 as males between sixteen and sixty as well as females between eighteen and forty-five were subject to compulsory labor in an agreement established between Marshall Pétain and Fritz Sauckel, the Plenipotentiary for the Employment of Labor for the Third Reich.[34] By 1944, therefore, it would have been almost impossible for Fall to avoid this expanding net for labor conscription. This totalitarian dragnet undoubtedly motivated Fall's decision to commit himself to the Maquis. After that, as he put it, "there was nothing except the endless tunnel."[35]

In Fall's case, resistance was a logical and pragmatic decision, as much or more than a patriotic indication of his anti-fascism.[36] As a young Jew, his decision to join the Resistance was also not an uncommon one. According to Robert Gildea, "Men and women of Jewish origin were an important part of the Resistance in France, fighting the war against Germany but also a 'war within the war' against both the Germans and Vichy to prevent their own

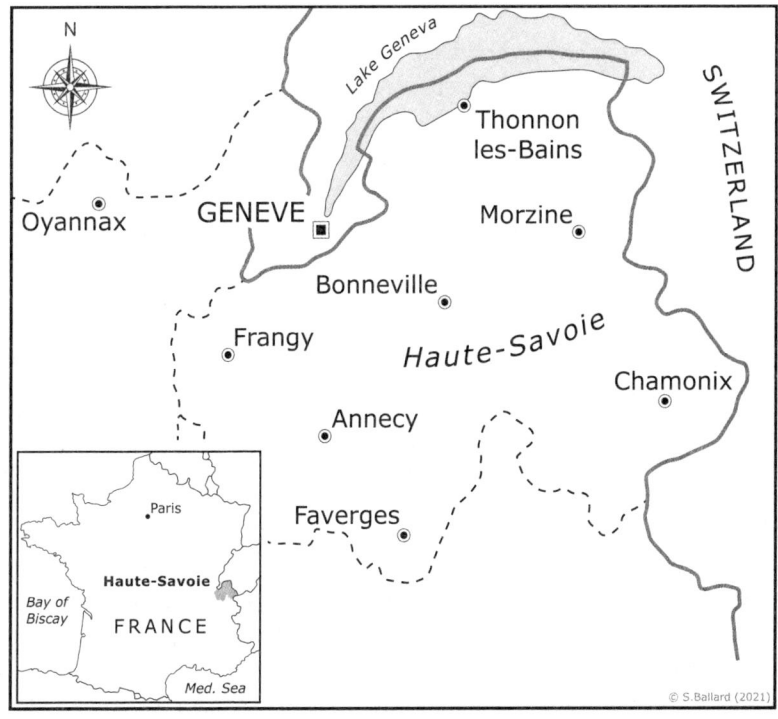

Map of Haute-Savoie

extermination."[37] Gildea claimed that these Jewish resisters constituted a historically marginalized and essential part of the diverse French Resistance. Fall's outsider status as an Austrian émigré, however, only added to his marginalization as a member of what Gildea perceived as an already-varied group resisting German occupation. Fall's status as a foreign Jew—which precipitated his family's denunciation by the French Jewish Council governing their kibbutz in southern France—strongly influenced his decision to join the Resistance after his mother's murder at Auschwitz and especially after the Gestapo murdered his father in November 1943.

In Gildea's view, Jewish Resistance members' agency and critical contributions against the Nazis were minimized and undervalued in scholarship on the subject because they conflicted with the massive victimization European Jews suffered. The memory of the Holocaust served as the predominant lens concerning Jewish individuals after World War II, whereas Jewish resistance was not a dominant narrative. Fall avoided describing his resistance as being Jewish in nature because his actions, like his father's, originated with his family's political denunciation by a Jewish Council. This betrayal, in Fall's eyes, repudiated what he might have earlier believed to be an assumed brotherhood of shared Jewish faith. As he likely quickly realized, however, he was only one of millions striving to survive in France and central Europe. Among Jews in the Baltics, Poland, Ukraine, Belarus, Romania, Bulgaria, and elsewhere further east, the chances of survival were generally far worse.[38]

After the Gestapo murdered his father in late 1943, Fall joined an alpine Maquis in Haute-Savoie and participated in combat in the Tarentaise Valley and Haute-Maurienne, one of the provinces of Savoy.[39] Fall fought at the mountain pass at Col de la Madeline in July and August 1944. At an elevation of almost 2,000 meters, Maquis groups and units of the *Forces Françaises de l'Intérieur* (FFI), along with French regular army units, joined to fight elements of the Wehrmacht.[40] Fall was valuable because he was bilingual in French and German, but also because he could ski.[41] Fall also appeared to extol the uncompromising commitment required among the Maquis, writing, "There was no such thing as living at home like a solid citizen and then going out to shoot up a few Germans and then go back home and stay camouflaged ... you actually fought all the way through."[42] His combat experience also occurred within an evolving political context in which the Maquis' outlaw status was in transition to a more conventional command structure under French FFI and French army leadership. On 4 September 1944, with the Allied armies' advance into Europe's interior, Fall transferred from the Maquis to join the FFI.[43]

Charles de Gaulle established the FFI in March 1944 to consolidate the Resistance, including clandestine units and the diverse Maquis, into the regular French military in anticipation of the Allied invasion in June.[44] In Fall's case, his experience of war in rugged terrain gave him firsthand insight regarding the importance of safe harbors and concealment in guerrilla warfare. Moreover, as noted, his French and German language capabilities and his ability to mountaineer and ski were additional positive assets.[45] In these crucial months during and after the Allied landing in Normandy and during the Allied operations in southern France and Italy, Fall contributed to the war effort in numerous ways. In one case during the autumn of 1944, Fall served as a guide for an officer of the Royal Canadian Artillery, possibly a Jedburgh team member. During this operation, Fall was wounded in his left leg and right arm by a grenade during an engagement with Nazi soldiers.[46]

Later in his life, it is unsurprising that he filtered his experiences of combat in ways that informed his scholarship. Fall retrospectively observed during his time in the Maquis that "Nobody had read Mao Tse-tung regarding political and physical training. Nobody had been to Fort Bragg and other Special Warfare Schools and the Americans from the OSS or the British from Special Operations Executive who parachuted in, weren't guerrilla leaders, but communications specialists or demolitions experts."[47] Fall's experience fighting guerrilla warfare in the late stages of World War II, unsurprisingly, was undiluted by Maoist influence, theory, or other doctrinaire concepts that informed irregular warfare. He had a raw basis of knowledge that was not ideologically oriented but driven instead by survival against a powerful adversary seeking to kill him and all his fellow Resistance members.

Fall's efforts fighting Nazis might have entailed a clear sense of purpose, but targeting civilian collaborators involved more complicated problems. Generally, rationales for killing collaborators ranged from "self-justifying to outright banditry and murder."[48] Collaboration and retribution became an even more severe issue after Fall's Maquis unit merged with regular French forces during liberation. Extrajudicial killings, and other vengeful acts, only intensified in the months after the war ended. By late spring 1945, after the Nazi defeat, approximately 10,000 individuals were killed in reprisals in France; in Italy, the number approached 20,000; in Yugoslavia, approximately 70,000 suspected collaborators were executed by partisans.[49]

During the liberation of France, and after his brief time with the FFI in September 1944, Fall was eventually assigned to the 1st French Army, led by General de Lattre de Tassigny, and then to the intelligence branch of the 27th Alpine Division because of his fluency in French and German. Subsequently, Fall transferred to the 4th Moroccan Mountain Division, 69th Pack Howitzer Regiment, as a mortar platoon leader and remained with this unit until demobilization on 19 March 1946.[50] Altogether, Fall's military experience transitioned through guerrilla warfare and independent units in the Maquis and FFI toward a more formal military structure that incorporated diverse personnel from France's empire, including North Africans and others in the 4th Moroccan Mountain Division. These formal military assignments undeniably supported Fall's credibility as a loyal son of France after the war. This was an important distinction, because Vichy's many and deep divisions continued to fester in French society for years after World War II. The same could not be said of those serving in Vichy units who, as a means toward rebuilding their careers after World War II, often deployed abroad with expeditionary forces to France's colonies.[51]

It is also essential to underscore how Fall chafed at military and political leaders who denigrated the irregular military contributions of groups such as the Maquis. Charles de Gaulle, whom Fall otherwise admired, described the Maquis "as composed chiefly of outlaws who had always to keep to the country. The only kind of warfare to be expected of them, therefore, was guerrilla warfare."[52] Fall was aware of De Gaulle's disparagement of "guerrilla bands" due to their perceived intractability. Some units could run wild, eliminating collaborators for reasons ranging from questionable necessity to outright vigilante justice. In de Gaulle's view, these guerrilla bands could only be effective if adequately controlled within the context of a professionally managed military command. De Gaulle's concern centered on ensuring unity of command within the French military when "at last—the landing of the armies came" on D-Day.[53]

Altogether, Fall's experience in the Maquis, FFI, and French regular army contributed to his understanding of the tension between irregular and conventional forces and the respective positive and negative capabilities and qualities each possessed. His perspective on cultural and bureaucratic differences within the French military and its allies also provided him with insight when organized armies' approaches to irregular warfare were in development. As exemplified in Europe by Jedburgh Teams, the "Devil's Brigade" of Canada's 1st Special Service Force, the British Special Operatives Executive (SOE), and the American Office of Strategic Services (OSS), these organizational innovations contributed to the war effort with a comparatively small footprint. They operated among civilian populations and belligerents alike, with a precision and focus that differed from conventional forces' undeniably more powerful and often less discriminating capacities.

Fall's awareness of condescension toward "guerrilla fighters" such as the Maquis by many French military leaders was an early and eye-opening insight into the realities of social constructions within military hierarchies. He appeared to learn quickly how cultural prejudices among services and units were not entirely unlike prejudice among civilian groups. He also recognized how balancing unity of command over irregular forces while granting them autonomy to conduct guerrilla-oriented operations was a serious challenge. Freedom to act provided opportunities, but such liberty could also become counterproductive in a larger operational planning sense and in complicated and worldwide conflicts. In the defeat of professional German forces, coordination and unity of effort mattered even more once conventional Allied forces gained a foothold in Europe. As historians invariably note, German forces were resilient and countered Allied advances unexpectedly, organized through advanced operational art and executed with intensity. Combat along the Gustav Line in Italy, let alone in other cases, demonstrated German capacity for counterattack.[54] In Fall's case, he came away from the war with a wide range of understanding that not only included an appreciation for conventional arms but also how irregular warfare contributed to the war effort.

On a larger social scale and as the war subsided, France's liberation marked the first time many Europeans encountered the culture of the United States, aside from in American films and music, through its troops. As Fall found them, Americans and the idea of America appeared as a revelation. In a 1966 interview, he described American music and how it epitomized a sense of optimism and freedom. The very liberation of France, Fall wrote, "to me is going to be forever just one vast orchestration of Glenn Miller."[55] In the same interview, Fall also described hearing "In the Mood" on a radio just before engaging in combat with the Germans in the winter of 1944, and, upon returning to his original position three hours later, he recalled hearing it still playing, "presumably after X-many station breaks ... this is exactly why it became really engraved in me."[56] "In the Mood," it appears, was the perfect metaphor for opportunities that American liberation seemed to promise. For many young Europeans, obviously including Fall, Glenn Miller's music hinted at an American-led future that looked immensely favorable in the light of the massive destruction he saw all around him in France. While Fall was fortunate to become naturalized as a French citizen because of his French military service, his subsequent engagement with American forces in postwar Europe demonstrated that his eyes were already on the west beyond the Atlantic.[57]

As the war concluded, Fall possibly envisioned America as a canvas onto which he could project his conflicted identity and recast himself. America's promotion of liberty was an opportunity for spiritual reclamation, perhaps, but it provided potential material opportunities as well. On a more day-to-day level, while Fall considered his taste in music as "a very happy lowbrow," Glenn Miller's music "so much represented the Americans in the confident, rich, lovable characters. You know, this was not an army of professionals—these were the American citizens—the guy on the street—the New York taxi driver—this was to us the first Americans whom we ever saw in our lives."[58] After he had disengaged from his Austrian upbringing and discarded what remained of his diminishing Jewishness, America offered Bernard Fall an opportunity for reinvention. Like millions of others, he saw the United States as a country that offered individuals an outlet to rebuild themselves as much as it offered material and financial resources to rebuild Europe.

After Fall's demobilization from the French army in 1946, he eventually received the *Médaille de la France Libérée*, and the medal validated his veteran status.⁵⁹ Importantly, it also verified his non-collaborationist credentials. In contrast to Vichy supporters who "claimed to have worked for the French Resistance" but could not prove their loyalty, Fall's award not only confirmed his allegiance to the anti-Nazi cause but also provided other benefits, including access to French military archives and other resources.⁶⁰ Fall's interest in pursuing his post-*lycée* education meant that these latter benefits were potentially handy, and he built upon his military experiences by beginning formal academic studies directly after the war. However, there was much for Fall to reconcile before commencing classwork at a university as a young veteran rejoining civilian society.

Consequences from the war, such as the targeting and destruction of civilian populations, shaped his outlook on the rules and politics of warfare. To fully understand his later views on revolutionary warfare, it is crucial to consider briefly Fall's perspective on killing. How did Fall's approach to warfare, particularly among civilian populations, qualify his understanding of the moral validity or legitimacy of violence? When was killing justified? During his experience in the Maquis, when, if ever, was violence justifiable against collaborators? Fall likely recognized that collaboration was often the only option many individuals possessed. According to István Deák:

> working for and thus "collaborating" with the Germans offered the only—mistaken—hope of survival for the members of the Jewish council, the Jewish ghetto police, and the ordinary Jewish workers ... critics of Jewish behavior overlooked the fact that a person under a death sentence could not uphold the same lofty moral standards as those who could choose between dying and not dying.⁶¹

Fall would have recognized distinctions among collaborators when there was freedom of choice to collaborate. In other cases, fear of harm or death compelled them to denounce fellow Jews or others. Civilian collaboration was an immense and critical issue for the Maquis and, more broadly, those resisting Germany's occupation of France. According to historian Robert Paxton, collaboration was especially critical in France because the French civilian population was "more collaborationist than resistant." In Paxton's view, this was an indictment against France that differed from other countries because "Vichy France was the only Western European country under Nazi occupation that enacted its own measures against Jews."⁶² More than in other occupied countries, therefore, and because of French complicity in the denunciation of foreign Jews seeking refuge, collaboration in France was deeply problematic. As Paxton indicates, the problem of collaboration added a consequential and violent dynamic to Europe's civil strife during World War II. Yet, in France, collaboration created additional and turbulent social undercurrents during liberation and far into its postwar history. As a result, Bernard Fall was situated in the center of an intensely and violently fraught society torn apart by civil conflict and anti-Semitism that only unraveled further in the context of World War.

In the case of the Maquis, a more clear-cut distinction was sought so that they might cast themselves as purely anti-Nazi and as a capable military-oriented unit. The Maquis actually expended significant effort in propaganda among the French populace "to show the population that the maquis were not the rabble of foreign bandits portrayed by Vichy propaganda" and that their operations against Germans and French traitors "were carried through with a military control and precision."[63] This message was symbolically conveyed, for example, in operations conducted in the village of Oyonnax, located in the region of Auvergne-Rhône-Alpes. In Oyonnax, the Maquis emerged as a consciously designed symbol of power when they defeated elements of the German army in the village in November 1943, the same month Fall's father was murdered by the Gestapo. French citizens in Oyonnax provided a dose of moral clarity regarding the Maquis' actions against the Germans and in punishing collaborators helping the Third Reich.[64] Oyonnax, in many respects, deservedly epitomized patriotism and resistance and served as a symbol for a type of purified French resilience against Nazi aggression.

In contrast to the clarity that anti-Nazi resistance in Oyonnax demonstrated, the issue of collaboration was significant during and after the war, and not just because of the moral questions it raised, but because of the prevalence of collaboration in French society. Robert Paxton and other scholars have demonstrated that collaboration seriously divided France with lasting effects that extended to France's colonies overseas, as well.[65] It is unsurprising that, after the war, Gaullists and other Free French military elements looked unfavorably, even critically, toward military personnel who served under the Vichy administration, whether in southern France or places like Indochina. Many officers who later influenced the French military's ideas on irregular warfare—such as Charles Lacheroy and Roger Trinquier, for example—served in Vichy-controlled military elements during World War II. Therefore, these individuals' past political allegiance to Vichy was of significance in France's postwar reoccupation of colonies lost to Axis forces during World War II, especially in Southeast Asia. Roger Trinquier, a figure who became more widely known as a result of France's operations in Algeria after 1954, served as a captain in Vichy forces during World War II, and Fall was well aware of this background. Trinquier, in one respect, was precisely the type of officer whom Fall would have fought against during France's liberation had Trinquier's Vichy outfit engaged with Fall's Maquis in Haute-Savoie.

After 1945, it was not uncommon to find former Vichy soldiers serving in French expeditionary forces in colonial theaters, such as Madagascar, Indochina, and elsewhere in Africa. Such personnel's past questionable loyalties were especially problematic in light of former Waffen SS soldiers who also served in Indochina as members of the French Foreign Legion.[66] It is inaccurate to claim that professional ostracization stemming from Vichy-associated service during World War II applied to all. However, it did exist and was an added dimension that complicated France's postwar efforts in its colonies and protectorates after World War II. Indeed, there were cases where soldiers specifically chose to serve abroad to salvage their military career, absolve themselves of past Vichy association, or clear social stains from alleged collaboration with Vichy and Nazi authorities.[67] Problems associated with collaboration, however, were lasting and difficult to untangle. Unlike Resistance efforts in villages like Oyonnax, targeting collaborators in France often failed to achieve precise and unambiguous righteousness: conflict stemming from collaboration would cast a long shadow over postwar France.

III—The Problem of Collaboration

The French Resistance's targeting of French collaborators created significant social problems in the later stages of the war as German forces, who had previously protected individuals who collaborated with them, surrendered or retreated. Stathis Kaylvas' analysis indicates that retaliation is part of the political economy of violence when constraints against retaliation are loosened or nonexistent.[68] The removal of constraints restricting revenge against collaborators, therefore, creates conditions for violent reaction—almost as a replication of Newton's Third Law of action and reaction—to perpetuate a cycle of violence. Horrifically during the war's conclusion the violence of revenge was not theoretical among French Resistance members, who targeted Nazi and Vichy collaborators. The subject of retaliation undoubtedly informed Fall's views on the perceived legitimacy of violence—or its illegality—in the conduct of warfare among civilian populations during and after World War II. At what point, after all, was war officially over? As Mary L. Dudiak has argued, wars do not always legally end with the signing of terms of surrender. In the case of the European war, Dudiak points out, "even as late as 1951, 'as a legal matter,' the nation [the United States] was still in a state of war against Germany. Truman didn't call for an end to this state of war until July 1951, but also stressed that this would not affect the occupation of Germany."[69] Targeting collaborators, whether the war was still on or not, raised other questions. Were civilians legitimate targets for retribution if they betrayed fellow citizens instead of information about military units? What about cases in which individuals denounced others to protect family members? Were there exceptions where collaborators deserved mercy? Context, social history, and personal relationships among local societies certainly factored in as well. So did ethnic considerations when a larger community or group was accused of collaboration.

Fall certainly encountered some of the complex problems related to political violence that retribution revealed, even when retaliation was potentially perceived as legitimate. The dynamics of violence found in denunciation, collaboration, and retaliation simultaneously indicate forms of selective violence, and this is a logic of violence that is emotional, cultural, and often but not necessarily ideological. Petty jealousies, for example, could factor into targeting local competitors, and this base characteristic prevalent in all societies does not require a specific ideology.

What is worth drawing attention to here, because of its relevance to Fall's later analysis of Vietnamese revolutionary warfare, is the subject of legitimacy in political violence. In the case of violence regarding collaboration, perceived legitimacy in targeting was a key issue related to retaliation. Without specific evidence of betrayal, for example, follow-on cycles of retribution and violence ensued to form a spiraling of violence at local levels.[70] This subject, in which civil violence could spiral out of control, was essential to Fall because perceived legitimacy determined whether targeting effectively separated the population from the enemy or if it would drive the population away, along with their critically needed support. If the Maquis' targeting of locals accused of collaboration was perceived as illegitimate, for example, or mistakes in identifying and targeting occurred, serious consequences could emerge that would create far more problems and more enemies. If the Maquis or other groups in the French Resistance sought to gain support while also eliminating Nazi sympathizers or collaborators, extreme caution had to be exercised in targeting individuals who were known or perceived by widespread consensus as guilty. Unsurprisingly, targeting collaborators was suffused with revenge motives of all kinds that blended into an unstable mix of rational and irrational decision-making.

Retribution against collaborators is challenging to delineate, since its relationship to governmental policies is ambiguous and it was not executed with the objectivity characteristic of military operations. Fall's understanding of legitimacy on this matter, and his recognition that legitimacy required verification of collaboration, depended on shared social, political, ethnic, and cultural conceptions of legitimacy among the French Resistance. Unquestionably, there were cases at one end of a spectrum in which vigilante justice against collaborators occurred without debate. Ultimately, like his familiarity with guerrilla warfare that added to his more conventional military experiences, his awareness of this social cycle of violence during World War II added to a growing and holistic comprehension of war.

World War II did not, of course, present simple binary distinctions between enemy combatants. All of European society was affected to different degrees, to be sure, yet the war included intentional targeting of civilians on a massive scale. In addition to violence inflicted by armies, as noted earlier, the issue of collaboration was extensive. Fall conducted research in 1961 on collaboration and noted that the French Resistance killed approximately 40,000 French pro-Nazi collaborators.[71] This number vastly exceeds Robert Paxton's 1997 account. Paxton determined that 9,000 suspected collaborators were summarily executed during the liberation, 1,500 collaborators executed after trial, and over 40,000 individuals received prison sentences.[72] While markedly different in their statistics of collaborators killed, Fall and Paxton's numbers are considerable and indicate the extent of collaboration. Vichy's moral drama and the crisis of collaboration raised questions that vexed Fall beyond World War II. Historian David Bell's analysis of the persistence of problems Vichy raised demonstrates that there are no complete answers to explain why so many French collaborated with Hitler, or why they rallied "so quickly to a regime pledged to an ultra-right ideology that had never prevailed at the polls."[73] Fall, it is certain, pondered similar questions, and the problem of collaboration seeped into his later writing in illuminating ways. In one case, Fall may have vicariously avenged his parents' deaths by writing a factual account of the vigilante justice enacted by Eliahu Ztzkovitz, published in his 1961 book, *Street Without Joy*.

Fall rarely commented on his own family, but his short history of this young Romanian Jew during World War II, who also lost his family to Nazi persecution, suggested Fall held an intense empathy with Ztzkovitz. Fall's account began with the Ztzkovitz's family's murder in a concentration camp during World War II in Eastern Romania by another Romanian, a "coldly efficient SS-type" named Stanescu.[74] An adolescent at the time, Eliahu had not been detained at the camp with his family and only learned of his family's death later. After swearing that "he would kill the man, Stanescu, if it took his whole life to do it," Eliahu Ztzkovitz found and killed Stanescu's son in 1947, was arrested and convicted, and then served five years in a reformatory for juveniles. Ztzkovitz then emigrated to Israel, where he served as a paratrooper in the Israeli army.

During his time in the Israeli army, Ztzkovitz learned from other Romanian émigrés that Stanescu had joined the French Foreign Legion and was in Indochina. Ztzkovitz decided to pursue Stanescu and, as a means of gaining access to him in Indochina without raising alarms, planned to join the French Foreign Legion. To facilitate this, Ztzkovitz transferred to the Israeli Navy, went absent without leave while on shore leave in Genoa and, in Fall's words, "crossed over to Menton, France, without the slightest difficulty. Three days later, Eliahu had signed his enlistment papers in Marseilles and was en route to Sid-bel-Abbès for service in the Foreign Legion." He eventually found Stanescu in Vietnam near Bac Ninh. Fall recounted the moment of confrontation between them, writing that Ztzkovitz stated to his family's murderer: "'Stanescu, I'm one of the Jews from Chisinau,' and emptied the clip of his MAT-49 tommy gun into the man's chest. He dragged the body back to the road: a Legionnaire never left a comrade behind." Fall did not avenge his parents by finding and punishing those who had denounced his family at the Villa Beauregard in Nice, France, let alone those who had murdered his mother and father. However, it is almost impossible to believe that he did not profoundly identify with Eliahu Ztzkovitz's motivation or mission. Fall's recounting of Ztzkovitz, years after his own parents' murders, possibly demonstrates an enmity and sorrow that never diminished. It also stands out in Fall's writing, not because it described a remarkable dedication to revenge, but because it disclosed his possible thoughts regarding his parents' deaths.

Fall's account of Ztzkovitz's targeting of Stanescu was not unique. Enzo Traverso described a similar historical case that involved Oskar Dirlewanger, a Nazi responsible for the murder of thousands of civilians in Russia and Poland early in the war. According to Traverso, Dirlewanger had woven a path of destruction as a member of the German Freikorps after 1918, and served in the Condor Legion. This group, the Condor Legion, was formed from the Nazis' air force and army who served with Nationalists during the Spanish Civil War from 1936 to 1939.[75] After the war, Dirlewanger was identified by a former concentration camp survivor, captured, and allegedly killed by former deportees. In an analysis which Fall would likely have approved, Traverso concluded that "In a war where risks were limitless, it was inevitable that partisans, who had suffered the most savage repression, should be in the front line of the epuration that settled accounts at the end of the war."[76] Neither Fall nor Ztzkovitz were alone in their desire for revenge. It was endemic to war.

Fall felt strongly about moral and legal limits separating belligerents and civilians in conflict. He may have conceived of war, perhaps as a youth, as that which only involved soldiers. However, the reality of World War II and the proliferation of often indiscriminate aerial bombing proved how shielding civilians from conflict was impossible. Moreover, the Nazis specifically targeted civilians because it was Nazi policy. Fall commented on the need for rules of warfare to contain violence against civilians, writing, "I'm not a pacifist, I'm sorry. I fought four years against the Germans and don't regret it one damn bit, so I can't stand here and say I condemn war as such. But I condemn the hurting of innocent and disabled people."[77] Determining innocence when it related to targeting collaborators or in pursuing revenge, however, was problematic because collaborationists' efforts were often intentionally obscured to avoid reprisal.

There is no evidence to suggest that Fall was personally involved with targeting collaborators, but his writings reveal a deep awareness of this problem in war, and it had a bearing on his later analysis of conflict in Southeast Asia. Moreover, as an individual who turned eighteen years of age in November 1944, it is unlikely that Fall was in a position to direct operations, let alone decide such matters as determining collaborators' guilt or innocence. In his writing and reflections on this subject, Fall did not portray Ztzkovitz as a hero. Instead, he only demonstrated Ztzkovitz's commitment to avenge his family, which included murdering Stanescu's son as well as Stanescu himself. In writing about violence against civilians and collaborators, Fall emphasized a principle regarded in current military law as "distinction." Distinction includes proportionality, honor, military necessity, and humanity, and it is used to describe legal differences between civilians, noncombatants, and combatants in conflict.[78] Fall's choice to focus on this concept likely originated with his innate decency and ability to empathize with others in a way that was possibly intensified through the loss of his family. Fall could empathize with Ztzkovitz, but perhaps not to the extent of becoming or acting like him.

The spiraling of violence that undoubtedly troubled Fall emerged from a dehumanizing process consisting of progressive desensitization, conditioning, and denial of defense mechanisms. These steps remain central to inflicting violence against innocent victims, and this process, termed "manufactured contempt," includes a purposeful psychological denial of and contempt for a victim's humanity.[79] This process invariably undermines the potential containment of violence enacted through laws and rules in the conduct of warfare. According to a study on the psychological effects of killing humans, manufactured contempt destroys efforts to mitigate violence, mainly when directed against vulnerable populations. This removal of limits to violence occurs whether contempt is manufactured through inciting revenge, through manipulating racial and ethnic prejudice, or through other exploitation of a population's potential proclivity toward violence.[80] Fall's statement condemning actions "hurting disabled and innocent people" indicated that he viewed distinction in the conduct of warfare as a fundamental condition holding humans to account for their actions, whereas targeting innocent humans was intentionally, and thus criminally, negligent.

These views are critical to consider in light of Fall's subsequent study of laws concerning warfare, a subject with which he became intimately familiar after World War II as a research analyst for the War Crimes Commission during the Nuremberg Trials. His views on distinctions between innocent civilians, confirmed collaborationists, and combatants evolved, but they undeniably originated in his service during World War II. His views gained further complexity through extensive study as a research analyst during the Nuremberg Trials after 1946.[81] When he later described his position on distinction after 1965, he concluded: "If total disregard of signed treaties is allowed to continue, then the Vietnam war will degenerate to an ignominious level of savagery far below that experienced in other wars since World War II." He added, "to me, the real moral problem which arises in Vietnam is that of torture and needless brutality to combatants and civilians alike."[82] Fall's humanitarianism is a critical component of his scholarship, its roots based on his experiences during World War II and the losses he endured as an adolescent.

Collaboration engendered a cycle of violence that was difficult to contain, yet Fall also recognized how cycles of violence could be manipulated to achieve specific goals. He explained how targeting collaborators was "a key activity of a guerrilla movement with cross-influences on undermining enemy morale and discipline" and that "guerrilla discipline is harsh in two fields: unit security and relations with civilian populations."[83] He built on this in a 1966 lecture in which he described the strategic effects of targeting collaborators in more detail.

> At first, the Maquis tried to kill German sentries, German soldiers. It seemed terribly heroic in the beginning. But the Germans would take fifty hostages and

execute them for each killed German soldier, which was unproductive in terms of kill ratios. The French population was tired of bearing the brunt of their guerrilla activities. That worked against the guerrilla. So finally, in 1943, by trial and error, they switched to killing French collaborationists. There was a triple advantage to that: (a) the French collaborationist would not be armed, which helped, (b) the French Vichy rarely would take hostages in reprisal for the killing of a collaborationist, (c) for every collaborationist killed, there would be another five thousand Frenchmen who wouldn't give the time of day to the German Army henceforth.[84]

Rather than targeting stronger German occupation forces, eliminating guilty collaborators was a tactic, but it required specificity and distinction to produce effects in the Resistance's favor. When guerrillas gained the local population's support through accurate targeting of proven collaborators, it consolidated and vindicated action against individuals assisting German soldiers. The legitimate targeting of collaborators, Fall wrote, "was the kind of deterrent effect we were actually looking for, the kind that would isolate the German troops from the population, in fact insulate them. There would be complete loss of contact with the population without creating any kind of adverse reaction toward us."[85] This statement, and how targeting collaborators "insulated" the German troops from the population, revealed an essential element in Fall's analysis of wars in which civilian support is critical. He later referred to this form of social insulation as part of a process of "competitive control" among populations in Southeast Asia. This indirect approach, through which insulation was generated between German troops and citizens, required deep knowledge of the local context and the participants involved. This was a simple but important lesson Fall learned to identify during World War II.

Fall described this "insulating" approach to conflict, writing, "any sound revolutionary warfare operator (the French underground, the Norwegian underground, or any other European anti-Nazi underground) most of the time used small-war tactics, not to destroy the German Army, of which they were thoroughly incapable, but to establish a competitive system of control over the population."[86] Insulating German forces from civilian-resourced intelligence, for example, was a step in the process. This competitive system of control was not about conventional military capability. It was about controlling a society politically through coercion and gaining widespread popular support in the face of powerful military opponents.

After liberation in 1945, Fall gained even more perspective on war among civilians following his discharge from the French military. At the age of nine-

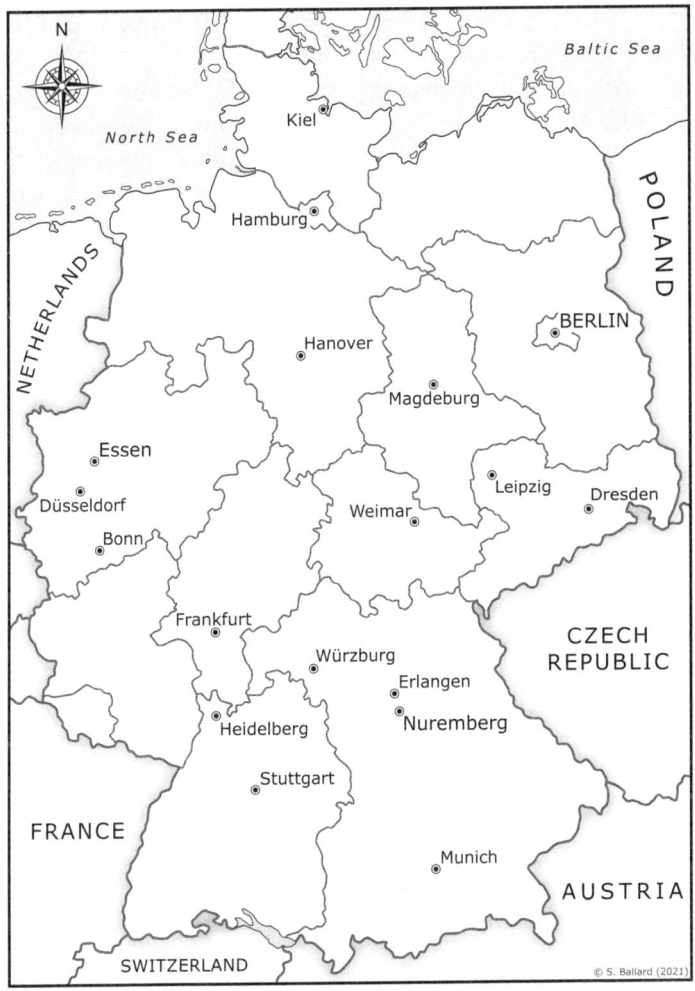

Map of Germany

teen, he began work researching Nazi aggression as a translator and then as a research analyst for the War Crimes Commission at the International Tribunal held in Nuremberg, Germany, between 1946 and 1948.[87] His employment as a translator, research analyst, and individual witnessing the Nuremberg Tribunals gave him time to reflect upon his wartime experience and the consequences of World War II upon civilians. It also provided him, primarily through his work as a research analyst, with an intense education in collecting, analyzing, and organizing evidence to support the prosecution staff in preparing their cases against Nazi leaders and organizations.

Fall's employment at this important point in the development of international justice formed a bridge between his subjective war experience and his future in developing objective research of war. Additionally, his presence at the Nuremberg Trials gave him a series of historical lessons and a vantage point to learn how the Nazis gained control of the Weimar Republic, manipulated its constitution to gain control of Germany, and then unleashed a cycle of violence in Europe. At Nuremberg, the international prosecution against German leaders began in 1946 with a description of what US prosecutor Robert H. Jackson called "the crime of crimes" that had destroyed Europe and so many of its inhabitants.[88]

IV—Nuremberg

Fall's contribution to the prosecution of Nazi war criminals during the Nuremberg Trials decisively shaped his understanding of war. His official title was "research analyst on the staff of the office of the Chief of Counsel for War Crimes," and he gained this position after working for the French delegation as a translator between April and September 1946.[89] The position enabled Fall to integrate his language skills in French, German, and English—he had acquired something of an American accent toward the end of the war—with an expanding ability to research warfare supporting the Tribunals' goals in establishing international justice. He shared these goals with the Chiefs of Counsel for War Crimes at the first and second series of trials, Associate US Supreme Court Justice Robert H. Jackson and US Army Brigadier General Telford Taylor, respectively.

Fall's promotion to the US research staff came about due to his previous hard work. According to Max Punch, the section chief for the French delegation who recommended Fall for the research position, "Bernard Fall is a serious and competent translator who works with assiduous effort. His perfect knowledge of German, which he speaks as a native language, makes him a valuable staff member."[90] As an Austrian émigré and naturalized French citizen—a reward for his service during the war—Fall's wartime experience had been a difficult road. In building on his abilities, however, he had transitioned to a position that required him to conduct field research throughout Germany in support of the Nuremberg Tribunals.

The Tribunals themselves were divided into two groups of proceedings. The first set—which began on 20 November 1945 and included French, Soviet,

British, and American judges—tried some of the most infamous Nazi leaders and was known as the International Military Tribunal (IMT).[91] The second series of trials was known as the Nuremberg Military Tribunal (NMT), and it commenced in December 1946 and concluded in April 1948. The specific case Fall researched during the NMT was against the Krupp Corporation, its activities supplying the German Wehrmacht with military arms, especially the Krupp Corporation's conscription and exploitation of slave labor.[92] As an observer during the first Tribunal, which judged the highest levels of Nazi leadership, he had a unique vantage on the overall series of Nuremberg Trials. That Fall attended the trials, let alone contributed to their prosecution, was remarkable: few young Jews who had lost their parents to Nazi persecution were physically present to witness the prosecution of Nazi leaders such as Herman Göring, Rudolf Hess, Albert Speer, Fritz Sauckel, and others.

The charter guiding the Nuremberg Trials was officially titled "The Charter of the International Military Tribunal—Annex to the Agreement for the prosecution and punishment of the European Axis' major war criminals."[93] US President Harry S. Truman appointed Associate Supreme Court Justice Robert H. Jackson to lead the American prosecution during the first International Tribunal. Telford Taylor, who had assisted Jackson and was promoted to Brigadier General in the US army and Chief of Counsel in October 1946, led the American prosecution team during the Nuremberg Military Tribunal.[94] Jackson, a former attorney general during Franklin D. Roosevelt's administration and Roosevelt's appointee to the Supreme Court, was critical in advocating that the prosecution's charges against Nazi leadership include criminal conspiracy.[95] The indictment of conspiracy was a critical distinction because the determination to try the cases as criminal acts, rather than acts of war, fundamentally changed international jurisprudence relating to war.[96] According to the Chairman of the United Nations War Crimes Commission, Lord Robert Wright, the goal was as lofty as seeking to change human nature or its basest elements.[97] Wright believed the world might gain improved and enforceable legal frameworks concerning restraining warfare from the Nuremberg Principles. However, he also believed more idealistically that "law by itself is not enough, unless it voices, and is inspired by, a change of heart among the nations, an active sense of justice, charity, and humanity."[98]

Wright's hope was commendable, but it did not offer the type of brutal realism needed to address Nazi atrocities in a way commensurate with the suffering of millions. The more concrete justice promised by the Tribunal's potential judgments moved closer to reality with the signing of the charter for the United Nations at the San Francisco conference on 26 June 1945, and the subsequent Nuremberg Charter, which was signed a little more than a month later on 8 August.[99] In turn, on 10 December 1948, "the United Nations recognized the Nuremberg Principles when the General Assembly adopted the Universal Declaration of Human Rights."[100] The Nuremberg Principles were thus always closely integrated with the UN Charter and UN Declaration of Human Rights: the legal origins of our contemporary understanding of human rights, in other words, share a compelling basis in the reestablishment of International Law at Nuremberg, as much as they do in the UN Declaration of Human Rights.

The idealism these rights inspired, however, was not entirely pure or unanimous. Despite the lofty goals the Nuremberg Principles inspired, the International Military Tribunal did not coalesce into a unified and ironclad agreement on legal principles regarding war crimes. Soviet involvement was critical, but Soviet participation also complicated an already complex basis for prosecution because of the Soviet Union's Molotov-Ribbentrop Pact, its brutality in Poland, and Soviet judges' role during Stalin's show trials preceding World War II. Francine Hirsch's scholarship revealed that, instead of an articulate conception of justice with a direct lineage to the Enlightenment or another human ideal, the International Military Tribunal was riven with disagreements, ambivalence, and compromises over what constituted justice.[101] Suffice it to say, these disagreements might have been difficult to parse among the rank and file working as researchers. Fall did not reference such disagreements in his papers, but they existed, as Hirsch indicates with ample evidence.

At the level Fall experienced them, how did the War Crimes Commission and the Nuremberg Tribunals inform his views on warfare and law related to war? Before discussing the trials' format in broader terms, and how the first and second series of trials differed in more detail, it is helpful to indicate a few core elements that shaped Fall's views on laws meant to regulate war. First, he learned about legal precedent concerning the distinction between combatants, collaborators, and civilians from the prosecution staff and General Telford Taylor, the Nuremberg Military Tribunals' chief prosecutor for whom Fall worked. While this Military Tribunal was technically the "second" set among the overall trials held, it also focused on issues, such as conspiracy and other problems, that were at the core of all prosecution efforts. Nazi Germany's corruption of laws of warfare, related to the principle of distinction and others, were violations Fall personally experienced. Distinguishing between soldiers and civilians, for example, was not an ambiguous matter: German soldiers' execution of 50 to 100 civilian hostages for every German soldier killed by partisans constituted war crimes. These punitive acts of retribution against noncombatants were illegal, and rules meant to punish military personnel's conduct were supposed to be in place and enforced by German military commanders. Collaborators' actions and the Resistance's retribution against those actions, however, and as indicated earlier, darkly clouded these distinctions, as Fall well knew.

In the case of German soldiers punishing civilians in response to the actions of partisans in the French Resistance, regulations against such actions were intentionally removed by the German high command.[102] The only legal exception to the removal of such regulations, according to Taylor, was in the unlikely case that "it was necessary for the discipline or security of the German forces."[103] In reality, restrictions prohibiting the targeting of noncombatant civilians were nonexistent, no matter what the civilian population did. Taylor was concerned about the Germans' removal of rules—which legally prevented the targeting of noncombatant civilians—because such actions specifically demonstrated conspiracy, implicating the German high command. In the sense of planned and organized criminal action, conspiracy was essential to prove because it was the basis for demonstrating criminal intent. Taylor remarked, therefore, that not only did targeting noncombatant civilians indicate of conspiracy, but that the Nazi annexations were also historically unique. As he explained in *Nuremberg and Vietnam: An American Tragedy*,

> The conduct disclosed at Nuremberg did not disclose new types of crime; murder, maiming, enslavement, ravage, and plunder are a familiar litany. What was unique about the Nazi conquests, especially in eastern Europe, was the enormous scope of the atrocities, and the systematic planning and meticulous execution of these hideous enterprises.[104]

Proving that concerted planning occurred, in terms of the prosecution of Nazi war crimes, remained central to Nuremberg's legal cases overall, especially concerning crimes that included targeting civilian populations. Differences between soldiers and civilians, according to Taylor, "together with the soldier's obligation to respect the rights of noncombatant civilians of enemy countries, remains to this day ... a vital part of the structure and content of the laws of war."[105] These were the types of lessons that critically informed Fall's views on warfare, especially since Taylor's arguments concerning protecting civilians related directly to the circumstances Fall's family suffered during the war. Taylor's points were also relevant to Fall's experience in the Maquis because of the prevalence of collaboration in French society. Fall learned that, to target collaborators legally, one had to affirm their status as a combatant. Ultimately, horrific waves of violence during World War II washed over distinctions between civilians and combatants. The point of the Nuremberg Tribunals was to reestablish the anchors mooring legal principles—such as distinguishing between civilians and combatants, among other principles—and to embed those principles in International Law.

The Maquis were combatants, but their attempt to blend into civilian populations increased civilians' vulnerability because Nazi German forces disregarded restrictions against targeting civilians. The irregular nature of the Maquis' efforts, which implicated innocent civilians who supported them by association, may have been another contribution to Charles de Gaulle's rationale for pulling the Maquis into his orbit of command and control. At their foundation, therefore, the Nuremberg Tribunals clarified civilians' rights and bolstered the development of human rights as a legally defensible concept in times of war.[106] It is not a coincidence that the London conference (held 26 June 26–2 August 1945)—which established the "London Agreement and the Charter of the International Military Tribunal" prosecuted at Nuremberg—directly followed the San Francisco conference (held 25 April–26 June 1945) establishing the United Nations Charter. Telford Taylor described the relationship between the two conferences in this way: "Different as the twins were, they shared the same two basic purposes: promoting peaceful rather than warlike settlement of international disputes, and humanitarian governmental policies."[107]

In terms of their overall effect on International Law, the trials were significant because they revealed the scale of Nazi criminality and illuminated earlier attempts to establish prohibitions limiting war. When World War I began in August 1914, no existing international law made an individual or state liable to criminal charges for declaring and engaging in war.[108] For example, at the individual level, the murder of civilians attempting to assist soldiers trapped behind enemy lines did not count as a war crime. In a well-known case at the time, Edith Cavell, a British citizen who served as a director of a nurses' training school in Belgium, was executed by German forces in October 1914 for her work in an "underground railroad" to help Allied soldiers avoid capture.[109] This case caused outrage in Britain because, under the Hague Convention of 1907, her execution was not codified as a war crime. For Londoners, this was a grave affront, and anger regarding Cavell's execution was exacerbated when zeppelin raids targeted civilians in the British capital. In Taylor's words:

The zeppelin raids ushered in the era of urban bombardment from the air, but violated no law of war—the Hague Conventions on land warfare forbade the bombardment of undefended cities, but London was not undefended; the separate 1907 Hague Convention prohibiting the discharge of explosives from "balloons, or by other new methods of a similar nature" was not in force, as neither Germany nor France had signed it.[110]

Despite efforts to clarify laws of war, an apparently endless amount of work remained for others to accomplish in post-World War I Europe. The 1919 Paris conference, as a prominent step toward improving laws regulating war, instigated the "Commission on the Responsibility of the Authors of the War and the Enforcement of Penalties."[111] This commission was created to investigate the Kaiser's accountability. The commission, however, eventually determined that, despite the Central Powers' guilt initiating a war of aggression, "this conduct did not provide the basis for a criminal charge under existing international law: it should, however, be strongly condemned and made a penal offense for the future."[112] World War II would make a mockery of this type of unenforceable righteousness.

The lack of any teeth to prevent such "penal offense for the future" indicated the weaknesses inherent to the Treaty of Versailles' articles. The former Allied Powers were unwilling to enforce them as they were subsequently whittled away after 1919. The commission's judgment, in short, did not indicate any call for enforcing terms established at the 1919 Paris conference. Instead, the commission's statement reflected only their willingness to kick the can of international frameworks—regarding the law of war—down the road until it finally reached Nuremberg in 1946. As part of his research duties into the historical background for relevant precedents, Fall documented the progression of the 1919 commission's work through a thirty-six-page report entitled "*Trois Rapports sur l'Armement et la Cavalerie du IIIe Reich*" ("Three Reports on the Armament and Cavalry of the Third Reich"). In the study, he focused on Germany's illegal rearmament after World War I, which violated numerous articles from the Treaty of Versailles.[113]

Fall was aware that the 1928 Treaty of Paris, from which the Kellogg-Briand Pact emerged, also provided a basis for a key argument made by the International Military Tribunal. This argument countered Nazi lawyers' criticisms that *ex post facto* justice—establishing laws to prosecute a crime after that crime has already been committed—was unfounded since Germany had signed the Kellogg-Briand Pact.[114] Fall was aware that Nazi lawyers sought several avenues in defense of their clients, and *ex post facto* claims were one of these critical and contested positions. Additionally, Fall referenced the Covenant of the League of Nations and the Hague Conventions of 1899 and 1907 (Articles 46–56 inclusive) as a basis for the London Charter, also known as the Nuremberg Charter.[115] After the UN Charter had been signed two months before in June, the European Advisory Commission completed the London-Nuremberg Charter (referred to hereafter as the Nuremberg Charter), and France, the United States, the Soviet Union, and the United Kingdom signed it on 8 August 1945.[116]

The background of World War II War Crimes Commission's mandates mattered to Bernard Fall at the time because they provided the legal framework guiding his research for the Commission's investigation of the Krupp Corporation during the second part of the Tribunals. Along with the training he gained during this period, the Tribunal's legal frameworks also guided his later criticism of war in Vietnam, and he consistently referenced the legal conventions he had studied at Nuremberg and directly after the trials in 1949. In one article from 1965, he explained:

> As personal questions to both American and Vietnamese unit commanders have shown, there is only the vaguest of ideas among them as to what is exactly covered by the 1949 Convention; in the few cases where the terms "rules of war" meant anything at all, the officer concerned very often confused the rules of land warfare of the Hague with the Geneva Convention on Prisoners of War of 1929, the 1949 Convention, the Red Cross Convention, and the American Code of the Fighting Man.[117]

As a solution, Fall added, "It should not be impossible to provide every American serviceman in Vietnam with a handy resume of his obligations under the existing laws and treaties toward the hapless civilian population as well as toward the enemy combatant."[118]

Promoting and adhering to clear legal guidelines was significant in Fall's eyes because doing so might limit retribution on a larger scale. When US military operations resulted in civilian casualties among the Vietnamese or mistreatment of prisoners, he stated that this led to the "September 29, 1965 announcement by Hanoi that henceforth American pilots caught in the North will be treated as 'war criminals' and this is a direct consequence of Washington's lack of foresight on the POW and civilian problem."[119] "War crimes" were not simply a single-sided problem, however. US pilots shot down over North Vietnam suffered at the hands of their captors not only because of legal disintegration in American conduct, but because North Vietnamese personnel also committed war crimes. Fall was not so naïve to think that one side following the laws of war would mean the other would follow suit. Fall's point was that the brutalization of American POWs might have been more limited or at least received greater unanimous international condemnation had Americans closely adhered to international laws of war. At the very least—through consistently holding US personnel accountable for adhering to international laws regulating war—Americans might more strongly and legitimately uphold the values they prosecuted others for violating at Nuremberg two decades before.

In studying legal changes attempting to address warfare in the early- to mid-twentieth century, he also learned of the cynicism with which the accused historically defended allegations against them. In a case from World War I, German military leaders "sought to justify their use of gas by the insistence that in the view of the explicit stipulation that 'projectiles' are prohibited, the use of gas from 'cylinders' was legal."[120] If any naïveté still existed for the twenty-year-old Fall before his work at Nuremberg, the trials and his awareness of bureaucratic maneuverings and manipulation of language from World War I likely removed his remaining illusions. In terms of the precedent set by the Kellogg-Briand Pact as an interwar-era restriction on war-making, Telford Taylor assessed that the Pact was "not intended to condemn resorting to war in self-defense, but what about launching an aggressive war? Opinions differed sharply at the time, and still did when World War II brought the question to a head in 1945—public and official *attitudes* toward the laws of war had undergone a sea change."[121] Other significant legal factors figured into the Nuremberg Trials. Among these, the legality of "Victor's Justice," the creation of law governing crimes after the commission of the crimes themselves (*ex post facto*), the determination of individual liability for "acts of State," immense financial costs, and the anticipated lengthy period required to collect evidence and conduct the trials were additional and prominent problems.[122]

The War Crimes Commission's mandate was significant. However, these numerous contentious problems were made more difficult because of the immense amount of work in collecting and analyzing staggering amounts of existing evidence. Penetrating the intricacy of the interdependent bureaucracies of the Nazis and the Krupp Corporation, as well as a vast network of other organizations, was one thing. Sifting through enormous amounts of data used to document the military-government-industrial complex in Nazi Germany, and to make sense of it coherently, multiplied the challenge. For example, Nazi Schutzstaffel (SS) documents detailing interactions between the SS, Gestapo, and the Krupp Corporation alone—not including documents Krupp employees intentionally destroyed to hide evidence—filled over six train freight cars.[123] Working through such immense amounts of documentation to support the prosecution's case during the trials provided a severe challenge for researchers. It is difficult, therefore, to overstate the task before the commission and its research analysts.

Ironically, the Nazis' extensive documentation charting the extent and speed of their imperial expansion throughout Europe and much of the Soviet Union formed the core sources of primary evidence used in prosecuting the Nazis and their associates.[124] The German Third Reich the Nazis envisioned required military might and labor to support it, and complex and expansive agrarian, economic, and foreign policies to gain support from populations in former British and French colonies.[125] Far-reaching bureaucracy required staggering amounts of documentation. The amount required to facilitate the Third Reich's massive war production effort within Germany alone was equally immense.[126] This evidence, of course, was precisely what Fall and an extensive team of research analysts and others were responsible for collecting and assessing in support of the prosecution's cases against the numerous Nazi organizations under indictment. Fall's employment in these circumstances was unique. These experiences in researching and investigating legal violations undeniably informed his subsequent outlook and study of warfare in Indochina after World War II. As Philippe Devillers noted: "B. Fall, who wanted to search for the truth, thus obtained membership in the war crimes commission at the International Tribunal from 1946 to 1948. These investigations, which are a milestone in contemporary history, have revealed, in all its scope, the horror of 'modern' war."[127] The horror of "modern war," as Fall knew it, began in World War II, but it continued far beyond it as well. Fall, as Devillers acknowledged, was working in a critical moment of world history that laid the groundwork for his later scholarship.

* * *

The International Military Tribunal opened against twenty-two leaders of the Nazi Party on 20 November 1945.[128] Although broadly considered a collective trial, the cases against Nazi leaders were individually deliberated and included the prosecution of Herman Göring, Rudolf Hess, Alfred Jodl, Albert Speer, Fritz Saukel, Joachim van Ribbentrop, and sixteen other defendants. The proceedings, led by Robert H. Jackson as lead prosecutor, concluded on 1 October 1946, with seven individuals being sentenced to imprisonment for terms ranging from ten years to life imprisonment, three acquittals, and twelve death sentences.¹²⁹ Fall attended the first and second Nuremberg Trial proceedings, but his research analysis primarily figured into the Nuremberg Military Tribunals, which began in December 1946. The Nuremberg Military Tribunal's legal mandate was different from the first tribunal because the case was prosecuted only by the United States under authorization corresponding to the Nuremberg Charter entitled "Control Council Law No. 10," enacted on 20 December 1945.¹³⁰ Among the twelve trials that made up the second component of the overall Tribunals, deliberations on the crimes of experimentation committed by Josef Mengele, known as the "Doctors' Trial" and the "Judges' Trial," which investigated illegality among the Nazi judiciary, figured prominently.¹³¹

Other cases included prosecution of the German Army High Command, known collectively as the "militarists." However, most of Fall's research effort was directed toward collecting and analyzing evidence related to "industrialists," a group that included the Krupp Corporation, the IG Farben Corporation, and Flick KG. Among these, Fall focused specifically on investigating the Krupp Corporation. On 16 August 1947, the Secretary-General of Military Tribunal III filed indictments against the Krupp Corporation, and the window for Bernard Fall to conduct research supporting this Tribunal's case opened. With others' help, Fall's work as a research analyst began with his digging into the Krupp Corporation's past to understand its leaders' criminal actions. His collection of evidence would close ten months later on 9 June 1948.¹³²

V—The Weapon Forge of the Reich

As early as October 1938, the German armed forces planned to utilize forced labor from prisoners of war and civilians in countries it planned to occupy.¹³³ Slave labor, known as *Slavern*, was central to conspiratorial planning between the Nazis, IG Farben, Flick KG, and the Krupp Corporation's executive leadership.¹³⁴ Fall himself learned of growing labor requirements after the June 1940 invasion of France by simply living in southern France while workers were being registered and later conscripted for labor. What was new information to Fall was the forced labor system's extensive reach throughout Europe, especially across Eastern Europe and into the Soviet Union.

For the armaments industry, forced labor was a critical factor required to achieve production quotas. By the middle of the war in 1942, one out of every five workers in the Third Reich was a forced laborer, and by January 1944 over ten million forced laborers worked for the Nazis and their industries. Of these laborers, 6.5 million were civilians, 2.2 million were prisoners of war, and 1.3 million were laborers either taken from or already working for German industries in concentration camps such as Auschwitz, Buchenwald, Ravensbrueck, and others.[135] What Fall learned was striking and horrifying, mainly because he was aware of his mother's deportation from Drancy to Auschwitz, where, as an older woman, her chances for labor conscription were nil.

Nazi leaders Albert Speer and Fritz Sauckel, who were judged in the Nuremberg Palace during the first series of the Tribunal's cases, oversaw the massive armament industry fueled by the Krupp Corporation and others that continued to grow until 1945. Despite massive Allied bombing, Nazi subterranean production facilities included over 300,000 square meters of underground workspace (equivalent to 74.13 acres) to predominantly produce fighter planes through 1944.[136] Until the Normandy landings gained a foothold, the Nazis developed plans to create over three million square meters of workspace for underground armaments production.[137] As a member of Hitler's inner circle, Speer served as the Armaments Minister while Sauckel, a Gauleiter in Thuringia, was the Plenipotentiary for the Employment of Labor. These individuals were directly connected to Alfried Krupp who personally oversaw his company's arms manufacturing and managed its internal operations as it filled Nazi armament orders.[138]

The Krupp Corporation, along with the other German industrialists, engaged in a complicated bureaucratic competition for conscripted labor. In addition to the Krupp Corporation, Flick KG, IG Farben, the Wehrmacht, and the SS also vied for slave labor, with significant political infighting among the organizations. Competition for labor between Heinrich Himmler's SS and Speer, as the Armament's Minister, was particularly strenuous.[139] Friedrich Flick, head of Flick KG, was part of a group known as the "Himmler Circle of Friends" (*Freundeskreis Himmler*) which made annual contributions to the SS that exceeded one million Reichmark to promote their requests for labor.[140] The bureaucratic struggle between these companies and the Nazi leadership over filling labor requirements demonstrated the type of details Fall learned while researching and during the early stages of the prosecution's investigation. His work provided him with formal experience conducting research, yet it also provided him with substantive knowledge of Nazi politics, Nazi documentation, and interdependence among the Nazis, German industry, and the German military. The firsthand knowledge he gathered from the field between 1947 and 1948 additionally served as evidence of these connections, and it was material upon which he built in later scholarship.[141]

The Krupp Corporation's history was complicated and extensive. It operated as a critical business cog in the German economy's armament and equipment fabrication sectors, and it remained a family-controlled enterprise throughout World War II.[142] Along with the militarists of the German General Staff after World War I, the German armament industry was a feature, according to Telford Taylor, "of the German landscape, pervasively feared and condemned in world public opinion."[143] The key actor in this overall armament landscape was Krupp of Essen, founded in 1811 and an industrial empire by 1914.[144] Due to a break in the male lineage of the family in 1902, ownership of the corporation passed to Bertha Krupp until 1906 when Bertha married a German diplomat named Gustav von Bohlen und Halbach, soon to be renamed Gustav Krupp von Bohlen und Halbach.[145] The couple oversaw massive and escalating armament manufacturing production, particularly in artillery, as Germany competed with the French and Russian militaries in 1913.[146] Infamously, shorter-range 420mm artillery were nick-named "Big Berthas," while 211mm Pariskanonen—siege guns with a much longer range, capable of throwing shells over seventy miles—were used to bombard Paris in 1918. An updated siege cannon, Schwerer Gustav, the "Heavy Gustav," was developed and unveiled in 1940. Its 80cm caliber and 106-foot-long barrel had a range between 24 and 30 miles. Affectionately or not, artillerymen called it "Dora."[147]

Fall's research was particularly meticulous in accounting for technical details concerning military arms' capacities and limitations. As a boy, he was fascinated with military subjects since finding a book called *Der Weltkrieg in Bildern* (*The World War in Pictures*).[148] Published by Johannes M. Meulenhoff Verlag in Leipzig, volume one appeared in 1914 and volume two in 1915: the books provided Fall with a trove of primary sources on the earliest stages of World War I.[149] Regarding the corporation's ownership, the birth of Bertha and Gustav Krupp's oldest son, Alfried, in 1907 rectified the Krupp's lineage issue.[150] Alfried, along with his father Gustav, were therefore prominent in Fall's research because their family history had consequences for the Krupp Trial at Nuremberg.

When World War II began, Gustav Krupp led the industrial giant, but he was sixty-nine in 1939 and suffered a stroke in 1941 that left him alive but incapacitated until his death in 1950. As members of the Reich Economic Council and President of the Reich Association of German Industry, the Krupp family was among the most devoted supporters of Adolf Hitler.[151] In November 1943, Alfried officially gained leadership of the Krupp Corporation, which had temporarily returned to Bertha Krupp after Gustav's stroke in 1941. A key event then occurred on 12 November 1943 when Alfried's leadership of the corporation was certified by Adolf Hitler in a document known as the "Lex Krupp," a specialized law codified as a federal law in Nazi Germany.[152] The law certified the Krupp Corporation's private ownership, and this decree mandated that "Krupp alone was enabled to continue as a family enterprise free from the manifold burdens of a corporate structure."[153]

The German public would not learn of the "Lex Krupp" until January 1950 when, after Gustav Krupp's death that month, Bertha Krupp attempted to disavow Hitler's certification of Krupp family control over the corporation. She manipulatively claimed that the Lex Krupp had been issued "in violation of the law of the land." However, Bertha's ultimate concern centered on regaining the Krupp fortune, worth approximately 500 million US dollars, which had been left in limbo after Gustav's death and forfeited to the Allies after the Nuremberg Trial ruled against Alfried.[154] The privileged relationship between the Krupp Corporation, led by Gustav, Bertha, and then Alfried, stemmed from an early, long-standing, and close personal relationship with Adolf Hitler, greased by massive financial contributions to the Nazi Party beginning in 1933.[155] "Lex Krupp," according to the prosecution's closing statement on the Krupp case, was "only one of many things which served to mark the special position held by the 'weapon forge of the Reich.'"[156]

Among the earliest of supporters, the Krupp family financed the Nazi Party in 1933, and this contributed to Hitler's seizure of power through the Reichstag Fire Act and the Enabling Act of 1933.[157] The Krupps even compelled other industrialists to support Hitler and the Nazi Party.[158] This industrialists' effort eventually coalesced into what was known as the Adolf Hitler *Spende* (the Adolf Hitler Fund of German Trade and Industry/*Adolf-Hitler-Spende der deutschen Wirtschaft*). According to Adam Tooze, the *Spende* was a critical institution supporting the Nazi Party in 1933 and after:

> In the years that followed, the Adolf Hitler Spende was to become institutionalized as a regular contribution to the maintenance of Hitler's personal expenses. In practical terms, however it was the donations in February and March 1933 that really made the difference. They provided a large cash injection at a moment when the party was severely short of funds and faced, as Goering had predicted, the last competitive election in Weimar's history.[159]

In Albert Speer's memoir, *Inside the Third Reich*, Nazi leaders requested that German business leaders contribute to this fund which Martin Bormann, the Nazi Reichsleiter—the second highest-ranking Nazi leader after Hitler between 1933 and 1945—distributed to Party leaders on Hitler's behalf.[160] In a 2012 revisionist history of the Krupp Corporation, Harold James mentions neither the *Spende* nor Lex Krupp.[161] James' assessment that the Krupps did not drive high-level Nazi policy is correct in the sense that they did not create Nazi policy. However, any claim that the Krupps were not responsible for contributing and directing others to provide much-needed infusions of capital into the Nazi Party is entirely absurd, as Adam Tooze indicates and as noted above. At the Nuremberg Tribunal, however, determining the responsibility of ownership pertaining to which Krupp to prosecute in the trial proved to be problematic, and this was a matter that involved Fall's research in particular. Even if he was incapacitated, should Gustav stand trial in Nuremberg, or should Alfried?

Initially, in the American prosecution's perspective, Alfried Krupp was considered the Krupp Corporation's sole owner. Therefore, his name was submitted as a defendant for the first series of trials to the US State Department, the entity responsible for constructing the overall defendant list, on 26 August 1946.[162] However, the British contingent, led by Sir Hartley Shawcross, believed that his delegation had a much stronger case against Gustav Krupp. This disagreement initiated a bureaucratic struggle over the correct person to stand trial. It is unclear why both individuals were not selected to stand trial in the first Tribunal, especially since both Gustav and Alfried led the corporation at critical points during the rise of Nazism in Germany. Sydney Alderman, a member of the American delegation to Nuremberg, was the first to recognize the problem concerning which Krupp, whether Gustav or Alfried, should stand for the trial. Alderman wrote on 28 August that there existed "confusion yesterday on the name of Krupp. We had Alfried, the son, on our list. The other three delegations seemed to have Gustav, the father. We ought to be certain of an agreement."[163] Unfortunately, an agreement was not specified. This ambiguity—over which Krupp would stand trial—bore powerfully on the prosecution's case.[164]

The result of this administrative confusion was that neither Gustav nor Alfried Krupp stood trial as part of the first International Military Tribunal before judges from England, the United States, France, and the Soviet Union. Alfried was eventually indicted, but because of the delay, he was prosecuted in the second Nuremberg Military Tribunal, by American judges only and not with prominent Nazi leaders, including Rudolf Hess and others. Telford Taylor reflected upon this bureaucratic mess and its implications in his memoir, explaining,

If the main emphasis was to be involvement in the conspiracy to initiate aggressive war, the obvious choice was Gustav … If the principal charge was to be war crimes, then the defendant should have been Alfried, for the principal acts of plunder, and exploitation of concentration camp and slave labor, had occurred after Alfried had replaced his father as actual head of the family and, in 1943, as sole proprietor of the Krupp enterprise.[165]

Evidence of criminal actions, whether conspiracy or plunder, were not matters of debate. The crux of the matter centered on determining which Krupp would face prosecution. In Taylor's judgment—and he was as familiar with the entire Nuremberg Tribunal process as anyone, including Robert H. Jackson—Alfried Krupp was as guilty of Nazi war crimes as Hermann Göring and the rest of the Nazis' most infamous leaders. As William Manchester described it, "the Fuhrer had not asked Alfried Krupp to take advantage of the victims of Auschwitz. Alfried Krupp exploited them voluntarily."[166]

With the indictment that Alfried Krupp and several other Krupp senior leaders stand trial during the Nuremberg Military Tribunal, Fall's research mission continued, and he completed numerous tasks as a research analyst for the War Crimes Commission. His research into the Krupp Corporation consisted of staff evidence analysis, research trips collecting evidence, interviewing and taking depositions from surviving laborers, and developing lines of inquiry for prosecutors questioning Krupp and his associates. It also included unconventional field research, such as collecting bricks at factories for evidence of the reconstruction of factories by slave laborers after Allied aerial bombardment during liberation. These diverse research-oriented experiences broadened and sharpened Fall's attention to detail.[167]

For example, Fall's research included several sources that documented the Krupp Corporation's specific violations of international agreements. The first Tribunal had already established that the Third Reich systematically violated multiple articles (46, 50, 52, and 56) of the Hague Convention of 1907 and several articles (2, 3, 4, 46, 51) of the Geneva Convention of 1929.[168] In Fall's research, the Krupp Corporation violated Article 52 of the 1907 Hague Convention and Article 6(b) of the Nuremberg Charter, which dealt with labor. This Article 6(b) stated, "the ill treatment or deportation of slave labor or for any other purpose of civilian population of or in occupied territory shall be a war crime," while Article 6 of the 1907 Hague Regulations added, "work done for the State is paid for at the rates in force for work of a similar kind done by soldiers of the national army, or, if there are none in force, at a rate according to the work executed."[169] The civilians compelled to work for the Krupp Corporation, it suffices to say, were not paid. It is unknown whether the Krupps' defense claimed that, since the Krupp Corporation was not "the State" but a privately held company, Article 6 in the Hague Convention did not apply. The Nuremberg Charter's Article 6(b), therefore, was critical since it specified slave labor in particular. Similarly, Article 2 in the 1930 Forced Labour Convention clarified the precise meaning of forced compulsory labor: "The term 'forced or compulsory labour' shall mean all work or service which is exacted from any person under the menace of any penalty and for which the said person has not offered himself voluntarily."[170] Fall's tasks, therefore, included documenting evidence that demonstrated violations of these various articles.

In gathering proof, Fall investigated how the Krupp Corporation had supplied, through coordination with the SS and Gestapo, slave labor in its armaments industries to support the Nazi war effort. To accomplish this task, Fall charted locations at which slaves had been incarcerated and worked, and he attempted to account for the frequency of violations when possible.[171] These research tasks almost certainly overwhelmed Fall and the trial research team supporting the prosecution because the Krupp Corporation privately owned and managed 138 forced-labor camps.[172] Fall sought to substantiate claims that, in addition to precedents set in the 1907 Hague and 1929 Geneva Conventions, Article 6b of the Nuremberg Charter had also been violated. In addition to his other research, Fall contributed to the Krupp prosecution team's findings that at least five million individuals in occupied territories were forced to work for the German war effort, including in armament production and other components of the German defense industry.[173] The prosecution team and its research analysts, including Fall, had significant work before them, and by this time he had experienced much that informed his thought and understanding of war. He had witnessed the complexity of war in irregular and partisan contexts and through the complicated environment of conventional warfare as a member of the regular French army. Now, his task involved studying the Nazis' disregard of rules of war and how Nazi positivist construction of power undermined democratic values.

As a young researcher, Fall contributed to a revitalized international understanding of human rights meant to protect civilians after World War II. The historical processes Fall lived through at Nuremberg contributed significantly to how he viewed justice and how warfare should conform to limitations that shielded civilians from being intentionally and directly targeted in war. The Tribunals especially informed how he viewed the United States as a beacon and protector of human rights after the United States helped establish those rights through the UN Declaration of Human Rights. It is useful, therefore, to describe in greater detail how his research and experience shaped his views on justice and war. As indicated in the next chapter, Fall's efforts were not typical tasks and experiences for a twenty-year-old individual; this was especially true for a young Jew, such as Fall, who had survived the war and was able to witness the process of justice firsthand. In this critical phase of his career, he learned how principles and rules of war, guided by the UN-mandated Nuremberg Charter, sought to reestablish order, justice, and international law regarding warfare. As Fall embarked on his research, he already knew war as a combatant, and he recognized the ambiguities of resistance and collaboration found among civilians. In researching the Krupp Corporation and gathering evidence to support the Nuremberg Military Tribunal, he would learn of the scale and intensity of civilian suffering through slave labor and the Holocaust, as well as the reality of legal prosecution of the Nazis.

2

GERMANY, 1946–1951

I—Evidence in Essen

In late 1946 and early 1947, Fall's field research took him to numerous locations in Germany, mainly to Krupp's factories in Essen, but also to Kiel and Hamburg.[1] This period and context, in which he conducted research for the War Crimes Commission's case against Krupp, broadened the development of his thought on warfare in several ways. First, he learned technical details about economics, the armaments industry in Germany, and the complicated bureaucracy and history of the Krupp Corporation's development. Second, using his knowledge of the Krupp Corporation, he developed skills in applied research creating analytical assessments using a format called staff evidence analyses to support the prosecution's case.[2] Third, he learned about the broader social and political consequences of World War II associated with the exploitation of slave labor. These laborers included not only men but also women, children, and prisoners of war who struggled to survive in horrific conditions. Fourth, he learned more about the importance of international law and its reestablishment in the judgment of war crimes.

Fall channeled these interrelated factors into an analysis of the political economy of war that integrated military experience with an empathetic understanding of war among civilian populations. His shared understanding of these civilians' circumstances and what they suffered depended upon his social and cultural intelligence. He already knew that war was much more than an aggregate of purely military-oriented components. However, his research for the War Crimes Commission deepened and expanded his comprehension of nonmilitary factors in war that were often of far greater importance and relevance than the military capacities listed in organization and equipment tables. These developments contributed to his understanding of politics, economics, and warfare during World War II. At the same time, his postwar research facilitated numerous skills and insights on which he would build and employ in later analysis of conflict in Indochina.

Fall's work began with collecting documentation to support the Tribunal's prosecution of Alfried Krupp and the Krupp Corporation. The tasks assigned to him varied. They included conducting interviews with witnesses, modifying questions posed to defendants by the prosecution staff, and providing detailed descriptions of the Krupp Corporation's annual production charts at its Essen plants, also known as the *Berthawerks* and *Gusstalhfabrik*, from prewar outputs up to 1943.[3] One of his reports, dated 24 December 1946, documented steel outputs, including "sheet-piling, rails, raw blocks," and other products such as "iron, ferrochrome and other materials." These were technical minutiae but demonstrated the type of detailed information Fall collected. His research was also prodigious, and he was held accountable for charting his analytical production by submitting weekly "screening work reports" to H. Russell Thayer, an attorney for the Military Tribunal prosecution team. In what appeared to be a typical week in early January 1947, for example, Fall listed his research products: "25 folders were screened; 10 folders were considered as relevant and classified; 2 documents were translated; 2 SEA's [staff evidence analysis] have been done; the "Krupp Folder File" has been completed and may be considered as ready to be used by the lawyers and (other) research analysts."[4]

Fall's tasks also included transporting film, captured in the Krupp files in its Essen plants by British armed forces to the prosecution's legal staff. These documents provided critical visual confirmation of Nazi operations and Krupp's production. Archival records indicate Fall certifying delivery, with an affidavit, of twenty-seven films to the British government's cinematography advisor, W.J.G. Maloney, in early 1947.[5] Fall also provided analyses of these films. In one case regarding "sequence 22" of film "2," Fall provided notes to accompany photos of Baldur von Schirach—the Nazi Party's National Youth leader and head of the Hitler Youth—with Baldur urging his charges at a torchlight meeting. Fall's analysis contextualized Schirach's role among German youth by noting "that Nazi ideology's aggressive aims were public knowledge."[6] This type of analysis demonstrated that he paid attention to social-political factors in the context of war while at the same time being attentive to technical details such as "sheet piling, rails, and raw blocks" produced by laborers in Krupp's factories.

His experiences in the Maquis, with Free French Forces, and in the French army also contributed a military-oriented technical knowledge base to his research into the Krupp Corporation's operations. In one staff evidence analysis he examined the strength and armaments of *Werkschutz* (Works Police) at Krupp AG, in Essen. At this network of factories forming the heart of the Krupp Corporation, Fall gathered evidence documenting 272 *Hauptamtliche* (major officials) and 422 "minor, or low-graded works policemen. Total: 694 men." Fall went on to note that their armament consisted of "3 Machine-guns, 8 Submachine-guns, 444 rifles of type '98,' Mauser, and Mannlicher, and 241 pistols, and revolvers, totaling 694 individual weapons and 3 MG."[7] His military background was conspicuous in his analysis of firepower wielded by the plant's security force and in his observation that this data "shows that the Works Police was of the strength of a light battalion."

This unit's armament and number of personnel suggested their potential capacity for light tactical maneuver, especially with the addition of more machine guns and mortars, such as the 5cm Leichter Granatwerfer 36 or other light mortar systems.[8] It undoubtedly exceeded security oversight of malnourished, weary, and often ill slave laborers. Moreover, many personnel in the *Werkschutz* were also *Schutzstaffel*, suggesting the plants may have served as an SS station or transit base for German personnel moving through the Ruhr.[9] According to the closing statement in the Krupp trial, "Krupp placed the dregs of Nazism, SA and SS men by preference, in charge of their camps and of their guarding."[10] The personnel manning Krupp's security elements indicated that Krupp did not bring in average German soldiers for the oversight of prisoners but that he relied upon fascists committed to Nazi ideology. Moreover, Fall's analysis of plant security's military armaments brought an intelligence analyst's perspective to the technical sides of his research. He demonstrated this analytical approach in his description of the Works Police's military capabilities, because analysis of organizational strength and signature weapon systems are specific concerns of military intelligence. The interdependence between the armaments' industry and the German military interested him greatly, but he was also repulsed by malicious actions of troops who served as guards over vulnerable laborers.

While he completed a diversity of tasks for the prosecution, Fall's research focused primarily on documenting the operations of forced-labor centers operated by the Krupp Corporation. Krupp's 138 work camps were too many for Fall to document by himself. He managed, however, to document data on 75 of these installations.[11] Most of these were in and around Essen and formed an extensive network of co-located factories and camps. At each installation, Fall documented camp surface area and, when possible, the number of workers, their nationalities, and the number of families living within the factories' concertina wire-encircled barracks.[12] These details and his fine-grained analysis of the camps demonstrated that he benefited from the apparent necessity of collecting evidence firsthand, but also from supervisors' demands and support for his field research. In examining Fall's staff evidence analyses, which he used to document Krupp manufacturing and other operations, one can see his methodical accounting and analyses are organized as if he were documenting a military operation's details. In many respects, Fall's research for the War Crimes Commission provided an analytical foundation, which he would build upon and continue to refine throughout his career as an analyst of war.

Fall's research in 1946 and 1947 indicated that, even though laborers were critical to production, Krupp meagerly provided only the barest of living essentials needed for a workforce that contributed to a quarter of the Third Reich's total workforce in all industrial production sectors.[13] Living and working in appalling conditions, slave laborers constituted 40 percent of all war production laborers under Nazi control.[14] Fall pointed out that Krupp's camps incarcerated large numbers of individuals and included social services because so many workers were women with children. In fact, by August 1944, women made up one-third of foreign forced laborers in Germany.[15] These services included nurseries for workers' children, and, as Fall explained: "As to Krupp's famous 'social welfare program,' it also included a clinic in Voerde, where female workers' [fetuses] were aborted so that they would not divert any of their time from Krupp's armament projects to the care of their newborn babies."[16] Due to his mother's murder, and as the brother of a younger sister who survived the war by gaining refuge in a convent, Fall was undoubtedly sensitive to women's plight during the war.

His comments on this abortion clinic also pertained to an unimaginably brutal camp the Krupp Corporation maintained called Buschmannshof in the city of Voerde, northwest of Essen on the Rhine River. This camp was a *Konzentrationslager* for infants born to Eastern European and Ukrainian women, where children were held under horrifying conditions so their mothers could work in Essen. As historian, William Manchester described it:

when eastern female workers employed at Krupp's factories were expecting a child, the confinement took place in one of the hospitals of Krupp. One part of the hospital was fenced off. There the women were delivered. After a certain time, it might have been three or perhaps six weeks, the women resumed work, while the children remained at the hospital.[17]

The children born at Buschmannshof were often transferred to other quarters at Voerde-bei-Dinslaken, near Essen, where they were "fed a slimy gruel from bottles; many had 'swollen heads,' and there was no child at all whose arms or hands were thicker than a thumb."[18] Toward the end of the war, these infants and young children died at a rate of fifty or sixty every day and these individual death rates remained consistent, because "every day, there was a constant influx of eastern female workers with children."[19] When the Allies finally encircled the Ruhr, significant numbers of infants were abandoned and died in a birch thicket in Voerde-bei-Dinslaken.[20] In 2012, the city of Voerde erected a memorial at Am Kindergarten, 46562, Voerde, to children who died at the Buschmannshof camp—which the city notes explicitly that the Krupp Corporation maintained—because of neglect and mistreatment.[21]

Fall allocated significant attention to these criminal actions by also analyzing German law. In one case, Fall sent an inter-office memorandum in 1947 to the attorney, Russell Thayer, with the subject line: "Legal considerations about the installation of an Abortion Station in the Krupp Hospital by Dr. Jaeger."[22] Through three dense, single-spaced typed pages, Fall analyzed Article 42 of the German Penal code. He concluded that, according to German law, "The criminal action of abortion was perpetrated in the Krupp works with the direct aid of Oberlagerarzt Dr. Jaeger and with the criminal knowledge of high-ranking Krupp officials and other organizations."[23] In addition to his extensive analyses of numerous other documents he collected, this evidence demonstrated how Krupp and his associates' actions violated German law in ways that added to the prosecution's overall case. Despite this evidence and other extensive documentation presented in the Nuremberg Military Tribunal's 1949 final report, Harold James argued that the case against Krupp did not rely upon actions that included abuse and neglect of laborers' children. Instead, James stated that: "The case appears to have been argued more on the level of the importance of Krupp as a symbol than on concrete actions."[24] James's statement reflects a lack of research into the evidence presented in the Nuremberg Military Tribunal's final report, Telford Taylors' papers held at Columbia University, let alone Fall's documentation used to prosecute Alfried Krupp and other Krupp Corporation directors.[25]

In addition to the children of laborers, Krupp's workers, particularly prisoners of war, also endured horrible circumstances.[26] In an extraordinary document presented against Krupp at his trial, a "Colonel Breyer" of the German High Command contacted Fritz von Buelow, the Gestapo liaison officer to Krupp, to complain about the treatment of Krupp's workers. The document indicated that conditions were so bad that they came to the attention of the army's high command through civilian reporting. As cited in the Nuremberg Military Tribunal final report, Colonel Breyer of the German armed forces wrote:

> The High Command of the Armed Forces has lately received from their own officers and recently also in anonymous letters from the German population a considerable number of complaints about the treatment of POW's at the firm Krupp (especially that they are being beaten, and furthermore that they do not receive the food and time off that is due them. Among other things the POW's are said not to have received any potatoes for 6 weeks.) All those things would no longer occur anywhere else in Germany ... the conditions at Krupp would be looked into either by the Army District Command or by the High Command of the Armed Forces themselves.[27]

This document served as evidence that the German military did not dictate conditions at Krupp's camps and factories. Instead, Breyer's statement revealed that conditions at Krupp's facilities resulted from concerted Gestapo-SS-Krupp planning. It is far from symbolic when a senior field-grade officer in the German army found conditions under Krupp's control so bad that he felt compelled to complain about them to his higher senior officers.

The level of coordination between Krupp and the Nazis' slave-labor services—through the forced-labor category system known as *Arbeitzeinsatz*—consisted of actions that required extensive planning and efforts to compete against other organizations for forced labor. The prosecution's case against Krupp maintained, "while the Krupp concern was eagerly seeking after concentration camp labor, other firms were refusing to employ such labor. Indeed, it was frequently difficult to obtain concentration camp labor and a firm had to have good connections with the SS in order to do so."[28] These kinds of details mattered because they supported the conspiratorial basis for Krupp's exploitation of labor with the Gestapo and SS, which aided the prosecution's criminal case against Krupp. These details were likely of interest to Fall personally, as avoiding conscription as a forced laborer had undoubtedly factored into his decision to join the French Resistance in Haute-Savoie in late 1943.

The "Compulsory Labor Service," an agreement between Vichy and the Nazis, included birth-year parameters that were very close to Fall's age group as early as 1942.²⁹ It is difficult to imagine that he could have perpetually avoided labor or worse, especially as a young and orphaned Jew. Additionally, if Fall had been caught as a member of the Maquis, it is unlikely he would have survived at all. Undoubtedly, Fall saw much of himself in the circumstances he studied in detail over almost two years of work as a researcher at Nuremberg: he knew the fate he had narrowly avoided was a daily nightmare for others.³⁰

Laborers began work at 4 am with 750ml of tea. Later, they received soup when their shift ended around 7 pm or 8 pm. They would also receive, if available at some point during the day, 240 grams of bread.³¹ During the Krupp trial, eyewitnesses also reported Russian workers catching mice and cooking them after skinning them with bits of glass and metal.³² The prosecution's Chief of Counsel, Telford Taylor, explained that such criminal liability "was not primarily charged on the basis of whatever government connections they may have had, but by reason of their responsibilities as directors of large, industrial concerns where 'slave' labor was extensively utilized under inhumane conditions."³³ Not only were the conditions in which the laborers worked abysmal, but the sheer number of individuals forced to labor was also overwhelming: by July 1942, 5,124,000 individuals taken from occupied countries were working in Germany, and, by the end of the war, total estimates of slave laborers in Germany ranged from seven to ten million people.³⁴

Not surprisingly, Krupp and other Nazi leaders contested evidence pertaining to slave labor at multiple points during the Nuremberg Tribunals. Like Krupp, Fritz Sauckel, the General Plenipotentiary for Labor Deployment, claimed that Russian slave labor was not illegal because the Soviet Union had never signed the Hague Convention of 1907.³⁵ In the case of Soviet citizens, Fall discovered multiple violations of war relating to Russian victims used to counter the defendants' arguments. In one case, Fall urgently telegrammed the prosecution team after discovering an admission written and signed by Peter Nohles, a Gestapo officer who had worked at Krupp's factories in Essen. Fall's telegram read:

URGENT HAVE FOUND AT ESSEN PSO WRITTEN AND SIGNED ADMISSION BY NOHLES CMA PRESENTLY AT NUREMBERG CMA THAT HE ORDERED THIRTY FIVE RUSSIAN WORKERS IN ESSEN TO BE SHOT BY GESTAPO AND SD IN A PARK IN THE TOWN STOP THAT THE RUSSIANS DID NOT HAVE TRIAL STOP AMONG DEADS [sic] WERE WOMEN STOP HANDS OF MURDERED WERE TIED BEHIND THEIR BACKS WITH TELEPHONE WIRE AND

THEY WERE KILLED BY PISTOL SHOTS IN THE NECK AT THE EDGE OF A BOMB CRATER STOP I BORROWED THE ORIGINALS FROM BRITISH PUBLIC SAFETY IF INTERESTED CMA PALLENBERG WILL BRING DOWN ORIGINALS ON WEDNESDAY STOP IN MEANTIME I WILL TRY TO FIND OUT IF RUSSIAN WORKERS SHOT WERE KRUPP SLAVE LABOR STOP ANSWER IMMEDIATELY PLEASE STOP BERNARD 241500Z[36]

The signed admission to which Fall referred in the telegram was added to other evidence, including an affidavit and seventy-one pages of documents Nohles left behind that the prosecution found.[37] Nohles's documents corroborated other evidence describing work conditions in Krupp's camps. It is unknown why Nohles left this detailed evidence, but it provided substance to criminal charges against Krupp.[38] Fall explained the conspiratorial nature and extent of such action, writing: "The Germans took elaborate precautions to keep their extermination operations a secret precisely because they knew that they were criminal."[39]

Fall's staff evidence analysis worksheets also included statements describing what happened to laborers as the Allies bombed German factories and Allied troops moved closer to Essen in 1945. In one case, Fall's interview with a former worker at Camp Humboldtstrasse in Essen after an air raid included a note that read: "this laborer mentions that the destroyed camp was occupied by 520 Jewesses and that, after the destruction of the barracks and the kitchen, the inmates were transferred to another camp, but they were still working for Krupp. The worker mentions no casualties caused by the raid."[40] In connection with this statement, Fall gathered evidence from other former Krupp workers, which remarkably included information provided by Elizabeth Roth, a young Ruthenian woman from Uzhhorod, who was one of these 520 "Jewesses."[41]

In 1947, Fall went to Essen with Roth to collect bricks—as evidence—which Elizabeth, her sister Ernestine, and other fellow workers had used to repair Krupp's buildings damaged by Allied bombing.[42] Roth and the "Hungarian Jewesses" to which her group was referred were often put to work after air raids, "moving rubble and carrying building material for the plant's reconstruction. Their principal task was the carrying of bricks and iron roofing sheets."[43] Roth's story was central to an article Fall would write in 1951 that condemned Alfried Krupp's actions and his treatment of workers.[44] The staff evidence analysis Fall completed on this trip with Roth was focused on technical details. However, their trip together to collect evidence from Krupp's bombed-out factories also likely provided an opportunity to learn of this woman's loss and suffering. Elizabeth Roth's experiences paralleled Fall's in some respects, and this connection possibly offered him added insight into the human dimension of war that women endured as victims of Krupp's and the Nazis' industrial policies. Fall learned of Roth's story directly from her and through her testimony against Krupp during his trial.⁴⁵

Elizabeth Roth was seventeen years old in 1939 when Hungarian armed forces invaded her city of Uzhhorod. She and her sister, Ernestine, were expelled from school because they were Jewish, and her family suffered occupation until May 1944 when all six members forming the Roth family were detained and deported to Auschwitz. Within moments of the army's arrival on 19 May 1944, her family was separated; one of Roth's sisters, her younger brother, and her parents were all murdered in Auschwitz's gas chambers. Elizabeth and Ernestine were selected as potential workers and subsequently sent to Gelsenberg-Benzin, where the sisters joined a large group of over 500 other women held for labor conscription.⁴⁶ Fall likely learned more about Auschwitz, to which his mother had been sent in late 1942, from Roth, whose initial experience of Auschwitz provided firsthand prosecution testimony in the case against Krupp.⁴⁷ From Gelsenberg-Benzin, Elizabeth was relocated, along with the group of other women, to Humboldtstrasse in Essen to work as *Kruppianer* [Krupp's workers].

In testimony to American prosecutor H. Russell Thayer, Roth provided a distressing description of her living and working conditions.⁴⁸ She had been assigned to work at a steel-hardening oven, while her sister Ernestine had mixed concrete to make bricks. During the winter of 1944, Ernestine had had to transport these bricks and other materials without gloves, using steel wheelbarrows.⁴⁹ Many women workers did not have shoes, let alone adequate clothing. Even other German workers were shocked at the conditions under which the sisters and their fellow 500 slave laborers worked, and the winter cold exacerbated the harsh treatment they endured. In one account, an elderly builder of tank turrets and World War I veteran, Peter Gutersohn, was horrified and "really ashamed to be a German when I saw what had been done to these young women." Gutersohn believed the Nazis would eventually kill them all, because "the work for which these women were used had never been done by any of the German women employed at our plant."⁵⁰ As Fall learned, the women were mistreated brutally, in part because their guards were SS soldiers.⁵¹ Roth singled out the particularly malicious *Lagerfuhrer* named Oskar Rieck, who specialized in attempting to whip workers in the eyes from eight feet with a dogwhip.⁵²

Elizabeth Roth's testimony also shed light on why Krupp's guards were SS soldiers. SS personnel assigned to the Krupp factories avoided direct administrative ties to the corporation because they were on SS payrolls and not those of the Krupp Corporation. SS brutality at Krupp's factories was unrestrained because, as the prosecution learned, there were no administrative restraints or other consequences for their actions. Krupp denied responsibility for the workers' treatment because the guards were not, at least administratively, personnel who constituted the Krupp Corporation's workforce. At most Krupp factories, many SS guards were either *Allgemeine* SS (a subgroup responsible for policing and internal security) or *Sicherheitsdienst* (SD) factions which, as Fall knew and as Roth testified, often murdered workers.[53] That many guards were SS soldiers instead of regular German forces possibly obscured the accountability for the treatment of slave laborers. This administrative coordination mattered because Krupp's foreign workers were consistently deported to camps when they were no longer useful, and the responsibility for overseeing deportations fell within SS mandate. As the death sentence and hanging of Ernst Kaltenbrunner, the SS *Obergruppenfuhrer* (Director of Reich Security Office), indicated, SS guilt for the deportation of Jews and foreigners in occupied regions was already extensively documented and established during the International Military Tribunal.[54] It possibly appeared to the prosecution that Alfried Krupp, who had knowledge of Kaltenbrunner's fate, was seeking to absolve himself of guilt by association with the SS and Gestapo by obscuring who provided security at his factories.

To establish the SS–Krupp connection, Fall's research targeted Friedrich von Buelow, one of the twelve defendants in the Krupp case. Von Buelow, notably, is one of the only Krupp defendants not even mentioned by Harold James in his history of the Krupp firm, even though von Buelow directed counterintelligence and the *Werkschutz* for the Krupp Corporation, and received—along with Alfried Krupp and Erich Müller—the most severe sentences among all Krupp defendants. Von Buelow maintained, as head of the *Werkschutz*, a liaison with the Gestapo to coordinate slave labor from prisoner-of-war and concentration camps in the manufacture of arms. Buelow, the court records and judgment demonstrated, sadistically trained special labor-allocation officers "to enumerate especially difficult and dirty work for which these foreigner workers may be used in groups of 50–60."[55] Additionally, von Buelow coordinated the Krupp firm's "furnishing of German, female workers who would be sworn into the SS and given 3 weeks' training at the women's concentration camp at Ravensbrueck and then assigned as guards for these concentration camps."[56] What mattered was the SS connection to Krupp, as Krupp's bureaucratic, obstructive efforts to avoid guilt became starker with evidence.

Statements provided by the German worker Peter Gutersohn assisted Fall's research by corroborating other sources. Locating forthcoming workers, such as Gutersohn, however, proved difficult. In March 1945, as the Allied invasion approached Essen, attempts to re-deport the women workers back to Auschwitz, thus removing evidence of their labor at Krupp's factories, occurred. In an affidavit made during his imprisonment, Alfried Krupp conceded that these women workers "very disagreeably affected him" and that he decided "to get rid of them as soon as possible."[57] While this statement was made after the trial closed, it validated Fall's research and the prosecution's argument against Krupp concerning slave labor. Krupp's defense attempted to manipulate such relocations as concern for workers' safety. However, these statements obscured the fact that the relocations consisted of transport to other work camps, including Buchenwald, and extermination camps such as Auschwitz.

In a rare case of fortune for Elizabeth Roth, her scheduled deportation was delayed due to disruption of train movement caused by an air raid. A few days later, on 11 March 1945, during another Allied air raid on Essen, Roth, her sister and a group of four other women escaped from their camp at Humboldtstrasse through a break in the wire and gained temporary refuge with a small number of sympathetic Germans.[58] Aided by the Allied air raid's extensive destruction and rapidly retreating German forces, Roth and her small group ultimately survived the war.[59] In contrast, the remaining 514 women were unable to escape, and a week later, on 17 March 1945, they were deported to Buchenwald where they were executed.[60]

When the Allies took over Essen, Elizabeth and Ernestine Roth found a Czech Displaced Person (DP) officer who directed them to a collection point in Essen. Eventually, after administrative processing determined that the sisters had worked as slave laborers in Krupp's factories, prosecutors called upon them to testify in the Tribunal against Krupp. Roth and Fall met at some point in 1946, before the sisters testified.[61] Fall's meeting and interaction with Elizabeth Roth were important to the Krupp trial because Roth's evidence contributed to spoliation charges against the Krupp defendants. Meeting Roth was also possibly important to Fall in that it enabled him to see, at a personal level, how his research into the plight of slave laborers connected to the broader goals of the Nuremberg Tribunal's prosecution of Krupp. In terms of substantive evidence, to which Fall had dedicated himself to locating, the prosecution believed the issue of slave labor was central to their case, so Elizabeth's testimony was a valuable component of their overall case.[62]

Remarkably, Fall met and recorded a deposition from Alfried Krupp. Fall's notes accompanying Alfried Krupp's deposition stated:

> Subject states that while he did not believe in a German victory in 1943, he expressed in an appeal to Krupp workers the hope in a coming retaliation for the Allied air raids on the Ruhr. Subject states that he could not do otherwise than to follow the German leaders. States that several common points existed between Nazi ideology and Krupp's tradition.[63]

The Tribunal's judgment of Krupp and his associates was delivered on 31 July 1948.[64] The sentences included one acquittal and eleven prison terms, with Alfried Krupp receiving a twelve-year prison sentence on the indictment's count 2: plundering—officially termed "spoliation" in the indictment—and count 3: slave labor.[65] Krupp's sentence would have been significantly more severe if the bureaucratic struggle placing Alfried Krupp in the second trial, instead of the first set of trials, had not occurred. Unlike Herman Göring and other Nazi leaders in the first Tribunal, Krupp's sentence stemmed from a ruling that, although complicit with Nazi ideology, industrialists—including Krupp and his business leaders—did not directly conspire with Hitler's overall strategy to subjugate Europe.[66] Nonetheless, the extent to which exploitation of slave labor occurred—the central issue concerning Fall, since it pertained to his research on Krupp—was undisputed, and senior Nazi leaders noted this in testimony. For example, Karl Otto Saur, the State Secretary in the Reich's Ministry for Armament Production, "swore under oath that Alfried's personal intervention with Hitler was directly responsible for Krupp's use of Auschwitz Jews in the Berthawerk [Krupp's factories]."[67]

Ultimately, Krupp and his fellow defendants received light sentences considering the extent of slave labor used in the Krupp factories. According to Telford Taylor, "Alfried Krupp was a very lucky man, for, had he been named to the first trial, he would almost certainly have been convicted and given a very stiff sentence by the International Military Tribunal."[68] Bureaucracy and politics saved Krupp. As William Manchester observed at the time: "Krupp was convinced that his future would be determined by statesmen, not jurists," because, toward the end of the trial proceedings, Krupp was aware that the "Four Power alliance was disintegrating at a meeting between Molotov and George Marshall in London."[69] The incipient Cold War was already changing Western powers' priorities in ways different from those that had established the Nuremberg Principles earlier at the San Francisco conference in 1945.

In Fall's case, his work as a researcher at the Nuremberg Trials informed his understanding of justice and war in a consequential way. He believed that the

United States possessed and executed serious responsibilities to administer and enforce justice after World War II. The question was: who would administer and enforce justice when it came to constraining American action after World War II? Over the next few years, this position of US primacy would remain significant in Fall's eyes, despite the contentious debates over US bombing in Dresden, elsewhere in Europe, and in Japan. What eventually became known as the Nuremberg Legacy transformed the application of justice pertaining to warfare and, according to Telford Taylor, established the fact "that the laws of war are superior to domestic law, and that individuals may be held accountable to them."

Similarly, according to the United Nations' History of the Commission: "the very essence of the Nuremberg Charter of 1945 is that individuals have international duties which transcend the national obligations of obedience imposed by the individual state. He who violates the laws of war cannot obtain immunity while acting in pursuance of the authority of the state if the state in authorizing action moves outside its competence under international law".[70]

This conception of international law, therefore, impinged on national sovereignty if the actions of that state, or individuals with "international duties," challenged or attempted to violate international law.[71] This development would become contentious but also obscured in years ahead. Instead of being even a matter of debate, the United States would neither subjugate its national jurisdiction or sovereignty in the years to come, nor would it face consequences for its involvement in future wars. Unlike those it judged as guilty during World War II—as so many Nazi and Imperial Japanese leaders were—leaders in the United States would not subsequently face any court of law with the power to punish American interventions in years to come. Debates over whether the United States would ever be subject to any severe or consequential jurisdiction over its national sovereignty would extend into the future, but far too quietly, long after the Nuremberg Trials concluded in 1949.[72]

Details explaining why the Nuremberg Principles were viewed as necessary in 1945 are critical to the debate between sovereignty and jurisdiction of international law before and during World War II. When the Nazis gained control over the Weimar Republic in 1933, their actions corrupted law by constructing fascist-oriented positivism to replace German constitutional law. National Socialist war, according to Michael Geyer, "was war for the sake of social reconstruction through the destruction of conquered peoples."[73] Through a nihilist dogma, the Nazis reduced law to an "act of will—to the identification of right with might ... where the doctrine of absolute sovereignty of the state gave rise to exaggerated nationalism in which the natural law was superseded by positive law."[74] The importance of this would undoubtedly have been evident to an observer and analyst as perceptive as Fall—it almost certainly drove Robert H. Jackson and Telford Taylor's prosecution during both the International Military Tribunal and the Nuremberg Military Tribunals.

In the trials at Nuremberg, the Nazis and their defense lawyers revealed how fascism operated in a legal world of the Nazis' making. The Nazis' defense pointed to many legal problems in the prosecutors' case, primarily because they were attempting to operate with an entirely opposing ideological—when it suited them—and through a legal framework which did not entirely mesh with that used by the prosecution. The Nazis' defense, in other words, indicated how the Allies' rules did not apply to them and where the Allies' legal indictments implicated Allied actions as much as Nazi Germany's. Between pointing out cases of *ex post facto* justice and *tu quoque* ('you also'), the Nazis' defense teams gave the Allied prosecutors many problems. Predicated on an extreme sense of autarky—which National Socialism created to isolate itself as a self-contained, thousand-year Reich—the Nazis' legal system ultimately sought to reify a self-interested state that ignored any universal or natural laws that might implicate Nazi governance. Significantly, the Nazi defense team demonstrated that their positivist approach to law prevented their state's subjection to higher laws due to the purported sovereignty of their actions. This epitomized, in short, the idea that might makes right, which was historically promoted in lyrics, such as "*Deutschland über alles*" and in the sentiment evoked in the NDSAP's party song, "*Horst-Wessel-Lied*." The Nazis' power to decide the exception, in the simplest terms, formed the heart of fascist legality.[75] The Nuremberg Tribunal, at which the Allies sought to defeat this positivist approach, revealed the criminal and fraudulent character of the Nazis' laws and sought to restore natural law as an internationally agreed-upon norm regulating war between nations.[76]

In the years leading to war and until Nazi control began to recede, the NDSAP possessed the power to enforce its ability to determine the exception and create a positivist legal framework to judge others. As perhaps all autocracies and dictatorships demonstrate, fascism functioned on the basis that determined who is above and who is under the law. As Michael Geyer described German objectives during World War II, "the war was fought to reorder the world rather than preserve or adjust existing structures of international relations" and to "establish a new national and international order through subjugation and extermination."[77] Mark Mazower similarly observed that Nazi Germany's colonization of Eastern Europe tore "down the whole noble façade of nineteenth-century international law."[78] Racial hatred leading to genocide, epitomized and consolidated through Nazi administrative unity, ultimately resulted in the Final Solution at the Wannsee Conference. Together, these steps of devolving/dismantling natural law demonstrated how Nazi planning was "the result of a well-considered, duly codified, and paragraphed public policy."[79]

The trials at Nuremberg, therefore, were a reaction to this and an effort to reestablish natural law. In doing so, the judgments rendered at Nuremberg sought to reestablish and develop more robust, institutionally backed norms to prevent and punish future crimes related to war.[80] The Genocide Convention, advocated by Rafael Lemkin, the Universal Declaration of Human Rights, and the Nuremberg Principles all constituted the trials' legacy, even if they were contested by some.[81] Fall contributed to and witnessed this legal rebalancing and attempt to reestablish natural law, mainly as it potentially related to international justice and relations after World War II. During this attempt to recalibrate legal codes regarding war at this early stage in his career, his presence at the trials was critical for his later scholarship. It was also submerged to an extent, but came to the forefront in 1965 with the large-scale aerial bombardment of Vietnam through Operation Rolling Thunder and other forms of indiscriminate warfare. Fall's background and this critical stage in his intellectual formation gave him insight into the functioning of international institutions, such as the Nuremberg Tribunals, and the importance of international cooperation on the one hand. On the other hand, it grounded his interest in international law intended to limit violence against civilians.

This legal recalibration after decades of war beginning in 1914, after all, was what the Nuremberg Trials attempted to reestablish, reimpose, and reinforce in the event of potential future conflicts. Most critically, international law constraining extrajudicial warfare centered on a supra legal oversight of state sovereignty based on the type of law Nazism attempted to destroy. Nazism viewed any supra legal system based on internationalist views, let alone religious values found in the Judeo-Christian tradition, as false and an imposition on the Third Reich's sovereignty. Fall's attendance at the Nuremberg Tribunals, and the arguments of prosecutors Robert H. Jackson and Telford Taylor, inculcated within him a sense of justice that was predicated on the Nuremberg Principles. The Nuremberg Principles, in turn, depended on principles that historically, at least since the Enlightenment, were conceived as natural law.

II—"Say I slew them not"[82]

After the War Crimes Commission concluded at Nuremberg, Fall briefly continued undergraduate study at the Sorbonne and then, returning to Germany, worked for the International Tracing Service (ITS) in Munich from November 1949 through March 1950.[83] According to Fall's CV, the tracing service was a "U.N. agency" created to reconnect children orphaned or lost during the war with their families.[84] Initially planned by the Allies while the war was in progress, the United Nations Relief and Rehabilitation Administration (UNRRA) and British Red Cross guided the program until its formal establishment on 1 January 1948 as the International Tracing Service.[85] Fall contributed to the organization as a "Child Search Officer, ITS," and his region, which included Munich and its surroundings, was known as "Area #7."[86] As part of this organization, Fall focused on helping others recover relationships—those between parents and children—of the type that he had lost during the war. Yet the job also pragmatically helped him put food on his table, while providing additional experiences and more time to refine his capabilities conducting field research. In March 1950, due to a reduction in staff, Fall left this position with ITS and returned to his studies for an undergraduate degree.[87]

In Munich, he studied at Ludwig Maximilian University for a semester while concurrently registering for the US Army Overseas European Program, administered by the University of Maryland.[88] Based in Heidelberg and initiated on 31 October 1949, the Overseas European Program also included centers in Berlin, Frankfurt, Munich, Nuremberg, and Wiesbaden. It grew to forty-two centers with an enrollment of 1,851 individuals by October 1950.[89] The program facilitated GIs' education in occupied Germany and mirrored a similar program undertaken in the postwar Pacific theater by the University of California. Fall enrolled in "History of American Civilization," taught by Dr. Verne E. Chatelain in the autumn of 1949, and then took "Government and Politics 105: Course in American Foreign Relations," taught by Dr. Martin Moser in the spring of 1950.[90] Fall's detailed, handwritten notes from these classes indicated an excellent command of English, as did his meticulously typed notes from Chatelain's course, in which he extensively recounted his professor's fourteen lectures.

A large amount of Fall's writing from this period was single-spaced and often typed on both sides of onion skin-thin paper. Notably, this often makes his papers difficult to read, but the level of detail Fall recorded in his typed notes from Chatelain's lectures suggests a profound, almost photographic memory, since it is almost certain he was not typing his notes from prerecorded lectures. He also demonstrated command over the typewriters he used, typing with fluency and minimal errors. In the rare cases where typos appear in his papers, he corrected errors in pencil or pen. In addition to mastery over his typewriters, Fall prided himself in his linguistic skills, and these certainly afforded him opportunities he rarely failed to embrace. He noted his linguistic capability in his earliest dated CV: "Accentless English (American), French, and German. Some Spanish and Russian. French Army staff interpreter diplomas in both English and German. Write all three languages with equal facility."[91]

During what would become a transition period in his life, and while taking courses in the US Army Overseas European Program, Fall supported himself by working as an assistant district manager for the US military's newspaper, *Stars and Stripes*. The job included delivering materials between offices and writing news briefs. One of Fall's pieces pointed out the availability of up-to-date legal doctrine among readers working in Nuremberg. In one of these, Fall wrote, "For those who wish to further their knowledge of courts-martial procedure, an 'Indexed Digest to the Uniformed Code of Military Justice' will be of great help."[92] Undoubtedly, these digests were not a hot item among GIs. With the postwar effort winding down, Fall turned to his studies and completed his undergraduate work in Europe at a fortuitous time. A scholarship opportunity, provided through the creation of the Fulbright Program, began in 1950. Fall sought to build upon his considerable experiential learning and ambition, and this was a trait that appeared to multiply with every opportunity seized. Therefore, with considerable momentum, he applied for a Fulbright-Smith-Mundt Fellowship for study in the United States the year the program began.

Financed with funds gained by selling surplus war property, Senator J. William Fulbright's bill creating the scholarship was brought before the United States Congress in 1945.[93] Its stated purpose was "the promotion of international goodwill through the exchange of students in the fields of education, culture, and science."[94] Fulbright, a lifelong champion of the exchange program that bore his name, later elaborated on its purpose. Writing in 1965, Fulbright explained that "important opportunities for encouraging habits of practical cooperation can also be found through international trade, business arrangements, and the settlement of financial claims—to say nothing of cultural and education exchanges, which to my mind are probably the most rewarding of all international cooperation."[95]

On 1 August 1946, President Harry Truman signed the bill establishing the Fulbright Program.[96] It soon gained prestige as a well-funded foundation for international and intellectual partnerships achieved through educational exchange. At the time, it was a remarkably innovative means of fostering the sharing of ideas, and, for Bernard Fall, it was an unprecedented opportunity to consolidate his recent achievements and find a new start in the United States. As his spouse, Dorothy Fall, reflected years later, Bernard's diary for 18 December 1950, concisely marked a happy occasion: "HURRAH, my application for fellowship has been accepted!!!"[97] This positive news was achieved through wartime service and several years of hard work assisting the United States during the Nuremberg Trials and as a UN Tracing Service officer. In the late summer of 1951, Fall moved to upstate New York as a Fulbright scholar and began a Master of Arts program in political science at the Maxwell School of Citizenship and Public Administration at Syracuse University.[98] Earlier in 1951, however, US officials in Germany had announced a political decision that frustrated Fall in ways that contrasted starkly with his enthusiasm for study in the United States.

On 31 January 1951, Radio Frankfurt interrupted its broadcast to announce the US High Commissioner for Germany's official statement on war criminal amnesties.[99] Among the amnesties announced, Alfried Krupp and most of the Krupp Corporation's board of directors were released from prison after receiving clemency that commuted their sentences to time served. This decision was made and announced by the US High Commissioner— John J. McCloy, the U.S. representative in Germany—after the Allies concluded their military governance under General Lucius Clay. The announcement, Fall quickly learned, reflected a rapidly changing worldwide political environment in the early 1950s. With Konrad Adenauer's election in 1949 as Chancellor of the Federal Republic of Germany, growing tension in Europe—and especially in Asia, with the outbreak of the Korean War on 24 June 1950—saw a change in policies affecting denazification. No longer perceived as the dregs of humanity, former Nazi leaders and collaborators were now among Germany's elite, believed by individuals such as McCloy to be key personnel in resuscitating West Germany into a bulwark against Soviet expansion in Europe. The decision to release Krupp et al. unsurprisingly outraged Fall. The news that Alfried Krupp would regain possession of all Krupp Corporation assets was especially reprehensible because Krupp's previously confiscated fortune was worth over US$500 million in 1951, and it had been significantly gained through slave labor.[100] In response to this news, Fall contended in part:

Although the "general confiscation of property is repugnant to American concepts of justice ..." to quote Mr. McCloy, it is nevertheless an accepted feature of American jurisprudence. Any pernicious use of private property on U.S. territory (firearms, etc.) may result in confiscation thereof. Likewise, Krupp misused that enormous empire of his for purposes that are beyond the law, both local and international.[101]

Fall learned of Krupp's release on 2 February 1951, two days after the radio announcement. His first published article, "The Case of Alfried Krupp," which condemned commissioner John J. McCloy's decision, was published that summer.[102] Fall argued that commuting Krupp's sentence was "politically as sound as making a major cash contribution to the Soviet propaganda war chest," and that the "only real beneficiaries from the move would be the Communists on either side of the Iron Curtain who will be able to tell their listeners: 'Remember? We told you so ...'"[103] McCloy's decision, it turned out, did stem from a reconfiguring of geopolitical calculations and a newfound reliance on German manufacturing as tension increased with the Soviet Union. Rearming Germany was the last issue facing the postwar Alliance, and until the outbreak of the Korean War, McCloy had opposed German rearmament.[104]

Fall's anger over Krupp's release was not due to his political alignment or belief in the Morgenthau Plan that aggressively called for Germany's deindustrialization after the war. Fall's enmity centered on the fact that Krupp's release was unjustified because the Korean War did not change the fact that he was a war criminal. The growing threat the Soviet Union posed did not change Krupp's guilt either. At the heart of the matter, offering clemency to Krupp undermined the Nuremberg Principles and the War Crimes Commission's work to prosecute Nazis like Krupp. Fall wrote:

> Without batting an eyelash, the Krupp works used the poor wretches from the concentration camps for the heaviest jobs that were to be found. The whole town of Essen saw every day the rag-clad column of five hundred concentration camp inmates, all girls from 15 to 20, march to their assigned places of work at Krupp's factories: twelve hours without food and without protective clothing in the armor plates rolling mill.[105]

Fall rhetorically added, "And what, Herr Krupp, happened to those girls?" Fall knew. Elizabeth and Ernestine Roth were two of the five hundred women that formed this "rag-clad" column in Essen every day. Fall might as well have asked what happened to the justice he worked so hard to support in the prosecution and sentencing of Krupp. How could the United States discard the

Nuremberg Principles for the sake of a convicted Nazi criminal who epitomized a slave overseer and robber baron in one person?

Fall was not a member of the postwar lobby group called "Prevent World War III" who published his first article, but he shared the organization's outrage and frustrations with the decisions made by American leaders. The most prominent associates of "Prevent World War III" included Lewis Mumford, William Shirer, Eleanor Roosevelt, Alfred Einstein, Eugene Rostow, and—most vocally—Henry Morgenthau, who advocated robust implementation of the Joint Chiefs of Staff [JCS] Directive 1067.[106] Based on the Morgenthau Plan to a degree, Directive 1067 sought to reduce Germany's territory and constrain its war-ravaged economy from potentially reigniting with the assistance of too much American-supplied oxygen. The postwar policy regulating the German economy, JCS 1067, was only slightly less strict than the Morgenthau Plan.[107] It was subsequently replaced as a reprieve for the German population by a more lenient policy, JCS 1779, that framed the Marshall Plan in July 1947.[108]

Fall did not criticize these more moderate policies supporting the German economy. Instead, his outrage centered on the politics of denazification generally and Krupp's release specifically. The problem of denazification remained contentious after Nuremberg, to the point that several journalists complained about lack of access to Telford Taylor's final trial report that was completed to inform readers of Nazi war crimes. When the Government Printing Office eventually released Taylor's report on 15 August 1949, Charles Van Devander, a journalist who later served as press secretary and executive to New York Governor Averell Harriman, complained that the report was intentionally "buried."[109] Other journalists, notably Thomas L. Stokes, who won the 1939 Pulitzer Prize for journalism and was a columnist for United Features Syndicate, criticized the US government for "our complete abandonment of plans to break up the giant Nazi cartels."[110] Motivation to investigate such complaints, however, appeared to dissipate with new and pressing Cold War concerns.

Van Devander, Stokes, and Fall undoubtedly pondered an array of questions. Among these, they might have wondered: why did the United States require the support of Nazi collaborators to defend against threats posed by the Soviet Union? How could the United States reverse its support for the long-deliberated verdict of convicted war criminals? It was not as if Krupp manufactured atomic bombs to protect Europe—what could his release offer western Europe that would be worth the price of undermining the Nuremberg principles that took so long to achieve? Reading between the lines in his article, it appears that Fall believed that the United States could address communist challenges without the support of convicted war criminals and do so while maintaining the integrity of the Nuremberg Principles.

Maintaining the Nuremberg legacy, Fall believed, would provide greater legitimacy for US policies elsewhere. Standing by the verdicts delivered at Nuremberg would also lend moral support to US authority in significant geopolitical contests, such as the Cold War, in which ideological superiority mattered. The moral grounding of US policy was relevant in this endeavor, in a central respect, because it legitimized US efforts to rid the world of Nazi fascism. At the same time, the Nuremberg Trials reestablished international justice and subverted the nihilistic positivism the Third Reich had inflicted on Europe and the Soviet Union. Why undermine these efforts by providing amnesty to war criminals like Krupp and others? In the Soviet Union's case, communist leaders pointed to the millions of dead and wounded, nearly 14 percent of the entire Soviet population, as proof of its antifascist commitment.[111] Was there no way to find a political solution with the Soviet Union? Was there no other way to resolve an escalating Cold War without kindling a global arms race that relied upon the support of former Nazi collaborators and their factories?

John J. McCloy, who commuted Krupp's sentence, came to his position as High Commissioner of Germany with significant experience. As the former assistant secretary of war (1941–5) and former President of the World Bank (1947–9), he became High Commissioner in the spring of 1949, replacing General Lucius Clay of the US army, who was retiring from service.[112] McCloy's decision-making centered on implementing economically favorable policies in Germany because an economically productive Germany was fundamental to European stability, mainly as political conflict with the Soviet Union and the outbreak of war on the Korean peninsula coalesced into the Cold War.[113]

Fall's anger with the decision centered on the failure to find other competent individuals familiar with industrial production who might lead German industry. In Fall's view, it was not a matter of pinning national war guilt onto Alfried Krupp and his directors: the Nuremberg Trials had already proved those facts. Fall appeared to ask: were former Nazi collaborators and war criminals the only ones capable of leading German manufacturing to the extent required to pull Germany out of economic peril? Why were war criminals the only ones capable of rearming Germany? Fall was incredulous that

Alfried Krupp and his directors were indispensable in reigniting and leading German industry during the early and tension-filled Cold War. Rearming Germany was a significant issue in Europe, to be sure, but was releasing Krupp as a means to facilitate rearmament the only option?

Evidence existed which demonstrated that Krupp was not essential to West German industry. In 1950, industrial production in West Germany reached 96 percent of what Germany had produced in 1936.[114] The only exception was industrial production in West Berlin, which was worse off than West Germany on a per capita basis because reindustrialization limped along at 38 percent of production compared to levels in 1936 during the depression.[115] It is undeniable that Berlin's stability was politically critical, especially after the airlift crisis only a few years before Krupp's release. Still, while Fall understood the logic of a revitalized Germany, he viewed Krupp's and his associates' release as a betrayal of the Nuremberg principles and a fracturing of the very values that gave a revitalized Europe a renewed meaning worth the cost of World War II.[116] Krupp's release was not a matter of economics, it was a matter of values. Specifically, it concerned the very values—namely justice and liberty—which the United States purported to protect in joining World War II.

The United States' decision to release Krupp, and other Nazis and collaborators, demonstrated a turn away from the Nuremberg legacy and belied the diplomatic and economic success embodied by the Marshall Plan. This appeared especially true because West Germany rebounded economically without convicted war criminals, such as Alfried Krupp, at the helm of the arms industry. As it mattered to Fall's early scholarship, Krupp's release contributed to a budding sense of political disillusionment and frustration that was undeniably grafted onto McCloy's decision. In Fall's perspective, Krupp's release demonstrated the reality that economic and political expediencies supplanted the values purportedly reintroduced to Europe by the justice served at Nuremberg. The United States' legitimacy in reestablishing and bolstering international law regarding warfare was damaged, therefore, in Fall's eyes. While Krupp's release may have been symbolic, it appears clear that Fall's disappointment was sharpened by the fact that it was the Americans who had ordered it.

To understand Fall's criticism, the political circumstances involved in Krupp's clemency are significant to recount. After his guilty verdict, Krupp wrote a letter to General Lucius Clay, the acting military governor of the sector in which Krupp was held at Landsberg Prison. Krupp's letter formally served as an appeal, which a review panel assessed and denied. Not only did the panel deny his appeal, the panel subsequently reconfirmed Krupp's guilty verdict on 1 April 1949.[117] Notably, Clay possessed profound acrimony for Nazis and advocated a "guilt by membership" principle during the Tribunals that, according to Telford Taylor, extended "far beyond anything that had been or ever was accepted at Nuremberg."[118] If Krupp sought clemency, Clay was not the one to ask. With the election of Konrad Adenauer as chancellor, Clay retired. As a replacement for Clay, Telford Taylor advocated that Charles La Follette be assigned the new US High Commissioner for Germany. La Follette, a strong advocate of denazification, was currently serving as military governor in Wuerttemberg-Baden when Clay decided to retire.[119] Instead of La Follette, and on Dean Acheson's recommendation, President Truman appointed John J. McCloy to High Commissioner for Germany in April 1949.[120]

Krupp only had to bide his time for another year before events on the Korean peninsula changed circumstances in his favor. When the Korean War broke out in 1950, Krupp and his attorneys were attuned to the geopolitical issues that it presented to the United States and its bearing upon the question of rearming Germany. William Manchester remarked on the circumstances of Krupp's release in 1964, writing, "the complex interweaving of Ruhr politics, NATO requirements and shifting military fortunes eight time zones away combined in a plural theme which, though unnoticed at the time, seems startling clear in retrospect."[121] In this shifting geopolitical context, Krupp and his lawyers sent another appeal to the new High Commissioner. With the hostile anti-Nazi Lucius Clay gone, and the anti-Nazi La Follette busy with another job, Krupp's reinvigorated appeal landed on McCloy's desk. The timing of McCloy's appointment as commissioner was serendipitous for Krupp: McCloy was less concerned with punishing former Nazis than "making Germany strong enough to resist the Soviets."[122]

McCloy was receptive to Krupp's appeal for clemency because of the rapidly changing geopolitical arena, including the outbreak of war in Korea in June and the evolving fear of communist expansion in Europe. McCloy saw these as problems, ultimately, in ways that US Army General Lucius Clay had not. As Adam Tooze explained, Clay's hardline position toward the German people was a consequence, in Clay's view, "of a war they caused."[123] Even with the changing geopolitical landscape, if Lucius Clay had remained High Commissioner, it is likely Clay would have looked for someone other than a convicted Nazi war criminal like Krupp to restart the German armaments industry.[124] John McCloy simply did not share Lucius Clay's views. McCloy appointed another board to review petitions for clemency in March 1950, only eleven months after the April 1949 reconfirmation of Krupp's verdict under Clay's leadership.[125] While individuals such as William Manchester saw the Korean War as a shaping event in McCloy's overall decision, the Korean War had not yet broken out. McCloy, Fall possibly believed, centered his motivations primarily on the changing context within Europe. Undoubtedly, McCloy might have viewed the Korean War as a related justification, but he could only point to it as *post hoc* evidence.

Ultimately, the review board re-evaluating the new petition advocated that McCloy release Krupp. In his statement announcing the amnesty, McCloy acknowledged that "Employment was illegal in the case of the civilians and contrary to the Hague Convention in the case of the prisoners of war."[126] However, McCloy believed, despite massive evidence provided by the tribunal against Krupp, that "slave labor was allocated by governmental authorities and the conditions under which the labor was confined were directed entirely by the concentration camp commanders in the case of civilians and by the army in case of the war prisoners."[127] McCloy was unaware of or dismissed evidence that the German Army High Command had investigated the treatment of Krupp's workers by the Gestapo within his camps and factories.[128] The claims of German officer Colonel Breyer that Alfried Krupp had failed to prevent the enslavement and mistreatment of laborers working in his factories was evidence that McCloy preferred to ignore.[129] It was not some ambiguous high command or authority that had placed "concentration camp commanders" or "the army" in Krupp's factories and camps to oversee its operations. It was Krupp and his directors.

As long as production quotas were met, Krupp undoubtedly did not think twice about the individuals meeting them. The mistreatment of workers was the fault of specific individuals, but the free hand given to those inflicting misery on Krupp's workers and overseeing the camps and factories in which they lived and worked belonged to Krupp. This attempt to distance himself from criminal actions, claiming that he had not personally mistreated workers, did not absolve him of responsibility. In Fall's view, McCloy ignored the fact that Krupp colluded with the Gestapo and SS in having them oversee his facilities, and he attempted to obscure his guilt through a complexly layered bureaucracy. McCloy's statement continued, "The judgment does indicate that several of the defendants were involved with certain of the illegalities, but it is extremely difficult to allocate individual guilt among the respective defendants."[130] This view contrasted the "guilt by membership" principle that

General Lucius Clay had advocated before McCloy replaced him as High Commissioner for Germany. As a result, McCloy determined that Krupp and his directors' offenses were no more significant than those of other firms, so he adjusted the Krupp terms to conform to "sentences in similar cases."[131]

The restitution of Krupp's fortune also stood out to the clemency board as an issue because Krupp was the only defendant to have property confiscated. While McCloy restored Krupp's fortune "to introduce a certain uniformity in the sentences," he did not explain why such uniformity mattered.[132] Most likely, according to Walter Isaacson and Evan Thomas, "McCloy was bothered by the arbitrary confiscation of the Krupp property; it offended his strong Wall Street lawyer's belief in property rights."[133] Fall found the confiscation of Krupp's property and fortune to be neither arbitrary nor inappropriate. It appeared to Fall that McCloy simply ignored the fact that Krupp had actively sought slave labor, as did other firms like Flick KG and IG Farben, built his fortune on the backs of slave laborers, and had treated them so brutally that even the German High Command had complained about Krupp's treatment of its workers.[134]

The facts, which Fall personally gathered, appeared not to matter. Fall's castigations of the clemency board and McCloy's decision demonstrated his exasperation that such a short-sighted and politically motivated decision would undermine the verdicts and legacy achieved at Nuremberg. Krupp's release provided one of the first indications, at least to Fall, that American principles—and the international principles of justice determined at Nuremberg—failed to override political expediency. In his terse article, Fall recounted Krupp's support for the Nazi Party, his illegal manufacturing, and his use of slave labor with evidence personally collected for the Tribunal, but to no avail.

"Nevertheless," Fall wrote on the subject of restoring Krupp's property and fortune, "the findings of the U.S. High Commission were 'that confiscation in this case constitutes discrimination against the defendant unjustified by any considerations attaching peculiarly to him ...'"[135] Fall's rebuttal of this claim cited the Nuremberg Trial's record. Allies, especially France, Fall knew, were not happy about the German arms industry's rebirth in the Ruhr. Older individuals, who had witnessed the dismantling of the Treaty of Versailles during the interwar years, had witnessed this progression of events once before, and even as late as 1951 fears of a militant and reinvigorated Germany had not subsided. These fears would have significant consequences in the relations between the United States and France as they pertained to collective defense and French participation in a proposed European Defense Community (EDC) in Europe.¹³⁶ Fall appeared to understand this, writing:

> The return of Krupp into the Ruhr spells labor trouble in this vital area, and also troubles with the Western European allies of the U.S. since they feel that they have a direct interest in the matter but have been bypassed by the completely unilateral decision of the U.S. High Commissioner.¹³⁷

Due to France's difficult financial situation after World War II, and its expensive involvement in Indochina and its other colonies, France "could not block the rearmament of West Germany." France's efforts to regain and keep its overseas empire in Southeast Asia while managing its participation in the EDC intensified after 1951. By 1954, according to historian Frank Costigliola, the "issues of German rearmament and the Indochinese war fused in a global crisis."¹³⁸ This, as Costigliola undoubtedly sought to underscore, was manifested eventually in the defeat of French forces by the Vietnamese communists at Dien Bien Phu in April and May 1954.

The "troubles with Western European allies of the U.S." to which Fall referred in 1951 affected, therefore, not just relations pertaining to the United States and Europe's continental interests, but also extended to US support for France's war in Indochina, which began in late 1946. US Ambassador to France Douglas Dillon warned that "Military defeat in Vietnam could trigger 'a neutralist government in France that would recreate the wartime Franco-USSR alliance in order to prevent German rearmament' and 'an angry Congress might pull our troops from Europe destroying NATO.'"¹³⁹ The "troubles" Fall perceived emerging from German rearmament—exacerbated in Fall's eyes if led by Nazi associates like Krupp—triggered his realization that German rearmament involved France in ways that had serious consequences for relations between the United States and France.

In a scenario that John J. McCloy appeared to support, the rearmament of Germany locked West Germany into the Western Alliance. Therefore, if the Nuremberg legacy had to be scuttled as the price for a stronger Western Alliance, which German rearmament provided, that was a price worth paying. However—and this perhaps was not a factor that McCloy envisioned as a consequence—German rearmament also contributed to France's demands for the United States to ensure its security against potential renewed German aggression. To ensure that the Americans would make good on their guarantee to do so, France could dangle the possibility that France might turn to the Soviet Union for protection, should the United States not follow through. In this case, awareness of early twentieth-century historical lessons was a serious factor at work. The idea of another Russia-France alliance—as a means to hedge against a strong Germany—was not appealing, not least because Russia had long since become the communist Soviet Union. Another option for France was to focus on its potential EDC commitment to ensure American guarantees.

The EDC angle entailed that the United States would consider French demands, including continued financial and diplomatic support for France's operations in Indochina, in exchange for France's acceptance of a potential EDC led by the United States. Only with the United States guaranteeing such support, which was understandable considering French–German history, would France comply with American demands allowing West Germany's rearmament. To be sure, these were evolving issues in 1951 when Fall's article condemning the decision to release Krupp was published. Nevertheless, given subsequent events involving Germany's rearmament, the United States, France, and the role of Indochina in US–French relations after 1951, Fall's concerns regarding German rearmament are notable.

The fact that Fall called attention to French concerns over German rearmament was either prescient or indicative of a growing awareness of the transactional nature of power. His understanding of how power functioned in the complex Cold War political context is critical to underscore because it demonstrated Fall's knowledge of political history in Europe and how overseas colonies might figure into contemporary decision-making. At the very least, his historical sensibility indicated that he understood how events affecting him and the world hinged on the catastrophic history between France and Germany, which played out during World War I and again in World War II. There were undoubtedly clear demarcations that one war was over, and, as Winston Churchill's "Sinews of Peace" speech indicated, that a new and different kind of war had begun.

These transitions also occurred with consequences that were undeniably difficult to discern in the moment. Fall knew neither what the future held, nor did he have inside information regarding serious political decisions that might determine possible outcomes. What he did possess was a strong background in reading history and applying it to events he saw unfolding around him. He might have not known this at the time, but the price the United States paid in supporting German rearmament led to an accommodation concerning US–French relations over Indochina. The consequences of this particular compromise also depended on the overall political context operating within France's many and diverse colonies. Among these, France had already redistributed many of its expeditionary forces from Indochina to Madagascar to put down the Malagasy Uprising in 1947–8. At the same time, committing these troops to Madagascar released critical pressure on Vietnamese communists in Southeast Asia, who had been undertaking a revolution against French control since August 1945 and through serious other efforts long before 1945. France's ability to retain control over Indochina, therefore, was growing worse by the time Fall perceived German rearmament as a serious problem. The idea that Krupp might lead the rearmament effort only made the problem worse.

As to Krupp's guilt, in a pithy dig characteristic of Fall's style, he wrote:

> Documented examples of Krupp's criminal activities abound. If a man's signature on a document means that he has at least held the piece of paper in his hands, the record of the Krupp trial shows beyond a reasonable doubt that through Krupp's hands passed requests for the looting of machinery from foreign countries, order for the "integration" of foreign factories into the Krupp Empire, as well as requests for considerable amounts of slave manpower.[140]

This echoed the Nuremberg Military Tribunal's closing statement that explained the importance of Nazi SS connections to obtain labor and that "the criminal record was not compiled under duress or fear; it is the record of voluntary acts of these who stand accused."[141] To this Fall added details regarding Elizabeth and Ernestine Roth's testimony which noted, "Alfried Krupp's order to begin anti-tank shell fuse production in the infamous Auschwitz death camp, in order to make the utmost of the cheap manpower available there."[142]

Others shared Fall's outrage over McCloy's decision to release Krupp in 1951. Articles in the *New York Times* and London's *News Chronicle*, *Daily Express*, and *Sunday Express* all demonstrated immense frustration with the High Commissioner's decision.[143] McCloy appeared either not to understand Krupp's guilt as deeply as Fall or Telford Taylor, or not to care, and holding German rearmament in such importance that it necessitated forgetting the past to move on. As William Manchester noted, the truth "seems to be that no one involved in the clemency decision had taken a really close look at the record."[144] Fall recognized that geopolitical concerns weighed heavily in the decision for clemency. Fast-moving global events also assisted in eclipsing criticism of Krupp's release, and, as a result of the brewing global crisis formed by German rearmament and the war in Indochina, interest in penalizing convicted Nazi war criminals was fading by late 1951. The Society for the Prevention of World War III, along with its arguments, had already lost significant influence by the late 1940s due to numerous positive reports on

German recovery. The Marshall Plan, as a driver for recovery, represented a sea change in global affairs because, in one view, "its successful implementation shifted the mainstream debate away from the wartime concern with emasculating Germany's industry."[145] What Fall could not accept was why denazification, and the release of specific war criminals, remained so critical to Germany's economic recovery. In a concluding paragraph in his article, he noted, "Western German industrial production has made an amazing recovery through the Marshall Plan without the personal help of war criminals like Krupp et al., and, therefore, stands no appreciable gain at this stage of the game from their reinstatement."[146]

A few final remarks on this pivotal moment in Fall's career are important because they concern the role of the United States in the world and US support for France's reoccupation of Vietnam after World War II. Senator J. William Fulbright, the founder of the exchange program that brought Fall to the United States, posed a question in late 1945 that anticipated problems Fall brought up in his article, "The Case of Alfried Krupp," in 1951. The United States' postwar foreign policy, Fulbright claimed, offered a choice between "either armed might and imperialism on the one hand or rules of law enforceable by the United Nations on the other."[147] Fulbright saw the United States, in the aftermath of World War II, at a crossroads. Either the United States' legacy of colonialism embodied in the Spanish–American War would continue, or the United States could choose a path that would demand subsuming its sovereignty under UN oversight according to the international rule of law. Samuel Moyn also described this complex turning point in America's relationship to international law, writing:

> The American state has always opposed a criminal prohibition on aggression, but for two opposite reasons. Before December 1941, it was because it could not tolerate a collective security system that might require global intervention. Thereafter, it was because it would not tolerate a collective security system that imposed risks of criminal indictment on global intervention ... Nuremberg mattered not primarily for the breakthrough to punishment of atrocity, but because it marked a passing moment in between eras when, for inverse reasons, the United States would not include, let alone prioritize, criminal punishment for warmaking as a task for international law.[148]

If the United States were to intervene in other countries, it would only accept an international system in which the United States would not be constrained, let alone penalized, for political or moral liabilities associated with such interventions. The United States would remain unfettered in its war-making when needed, and if this entailed dismissing the Nuremberg principles, then that was the necessary compromise. As Moyn so astutely observed, this moment would have significant consequences for the United States and its ability to rationalize intervention abroad for the remainder of the twentieth century—and well into the early twenty-first as well.

In this regard, Fall viewed McCloy's decision with a great deal of anger. Yet McCloy's decision was also symbolic of American shortsightedness and willingness to compromise its central values, such as justice and liberty for all. These were the very values that the United States claimed to be promoting in the world, values which—eventually along with equality—the United States continued to struggle to achieve within its own borders. These, more than anything, were undeniably central to what Fall conceived of as the most complete fulfillment of what the United States represented in the world and what it offered to immigrants, such as himself. In Fall's eyes, McCloy's decision indicated "the passing moment," as Samuel Moyn describes it, when the United States would hold itself above condemnation or punishment for potential future war-making as a criminal act (at least, as a criminal act enforceable under international law).[149] Instead, the United States had chosen another path. This path, as Fulbright described it, "was the course of armed might and imperialism."[150]

Moyn further described this shift in American foreign policy after World War II: "Nuremberg's true significance is thus not simply as an aggression trial but that it took place in a passing window of plausibility that opened then shut."[151] The "passing window of plausibility," in which greater enforcement of rules governing warfare under international law, was at stake. Senator J. William Fulbright anticipated this kind of turning point in 1945 and perceived this as one of two possibilities for America's future foreign policy. As Fall understood it in 1951, this was not a passing window but more of a door slamming shut. This paradigmatic shift, if it is considered as such, would create a series of consequences stemming from US intervention in other countries during the post-World War II era across the globe.[152]

Despite Fall's frustration, his research documenting Krupp's actions during World War II was important. Even though Krupp was released, Fall could be satisfied that he had documented Krupp's guilt and that politically expedient decisions could not wash away the permanence of that guilt. In this way, Fall agreed with Associate Justice Robert H. Jackson's summation for the prosecution, made 26 July 1946, because it spoke volumes on the inviolable veracity of the trials' judgments. Jackson closed his opening statement during the International Military Tribunal by referencing Shakespeare's *Richard III*:

It is against such a background that these defendants now ask this Tribunal to say that they are not guilty of planning, executing, or conspiring to commit this long list of crimes and wrongs. They stand before the record of this Trial as bloodstained Gloucester stood by the body of his slain king. He begged of the widow, as they beg of you: "Say I slew them not." And the Queen replied, "Then say they were not slain. But dead they are…" If you were to say of these men that they are not guilty, it would be as true to say that there has been no war, there are no slain, there has been no crime.[153]

III—The Keystone of the Arch

In contrast to his short first article, Fall's 1952 Master's thesis at Syracuse University, "The Keystone of the Arch: A Study of German Illegal Rearmament, 1919–1936," was a 266-page dissection of Nazi Germany's dismantling of the post-World War I order constructed at Versailles.[154] The extent to which Fall devoted himself to study of rearmament during the interwar years indicated his drive to understand how power functioned politically and how the Treaty of Versailles had failed to prevent subsequent conflict leading to World War II. His study assessed how the Treaty created the League of Nations, punished Germany, allowed for Allied occupation of the Rhineland, and provided extensive national self-determination within Europe, but still could not prevent future upheaval. Moreover, "The Keystone of the Arch" demonstrated that Fall's academic work had sensitized him, conditioning the way he viewed social and political factors. He viewed conflicts as complex socio-political landscapes early on, but did so without universalizing them out of only his lived experience.

As a young academic, Fall integrated political analysis with other war-planning levels involving the armaments industry and the German military to reveal a far more complex picture. For these reasons, the study demonstrated an essential progression in his thought. It revealed how he used his experiences in the French Resistance and as a research analyst at Nuremberg to infuse his academic analysis with details that could not be obtained vicariously or solely through academic research. Fall was hardly a removed spectator to German expansion, and his ability to integrate firsthand knowledge while retaining academic objectivity is notable. In knowing Fall's background, it is difficult to read his thesis and perceive him as somehow disconnected from his topic, as if he were writing about the Congress of Vienna of 1814–15. Altogether, his thesis indicates an applied analytical approach and synergy of skills that distinguished his early and precocious scholarship. In this regard, his work might have differed—at the time—from more deskbound peers he encountered at Syracuse University who had not fought in World War II or who had more prosaic backgrounds.

Fall came to his MA thesis well-prepared and well-informed. At Nuremberg, he had already completed study of German rearmament for the War Crimes Commission, so building upon his previous knowledge and work to finish a graduate degree efficiently made sense. Consequential events leading to World War II, however, were not the only subjects he studied at Syracuse. Among other issues in the world in 1952, Fall wrote about the political conflict between Britain and Egypt that would eventually culminate into the Suez Crisis in October 1956.[155] The range of topics he studied demonstrated a general interest in geopolitics, especially pertaining to colonial issues as decolonization gained momentum, but these were ancillary subjects to his primary focus on German rearmament and Nazism.

Fall's thesis was significant at the time because few other studies existed on the subject. He remarked, "No major work has come to this student's attention which—with the new documentary evidence at hand—satisfactorily explains the decisive role played by the German armed forces in shaping the events which ultimately led Republican Germany to its ruin."[156] He allocated much attention to the dismantling of the articles of the Treaty of Versailles, contributing to a field that has been even more thoroughly studied in the decades since.[157] With his specific interest in the German military's role in the subversion of the Treaty's articles, however, Fall was breaking new ground. He argued that his contribution:

> to the field of political science should lie in the fact that it shows the ways and means used by the military establishment of a country to subvert to its own purposes the whole apparatus of constitutional government until it became "the state" itself; in the same manner in which a parasitical growth will gain control of the body which carried it—until it eventually will kill the very carrier which is its source of life.[158]

This form of subversion, in which an organization parallels an established power to displace and then eventually replace it, fascinated Fall. In his writing on this subject in 1952, what concerned Fall was the lack of attention given to the military's role in undermining democracy in Germany. He observed:

> It is the German military who may safely be termed the "Grave-Diggers" of the Weimar Republic. The military paved the way for Totalitarianism; for the "Rule by Decree." They held the "Keystone to the Arch," the necessary military power which could have dispersed Hitler's private armies (the *Sturmabteilung*) into the

four winds and could have saved the Republic as it had saved itself from left-wing elements in the early post-war years.[159]

His examination of German rearmament after 1919 and his detailed analysis of the events that finally unraveled Weimar in 1933 reveals an early and illuminating dimension of his scholarship that may be unknown to scholars and readers who are only familiar with Fall's later writings on Southeast Asia.

Fall identified three main stages in the subversion of the Treaty of Versailles and in German rearmament between 1919 and 1936. The first stage included "the years immediately following the German Surrender after World War I"; the second consisted of "the period of illegal rearmament"; and the third stage Fall defined as the "period of open violation of the rearmament clauses of the Treaty of Versailles."[160] Through his analytical progression of these stages, his broader assessment revealed how Germany's forces capitalized on Allied disunity and other weaknesses. Second, it revealed how the United States and democracies in Europe were unwilling to enforce the treaty's provisions or resist challenges to its legitimacy. Fall knew the rise of Nazism was a manipulation of interdependent factors, including the Weimar Republic's internal political weaknesses, dissatisfaction within German society, and concerns regarding German industrial capacity. After 1929, the Great Depression inflicted such severe stresses on the German people that previous cracks in society and the economy were only pried open further.

Within Germany, Fall also analyzed the critical role the *Sturmabteilung* (SA) played in the NSDAP (National Socialist German Workers' Party) gaining a majority in the Reichstag during the March 1933 elections, mainly through the SA's physical intimidation of communist and socialist competitors. What appeared to fascinate Fall the most in his study of the "third stage of open violation of the Treaty of Versailles," based on the amount of space he allocated to the subject, was the internal competition for power among the NSDAP, its proxy the SA, and the German military. While the Nazi Party initially relied on the SA for support and manipulated the SA's proclivity for violence against communists in particular, the Nazi Party eventually subverted SA leadership as a potential threat to its political power and policies.

After the Nazis secured a majority in 1933, Operation Hummingbird—*Nacht der langen Messer* (the Night of the Long Knives)—purged SA leadership under Ernst Röhm in mid-1934. This event was a progression in the Nazis' overall strategy for political subversion of Weimar that transfixed Fall.[161] He perceived the Night of the Long Knives as the political action, through the assassination of Nazi competitors, that caused the "German

Army's Generals to climb onto the Nazi bandwagon. No doubt they hoped later to take over direction themselves. That exactly the reverse happened is one of the ironies of history."[162] Eliminating SA leadership, Fall knew, helped Hitler consolidate the German military's support, because military leaders despised Ernst Röhm and the SA and viewed them as serious, even if far less capable, competitors.[163] This was the type of historical lesson from which Fall drew a great deal of insight. The development, manipulation, and eventual forsaking of the SA—as a parallel organization that initially assisted the NSDAP's plans to gain power over the German army and other rivals—provided a hard lesson in the transactional nature of power that could cut in multiple directions.

Fall's capacity to analyze the NSDAP's incremental subversion of the Weimar Republic is a striking feature in his early scholarship. Subversion of Weimar required, Fall noted, a hard-core cadre with external support, especially in the form of enormous financial assistance provided by German industrialists, led by the Krupp Corporation and others. The Krupps were particularly vital because of their dominance in the business sector of arms manufacturing. Politically, the focus of Nazi leadership centered on deploying ideologues to penetrate existing organizations to challenge and eliminate weaker factions. This process created a divide-and-conquer form of organizational integration which Fall described simply as infiltration.[164] Fall recognized the unique context and circumstances leading to Nazi consolidation of power. His identification of political processes, including subversion and infiltration, also provided substantive foundations for his thought on warfare. He was increasingly coming to recognize that war incorporated far greater interdependence between its socio-political-military-economic components than what he had experienced through guerrilla warfare with the Maquis and French Resistance or with conventional operations with the French army during the liberation of Europe. The primacy of political factors appeared to gain ascendency in his thought on warfare, even at this early stage in his scholarship.

In his thesis, Fall also recounted how Hitler's government became a legal dictatorship through subterfuge masked as democratic processes, resulting from a consequential series of events in 1933.[165] The Reichstag Fire Decree, issued on 28 February 1933, gave the NSDAP legal power to dismantle civil protections and undermine internal competitors, such as SA leaders and external political competitors, which included Social Democrats (SPD) and the German Communist Party (KPD).[166] Depicted as an "emergency presidential decree," the Fire Decree was a watershed moment. The decree and those issuing it were critically aided by individuals whose political and economic interests aligned with those of the NSDAP, which as an organization, eventually followed through on its promises for booming economic growth through the dynamic rearmament of the German armed forces.[167] Gustav Krupp's financial support for the Nazi Party at this crucial point included over a million Reichsmarks disbursed on 20 February 1933, eight days before the proclamation of the Reichstag Fire Decree.[168] This vital financial infusion facilitated Nazi operations until the last election of the Weimar Republic was held on 5 March 1933, almost two months after Hitler was appointed Chancellor.[169]

The Enabling Act of 1933 followed closely on 24 March 1933.[170] It abolished remaining civil liberties in Germany and allocated state power to the German Cabinet, led by Chancellor Hitler, thus enabling the passage of laws without involving the Reichstag. Through a corruption of Article 48 in the Weimar Republic's constitution, the "Enabling Act," renewed in 1937 and again in 1941, provided Hitler constitutional authority to enact law and policy by decree.[171] The Nazis retained the constitution, it is important to stress, as the "legal constitutional basis" for the Third Reich in order to legitimize its promises for territorial expansion among the German electorate who supported Nazi-led imperialism in Europe.[172] The Nazis' actions after 1933 followed laws, but, unsurprisingly, they were laws devised through a perversion of democracy. This epitomized a form of legal positivism in which laws are not formed or judged by questions of justice or humanity but by those who make them, and who, as a result, determine the exception. This process explains how the Holocaust and the exploitation of slave labor were not a matter of morality for the Nazis. They were a matter of policy.

The German military was critical in making such policy a reality and implementing it beyond German borders. The promise for *Lebensraum* was tied up with this because geographical enlargement would "secure" Germany and fulfill its aspirations as the Nazis envisioned them. According to Michael Geyer:

> At last, German society was to be autonomous, free from the vagaries of the market, and secure behind its extended imperial borders. The National Socialist answer to the challenge of mass participation in politics and war and their response to the economic and social crisis of the interwar years consisted of a populist and militant form of hegemony. The resulting ideological strategy fused with the operational opportunism of the German military.[173]

Nazi leadership required control over the German army through its leaders, even though the military's general staff was an organization banned by the Treaty of Versailles. In turn, the general staff depended on rearmament as a condition for its capacity to wage war. In the Third Reich, state-making and warmaking were entirely symbiotic.

Reflecting in 1966, Fall suggested that his Master's thesis, "The Keystone Arch," was "perfectly esoteric and something that no one has heard from since."[174] While his evaluation might have been correct for a time, it is now no longer accurate. The thesis was and remains insightful because it described how Germany came to power between 1919 and 1936, but also because it marked the end of Fall's sole preoccupation with World War II, and his turn to the study of Southeast Asia. His concluding statements in the thesis centered on the World War I Allies' lack of resolution when they forced Germany to sign, in 1919, "a treaty whose application these powers were unwilling to enforce."[175] He added:

> Allied action on behalf of the Treaty (of Versailles) is one long series of lamentable capitulations. In comparison, a complete abrogation of the Treaty by unified Allied action would have been far less harmful to postwar relations than the whittling down of it, paragraph by paragraph, until it was but a ridiculous and meaningless sham of the original.[176]

Fall argued that the enforcement of the articles of the Treaty of Versailles demanded action and a stronger sense of political realism by Allied leaders after World War I. When withdrawal and appeasement "morph into an unwillingness to defend an existing order under assault," as Hal Brands and Charles Edel argued, "the results can themselves be tragic."[177] Brands and Edel's powerful assessment certainly echoes a view Fall also shared in his 1952 thesis. The paralysis and emerging dangers leading to World War II, however, were far more than tragic. They led to catastrophe. About the Allies' failure to enforce the Treaty of Versailles, Fall observed that "in International Politics, to paraphrase Talleyrand, there are acts that are sometimes worse than crimes: mistakes."[178] This insight was critical to Fall's later scholarship because it indicated his understanding of how mistakes led to war. Crimes, as brutal and horrendous as he knew they could be, only made war worse.[179]

3

FIRST REFLECTIONS ON A WAR

I—Washington, DC, 1952

Bernard Fall was averse to going on summer break while completing his MA at Syracuse University in 1952, so he enrolled in a class taught by Dr. Amry Vandenbosch at the School of Advanced International Studies (SAIS) at Johns Hopkins University.[1] He rationalized the choice, writing: "I had more time on my hands than I thought I would have and decided to do some work in a different field ... they offered an Asian concentration and for the first time there was a part of a course devoted to Indo-China and I took that."[2] Fall's decision determined the direction of his career, and Indochina subsequently dominated his scholarship. This period also marked a turning point in his study of warfare because the conflict in Indochina was a war of decolonization, and that provided unfamiliar challenges after World War II. The convergence of Fall's experience, decision, and changes in warfare positioned him as the foremost author describing the conflict in Indochina in English in the 1950s and 1960s.

As a career move, Fall's decision and timing was propitious. The rupture of power in the Indo-Pacific early in World War II, created by the Japanese occupation of European colonies in the region, initiated decolonization and encouraged anti-colonial movements that had been quietly simmering—some of them approaching a boil—for decades before the war. Communist-led anti-colonialist movements in Indochina and elsewhere were incompletely understood in America. And Indochina, a region immensely diverse in both its population and ecology, was mostly unknown among the American civilian population. In contrast, French citizens generally had a greater awareness of Southeast Asia because of France's colonies, protectorates, and overall economic stake in the region, which originated in the mid-nineteenth century as Western colonialism began to tighten its hold on the region. French interests broadened in earnest in 1887, when France integrated the colony of Cochinchina in Southern Vietnam together with France's neighboring protectorates in Annam, Tonkin, and Cambodia to become French Indochina. Several years later, France further consolidated its position in Southeast Asia, adding Laos as a protectorate after the Franco-Siamese War of 1893.[3]

World War II and the early Cold War dramatically altered American interest in France's Southeast Asian colonies. John T. McAlister and Paul Mus claimed that Americans' awareness of the region was, in fact, negligible until containing communism and people's revolutions associated with Marxism became a priority.[4] After the formation of the communist People's Republic of China on 1 October 1949, Americans, and especially those in political positions of power, increasingly began to take an alarmist view of the conflict in Southeast Asia.[5] This event was geopolitically significant, yet Fall would later contextualize communism in Asia without exaggerating its rarity as a phenomenon. Writing in 1966, he noted:

> Communism has not added a thing that participants in other doctrinal wars (the French Revolution or the religious wars) did not know just as well. But communism did develop a more adaptable doctrine. The merit of communism has been to recognize precisely the usefulness of the social, economic, and political doctrines in the field to diminish as much as possible the element of risk inherent in the military effort.[6]

Fall recognized that the Chinese Communists triumphed not necessarily just because of ideology in their war with Chinese Nationalists, but because of their ability to adapt and survive against the much more powerful Chinese Nationalist forces supported by the United States. Fall's decision to focus on Indochina in 1952, becoming one of the first writers to describe the region and events there in English, did indeed prove timely. It was a moment in which his wartime knowledge of guerrilla tactics from the Maquis and French Resistance, his formal educational training, and his research skills gained as an analyst at Nuremberg converged with the opportunity to study and write about war in a region that was of growing geopolitical interest. After the founding of the Democratic Republic of Vietnam (DRV) in Hanoi on 2 September 1945, and especially after the establishment of the People's

FIRST REFLECTIONS ON A WAR

Republic of China in 1949, France's conflict with the Viet Minh evolved into a war with much greater strategic importance. According to Fall's friend Philippe Devillers, Fall initiated his study of Indochina at this critical time because "the problem of Vietnam appeared to Fall, already, as the most important and the most serious dangers of the era."[7] Studying the development of communism in Southeast Asia, therefore, made sense to him. Meanwhile, aside from scholarship generated by specialists, Americans' general lack of knowledge of the region and their latent interest in potentially wanting more created a professional opportunity which Fall could and did pursue.

The catalyst for Fall's decision to study Indochina was a class on Southeast Asia with a visiting professor at SAIS, Dr. Amry Vandenbosch, affectionately known as "Dr. Van."[8] Fall's course with Vandenbosch during the summer of 1952 was fortuitous. Aside from this one year in which he was a visiting professor at SAIS, Vandenbosch otherwise spent his entire academic career at the University of Kentucky. In Lexington, Vandenbosch taught political science from 1933 to 1958 and then directed the Patterson School at the university from 1959 to 1965. It is possible that Fall would have eventually determined Indochina was the right subject for him, and he might have met other instructors who could help him, but Vandenbosch was a good match. Additionally, Fall's decision to study Indochina in 1952 included an advantage not widely available to Americans. Because Fall was a French citizen and a World War II veteran of the French army, he was permitted to travel to Indochina and received material support for lodging, food, and transportation within Vietnam, Cambodia, and Laos while accompanying French troops on missions. Furthermore, military operations in Indochina were at an intense level and, although Fall hadn't known this at the time, would reach a critical turning point in early 1954. Had he waited, he might not have studied Indochina, or seized the opportunity he did, after France's defeat in 1954. Fall was also fortunate to work with Vandenbosch because of the experience and expertise Vandenbosch brought to the classroom. In Dr. Van's class, "Colonialism and Nationalism in Southeast Asia," Fall learned from Vandenbosch's experiences in the US military as well as his diplomatic service for the US State Department between 1943 and 1946.[9]

In Vandenbosch, an expert on Indonesian politics, Fall found a mentor who wove knowledge gained through field research, as well as personal experience with war and politics, into academic study. According to scholar Vincent Davis, Vandenbosch was "never without well-peppered and sometimes well-salted views on a wide range of public issues both domestic and international."[10]

Davis was a colleague of Vandenbosch's at the University of Kentucky and later led the Patterson School himself. Writing in 1991, Davis added that Dr. Van "could quickly smile during and after loud exchanges of views, often proposing a beer and a game of pool as the denouement for a vociferous shouting match."[11] Vandenbosch's verve, knowledge, and maybe even his skills shooting pool grew out of the diverse experiences that shaped his life.

During World War I, Vandenbosch served as an intelligence officer in the US army because he was fluent in French. He was soon assigned to US Army General John Pershing's Allied Expeditionary Force staff and directly worked with Pershing as his translator. After the war, Vandenbosch returned to his home in Michigan, resumed undergraduate studies at the University of Chicago, and later completed his PhD in political science at the University of Chicago in 1926.[12] Coincidentally, Vandenbosch was a peer of Harold Lasswell, an interdisciplinary and innovative scholar working in political science, sociology, and psychology. Lasswell worked predominantly on the politics of violence and propaganda in autocracies and, in 1941, produced an influential study of totalitarianism.[13] According to Gabriel Almond, Lasswell's expertise began with his 1927 dissertation "on propaganda in the 1914–1918 war which was a systematic effort to place World War I propaganda experience in the theory of politics."[14]

Lasswell's scholarship undeniably influenced Fall's thought and writing. In later scholarship, Fall cited themes Lasswell had assessed in 1941, particularly those related to the subversion of political administrations. Fall even used the title of a Lasswell article for a chapter in his 1963 book, *The Two Viet-Nams: A Political and Military Analysis*.[15] It is almost certain that Vandenbosch introduced Fall to Lasswell's work during their class together at SAIS in 1952. Methodologically, Lasswell's academic approach, which included sociology, political science, and economics—the latter being Lasswell's undergraduate major—resulted from an interdisciplinary outlook fostered in the intellectually progressive and creative environment simmering at the University of Chicago during the interwar years.[16] This environment and the multidisciplinary approach it encouraged certainly informed Lasswell's scholarship, enabling him to focus upon interwar political troubles, first in his 1936 political-theory formula, "Politics is the study of who gets what, when, and how," and later in his 1941 article, "The Garrison State."[17] This latter work focused upon "the supremacy of the specialist on violence, and the dictatorial, governmentalized, centralized, and integrated, nature of authority."[18] Fall's direct experience with violence and authority in Nazi-controlled Europe predisposed him to be receptive to Lasswell's arguments and other theoretical approaches to understanding violence. Lasswell's analysis on the logic of violence in authoritarian settings, inspired Fall—and may have even served as a potential model on which to build in some respects—to integrate theory and practice into his work to create a more unified and descriptive analytical framework to assess how power functioned through violence.

Fall and Vandenbosch's intellectual connection also likely stemmed from a mutual appreciation for each other's wartime experience, which both individuals drew upon for their academic studies. They, after all, were both veterans and almost certainly shared a sense of camaraderie as such. In addition to his education and World War I service on Pershing's staff, Vandenbosch also served in the Office of Strategic Services (OSS) in the Southwest Pacific in 1941–2 and then conducted diplomatic work for the US Department of State between 1943 and 1946. Working for the State Department, Vandenbosch served with the delegation to the San Francisco Conference in 1944–5, at which the United Nations Charter was drafted and approved.[19] It was here that Vandebosch and Fall had yet another connection.

A basis for Fall's research as an analyst for the War Crimes Commission at Nuremberg came about, in a key respect, because the development of the UN charter on 26 June 1945 contributed to establishing the International Court of Justice.[20] Later, on 8 August 1945, the International Court of Justice created and legally grounded the Charter of the International Military Tribunal's authority, which was also known as the Nuremberg and London Charter.[21] Fall was intimately familiar with the Nuremberg Charter because it guided his research as an analyst for the War Crimes Commission between 1946 and 1948, and because the Charter provided a framework for the overall prosecution of Nazi defendants. Fall and Vandenbosch's past experiences, at least as it concerned the Nuremberg Charter, therefore, genuinely intersected. While Vandenbosch participated in the creation of the Charter at San Francisco, Fall's efforts supported the implementation of the Charter's principles at Nuremberg. The Nuremberg Charter, and the subsequent war crimes trials prosecuted under the UN International Court of Justice's authority, was a shared connection. This suggested they shared an abiding concern for principles that would ensure the rule of law in international relations and in times of war.

Vandenbosch's work for the State Department also consisted of his membership on the "Subcommittee on Territorial Problems." President Franklin Roosevelt directed this organization to study and create plans for an international trusteeship for Indochina in November 1943, which was intended to guide the implementation of self-determination for subjects in European overseas colonies.[22] Unfortunately, the US-led international trusteeship idea failed due to numerous obstacles, one of which had a historical basis in 1919. Point Five in Woodrow Wilson's Fourteen Points, published in January 1918, endorsed self-determination among colonized peoples, but it was never realized after World War I.[23] This was an initial point of failure, but another came along two years after the United States entered World War II. Point Three of the Atlantic Charter, pronounced in August 1941 to clarify war aims between the United States and Great Britain, revived the idea that self-determination might extend to Europe's colonies, and it served as a source of inspiration for colonial subjects seeking independence.[24] When the Atlantic Charter failed to support self-determination in the colonies, it appeared to be a false promise to colonial peoples looking to the United States as a champion that might ensure, or at least aid them in their fight for, freedom from colonial rule. The failure to realize the hope inspired by the Atlantic Charter toward the end of the war did not mean Roosevelt had forgotten pledges supporting self-determination or that he was obligated to the other Allies on this issue. As Roosevelt explained in a late 1944 memorandum to Secretary of War Henry Stettinius, "I have made no agreement, definite or otherwise, with the British, French, or Dutch to retain their Far Eastern Colonial possessions."[25] The creation of the Subcommittee on Territorial Problems, in many respects, indicated Roosevelt's sincerity and support for the achievement of self-determination in European-held colonies across Southeast Asia. This, of course, included France's colony and protectorates in Indochina.

Aside from the Netherlands' position regarding Indonesia, European countries and their far-flung colonial administrations unsurprisingly resisted the Subcommittee and Roosevelt's concept and undermined even the idea of the potential implementation of a trusteeship for Indochina. Vandenbosch and his fellow State Department planning team recognized that France was exceedingly unwilling to support self-determination and that its position, perhaps because France had been weakened by World War II, was resolute. Independence for any of the countries forming Indochina would undermine France's exploitation of Indochinese resources, especially rubber, the demand for which had surged due to growing bicycle and automobile sales during the twentieth century.[26]

Private concerns, often led by joint-stock companies and plantation owners, also undermined the French government's attempts to centralize control of their operations, except when it benefited the plantation owners' operations and their financial bottom line. Additionally, as Michitake Aso has trenchantly argued, planters' economic and political interests drove the ongoing scientific development of valuable agricultural production practices, and these, in turn, increased latex production through much of the early twentieth century.[27] Planters, therefore, generally had much to lose should they concede to Roosevelt's idealistic plan for an International Trusteeship guiding independence in Indochina. In places where extensive forests thrived in southern and central Vietnam, agricultural successes yielding valuable latex provided tangible evidence and ample reason for France to protect plantation owners' interests. Undeniably, supporting self-determination in Indochina was not one of them.

Modernizing agricultural production through advances in equipment, drainage, and canal building had changed Indochina's political economy in ways that a trusteeship would have found difficult to channel in alignment with American economic interests.[28] Indochina, in short, did not yield much that America needed in any existential sense, either before or after World War II. Instead, the idea of supporting self-determination in Indochina was supposed to be about what was good for Vietnamese, Laotians, and Cambodians ... not about what was good for America. The United States issuing strong declarations about the importance of liberty and militarily prosecuted the protection thereof as a central rationale for going to war in the Pacific after the Japanese attack on Pearl Harbor. However, a far more pressing concern than Indochinese goods and resources controlled by France, which were increasingly threatened by Imperial Japan well before December 1941, was protecting US economic interests in the region—and especially protecting access to and from those markets through ever-increasing shipping capability. Ensuring that aggressive imperial powers did not shut off half of the world to the United States, in other words, was a basis for World War II in the Pacific, and this embodied liberty more than anything else that only possessed non-material or moral value. "Liberty," perhaps, did not equate self-determination as much as it did ensuring economic imperatives.

Like Americans who saw defeating Japan—and Nazi Germany as well—as ultimately about preserving economic interests, French officials in Indochina could argue that the same argument held for France's regaining control over Indochina after World War II. Additionally, a French plantation owner might argue that France had "built" Indochina, and that French colonialism, therefore, could hardly compare with Imperial Japan's destructive attempt to dominate the entire Indo-Pacific. Thus, when French colonialism differed from

Japanese Imperial aggression so significantly, how could the United States credibly undermine French plantation owners and France's economic interest in Indochina? After all, didn't the United States benefit in some ways from French control? Was it not accurate to say that the United States indirectly supported France's empire by purchasing most of the tires that Michelin produced, which relied on Indochinese-sourced latex before World War II?[29]

Vietnamese workers, more than anyone, had a vested interest in whether French control would eventually wither in Indochina or if World War II had unalterably loosened France's clampdown on Vietnamese aspirations for self-determination. As a former Vietnamese plantation worker, Tran Tu Binh recounted in his memoir his life as a worker at Michelin's Phu-Rieng plantation in the late 1920s and early 1930s. Tran Tu Binh's valuable account describes how, before World War II, Michelin's extensive network of plantations were already fertile breeding grounds for anti-French sentiment because of the brutal treatment by French employees and horrendous living conditions the Vietnamese workers were forced to endure.[30] While Roosevelt might not have known the specifics of the Phu-Rieng plantation, or in the many other places Vietnamese were brutally forced to work, he knew enough to excoriate French policy in Indochina and France's exploitation of the Indochinese people, despite Americans' need for French-made tires.

France's arguments that its "civilizing mission" critically opposed Imperial Japan and its "Greater East-Asian Co-Prosperity Sphere" did not seem to get far with the White House, even with the decline of Japanese control of French colonies in Southeast Asia as World War II ended.[31] Certainly, Vichy France's complicity with Imperial Japan during the war was a significant factor that angered Roosevelt and others. In the spring of 1945, before Roosevelt died in April, it soon became apparent that appealing to France's better angels would not work, and forcing France to comply with American demands was hardly an option. Guiding French planters and others—who were uncompromising in their aim of returning to Indochina for numerous self-interested reasons—and directing such people toward the idealistic ends that Roosevelt's trusteeship plan envisioned would be impossible, no matter what Roosevelt thought or said.

France, however, also avoided a United States-led trusteeship because it valued Indochina for more than just economic reasons. Strict economic rationales for regaining French control of Indochina did not always create, let alone guarantee, large net profits. Colonialism was expensive to maintain, and balancing business practices in Indochina with economic and political policies in metropolitan France was difficult after World War II. So, while economic reasons certainly motivated France's return to Vietnam—and were still a priority among many French factions—so did other compelling reasons. National pride and a nostalgia for a diminishing empire perhaps offered intangible but still strong reasons for reclaiming control over Indochina. Moreover, World War II created an existential malaise for France that might be fixed by returning to an antebellum status quo, at least with regard to France's colonies. In other words, France's desire to recover from the humiliation of defeat in 1940 and the brutal occupation by Germany during the war—along with surmounting the indignity created by Japan's displacement of French power in Southeast Asia during World War II—all contributed to arguments made in favor of regaining Indochina.

As Mark Mazower explained, France's desire to re-colonize Indochina grew out of a crisis of credibility: "the humiliation [the French] had all suffered at the hands of the Germans or Japanese only increased their determination to demonstrate their power."[32] These were substantive concerns. Potential concessions to a trusteeship for Indochina would have numerous implications, none of which were viewed favorably at the time. France might retain a place as a world power, but regaining its empire improved the viability of this standing for French leaders, such as Charles de Gaulle. Even while it conferred prestige among some, empire's extractive nature antagonized Roosevelt ideologically and Vietnamese, Laotians, and Cambodians physically. Étienne de Durand, a scholar of security studies and international relations, writes that France's return to Indochina was "taking place after the 1940 trauma and in a decolonization context."[33] For France's military, in particular, "it was therefore very difficult for them to accept another defeat or to acknowledge the fact that the locals had legitimate grievances."[34] Antipathy for the idea of granting its colonies local self-determination, or conceding to any part of Roosevelt's trusteeship, therefore, typified France's position. In developing the US State Department trusteeship for Indochina, Vandenbosch learned firsthand that there were simply too few reasons for French authorities to support such an idealistic plan.

Other problems bristled against the trusteeship. The overall concept relied upon assumptions that it could discredit long-held racist and paternalistic policies, shaped by a civilizing mission ethos that held that individuals in Indochina did not possess the capability or means to govern themselves. The opportunity to undermine this kind of imperial racism was perhaps one goal Roosevelt sought to achieve in establishing a trusteeship for Indochina.

Roosevelt possessed a genuine interest in disrupting the exploitation of local populations in Indochina, and he voiced his anger over France's actions in a memorandum to Secretary of State Cordell Hull in January 1945:

> I had, for over a year, expressed the opinion that Indo-China should not go back to France but that it should be administered by an international trusteeship. France has had that country—thirty million inhabitants—for nearly one hundred years, and the people are worse off than they were at the beginning ... the case of Indo-China is perfectly clear. France has milked it for one hundred years. The people of Indo-China are entitled to something better than that.[35]

Despite Roosevelt's well-founded point, until the United States fixed its own problems regarding race and disenfranchisement, his position hazarded being hypocritical. Undoubtedly, these were problems Vandenbosch recognized. As it pertained to his interaction with Bernard Fall, Vandenbosch's past support for Indochina's trusteeship likely influenced the content of his course at SAIS, which Fall took in the summer of 1952. Unfortunately, the opportunity to implement Franklin Roosevelt's idealism and implement some form of self-determination—even if imperfect—in Indochina died with the US President in April 1945. Nevertheless, Vandenbosch carried Roosevelt's antipathy for French colonialism. He certainly supported Roosevelt's intent to establish a stronger form of self-determination in Indochina, and like FDR Vandenbosch believed that far better options than colonialism existed for the people of Vietnam, Laos, and Cambodia. This was significant for Fall, who was learning about Indochina from a man who had direct experience in confronting some of the difficulties colonialism created in the region. Additionally, while Fall did not have to be told why self-determination was valuable, he undeniably assimilated Vandenbosch's progressive outlook. In his view, Fall regarded Vandenbosch as "one of my good professors at the time," and it is almost certain that his study with Dr. Van contributed to a sense of liberal values and tempered realism he developed during the early and mid-1950s.[36]

In the context of the 1952 summer course at SAIS in Washington, DC, "Colonialism and Nationalism in Southeast Asia," Fall's first paper was called "Political Development in Indo-China," and he submitted it along with a thirteen-page essay for the class's final exam.[37] Fall was frustrated by a lack of accessible primary and secondary sources to consult for these assignments, and he had to rely on the Information Division of the French Embassy in Washington, DC for periodicals, reports, books, maps, and photographs.[38] Despite this lack of research material, Fall's paper emphasized his understanding that Vietnam, due to its long and contentious history with China, was independent of and often at odds with its immense neighbor. Additionally, he displayed an interest in the Vietnamese government in the north, the Democratic Republic of Vietnam (DRV). It was led by the Indochinese Communist Party (ICP) that was later rechristened the Worker's Party, the *Lao Dong*, after 1945. It was this political party that guided the DRV's policies through the Viet Minh political front. Fall's paper also identified competition between nationalist and communist factions within Vietnam. In contrast to the French-sponsored and controlled State of Vietnam founded in 1949, the DRV worked to develop a capacity for self-government while also integrating select nationalist elements that communists controlled to achieve political legitimacy among numerous, but certainly not all, Vietnamese. The comparison of, and the competition between, the two different Vietnamese administrations in North and South (the DRV and the Associated State of Vietnam, respectively) was the focus of Fall's earliest analysis on Indochina in 1952.[39]

The DRV's communist leadership's integration of nationalist elements related to independence were consciously chosen to obscure an uncompromising Marxist–Leninist ideological orientation. Fall certainly recognized early on that the DRV was guided by one-party communist rule. And while he held anti-communist views, he was neither blinded by anti-communist fever, nor did he dogmatically critique the DRV's ideological mix that often incorporated a tinge of nationalism to widen the DRV's appeal among uncommitted Vietnamese. Fall's anti-communism was more anti-authoritarian than a rigid antipathy directed against socialist ideology, however, he never laid down a specific theoretical explanation for his anti-communist views. In any case, Fall never harbored communist sympathies. Those parts of his paper that criticized aspects of the Viet Minh's communist-led control mainly indicated academic objectivity. The paper, after all, was not an opinion piece. Rather, it was merely Fall's earliest attempt to figure out what Vietnamese communism was about and what were some of the most important political developments occurring in Vietnam at the time. If Fall despised colonialism because it exploited people, he equally condemned communism because of its authoritarianism.

In contrast to the focus on Indochina in his paper for Vandenbosch's class, Fall's final exam was regionally oriented. In the exam, he recounted problems colonialism created in Southeast Asia more broadly, while also assessing the legacy of colonialism legacy on the Asian mainland through, for example, European concessions along the Chinese coast.[40] In one of the exam's questions, Vandenbosch asked his students to analyze the viability of an independent "Southeast Asian Federation." Fall argued that such a federation was "most unlikely due to geographic obstacles and the diversity of experience with colonialism taking place in the region."[41] It is unclear whether Vandenbosch created the question in anticipation of a possible future federation in Southeast Asia or whether he just wanted his students to engage with the diversity of history and political outlooks in the region. It is also possible that Vandenbosch wanted his students to address the compatibility, or lack thereof, of the varied political views existing across factions and colonies undergoing wars of decolonization.

Fall regarded regional diversity as an obstacle that precluded a federation, regardless of political or ideological orientation. In his view, ethnic and territorial differences varied to such an extent that a potential communist-bloc federation was not likely. Similarly, a large diversity of views precluded a unified anti-communist bloc. These kinds of views might have served as a counterpoint to the type of domino-theory thinking brewing in Washington at the time, but the exam was not being developed into commentary for publication in the *Washington Post*. It was only an exam response by a twenty-six-year-old student and World War II veteran working at the entry level of a budding career in policy and military analysis. Even so, his exam responses were perspicacious and indicated a firm grasp of international politics and history. In one response, Fall expressed skepticism regarding the viability of a federation allied with the West.

The later establishment of the Southeast Asia Treaty Organization (SEATO) in 1954 proved that Fall was only partly wrong in his prediction, because SEATO only incorporated two Southeast Asian partners: the Philippines and Thailand. The challenges a potential Southeast Asia Federation faced in 1952 were obstacles Fall could only speculate about when he composed his exam responses for Vandenbosch. However, the potential for a SEATO-like organization—which was a topic of discussion in policy circles at the time—inspired Vandenbosch to ask his students to consider the possibility. After the formation of SEATO in 1954, problems did surface quickly. The alliance faced charges of "being a new form of Western colonialism," despite its intended function in support of the broader strategy of containment advocated by George Kennan.[42]

The class with Vandenbosch was a critical turning point in Fall's life and work. Vandenbosch knew something of Fall's views on politics—because Fall described them in his course assignments—yet Vandenbosch also saw that Fall was uniquely positioned to study Indochina as a French citizen and as a veteran of the Maquis, FFI, and French army. On this basis, Dr. Van suggested to Fall, "You know, Bernard, you with your French background—you ought to get specialized in that area—you know, nobody knows much about it."[43] Fall took Vandenbosch's career advice to heart. In taking the next step toward conducting field research in Indochina the following year, Fall reflected, "I found the area rather interesting ... the French no longer owned it as a colony, but French troops were fighting there ... this was actually getting to be a pretty nasty war except nobody knew anything about it."[44]

Fall explained, "And this is how by pure accident, one sunny day in Washington D.C., of all places, in 1952 I got interested in Viet-Nam ..."[45] Fall must also have recognized that study of Asia was a nascent professional field for academics, rife with partisan politics in the United States because of the establishment of the People's Republic of China (PRC) in late 1949. Conservatives condemned liberal views and policies toward China and blamed their proponents for losing the country to communism. Anti-PRC factions then pointed at such allegedly "pro-communist" policies "as a justification for the investigations and recriminations which followed in the early 1950s as part of the general atmosphere of 'McCarthyism.'"[46] Vandenbosch's claim that "few knew much about [Indochina]" was partly valid but less accurate when it came to China. Interest in China was prevalent in America, and newsreels preceding movies across the country often included updates with depictions of the brutalization of the Chinese civilian population by the Japanese army. After the Second Sino-Japanese War began in 1937, American interest in China surged, echoing an earlier upswing of interest that had occurred "during the winter of 1921–22 when China was the focus of greater international attention than at any time since the Siege of the Legations by the Boxers."[47] In contrast to China, Fall's opportunity centered on illuminating an area that was comparatively unknown among most Americans in 1952.

After completing his MA at Syracuse in late 1952, Fall decided to finish a doctorate. In a big step toward building his knowledge of Southeast Asia, he planned a ten-month long research trip to Vietnam in 1953, which he funded with hard-saved money. It was a considerable expense for him, and he continually referenced its cost.[48] This research trip would be critical in enabling Fall to gather primary sources, interview government officials in Indochina, and collect other information he needed to write and complete a dissertation en route to his PhD in International Relations at Syracuse University. Crucially, a research trip to Vietnam would provide the critical information he could not access in the United States. In planning for his research in Vietnam, Fall claimed that his investment also provided him with the independence to provide objective analysis without institutional constraints. At least, that was how he explained his view in a 1966 interview.[49] More likely it was difficult to find external financial support on top of the resources his Fulbright scholarship provided for academic research conducted in a war zone. Fortunately, Fall had multiple connections with French military authorities who would provide food, lodging, and transportation that allowed him to travel to places in Indochina few independent scholars could otherwise visit.

It was during his first trip to Indochina that Fall's new intellectual interests would begin to coalesce. His experience and education in an extensive range of subjects at several institutions would prepare him for research in an area that was relatively unknown in the United States. Fall was soon on his way to Indochina with a "new short-wave radio and precious Leica camera" packed into a military duffel bag, along with a letter of recommendation from the French Embassy in Washington, DC to the political advisor of the Vietnam National Government, which Fall would use to build upon his already established contacts in the French military.[50] Perhaps Dr. Vandenbosch was right to claim that few in America knew much about Indochina in 1952. He was undoubtedly correct that Bernard Fall would address the need for information with alacrity and aptitude. Fall concisely described the task ahead of him in a letter to his fiancée, Dorothy Winer, after arriving in Vietnam in 1953:

> From the general point of view, this place is a hotbed and a more likely spot to start a general war than ten Koreas. Any knowledge we get out of it soon might help a few bigger people than you and I keep things on an even keel, and I happen to be one of the guys trained to present such knowledge intelligibly.[51]

II—Vietnam, May 1953

> It looks just like one big garden, with all the little villages very neatly surrounded by trees and shrubbery, and French military roads showing their regular tracings against the erratic boundaries of the fields. As we lowered through the overcast for the landing, you began to see the scars and the marks of the watchtowers, gun emplacements.[52]

This is how Bernard Fall described Vietnam as he descended upon Hanoi in mid-May 1953. Fall quickly learned that French fortifications, despite their dire appearance, possessed "architectural periods" based "on the local terrain, the availability of building materials, the enemy's combat potential, and the state of the art of military engineering."[53] In 1950–1, General de Lattre de Tassigny, the commander of French troops in Indochina, had brought two new approaches to his military command. The first "included the installation of *béton armé* [reinforced concrete] as a defensive barrier forming the de Lattre Line and the second was ordering the implementation of *vietnamisation* [Vietnamization]," a program to upgrade and expand Vietnamese militias for pairing with French units "for training and joint operations."[54] The latter of these two developments, Vietnamization, formed a significant precedent for subsequent operations in 1953 and 1954 when the Associated State of Vietnam's troops assumed greater responsibility for the war effort against the communist Viet Minh. Increasing Vietnamese troops' operational tempo and assigning them more missions also provided French authorities with space and time for the political maneuver of reducing its troop deployments as the war became increasingly unpopular in metropolitan France.

The initial development of the de Lattre Line, into which Foreign Legionnaires and Vietnamese auxiliaries "poured 51 *million* cubic yards of concrete into 2,200 pillboxes," served as an indication of the nature of French warfare in Vietnam and its attempt to "seal off the 7,500 square miles and eight million inhabitants of the Red River delta from the Communist areas," but "all to no avail."[55] As Fall noted in 1953, "Battles involving near a whole Vietminh division were fought last year well within the fortified line and conservative intelligence estimates place the number of Vietminh troops operating within the Red River Delta at around 30,000 men."[56] The fortifications reflected how swiftly the Viet Minh adapted to them, to the point that they were even conducting operations within the so-called "fortified area." In a futile sense, the French army's fortified structures themselves changed on a somewhat frequent basis because "even those standardized bunkers had their architecture and yearly style changes, as the enemy's attack patterns altered, or his weaponry improved."[57] In late May 1953, while on a tour of northern provinces with Vietnamese officials, Fall described the contrast between the land and France's numerous fortifications:

> The countryside has a charm of its own: the rice which is nearly ripe, the little fields full of water with their little dikes around them, the buffaloes wallowing in the mud to get the flies off their back, the farmers (call them Viet-Minh after working hours) with their cone-shaped hats—and then, a new element that looks as strange here as an armoured knight riding down Fifth Avenue, the French forts. Built along strictly functional lines, high square towers of concrete pillboxes, they have an air of early-gothic castles and give the whole place an eerie-out-of-this-worldliness.[58]

François Sully, a former French soldier and journalist Fall befriended in 1957 in Vietnam, also commented on France's defensive infrastructure and mindset among personnel. Writing in 1968, Sully reflected: "On the French side, barbed wire, sandbags, and fortifications were the visual evidence of a Maginot line mentality, a poor substitute for aggressive patrolling and alertness ... I learned that the amount of barbed wire used by an army is a good indication of its lack of fighting spirit."[59] Like Fall, Sully studied Viet Minh operations, and they shared similar respect for the Viet Minh's capacity for war. As a journalist for *Sud-Est Asiatique* and *Time-Life* in 1954, Sully reported from the French garrison at Dien Bien Phu for *Time-Life*. In April, he managed to leave and thus narrowly missed becoming a prisoner of war when the Viet Minh defeated French forces at the extensive network of forts. The French fortification in the valley of Dien Bien Phu certainly contrasted with the cover and concealment Viet Minh troops relied upon in their assault on the garrison. Inbound to Dien Bien Phu, Sully commented:

> I flew into Dien Bien Phu and over the forests where (Vo Nguyen) Giap was massing his divisions for the assault. Unbelievably, although flying low, we could not spot a single Viet Minh bivouac or gun emplacement; everything was concealed under trees or underground. The dark brown jungle looked empty, and still we knew the Viet Minh were there![60]

France's troops were painfully aware of the Viet Minh's aggressive fighting spirit by April 1954. Yet Sully was wrong to believe that the garrison's barbed wire, sandbags, and fortifications indicated a weaker fighting spirit among soldiers defending their besieged positions. Poor decisions by senior leaders, more than the flagging resolve of the soldiers fighting for France, led to their defeat at Dien Bien Phu. Fall studied and knew this as well as anyone.[61]

Before he met Sully, Fall had a personal connection among those fighting for France in Vietnam. Remy Malot, a friend from the French Maquis in Haute-Savoie during World War II, wrote to Fall:

> We are fighting against the Vietnamese regulars, perfectly equipped and armed à l'américaine, that is, with American arms captured in Korea, supported by the Chinese Communists. We didn't come out of it unscathed and in the final analysis ... I believe that Indochina will only be pacified after a third world war ... or she will be completely lost for us.[62]

From his research in Indochina in 1953, Fall confirmed Malot's point, noting, "Human losses have been heavy—43,000 dead, 40 percent of these casualties were regular French officers and noncommissioned officers who are sorely needed for the infrastructure of the new French North Atlantic Treaty divisions."[63]

France's operations in Vietnam degraded its ability to contribute to NATO. However, France's attempt to maintain its empire also revealed why fighting for colonialism was fraught with paradoxes for those doing much of the fighting. The situation in Vietnam was bleak for France and its soldiers in 1953 and 1954. However, the conflict was also generating new and stirring old nationalist aspirations among African soldiers who questioned their service for France's empire as the vibrancy of decolonization intensified across the globe.[64] Aside from elites with economic interests, many French civilians in Vietnam also felt forsaken. In his first article on Indochina, published in the October 1953 issue of *Military Review*, Fall noted this frustration, writing, "as a French civilian over here put it: 'How do you think it feels to fight alone for 7 years a war that is militarily hopeless, politically a dead-end street, and economically ruinous?'"[65] The despairing nature of the question, Fall realized, was one the French government could not coherently answer.

During his ten months of field research in 1953, Fall cast a wide net and gathered as much material on the ongoing First Indochina War as possible. Military documents, interviews, maps, photographs, economic and agricultural reports, studies of religions, and newspapers provided him with the information he had been hard-pressed to find in the United States. He prioritized collecting materials on the Viet Minh's political formation and the Democratic Republic of Vietnam in the north. However, he also gathered extensive information on the fledgling Vietnamese administration in the south, supported by France and known as the Associated State of Vietnam (SVN), formed in 1949. Using military transportation, Fall traveled extensively. He visited sites such as Tay Ninh, where he met with religious leaders, including the Cao Dai Ho Phap [Pope] Pham Cong Tac. Fall did this, as he acknowledged in the preface to a large study he published the following year, with the help of the French High Commissioner, Guy Merlo, and State of Vietnam leaders, such as Dr. Le Van Hoach, the Vietnamese Minister of Information who was also an adherent of the monotheistic and syncretic Cao Dai religion.[66] It was likely that Dr. Le Van Hoach introduced Fall to the head of the Cao Dai faith.

Pham Cong Tac was one of the most important non-government-associated leaders in Vietnam because he largely developed and consolidated the Cao Dai faith after it was founded in 1926. As it initially mattered to Fall in terms of political developments in Vietnam, Pham Cong Tac's political clout was significant, and was reinforced by a Cao Dai army that numbered over 10,000 personnel in 1948 and continued to grow in subsequent years.[67]

Pham Cong Tac, along with the profuse Hoa Hao millenarian Buddhist organization in the western Mekong Delta region, figured more prominently in Fall's later research, but he was introduced to these belief systems, and became aware of their convergence with politics, in 1953. During this first research trip, he built a considerable network and emphasized meeting Vietnamese leaders in the State of Vietnam. A partial list of those he interviewed included the Governor of North Vietnam, Nguyen Huu Tri; the President of the T'ai Federation, H.E. (His Excellency) Deo Van Long; and Vu Quoc Thong, a professor of administrative law at the University of Hanoi who became the Minister of Social Action and Health in the Republic of Vietnam in 1955.[68] These leaders were vital sources of information, and they were important because they facilitated his research. Once Fall gathered enough material for his doctoral dissertation at Syracuse University, he would focus on writing after returning to the United States in late 1953. Fall also managed to meet Nguyen Van Tam, the Prime Minister of the State of Vietnam, in late August 1953.

Nguyen Van Tam exemplified the complex dimensions of civil conflict in Vietnam both during and immediately after World War II. Tam had fought against the Japanese and then against other Vietnamese factions as the war ended. In meeting the Prime Minister and learning of his experiences, Fall was provided with a detailed (and likely one-sided) background that illuminated the long-standing animosity between communists and nationalists in the war-torn country. Tam himself contributed to this animosity by persecuting Vietnamese communists. As a result, he and his family suffered from the vicious cycle of violent retribution characteristic to civil wars. In a letter from 24 August 1953, to his fiancée, Dorothy Winer, Fall described Tam's background:

> He's a nice, old but very active man with a crew cut whose own family is a nice example of the tragedy that goes on here. 2 of his 3 sons were killed (chopped to bits in a scientific slow way) by the Viet-Minh. His last son is the V-Nam Commander-in-Chief. But, the husband of his oldest daughter ironically is surgeon-general for the Viet-Minh. This Prime Minister, too, spent years in a Jap concentration camp. But you should see him! He's outspoken for Vnam independence and certainly no French puppet, though he's realist enough to know that V.N. can't stand alone yet.[69]

While he knew a great deal about the broader political dimensions in the region, Fall was beginning to learn more about key individuals and their histories during and after World War II. In describing Tam in his letter, Fall did not provide more details to explain why Tam's two sons died in such an atrocious manner. Obviously, the Viet Minh did not perceive him as the "nice, old

FIRST REFLECTIONS ON A WAR

man" who Fall met in 1953.[70] In 1948, Nguyen Van Tam held several ministerial posts in the Provisional Central Government of Vietnam before the Associated State of Vietnam was established in 1949. Before becoming Prime Minister under Bao Dai, Tam was "nick-named the Tiger of Cai Lay for eliminating Communist resistance groups" in My Tho and Tien Giang provinces in South Vietnam.[71] As his nickname suggested, Tam was ruthless in his approach, but he was also treated ruthlessly in return. He had been captured and tortured by the Viet Minh for his loyalty to France, and his two sons were gruesomely murdered as revenge for Tam's persecution of the Viet Minh. This cycle of violence and retribution, and local-level spiraling of civil conflict, Fall would have identified from his days in the Maquis during World War II. Fall might not have known the details and complexity of the regions he studied in 1953, but he was learning more daily. In broader terms, however, he was able to identify certain processes that civil wars shared. Whether it occurred in France during liberation or in My Tho province, retributive violence characterized the brutal and vengeful sides of human nature, which existed wherever humans were found.

That Fall acknowledged divisions in Nguyen Van Tam's family indicated his awareness of critical social dimensions at work. Conflict in Vietnam was not only a growing geopolitical problem that nation-states like France, China, and the United States imposed on the region. It equally emanated from the interpersonal level up. Meeting individuals such as Nguyen Van Tam was vital to Fall's research because it informed and enhanced his study of conflict and society in Vietnam. Firsthand information, such as that he gained from Tam and others, was not available in books and seldom in news reports. This, of course, was why Fall had traveled to Vietnam; he simply could not find the primary sources he needed for Vandenbosch's class, or for the doctoral dissertation he planned to finish, at Syracuse. Undeniably, through meeting with Pham Cong Tac, Nguyen Van Tam, and others, Fall learned more about Vietnam than the kind of vicarious material that books could teach. In Tam's case, he had initially sought a separate and independent Vietnam but then decided to join the anti-communist Associated State of Vietnam under French control. He became Director-General of the National Police and Security in June 1950 and played an essential role in defeating the Viet Minh's urban offensive operations in Cholon, a section of Saigon, during that summer.[72] He later became Minister of Public Security in February 1951 and, in recognition of his counter-terror pacification programs, was made an *Officier de la Légion d'honneur* in May by General Jean de Lattre de Tassigny.[73]

Nguyen Van Tam eventually became disillusioned with France's colonial policies, even within the liberalizing French Union formed in 1946. He later announced his frustration with the French Union in a radio broadcast, stating, "it is important that we no longer remain in this Union as tenants of a house built without us."[74] He emigrated to the United States in 1955 and remained a stalwart opponent of Vietnamese communism for the rest of his life, writing: "one does not come to terms with the Indochinese Communist Party. One beats it down, or it beats you down."[75] Fall's understanding of Tam's hatred for the Viet Minh, his anger with the French Union, and his later disillusionment with Ngo Dinh Diem—who led the successor to the State of Vietnam—could only be gained through personal interaction at the time. Including this material in his early scholarship enriched it in ways others had difficulty equaling without similar access. Fall was living through and recounting events, in other words, that were typically documented by historians. In order for Fall to understand war in Indochina, he recognized that he had to gain a comprehensive understanding of how political legitimacy in Indochina functioned. Gaining such knowledge depended on achieving a detailed understanding of the region's history, culture, and diverse and contentious politics. These tasks would consume the next fourteen years of Fall's life.

Fall's interactions with various institutions and individuals, such as Nguyen Van Tam and others, in Vietnam provided him with unique access to documentation on the two Vietnamese governments, the Democratic Republic of Vietnam and the State of Vietnam. Moreover, his veteran status and contacts within the French army enabled him to participate in operations during the months of his field research in 1953. In a reflection on Fall's research, US Congressman James Grant O'Hara later remarked that Fall possessed "in his pocket," access to information in Vietnam that "permitted the inspection, appreciation, and the ability to question and examine each act, and the ability to bring out the nuance of actions until the moment he assembled the fragments and threads into this fabric we call history."[76] Fall's earliest publication on Southeast Asia, "Indochina: The Seven Year Dilemma," exemplified such an assembling of information and was published while he was still conducting field research. The article provided a detailed analysis of *le Viet-Minh*—the term French authorities insisted on using for their adversaries instead of the terminology "Democratic Republic of Vietnam" or "the North Vietnamese"— because referring to their administrative apparatus might confer legitimacy the French authorities did not want to provide.[77] The article, published in *Military Review* in October 1953, also indicated that French options were narrowing as the French metropole's disenchantment with the "dirty war" (*la guerre sale*) increased, French army morale dwindled, and Viet Minh capacity gained traction in northern Vietnam. These factors contributed to France's General Henri Navarre developing an aggressive military offensive to pursue the Viet Minh into open terrain in northwestern Vietnam at Dien Bien Phu in late 1953 and early 1954. The reason for the Navarre Plan, Fall knew, was to achieve a knockout blow through a set-piece military victory, but it stemmed equally from dissatisfaction in France with the war and a sense that time was running out.

Fall's article, "Indochina: The Seven Year Dilemma," also relied on Viet Minh publications and other sources that French forces either retrieved during operations or confiscated from captured Viet Minh personnel. One source included the Viet Minh newspaper, *Cu'u Quoc*, published to propagate the Viet Minh's revolution against French control.[78] Even more remarkable, Fall had access to the *Vietnam National Gazette* (*Viet Nam Dan Quoc Cong Bao*), considered an official journal of the DRV in which government decrees and edicts were published. According to Dr. Lauriston Sharpe, the director of the Southeast Asia Program at Cornell University, who edited Fall's first book-length study of the Viet Minh in 1954: "no complete set of this journal is known to exist in a location accessible to Western students," but all of these "sources of information were open to Mr. Fall during his stay in Vietnam."[79] At Johns Hopkins University in 1952, Fall had had trouble finding the documents he needed to understand war in Indochina; in 1953, he found as much material as he could absorb, and he wasted no time crafting this abundance into a manuscript upon his return to upstate New York.

These "sources of information" formed the basis for Fall's first book, *The Viet-Minh Regime: Government and Administration in the Democratic Republic of Vietnam*, published in 1954.[80] Despite his incorporation of illuminating, extensive, and difficult-to-obtain Vietnamese communist documentation, Fall's early analysis of the Viet Minh and its administration is rarely cited as critical source material in contemporary scholarship. Until 2013, few, if any, Western scholars produced a detailed analysis of the Democratic Republic of Vietnam's formation comparable to Fall's 1954 study.[81] Notably, he was also assessing the Viet Minh state at a time when his work might have made a positive difference in Western policy development toward Vietnam. Nonetheless, Fall's account of the Viet Minh's history was remarkably detailed, and it deserves its recognition as the first study of the formation of the DRV state in English, even if it is shorter than work completed fifty-nine years later with the aid of far more source material than what Fall had available to him.[82]

In a rare case, the value of Fall's analysis was not lost on at least one contemporary scholar. In 1967, historian Joseph Buttinger regarded Fall's book as "The most comprehensive study of the evolution, military organization, and government of North Vietnam."[83] Moreover, what Buttinger did not mention in his description of *The Viet-Minh Regime* was that it was only the first volume of what would become Fall's three-volume, 1,107-page dissertation for the doctoral degree he completed at Syracuse University in 1955.[84] The publication of the first volume of Fall's work, *The Viet-Minh Regime*, preceded Fall's dissertation defense and was, by itself, over 180 single-spaced pages in length.[85] According to Lauriston Sharp, the Director of the Southeast Asia Program at Cornell University in 1954, Fall's scholarship in *The Viet-Minh Regime* positioned him as "among the first to identify and organize such data into a systematic account of the structure and functioning of the government of the Democratic Republic of Vietnam."[86] Sharp's and Buttinger's comments remain relevant and indicate why Fall's earliest scholarship on the Viet Minh deserves detailed analysis on top of the work itself.

In the United States during the early 1950s, as Fall quickly realized, public knowledge and debate concerning Indochina after World War II was meager at best. Profound analysis of policy formulation related to Indochina, aside from that among policymakers directly involved with the region, did not appear to penetrate academic scholarship in the United States in the postwar era, with a few exceptions.[87] For readers today, it is helpful to provide brief historical context of the political environment Fall encountered when he arrived in Vietnam in 1953. A fundamental understanding of the events leading to the division of Vietnam after World War II is critical because they contributed to France's reoccupation of Indochina after Japanese defeat in 1945. Indeed, Vandenbosch was correct to say of Indochina that "nobody knows much about it." There was much for Fall to learn on top of what he had read from afar in Washington, DC.[88]

A result of the Potsdam Conference in July 1945—which did not include French participation—the division of Vietnam at the sixteenth parallel was a starting point in Fall's historical analysis. Following the defeat of Imperial Japan, Chinese nationalist forces occupied the north of Vietnam while British troops occupied the southern zone. In October 1945, the first French elements arrived in Saigon, led by General Philippe Leclerc. These French troops supported British forces under Major General Douglas Gracey's command, which "began to reconquer and pacify the region south of the 16th parallel."[89] According to terms agreed to at Potsdam, Chinese troops would leave and

French troops would be allowed to return to northern Vietnam. By agreeing to the March 6 Accords—viewed as a compromise solution to ensure Chinese nationalist forces did not remain in Vietnam because of Vietnamese concerns over Chinese encroachment—Ho Chi Minh, the Viet Minh leader, settled for the return of French troops to northern Vietnam. The agreement stipulated that "the French recognized the 'Republic of Vietnam' as a 'free state' within the Indochinese Federation and French Union."[90] In exchange, "the Vietnamese agreed to welcome the return of twenty-five thousand French troops for five years to relieve departing Chinese forces."[91] Subsequent negotiations at Dalat and at Fontainebleu, which focused primarily on south Vietnam, failed, and continued antagonism between Vietnamese and French troops set conditions for conflict between the Viet Minh and France in December 1946.[92]

Fall's trip to Indochina in 1953, therefore, came toward the end of a complicated war of decolonization which had roots in World War II and several complex postwar agreements. Furthermore, his research was conducted while the war was still on, so his ideas on warfare during this time were protean and an accurate reflection of a still-undecided conflict. His intellectual reckoning of warfare was thus a work in progress, and, while it was a tremendous scholastic opportunity, it was also a challenging subject to study firsthand. As a result, his writing oscillated between documenting the history of the aftermath of World War II in the region and chronicling current events in 1953.

Notably, he did add further analysis of events in 1954—when the First Indochina War ended in French defeat—after returning to Syracuse. In many respects, the division of Vietnam in 1945—as agreed to at Potsdam without French participation—was one intellectual bookend marking a starting point for much of Fall's analysis. While he did delve further back in time to chart the Indochinese Communist Party's formation and the Viet Minh's origins as an anti-colonial front, this critical material added important context and background information to his work.[93] The other bookend marking this early tranche of his scholarship was the status of conflict in 1953 and 1954. It is important to add that Fall was especially mindful to account for the multi-leveled war within Indochina as a conflict also implicated in the Cold War's broader geopolitical context.

After Ho Chi Minh's proclamation founding the Democratic Republic of Vietnam in Hanoi on 2 September 1945, its primary competitors included nationalists and others who later coalesced into the French-supported State of Vietnam (SVN), formed in 1949 under the leadership of Emperor Bao Dai.

For years, the State of Vietnam had difficulty, and Fall concluded, even as late as August 1954, that "National representative government is entirely non-existent despite local and regional elections."[94] The problem was twofold: elections had not been held for four years after the government had been declared in 1949, and, once they were held, they took place during the rice-planting season in January when few peasants had time to participate.[95] Fall determined that these issues and others culminated in preventing a legitimate and representative government from forming, and it provided opportunities for the Viet Minh to compete with the State of Vietnam.

Other problems obstructing the consolidation of a robust, indigenous, and anti-communist Vietnamese government existed as well, but they were harder to pin down. Shortly after landing in Hanoi in May 1953, Fall checked in with a French briefing officer and asked about the situation in the Red River Delta. He was told:

> Well, we hold pretty much of it: there is the French fortified line around the Delta which we call the Marshal de Lattre Line—about 2200 bunkers forming 900 forts. We are going to deny the communists access to the eight million people in the Delta and the three million tons of rice it produces.[96]

Fall questioned if the communists held anything within the Delta, to which the officer, referring to a map of the region, replied, "Yes, they hold those five black blotches." Within days, Fall began documenting this competition over control within the Red River Delta. He described his methods, writing:

> I used a working hypothesis: I went to the Vietnamese tax collection office in Hanoi to look at the village tax rolls. They immediately indicated that the bulk of the Delta was no longer paying taxes. As a cross-check on my theory I used the village teachers. The school teachers in Viet-Nam were centrally assigned by the Government. Hence where there were school teachers the Government could be assumed to have control. Where there was none, there was no Government control. The resulting difference between military "control" and what the Communists controlled administratively was 70% of the delta inside the French battlelines.[97]

He concluded, "the military situation was complete fiction and had absolutely no bearing on the real situation inside the Delta ... the area was solidly Communist infiltrated and, of course, collapsed overnight." Years later, he described this type of subversive warfare, writing, "that is Revolutionary Warfare."[98] Therefore, as early as 1953, he had already assessed that the Viet Minh focused on actions, such as controlling tax collection, teacher placement, and other similar socially oriented points of control in Vietnamese villages. More critically, these were essential indicators that eluded French officers, whose military-focused operations analyses did not adequately account for things such as tax collection or who was actually controlling village schools. Instead of military-focused metrics, more socially oriented and politically attuned evaluations were needed to provide accurate indications of control. Fall realized that too many French officers relied upon the number of defensive positions held by bunkers and forts, and they measured territorial control by counting the number of attacks French forces initiated against the Viet Minh.

In contrast, Fall's earliest research on warfare in Indochina demonstrated that the space between reality on the ground and what French military officials believed was wide and becoming more inaccurate as time passed. His work demonstrated how the Viet Minh's form of warfare relied on competitive control over society instead of a preponderance of power found in military strength. Moreover, this was an essential point in Fall's thought because of parallels between what he experienced in the Maquis during World War II and what he observed in such a different context as Indochina. A defining and increasingly evident characteristic of his analyses centered on his ability to connect his past experiences with war with what he began to recognize in Indochina. Over the course of ten months of research in 1953, he would devote himself to determining how and why the truth on the ground was different from what French military officers and their commanders believed.

4

SEVEN YEARS OF WAR IN INDOCHINA

The Viet Minh's organizational structure and its application of communist doctrine to war contributed to their victory over France in 1954. The Chinese Communists' defeat of Chinese Nationalist forces in 1949 provided a critical geopolitical development that worked in the Viet Minh's favor by providing sanctuary and supplies. However, before the French defeat was assured, Bernard Fall began his research on the Viet Minh in 1953. He analyzed how the combination of doctrinal flexibility, organization, the mass mobilization of Vietnamese civilians to support its operations, and an unremitting commitment, aided by Chinese Communist forces and materiel, helped the Viet Minh. These factors built upon the subversive nature of the Viet Minh's earlier guerrilla tactics that had done much to weaken French authorities and their Vietnamese allies, as well as other anti-communist and nationalist factions, such as the Vietnam Quoc Dan Dang (VNQDD).

The post-World War II era in Southeast Asia was multi-layered with conflict among communist, nationalist, and anti-colonialist Vietnamese. As Mark Atwood Lawrence forcefully argued, it was also politically contested among Western allies who held competing views for the region's future.[1] According to Lawrence: "Instead of completing the process of colonial recovery begun in the last months of 1945, the Franco-Viet Minh war quickly exposed French weakness and generated a new sense of crisis among French policymakers about their ability to remaster Indochina. Most significant, the outbreak of war rendered the French government once again dependent on its allies."[2]

Fall recognized how the United States had a much different goal for Indochina, as indicated by their hope for a potential trusteeship, than French authorities seeking to reclaim their position. Between 1950 and 1953, war in Korea added further critical dimensions to the numerous levels of conflict in Indochina.

Fall initiated his analysis of these events by studying Indochina's recent history during World War II and assessing how the North Vietnamese State, the Democratic Republic of Vietnam (DRV), was formed on 2 September 1945. Having served as a member of the French army as well as the Maquis, he undoubtedly sympathized with French forces returning to Indochina in 1946. At the same time, he also understood that the Viet Minh's efforts were as much anti-colonial as they were communist. In a critical respect, the Viet Minh were neither threatening civilians in Haute-Savoie or Nice, nor were they threatening to overrun France or take and hold Alsace-Lorraine. Conflict in Indochina was further complicated by the establishment of the French-supported Associated State of Vietnam. From his study of the interwar period in Europe, Fall was alert to how interconnections between past and current conflicts invariably overlapped. The war he found in Hanoi, already entering its seventh year, was no different because its roots preceded World War II.[3]

Fall came to Indochina relatively late in the war. However, during his ten-month-long stay, he gathered the research for his first book, *The Viet-Minh Regime*, and other material for the doctoral dissertation he would complete in 1955. Also, he collected significant research that later provided a basis for his most well-known work, *Street Without Joy*. More broadly, he was mindful of geopolitical factors contributing to France's recolonization of Indochina. France's reclamation of its colony in South Vietnam and its protectorates, Tonkin in northern Vietnam and Annam in central Vietnam, was assisted by the United States, who committed to reconstructing France through the Marshall Plan.

As Fall well knew in the early Cold War era, anti-communism could induce a powerful and far-reaching political paranoia, and he demonstrated this awareness in a 1955 article for *Foreign Affairs*, published by the Council of Foreign Relations.[4] In it, he explained how the French Communist Party posed an encroaching threat to post-World War II France and why this created a robust need for US support. Moreover, preventing communist control of France required resources that barely exceeded France's demands for US support of its anti-communist war against the Viet Minh. As Fall and other contemporary researchers would discover in 1955, France's operations in

Indochina cost almost as much as all Marshall Aid to continental France.[5] Why, after all, was France's war in Indochina even necessary? Did war in Indochina somehow prevent war between communists and anti-communists in France? These were only two among the many questions the First Indochina War evoked.

This chapter's first section presents a historical overview of the war's origins and key events. The latter part of section one also focuses on Fall's *Foreign Affairs* article because it helps explain why France appealed to the United States to support its operations in Indochina. The chapter's second section recounts the development of the Viet Minh and the formation of the Democratic Republic of Vietnam. This section does not seek to provide a comprehensive history of the Viet Minh and DRV's origins. Instead, it provides a guide based on Fall's research to indicate how he viewed these developments when his work was published. Fall's opportunity to study Indochina in 1953 gave him a perspective that many American scholars could not match when the Cold War in Southeast Asia began to take on greater significance. The First Indochina War's origins, he soon learned, were part of a series of complex waves initiated by imperialism in Indochina and magnified by World War II.

I—The Road to the First Indochina War

> *"It would take 500,000 men to do it, and even then, it could not be done."*
>
> – Philippe Leclerc de Hauteclocque, Commander of the French Expeditionary Force Far East to Paul Mus on France's recolonization of Indochina in 1945.[6]

On top of the bitterness dividing Vietnamese society, the First Indochina War embittered the French public's relationship with the French military.[7] The war was not based on the same motivations Fall and so many others fought for during World War II. Instead, as he would later write, it "was one of colonial reconquest."[8] At the heart of this imperialism, territory was a central factor, and land reform initiatives were one of many factors contributing to Fall's analysis of the DRV and the French-sponsored Associated State of Vietnam (SVN). An average French citizen in metropolitan France might have had little interest in France's reoccupation of Indochina because of the expenses associated with colonialism and the difficult postwar challenges involved in rebuilding French infrastructure and society. Considering the massive amount of US financial support required to reoccupy Indochina, let alone rebuild France, returning to Indochina mattered more in terms of prestige than in terms of economic necessity. An average French citizen might have had little interest in Vietnamese farmland and likely only saw French reoccupation as a means to increase his or her taxes. In contrast, land was the most critical resource among the Vietnamese in the Democratic Republic of Vietnam (DRV). For this reason, the DRV undertook initiatives regarding land to help facilitate the mass mobilization of Vietnamese society against French conventional operations in 1953. Vietnam was not the only country forming Indochina, so Fall's analyzing sanctuaries in Laos and Cambodia from before war broke out between France and the DRV in late 1946 added important dimensions to his work.

The result of this research was published as *The Viet-Minh Regime* in 1954, and it provided a comprehensive examination of the DRV administration and the serious challenges it faced for over a decade.[9] Fall began his study by examining the historical circumstances that led to the formation of the Democratic Republic of Vietnam. At a May 1941 congress in Chinghsi (Kwangsi Province, China), the Vietnam Revolutionary Youth League, elements of the Nationalist Party (Viet-Nam Quoc Dan Dang), and various National Salvation organizations (Cu-u Quoc) "banded together to create the League for the Independence of Vietnam [*Viet Nam Doc Lap Dong Minh Hoi*], known as the 'Viet-Minh.'"[10] The group met in China because Japan had conquered the port of Haiphong and towns and cities bordering China earlier in September 1940.

Japanese forces targeted French-held border towns, such as Lang Son, Dong Dang, and others, seeing control of the supply routes from Haiphong to Yunnan province, through which Chinese Nationalists received American aid.[11] These main supply routes were vital in the early stages of World War II. As Fall wrote, when they fell under Japanese control, this led the United States to "freeze all Japanese assets in the United States and place an embargo on petroleum exports to Japan."[12] Japan then moved quickly to gain control of this supply corridor, and the French government was forced to abandon its colonial troops in Indochina during the autumn of 1940. Having been overrun by German forces earlier in June, France had nothing to reinforce its position in Vietnam as Japanese troops entered Indochina. In Fall's description, the French "had their own miniature Pearl Harbor a full fifteen months before the United States, and the only outside attention the event attracted was a tongue-in-cheek editorial in an American newspaper entitled: 'Who Wants to Die for Dear Old Dong-Dang?'" To which Fall added, "The answer, apparently, was obvious."[13]

After Japan invaded and gained control of French Indochina, it retained a weak French colonial bureaucracy to assist in the region's administration. Fall recounted that "on July 29, 1941, Japan further occupied naval and air bases at Saigon and Tourane [Danang], and shortly after Pearl Harbor, Indochina was as much a Japanese-occupied territory as any of the other southeast Asian countries which were overrun by the Japanese forces," except "the French still maintained their internal administration and lightly-armed military forces."[14] While resisting calls to support Japanese aims, the Viet Minh perceived an opportunity in France's weakened position. The dissolving of the Third Republic in July 1940, and its replacement by the Vichy administration, provided the Viet Minh with an opportunity to support Allied objectives in Southeast Asia. As one result, the Viet Minh cooperated with the Office of Strategic Services (OSS) by providing tactical intelligence and other support. In return, the Viet Minh gained limited material assistance from the United States.[15] Fall described this, writing:

> The elimination of the French brought about a complete breakdown of Allied intelligence which, hitherto, had mainly relied upon its French contacts and the factor favored the activities of these groups ... As it happens, it was the Communist groups under the Moscow-trained leader Ho Chi Minh which possessed not only the necessary strength but also the adequate purposeful leadership necessary to exploit the situation to the fullest.[16]

With Japan's defeat and the Vichy administration's downfall in 1945, circumstances for France had changed. The Viet Minh's goals, in contrast, had not. While France would soon take steps to return to Indochina, the Viet Minh's long-term strategic plan remained focused on ensuring the complete elimination of French colonialism in Indochina after World War II. The Viet Minh also faced domestic threats, yet eliminating competitors also allowed them to consolidate its control among the Vietnamese. In the interim period between late 1945 and into 1946, after unity with other Vietnamese factions was no longer needed to defeat Japanese forces, the Viet Minh moved quickly to fortify their grip over Vietnamese societies, especially in northern Vietnam where the Viet Minh were stronger than in the south. General Vo Nguyen Giap described the political context when the French Expeditionary Corps determined their next steps in reoccupying Vietnam. In his "Summary of the Progress of the War of National Liberation," Giap explained:

> It was thus that negotiations which ended in the Preliminary Agreement of March 6th, 1946, took place between the French colonialists and our Government (the DRV). According to the terms of this convention, limited contingents of French troops were allowed to station in a certain number of localities in North Viet Nam in order to co-operate with the Vietnamese troops

in taking over from the repatriated Chiang Kai-shek forces. In exchange, the French Government recognized Viet Nam as a free state, having its own government, its own national assembly, its own army and finances, and promised to withdraw its troops from Viet Nam within the space of five years.[17]

During the remainder of 1946, Giap claimed that French colonists consistently breached the terms of the March 6 Accords, provoked anti-French Vietnamese, and attacked numerous Viet Minh-held provinces. These accusations may have been accurate, but the reality of the internal dynamics among Vietnamese anti-colonialist factions added significant complexity to the situation. Between March and November 1946, the Viet Minh bitterly denounced Trotskyist anti-colonialist factions, Vietnamese in the Dai Viet political party, and what was known as the Revolutionary League. However, these non-Indochinese Communist Party factions were not the most serious domestic challenger. In late 1945 through 1946, DRV leadership in the Indochinese Communist Party (ICP) "judged that the Vietnam Nationalist Party posed a more substantial challenge to them than the Dai Viet parties, Trotskyists, and the Revolutionary League put together."[18] When Nationalist factions, especially Vietnamese Nationalists known as the Viet Nam Quoc Dan Dang (VNQDD), refused to accept the negotiated truce allowing French troops to return to Hanoi temporarily, the Viet Minh attacked the Vietnamese Nationalists of the VNQDD. The Viet Minh did not on principle oppose anti-colonialist agitators, and in fact they worked hard to create an appearance of a unified Vietnamese front against French imperialism. However, by 1946, after a complex series of exchanges over the years—that differed significantly in the south from developments in the north of Vietnam—the Viet Minh's strenuous efforts to eliminate the VNQDD was ultimately a matter of power.[19] In achieving dominance over other factions, the ICP ensured one-party control over the DRV and as much of other parts of Vietnam as possible. No matter how much they shared a hatred of the French, eliminating competitors was the party's path to power.

The Viet Minh's effort to undermine competitors did not become explicit until the summer of 1946, but it was entirely ruthless all the same. According to Vo Nguyen Giap: "The liquidating of the reactionaries of the Viet Nam Quoc Dan Dang was crowned with success and we were able to liberate all the areas which had fallen into their hands."[20] The Viet Minh's internal security forces, including the Cong An, were key organizations in "liquidating"—to use Giap's choice of words—Vietnamese nationalists. According to David Marr, "From late July 1946 to the end of the year, the majority of persons

SEVEN YEARS OF WAR IN INDOCHINA

detained by the Cong An for political reasons bore a Nationalist Party label, whether real or assumed."[21] This was a campaign of denunciation and elimination that echoed the complexity and violence of internal divisions among the Bolsheviks, which the Cheka rooted out during the Red Terror during the Russian Civil War, as well as the extreme violence against and within anti-Bolshevik factions carried out by the White Army during the White Terror. While hardly as extensive as either the Red or White Terror, the denunciation and violence among the Vietnamese established what Fall regarded as "competitive control" over domestic adversaries. This contributed to a war-within-a-war aspect that added a multifaceted complexity to the First Indochina War.

The Viet Minh's elimination of their Vietnamese competitors demonstrated that power and Marxist–Leninist ideological purity drove political action in uncompromising terms. Even though many groups shared an anticolonial agenda, the Vietnamese communists demanded complete control of the agenda. This formed a brutal undercurrent that fermented for a time, but could settle into genuine cooperation between factions with the emergence of existential crises, such as against Japanese forces during World War II. Then, after they had achieved that shorter-term goal, the appearance of unity would unravel, as occurred when war broke out between the French and the Viet Minh in late 1946. The violence of inter-Vietnamese politics, along with the breakout of war, all contributed to the Indochinese Communist Party's consolidation of control, even as it was seriously beleaguered early in the First Indochina War. War-making, ironically but crucially, was essential to state-making in the DRV. Fall recognized this and strove to understand further the historical context for conflict between Vietnamese Communists and Vietnamese Nationalists. After all, he had already survived one of the most violent eras in which state- and war-making had formed two sides of the same coin, and that coin had been a Reichsmark.

In Asia during World War II, Chinese Nationalists in the Kuomintang Party worked to support a "Vietnamese government-in-exile on the model of such governments as existed in Europe during that time."[22] In 1941, the Kuomintang empowered its preferred Vietnamese proxy, Nguyen Hai Than, over Vietnamese Communist leaders also living under protection in Chinese Nationalist sanctuaries during China's war with Japan during World War II. Among these Vietnamese Communists, Nguyen Ai Quoc, who later changed his name to Ho Chi Minh, was the most prominent. When Chinese leaders sought to foster a type of pan-Vietnamese unity among Vietnamese under their control, the results were unsatisfactory, as unity was not achieved.

143

Instead of unity, Ho sought to establish dominance over the Vietnamese factions, and a political struggle among Vietnamese Communists and others persisted through World War II and through the August Revolution of 1945.

As a result, "Ho and several other Vietnamese political leaders were jailed by the Kuomintang for nearly eighteen months, hoping that this would bring about a more harmonious cooperation, but to little avail."[23] Fall added, "Nguyen Ai Quoc was to remain in jail until early 1943, at which date Chinese Kuomintang General Chang Fa-kwei recognized the failure of Viet Minh rivals over the Viet-Minh league." After Ho's release, Fall added, "this gave Nguyen Ai Quoc, the man who was now introduced to Chungking as Ho Chi Minh, a practically free rein in the reorganization of the Vietnamese nationalist revolutionaries."[24] This was an important moment in which Ho Chi Minh regained not only his freedom and recovered a leadership role, but in which he received support from Kuomintang authorities who had previously held him as a political prisoner.

After Ho Chi Minh's release, "another congress was held at Liu-chou, China between March 25–28, 1944 and a Provisional Republican Government" was formed. In Fall's words, "The program of the newborn government was brief: (a) liquidation of both the French and the Japanese grip on Vietnam; and (b) independence for Vietnam with the help of the Kuomintang."[25] Fall described the Viet Minh's considerable efforts in 1943 and 1944, during which time it consolidated its strength with the support of the OSS and through Kuomintang materiel aid and training. He added:

> It cannot be denied that the Viet-Minh showed an amount of political foresight which the other Vietnamese parties were far from sharing. The Viet-Minh mounted extensive recruiting campaigns and acquired a well-known reputation throughout the back areas of North Vietnam. They won many recruits, particularly among the Vietnamese soldiers of disbanded French colonial forces, who became the hardcore of the Viet-Minh's nascent army and who are today the elite of the military cadres of the DRV.[26]

This statement, made in 1954, also singled out the Viet Minh's top leadership: "While the old nationalist party leaders preferred the comparative safety and comfort of Yunnan and Kwangsi, Ho Chi Minh was the only cabinet member of the Provisional Government who volunteered to enter Vietnam in 1944 in order to intensify the struggle." Fall concluded, "Joining up with the partisan groups of Vo Nguyen Giap, a young Communist history professor who had held out in the various North Vietnam mountain areas since 1942, Ho Chi Minh soon controlled the vital Thai Nguyen area which, until the Geneva cease-fire of 1954, remained a major Viet-Minh stronghold."[27]

SEVEN YEARS OF WAR IN INDOCHINA

Despite Japan's occupation of Indochina in 1940, the Viet Minh continued to build its strength in rural North Vietnam until 9 March 1945. In a coup that day, the Japanese removed the Vichy-controlled colonial administration and imprisoned French civilians and soldiers to remove the potential internal threat they represented as the Allied Island Campaign in the Pacific progressed. This action, a coup against French bureaucratic control, eliminated the French administration. According to Fall, France's security forces were disarmed and incarcerated in camps that "achieved a notoriety in the Far East comparable to that of Dachau or Buchenwald in Europe."[28]

The power vacuum created by the 9 March coup pervaded local levels and disrupted French administrative control throughout the protectorates of Tonkin, Annam, and in the colony of Cochinchina in South Vietnam. This change in the political situation enabled the Viet Minh, founded earlier in the war in 1941, to coalesce further as an anti-Japanese organization; build its political and military strength even more; and co-opt, eliminate, or coerce competitors to join its ranks. To minimize the appearance that they might reassert a firm political grip over the Vietnamese as a communist vanguard, the Viet Minh appealed to nationalists by emphasizing revolution through unified action. This was precisely the type of unity the Viet Minh would eventually discard when political circumstances changed after World War II, leading to their subsequent targeting of nationalists in 1946.

With the defeat of Japan in August 1945, "Ho Chi Minh's guerrillas became the 'Vietnam Liberation Army,'" and "a shadow government, called the 'Vietnam People's Liberation Committee' was set up during the following days."[29] This event's groundwork had been ongoing for much of World War II with support from both the United States and Chinese Kuomintang. In the closing days of the war, and through what became known as the August Revolution, the Viet Minh emerged as the Vietnamese primary independence leaders. In the next week, a series of steps then quickly consolidated the Viet Minh-dominated government under Ho Chi Minh. First, on 25 August 1945, the "Emperor of Annam (Bao Dai) abdicated and handed over his powers to Ho Chi Minh and on the same day, a 'Provisional Executive Committee for South Vietnam,' including seven communists among its nine members, took control of Saigon."[30] This step notably attempted to consolidate gains the August Revolution sought to achieve in the south and was an important step for communist agitation.

Another step was taken a few days later, and "a new Provisional Government of the Democratic Republic of Vietnam was formed in Hanoi on August 29, 1945."[31] Finally, Fall explained:

One last step remained to complete the impressive list of bloodless political successes: the declaration of independence of the Democratic Republic of Vietnam (DRV). It followed on September 2, 1945, hardly one week after Ho Chi Minh had consolidated his internal position. The proclamation announcing the DRV was carefully designed to appeal to the anti-colonialist leanings of the United States, from which Ho expected to receive most of the help he needed.[32]

The second day of September was also auspicious in other respects that genuinely mattered to the United States and its allies in Asia. It was no coincidence that Vietnamese independence was proclaimed on the same day as the Japanese surrender aboard the USS *Missouri* in Tokyo Bay. This was a historically critical event marking the end of one war, but it also formed a foundation for another soon to begin.[33]

After proclaiming their government's independence on 2 September 1945, the Viet Minh worked to build strength as decisions determining the postwar European order unfolded at the Potsdam Conference. Gaining popular support also grew in importance and, in September, the Viet Minh eliminated a series of taxes, including individual income tax and professional taxes. These, Fall wrote, "were obviously popular but put the fledgling government into a disastrous financial situation."[34] Quickly, taxation was reimposed, along with other means of generating income, including "the famous 'Gold Week' during the second week of September 1945 when the population was asked to contribute gold so that arms could be purchased abroad."[35] The more significant problem Ho Chi Minh faced, however, centered on decisions determined at the Potsdam Conference. It was decided by the "Big Three" (the Soviet Union, Great Britain, and the United States) that Chinese forces would return to Vietnam to oversee the withdrawal of Japanese troops, and this reduced "the Viet-Minh's sphere of authority to Hanoi and the southern part of North Vietnam."[36]

In November 1945, "a decision by the Central Executive Committee of the Indochinese Communist Party stated that: 'so as not to harm National Unity, the members of the Communist Party of Indochina have decided to dissolve the Party.'"[37] In Fall's view, "This measure was seemingly designed to have the double effect of reassuring the Chinese, Southeast Asians, and the West as to the primarily nationalist aims of Ho Chi Minh, and of considerably broadening the base of internal popular support upon which the Viet-Minh had to depend for the time being."[38] It was a move, Fall recognized, developed to dissuade Chinese Nationalist troops from staying in Vietnam under the pretext of an anti-communist agenda. Moreover, he acknowledged antagonism in Vietnamese–Chinese relations because they had a historical basis in

Vietnamese apprehension over long-term Chinese interests in Vietnam. The potential for Chinese encroachment into Vietnam was, in fact, a greater fear for the Viet Minh after World War II than even the potential return of French troops. If there was an Asian version of the domino theory that the Vietnamese feared, it was Chinese territorial expansion at the expense of Vietnam, Laos, Cambodia, and elsewhere in the region. Regardless of the Viet Minh's hopes, Chinese Nationalist troops remained in North Vietnam for the time being while British troops occupied the country's southern half. After agreements were made at the Potsdam Conference, French troops were allowed to return to Indochina in 1946.

In *The Viet-Minh Regime*, Fall briefly recounted these broader developments before articulating an extensive political analysis of the Viet Minh. His subjects ranged from the "Statutes of the Lao Dong Worker's Party," which replaced the Indochinese Communist Party in 1951, to a minutia-filled analysis of the Lao Dong Party's organization. He assumed, it appears, that his readers understood the larger contours of post-World War II developments in Indochina. The fact that Fall published *The Viet-Minh Regime* through the Institute of Pacific Affairs and Cornell University's Southeast Asia Studies Department indicates that he composed it with a specialist reading audience in mind. However, even among specialists, *The Viet-Minh Regime* is rarely cited and, previously, has never been assessed in detail by contemporary historians of Indochina or by other scholars assessing the wars that occurred there. Nonetheless, it is one of the first books published to examine events during and after World War II in Indochina, mainly as these events were related to the Viet Minh's history.

After World War II, with Chinese Nationalist forces and French troops stationed in Indochina, Ho Chi Minh and the Viet Minh were faced with a decision. Due to the Viet Minh's weakness confronting reestablished French military power, a compromise was developed between the Viet Minh and France on 6 March 1946. This agreement permitted French troops to remain in Indochina, replacing Chinese forces who then returned to China. The March Accords, also known as the Ho-Sainteny Agreement, was a concession Ho Chi Minh made because of his pressing concern that Chinese Nationalist forces would perpetually remain in Vietnam.[39] It helped that the Chinese Nationalist leaders were preoccupied with war against the Chinese communists—led by Mao Tse-tung and Generals Chen Geng, Wei Guoqing, and Chu The—and this added urgency to their motivation for withdrawing from Vietnam.[40] Fall recognized that the March 6 Accords were a precarious compromise for the Viet Minh, but the agreement was made to accomplish the strategic goal of consolidating a tenable DRV administration for the long term. However, along with agreements made at the July 1946 Fontainebleau Conference, these efforts to achieve a political solution failed to resolve the continued animosity between Vietnamese and French authorities.[41] Later, on 26 November 1946, conflict broke out between the Viet Minh and French forces in Haiphong, and, after a Viet Minh attack on French installations in Hanoi the next month, the First Indochina War began on 19 December.[42]

In the early stages of the war, French forces focused efforts against the Viet Minh in the north and operated with an economy of force in the South.[43] Despite efforts to promote an aligned administrative apparatus in the south early in the war, the Viet Minh never held much sway in southern regions. The Cao Dai and Hoa Hao, along with Vietnamese anti-communists, such as Nguyen Van Tam and many others, all mitigated Viet Minh potential to establish a vibrant communist base at the time. According to Shawn McHale, the Vietnamese population's diversity in southern and central Vietnam was extreme, and "in the South, the Viet Minh faced legions of local competitors."[44] In the late 1940s, as war went on, France maintained corridors between cities, such as Hanoi, Haiphong, and border cities, but the Viet Minh maintained a hold on rural, northern areas. After the Chinese Communists' victory over the Chinese Kuomintang in late 1949, the Viet Minh gained much-needed resources from their communist allies, which they quickly put to use to defeat French border garrisons in Cao Bang, Dong Khe, and Lang Son in 1950.

In the years leading to the battle at Dien Bien Phu in late 1953 and early 1954, Viet Minh forces led by Vo Nguyen Giap continued to build strength and launched attacks against French garrisons in the north, such as Nghia Lo, a town in Yen Bai province, northwest of Hanoi. Conflict there resulted in French forces undertaking a massive operation called Operation Lorraine in late 1952 to relieve pressure against its many beleaguered outposts. Operation Lorraine ended in disaster, and in 1953 the Navarre Plan initiated even more aggressive operations against the Viet Minh by seeking to draw the Viet Minh into open conventional battle.[45] This strategy led to the establishment of the large garrison of forts at Dien Bien Phu in November 1953.[46] After Viet Minh assaults intensified in March and April, French forces were defeated on 7 May 1954. During this final wave of Viet Minh attacks that ended in victory for the DRV, the Geneva Conference—established to resolve conflict in Vietnam even while the battle at Dien Bien Phu raged—established a ceasefire and call for subsequent diplomatic discussions to chart Indochina's future.

The First Indochina War, through the seven years it was fought, significantly changed France's and America's broader geopolitical calculus during the early Cold War. While it is essential to draw attention to the formation of the People's Republic of China in 1949, which provided a critical basis for the Viet Minh's victory, it is also critical to note that the Korean War added to the overall intensification of international relations. Fall acknowledged essential developments in China and on the Korean Peninsula in several early journal articles, but only to the extent that key incidents in China and Korea might relate to his focused analysis of events in Indochina. Notably, however, Fall briefly turned his attention to French politics in 1955. In a rare article that explained why France had committed itself to reclaiming Indochina after World War II, Fall described reasons why the United States gravitated—almost as if no one was at the wheel in the United States—toward Indochina after the immense amount of bloodshed caused during the Korean War.

In "The French Communists and Indochina," an article published in *Foreign Affairs* in April 1955, Fall described how the challenges of confronting the Viet Minh between 1946 and 1954 increasingly divided French politics.[47] These types of blurry lines between politics and military operations were apparently a theme in this particular issue,[48] With Henry Kissinger's "Military Policy and Defense of the 'Grey Area'" also appearing alongside Fall's article.[49] The most prominent point in Fall's article, however, was the ironic nature of relations between France and the United States, and the role Indochina played between them. In a twist that might have added a new dimension to thinking about Indochina, Fall recounted how the French Communist Party (PCF) supported France's return to Indochina in 1945 and actively worked to reestablish French control over Vietnam.

In many respects, this might have created cognitive dissonance among some in the United States who exclusively framed France's intentions in Indochina as entirely exploitative. In contrast to this view, the PCF's motivation was not to exploit the Vietnamese. Rather, the PCF wanted to regain control over Indochina to ensure that French colonial possessions in Asia and Africa transferred to a unified communist bloc, led by the Soviet Union, that would also include France. As a politically astute French citizen, Fall was personally aware of the degree to which post-World War II French politics were contentious. Political instability in the French Fourth Republic was so endemic that twenty different governments attempted to govern between 1945 and 1958. That so many administrations rose and fell over the course of thirteen years was undoubtedly a key indicator of widespread political dissent.[50]

While the early goal of France reclaiming its empire soon prevailed after World War II, the sheer number of different governments indicated a troubling lack of unity that might have helped produce consistent policies related to France's former colonies. The revolving cast of political leaders also indicated how differing political aspirations resulted in fluctuating views on how to achieve financial and political stability in France, let alone develop coherent policies for French administrations overseas. Even in 1945, the decision to return to Indochina remained contested among French politicians with differing ideologies. According to Fall, "The quasi-colonialist enthusiasm of the French Communist parliamentarians was evident in the Constituent Assembly of 1946."[51] Édouard Herriot, a leader of the Radical Party (PRV) and three-time prime minister in the Third Republic, "insisted upon tight French control of outlying French imperial bases in Africa and Indochina."[52] Fall cautioned his readers that:

> We must remember, however, that for Viet-Nam to break away from French influence would have been a step backward given the imminent integration of France herself into the Communist orbit; and this would have been so even if the Ho Chi Minh regime had been 100 percent Communist. It would have been comparable to what Tito did later in Yugoslavia, for it would have separated the Vietnamese and French Communist parties and set them on divergent paths.[53]

Thus, French Communists were interested in retaining France's colonies, but not because they wanted France to regain its pre-World War II status as a bourgeois power. Instead, they wanted to reclaim Indochina so that France could join the communist world unified with its (ideally) communist colonial holdings intact. Paul Mus, an influential scholar and diplomat who served in the French Colonial Apparatus and was with the French delegation at Japan's surrender ending World War II in Asia, provided a key account on this view. Writing in 1952, Mus explained:

> I remember how, upon our arrival in Saigon in 1945, General Jacques Leclerc (the commander of French Forces) met the local group of French Marxists and asked them about the feelings of the French Communists in Indochina toward the '"Annamite" Communists. We were answered: "There are no French and Vietnamese Communists. There is one Communist Party, and here we happen to be in Indochina."[54]

French Communists, such as these, were possibly more problematic in Mus' and Leclerc's eyes than Vietnamese Communists. In other words, if there was an internationalist Marxist ideology held by communists in Asia, it might have been held more virulently by French Communists than by Vietnamese

Communists. Many Vietnamese Communists argued over the degree to which they should include patriotism or nationalism in achieving their political goals for independence. To be sure, the story of Vietnamese political ideology in the twentieth century is characterized, and even dominated, by communist ideology. However, it is also a real-life story with consistent and robust differences in political opinion.[55] As Mus and LeClerc likely realized, and as Fall pointed out in *Foreign Affairs*, the problem of decolonization was as contentiously debated among communist parties after World War II as it was among anti-communists.[56]

Wary of the French Communists' plans, US policymakers and anti-communists in the French political class felt compelled to hold onto a critical, even existential, goal: to prevent France from becoming a member of the communist bloc. In addition to helping French citizens rebuild their country, this political demand indicated why post-World War II aid to France through the Marshall Plan was perceived as abundantly urgent.[57] It also explains, in part, why non-communist and anti-communist political elements in France demanded control of French colonies and continued US assistance after 1952 when Marshall Plan aid subsided. In short: preventing communist infiltration of France's colonies was perceived to be a means to prevent communist infiltration of France. The potential communist threat within France might have been the primary concern, but France's colonies and protectorates were undoubtedly perceived as important extensions of France. They might not have been a part of France in the same way Algeria was, but they were still crucial to various political factions, just in different ways and for different reasons.

What was the basis for Western fears concerning communist control over Indochina, and how were they historically linked to potential communist subversion in Europe? A central reason was based on a fear of "Tripartism and communist hopes of being able to get control of France and her overseas possession in one swift sweep."[58] The plausibility for such a political shift was perceived as severe after World War II because the loss of Indochina might accelerate this progression. At the very least, losing Indochina revealed France's political vulnerabilities on top of dealing a serious blow to France's military power in terms of personnel lost. Instead of the "one swift sweep," Fall pointed out as conceivable earlier in 1945, by August 1947, "The old tactic of 'Communism in one country' came again to the fore, and now the country in question was Viet-Nam and not France."[59] Previously, French Communists had viewed control of Indochina as a step toward eventual communist control of France. The eastern bloc's absorption of Czechoslovakia in 1948, for example, was the type of victory that French communists had hoped for but failed to achieve for France. Among anti-communists, however, lingering fears over which way France might tilt was a problem, and the numerous and rotating cast of French governments in the Fourth Republic demonstrated continued instability. Moreover, in the United States, the question of "Who lost Czechoslovakia?" in the late 1940s laid a foundation for the far greater accusatory power of "Who lost China?" the following year in 1949.[60]

The idea that the French colonies in Indochina served as potential bridges to communist infiltration in Europe created a vicious cycle beyond 1947. Fall, observing this development, wrote that "the Indochina issue became rapidly involved in the broadening rift between the Soviet Union and the West following the creation of the Marshall Plan and the beginning of American military aid to Greece under the Truman 'containment policy.'"[61] Complex post-World War II French politics aside, American interests were also involved, and US financial support for rebuilding war-torn France became the most significant factor for enabling France to return to Indochina. Fall described this support, writing, "France spent twice as much on the Indo-China war as it has received under the Marshall Plan for its own rehabilitation, and America has furnished much more military and economic aid—calculated on a per capita basis—than it ever gave to Chiang Kai-shek's Nationalists."[62] In effect, the United States supported France's recolonization in Indochina in order to maintain its influence over France. Preventing potential communist subversion within France surely played a part in this, but it more clearly played a part in preventing Indochina from falling under communist control. This crossover between France and the United States—with Indochina in the middle—was the critical overall basis for Fall's *Foreign Affairs* article. While he might have focused primarily on France's internal politics, his larger purpose was to explain how the United States became tied to France's future in Southeast Asia because it was committed to France's rehabilitation in Europe.

US support for France's renewed colonial enterprise in Indochina was a problem in Fall's eyes for two reasons. First, it wove the United States into France's colonial past and contemporary aspirations to reoccupy Indochina. Strategically, the United States' decision to support France's goal to return to Indochina was made to ensure that France did not tilt too far toward the Soviet-led bloc. Yet, in supporting France, the United States tied its prestige and anti-communist leadership of the free world to the outcome of France's support for a non-communist Vietnamese national government, the State of Vietnam. Second, there was a lack of transparency because, while France rebuilt its domestic economy through Marshall Aid funds, it directed nearly the same amount to fund its operations in Southeast Asia.[63] This might not have been well-known information at the time, but it demonstrated the trilateral nature of relations between France, Indochina, and the United States. While Fall's analysis in *Foreign Affairs* did not offer any solutions, it did attempt to explain the larger political forces at work which were drawing the United States to become more involved in the region.

Of all the points Fall made, the most remarkable fact was that the United States provided so much for France to reclaim Indochina. Irwin Wall emphasized this same issue in 2001, writing, "In France, skillful politicians proved adept at manipulating American aid to their own uses and to the furtherance of their own policies. In fact … in France the Americans became accomplices, indeed mainstays, of French colonial ambitions in Indochina and paradoxically, Algeria."[64] The idea that the United States might support self-determination after World War II was entirely a ghost of an idea by the time the Marshall Plan changed Europe. Frank Costigliola was correct to point out that "American officials felt confined by the transatlantic ties they had fostered," but many of these downsides were because of France's ties to Indochina.[65]

Richard Hunt has also commented on the implications of this connection in subsequent France–US relations. When divisions in public opinion and differences among policymakers began to appear in the later stages of the First Indochina War, this contributed to a growing political aversion to France's experience in Indochina among US decision-makers: "The occasionally contentious Franco-America relationship that emerged helps explain why [later] the U.S. military in Saigon and Washington was little influenced by French methods and experience," even though "American officials felt they remained largely ignorant of French plans and programs for Indochina."[66] Meanwhile, in the United States, the "Second Red Scare" promoted narrow-minded views that demanded continued support for France as a necessary action to prevent global communist subversion. According to George Herring, these dynamics took place while a "Cold War culture of near hysterical fear, paranoiac suspiciousness, and stifling conformity began to take shape."[67]

Fall was undoubtedly an anti-communist, but he did not buy into communist fearmongering when it was wielded as a tactic to increase political standing. Instead, while he believed communism posed a serious threat, he also believed that the United States overemphasized Indochina's importance within the broader Cold War at the time. He explained this in 1954, writing:

We need have no illusions about Ho's regime; it is of course communist-dominated. But so are North Korea and Red China, with whom the United States sat at the conference table for two years; and so is the U.S.S.R. and its satellites, with whom the United States, and France, maintain normal diplomatic relations.[68]

Since these statements were accurate, he seemed to ask, why did Indochina matter so much? And what were the best solutions for problems there? In a 1954 article for *The Nation*, he concluded with some considerable understatement: "A farsighted policy in Indochina based on well-administered aid might do more to stem the communist tide in Southeast Asia than the sending of a few technicians or of a few additional planeloads of napalm."[69]

Fall was not alone in thinking that Indochina was overblown as a matter of serious political consequence. He was also accompanied by others who did not see how military operations would effectively counter decolonization. In a 28 May 1954 letter to Texas Senator Lyndon B. Johnson, Austin resident, Mr. J.A. Dennis shared a view similar to Fall, writing: "Communism, though a very real threat, cannot be stopped by bullets or H-bombs, but must be met by winning the minds of men by showing them something better in deeds, not words."[70] If a citizen in Texas could see this, what was different about Fall's observations? Ultimately, not much, because individuals like Mr. Dennis and Fall both agreed on the importance of promoting a robust liberal ideology that supported self-determination and independence. This precise point, after all, was why Fall had such a difficult time when John J. McCloy offered amnesty to Nazi associates, such as those in the Krupp Corporation. If the United States was to make a difference in the world, it would be through promoting its self-professed values domestically and with others through its foreign relations overseas.

At the same time, Fall recognized that developing policies to counter the Viet Minh was complicated, given the challenge of providing the Vietnamese with "something better in deeds." A central question at that point was whether a farsighted policy was even possible, and whether wisely planned financial assistance might be provided to Vietnam without crippling its predominantly agriculture-based economy. For Fall, and likely for Mr. J. A. Dennis in Austin, Texas as well, the values of life, liberty, and equality mattered a great deal. Also important, however, was whether enough senior political leaders in Washington shared those convictions when it came to intervening in a manner that strengthened, rather than compromised, life, liberty, and equality among the Vietnamese. Whether those leaders could ensure that these values were fulfilled in the United States, and whether they could promote them abroad without using H-Bombs and bullets, were questions that mattered even more.

* * *

In 1953 and 1954, Fall understandably gained more nuanced views about Indochina's history and the development of Vietnamese communism. He recognized that Ho Chi Minh sought Vietnamese independence first and foremost and had joined with the Communist International movement before the Cold War primarily because he had few other practical options in furthering this aim. Writing in 1966, Fall explained:

> It would be quite inaccurate to say, as have some Western scholars, that Ho has let his Communist allegiances override his Vietnamese patriotism. The contrary, in fact, is true ... throughout the 1920s and 1930s, Ho makes anti-colonialism such a central issue of all his public statements at Communist Party congresses, to the almost total exclusion of any other consideration, particularly those of Soviet diplomatic requirements, that one can well wonder where he would have stood politically had any strong nationalist Vietnamese party existed in Viet-Nam, or had any French political party other than the Communist Party espoused a deliberate policy of eventual independence for the colonies.[71]

This statement was important because it demonstrated, in Fall's eyes, that Ho Chi Minh's primary goal was Vietnamese independence. Yet, the means to achieve the goal of independence, which was ideologically based in Marxist–Leninist thought, was critical even if the means to achieve independence were sometimes and intentionally obscured by a nationalist cover to increase the appeal of communist policy and programs. The "national vs. communist" debate was a subject with which Fall continued to wrestle, even though, as early as 1954, he was already convinced that Vietnamese leaders retained an uncompromising position based in one-party communist control.[72]

Fall was not the only one eventually pointing out the complexity of Ho Chi Minh's position. Writing in 1981, David Marr explained:

> By his own admission, Ho Chi Minh was attracted to the Communist Third International in 1920 not by ideas such as the historical dialectic, surplus value, or modes of production, but by Lenin's attack on imperialist oppression and support for revolutionary movements of national liberation. Both then and thereafter, the first question Ho Chi Minh would address to foreign comrades was, "If you do not condemn colonialism, if you do not side with the colonial people, what kind of revolution are you waging?"[73]

Similarly, as Fall pointed out earlier in 1966, "Ho's most important work, *French Colonialism on Trial*, originally written in French, is in reality a series of highly emotional pamphlets denouncing the various abuses of the French colonial system."[74] He added, "throughout his whole life, Ho has never quite reconciled within himself the conflicting demands of over-all Communist strategy and his love for his country."[75] The Vietnamese leader adopted communism, in part, because of the anti-imperialism it exemplified while, in contrast, liberal democracies failed to assist the Vietnamese in achieving self-determination. Fall's willingness to point out Ho Chi Minh's political flexibility well before World War II was an important point. It demonstrated his understanding that Ho Chi Minh had other options than just a communist road to power in Vietnam. Undoubtedly, victory over Czarism through the Russian Revolution and Woodrow Wilson's unwillingness to hear Ho Chi Minh's pleas for Vietnamese independence in 1919 contributed to steering him toward his chosen path. Among rank-and-file Viet Minh, historical ties to other past successful revolutions also provided models to emulate.

Vietnamese individuals who were connected to the Russian Revolution were central in establishing the Viet Minh's broader association with a communist-aligned past. Ton Duc Thang, Ho Chi Minh's second-in-command in the DRV, born in 1888, was encouraged by other leaders to emphasize his ties with the Russian Revolution, even though the veracity of his connections later came into question.[76] Yet, Ton Duc Thang's proven commitment to communism and world revolution—he had served seventeen years in prison, including confinement at Con Son Island for his anti-colonial activities—gave him added credibility as a symbol of communist uprising, linking the Viet Minh to the October Revolution.[77] Undeniably, he was also among the anti-colonial pioneers who took up the revolutionary fervor—Pham Boi Chau, Phan Chu Trinh, Nguyen An Ninh, and others—promoted in the early twentieth century. Christoph Giebel has also argued, like Fall, that Ton Duc Thang might have become Ho Chi Minh's mostly symbolic second-in-command precisely because of his reputation as an alleged mutineer in the "Black Sea Mutiny" in support of the Russian Revolution in 1919.

In 1963, Fall first wrote about the debate surrounding the authenticity of Ton Duc Thang's connections to the mutiny.[78] However, it was clear to him that Ton Duc Thang served as an essential element in cultivating significant, symbolic ties between the Russian and Vietnamese Revolutions.[79] This history was essential to explain but also politically risky to contextualize for Western audiences at an intense stage in the Cold War during the early 1960s. Open-minded political discussions hardly characterized American discourse in the 1950s and early 1960s. It was a tall order to provide nuanced views on the Russian Revolution's relevance or explain why the Black Sea Mutiny might inspire young communists in places like Vietnam. While Ho might have been still ideologically open-minded in the 1920s or 1930s, he was undeniably committed to communism in the 1950s and 1960s, to the extent that Nikita Khrushchev thought of Ho Chi Minh as "an apostle of the revolution" and as "one of communism's saints."[80] This was undoubtedly clear to many Americans, but Vietnamese Communism was also interwoven with threads of patriotism, nationalism, anti-Francoism, and numerous other strings. Unless they were reading Bernard Fall's books closely, it is unlikely that many Americans carefully considered Ho Chi Minh, Ton Duc Thang, Truong Chinh, or Vo Nguyen Giap's views on communism as a path to freedom against colonialism rather than a monolithic crusade against Western-oriented liberalism.

II—The Democratic Republic of Vietnam

After the First Indochina War, the Viet Minh and the DRV underwent significant transformation. In describing this postwar transition, Fall recounted a key Viet Minh characteristic: the ability to adapt to change. "This reorganization—mostly dealing in personalities and designed to make use of the Communist leaders who had been evacuated from the southern guerrilla pockets to North Vietnam—took place in the fall of 1954."[81] These moves also consolidated communist control of the north after the bitter war with France and its Vietnamese allies in the Associated State of Vietnam. The DRV's ability to endure, as Paul Staniland observed, had been "forged by decades of shared experiences, stabilized central institutionalization and made possible by the increasing mobilization of local society."[82] Numerous factors, thus, contributed to the staying power of the Viet Minh and their government. Among these, the "mobilization of local society" was critical. Land reform was also essential to this effort because it mobilized Vietnamese supporters to the Viet Minh cause. However, land reform efforts also alienated vast numbers of Vietnamese and led to the deaths of thousands.[83]

Complications associated with land reform indicated to Fall that the Viet Minh was far more than an insurgency. The cause they fought for encompassed far more than changes in governmental administration, such as new leadership in the French-supported government or comparatively less impactful changes in French policy toward Indochina and Vietnam. Land reform changed the entire social fabric of Vietnam. Compromises sought through the

March 6 Accords or other failed agreements were long a thing of the past. Fall viewed land reform as a collective effort of such magnitude that it more closely resembled revolution than past uprisings in Vietnam or insurgencies against French authority in other countries, such as the Malagasy Uprising in Madagascar in 1947 and 1948. Land reform permeated Vietnamese society comprehensively because, as he observed, "the institution of agrarian reform, particularly in a nation where 90 percent of the population lives by agriculture, is bound to have deep repercussions upon the development of the country at large."[84] Due to the potential land reform had to affect such large numbers of the Vietnamese population, the fact that it was often implemented by fanatical cadres also revealed serious problems regarding how Vietnamese society's mobilization might be achieved.

The DRV mobilized the Vietnamese under its control, but Chinese ideological influence and supplies, advisors, diplomatic support, and contribution toward the development of the Vietnamese People's Army (PAVN) also contributed to mass mobilization in an interdependent manner. Land reform in 1953 was critical to this because "in a peasant country the most effective way to mobilize the population for social change was land reform," and mobilizing Vietnamese peasants relieved the "organizational and economic burden on the Lao Dong party."[85] Land reform also strengthened the DRV and Lao Dong Party (formerly the Indochinese Communist Party) through its associations with the Chinese Communist Party. Negatively, numerous cases of repression ensued due to class struggle and fanaticism targeting non- and anti-Viet Minh and bourgeois Viet Minh leaders of local party committees.

According to Fall, the "DRV's Mass Mobilization Movement's problems occurred because it was an almost exact copy of similar measures undertaken in Communist China from 1950 to 1952."[86] He observed that the DRV was unable to successfully transplant Chinese policy to Vietnam, at least not in 1953. Instead of copying a Chinese model, the DRV had to readjust its implementation of land reform. However, when they failed to do so, Vietnamese land reform efforts resulted in often inaccurate targeting of "kulaks who were feudal landowners, and through expropriation and extermination of other Vietnamese."[87] To change course, the Lao Dong party issued over DRV-controlled radio networks a "new directive on Mass Mobilization and its New Relations with the Rich Farmers" on 22 September 1953.[88] As directed by DRV authorities, and because it was initially based on the Chinese model of land reform practices, land reform started poorly, was too indiscriminate, and antagonized far too many Vietnamese.

Fall was angered by the cruelty, social discord, and refugee problems created by the Viet Minh's communist-driven land reform before implementing the September 1953 adjustments. Social unrest crested to the point that on 22 September the entire National Assembly of the DRV assembled for the first time in six years specifically to pass decrees on agrarian reform, which were then immediately announced. This series of actions demonstrated how DRV authorities perceived the unrest created by earlier land-reform directives and understood it needed to be dealt with urgently. One example of how the directives had alienated the Vietnamese were the mass mobilization mandates issued earlier on 12 April 1953, which destroyed the landowning class of "feudal" landlords, eventually redistributing over 500,000 acres of land by 1956 and 1957. Then, in the late 1950s, one-year economic plans created "economic, administrative bases for the later longer-range plans."[89] Amid these bureaucratic and sometimes confusing changes, Fall excoriated the Viet Minh for creating "People's Agricultural Reform Tribunals" that "delivered verifiable quotas of landlords and rich peasants even in areas where the difference between the largest and the smallest village plots were a quarter-acre."[90] Communist fanatics' indiscriminate targeting on Vietnamese civilians based on marginal material differences between the "haves and have nots," was counterproductive as much as it was cruel.

Fall estimated that possibly 50,000 individuals were executed in connection with land reform in 1953, and "that at least twice as many were arrested and sent to forced labor camps."[91] These included not only thousands of landlords and other Viet Minh enemies but also "individuals who in many cases had loyally served in the war against France or had even been members of the Lao-Dong."[92] The indiscriminate nature of such targeting, especially against former Viet Minh soldiers, outraged Fall because it indicated a mechanistic, bureaucratic, administrative approach to governance by which innocent individuals were victimized. His calling attention to the DRV's failures in 1953 was based not on a rigid anti-communist ideological position but rather a committed anti-authoritarian outlook. In North Vietnam, Vietnamese anger against the Viet Minh over land reform eventually reached such severity that an extensive rebellion broke out in November 1956 in Nghe An, Ho Chi Minh's home province.

The ensuing repression against Vietnamese farmers in Nghe An was draconian and, as Fall observed, "Hanoi responded in exactly the same way as the colonial power had, sending the whole 325th Division to crush the rebels. It did so with typical VPA [PAVN] thoroughness; allegedly, close to 6,000 farmers were deported or executed."⁹³ Additionally, Fall was appalled, in his words, "that no U.N. member—neither of the always touchy Bandung bloc so concerned about the fate of its brothers in colonial shackles nor of the habitually anti-Communist nations—mustered sufficient courage … to present the Nghe An case to the conscience of the world."⁹⁴ In Fall's eyes, this was a hypocrisy that required denunciation. By his reckoning, UN and Bandung members criticized other governments only when it was in their political interest, not because criticizing repression was the right thing to do. If the UN and members of the Bandung Conference were to retain moral authority or validity as anti-colonist crusaders, they would have to be consistent and indict the DRV's repression of its people.

A vital component of Fall's analysis is his calling attention to this insincerity, or non-action, on the part of the non-aligned movement over the DRV's repression enacted in Nghe An Province in late 1956. In doing so, he demonstrated a commendable willingness to criticize any organization that failed to condemn repressive policies, regardless of that organization's political outlook. Fall was critical of anyone, in other words, who averted their gaze from Viet Minh aggression against other Vietnamese. Pointing out the repression in Nghe An to others indicated his enmity toward authoritarianism—of any kind—as well as his unwillingness to turn away from what he perceived as injustice, no matter who perpetuated it.

Fall despised the authoritarianism on display in these land-reform efforts, especially since the Viet Minh sought to portray themselves as victims of colonial abuse. He condemned such hypocrisy, writing:

> the indiscriminate lumping together of practically all land-owning groups down to the middle-class farmers into the category of "exploiters" brought about a dangerous condition in which the regime risked alienating more farmers than it could afford to in time of war, for the poor farmer who knew that he was about to obtain a better piece of farmland, or conversely, the landowner who knew that he was about to lose all of his, hardly did any fieldwork but rather waited for events to develop.⁹⁵

As a result of war and land reform, he added, "the state of insecurity prevailing in the open country created a movement of large numbers of homeless refugees towards the urban areas," and even before 1954, "Saigon and Hanoi's populations increased five-to-eight-fold in comparison to pre-World War II figures."⁹⁶ He knew these details well because he had been in Vietnam in 1953 when refugees began streaming to the cities. In his 1954 study, he comprehensively recorded land-reform implementation chronologically and described every single DRV policy article that made up the "Agrarian Policy of April 20, 1953," which the Viet Minh later announced on 20 May 1953.[97] Similarly, he analyzed Viet Minh land-reform policies again in late November and December 1953, but with broader contextual analysis describing how "land reform patterns of the Asian People's Republics of North Korea, China, and Viet-Nam" differed from "Soviet practices in the matter."[98]

DRV leaders knew problems existed, even with the enacting of reforms and new directives in September 1953. Two years later, Ho Chi Minh recognized the trauma land reform had caused in Vietnamese society, and on 17 August 1956, he renounced the Viet Minh's mistakes in the "Rectification of Errors Campaign."[99] After Ho Chi Minh's highly public act of contrition, however, the DRV resumed the final phases of agricultural land reform that indicated a less than forgiving Chinese influence concerning the peasantry. The Viet Minh's problem, Fall observed, was its over-direct adoption of Chinese practices, and he noted, "Great emphasis was placed upon Mao Tse-tung's report on farm collectivization in Red China in October 1955, and the Lao-Dong's party newspaper of November 3, 1955, after lauding the achievements of Red China in the field of collectivization, asked its readers 'to buy this document at the People's Bookstores.'"[100]

Despite the victimization of the Vietnamese peasantry in 1953, Fall wrote, by late 1955 "the situation was considered propitious for the beginning of the final liquidation phase of large agricultural ownership and for the start of collectivization."[101] He may have been disgusted by the harsh measures the Viet Minh took in executing land reform, but he understood that the resumption of efforts in late 1955—which were an adjusted continuation of the DRV's already extreme and indiscriminate agricultural policies from 1953—proved that the DRV would not be deterred from creating an authoritarian state. Fall saw this, writing:

> the Agrarian Reform Committee in Hanoi launched an appeal to the peasants themselves, that "the Committee is resolutely proposing to abolish the regime of appropriation of lands and rice fields by the landowner class. The peasant comrade of the laboring class must favorably respond to the agrarian reform policy of the Party and Government."[102]

By 1955, the road to one-party rule in the DRV had already long been established. The DRV and Lao Dong Party devoted so much attention to land reform for the simple reason that land and the rice it produced was Vietnam's lifeblood. Not only was land valuable for its agricultural virtues in producing rice, but because so much of the population was primarily rural.

Moreover, land reform was a tool that would initiate a critical series of stages toward social revolution against colonial land-holding practices. It was social engineering of a kind that transcended politics. However, Fall recognized that land reform was one thing; land collectivization would be a far more difficult challenge to overcome. The "crux of the problem," he observed, "lies in the apportionment of available land."[103]

In an important lesson he appeared to recognize in 1954, he added, "Retrospectively, it might be said that one of France's most serious errors of policy was to let the communal lands fall prey to speculators and to dishonest village chiefs despite the warning of experts of the importance of the maintenance or even increase of communal holdings."[104] These errors were especially onerous in southern Vietnam, where France's colony, Cochinchina, was under greater French control than its protectorates of Annam and Tonkin farther north. Cochinchina was critical, above all, because southern Vietnam was one of the most important rice-producing regions in all Southeast Asia.[105] France's significant economic interests in the south, reflected in its more aggressive security posture protecting commodity production—rice, and especially rubber—partly explains why Viet Minh efforts were generally weaker there when compared to their greater political reach in rural areas of central and northern Vietnam.[106]

French failure to protect communally held land, wherever it existed, was a critical lesson Fall absorbed. As others, such as Paul Mus also contended, dismissing evidence-based advice—which advocated greater cultural and historical attention and respect for Vietnamese communal-agricultural life based in the Vietnamese village—had strategic significance in either gaining or losing Vietnamese political support or allegiance to a specific political cause. Agricultural fields were undeniably the most central and crucial contested ground on which political legitimacy among Vietnamese mattered. That Fall pointed this lesson out in *The Viet-Minh Regime* in 1954 was significant. It indicated his awareness that the Vietnamese people's long-held socio-cultural practices were critical to understanding the nature of political and military conflict in the region. Fall appeared to recognize this importance intuitively. Although he did not grow up in a rural environment, let alone in Southeast Asia, he sympathized with people's concerns as a humanitarian, and he understood how control or disruption of long-held patterns of daily life was strategically important.

Moreover, Fall demonstrated how French authorities ignored the issue of land to their detriment. Control over this all-critical center of Vietnamese life created strategic effects because many Vietnamese would look to the Viet Minh to protect what the French allowed to be spoiled through speculation and theft. As indicated earlier, Fall knew that the DRV failed to manage land reform in profound ways, and the problem of land allocation equally complicated the Viet Minh's appeals to be accepted as a legitimate accepted organization. The Viet Minh's fanatical efforts to eliminate landlords, as well as some non-landholding individuals who challenged communist rule and other innocent Vietnamese, antagonized large numbers of the civilian population, not just those who openly revolted in Nghe An Province in late November 1956.

Distributing land equitably was undoubtedly an arduous task. The attempt to recreate the type of communally shared land that had existed in Vietnam before World War II was perhaps impossible, even after new distribution-related decrees. Additionally, tying long-held Vietnamese historical farming and social practices together with the Lao Dong's Marxist orientation was incongruous. Fall argued that reclaiming collective ownership over tillable land and weighing it down with the ideological baggage of economic theory originally conceived for industrialized countries had massive downsides.[107] Communalization of land, in the sense that the Lao Dong conducted it in 1953, was a process of modernization that failed to produce political, social, or economic stability. However, an exception existed, and this was the reduction of rent.

Fall emphasized that "reduction of high and excessive land rents and other usurious practices were eventually realized by the Republican government, the DRV."[108] Therefore, reducing rent was a last-ditch effort by the DRV to deliver some benefit to the people it governed after recognizing its land reform problems in 1953. He was determined to provide an even-handed evaluation of what he saw the DRV getting right, at least according to Marxist ideology principles as he knew them. However, he also saw more problems than commendable socialist glories created by their communist ideology put into practice. Surprisingly, Fall did not explicitly ask whether the DRV pursued land reform to mobilize Vietnamese society for personnel needed to support conventional military operations against French Union forces. Nor did he question whether land reform was implemented to solicit more significant popular support among Vietnamese farmers, at least initially, before fanatical low-level Can Bo (cadres) undermined this possibility. A tentative answer is that both of these were intended of land reform, although to different extents.

Fall also noted that the effectiveness of land reform depended on where it was implemented. He viewed land reform as "improving the status of small farmers in the Republican zone" (the DRV-held zone), whereas, in Nationalist-held zones, along with those held by other Viet Minh competitors, "DRV enthusiasm for land reform was created more for its propaganda effects."[109] The amount of communally owned arable land also differed significantly from region to region in Vietnam during the 1930s, an interval Fall used as a baseline because of its pre-World War II, pre-Cold War, and pre-divided status between the two competing Vietnamese governments. Communal lands in the north represented about "20 percent of the total arable area of North Vietnam; 25 percent in Central Vietnam; and only 3 percent in South Vietnam."[110] The percentage of land tilled by owners in North, Central, and South Vietnam was also significant to consider in this overall context because, in the 1930s, "owner-tilled land was 98.7% in the north, 90% in central, but only 64.5% of owners tilled land in the south."[111] He did not, of course, make these numbers up or cite an unreliable source. Instead, he referenced this data from a 1950 US Department of Agriculture report, which he integrated with other Vietnamese sources gathered during his field studies.

Predatory speculation and fraud were problems wherever they occurred, but they were acutely felt in areas where less land was available to farmers.[112] Fall believed these offenses created an especially severe problem in the south because smaller amounts of arable land and relatively smaller percentages of tilled land were available when compared to central and north Vietnam. Cases of theft and agricultural malpractice certainly did occur in north and central Vietnam. However, with more arable owner-tilled land in these regions, social disruption caused by depredation associated with France's control over Indochina could be somewhat mitigated compared to depredation in the south. In addition to there being more extensive tillable land, a more substantial Viet Minh presence and control in the rural north also enabled increased targeting of land speculators or fraudsters. Initially, this created a Robin Hood-like reputation for the Viet Minh and DRV among Vietnamese farmers, until the Viet Minh's land reform excesses drove Vietnamese farmers against them, as reflected in the revolts based in Nghe An Province later in 1956.[113] In Fall's words, the only difference between Robin Hood and the DRV was that, while Robin Hood robbed from the rich to give to the poor, "the DRV robbed from the rich to make outright gifts of their estates to the State."[114]

Land reform was complex and of such importance to Fall that he devoted two chapters of *The Viet-Minh Regime* to the subject.[115] He utilized presidential decrees; the Viet Minh newspapers, *Nhan Dan* and *Cu'u Quoc*; and the "Manifesto and Platform of the Vietnam Lao Dong Party" as primary sources for his descriptions and analysis of land reform. Additionally, he supported his arguments and analysis with documents produced by France and the State of Vietnam that recorded reactions to the Viet Minh's efforts. Based on the materials he assessed, Fall viewed DRV-controlled land reform and collectivization movements as a turning point in the DRV's modernization of Vietnam and a critical factor in the Viet Minh revolution, at least as he saw it in 1953–6.

As published in *The Viet-Minh Regime* in 1954 and revised in 1956, these findings formed the most detailed analytical account of DRV land reform in English at the time, which would not be supplanted until much later.[116] The attention Fall gave to land reform demonstrated how seriously he took political, economic, and social affairs in Indochina. His commitment to these issues reflected how his understanding and analysis of war was shifting. Yet, Fall allocated extensive analysis to land reform in *The Viet-Minh Regime*, so much that it even exceeded the attention he gave to military developments in the People's Army of Vietnam (PAVN). By prioritizing analysis of these socioeconomic-political constructs over martial ones, Fall demonstrated a progression in his thought. He was beginning to view conflict even more holistically than he had before coming to Indochina in 1953.

III—The Associated State of Vietnam

In *The Viet-Minh Regime* and articles published in 1954 and 1955, Fall devoted most of his research and analysis to subjects ranging from land reform, the formation of the DRV, and history in Indochina during World War II to the implications of communist influence in France and Indochina. In addition to addressing the formation of the DRV, Fall also gathered research on the DRV's anti-communist administrative competitor, the Associated State of Vietnam (SVN). Bao Dai led this government as Chief of State of Vietnam between 1949 and 1955. Notably, Bao Dai was also previously the former Emperor of the Nguyen Dynasty between 1926 and 1945.[117] In "Representative Government in the State of Vietnam," an article published in August 1954, Fall recounted how the State of Vietnam was perpetually in a state of disarray and had been since its formation in 1949. It eventually established a "Provisional National Council" on 8 July 1952, but even this represented "a rather regressive step on the path towards national representative government in Vietnam."¹¹⁸ He assessed that State of Vietnam leaders were unable to gain sufficient control over the population in government-held areas and how they had, in reality, limited power over the State of Vietnam's future. Moreover, they competed against other Vietnamese in communist-held areas ruled by the DRV and internally against French authorities.

Concerning the State of Vietnam's lack of control over its economy, Fall based his conclusions on evidence that indicated that French administrators imposed strict limitations on the Provisional Council's actual command over its national budget.¹¹⁹ Despite outward appearances and the French authorities' claims that they supported expanding Vietnamese executive power and responsibility for financial decisions, little administrative control was actually left for State of Vietnam administrators to wield. Fall concluded that Bao Dai and the Vietnamese government, led by Prime Minister Buu Loc, could not overcome these obstacles limiting Vietnamese authority. French support for a Vietnamese administration with actual power, required to form policy and control government through decision-making, was just not forthcoming. Moreover, Fall concluded by 1954 that obstructing Vietnamese self-determination had been a key source of self-defeat for France. If France had sincerely sought to maintain a long-term and viable position of power in Vietnam, it would have required providing greater autonomy to the State of Vietnam. Potential staying power entailed, in other words, France providing genuine support for a more capable and functionally enabled Vietnamese State as a partner. As it was, the State of Vietnam might not have been the complete lackey communists derided it for being, but that accusation had too many accuracies to deny. Authentic support for anti-communist Vietnamese political and economic self-determination was what was required. This problem was consequential to the State of Vietnam, France, and the United States, as well as other countries with a stake in the State of Vietnam's future. Fall described this, writing:

> It remains to be demonstrated whether a timely establishment of even a limited amount of representative government, particularly at the national level, would not have helped greatly to give the Bao Dai regime some stronger basis of popularity in the country. As the situation stands at the present moment [in August 1954], neither large-scale American economic aid nor French military efforts have succeeded in doing this.¹²⁰

Fall believed that supporting earnest enfranchisement and self-determination at the State of Vietnam's founding in 1949 might have conferred upon it legitimacy. Military support, which French authorities opted to prioritize, would not provide this; only authentic Vietnamese leadership could. Fall suggested, in other words, that had France enabled and supported self-determination, the State of Vietnam might have potentially garnered enough popular Vietnamese support to compete more resolutely against the communist administration of the DRV. As it appeared to Fall in August 1954, this was a missed opportunity that could not be regained, even with "large-scale American economic aid" or presumably through increased military assistance. After all, the United States had already provided France with vast amounts of aid for Indochina between 1948 and 1954. The only result it had to show for this massive expenditure was an even weaker French ally. Undeniably, the price the French state paid was tallied in terms of blows to its prestige. More consequentially, the people of France and its colonies from across the French empire were the ones who paid for these failures through tens of thousands of casualties.

US-supplied assistance often camouflaged underlying weaknesses among those receiving it, such as political problems and lack of legitimacy among recipients who did not possess popular support. Fall suggested that future military and financial assistance, without legitimate governance—as perceived by a majority of the Vietnamese people—would not only be too late, but it would also be detrimental. It would fail to address the central problem of achieving a "stronger basis of popularity in the country." He believed that the chance to achieve such legitimacy had only viably existed at the point when the State of Vietnam was established in 1949. After that, too many other factors were coming into play that made a legitimate and sustainable autonomous Vietnamese government unrealistic. In part, French obstructions and internal conflicts among the Associated State of Vietnam's authorities were significant problems, but timing mattered. In failing to unify sufficiently, "the State of Vietnam hesitated for more than five years before even the beginnings of local democratic government were implemented."[121] In contrast, DRV leaders imposed their will over Vietnamese under their control with no hesitation, no regret, and, after mid-1950, with materiel aid provided by Chinese Communists.

In contrast to the ease with which the Viet Minh received support from China, supporting the State of Vietnam entailed serious logistical problems. Geopolitical challenges by 1950 were even more consequential. Even if a more vigorous government existed in 1949, the State of Vietnam would still face a considerable opponent in the DRV, and its potency was further magnified with the formation of the People's Republic of China. Therefore, the overall problem had two facets: French restrictions were part of the problem while changes in the broader strategic environment exacerbated problems with France's control over the State of Vietnam. As Fall knew, French obstructions preventing self-determination drove former Prime Minister Nguyen Van Tam to abandon the State of Vietnam and emigrate to the United States in 1955. In some respects, Tam embodied a set of conflicting views regarding France and its role in constricting Vietnamese self-determination. Tam was a French citizen and had given himself entirely to France's cause, and he had lost two sons in the process. Yet, French policies antagonized him because they never permitted authentic levels of governance based on equality. Instead, France's position remained entrenched in a thoroughly colonialist worldview.

The State of Vietnam's lack of perceived and real political legitimacy was undoubtedly a serious matter, but it was overshadowed by events further north. The establishment of the People's Republic of China (PRC) on 1 October 1949, drastically changed the regional balance of power. On the one hand, this development soon provided the DRV with the resources it needed to endure its war with France. On the other hand, the PRC's formation enormously complicated France's position regarding the threat of enhanced Viet Minh military capabilities, and this led to France increasing its efforts to restrain Vietnamese self-determination even more. According to Mark Atwood Lawrence, "the mounting threat from Communist China lent credibility to the French position that it was impossible to concede more autonomy to Bao Dai as long as a grave state of emergency persisted in Vietnam."[122] On the DRV's side, the formation of the PRC was a double-edged sword in some respects. On the positive side, the Viet Minh received much-needed supplies, but on the negative side, relations between the Viet Minh and Chinese leaders were rarely perfectly aligned.

In 1950, Mao Tse-tung was more concerned with eliminating remaining Chinese Nationalists than attempting to dictate policy to the Viet Minh. According to Qiang Zhai, Viet Minh victories in 1950–51 in northern Vietnam proved consequential because they would "strengthen China's border and consolidate the position of the People's Republic of China."[123] The Korean War certainly added a critical dimension—and threat—to Chinese requirements for strategic territorial depth. While the position of the Democratic People's Republic of Korea was so essential that, following the outbreak of war on the Korean Peninsula, it required massive Chinese support, Chinese Communists similarly viewed the DRV as critical terrain. Political relationships among these three states formed a trilateral form of codependency, however, that was rarely harmonious. In subsequent years, internal political disagreements over which should be followed—Maoist versus Stalinist visions of communism—would also exacerbate divisions within Vietnamese communist leadership. These debates would eventually complicate the DRV's relationship with the PRC. These and other challenges to the historically contentious relationship between Chinese and Vietnamese leaders would eventually have to be hammered out in years to come. As it stood in and after 1950, the DRV certainly relied on the PRC, but the DRV was an autonomous communist state. In the PRC's eyes, while the DRV might be an autonomous state, its primary value was in providing a means to defend China's strategically critical southern border.

In the earliest years of the Cold War, to be sure, the DRV and China had a close relationship. On 18 January 1950, the PRC became the first country to recognize the DRV. Six months later, at a meeting on 27 June 1950, the Chinese Communist Party (CCP) and Chinese Military Advisory Group (CMAG) decided to provide materiel support to the DRV in accordance with Mao Tse-tung's platform advocating internationalism.[124] These steps consolidated the DRV state in North Vietnam. However, they also served an important national security function in that supporting the DRV provided an insulating, allied border area, a goal driven by security concerns related to events in Korea. The Korean War, which broke out on 25 June 1950, undeniably crystallized the need for a strong DRV. The simple fact that the PRC locked in its decision to provide aid to the DRV only two days after the Korean War began indicates a critically close correlation. Problematic relations between North Korea and the PRC added further pressure and motivation for the PRC to support the DRV under the blanket of internationalism. According to David Halberstam, the surprisingly thin levels of mutual trust between North Korean and Chinese leaders that June added further motivation for the PRC to maintain defensive depth along their shared border with North Vietnam.[125]

These developments formed the broader political circumstances encountered by the State of Vietnam soon after it was formed. While France's concerns certainly focused on maintaining control over its Vietnamese allies, these changes deeply complicated France's position and, importantly, America's position as a key financial source of support. US President Dwight Eisenhower recognized how France was in a bind because it would not accord "independence and the right of self-determination upon the Associated States until military victory could be attained" against the Viet Minh.[126] Accomplishing this, however, soon became a serious problem for

France and the Associated State of Vietnam because of changing circumstances in China. It was improbable that the PRC would allow the US-supported and mostly French-controlled State of Vietnam to defeat the Viet Minh. The problem of creating an effective and legitimate State of Vietnam was, by itself, an arduous and maybe even insurmountable task. The State of Vietnam's efforts to achieve political coherence in 1949 and 1950, as Fall pointed out, certainly indicated significant instability. Nevertheless, the idea that the State of Vietnam could somehow hold out against a Chinese-supported Viet Minh for longer than a few years, even with massive American financial assistance, pushed the bounds of credibility past a breaking point. In turn, the battle at Dien Bien Phu powerfully reflected this breaking point of belief in France's cause. The battle, moreover, provided further proof that the Viet Minh and their approach to revolutionary warfare was not only politically well-organized, but also militarily planned with strategic art and patience. In the execution on their side of the battle, Viet-Minh military planners, led by Vo Nguyen Giap, harnessed the uncompromising resolve that tens of thousands of Vietnamese civilian porters provided and channeled all these factors toward the Viet Minh's victory.

France's lack of support for Vietnamese self-determination plus the establishment of the PRC were monumental problems, but what was wrong within the State of Vietnam that rendered it so vulnerable after it was formed? The State of Vietnam eventually did create a national assembly and representative government, but far too late after its formation in June 1949. The first national elections were not held until four years later, on 25 January 1953, and provincial elections were not held until 25 October 1953.[127] In Fall's eyes, it was no wonder that the State of Vietnam was nonexistent as a government for many Vietnamese. Additionally, Fall was incredulous that French authorities believed that military victories could fill a void where Vietnamese self-determination should have existed. On top of these problems and other French obstructions, Fall identified two other significant factors contributing to the electoral ineptitude and political lethargy which prevented a representative government from forming. First, three anti-French Vietnamese factions in the State of Vietnam could not agree among themselves on the way forward. Second, and broader developments in Korea and China aside, the Viet Minh mounted serious and effective efforts to defeat electoral processes wherever possible.

The Vietnamese blocs preventing the formation of a representative government included, in Fall's analysis: "(1) the Government and the hordes of

Government jobholders and their families: (2) the largely neutralist bourgeoisie who wished to express their disapproval of the existing state of affairs; and (3) the 'neutralists by fear'—that large segment of the population which did not vote for fear of reprisals by the Viet-Minh."[128]

These Vietnamese groups formed a possibly significant portion of the Vietnamese population in areas held by the State of Vietnam, but Fall did not provide statistics supporting this data. Adding further qualitative input, he added, "The press was almost totally indifferent, with the exception of a newspaper, *Gian-sang* in Hanoi, which backed 'an ebullient French-trained dentist with American sympathies, Hoang Co Binh,' along with a few other papers in Saigon."[129] Fall possibly believed that an apathetic press was an accurate indicator of the popular mood, especially in an otherwise vibrant print culture.[130] Most telling, weak support for the State of Vietnam reflected a failure to create genuine grassroots legitimacy. The Viet Minh's targeting of potential Hoang Co Binh supporters and others undoubtedly also contributed to an aversion toward electoral participation among the Vietnamese. Fall pointed this out, writing, "even the candidates were not too eager to have their names on posters or to appear in public, for fear of being branded *Viet-gian* (traitors) by the Viet-Minh."[131] Even if he did not provide complex data and electoral statistics, the kind of electoral process he described occurring through provincial elections held in October 1953 did not appear to evoke much confidence in the results.

Other problems also existed. In Fall's description, "When the elections were finally decided in desperate haste ... this gave little time to the weak Vietnamese political parties to rally sufficient following." To this, Fall added a point of emphasis:

> The Government held the elections in the middle of the rice-planting season when time is a vital commodity and the Vietnamese farmer is less willing than ever to listen to political speeches, no matter how much entertainment they might provide to break the monotony of life in small villages of the Red River Delta.

Finally, he concluded: "As a village notable told this writer: 'Any government that did not transact its business from a health resort in the mountains should have known that ...'"[132] In referring to Bao Dai, who often retreated to Dalat, the villager's point reflected the serious problems facing the State of Vietnam. Between the pressures inflicted by the Viet Minh and the obstructions emplaced by French authorities, there were simply too many factors stacked against the anti-communist Vietnamese state.

NUMBER ONE REALIST

In light of these problems, Fall publicly advocated a solution to the First Indochina War in March 1954, writing: "Negotiations offer the only solution, and the first step, as Jawaharlal Nehru has suggested, must be ceasefire ... Any solution that accomplishes the effective neutralization of Indo-China would be more desirable than this hopeless stalemate in the jungle swamps."[133] These were views shared by American citizens, who were also concerned by the potential for increased US participation in Indochina. In Texas, for example, hundreds of individuals sent letters to US Representatives and Senators urging negotiations. In one letter from 10 April 1954, Mrs. William R. Chappell of Dallas wrote Senator Lyndon B. Johnson, urging him to negotiate and avoid further US entanglement:

> Dear Senator Johnson: France's colonial policy is responsible for the current crisis in Indo-China, and I agree with the position of Senator Kennedy that it would ill behoove the free nations to come to the defense of a backward colonialism. The true enemy is communist imperialism, but the native peoples of Indo-China have evidently felt that the choice between what France offered and what the rebels offered was equally bad.[134]

The ongoing battle at Dien Bien Phu in April 1954 had the attention of America's heartland. The central reason for this attention was concern that the Korean War might reignite and pull the United States, once again, into a land war in Asia but with an additional front somewhere in Indochina. After the massive amount of bloodshed in Korea, the last thing anybody anywhere likely wanted was a wider war involving Vietnam, China, Korea, France, the United States, and other UN countries. While actual fighting in Korea ended in 1953, war on the Korean Peninsula remained officially unresolved. For this reason, Indochina had the attention of Texans like Mrs. Chappell. Maury Maverick, also of Dallas, seconded Mrs. Chappell's view. In his letter to Lyndon Johnson, Maverick pointed out:

> The radio says you have joined [Senate Majority Leader Senator William] Knowland in asking for action against Indo-China with other nations. This is wrong and we should negotiate. There must be some reason to have the Geneva Conference. John Foster Dulles is a thousand times worse than Acheson and he will get all our kids killed off if we just let him.[135]

Other Texans offered their views. In another letter, Thomas Hudson McKee added, "The French exploiters have asked for the revolution of their underlings in that area and it is time (long overdue) for the Republic of France to decree the independence of those people or take a damned good licking from them, which they deserve." Mr. McKee further emphasized: "Our family wants America to keep hands off until independence is given these people and justice is done. I'm a proponent of freedom and independence for exploited people. Are you? This is a case of lousy power politics and it is disgraceful."[136] A letter from Mr. and Mrs. R.G. Nabors of Abernathy, Texas offered a poignant representation of what American mothers and fathers saw at stake to them as parents:

> Dear Senator, We are farmers. Not very big farmers. We have a son in Korea. He is about like other boys. Between the cotton patch and Texas Tech he got a degree in chemical engineering. We do not ask favors for him. If we get mixed up in Indo-China we think the chances of him getting back are less. We think the United States might be meddling in Indo-China. You do not need to answer this letter. We just thought it might do some good to write you.[137]

To his credit, Johnson responded to the Nabors and everyone else writing to express concern. Whether he ever received the more critical and essential messages they urgently conveyed to him was another matter.[138] In April 1954, these and hundreds of other letters calling for American politicians to reduce and even eliminate American support for France in Indochina were widespread. As disaster at Dien Bien Phu became more apparent in late April and early May, the United States considered deploying even more resources to the conflict. Ironically, diplomatic efforts related to the Korean War were underway at the Geneva Conference in April and May 1954, and these intersected with negotiations to determine a solution for the war in Indochina. Article IV of the Korea Armistice Agreement, intended to resolve the Korean conflict politically, was one of the key topics for discussion.[139] Thus, the negotiators' focus on resolving both the Korean War and the First Indochina War was a reason why so many individuals in the United States saw connections between those conflicts, especially among those Americans who had already lost sons or daughters in Korea.

IV—The DRV at the End of the War

Fall's analysis of the State of Vietnam was extensive, but his study of the Democratic Republic of Vietnam was even more detailed. That the Viet Minh and DRV survived the First Indochina War against France and that they managed to form a revitalized and reorganized government in 1955 were achievements he found remarkable. Over the next several years, Fall would devote considerable effort to understanding how the Viet Minh had prevailed against France's militarily superior forces between 1946 and 1954. Relying on knowledge gained from his experiences during World War II and through analysis of the Viet Minh during 1953, Fall integrated these lessons into his understanding of warfare in Indochina. Viet Minh survivability depended, he was learning, on their capacity for a socio-political anti-colonial revolution to compensate for France's military power, which was supported mainly by massive American financial and materiel aid. The Viet Minh's success also depended on Chinese sanctuaries and Chinese, North Korean, and Soviet aid that flowed into the DRV after its recognition by these states in the early 1950s. Fall's friend, François Sully, went so far as to write, "the French did not know it then, but they had already lost Indochina in December 1950, as the first Chinese Communist soldiers reached the Vietnamese border. From that day, Vo Nguyen Giap could use China's immensity as his sanctuary, and China would never have permitted a French victory in Indochina."[140]

In addition to these developments, Fall gave a renewed focus to the DRV's reorganization on 20 September 1955 for his revised 1956 edition of *The Viet-Minh Regime*. The DRV's reorganization was significant because Ho Chi Minh relinquished part of his "prerogatives to Pham Van Dong who became the D.R.V.'s first Prime Minister."[141] Ho Chi Minh's authority in the DRV was not dissipating, but power was increasingly distributed among other important Vietnamese Lao Dong Workers' Party members. Le Duan, who became the DRV Secretary of the Politburo in 1956, commented that the Lao Dong Party's leadership was "constantly based on the principle of collective leadership."[142] However, leaders such as Pham Van Dong, and especially Le Duan, continued to gain critical powers in leading that collective leadership after the 1955 reorganization.

Still, Ho Chi Minh remained the DRV's central leader as the Lao Dong Party Chairman. Along with Pham Van Dong, Ho certainly exemplified the long-term commitment to anti-colonialism that enabled the Viet Minh to organize its victory against France. Fall also cited the importance of other Central Executive Committee members—Ton Duc Thang, Truong Chinh, Vo Nguyen Giap, and Le Duc Tho—as other key leaders at that point in 1955.[143] In late 1956, however, dissent in the Lao Dong Party would increase because of anger over the implementation of land reform "when the brutal land-collectivization policy backfired in the fall of 1956."[144] Hard-line divisions among Vietnamese Communist leaders, arising over interpretations of Marxism–Leninism, would not become more apparent in Fall's view until later, but he began to recognize them in 1956. In the second edition of *The Viet-Minh Regime*, for example, Fall cited the communist newspaper *Nhan Dan*, which openly discussed corruption, ideological divisions, and other problems in the DRV in late 1955 and 1956.[145]

At the time, Fall was the only Western scholar to rely on communist papers, such as *Nhan Dan*, to analyze the Viet Minh and DRV. Land collectivization in 1956, moreover, was a breaking point in which "the Chinese view of Communism," as advocated by Truong Chinh, demonstrated that communism was not a monolithic nor a united ideological power.[146] Divisions between communists in Hungary and the Soviet Union in 1956, and communists in North Vietnam in the same year, interested Fall considerably. North Vietnamese Communists, he almost certainly realized, had a much more complex and turbulent history with communists in China than he might have earlier believed. Between 1950 and 1953, the Korean War had revealed serious distrust among communists in Asia, while the Hungarian uprising in 1956 indicated dissent in Eastern Europe against the Soviets. Violence in Nghe An Province, North Vietnam, where farmers revolted against collectivization in 1956, also indicated serious problems. As a result, divisions in the communist bloc would merit special attention in Fall's eyes in subsequent years.

In addition to ideological divisions within communist factions, Fall assessed the Viet Minh's provisional government and the DRV's constitutional structure. He also analyzed the DRV's judiciary and the Ministry of the Interior's organizational structure, including the DRV's state police and security.[147] The study of political-social control, such as that administered by the DRV's security forces, later deeply informed Fall's understanding of Vietnamese revolutionary warfare. He was beginning to recognize that this form of warfare was a holistic, multi-faceted, and culturally infused phenomenon based on anti-colonialism and wielded by the DRV leadership in order to pursue its political goal of a unified communist Vietnam. Fall's focus on revolutionary social practices, such as land reform in 1953 and land collectivization in 1956, became increasingly relevant as the DRV consolidated itself after its total war against the French Union Forces during the First Indochina War.

Some of the set-piece battles during the war were preceded by subversive political action, such as in Nghia Lo in 1952 and at Dien Bien Phu in 1954. This preparatory agitprop-oriented groundwork figured prominently in Fall's writing. He explained, "As in every Communist state, the police network of the DRV was extensive and efficient and, directed centrally by the State Secretariat to the Ministry of the Interior, it reached down to the tiniest village and hamlet."[148] In another description from 1954, he added, "The arrival of the young revolutionary elements of the Viet-Minh in the villages had the effect of the proverbial stone in the village pond, and armed adolescents replaced the peaceful councils of notables. This was not necessarily an improvement."[149] Fall collected evidence of these developments from the DRV's official journal, *Viet Nam Dan Quoc Cong Bao*; Viet Minh newspapers *Nhan Dan* and *Cu'u Quoc*; and other DRV decrees and regulations he obtained between May and December 1953.[150] In addition to personal observations made during his time in Indochina, these documents formed a credible collective of rich primary resources. When processed through Fall's analytical intellectual machine, the outcome forming his first book, *The Viet-Minh Regime*, was an authoritative and extensive analysis of the origins of the Viet Minh and DRV rooted in the aftermath of World War II.

Fall was familiar with internal security organizations from his time in the French Resistance and working as a researcher during the Nuremberg Trials. He brought this knowledge to bear in his work on the Viet Minh and, in the case of the DRV's security apparatus, he assessed that their purposes included: "(1) to protect government agencies and property, communication lines, and troop movements; (2) to insure public safety and the property of the population; and (3) to repress any act of a nature likely to be harmful to the interests of the State."[151] The DRV organized its security services into several sections: Political and Protection; Administrative Police, in charge of issuing identification cards, passports, automobile registrations, and similar tasks; and an Administrative Section for the everyday activities of running a police headquarters. Fall emphasized that the DRV's internal security units prioritized protecting the state. At the most local level, he explained, "finally, every village and hamlet had its own 'Section for the Repression of Traitors' composed of most of the local party or government officials."[152]

Internal security, often achieved by eliminating collaborators or others who posed a threat to any level in the hierarchy of state control, was essential in establishing competitive control over the population. The problem of collaboration was, of course, an issue with which Fall was familiar from his time in Haute-Savoie, France. In many respects, collaboration was a socio-political problem rather than a military one. That they were entwined was evident. Yet, Fall also acknowledged that targeting collaborators evoked complicated issues in analyzing political and military distinctions in establishing control over a population.

> In order to do this, here and there the Maquis had to kill some of the occupying forces and attack some of the military targets. But above all they had to kill their

own people who collaborated with the enemy. But the "kill" aspect, the military aspect, definitely always remained the minor aspect. The political, administrative, ideological aspect is the primary aspect. Everybody, of course, by definition, will seek a military solution to the insurgency problem ... the insurgency problem is military only in a secondary sense, and political, ideological, and administrative in a primary sense.[153]

François Sully, who narrowly escaped the Viet Minh's siege at Dien Bien Phu while reporting on the war as a journalist for *Time-Life*, had a similar background to Fall as a member of the French Resistance.[154] Writing in 1968, he commented on Fall's capacity to connect intellectually with problems the Viet Minh faced because they were problems he had encountered during World War II. In Sully's view:

> because of his experience in the French Underground, Fall thought that he was better equipped than anyone else to capture the essence of a guerrilla-resistance movement, and he would say, "The hardcore guerrilla, the one fully committed does not need hope to keep him going. In Europe, we would have fought to death, even if German Armies had been victorious. People generally do not understand why guerrillas, even those animated by a just cause, sometimes resort to terrorism, sabotage, and intimidation. It is a harsh necessity for survival.[155]

The Viet Minh's commitment against colonialism and in fighting French forces had parallels with Fall's experience in World War II. He knew the circumstances of France's empire in Indochina were entirely different from those he had fought against, but the Viet Minh's commitment to their cause was a quality he recognized. In broader geopolitical terms, Fall believed that Indochina was of minimal importance by itself, and he questioned the validity of domino-theory thinking as it applied to Southeast Asia. Nonetheless, Fall understood that the United States was increasing its commitment to the defeat of communism. As part of the broader Cold War in development, Indochina was becoming more critical to the United States, primarily because of conflict in Korea, the threat posed by Communist China, and the looming power of the Soviet Union. In this context, with the growing concern over Indochina and its relation to the broader Cold War, further analysis of the different governments in Vietnam was increasingly important.

5

THE ENDING IS A BEGINNING

The Viet-Minh Regime was published during an intense, politically charged era. In addition to conflicts in Indochina, diverse revolutions against colonialism in numerous places worldwide merged into a bipolar competition between communist and non-communist spheres of influence. In his book, which would form the first volume of a three-volume doctoral dissertation completed in 1955, Fall focused on Indochina. He analyzed the Viet Minh's socio-political-military doctrine and how its administration in the DRV competed with the State of Vietnam and French forces. Broader questions concerning the Cold War's intersections with Indochina interested him, and they informed his overall writing output, making their way into his published articles and parts of his dissertation. In many respects, Fall's assessment of Indochina's relationship to broader geopolitical developments had much in common with other scholars' work at the time.[1] However, instead of a geopolitical analysis of Vietnamese Communism's role in the Cold War, *The Viet-Minh Regime* focused exclusively on the Viet Minh's anti-colonial war in Indochina. It also stands out because of the detail Fall allocated to the Viet Minh's history, its organization, and its ability to adapt in its war against France's military forces.

As the only detailed assessment of the Viet Minh available in English at the time, *The Viet-Minh Regime* described how the political organization and adaptable nature of the Viet Minh made up for materiel shortfalls and other deficiencies before 1950. After the success of Mao Tse-tung's communist forces in China, the Viet Minh were better positioned to confront French forces. They were also provided with the equipment and technical assistance required to succeed against French forces in conventional battles in late 1952 and early 1954. The "loss of China" to communism in 1949 and the ongoing Korean War between 1950 and 1953 also contributed to geopolitical concerns among Western nations over communist expansion. These early Cold War developments received no lack of attention from scholars, including Fall, but the subjects he assessed in *The Viet Minh Regime* were not well-known among English-speaking audiences. Moreover, his work demonstrated a comprehension of numerous factors forming a type of warfare he would identify as "Revolutionary Warfare" not long after the book's publication in 1954.

Among the many topics Fall analyzed, the Viet Minh's organizational structure stands out. He especially gave considerable attention to the internal security structure that protected the Democratic Republic of Vietnam (DRV). The study of internal security made sense in many respects. First, the Viet Minh's existence relied on ensuring the security of their vulnerable state against infiltration by both Vietnamese and external French threats. Second, through personal experience, Fall had an intuitive sense of internal security's critical importance. He had endured the liberation of France as a member of the Resistance and Maquis, and maintaining internal security had been a critical contributing factor to his own and others' survival. In a sense, internal security and the subversion and elimination of German forces and French collaborators were mutually enforcing priorities. Eliminating collaborators, in other words, achieved multiple effects. It prevented collaborators from providing local intelligence to German forces, and this protected Resistance fighters while rendering German forces more vulnerable to attack and other subversive practices. Third, as a member of the War Crimes Commission at Nuremberg, Fall had studied how security units functioned in Nazi Germany, in the Krupp Corporation's factories, and how internal security forces, such as the *Sicherheitsdienst* (SD), mercilessly used coercion. Subsequently, in his graduate thesis at Syracuse University in 1952, Fall focused on how German organizations, such as the *Sturmabteilung* (SA), had subverted socialist and communist German competitors in the Weimar Republic. The SA and others formed a type of parallel administrative and security framework that contributed to the undermining of the Weimar Republic and the Treaty of Versailles.

In the case of the DRV, the Viet Minh's internal security system was divided among many different groups. Units known as Cong An, Trinh Sat, and Dich Van were vital among them. Fall's analysis of these groups revealed an ability to identify subversive warfare patterns in Indochina that he recognized from his past. He applied this aggregate of experience to his analysis of Viet Minh doctrine, internal security, and the development of shadow government capabilities in organizations which he later regarded as parallel hierarchies. These and other factors contributed to the Viet Minh's subversion of French administrative power. Moreover, the development of parallel hierarchies of power contributed to the Viet Minh's success in conventional battles, such as Operation Lorraine, which took place in late 1952 in northwestern Vietnam. Operation Lorraine was France's largest military operation in Indochina, and one of its most significant defeats before Dien Bien Phu.

Operation Lorraine was also critical in another way. Fall began to notice how the Viet Minh's mode of conducting of subversive activities before conventional battles indicated a critical relationship between political subversion and military engagement in their approach to warfare. The Viet Minh's use of parallel hierarchies of power to wield political control over local populations conditioned their chances for achieving military success. This was critical because it took the reverse approach from France, which emphasized military conquest as a condition for political victory, a tactic which was similarly unsuccessful. The political preparation of the battlefield was the critical lesson Fall gained from studying parallel hierarchies and battles, such as Operation Lorraine. In France's eyes, their enemies' most dangerous course of action was political preparation. However, all too often French commanders and their forces could neither see this preparation nor quantify it. They were often unable to counter or repel it, no matter how much American money backed their efforts.

Viet Minh doctrine, subversion of competitors, increasing materiel strength, and the critical contribution of mass mobilization among Vietnamese serving as equipment porters all worked in concert to undermine French authority. Despite France's superior military strength and extensive American financial support, the Viet Minh were succeeding. Fall was determined to understand how and why this was accomplished, and he was beginning to formulate a more comprehensive understanding of warfare. Moreover, the Viet Minh's way of war incorporated an operational art and vision based on tried-and-true military principles, such as decisive action against chokepoints. Such concepts had origins in the Napoleonic era and the thought of Antoine-Henri Jomini.[2] Vietnamese General Vo Nguyen Giap used historical lessons Jomini and many others provided to capitalize on opportunities that aggressive French military planning offered. After the French garrison at Dien Bien Phu was established in late 1953, as a result of the Navarre Plan, Giap's forces exploited what French military commanders gave them: the opportunity to attack a vulnerable garrison that the Viet Minh could defeat. This, in turn, gave the Viet Minh a strategic victory and contributed to French defeat in the First Indochina War. As a former soldier and current scholar studying war in Indochina, Fall was well-positioned. The large-scale battle during Operation Lorraine and the subsequent disaster at Dien Bien Phu were culmination points that resulted from long-term subversive practices he would regard, overall, as essential factors in Vietnamese revolutionary warfare. Subversion of France relied on the Viet Minh's own internal security, manipulation of Vietnamese socio-political grievances, and a host of other considerations. As Fall described in *The Viet-Minh Regime*, these were all factors to which he called attention as a young soldier-scholar studying war in Indochina.

I—The Viet Minh Regime

> *"What we have here is a sort of gouvernement crepusculaire—a twilight government," said the French colonel in charge of the Pacification Bureau in Hanoi, "In our own area we control the cities and major roads from daybreak till nightfall. Thereafter the Vietminh has the country to itself to levy taxes, attack our posts, and execute the 'Vietnamese traitors,' that is, the Nationalists who still profess to believe in victory for our side."*
>
> – Bernard Fall, 6 March 1954[3]

The first edition of *The Viet-Minh Regime* was co-published by Cornell University's Southeast Asia Program and the Institute of Pacific Relations. Since its founding in 1925, the Institute of Pacific Relations had dominated the study of contemporary Asia through its sponsorship of publications and research funding. Its coordinating committee, the Pacific Council, served as an umbrella organization composed of a dozen national councils for the study of Asia across the Indo-Pacific Region.[4] However, the Institute of Pacific Relations was also the target of conservative fire after 1949 because its councils had contributed to perceived liberal policies, especially pertaining to China. In addition to the insecure peace concluding the Korean War, the Viet Minh's successes against the State of Vietnam and French authority in Indochina increased Western concerns that communism was expanding beyond the region.

In the United States, social and political conservatism and a vocal anti-communist lobby grew in the early 1950s following Mao Tse-tung's triumph over Chiang Kai-shek's Nationalist government in late 1949. A central argument of the anti-communist agenda among government officials and likeminded intellectuals, as historian Ben Martin explains, "was to unseat and discredit those who had presided over policy formulation and opinion-making with respect to Asia in the late 1940s."[5] Anti-communists could easily lambast officials for pursuing "liberal" agendas, but criticizing was undoubtedly easier than prioritizing and committing resources to the serious study of colonialism and other policies which caused grievances in countries where communism prevailed. All too often, anti-communist officials failed to assess how and why anti-colonial agendas, which often integrated communist ideology, were succeeding. Moreover, in countries with diverse histories, anti-colonialism merged with communism in complicated ways. Each "colonial" case possessed unique historical and political contexts that there was significant risk in disregarding.

The Institute of Pacific Relations took on the challenge of revealing these problems, and the organization served as a proxy for liberal policy related to Asia. Because of its prominence "as a forum for interaction among liberals" studying such subjects, the Institute became "a natural target for investigation."[6] Therefore, the Institute of Pacific Relations operated under a political cloud at the time of Fall's first publication, when anti-communism factored prominently in the dynamic American national-security state that emerged with the National Security Council policy, NSC-68, in April 1950.[7] As it related to communism in Southeast Asia, George Herring observed that "the collapse of Chiang Kai-shek's government in China in 1949 and the southward advance of Mao Tse-tung's army raised the ominous possibility of Chinese Communist collaboration with the Viet Minh."[8] This had already materialized through Chinese support for North Korean forces. In North Vietnam and Laos, communist collaboration conspicuously culminated at Dien Bien Phu. The defeat of French forces there only increased anti-communist rancor and political antagonism—centered in part around Senator Joe McCarthy's censure, but for other reasons too—among competing US foreign policy circles.[9] In such a toxic political environment, was it possible to formulate and publish analysis of communism in such a way that the subject could be discussed objectively? In 1954, undertaking a detailed and objective study of the Viet Minh was a fraught endeavor, but it was also a vitally important one so that others could understand how the Viet Minh had succeeded. As a young French citizen based in the United States at Syracuse University, but conducting research with French forces on the Viet

Minh in Indochina, Fall was practically the only young scholar studying these developments during the war.[10]

When *The Viet-Minh Regime* was published, the political establishment's anti-communist paranoia was not immediately or personally problematic for Fall because his work was not yet well-known. However, knowledge of his scholarship was growing, and he would come to publish in prominent journals, such as *The Nation* in 1954 and the Council of Foreign Relations' journal *Foreign Affairs* in 1955.[11] He did, however, have some problems in Indochina as he neared the completion of his research in 1953. In one case, he wrote to his fiancée, Dorothy Winer, that he had not been invited to the US Consulate in Hanoi for the Fourth of July celebrations. He had expected an invitation because of his status as a former Fulbright Scholar at Syracuse University, and because he was known to the consulate staff. The reason behind the consulate's dismissal was because Fall had antagonized the "vice-consul over lunch by telling how [Fall] and many Frenchmen felt about the execution of Julius and Ethyl Rosenberg, the alleged atomic spies, two weeks earlier."[12] Fall concluded his letter: "Better apply for my re-entrance visa to the U.S. from another consulate now, I guess." Despite offending the US vice-consul in Hanoi, Fall managed to secure a visa, and he returned to the United States in late 1953.

Bothering a US official was the least of Fall's concerns. He was occupied with his study of the use of subversion and competition among Vietnamese organizations as they struggled for legitimacy and dominance. These factors were further complicated because Vietnamese Communists and Vietnamese anti-communists simultaneously struggled with French forces but for different reasons. Personally, Fall was interested in political violence and internal competition within Vietnamese society because it was a phenomenon he could identify out of his own experience. It was also a political problem that presented an academic opportunity, since it was an insufficiently studied subject. Finally, the competition between different Vietnamese organizations and between the Viet Minh and France had relevance in world affairs because the group that succeeded would dominate and chart the future of Vietnam after French defeat.

Fall's research on these subjects, he believed, would interest American policy-makers who potentially knew little about the Viet Minh as an organization and, after 1954, would want to learn more because of Indochina's relevance in the growing Cold War. To develop his study, Fall had to examine how the Viet Minh succeeded, despite considerable odds. He needed to be able to explain how their success included eliminating political competitors, prevailing militarily over American-supported French forces, and co-opting or coercing the Vietnamese peasantry to meet logistical, financial, and personnel requirements for military service.[13] To achieve these goals, Fall recognized that the Viet Minh's internal security apparatus was fundamental—and not well-known at the time—so he turned his attention to these components of the Viet Minh's state.

To wield influence internally among the Vietnamese population and to protect the DRV, the Viet Minh's intelligence and security infrastructure was critical. As an anti-colonial organization seeking to avoid infiltration by colonial authorities, the Viet Minh "developed compartmentalization techniques, secrecy, deception, counterintelligence, internal punishment, and elimination of enemies."[14] Intelligence personnel in the Viet Minh refined these skills, with assistance from Chinese Communists, to form a comprehensive and capable security service. Previously, the DRV's intelligence and security apparatuses were limited in what they could accomplish without external logistical and advisory support. With the Viet Minh receiving Chinese assistance, 1950 served as a transitional period for the intelligence-security apparatus, and it was a year during which the Viet Minh's capabilities flourished.

Direct military assistance also dramatically enhanced the Viet Minh's military forces. Writing in 1954, Fall explained, "While it has not been officially verified, mention was made of a lend-lease agreement contracted by the Democratic Republic of Vietnam with People's China during Ho Chi Minh's visit to Peking in April 1950."[15] Materiel aid emerging from this agreement consisted of extensive military equipment to support the Viet Minh's offensives against French posts strung out along the Tonkin–Chinese border in September 1950. Fall also stressed that aid from China included the refinement of a "successful politico-military doctrine."[16] DRV doctrine was codified in statutes and decrees, especially those promulgated in *Viet Nam Dan Quoc Cong Bao* (the DRV's official journal) and in articles forming the DRV's constitution.[17] In some of these documents, doctrines directed security and intelligence units' tasks and defined their purpose. The most basic of these centered on their role as protectors of the Viet Minh's administration.

Viet Minh leadership also sought to adapt when problems surfaced.[18] Due to their centralized control, adjustments after land reform problems in 1953 demonstrated how single-party political control allowed for doctrinal flexibility. It was not the case that solutions always solved problems. The dramatic turn to collectivization in 1956, even after land reform problems surfaced in 1953, indicated how doctrinal flexibility did not guarantee wise decision-making. However, Viet Minh doctrine provided a basis for integrating a mix of social-political-military factors when subverting Vietnamese competitors or preparing for a particular campaign against French forces. What interested Fall was how the Viet Minh could adapt to changing circumstances, even if those adaptive strategies did not always work. Quoting a statement by Lao Dong Secretary-General, Truong Chinh, Fall cited the October 1951 Congress of the Workers' Party's revised doctrine as consisting of several parts: "intensifying struggle behind enemy lines; ideological reformation of the party; ideological and technical reformation of the army; and readjusting the work of mass organizations."[19] It is worth noting that changing the culture in any large organization is a serious challenge. That the Viet Minh were able to change and reorient Lao Dong thinking, as long as they held to perceived correctness according to Marxist–Leninist thought, was not something Fall merely glossed over.

Materiel aid and Chinese advisors also assisted the Viet Minh in accomplishing Truong Chinh's directives. Notably, the Viet Minh were hardly starting from scratch when Chinese assistance began. Instead, they built upon baseline organizations developed well before Chinese external support became feasible in 1950. As Fall was beginning to realize, Maoist thought inspired the Viet Minh's socio-political-military doctrine as it evolved, but Maoism did not dictate it. Viet Minh supporters possessed a range of communist and anti-colonialist ideologies, and these existed along a continuum of varying degrees of support and antipathy for Chinese Communist ideology. A monolithic "Asian Communism," Fall would learn, did not exist. Instead, while communist movements in Southeast Asia shared many similarities, they each had a unique history, diverse ethnicities, and differing historical relations.

In the case of Vietnam, Vietnamese Communism was perhaps even more diverse than it was in other places because of the rich regional diversity within Vietnam. Differences between northern and southern Vietnam preceded the introduction of communism, and many of those differences persist to this day. In other words, a monolithic form of communism did not exist in Vietnam, let alone across all of Asia. Vietnamese Communism integrated a blend of patriotism, nationalism, and anti-colonialism in ways that, it turned out, had to be modified to gain supporters whose interests and needs might vary from place to place. Members of the Lao Dong party integrated their approaches to appeal to as many Vietnamese as possible. However, they also worked to ensure that the cumulative effects of anti-colonial efforts remained entirely under communist party control.

THE ENDING IS A BEGINNING

"Parallel hierarchies," a term that originated out of France's occupation of Indochina, was a critical analytical concept developed to describe how the Viet Minh's way of war functioned. Fall learned of this term from French officers, particularly Charles Lacheroy and Roger Trinquier, the latter whom Fall met in 1953.[20] Along with Jean Hogard, Jean Nemo, and others, these officers formed an intellectual collective based on shared experiences of war with the Viet Minh as the First Indochina War drew to a close and as they reflected on French defeat after 1954. The primary vehicle through which they published their ideas on parallel hierarchies, and later, on revolutionary warfare, centered around the French journal *Revue Militaire d'Information*. This journal, especially those issues published in early 1957, greatly influenced Fall's views.[21] A critical difference between Fall and these French officers, however, was that he built on their work but remained focused on developments in Vietnam, while they moved on to other theaters and conflicts. French officers, such as Lacheroy, Trinquier, Hogard, and others sought to implement lessons they had learned from Indochina and apply them in Algeria. France's military forces had little time to waste in making operational and strategic improvements. The Algerian revolution erupted in September 1954 and pitted Algerian Nationalists in the National Liberation Front (FLN, founded on 1 November 1954 in Cairo), French colonists (the *Pieds-Noirs*) in Algeria, and French forces.[22] French officers gleaning lessons from their experiences in Indochina did not concern themselves with how Vietnamese Communists adapted in the months and years after Dien Bien Phu. Fall, in contrast, did.

According to Peter Paret, French officers like Lacheroy and Trinquier were foremost among those "whose experiences in Indochina led them to seek new ways of countering anticolonial insurrections."[23] Aside from combat, their significant theoretical contributions consisted of describing parallel hierarchies as the complex organizational networks the DRV wielded through its security apparatus and the other alternative administrative networks they constructed to achieve their goals. French officers' analysis of the Viet Minh and the DRV was ironic, in an important respect, because they were busy transferring and attempting to implement their knowledge within the very different revolutionary, historical, and cultural context of North Africa. Nevertheless, their work on Indochina was insightful. In building on their efforts, Fall was uniquely positioned to benefit as he developed his analysis on warfare in Vietnam after 1954.

As it pertained to parallel hierarchies, in one of the most straightforward descriptions produced, Jean Hogard regarded them as a series of "social networks or grids in which the control of people are principally obtained."[24] Similarly, "the individual is enchained in several networks of independent social hierarchies," but, most importantly, that these "networks are layered in different associations according to their age, their sex, their profession, and so on."[25] Parallel hierarchies, therefore, were specifically developed and targeted toward discrete social groups, as Hogard noted, but he also pointed out how these parallel hierarchies intentionally overlapped. Different organizations could and often did come into contact through shared values, interests, or ideologies. In a key respect, these interactions would then form a broader network of social cobwebs in which an individual or group might find themselves placed within several shared categories, as if they were within a Venn Diagram composed of multiple circles.

More broadly, parallel hierarchies could be construed as two organizational systems approaches centered on social control over civilians. To use an analogy, these approaches might be thought of within a framework related to the Cartesian coordinate system with its horizontal x-axis and its vertical y-axis. In the case of the Viet Minh, the first approach was a vertical-oriented administrative system that consisted of organizational levels from interzones (in Vietnam, this level was called *Uy Ban Hang Lien-Khu*) down to village administrations (*Uy Ban Hanh Chinh*). Viet Minh-controlled administrative committees, in turn, directed and oversaw this vertically oriented network of networks. In the second branch of hierarchies, Vietnamese Communists organized a series of Fronts (such as the Lien Viet and Fatherland Front, which were more horizontally oriented). The Viet Minh used these fronts to consolidate the numerous vertically oriented associations and organizations under communist control to achieve broader strategic goals.

This network-of-networks approach included a vertical system of organizations and a horizontally oriented front to help direct them. In turn, the convergence of administrative, organizational structures provided flexibility, corralled civilians for political-military agitation, and, together, formed population-centric warfare during military engagements that the French military found challenging to overcome. Parallel hierarchies are perhaps even more accurately represented as a type of three-dimensional Cartesian coordinate system. The Cartesian coordinate system analogy is also helpful because of its relevance to other branches of mathematics in which algebraic combinations result in dynamic results. The Viet Minh harnessed multiple sources of power that, when multiplied together, created more potent effects than many French officers might have anticipated. As it related to Fall, this type of complex and

THE ENDING IS A BEGINNING

multiplicative effect—which parallel hierarchies helped produce—was a key and powerful functional characteristic in what he would regard as Vietnamese revolutionary warfare.

Identifying the social phenomena of parallel hierarchies at work in Indochina was similar to delineating a thicket of trees in a forest. Doing so required educated observation built upon social knowledge of the local environment and people. Moreover, understanding how and why different social networks tended to form relied on historical and sociological comprehension of the social context generating the parallel hierarchies. As a member of the French Resistance, Fall had gained insight into how and why different groups of individuals cooperated or competed. Besides simply seeking to survive Nazi persecution, social cohesion (or fracturing) depended on numerous factors, such as interpersonal history, motivations, and goals or values. Fall's ability to survive, in other words, depended on a street-smart capability to "read" his social environment. This conditioned him to see competition among social groups caught up in other conflicts with a similar, insightful mindset. It is almost certain that Fall's humanitarian outlook, shaped through the pain of personal loss, heightened his ability to read social groups in competition or conflict with each other. His ability to sympathize and even empathize with others who faced brutal military forces was critical in his work, especially as it intersected with his formal training and practical experience in analyzing population-centric warfare.

For French forces, shortcomings in analyzing this complex system of parallel hierarchies, not to mention their indiscriminately targeting individuals within these networks, could lead to severe problems. French officers' ideal goal was to outmaneuver the Viet Minh by leveraging or subverting control of these parallel hierarchies away from Viet Minh control. The competition for control over the Vietnamese population had to be achieved without creating more problems than the hierarchies created for French forces themselves. None of the French officers Fall studied nor Fall himself suggested that these tasks were simple, or that the French military was effective at accomplishing them. Nonetheless, these officers and thinkers, and certainly Fall, recognized that successfully defeating the Viet Minh's socially based form of warfare demanded these types of social skills. To break the Viet Minh's control over society, French officers writing in *Revue Militaire d'Information* recognized that this phenomenon of social-networked warfare demanded serious analysis, historical and cultural understanding, and wise cultivation and use of intelligence. Second, it all had to be put together into effective operational design and careful execution. Failure in any of these tasks meant conceding control to the Viet Minh.

When multiple administrative hierarchies were combined, these Viet Minh-led social administrative apparatuses were highly effective at subverting and replacing competing governments' control over society. Fall explained that the establishment of parallel hierarchies primarily took on two forms: "the utilization of existing administrative structures through the infiltration of subversive individuals, or the creation of altogether new clandestine structures designed to take over full administrative responsibilities when political and military conditions are ripe."[26] Fall added, in acknowledgment of all the French officers who contributed their ideas in *Revue Militaire d'Information*, that this series of topics was "thoroughly studied by the French Army and reported on in 1957." It was one thing for captains, majors, and colonels to recognize these lessons. It was, with intentional understatement, an entirely different issue for those formulating policies to keep them in mind.

Parallel hierarchies were essential features of Viet Minh warfare, and Fall undoubtedly recognized them as a phenomenon from his experience during World War II. However, learning from officers such as Charles Lacheroy and Roger Trinquier also introduced him to a shared vernacular to describe the Viet Minh's actions in Indochina. Fall explained the nature of parallel hierarchies further: "Starting in World War II, both systems [of parallel hierarchies] have been used extensively, sometimes simultaneously with, but more often subsequent to, the infiltration of subversive individuals preceding the creation of an independent apparatus."[27] Fall was able to identify parallel hierarchies in Vietnam because he recognized them as organization tools the French Resistance had used against Nazi forces in occupied France.[28] His ability, therefore, to integrate his personal experience and education and intellectually channel it all together into an objective diagnosis of the Viet Minh's way of warfare was a distinguishing characteristic in his thought between 1953 and 1957.

Parallel hierarchies were also crucial to understand because the Viet Minh began to make effective use of them even before receiving external aid from communist forces in China. The role of psychological operations and direct-action units that employed terrorism and propaganda to control the perceptions and actions of Vietnamese villagers were notable features in this framework. Most importantly, parallel hierarchies involved in the security of the DRV were necessary to eliminate dissent and ensure compliance with communist party rule.[29] In broad terms, according to Paul Staniland, "organizational dynamics remained crucial: the Indochinese Communist Party needed to elbow aside competitors, bargain with and co-opt powerful local actors, and figure out how to govern under fire."[30] As Fall and many French officers recognized, parallel hierarchies were essential to guide these dynamics as they unfolded. Through leaders—including Ho Chi Minh, Ton Duc Thang, and others—the Viet Minh learned to apply such strategies by incorporating their country's history with organizational practices from Bolshevism and other ideas they perceived as relevant to freeing Vietnam from colonialism.[31]

Conflict Within the Viet Minh Regime

Fall was increasingly aware of the Viet Minh's internal security, intelligence, and reconnaissance units' political action on the ground and how these organizations contributed to the development of parallel hierarchies. Their actions became more pronounced as the Viet Minh gained local-level support, eliminated Vietnamese competitors, and subverted French authority. These units were not the only tools used. However, the actions of internal security units succeeded in gaining competitive control for the Viet Minh over Vietnamese society, and the development of parallel hierarchies functioned as competing administrative structures to facilitate this process. As an organizational means to administratively overcome competitors, parallel hierarchies consolidated the DRV's legitimacy and power by forming a shadow-structured government that physically paralleled French and the State of Vietnam's control in cities and some rural areas.

Instead of attempting to destroy French units and the State of Vietnam's military forces directly, the Viet Minh used parallel hierarchies to compete with, undermine, and eventually replace French and State of Vietnam control.[32] For example, taxation was a key indicator in demonstrating an organization's control over society; as Fall put it, "to the last breath a government will try to collect taxes."[33] Fall recognized that the Viet Minh possessed administrative control over a region if they eliminated government taxation and instead collected those revenues themselves. By interdicting and collecting taxes, the economic lifeblood of the state, the Viet Minh created economic and political conditions for controlling much of rural North Vietnam well before the battle at Dien Bien Phu.[34]

Moreover, the physical act of Viet Minh tax collection embodied propaganda by the deed. This was the type of "political" domination Fall saw as holding far greater relevance than military power in the context of the conflict in Vietnam. Once security lapsed in oversight of governance—which included taxation, education, and other administrative functions—the Viet Minh's parallel hierarchy would infiltrate that gap in governance, replace it with a Viet Minh-controlled authority, and continue to build other parallel hierarchies in surrounding areas to connect them. Importantly, this was a counter-revolutionary *tache d'huile* (oil spot) tactic in reverse. In Fall's eyes, the Viet Minh's ability to collect taxes was one of the more significant indications that a Viet-Minh parallel hierarchy had replaced French or State of Vietnam authority in a given area. The political power was certainly a priority, but collecting taxes undoubtedly helped address the Viet Minh's serious need for economic infusions of funds.

Arguments over whether security must precede political stability, therefore, miss an important point. In conflicts where military officers and politicians debate which should be secured first, it is often already too late to stabilize an environment. To fix a degrading security environment requires far greater infusions of troops and resources, which invariably requires political support to requisition and deploy. The battle at Dien Bien Phu was a classic case where French decision-makers had little to no political capital to remedy their losses. It was also a classic case in which the United States saw further support as a waste. Despite debates over whether the United States should deploy tactical atomic bombs to destroy assaulting Viet Minh forces through Operation Vulture, a contingency operation in case the garrison was overrun, President Eisenhower decided against further support.[35]

Before 1954, Fall pointed out other indicators of actual Viet Minh control, such as their control over local judicial and educational functions, especially curriculum development and teacher assignment.[36] Instead of military indicators such as troop strength, fortification defense, or possession of signature weapon systems, Viet Minh control over civil-political functions indicated competitive control over the population. For example, social control over teacher selection and what was taught on the curriculum more accurately revealed those areas in which the Viet Minh's socio-political-military doctrine was at work. This was a type of "warfare" and "control" that Fall found fascinating and effective, despite the competition the Viet Minh had from their opponents.

A local farmer did not need to know the intricacies of Marxist dogma to know who controlled his or her village. The most authentic test was whether the individual demonstrated adherence, whether willing or pressured, to whoever the community recognized as the authority controlling taxes, education, or the local judicial system. If individuals believed the taxation was fair, or that they were treated fairly in terms of accessing land to farm, that was likely to elevate the authorities' legitimacy. Such recognition might even eventually develop into genuine support. In contrast, and in cases where farmers disagreed with policy, they could and did revolt. However, like angry citizens in Budapest at about the same time in later 1956, Vietnamese farmers also paid a serious price for challenging communist policy. Overly repressive measures, such as in the Viet Minh's draconian response in suppressing the Nghe An revolts in 1956 indicated—like the communist authorities' heavy-handed response to the revolts in Hungary—that Vietnamese communists could overplay their hand and spiral into fanaticism. However, local civil, administrative control was where legitimacy originated. Unless one was willing to destroy everything and everyone in a village, military-oriented assets were mostly irrelevant in comparison to more quotidian tasks, such as controlling teachers and school curriculum development. To be sure, when Fall discussed the irrelevance of military control, he meant that it was irrelevant in the face of administrative and ideological functions that military authorities did not regard as military targets or within their mandate. What mattered were the mechanisms of social control, whether they were taxation, policing, education, the legal system, or other structures. If the Viet Minh controlled those, they controlled society, and that was where power resided.

Fall provided a detailed account demonstrating his point.

> When I first arrived in Indochina in 1953, the French were mainly fighting in the Red River Delta ... I checked in with the French briefing officer and asked what the situation was in the delta. He said: "Well, we hold pretty much of it; there is the French fortified line around the delta which we call the Marshal de Lattre Line—about 2200 bunkers forming 900 forts. We are going to deny the communists access to the 8 million people in this delta and the 3 million tons of rice it produces. We will eventually starve them out and deny them access to the population."[37]

Fall asked, "Do the communists hold anything inside the delta?' The answer was, 'Yes, they hold those five black blotches.'" Later that year, while researching at the University of Hanoi under national Vietnamese control, Fall brought up this story to other Vietnamese, who said "that their home villages inside the delta were Communist-controlled and had Communist village chiefs ... that both the French and the Vietnamese Army simply did not know what was going on."[38] In his point about a government "fighting to collect taxes, even to its last breath," Fall explained his thoughts on the matter in detail:

I used a working hypothesis: I went to the Vietnamese tax collection office in Hanoi to look at the village tax rolls. They immediately indicated that the bulk of the Delta was no longer paying taxes. As a cross-check on my theory I used the village teachers. The village teachers in Viet-Nam were centrally assigned by the Government. Hence, where there were school teachers the Government could be assumed to have control. Where there were none, there was no Government control. The resulting difference between military "control" and what the Communists controlled *administratively* [italicized in original] was 70% of the delta inside the French battlelines! In fact, the military situation was complete fiction and had absolutely no bearing on the *real* [italicized in original] situation inside the Delta. The area was solidly Communist-infiltrated and collapsed overnight.[39]

This kind of social control and not military power, Fall believed, prepared the way to disaster for French forces at Dien Bien Phu. The Viet Minh's strength resided primarily in its functioning as a social and political force among Vietnamese. As Fall put it in a letter to his fiancée, "Funny when you think that every Vietnamese around you, that grimy beggar, the flower girl, the vagabond salesman of odds and ends, they may all be part of the fanatical group that does more to keep the Viet-Minh alive as a political force than any of the Chinese-delivered Soviet (and U.S.) made guns ever could."[40] As Fall clearly understood, these often-disregarded individuals formed the type of networked parallel hierarchies that several French officers, including Jean Hogard and others, recognized in their work for *Revue Militaire d'Information*. In an important sense, Vietnamese societies' weakest and most vulnerable members made the Viet Minh much stronger. Winning over beggars, salesmen, and flower girls enabled the Viet Minh to withstand far superior military might in terms of their political legitimacy. In contrast, the French failed to develop control, let alone legitimacy, through force. Moreover, the Viet Minh developed political and social control by providing governance and services and, when needed, through force that was violent and swift. Technological innovations such as jets, tanks, and other tools often obscured revolutionary warfare's overall asymmetry. However, it is almost certain that nineteenth-century French officers, such as Gallieni and Lyautey, would have seen and understood this kind of Viet Minh administrative strength right away.[41]

In the late stages of the First Indochina War, the French military attempted to increase civil affairs operations to pacify areas where Viet Minh control might be contested. In one case, French General Raoul Salan created teams of civil affairs teams, *Groupes Administratif Mobile Opérationnel* (GAMO, translated as Mobile Operational Administrative Groups). Also, a progression of "Morale and Information Service" sections evolved into psychological warfare sections by April 1953, but these units were "hampered by a lack of adequate personnel."[42] In contrast to the Viet Minh's efforts, such initiatives were probably perceived for what they were: weak and superficial attempts to sway a local population. In what was perhaps his most succinct statement on the matter of social-oriented control, Fall concluded: "when a country is being subverted, it is not being outfought: it is being out-administered."[43] Ultimately, legitimacy mattered far more than militarily "securing" an area, and the Viet Minh gained power through social functions the French military were insufficient at addressing.

In contrast to French efforts, Viet Minh leadership rigorously prioritized the selection of personnel in control of local populations. Party members were typically assigned positions of primary importance, while sympathetic party affiliates assumed less critical positions. Fall described the effects of their work in 1956, writing, "All [French and Vietnamese] agreed that the Red River Delta area was actually under the administrative control of the Communists, that is, the area where they collected the taxes, ran the village government, and indoctrinated the children in the schools, this was far greater than even the extent of VPA [Vietnamese People's Army] military control."[44] Overall, taxation, schools, and local government were the "battlegrounds" in which the Viet Minh out-administered its adversaries. In the context of post-World War II Vietnam, the DRV's efforts to eliminate Vietnamese nationalist groups and French authorities utilized parallel hierarchies that grew as the DRV confronted increased numbers of French forces after late 1946.[45] In addition to administrative control through acts like taxation, the Viet Minh sought to increase its own symbolic legitimacy and achieve social cohesion by controlling Vietnamese national. However, the Viet Minh's success in achieving administrative control among Vietnamese varied widely across the country.[46]

In contrast to the north of Vietnam, administrative dominance was challenging to achieve in southern Vietnam. For one thing, the former colony of Cochinchina in South Vietnam had a more diverse population than in the north. This included Buddhist religious organizations, such as the Hoa Hao, which violently opposed the Viet Minh, and many others. As Shawn McHale described, the Mekong Delta region was environmentally and a socially complex region, in which "shifting tactical alliances, ethnic, political, and religious conflict" reflected a formidable social environment. It was the region, according to McHale, with "the most extreme range of beliefs of any part of

Vietnam."[47] In this area, where Hoa Hao, Khmer minority groups, and Cao Dai believers spread from their main headquarters in Tay Ninh, the Viet Minh was the most potent organization fighting the French.[48] The complexity of Vietnamese society and important differences between north, central, and southern regions, not to mention the diversity of societies sympathetic to anti-imperialism in Laos and Cambodia, explains why war in Indochina differed from place to place and why it was difficult, if not impossible, to analyze categorically for Western scholars.

In those areas where Viet Minh control was contested, there was competition over power through violent means, but also through assimilating the legacy of national identity associated with the Nguyen Dynasty represented by Emperor Bao Dai. Although the Viet Minh rejected the monarchy, they understood the importance and legacy of imperial power. Viet Minh historian Tran Huy Lieu demonstrated this respect when he traveled to the "Nguyen capital in Hue to claim the imperial seal and imperial regalia from the ex-emperor."[49] While Frances FitzGerald interpreted this event as the Viet Minh literally and figuratively tearing the Vietnamese Mandate of Heaven from its dynastic forebears, this view possibly overemphasized ownership of the "Mandate of Heaven" as a material-oriented transfer of power.[50] The Viet Minh more likely took the regalia to buttress its position among Vietnamese still under imperial influence. Nonetheless, it suggests that the Viet Minh regarded Confucianist order associated with the monarchy as something worth accounting for and controlling. These changes in Vietnamese society—propelled by modernity and war from the early 1940s that piled upon decades of colonial exploitation that had existed since the nineteenth century—contributed to a weakening of the Confucianist-Taoist-Buddhist social order in Vietnam.

These social changes occurred rapidly. According to David Elliott, "the whole texture of rural society was dramatically transformed between 1930 and 1975."[51] However, the work of nationalist firebrands from the early twentieth century, such as Phan Boi Chau, indicated that these revolutionary transformations preceded 1930 and went back to the Russo-Japanese War and the Dong-Du (Eastern Movement) initiated in 1905.[52] As David Hunt also explained: "Destabilizing dynamics associated with the political and military history of the region of South Vietnam were only part of the story, for even without war and revolution, modernizing trends were refashioning the social order of the countryside."[53] In another view, Dan Van Sung, a nationalist and former leader in the Dai Viet, also known for publishing the Saigon-based daily *Chinh Luan*, more forcefully claimed in agreement with David Elliott that "Vietnam has probably changed more in the last three decades than in the previous twenty centuries."[54] Even if modernization occurred before 1930, Sung's point suggested not only a widespread cognizance of change across Vietnamese society during the twentieth century but a rapid intensification and acceleration of those changes.

Fall recognized that technological advancements associated with modernity drove social transformations in Vietnam.[55] However, he also recognized changing political currents evolving from nationalist struggles in the early twentieth century and with the growth of Vietnamese radicalism in the decades before World War II. Much earlier, and before the formation of the Indochina Communist Party in 1931, Vietnamese intellectuals such as Phan Boi Chau, Nguyen An Ninh, and others promoted Vietnamese nationalism and independence with varying degrees of intensity.[56] Pham Boi Chau argued in favor of the radical transformation and complete liberation of Vietnam. Other leaders, such as Phan Chu Trinh, appeared to accept French rule while demanding better treatment and reform of French colonial policies. More moderate nationalist positions also existed, while other pro-French Vietnamese contributed to and directly supported France's position. Elites, like Bui Quang Chieu of the Constitutionalist Party, accepted and accommodated French policies to a fault. The Viet Minh in the north and Vietnamese Communists in the south, not surprisingly, viewed Chieu's relationship with French authority and with the Japanese-controlled Empire of Vietnam as blatant collaboration.[57]

When Japanese forces invaded Indochina during the early stages of World War II, Vietnamese Nationalism became even more complicated because Indochina was under dual control of Vichy France and Imperial Japan. With the end of World War II and the relinquishing of Japanese and Vichy control, the August Revolution led to the establishment of the DRV but also unleashed an internecine settling of scores against collaborators as well as among Vietnamese competing for political dominance in the south of Vietnam. This chaos was especially prevalent in the south because Viet Minh control was not as strong as in the north. Not only were collaborators killed, communist factions, such as those allied with Trotsky's internationalist-oriented ideology, were also targeted as competitors. Along with prominent Trotskyist leaders Ta Thu Thau and Phan Van Hum, Bui Quang Chieu was assassinated by Vietnamese Communist "Honor Squads to Eliminate Traitors" (*doi Danh du tru gian*) in September 1945.[58] These squads were associated with South Vietnamese Communist leader Tran Van Giau, and they eliminated these individuals and other competitors because of links (alleged and actual) to the Japanese occupation, for being French minions, and because of divisions within communist ideological orientation.

It is important to emphasize that in this period surrounding the August Revolution in 1945—during which Vietnamese Communists gained a predominant position—there were divisions between North and South concerning Vietnamese Communist organization. South Vietnamese leader Tran Van Giau was neither a member of the Viet Minh nor in contact with DRV leadership during the August Revolution.[59] During the later stages of World War II, South Vietnamese Communists like Tran Van Giau actually contacted French Gaullists in Vietnam to defeat the Japanese in exchange for greater independence in the South. After the establishment of the DRV in September 1945, Tran Van Giau served as the chairman of the Provisional Administrative Committee for South Vietnam. It would have been at this point, as a critical South Vietnamese Communist leader, that Tran Van Giau coordinated the targeting of those perceived as collaborators with the Japanese, such as Bui Quang Chieu and others.

In the following years, Tran Van Giau took on several positions supporting the DRV, such as coordinating activities in Thailand and serving in other leadership positions related to communication and education. As a communist leader in the south, it is important to note that Tran Van Giau's position was taken over by Le Duan, who led the Territorial Committee for South Vietnam. In 1948, the DRV, seeking to exert greater control over the south, sent Le Duc Tho—who was later a key leader during peace negotiations with the United States in the 1970s—to assist Le Duan in neutralizing Vietnamese opponents and fighting a war against French forces.[60] In a way, the August Revolution in 1945 could be viewed as the starting point for a schism between North and South Vietnamese Communists. These divisions became more pronounced with the formation of the National Liberation Front in 1960, and even more so in subsequent years after the United States intervened in 1965. Scholarly debates over whether North Vietnam controlled the National Liberation Front, or whether Ho Chi Minh and his colleagues were primarily communists or nationalists in terms of ideology, have origins in the chaotic post-World War II era in Indochina.

The efforts of Tran Van Giau, among others, to eliminate Vietnamese competitors added chaos to the anti-colonial resistance emerging in Cochinchina, the former French colony in the south. It is important to clarify: while inter-

The Ending is a Beginning

Vietnamese violence between the Viet Minh and the Vietnamese Nationalist Party (VNQDD) was one set of problems in the north, Vietnamese Communists in South Vietnam faced different problems. These divisions became clearer when French forces returned, and a temporary truce was established in early 1946. In the south, and according to Ellen Hammer, the March 6 Accords did not apply, at least in reality. In her view, "When the disorganized resistance in the south refused to lay down their arms ... the French attacked them in the name of mopping up and police operations."[61] The potential for cooperation among Vietnamese and anti-Vichy French forces against a common Japanese enemy during World War II was long over. The political circumstances of mid-1946 were vastly different from what they had been mid-1945. While the Viet Minh were significantly weaker in the south, this did not prevent their allied communists in the south from targeting Vietnamese opponents, as the assassination of Bui Quang Chieu demonstrated. Ellen Hammer described this:

> The fact that many of the guerrillas and a number of their leaders were not Communists did not prevent Tran Van Giau from attempting by force to neutralize, eliminate, or replace individuals who challenged Viet Minh domination of the resistance. The Viet Minh did not scruple to use terror not only against traitors but also against its political opponents; it was dangerous for a non-Communist to become too well known in the resistance.[62]

* * *

Fall came to Vietnam at the peak of the anti-colonial agitation that had spurred and accelerated social transformation for decades. Groups that had preceded the Viet Minh, such as Vietnamese secret societies, were of particular interest. He suggested that these groups' tactics of secrecy were appropriated by Viet Minh internal security and intelligence units. Fall wrote, "It was a combination of Marxist ideology and the secret societies of Vietnam that produced the *one* effective political organization the country has ever had—the Indochina Communist Party."[63] This kind of statement was revealing, not because he suggested a direct link between secret societies and the Viet Minh, but because the groups shared similar approaches. The Viet Minh, like secret societies, used external threats to defend themselves against infiltration by external threats, as well as enforcing internal compliance with rules through direct personal connections among members.

In Fall's view, the Viet Minh's internal security-intelligence apparatus—especially the Cong An, Trinh Sat, and Dich Van—was critical to the DRV and the Viet Minh's survival. Among its many tasks, it protected the Viet Minh against infiltration, provided intelligence and counterintelligence, eliminated collaborators, and infiltrated opposition groups. These operations were crucial because initially the DRV was internally fragmented, targeted by French Union forces as it initially struggled to consolidate its strength. These struggles, especially between 1946 and 1950 before Chinese support, explain why Fall described the DRV during this period as "a government in the bush," focused on reducing the risk associated with military effort whenever possible.[64] Organizationally, Viet Minh security-intelligence units, such as Cong An, Trinh Sat, and Dich Van, not only provided state security. They also offered an advantage in competitive control by providing space for the Viet Minh to administer taxation, decide judicial questions, and dominate education more effectively than other Vietnamese competitors.

These Viet Minh groups also gained political control through violence, while minimizing Viet Minh vulnerabilities because their actions usually affected small numbers of Vietnamese. In contrast, when French authorities targeted Vietnamese, even small mistakes could be magnified because of colonialism's racist legacy and France's history of exploitive practices in Indochina. In cases where French authorities punished innocent Vietnamese for being alleged Viet Minh, usually gruesomely in front of the accused's family, this only increased antagonism against French and State of Vietnam forces.[65] In other cases, when Vietnamese were targeted in reprisal for Viet Minh attacks, individuals and communities would often subsequently join or provide material support to the Viet Minh cause. Henry Ainley, a French Legionnaire during the First Indochina War, offered numerous eye-witness accounts of cases in which Vietnamese pursued vendettas against those, especially French officers, who had wrongfully targeted their family or friends.[66] This was calamitous for Vietnamese society, which predominantly consisted of innocent civilians and their families. However, in an honor-bound society with close-knit familial ties, violent retribution and cycles of violence characterized the brutality of war in Indochina, and the Viet Minh were effective at making this work to their advantage.

II—The Cong An, Trinh Sat, and Dich Van[67]

The Cong An, Trinh Sat, and Dich Van contributed to a parallel hierarchy of Viet Minh security that was flexible and effective. Their collective purpose was to "create unity of command at every level from the village up … via the ever-present members of the Party to conduct the war as they please, without fear of the opposition or of 'deviations.'"[68] Bernard Fall described the Cong An as a civilian secret police, comparable to the French *Sûreté* and regulated by a centralized authority in the DRV government.[69] In February 1946, five months after the DRV was proclaimed in September 1945, a merger between the DRV's earliest security service and various police units resulted in the Cong An, technically the Vietnam Public Security Department (*Viet Nam Cong An Vu*).[70] The unit was created, therefore, before the Indochinese Communist Party was dissolved in November 1946, long before the Vietnamese Communist leadership reestablished its political party later as the Worker's Party (*Viet-Nam Dang Lao Dong*) in February 1951.[71]

Security organizations like the Cong An were led by individuals with long-standing ties to the Party's core members, or who were themselves Party cadre. Fall identified the civilian "Director-General of the Police and Security Services" and his deputy as "members of the Indochina Communist Party (ICP) for more than twenty years" which, considering the founding of the ICP in 1930, demonstrated the importance of commitment and trust when it came to how ICP/Lao Dong leadership staffed these positions.[72] During the post-World War II years, roles and tasks were in flux. By 1951, according to Christopher Goscha, the Public Security Department "was assigned a new and clear role in the strengthening of the party, the state, and people's democracy (meaning communization)."[73] The Cong An also conspired with the military structure of the DRV at the regional level when seeking out and eliminating Vietnamese competitors, such as nationalist factions or collaborators and other traitors. Fall's detailed organizational chart, "Structure of the State Secretariat to the Ministry of the Interior (Police and Security)," first illuminated this security apparatus's complexity in 1954.[74]

Trinh Sat were intelligence teams primarily tasked with monitoring French units and forts along the De Lattre Line around the Red River Delta in northern Vietnam. Their assignments consisted of active intelligence collection, which included intercepting documents, reporting enemy movements, and preparing analysis and reports to plan potential attacks against French posts.[75] In contrast to the Cong An, Trinh Sat functioned as an intelligence component of the Viet Minh's military. They could be task-organized, or assigned, as an attachment to conventional DRV troops from company to division levels of command. According to Fall, Trinh Sat personnel operated as politico-military sappers probing for vulnerabilities along the de Lattre perimeter. In addition, they especially sought out angry Vietnamese willing to provide information on French and State of Vietnam troops and their potential operations.

In their role soliciting informants, Trinh Sat were even more prominent after 1950, when Chinese material and advisory support significantly increased the Viet Minh military's capacities.[76] The completion of the De Lattre Line in 1951, which the Viet Minh subsequently infiltrated over the subsequent three years, provided only an illusion of control to French authorities. French officers' inability or unwillingness to confront Viet Minh infiltration bewildered Fall. However, he rarely denounced French operations and commanders while the First Indochina War was in progress, with few exceptions.[77] In another instance in which he documented Viet Minh control, after visiting "nearly every North Vietnam province in May and June 1953," Fall created a situation map depicting Viet Minh control over the region. Accompanying it was included a map of the same terrain, with the territory marked out that was purportedly under French control. The contrast Fall sought to illustrate, in his words, represented "what a well-organized guerrilla force which enjoys at least the partial support of the population can do behind the lines of even a well-equipped enemy."[78] The extent of Viet Minh activity was clear to Fall, and he commented on the Trinh Sat as a vanguard unit: "Infiltrators of the Trinh Sat precede every movement of the Vietnamese People's Army's (VPA) regular units, often by months."[79] Such preparation invariably demonstrated the Viet Minh's effective use of local intelligence in preparation for larger-scale attacks on French posts.

A Trinh Sat specialty was inflicting revenge on French officers and non-commissioned officers (NCOs) who tortured Viet Minh suspects and victimized communities accused of providing local support to the Viet Minh. Henry Ainley, an Englishman serving with the French Foreign Legion, provided extensive firsthand accounts of rape, torture, and theft by French military personnel and Vietnamese collaborators. These offenders were invariably targeted for revenge and often suffered vicious retribution at the hands of the Trinh Sat. Ainley pointed out that French soldiers were aware that "the Viet maintained a first-class filing system in which were included not only Europeans renowned for brutality but also the officers, NCOs and men who worked in key positions."[80] In Fall's evaluation, the Trinh Sat played an important role in maintaining this filing system and "did excellent reconnaissance work."[81]

Thinking back to his military background, Fall drew historical comparisons between "anti-Vichy Resistance members' work in Nazi-occupied France" with his contemporary analysis of the Viet Minh's development of parallel hierarchies.[82] Building on his knowledge from previous experiences by reading *Revue Militaire D'Information*, he envisioned parallel hierarchies as complex organizations. However, he also regarded them as operating primarily along two relatively simple lines of action. The first of these centered on tasking individuals to infiltrate existing administrative structures and subvert them from within. The second main line of action was the "creation of altogether, new clandestine structures designed to take over full administrative responsibilities when political and military conditions are ripe."[83]

Fall's time with the Maquis in Haute-Savoie helped him recognize these processes. Writing in 1963, he recalled how "the infiltration of subversive individuals preceding the creation of an independent apparatus" led to the "establishment of the CNR (*Conseil National de la Resistance*) in 1942, which began the creation of a full-fledged nationwide parallel network of underground administrative organs."[84] The CNR, to be sure, initiated a web of resistance units with distinct characteristics that were unique to their local circumstances. Yet it was a phenomenon that Fall identified in Vietnam, too. The above statement demonstrated how Fall drew upon his experience and applied it as an early critic of warfare in Vietnam. The murder of his father by the Gestapo in November 1943 undoubtedly heightened his sensitivity and awareness of retaliatory tactics that called to mind the Nazis' aggression in the name of protecting against anti-Nazi subversion. He knew that the Gestapo, along with the Soviet Union's People's Commissariat for Internal Affairs (NKVD) and the Bolshevik Cheka before it, epitomized brutality under the auspices of maintaining security and "protecting the state."[85] It is not surprising that he would notice similar phenomena elsewhere, including those found among Indochina's diverse and complex societies.

Fall also explained how the concept and methods found in parallel hierarchies possessed wider, even global, applications when subversion of established power was a goal:

> By trial and error all insurgent movements eventually concentrate on some forms of population control—and both the Communists and the John Birch Society by and large agree on the methodology; at least, on the basic level. The French specialist term for that stage is *noyautage* or the creation of nuclei of hard-core activists who will penetrate existing organizations and slowly change their character.[86]

It is critical to note Fall's ability to perceive relationships between an organization's structural characteristics—where its vulnerabilities were located, for example—and principles for subversion that would work best to infiltrate a targeted organization. In broader terms, he also recognized how the function of infiltration was entirely context-dependent, and that different groups could share similar but not identical methods. This required, notably, qualitative assessments more than quantitative ones. Circumstances and historical context could vary to such a degree that exceptions always existed. He could call out patterns in his writing, but he did not bother to theorize them through analytical approaches such as linear-regression analysis or other means.

That Fall pointed to the common approach of forming a nucleus (or vanguard) for infiltrating an organization—used by far-left communists as well as the far-right John Birch Society—was a notable insight at the time. In the United States in the 1950s and early 1960s, these kinds of nuances might have been lost in an ideological haze clouded with bias, self-interest, and old-fashioned ignorance. The idea that the John Birch Society and communists might share similarities, at least in how they sought to gain power, was undoubtedly a difficult one to get across, given the intense political divisions in American society in the 1950s and early 1960s. Fall's overall intent was to demonstrate how the concept and specific actions involved in infiltration were non-ideological: it was a tool. It was only ideological in the ends achieved. In short, communists and John Birch Society members could use the same vehicle to achieve political goals even when those goals were opposed to each other. As a means to study contemporary conflict, applying Fall's qualitative-analytical approach to other contexts is appropriate but requires careful historical contextualization. Unlike theory-based analysis, which relies on less ambiguous data sets, the qualitative characteristics comprising his analytical approach makes his work challenging to apply to other contexts in a prescriptive manner. He never formulated a dogmatic doctrine. Instead, he focused his attention on diagnosing and analyzing Viet Minh subversion to create a context-dependent net assessment of warfare.

Dich Van units were a third component to Fall's analysis of the Viet Minh security apparatus, and the one to which he gave the most attention. In contrast to Cong An and Trinh Sat units, Dich Van specialized in espionage, propaganda, and infiltration of Vietnamese auxiliary units. While Dich Van actively collected intelligence, they also targeted individuals, capabilities, and resources. Fall did not consider them military intelligence-reconnaissance assets in the same manner as Trinh Sat.[87] Trinh Sat generally adopted more conventional approaches to operations, whereas Dich Van typically used unconventional means to accomplish their aims in a clandestine manner. Still, they were also used to wage psychological warfare, and they inflicted brutal violence to evoke terror through symbolic messaging when necessary.

Dich Van were distinct organizational units, and they were comparatively more autonomous than Trinh Sat. However, the term *dich van* is the predicate form of the verb "to proselytize," or effectively to convert enemies to the Viet Minh cause. According to Christopher Goscha, Dich Van's actions were an institutional and intensely political part of the North Vietnamese army toward the later stages of the First Indochina War. Goscha recounted, "It became very controversial when the army's *dich van* services went to work on thousands of prisoners from France and its empire in a bid not to hurt them necessarily physically, but to change them psychologically."[88] Goscha also acknowledged that Dich Van processes and units had an influence on later French appropriation of Viet Minh methods. As he described it, "Paradoxically, *dich van* not only transformed Vietnamese intelligence, but it also influenced the development of French and American counterrevolutionary tactics and methods to this day."[89] In Goscha's view, "this emphasis on *dich van* in particular distinguished communist Vietnamese, North Korean and Chinese intelligence services and security cultures from their non-communist postcolonial counterparts in other parts of the non-Western world."[90]

The unique capabilities and often brutal approaches Dich Van units adopted, as Fall observed, did influence French counterrevolutionary practices, especially against the FLN in Algeria. Dich Van units were also breeding grounds for fanaticism. A distinct type of socially induced radicalism came about, in part, through self-criticism sessions known as Kiem Thao that were typical of communist movements in Vietnam. Together, narrow-minded adherence, hatred of French soldiers and their allies, and the type of peer pressure Kiem Thao sessions encouraged brewed a toxic and violent mix. In Eric Hoffer's view, "The proselytizing fanatic strengthens his own faith by converting others."[91] This was certainly the case with the Dich Van. Yet, like infiltration, this kind of radicalization was as endemic to far-left communist political factions as it was to far-right political organizations.

Fall commented on the Dich Van's ability to "make themselves felt at a specifically 'Vietnamese' level of fighting upon which the foreigner has no effect." He added:

> It will be a Dich Van group that will capture the mayor of a recalcitrant village and cut his body to ribbons, or leave his head dangling from a bamboo pole in the middle of a village (with a note attached to it warning that anyone who takes it down will suffer the same fate).[92]

Dich Van violence and psychological operations were enhanced through the dissemination of their message through print and radio, and they were further distinguished by unit personnel's advanced linguistic capabilities in French and the employment of women as operatives. Dich van operatives worked in groups of three, like other security units, each group with a specialist in anti-French propaganda, a second member who focused on infiltrating auxiliary troops and connecting with Europeans for information, and a third member who "acted as a liaison agent between the group and headquarters and contacted local agents."[93]

All specialists were selected for their fluency in French, and the task of infiltration of auxiliary Vietnamese or French units "was frequently given to women: clever and attractive physically, they tried to become either the congäie of European soldiers or else the wives of auxiliaries."[94] The commitment to and nature of these operations is self-evident. In a sense, marital and carnal relationships served as small scale-parallel hierarchies that added to an overall subversion of authority. These practices also embodied a type of infiltration that avoided military categorization, as it was a challenge to defend against agents infiltrating a community through marital or carnal connections. Physically tangible obstacles, such as barbed wire, massive amounts of poured concrete, and establishing clear fields of fire along a perimeter did not count for much against agents whom other young adults in military units might find irresistibly attractive.

Preventing attractive and intelligent women and men from purposely crossing paths with young French and Vietnamese soldiers was difficult, especially given the circumstance of the First Indochina War. Fall pointed out that one solution included establishing military brothels called BMC (*Bordel Mobile de Campagne*, or Mobile Field Bordellos). He recalled similar units from World War II when he had served with the 4th Moroccan Mountain Division, and in Indochina these units included Algerian women from the Oulad-Naïl tribe.[95] However, historian Ruth Ginio cites Vietnamese women as being the majority of workers in military brothels.[96] Infiltration through sexual allure was a known and prevalent problem. Douglas Porch claimed that Dich Van units were 70 percent female and predominantly employed as informers. Male operatives were typically "recruited through fear of reprisals against their families and instructed to be model soldiers and earn promotion."[97]

Dich Van used printed propaganda, such as leaflets and night letters, together with physical infiltration, especially among colonial troops. Fall devoted several sections of a chapter in *The Viet-Minh Regime*, "The Party in

THE ENDING IS A BEGINNING

Power," to this subject and stressed that "the Democratic Republic took into full account the ethnic and national differences between the various component units of the French Union Forces."[98] This was a highly significant effort because French forces relied heavily on colonial troops from West and North Africa, including 60,000 Moroccans. Michel Goya pointed out that over 350,000 troops from all over the French empire served in Indochina, while French troops from metropolitan France did not exceed 60,000.[99] As Fall knew well, this created an environment rich in opportunities for the Dich Van to stir up agitation among indigenous troops who might bear grudges against a condescending civilizing mission.

As such, Dich Van often distributed leaflets received in China from, for example, the East German Social Unity Party and the French Communist Party.[100] The leaflets' purpose was two-fold: (1) to influence morale at the tactical level, and (2) to change soldiers' behavior by fostering long-term discontent with racial inequality, especially in the event they survived and eventually returned to their home countries. Fall analyzed multiple leaflets designed to change behavior among French forces and, likely due to his service with the 4th Moroccan Mountain Division toward the end of World War II, he paid close attention to a Viet Minh leaflet targeting Moroccan troops printed in Arabic:

> Moroccan soldiers—You fight for an unjust cause at the service of your oppressors ... The Americans and French carve up your country. Moroccan soldiers, the Vietnamese are your brothers ... the soldiers of the Vietnamese Army fight against your oppressors for the liberty and independence of their country ...[101]

Fall's military experiences working with Moroccan soldiers during World War II informed how he understood the conflicted historical circumstances in which they served with French Union Forces. He saw the indirect means through which the Viet Minh exploited imperialism in Morocco and how the Viet Minh sought to change Moroccan soldiers' perceptions of France before they returned home. The ultimate goal of convincing North Africans to subvert French interests was to weaken the French colonial empire as a whole, which would aid the Viet Minh's subversion of French administration in Indochina. Rising political unrest in Algeria during the 1950s unquestionably also contributed to the Viet Minh's emphasis on agitating North African soldiers concerning France's colonialist history of exploitation in their homelands.

Sub-Saharan African troops, along with North Africans, were also the target of anti-colonial propaganda. However, Viet Minh propaganda did not always appeal to African soldiers as part of a unified anti-colonial brotherhood. Instead of attempting to gain their sympathy or support for the Viet Minh cause, the Viet Minh sometimes portrayed racial and ethnic differences among soldiers serving with French Union Forces in denigrating ways, and often distributed leaflets and other propaganda with racist portrayals of African soldiers. One possible goal in doing so was to evoke fear among Vietnamese villagers, or to prevent potential cooperation between Vietnamese and locally based French Union troops. Used as an agitprop tool, propaganda developed for Vietnamese consumption often vilified Africans, portraying them as demonic and even cannibalistic.[102] This type of racialized psychological warfare was not exclusive to Indochina; race-oriented propaganda was an endemic and toxic practice during World War II.[103] It also extended even further into the past and was a sick tactic employed in the Philippines through the late-nineteenth and early-twentieth centuries. As Christopher Capozzola explained, "African American soldiers, about 5,000 of whom served in the Philippines with the 9th and 10th Cavalry and 24th and 25th Infantry, encountered revolutionary propaganda that pointed out the ironies of their service."[104] The Viet Minh attempted to take a similar course but focused primarily on stoking fear and prejudice among Vietnamese who might be encountering soldiers of a different race for the first time.

Viet Minh propaganda posed a serious problem that threatened to undermine French Union soldiers' loyalty to France. Military authorities reasonably doubted commitment of African soldiers in particular, so they expended significant effort to increase Africans' sense of belonging to their units and to the anti-communist cause. Ruth Ginio, like Fall did earlier, contextualized the problems French authorities encountered when using colonized subjects. Ginio explained, "it was difficult to ignore the fact that African soldiers were being sent to fight against national movements seeking to end colonial rule—the same colonial rule under which they themselves lived."[105] Fall also devoted analysis to the Viet Minh's efforts to convert prisoners of war into anti-colonialists. This was a powerful tactic, and African soldiers who survived the war and returned home, in Fall's words, "were ideologically indoctrinated through treatment similar to that received by United Nations prisoners of war captured in Korea."[106]

As another intellectual thread through his work, Fall's early scholarship on Indochina and the DRV consistently returned to the Viet Minh's organizational capacity and adaptation as the DRV confronted Vietnamese competitors and French forces. Units such as Cong An, Trinh Sat, and Dich Van were critical because they enabled the Viet Minh to subvert opponents at little cost when compared to set-piece conventional battles. For these reasons, Fall spent a great deal of time working to understand the organizational structure of the DRV's security apparatus. His analysis emphasized the DRV's organizational development horizontally, through front organizations which were spread across territory held by the Viet Minh, and vertically as the Viet Minh consolidated power in depth at multiple levels ranging from villages to large interzone administrative echelons.

In later stages of the war, Fall determined that similar techniques were spreading geographically and beginning to appear in Central and South Vietnam. In the early period after the DRV's founding in 1945, such flexible organizational capacity was critical. While the Viet Minh had widespread support in many areas, there was considerable opposition to them from Vietnamese Nationalists, other political-religious organizations, and among ethnic groups such as Nung Chinese. The Nung, who detested the Viet Minh, were also termed the Hoa Nung, or Tau Nung, and lived in modern-day Quang Ninh and Lang Son Provinces in Northeast Vietnam.[107] Like the Meo (Hmong) population in Laos, Nung Chinese resented communist expansion in their territory.

Land reform and collectivization in 1953 and 1956, in two of the most severe cases, also created significant opposition to the Viet Minh after the Viet Minh military repressed and killed tens of thousands of Vietnamese. Fall believed that, in the immediate post-World War II era, in a bid to mitigate possible anti-communist feeling, "Communist coloration of the Viet Minh leadership was not as yet directly evident to the vast majority of supporters," so the Viet Minh sought footholds before its ideological communist orientation dissuaded potential supporters.[108] Internal propaganda, the establishment of parallel hierarchies to subvert competitors, and the elimination of enemy collaborators were preconditions for transitioning, in the later stages of the First Indochina War, beyond a Maoist-inspired second stage of equilibrium and toward fulfilling the third stage of conventional warfare.

Contemporary theorists also draw attention to the relationship between organizational structure and violence. Jeremy Weinstein has delineated how control of populations through violence manipulates multiple social mechanisms, such as pressure from peer groups, bias, or others. However, in political violence that subverts competitors, organizational configuration is a crucial facilitating characteristic that distinguishes organized violence from unorganized mobs. As Weinstein writes: "violence can be an effective strategy because it is both persuasive and selective, but the strategic use of violence requires effective organization."[109] In the Viet Minh's case, wielding effective organizations was a notable characteristic of their security services. When Dich Van units inflicted violence upon recalcitrant village leaders, it epitomized strategically oriented subversion to gain control at local levels.

Public violence meted out by the Viet Minh might have been even more strategically effective had they possessed the capability to disseminate the effects of their violence beyond word-of-mouth. Still, as small, well-organized networks, Dich Van units were well-positioned to inspire fear and gain control over local populations. Fall recognized that local Vietnamese villagers and potential targets of Dich Van repression knew what Dich Van messaging meant and often personally knew, or were related to, the Dich Van's victims. In the case of Dich Van personnel entering into long-term relationships with French or State of Vietnam personnel for the purpose of subversion, it may be dehumanizing to regard an attractive Dich Van member as a small, networked structure. However, the Viet Minh's socio-political-military doctrine counted "martial-infiltration techniques" as one effective method among many. The plurality of relationships Dich Van had with French and State of Vietnam authorities demonstrated flexibility in its organizational design. Altogether, the cadre of security and intelligence units were critical in gaining and coordinating control over the Vietnamese civilian population through selective and strategic violence.

Fall studied the Viet Minh's internal-security apparatus while its tasks were evolving and the Viet Minh was improving its conventional-oriented military capacities. On the one hand, Chinese-supplied arms, which primarily consisted of American military equipment captured in Korea, improved materiel capacity. On the other hand, the mass mobilization of the Vietnamese population between 1951 and 1954 was as critically important as it was challenging because of its monumental scope. Initiating mass mobilization depended on patriotic appeals but was also achieved through the carrot of land reform incentives and, when needed, the stick of brutal coercion.[110] However, it is critical to emphasize that these distinctions and changes were about improving organizational effectiveness and ensuring communal cohesion whenever possible. Since the DRV's founding, according to Merle Pribbenow, "The Vietnamese communists rejected the common Western concept of separating national security (political security) functions from civil (criminal) police functions … all disruptions of internal stability, including both social and political stability, were viewed as threats to the Party's hold on the reins of power."[111] While Fall might have perceived a Viet Minh security apparatus in flux at the time, primarily through adopting directives issued in 1951, its overall task was to ensure the state's security.

As the Viet Minh consolidated control and built power through 1952 and 1953, the northern region became "the revolutionary base area for the entire nation, a firm foundation on which (the Viet Minh) army could build and expand."[112] Conversely, in a critical development with long-term implications after 1955, "the (pro-communist) people of South Vietnam quickly shifted from armed struggle to political struggle."[113] Sympathetic populations certainly facilitated the success of the internal security units as well as the recruiting drives for the People's Army of Vietnam (PAVN), but so did abuse by French troops and violent reactions against such treatment. Invariably, French torture of villagers and the mistreatment of Vietnamese auxiliaries did more to solicit support for the Viet Minh's cause and its security units' missions than the Viet Minh could accomplish themselves. Henry Ainley's firsthand accounts of atrocities committed by French troops, and those perpetrated by anti-communist Vietnamese collaborators known as the *Bande Noire*, are vivid and horrifying.[114]

The French military's use of Vietnamese proxies to inflict violence upon other Vietnamese exacerbated the viciousness of civil conflict, but it was also counterproductive. As Stathis Kalyvas has argued, indiscriminate cruelty is "much less likely to achieve its aims during a civil war, where the presence of a rival makes defections possible."[115] In a related sense, Ainley's accounts of brutality also indicate that Vietnamese auxiliaries, and the French soldiers responsible for mistreating Vietnamese, neither thought nor acted in rational terms, nor did they care about the tactical or strategic implications resulting from their mistreatment of others. The *Bande Noire*, Ainley explained, "were usually instrumental in the application of torture or beatings employed during the interrogation of Viet suspects." Ainley spared nothing in his accounts of sadistic punishments inflicted on mostly innocent Vietnamese individuals by French officers and soldiers.[116] Fall was familiar with Ainley's work, and he was certainly familiar with similar cruelty from his research on the Gestapo and Krupp Corporation leaders' treatment of slave laborers during World War II.[117] Fall did not describe the inhuman acts inflicted upon Vietnamese in the nauseating detail Ainley provided, but he nevertheless recognized how Vietnamese auxiliaries' abuse of other Vietnamese contributed to a socially destructive cycle of violent retribution characteristically found in civil wars.

The brutalization of Vietnamese peasants was also self-defeating for French forces because it denied them access to tactical intelligence. According to

Douglas Porch, this failure "had a direct effect on French morale and combat performance and made a significant contribution to the French army's high casualty rates in Indochina."[118] In Ainley's perspective, "The French were justly and universally unpopular and nearly every native was willing to pass on to the Viet the slightest piece of information, no matter how unimportant."[119] The brutality inflicted upon noncombatants was thus self-defeating in a practical military sense, as much as any other reason. Moreover, Ainley criticized the lack of operational security among French troops who underestimated the Vietnamese, noting that the "Europeans as a whole were shockingly indiscreet and carried on conversations about past and future operations as though the Viet had never thought of sending out agents who were trained linguists."[120]

Acknowledgment of the counterproductive effects of brutality was mainly lost in subsequent years. During the Second Indochina War, anti-communist units, such as Republic of Vietnam Rangers and Provincial Reconnaissance Units (PRU), continued to brutalize civilians. As Neil Sheehan pointed out, Vietnamese companies which "had been taught how to soldier in the French colonial paratroops" cruelly tormented innocent Vietnamese with tortures that ranged from wrapping a suspect in barbed wire to beating a suspect's stomach until it collapsed and the individual vomited it out.[121] Vietnamese auxiliaries' living conditions and their treatment by French personnel also percolated into a toxic stew that permeated local societies. According to Ainley:

> [auxiliaries] received starvation wages, held grudges against the French who treated them like dirt, even when they were NCOS or commissioned officers ... All too frequently auxiliaries were hit, kicked and generally roughed around by the European commanders, and in each case it left behind a violent and lasting resentment which was easily turned to active hatred.[122]

Unsurprisingly, such animosity often increased Viet Minh-PAVN membership, fueled and validated its propaganda, and generally intensified anti-colonialism thought and action propagated against French and State of Vietnam personnel. Nonviolent mistreatment and the humiliation of colonial troops revealed another dark angle of colonialism in Indochina. During a stop in Cambodia in 1953, Fall noticed French officers' paternalism toward a Cambodian master sergeant of the French Marines, *Les Troupes Coloniales*. The story demonstrated not only the French officers' arrogance but also their apathy toward the French cause. Fall described this incident, writing:

> When I went to the Transportation Office, a Cambodian orderly told me apologetically that the [French] Lieutenant had gone to the mess to play tennis with the Captain. Since a convoy which I expected to catch was supposed to leave at

dawn, I decided to stroll over to the mess in order to get my travel documents signed there ... Since the men were in the midst of a set, I had little else to do, I sat down at a neighboring table. Then emerged from the verandah a soldier in French uniform. His small stature, brown skin and Western-type features showed him to be Cambodian ... On his chest above the left breast pocket of his suntan regulation shirt were three rows of multi-colored ribbons: *croix de guerre* with four citations, campaign ribbons with the clasps of France's every colonial campaign since the Moroccan pacification of 1926; the Italian campaign of 1943 and the drive to the Rhine of 1945.[123]

Fall added, "In his left hand, he carried several papers crossed diagonally with the tri-colored ribbon; travel orders like mine, which also awaited the signature of one of the officers." During a break in their game when the officers joined their wives for drinks, the master-sergeant "strode over in a measured military step, came stiffly to attention in a military salute, and handed the orders for himself and his squad to the captain ... [the captain's] eyes narrowed suddenly as he understood that he was being interrupted."

"Sergeant, you can see that I'm busy ... wait until I have time to deal with your travel orders. Don't worry. You will have them in time for the convoy."

Fall described the sergeant standing at attention and then stating, "'*A vos orders, Mon Capitaine*,' and resuming his watch near where the Cambodian mess boys were following the game." Fall continued:

The sun began to settle behind the trees of the garden and a slight cooling breeze rose slightly from the nearby Lake Tonlé-Sap, Cambodia's inland sea. It was 1700 ... All of a sudden, the beautiful bell-clear sounds of a bugle playing "lower the flag." Nothing changed at the tennis court; the two officers continued to play their set ... Only the old sergeant moved. He was standing stiffly at attention, his right hand raised to the cap in the flat-palmed salute of the French army, facing in the direction from which the bugle tones came; saluting, as per regulations, France's tricolor hidden behind the trees.[124]

Fall concluded:

Something very warm welled up in me. I felt like running over to the little Cambodian who had fought all his life for my country, and apologizing to him for my countrymen here who didn't care about him, and for my countrymen in France who didn't care even about their countrymen fighting in Indochina ... And in one single blinding flash, I *knew* that we were going to lose the war.[125]

This anecdote demonstrated Fall's frustration on many levels. Juxtaposed against the commitment prevailing among the Viet Minh, the story shredded the illusion that France's cause mattered, even to the French officers who were supposed to be leaders. For Fall, as a veteran who had served toward the end of World War II, these officers' treatment of a master sergeant and their disregard for France was beyond disillusioning. The officers embodied a disdain for devotion to duty. The anecdote also revealed an insulting condescension toward enlisted personnel, let alone colonial troops, among French military leaders, who Fall anticipated would be the primary audience for his books. The fact that the Cambodian soldier was a master sergeant is critical. Along with sergeant major and command sergeant major, this rank is earned by the most experienced, knowledgeable, and competent members of Western armies. In terms of training, execution of orders, and oversight of troops and their welfare—in contrast to officers occupied with planning—senior NCOs were critical, and Fall knew that non-commissioned officers were the backbone of any well-prepared military force.

More broadly, Fall's account of the incident between the Cambodian master sergeant and the French officers was only one incident illustrating the racial enmity which colonization fostered. In Frantz Fanon's perspective, "the native is an oppressed person whose permanent dream is to become the persecutor" because the agony the oppressed experiences drives them to revenge. Fanon's more significant point was that colonialism initiated cycles of violence and essentially devolved into a type of nihilism: "a non-thinking machine, a body without reasoning faculties."[126] These factors revealed colonialism to be "violence in its natural state," which only yielded "when confronted with greater violence."[127] Stathis Kalyvas' descriptions of cycles of violence in civil wars share many characteristics with Fanon's assessment of colonialism. Yet it is important, in Kalyvas' perspective, to not "overlook a critical dimension of civil wars: the fact that they provide powerful incentives for the production of 'indirect' violence by 'ordinary' civilians ... civil wars offer irresistible opportunities to harm everyday enemies."[128]

The indirect and direct violence that Kaylvas described was not restricted to Westerners inflicting violence on Asians It also incorporated itself in conflict among and within Asian societies with competing visions for the future. The anguish inflicted through French colonization was only the most apparent undercurrent to war in Indochina. All too often, indigenous, colonial practices preceding France's occupation of Indochina were forgotten or unknown, even though they were powerful contributions to deep-rooted ethnic divides among communities in Southeast Asia. For many Americans and others in the 1950s and 1960s, the relatively unknown legacy of indigenous colonization among Chinese, Vietnamese, Laotians, and Cambodians formed often unseen layers of complex animosity that did not include Western

THE ENDING IS A BEGINNING

forms of imperialism. As Christopher Goscha has argued, "Vietnamese were colonizers, too."[129] When French colonialism introduced its brand of imperialism to Southeast Asia in the nineteenth century, it only piled on another vicious layer.

III—Operation Lorraine: The Entrance to the Valley of Dien Bien Phu

During World War II, the disorder in Vietnamese society, the outbreak of the First Indochina War in late 1946, and problems created through land reform in 1953 and collectivization in 1956 were disastrous in almost every respect. These problems, however, also contributed to the Viet Minh's demands for mobilizing Vietnamese society against French forces in the years before French defeat. A critical component of the Vietnamese Army, one that Fall emphasized at length, was its civilian logistical transportation corps of porters. This supply system requiring mass mobilization facilitated the Viet Minh's capacity to wage strategically significant battles, and contributed to their defeating French operations as early as late 1949 and later on through 1953 and 1954. In Fall's view, massive numbers of porters supporting the Viet Minh exemplified "total war in which men and women over eighteen were mobilized throughout the territory of the DRV in November 1949."[130] He added that those "who were recruited into the People's Army often served with village-level guerrilla forces (*Du Kich*) to gain sufficient training before joining main force units (*Chu luc*)."[131] Viet Minh leadership approved additional obligatory labor legislation on 1 September 1952, and these decrees required that all healthy citizens between eighteen and fifty years of age were required to serve as porters.[132] Fall, who had been only ten years earlier a young Jew facing deportation for labor in Vichy France, was incisively aware of such decrees and how they affected others.

His emphasis on the Viet Minh's use of civilian porters underscored a profound appreciation for their immense numbers and the practically Sisyphean tasks before them. Civilian porters were critically important to conventional operations, but their recruitment indicated a serious collapsing distinction between combatants and the hundreds of thousands of civilians required to carry out the Viet Minh's way of war against France. If an eighteen-year-old carried a box of supplies, was he or she still a civilian, or was that person now a legitimate military target? One effect of mass mobilization was pulling whole swaths of civilians into the crosshairs of potential military action in ways that added another level of meaning to population-centric warfare.

Mass mobilization also typified a scale of political and social effort that undermined French military planning which lay behind ideas such as the De Lattre Line and its strings of fortifications, which Fall had encountered when he first came to Vietnam. In tactical situations where Viet Minh forces had previously attacked bunkers and blockhouses along the De Lattre Line, breaches were soon "abandoned in favor of a thorough political and guerrilla infiltration of the Red River Delta, while the main forces of Giap proceeded to further consolidate their hold upon northern Laos and the tribal Thai territory of North Vietnam."[133] The De Lattre Line, it was clear to Fall, might as well have been invisible.

"People's Workers" (*Dan Cong*), in Fall's words, were not only crucial as supporters but "constituted the logistical backbone of the Republican forces."[134] Modified bicycles, designed to carry heavy loads, contributed in areas, yet "it was chiefly with the help of such primitive means of individual human labor multiplied by a huge number of individuals that the Viet-Minh actually succeed in winning its battles, which were first and foremost logistical victories."[135] Christopher Goscha seconded Fall's point by noting that the DRV "initiated from 1950 what became one of the most 'totalizing' wars in the history of the twentieth-century decolonization, profoundly transforming its state and the society it sought to mobilize."[136] In a Viet Minh operation in June 1953 in Laos, Fall confirmed that women and men carried loads up to 45 lbs., traveling an average of fifteen to twenty miles a day.[137] It is worth pointing out that the terrain covered was rarely level, if ever, and was obstructed by jungle growth that scouts had to remove.

The will to endure was undeniably a staggering feat. Because these carriers consumed between "2 and 2.2 lbs. of rice per day on a 300-mile haul of fifteen days, the porters' final payload was reduced to 12 lbs."[138] The wherewithal to transport a final delivery consisting of only 12 lbs. after a 300-mile journey on foot testifies to a kind of tenacity and sheer physical endurance that even exceptional and highly motivated soldiers likely have to dig deep in their reservoir of willpower to locate. The vast numbers of individuals contributing to this specific operation in Laos in 1953 were also astounding: "the two Republican [Viet Minh] divisions operating in the area had an aggregate supply column of 95,000 porters. Similar figures were frequently cited by both friend and foe and may even be considered as conservative."[139] Even if the numbers were lessened by thousands, the magnitude of the human effort involved in the military operation Fall referenced in Laos in 1953 is difficult to fathom in many respects.[140] However, even more massive numbers of indi-

THE ENDING IS A BEGINNING

viduals were involved in this overall human porter system between 1950 and 1954. Bernard Fall was not the only one to describe the magnitude of mass mobilization. Writing in 2012, Christopher Goscha pointed out that, in the overall context of civilian labor between 1950 and 1954, the "DRV mobilized 1,741,281 people as civilian porters, almost all of them peasants."[141]

This human effort was astounding, but so was the Viet Minh's creativity and industry. In an interview Fall conducted in 1953, a former construction worker and prisoner of war recounted how he and his unit were ordered to build twenty supply buildings in five days. He recalled how, "Lacking tools, they had the initiative to cut tree trunks into flat slivers for use as spades to dig into the ground."[142] French Legionnaires were also aware of the Viet Minh's ingenuity, yet many French officers underestimated the use of tens of thousands of "coolies" to carry disassembled arms, including artillery and mortar systems, and their ability to reassemble them to engage French forces.[143]

Like their French counterparts, leaders in the United States were aware of the Viet Minh's military organization and increasing materiel capacity. Still, the synergy between political and military factors and the massive numbers of civilian porters who hauled equipment through places vehicles could not reach were challenging to understand or fully appreciate. Viet Minh operations that involved tens of thousands of porters often exceeded US Works Progress Administration initiatives, if not in their duration or products, then in their size and scope. While the Viet Minh did not leave bridges and roads behind in the same way the WPA did, it was a similar social-based mobilization undertaken by Vietnamese, but for no pay, with severe risks to life and limb, and for the sole purpose of defeating French Union forces.

Also contributing to the Viet Minh's strength was a series of political networks extending beyond Vietnam. Fall explained that the Viet Minh and the Worker's Party (Lao Dong) "made a serious attempt to assume the leadership of other Communist-inspired 'national liberation movements' in Thailand, Burma, and Malaya-not to speak of those of Cambodia and Laos which are totally under the Party's control."[144] Three organizations, in succession, developed local administrative networks according to the Viet Minh's direction. According to Fall, these included the following:

> Southeast Asia League, which collapsed in 1948 after a brief appearance in Thailand before Marshal Phibun's return to power [on 8 April 1948]; the Ku Sap Be, which operated under Nguyen Van Long, another Moscow-trained Vietnamese; and lastly, the Communist Co-ordination Committee in Southeast Asia which, as its name implies, supposedly coordinates the operations of the Communist parties on the whole Southeast Asia mainland and Indonesia.[145]

Fall initially identified these organizations and the Viet Minh's physical sanctuaries in Thailand, Laos, and Cambodia through his research in 1953. Yet, these connections and sanctuaries had deeper roots that preceded the formation of the Indochinese Communist Party (ICP), and the groundwork for them had begun earlier in the twentieth century.[146]

Organizational dynamics that helped the Viet Minh eliminate competitors, achieve a functioning administration, and gain mass support among the Vietnamese population were critical. However, their horizontal expansion into neighboring states reinforced Vietnamese-based networks and provided space and time for alternative and contingency plans, or for when emergencies developed. The essential support that external connections and sanctuaries provided was especially evident among those agitating against French colonial powers. Unsurprisingly, these backstops were existentially relevant for weak organizations to develop when facing stronger opponents.

As Jeremy Weinstein explained, "In the absence of economic endowments, leaders must build networks rooted in identities and ideologies to succeed."[147] At face value, French Union Forces and their associates exerted pressure on Vietnamese nationalist and communist groups, especially in South Vietnam, and they responded by simply relocating and expanding elsewhere. However, the development and extension of organizational frameworks into other places—through familial, tribal, social, ideological, ethnic, or other linkages—also helps to explain broader political changes in Southeast Asia during the Cold War.[148] While researching in 1953, Fall identified a series of networks extending into Laos that the Viet Minh established after joining with former members of the Lao Issara. This integration of Lao individuals assisted by Viet Minh led to the formation of the Pathet Lao in 1950 under the leadership of Souphanouvong.[149] Fall believed that the Pathet Lao's headquarters in Viengxay—essentially a network of limestone caves in Northeast Laos—provided North Vietnamese Communists with a haven for planning and staging their Spring Offensives between 1952 and 1954.[150]

Fall also viewed Cambodia as an important sanctuary. Writing in 1954, he noted, "Vietnam has a more direct interest in Cambodia since the latter has been Vietnam's favorite overflow area for the last 150 years."[151] This kind of overflow, however, was not always welcomed. Khmer populations in Cambodia had opposed incursions from the 1830s, and ethnic assimilation policies enacted by the Vietnamese Nguyen dynasty, which ruled the region for much of the nineteenth century, led to uprisings against the Vietnamese empire during the 1840s.[152] While Fall was generally correct in much of his analysis related to this area of study, relations between Kinh (ethnic Vietnamese) and other ethnicities were never uncontested. The ethnic relations in Southeast Asia and their history were diverse and complex, and Fall continued to study them in subsequent years. However, he did work to develop a more sophisticated understanding of the subject, especially as it concerned relations among lowlanders and highlanders in Central Vietnam. Much of what he learned was through personal study but also through meeting and learning from anthropologists, such as Gerald Hickey and others, who specialized in this field of study.[153]

As it concerned his research in 1954, the Viet Minh's inroads to and from Cambodia were consequential enough that Fall detailed these connections in a section on the DRV's foreign relations, entitled "The Worker's Party and the Khmer Issara," in the third part of *The Viet-Minh Regime*. This entire section, "Part Three: The Party in Power," consisted of forty pages of analysis into relations among Vietnamese Communists, non-Vietnamese ethnic minorities, religious groups, Lao (including the Lao Issara, Pathet Lao, and other groups), and Khmer (also including the Khmer Issara and others). He concluded in 1954 that connectivity between the Viet Minh and these neighboring groups and regions had in fact been planned and developed before World War II. Later, scholars provided evidence that corroborated Fall's conclusions.[154]

Laos and Cambodia, accordingly, stood out as critically important in Fall's earliest scholarship on Indochina. In a section entitled, "Relations With the other Indochinese States," he remarked on the Viet Minh's connections to Cambodia in 1950, writing, "The young Democratic Republic of Vietnam had learned its lesson well. Hardly five years after its own liberation from the chains of colonialism, and in the midst of a war for its own survival, it had created a full-fledged satellite of its own."[155] Fall's early recognition of networks among the Viet Minh, Pathet Lao, and Khmer Issara demonstrated that the Viet Minh was an expansionist power, but only in the sense of expanding into rugged terrain to survive against stronger French Union forces. In much the same way that the People's Republic of China sought buffer zones along its borders with North Vietnam and North Korea, the DRV sought a type of insulation along its borders with Laos and Cambodia.[156] Cambodia and Laos, therefore, were separate from the DRV, but were of far-reaching significance. This was not so much a matter of falling dominoes as it was a shoring up of a safety net that would prove existentially crucial for the DRV in coming years.[157]

In late 1952, Laos especially preoccupied government authorities in Paris and Washington because of the Viet Minh's incursions into Laos from neighboring northwest Tonkin (North Vietnam). These concerns, and France's expensive efforts in Indochina, were already severe problems in President Eisenhower's view. Since 1951, collective security in Europe depended on France's support and participation. However, France's inability to contribute sufficiently stemmed from losses and costs incurred in Indochina, despite the massive amounts of aid provided through the Marshall Plan that continued well into 1952.[158] Diplomatically, France was also recalcitrant: it would neither adjudicate the Indochina question at the United Nations, nor would it grant independence to the Associated States of Laos, Cambodia, or Vietnam unless it achieved a military victory over the Viet Minh first. As Eisenhower claimed, France tied "the fate of the European Defense Community (EDC) to our willingness to do things in Indochina as the French government desired."[159]

Eisenhower maintained that the United States was bound to France's problems in Indochina because the United States was bound to France. "The decision to give aid [to France] was almost compulsory," Eisenhower later reflected. "The United States had no real alternative unless we were to abandon Southeast Asia" and, in doing so, risk losing French commitments to collective defense in Europe as the Cold War intensified.[160] For these reasons, the United States was as concerned as France about the Viet Minh presence in Laos. If the Viet Minh and their socio-political doctrine spread to other areas, France's diminishing control over Indochina would become entirely untenable. The Viet Minh's presence in Laos and their assaults against French garrisons in Tonkin posed such a threat that France initiated operations against the Viet Minh in the region to preempt further communist attacks.

A year and a half before the Viet Minh's victory at Dien Bien Phu in 1954, another French military operation gave Fall insight into how the Viet Minh responded to French planning. Operation Lorraine was the largest one French forces had unleashed in Indochina to that point. Ironically, it was inherently defensive and was initially developed to save a beleaguered garrison at Gia Hoi, southeast of Nghia Lo, in late October 1952.[161] The operation demonstrated that the Viet Minh's doctrine, sanctuaries, and use of human porters all coalesced into a critical step toward France's defeat in Indochina. The days of the DRV existing as a "government in the bush" were long past. Planning against the Viet Minh was far more challenging than French officers had ever envisioned.

* * *

THE ENDING IS A BEGINNING

Operation Lorraine sharpened French military and political leaders' focus, but not their ability to learn. The operation's questionable planning did not center around the intent or merit in rescuing the Gia Hoi garrison after a Viet Minh attack. Instead, the retrograde element of the plan was the problem. In returning from the garrison's location, French forces in Groupe Mobiles 1 and 4 were ambushed after the operation was canceled on 14 November 1952.[162] French Defense Minister René Pleven attempted to explain the operation's outcome before the French National Assembly because the result was "a miserable failure, costing some 1,200 Expeditionary Corps casualties altogether and failing to draw [General Vo Nguyen] Giap into major combat."[163] Criticism mounted, however, because Lorraine was the largest military operation to date, including over 30,000 troops which consisted of three parachute battalions, two infantry battalions, *Dinassaut* naval forces, two armored groups, two artillery battalions, engineering units, and two tank destroyer squadrons.[164] According to Fall, Operation Lorraine was "disastrous" because "practically all French troop movements in Indochina took place in a 'fishbowl.'"[165] Fall's account of Operation Lorraine is one of the most dramatic narratives in his writing, and the operation was consequential because "the desperate search for the set-piece battle became an obsession of the successive French commanders-in-chief in Indochina until the end of the war."[166] He added, "The set-piece battle had become the credo of not only the French who were fighting the Indochina war but of the United States which, after 1952, had become more and more directly involved in its financial and often in its strategic aspects."[167]

Despite Operation Lorraine's failure, Fall was bewildered that even more aggressive French operations were planned in 1953 to entice Viet Minh forces into a conventional battle. Years later, he recognized the intent behind such planning, but he noted in 1961:

> The now-famous "Navarre Plan," named after the unlucky French commander-in-chief in Indochina in 1953–54, provided, according to as authoritative a source as the late Secretary of State John Foster Dulles, that the French forces were intended to break "the organized body of Communist aggression by the end of the 1955 fighting season," leaving the task of mopping up the remaining (and presumably disorganized) guerrilla groups to the progressively stronger national armies of Cambodia, Laos, and Viet-Nam.[168]

Even with the benefit of hindsight, it still seemed incredible to Fall in 1961 that French leaders had failed to learn from Operation Lorraine. Instead, they remained overoptimistic that weather would not interfere with aerial operations and moved forward with garrisoning troops in the middle of the "fishbowl" forming the Dien Bien Phu valley. Thus, the Navarre Plan epitomized the desperate search for a conventional set-piece battle that over-relied on uninterrupted aerial supply and support to bomb Viet Minh positions.

The plan, perhaps most notably, underestimated a Viet Minh logistics system that involved tens of thousands of human porters who could transport supplies through otherwise inaccessible terrain. The Viet Minh's operational plan, which included unleashing its artillery on the French garrison from the hills surrounding Dien Bien Phu, was also intelligently conceived. It included emplacing artillery in well-covered areas on the front slopes of hills facing French positions and in reverse-slope positions that offered protection from French artillery. Ultimately, the sheer amount of Viet Minh firepower proved overwhelming. On the battle's outcome, Fall remarked: "Communist commander-in-chief, Vo Nguyen Giap, explained that the French Expeditionary Corps 'was strategically surprised because it did not believe that we would attack-and we attacked; and it was tactically surprised because we had succeeded in solving the problems of concentrating our troops, our artillery, and our supplies.'"[169] With regret since he knew soldiers at the garrison, Fall remarked, "the French already had extended themselves a great deal by attempting 'Operation Lorraine' at all."[170]

In contrast, Viet Minh leaders recognized that their attacks upon isolated garrisons like Gia Hoi served as bait. Rescue attempts rendered French forces vulnerable to launch ambushes in locations ideally suited for such pre-planned assaults. In this, Viet Minh leaders had "decided upon a military strategy from which no French initiative and no amount of American military aid were going to cause it to deviate until the end of the war."[171] It is clear that, before Lorraine, French leaders were overoptimistic in their military's capabilities. To explain one of several reasons for this, it is useful to briefly describe the French military innovations that led French leaders to develop aggressive operations, such as Operation Lorraine and the Navarre Plan in 1953. *Groupement de Commandos Mixtes Aéroportés* (GCMA), later known as *Groupement Mixte d'Intervention* (GMI), was a key innovation supporting French operations in northwest Vietnam in 1952. These commando units, Fall wrote, "were organized on the basis of the experience gathered during World War II by the European *Maquis* and by such Allied long-range penetration groups as the British 'Chindits' of General Orde Wingate in Burma, and the United States 'Marauders' of Brigadier General Frank D. Merrill."[172] By 1952, they assumed what Fall regarded as "strategic importance" because of their capability and proven effects.[173] GCMAs typically parachuted into Viet Minh-held territory, were left to their own devices to destroy what they could, and, if possible, would exfiltrate back into French-held territory.[174]

THE ENDING IS A BEGINNING

In the riverine environment, *Dinassaut* naval forces were another critical innovation. As part of a brown-water navy, Dinassaut were "one of the few worthwhile contributions of the Indochina War to military knowledge," according to Fall.[175] Dinassaut were *division d'infanterie navale d'assaut*, often translated as "naval assault divisions," and they were composed of joint forces that included army infantry and marines, and also sailors for ship handling and navigation.[176] Dinassaut tasks consisted of transporting infantry, blocking Viet Minh retreat across waterways, and providing logistical and fire support. Initially developed in 1945 with fourteen landing craft "purchased from the British and modified with additional armor and armament," the concept behind the Dinassaut later contributed to US "brown-water" naval operations across the Mekong River Delta after 1965, helping to provide "gunfire support and logistics for these forces once they engaged with the enemy."[177] These kinds of units, along with GCMAs, were effective, and they increased French leaders' optimism that their forces could overcome the Viet Minh, before Operation Lorraine and Dien Bien Phu proved them conclusively wrong.

French forces' consequential defeat at Dien Bien Phu, to be sure, resulted from brilliant operational planning on the part of Vo Nguyen Giap and his staff, as well as the tenacity of tens of thousands of mass-mobilized Vietnamese and Viet Minh military forces. It also revealed the Viet Minh's long-term political action. Fall pointed out that the infiltration of the Red River Delta in the years before Dien Bien Phu was the critical groundwork that made Viet Minh strategic victory possible: "Warfare behind French Union lines had already weighted the scales of war heavily in favor of the Vietnamese People's Army before Dien Bien Phu, and even before the development of the Navarre Plan."[178] This was achieved through many other factors as well: external Chinese support, the development of sanctuaries in Laos and Cambodia, an often brutal socio-political-military doctrine, numerous networks of parallel hierarchies, and operations undertaken by the Cong An, Trinh Sat, and Dich Van. Western forces' underestimation and inability to understand the Viet Minh's way of warfare led to the Viet Minh's victory. It would be left to individuals like Bernard Fall to figure out how all these factors consolidated into a type of warfare that military force could not defeat.

IV—Upstate New York

After almost a year in Indochina, Bernard Fall returned to Syracuse, New York in late 1953 and began writing. In the field, he had drawn on his experience in the Maquis and French army during World War II and applied analytical abilities developed during the War Crimes Commission at Nuremberg and through graduate study. He recognized that many aspects of warfare he remembered from his time in Haute-Savoie were also at work in Indochina: sanctuaries provided refuge for beleaguered soldier-citizens and the Viet Minh built on this development from networks established in Cambodia and Laos before World War II. The depth of Fall's organizational analysis of the Viet Minh and the DRV would likely have been less impressive without the skills he had developed from his work at Nuremberg and through graduate study at SAIS and Syracuse University. After over ten months of intense research in Indochina, Fall's thought and understanding of warfare had grown exponentially, and his efforts produced a prodigiously strong and extensive foundation for his subsequent scholarship. In the short term, material he gathered from spending the majority of 1953 in Indochina provided a wealth of information from which to draw for the dissertation he would soon complete at Syracuse University in 1955. In addition and in the long term, much of the material in his later books, *Street Without Joy* and *Hell in a Very Small Place*, was also based in the research he gathered in 1953.[179]

There were, however, physical downsides to fieldwork in Indochina. While conducting research, he developed a case of jungle rot on parts of his back, groin, and along one arm and leg. As he wrote to Dorothy, he was earning his PhD "the hard" way, and he described his painful home remedy in a letter:

> the treatment consisted of ripping open the pores where the fungus is lodged, and then kill the stuff inside. This is done by first shaving the body hair in the area affected, then using a nylon finger brush on the sore area until it breaks. Then taking some cotton and rubbing the entire area with a solution combining salicylic acid, benzoic acid, iodine, sulfuric ether, and pure alcohol. Together, you ought to be able to melt metal with it.[180]

Other difficult situations did not inflict such acute pain as the acidic concoction he described, but they were often less treatable. Fall's experience with French and Vietnamese soldiers in the field "along the defense perimeter, wet and afraid" revealed an empathetic awareness that stands out in his writing. He undoubtedly did not want to return to the traumatic time he spent in the Maquis and French army as a youth. However, it is possible he pursued opportunities to share in the plight of soldiers, perhaps even enduring combat as a means of reliving the camaraderie of soldiering he had once known.

Getting to know Vietnam and Cambodia were also powerful experiences for Fall. As he consistently explained, he had committed himself to the region,

THE ENDING IS A BEGINNING

and Indochina would remain his intellectual focus for the remainder of his career.[181] He wrote to Dorothy in 1953, these interactions combined to "knock the intellectual superciliousness out of me."[182] This reflection is telling in its implication that Fall's background and experiences doing field research had inoculated him against becoming an armchair analyst, removed from the realities he described. His field research gave his work authenticity and practical utility that abstract intellectual reflection would have lacked. Moreover, if he was to be authentic, Fall had to be honest in describing what he saw.

Before returning to the United States in November 1953, Fall offered a further reflection on his first trip to Indochina. In the same letter to Dorothy describing the treatment for jungle rot, Fall wrote, "Mixed feelings about leaving? Sure. With all my bookish air and with my highly peaceable education, I nevertheless enjoy a good tough scrape, just to prove to myself that I'm no sissy. I guess that I've been trying to prove a point to myself ever since my parents died."[183] The intimacy of the statement was rare. In Dorothy's perspective, as someone who knew Bernard Fall better than anyone else, it was "a profound piece of self-analysis."[184] François Sully, who also knew Fall had lost his parents to Nazi persecution, once pointed out that "Fall never talked about his father who was captured and killed by the German Gestapo in France."[185] It is possible that Fall found in Indochina, especially in Vietnam, something that enabled him to cope with or somehow mitigate the loss of his parents. The war in Indochina certainly provided a professional academic opportunity, but Fall's dedication to his study was all-consuming. His teacher, Amry Vandenbosch, had been correct: nobody knew much about Indochina, at least among English-speaking audiences, and so Fall set about filling this gap for the rest of his career. The first trip proved, in any case, that Fall had found a calling, and he would study and write about Vietnam, Laos, and Cambodia with fervor after 1953. He would do so with a "tireless effort to secure the facts and data as they are, and not as one wishes them to be."[186]

Syracuse University and the goal of completing his doctoral requirements, however, were not far from his mind. After leaving Vietnam, and a short stop in Paris to spend time with an aunt and uncle, Fall returned to the Maxwell School to develop his research into a dissertation for his political science advisor, Dr. W.W. Kulski. Before he left Vietnam, a reminder of the academic life waiting for him in Syracuse reached him in the field. He recalled:

> While in Lai-Chau, the airhead behind Communist lines, a mailbag was parachuted in to us, since the airfield was flooded. It contained a letter for me which had followed me, through all my changes of address, from Syracuse,

225

N.Y., to France, Hanoi, and the postal unit of our Airborne Resupply Group. It was a court summons issued for a parking violation committed while a graduate student at Syracuse. (P.S. I went back to pay it one year later, but the judge dropped the matter when he heard under what circumstances the summons had been delivered.)[187]

With a dissertation to complete, the parking ticket served as a reminder that Fall had a very different type of work ahead of him.

6

THE WIND AND THE WATER

After earning his doctorate in International Relations at Syracuse University in 1955, Fall completed numerous additional articles and projects while seeking long-term employment.[1] His publications of this period included an analysis in *Pacific Affairs* that assessed the 1954 Geneva Agreements resolving the First Indochina War. Another example for *Politique Etrangère* analyzed the Republic of Vietnam's formation in Saigon, under the leadership of Ngo Dinh Diem. Finally, Fall produced another article for *Pacific Affairs* assessing the Cao Dai and Hoa Hao and their contentious relationship to Diem's government in 1955.[2] These articles depended on primary sources and interviews he had collected in 1953, and on research conducted in Ithaca, New York as a participant in Cornell University's Southeast Asia Program in 1954.

As for his personal life, on 20 February 1954, Fall and Dorothy Winer were married in Manhattan's City Hall in a ceremony officiated by a justice of the peace.[3] They also had a traditional Jewish wedding on 28 February, which Bernard agreed to despite initial resistance stemming from a rejection of his Jewish faith. In her biography of her husband, Dorothy recounted that Bernard explained why he did not want a Rabbi-officiated wedding, stating: "It was the Jewish Council in Nice that gave the names to the French police, which came after us, who did the bidding of the Nazis." Later, he told her, "I don't want my children raised as Jews. I don't want anyone coming after them the next time."[4] These comments indicated the complexity of his feelings around his Jewish identity, and how it remained a complex internal struggle for him long after World War II.

Together, after living in Ithaca as Bernard completed his degree, the Falls moved to Washington, DC. Initially, he found work as an associate at Systems Analysis Corporation, and then at American University, where he worked as an assistant professor contributing to the Human Relations Area Files (HRAF) consortium.[5] These terms of employment were brief, so he filled his schedule as a guest lecturer at Johns Hopkins University's SAIS, George Washington University, and as a lecturer for the Department of Government at Howard University, beginning in 1956. Like many young, ambitious scholars, he pursued numerous opportunities and rarely passed on any, which quickly filled his CV. However, Fall's employment at Howard University marked the beginning of his long-term intellectual home. In 1957 he became an associate professor. This provided him a measure of professional security, and his role at Howard became a rewarding commitment that lasted the remainder of his scholarly career.

In his articles, Fall felt compelled to tell the truth of what he saw in Indochina, and he backed his claims and conclusions with evidence which he had often personally gathered. One issue he called attention to included US foreign assistance to the Republic of Vietnam, which had been established in 1955. Unsurprisingly, his outspoken criticism created problems for him because the truths he published did not support the current course of US and Republic of Vietnam policy. He would pay a price for his candor, ultimately being rejected by policymakers and professionally blocked from future employment with the US State Department. Fall would be forced to find other external research support, in addition to his employment at Howard University, by which to fund continued field research in Southeast Asia. The First Indochina War was over. However, Fall could see that the conflict was ongoing, even though it flowed like an undercurrent beneath the waves on the region's surface.

This chapter assesses the growth of Fall's scholarship between 1954 and 1957. It focuses primarily on his analysis of political developments in South Vietnam in 1956 and his second research trip to Vietnam and Cambodia in 1957. Foremost among the issues he studied was Ngo Dinh Diem's decision to remove elected village leaders in South Vietnam in 1956 and replace them with Republic of Vietnam (RVN) officials, personally appointed by Diem and his brother, Ngo Dinh Nhu. Fall's friend, scholar Paul Mus, referenced a Confucian proverb to illustrate how the village was the foundation of Vietnamese society, and how replacing the leaders of South Vietnamese villages was Diem's most consequential mistake. These leaders, according to Mus, "were the expression of the country, as they say the 'Wind and the Water' of the locality." Mus claimed that Diem's decision was effectively an "extinguishing of the light of the Vietnamese."[6] Diem's determination to disrupt these critical relationships, along with other troubling decisions, created the type of social instability that the Viet Minh had purposely created and exploited during the First Indochina War. As both Mus and Fall recognized in 1956, Diem's decision-making was doing the Viet Minh's work for them.

However, the Viet Minh could hold their own when it came to acting as a destabilizing political and social force. The Viet Minh were persistent in crushing dissent in North Vietnam, and they were not beyond destroying villagers and their long-held historical communal farming practices. Calamities associated with DRV land reform and collectivization were issues Fall criticized as vigorously as he criticized problems created by the RVN. The Viet Minh disrupted local society and violently removed village elders whenever such leaders were deemed unsupportive of their cause, and they did so in the name of anti-feudalism or other communist tropes.

Fall might have been inclined to understand why the Viet Minh succeeded in northern Vietnam, primarily because of their anti-colonial political outlook, but he also saw how DRV policies could be counterproductive. Compared to the intuitive approach he had taken to building his understanding of North Vietnam before 1955, Fall found it more challenging to comprehend the Viet Minh's efforts to revolutionize society in the south. Different anti-communist and communist factions, diverse religious organizations, and a large number of ethnic groups contributed to a far more varied social fabric. This posed a broader challenge to Vietnamese Communists attempting to establish themselves as viable organizations after the First Indochina War. Even though frustrations which fostered pro-communist organizational networks grew significantly after 1955, because of Diem's policies and as a result of his antagonizing Buddhists and others, it would not be until late in the decade when the National Liberation Front began to swell. A turbulent stream of often crisscrossing and converging currents, therefore, contributed to a tidal wave that eventually crested as the Second Indochina War.

Fall's frustration with the Republic of Vietnam's leadership centered on Diem's policies, which he perceived as illiberal and among Diem's worst options. Fall appeared to recognize that factionalism in South Vietnam was profoundly diverse and that, while almost all anti-communists favored some form of democracy, their conceptions of democracy differed significantly. These divides were especially potent when it came to the amount of democracy that should exist for average Vietnamese citizens and the amount of religious freedom and equality afforded by the new Republic, which was based in Saigon. Considering internal dissent a threat, especially that posed by Buddhists and any others who argued against the Republic of Vietnam's policies, Diem turned to repressive measures as soon as his administration was established in 1955. Despite his strong anti-communist views, Fall's earliest critiques of Diem centered around the Diem administration's authoritarian interpretation of democracy.

Was Fall biased in his early criticism of the Republic of Vietnam and in criticizing Diem's decision to remove village elders? With the benefit of hindsight and a more comprehensive outlook on his writing, one can clearly see that he criticized DRV policies as vehemently as he criticized those issued by the RVN in Saigon. After 1955, however, he simply had greater access to information to criticize what he viewed as counterproductive decisions in the south. Fall had also spent more time studying the Democratic Republic of Vietnam than the new South Vietnamese administration as it attempted to consolidate. If a bias existed, it is likely that a degree of prejudice in his analysis may have been based on his greater familiarity with the DRV, which despite its many problems, also had a history of anti-imperialism against Japan and then against France.

And even though Fall was ideologically committed to anti-communism, his views were complicated by his anti-colonialism and humanitarian sympathy for nationalist movements of independence. Anti-imperial conflicts in other countries—such as Guatemala, Iran, and the Congo—in 1954 and 1955 undoubtedly contributed to Fall's dynamic and conflicted perspective. Each of these troubling cases had gruesome histories that the Cold War compounded by adding another overlaying struggle. These more localized regional conflicts thus contributed to a broader and more complicated global struggle. They were, to be sure, communist-inspired movements, but they were also ones that called for national independence against exploitation inflicted by European colonialism. The repressive administrations and subsequent illiberal democracies established in each of these countries were also a reason for serious concern. Thus, it is not surprising that Fall—who maintained a profound and comprehensive interest in International Affairs but remained primarily focused on Indochina in his writing—would exhibit frustrations with similar illiberal repression in South Vietnam, especially in light of the enormous assistance provided by the United States to the former French colony. Ngo Dinh Diem's policies and other troubling problems with the delivery of US assistance, therefore, drew Fall's attention far more than the Viet Minh's self-inflicted wounds, such as land reform disasters and brutal repression of peasant revolts.

Fall conducted his second visit to Southeast Asia in 1957. This research trip originated with an Institute of Pacific Relations commission that charged Fall to study South Vietnam's economy and changes in the country since 1954. US assistance to South Vietnam was his focus, especially programs administered by the International Cooperation Administration (ICA), an organization led by the US State Department which was subsequently replaced by USAID in 1961. As a result of his analysis of US assistance to South Vietnam, Fall produced an article, "Will South Viet-Nam Be Next?" which was published in *The Nation* in May 1958. The second section of this chapter examines this critical, even scathing, analysis of US economic aid programs to South Vietnam. The article also marked a crucial turning point in Fall's career for two reasons. First, he used the article to chart differences in Indochina between 1953 and 1957, but with a specific focus on problems stemming from flawed US assistance that undermined South Vietnam's agricultural-based economy. Second, the article led to serious professional repercussions for Fall, the price he was forced to pay for describing what he saw as consequential problems that undermined both the Republic of Vietnam and US policy supporting Diem's administration.

In late 1957, before his article for *The Nation* was published the following year, Fall secured an International Cooperation Administration (ICA) contract to teach at the Royal Institute in Phnom Penh, Cambodia. However, that contract was rescinded by authorities in the US State Department in reaction to Fall's outspoken criticism in "Will South Viet-Nam Be Next?" along with other critical comments he made at a New York speech before the Association of Asian Studies in April 1958. The third section of this chapter describes the subsequent events following Fall's New York speech and the publication of "Will South Viet-Nam Be Next?" This frustrating experience compelled him to find other institutions to support future research, and to rely further upon Howard University as his academic home institution.

Despite accusations from the US State Department that alleged political bias in his analysis of faulty foreign-assistance programs, Fall did not call attention to widening and increasingly evident problems in South Vietnam for partisan reasons. Rather, he did so because he knew the Viet Minh possessed significant capability to exploit security and economic problems in non-communist-held areas. Historically, as he had shown through his extensive and earliest reporting, the Viet Minh were adept at securing victory against the French, despite France's superior military strength. In the mid- and late 1950s, Fall did not want to see the history of the Viet Minh's war against the French possibly repeating itself against American interests in the region. He wanted to apply the history he knew to assist anti-communist authorities in crafting stronger policies that might appeal to vast swaths of the South Vietnamese population. In a similar line of effort, he worked to develop his analysis so that it might inform those responsible for the growing US presence in Southeast Asia as the United States sought to support its ally, the Republic of Vietnam.

I—"The Village Is the Spirit of a Place"

In moving to Washington, DC and weathering a progression of changes in his professional life, Fall was now fortunately anchored to a strong and supportive foundation. Not only did his employment at Howard University provide stability, but the intellectual environment there provided him the freedom to think seriously about warfare in Indochina, civil rights in America, and the role of the United States in the world. Fall came to the Pleasant Plains neighborhood already well-prepared as a scholar and a bold writer and thinker. At Howard, he now received the professional support and encouragement to progress further, and to do so within an intellectually vibrant setting. Furthermore, it was an academic climate suited to Fall as he considered the colonial contexts of Indochina in more detail. According to Robert Vitalis, in addition to Ralph Bunche, Merze Tate, Toni Morrison, and other faculty members, these Howard University-based "thinkers stand out for the early and relentless critiques of the supposed truths of racial science and the role racism played in sustaining imperialism."[7] In key respects, Bernard Fall contributed to this environment of intellectual inquiry as both faculty and students applied ideas to effect change in the United States and abroad. In addition to working with such individuals as Tate, Morrison, and others, Fall taught a new generation of students, including his students Stokely Carmichael, Acklyn Lynch, Hanes Walton, and many others.[8] Ralph Bunche, who taught at the university and founded the political science department before Fall arrived, served as a world-recognized diplomat and role model for Fall and others.

Fall also fit in because he was not content to study his subjects from a desk. Moreover, because his teaching and research addressed contemporary problems in foreign policy, few cities were better than Washington, DC to complete such study. Fall also never forgot his experiences during World War II, and he worked to ensure others did not forget Nazi crimes either. At the Human Area Relations Files, and as a guest lecturer, he often showed his colleagues films he had obtained from the US Army on Nazi atrocities. As Dorothy Fall explained: "He thought [the films] were the best way to make people understand the reality of Nazism." She added, "The films were somewhat subversive in Washington, at a time when our government mainly wanted to forget about the Nazis and concentrate on our ties to West Germany."[9] Fall believed that Americans could not justifiably obscure, let alone forget, criminal actions and lessons from World War II when developing foreign policy. Membership in the Washington, DC branch of the French War Veterans group, *Les Anciens Combattants Français*, and an award for valor during the German occupation presented to him by the French government in October 1955, reinforced his resolve to remember.[10] In addition to volunteer service with French veterans and his teaching at Howard University, Fall found time to work as a research associate for Systems Analysis Corporation, which was under contract to the US Senate Committee on Foreign Relations.[11] Henceforth, Fall would pursue two parallel career paths: one in academia at Howard and the other in government-supported research.[12]

During this period of sea changes in Fall's professional life in DC, dynamic events were still ebbing and flowing in Indochina. After the Geneva Conference convened and a ceasefire was finally established, Vietnam entered a new era.[13] Fall described these developments in an article in March 1955 called "Indochina Since Geneva." In it, he noted that one of the most critical aspects of the agreement was that "Nationwide elections are supposed to be held in both sections of divided Vietnam sometime between March and July 1956."[14] As agreed to at the conference, the elections planned for 1956 would unify the country after establishing a temporary division along the demilitarized zone straddling the 17th parallel. After the State of Vietnam's (SVN) demise, Ngo Dinh Diem assumed the presidency of the Republic of Vietnam (RVN), contingent on later elections determining governance within South Vietnam in 1956.[15] Fall focused on the predicament of the Republic of Vietnam: "The overall difficulty which faces the Diem government is that of a rapidly-disintegrating regional, provincial and local administration."[16]

Fall drew on his observations and those of journalists whose judgment he trusted, such as C.J. Sulzberger of the *New York Times*. Sulzberger described Diem's administration scathingly in 1955, writing: "Largely through the obstinate insistence of our own State Department the inept and chaotic Ngo Dinh Diem Regime remains in power. But anarchy, rather than Diem, governs ... Experts are betting that South Vietnam will fall of its own corrupt weight."[17] Sulzberger may have rightly perceived such chaos, but historians have also challenged these kinds of one-sided understandings of Diem to develop a more nuanced analysis of his ideology and the political context in which he formed the Republic of Vietnam.[18] Yet, whether viewed by Sulzberger in 1955 or by historians decades later after mountains of evidence had been gathered, nearly all could agree that the genesis of the Republic of Vietnam was inauspicious, forming as it had in the still stormy postwar environment as France's troops and administrators packed up and finally left.

Out of the ashes of the State of Vietnam, the Republic of Vietnam's emergence proved to be a rocky transition. Ngo Dinh Diem, a Catholic in a country where most Vietnamese were Buddhists, was initially appointed the sixth and last prime minister of the State of Vietnam by Bao Dai in June 1954. But Diem demanded greater military control than previous prime ministers, who included Buu Loc and Nguyen Van Tam.[19] Bao Dai announced Diem's position on 17 June, explaining, "I have charged Ngo Dinh Diem with forming a government, ... an almost symbolic task which consists in galvanizing, binding, and merging the national energies. He accepts this role. It is up to the country to respond by a vast movement of unanimous adhesion."[20] In Seth Jacob's most succinct assessment, "The country did nothing of the sort."[21] That the Republic of Vietnam was not necessarily a democracy early on was evident to Fall, who claimed that "the South Vietnamese regime rose out of the shambles of the State of Vietnam in 1954."[22] Diem's demand for a wider range of control enabled him to build further executive power, and he consolidated this in the second half of 1954 through two elections: one to determine the executive in 1955, and the other to decide the national assembly in 1956.[23]

On 23 October, after a falling out between Bao Dai and Diem, the first election was a runoff, which Diem masterfully maneuvered to gain power. Fall was particularly critical of this election, mainly because he believed Diem had assumed control over the Republic fraudulently after receiving 98.2% of all cast ballots over 1.1% in favor of Bao Dai.[24] Two days later, Diem established the Republic of Vietnam on 25 October 1955, and he announced his administration as its executive.[25] Later, on 4 March 1956, elections for the 123-member national assembly occurred under a cloud of political suspicion. Anti-Diem Vietnamese claimed "that the [national assembly] elections were unfair and were merely designed to find Diem a puppet legislature which he could dominate."[26]

On the national stage, another referendum initially conceived at Geneva and intended to determine Vietnam's future after the First Indochina War was never held. As stipulated in Article 6 of the Geneva Agreements, preparations to unify Vietnam through a referendum were supposed to begin on 20 July 1955, with the referendum scheduled for 1956.[27] Pham Van Dong, the North Vietnamese Vice Premier and Foreign Minister, sought to initiate this overall process, but Diem rejected his efforts. Instead, Diem refused to hold elections, preferring to hold out until "true liberty" was established over North Vietnam.[28] Diem's position was that the new Republic of Vietnam was "not a signatory to the Geneva agreements of July 1954, and so was not bound to honor them."[29] The United States also had not signed the agreements, nor did it encourage Diem to hold national elections in 1956. According to George Herring, "[President] Eisenhower and [Secretary of State John Foster] Dulles agreed ... that if elections were held immediately Ho Chi Minh would be an easy victor."[30] On the one hand, the democratic election of a communist leader was not the type of outcome that democratic processes were supposed to produce. On the other hand, democratic processes were also not supposed to install authoritarian anti-communist leaders whose policies directly and intentionally undermined democracy.

Diem's fraudulent election over Bao Dai on 23 October 1955 was a first and ominous development in Fall's perspective. However, the failure to hold elections in 1956 created even more significant problems when opposing sides blamed each other for failing to abide by the 1954 Geneva Accords. Fall criticized the North Vietnamese, South Vietnamese, and Americans for the failed elections in an evenhanded judgment. He believed it was critical to support the new Republic, but he was deeply concerned about its many weaknesses, most of them resulting from Diem's narrow-minded and exclusive vision for South Vietnam's future. In one assessment from 1958, Fall explained:

> South Viet-Nam, created in the chaos of division, faced the bitterest struggle for survival. It would not be unfair to say that without a most generous measure of American aid in every field South Viet-Nam could not have survived long enough to face the communists in an electoral test.[31]

Most critically, Fall was concerned that South Vietnam's security was at risk, regardless of its failure to avoid national elections unifying the country. He described the volatile security situation, noting "within a few months after the election deadline had passed in 1956, the killing of village chiefs in South Vietnam began—by stay behind guerrillas, not 'outside aggressors.'"[32] These assassinations were significant, because Fall had seen these types of actions perpetrated against Vietnamese who collaborated with the French during the First Indochina War.

Diem's path to increasing power corresponded with repressive policies implemented to ensure the State's security. His fraudulent election over Bao Dai, in particular, was an event Fall often revisited in his analysis concerning the establishment of the Republic.[33] It was not an intellectual leap for Fall to remember how the National Socialists in Germany had undermined democracy in the Weimar Republic in 1933 through democratic means, and how the *Sturmabteilung*'s domestic terrorism had intimidated competitors. Repressive policies in the name of state security had been fundamental to authoritarianism in Germany in the 1930s. These kinds of approaches to consolidating and holding fast to power were already tried and true mainstays in contemporary politics by the time Fall critiqued them in Vietnam through his 1955 article, "Indochina Since Geneva," for *Pacific Affairs*.[34] He knew these characteristics applied to the Democratic Republic of Vietnam in Hanoi, but he was especially troubled to see American aid supporting an equally repressive authoritarianism in South Vietnam. Diem's "election" demonstrated this, as did his refusal to support a national referendum to unify the country in 1956. Authoritarianism, masked as democracy in South Vietnam, raised far too many ghosts for Fall.

In the contested political environment of South Vietnam, anti-communist factions struggled against anti-democratic procedures put into place by Diem's new government. The political-religious organizations, the Cao Dai and Hoa Hao, with centers in Tay Ninh province and the western Mekong Delta region, initially supported Diem's administration. However, they soon resented what they perceived to be a pro-Catholic bias in his policies. Another even earlier challenge to Diem's authority existed while Diem was the Prime Minister of the State of Vietnam, before the Republic was even established. The actions of the Vietnamese National Army's leader Major General Nguyen Van Hinh, son of former State of Vietnam Prime Minister Nguyen Van Tam, were among the earliest signs of anti-Diem political chaos. Fall described Hinh's attempted coup against Diem, stating: "Diem's rift with the Vietnamese National Army and its chief of staff Hinh, resulted in several bloody clashes between Army units and police groups loyal to the Premier [Diem], and these further underlined the weakness of the regime."[35] Hinh was dismissed in November 1954 and emigrated to France, where he continued to support anti-Diem factions.[36]

Fall did not provide details into the origins of Nguyen Van Tam and Hinh's antagonism toward Diem and his administration. Undeniably, they both viewed

Diem as incapable of consolidating a genuine consensus among the Vietnamese people, which they believed was necessary to create a legitimate representative government in South Vietnam.[37] After Diem's election, which they viewed as fraudulent, they equally resented the formation of a "rubber stamp" national assembly in March 1956. Nguyen Van Tam, already profoundly frustrated with France's dismissal of Vietnamese autonomy during his days as a leader of the State of Vietnam, had resigned as prime minister because of this in December 1953. The extent of his frustration with Diem over South Vietnam's future was indicated by his decision to leave Vietnam for good in 1955.[38]

Fall saw other problems with Diem's leadership that were perhaps more consequential than internal conflicts between Diem and his former army chief of staff, Hinh, or former prime ministers like Tam. Fall described Diem:

> he is highly cultured, but he neither knows nor trusts the masses and does not know how to use them. He does not, like [Philippine leader Ramon] Magsaysay, visit the villages dressed in ordinary soldier's uniform or an open-collared shirt. On the contrary, photographs of his visits to the ragged refugees who have just escaped the Viet-Minh and have lost everything have pictured him and his aides in immaculate white suits in the best "colonial" tradition.[39]

Geopolitically, American support for Diem also had strategic implications because US officials blamed France for, in Fall's assessment from 1955, "sabotaging the pro-American regime of Ngo Dinh Diem and of supporting the Vietnam Army clique which, under Major General Nguyen Van Hinh, defied the authority of the Diem Regime."[40] In Fall's perspective, this distrust formed one of many deterrents that prevented the United States from learning from France's experiences in Indochina.[41]

By the late 1950s, American skepticism concerning France had developed further, and Fall was alarmed as US political authorities continued to discount the many lessons the French military had learned during seven years of war against the Viet Minh. As he recognized from his reading of French military journals, especially *Revue Militaire d'Information* in 1957, many French officers put significant effort into understanding how they had misread the Viet Minh's way of warfare. Issues of *Revue Militaire d'Information* revealed how France's military acknowledged how badly the Viet Minh had beaten them, and how the Viet Minh manipulated the Vietnamese population in ways French authorities could not sufficiently counter. The kind of analysis and assessments officers such as Lacheroy, Hogard, Nemo, and Trinquier offered revealed a willingness to learn that Fall found commendable, and he was a primary analyst, and perhaps one of the only ones writing in English, to pick up on the lessons they provided at the time. This factor combined with his background, timing, and profound ability to memorize vast amounts of information distinguished Fall from any other analyst at the time.

Articles in the *Revue* also indicated how many officers were disgusted by the lack of support from the many governments which formed the Fourth Republic between 1946 and 1954. Fall explained that French reliance on American support further added to the officers' frustration, and contributed to ruptures between the United States and France. In 1954, the French government of Prime Minister Pierre Mendès-France, "wanted American full-scale involvement in the area in order to prevent the United States, 'as she already did before the cease-fire', from deserting France, and leaving to France 'alone the responsibility of a failure in South Vietnam.'" Fall quoted Mendès-France again, stating: "If failure there is to be, let us make sure to see to it that the United States carries at least a half share of the blame."[42] The Prime Minister's comments reflected his country's concern that the United States could not be relied on as an ally, despite the massive financial support the United States provided France for its operations in Indochina. Among already complex security and cooperation agreements in Europe, such geopolitical clashing within an alliance of great importance was not something to gloss over. Fall could only call attention to these problems in the hope that the United States might gain lessons from France's war against the Viet Minh. Even if the United States could not abide by what it perceived as France's political failures, surely there was much Americans could learn if South Vietnam was so important to defend.

In 1953, Fall had gained a firsthand view of the origins of many of the problems which manifested between 1954 and 1956. Not only had he met with Nguyen Van Tam, but he was also able to meet other leaders. Foremost among these was Pham Cong Tac, a figure of importance in Tay Ninh and beyond because of his stature as the Ho Phap (Pope) of the Cao Dai. Tac was more than a religious figure. His political and nationalist views made him one of the most influential leaders throughout South Vietnam. According to historian Jayne Susan Warner, "The Superior's [Pham Cong Tac's] moral and political influence among southern peasants probably exceeded that of any other Vietnamese leader, except Ho Chi Minh."[43] Fall empathized with the Vietnamese' perspective on the man because, after spending three hours with him in 1953, Fall wrote to his fiancée, Dorothy:

> Pham Cong Tac had a piercing intelligence and his approach to things are very realistic. I learned more about Indochina than I'd learned before in 3 ½ months.

1. Fall, second from right, Nuremberg

2. Circa 1945

3. Circa 1945

4. Fall (left) and Remy Malot, 1945

5. Member of Maquis, circa 1944

6. Fall, top row, center, circa 1944

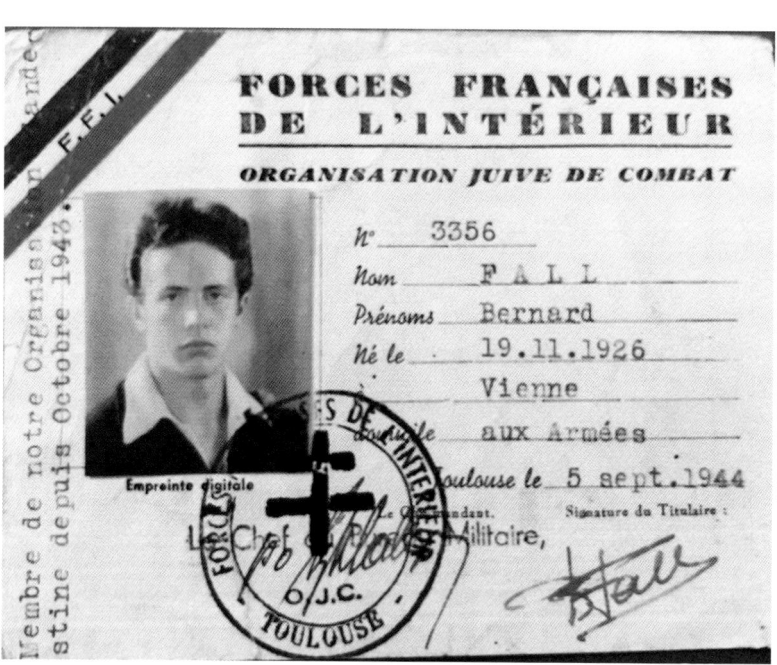

7. F.F.I. Identity Card

8. Bernard with sister Lisette, circa 1945

9. Bernard with sister Lisette, circa 1945

10. Fall, top center with hand on chin, Nuremberg

11. Nuremberg, Identity Card

12. Fall, ROTC instructor, Syracuse University, 1951–1952

24. February 1967, photo credit, USMC

25. February 20, 1967, photo credit, USMC

26. Fall, February 1967

27. Fall, circa 1967

To think that he was sitting there with me talking about the need for French help after he'd spent 5 years in French banishment in Madagascar. The man was fascinating and I can see why 2 million people think he's the next thing to God himself—and that includes a lot of educated Europeans.[44]

Fall's interest in Pham Cong Tac, the Cao Dai, and the Hoa Hao rippled through his 1955 article, "The Political-Religious Sects of Viet-Nam."[45] In addition to the Cao Dai and the Hoa Hao, a millenarian Buddhist revival movement in the western Mekong Delta region, Fall also assessed the Binh Xuyen, a crime syndicate controlling prostitution and gambling establishments in Cholon, a Chinese-dominated area in west Saigon. The article was notable for several reasons. First, the level of analytical detail on the Cao Dai and Hoa Hao was a considerable early achievement in an English-language article. Generally informed readers and other scholars could look to Fall's study to improve their understanding of these organizations' history and motivations. In turn, improved awareness could undermine biased arguments about these religious groups in Vietnam, which might be perpetuated by ignorant individuals who chose to spew racialized critiques of societies that they were too obtuse or lazy to understand.

The type of cultural anthropology-oriented knowledge and information Fall accumulated from working with the Human Relations Area Files (HRAF) helped him access difficult-to-find material and broaden the scope of his analysis. HRAF, by 1955, was an inter-university organization with sixteen branches, including offices at the Universities of Iowa, Colorado, Hawaii, Michigan, Utah, and Washington, as well as at Harvard, Yale, and the University of Chicago, along with many others. HRAF later established its headquarters at Yale University in 1964.[46] When Fall researched and wrote his article on the Cao Dai and Hoa Hao, HRAF had a branch office at American University. After the development and completion of manuscripts, as organized through the various home offices among the HRAF network of institutions, many of the manuscripts were sent to the American University branch, where they were prepared for use by the US Army. American University was vital in the process because, as a subcontracted site, it coordinated efforts with the Department of Defense to integrate classified material with university-produced unclassified research. Accomplishing this in Washington, DC prevented the other "universities and HRAF from being hampered in any way by security precautions" because of the mix of classified and unclassified material that was published in handbooks for readers with security clearances.[47] In addition to his individual research, Fall's contributions to HRAF were rather extensive, and he contributed to a handbook on Iraq for which Johns Hopkins University was the lead institution.[48] He also collaborated on the HRAF book *Cambodia: Its People, Its Society, Its Culture*, which appeared in 1957 and was published as a revised edition in 1959.[49]

Fall's article on the Cao Dai and Hoa Hao was notable for a second reason as well. Instead of focusing his studies on prioritizing centralized power among elites and urban centers, such as Saigon or in RVN-controlled provincial centers, he devoted the majority of his analysis to the political and military influence of these religious groups in predominantly rural areas of western South Vietnam and other geographical pockets throughout the country.[50] This was a significant contribution because it demonstrated the diversity of power centers in South Vietnam and how they challenged the South Vietnamese government. The Cao Dai, in particular, was a prominent and powerful organization based in Tay Ninh province outside of Saigon. In Fall's description, "Pham Cong Tac was exceedingly sensitive to changes of the political atmosphere in the country, and Tac in 1953 steered the Cao-Dai movement on a strictly Vietnamese nationalist basis."[51] When conflict between Diem and Vietnamese army forces led by Nguyen Van Hinh erupted, Pham Cong Tac wisely maneuvered the Cao Dai away from potential involvement. As Fall explained, "Tac adroitly succeeded in avoiding a head-on clash between the Cao Dai Sect—backed by a well-disciplined hierarchy and a devoted following of more than two million faithful—and the Diem regime during the brief civil war of April and May 1955."[52]

Instead of directly threatening the Diem administration, Pham Cong Tac's primary interest was twofold. First, Tac sought to ensure the Cao Dai's longevity. Second, his role was to defend the Cao Dai's autonomy as a spiritual organization and help it maintain its vibrant support system through community-assistance associations. In providing public-oriented services in various forms of assistance, the Cao Dai religious hierarchy could and did fulfill social functions which the Republic of Vietnam otherwise struggled to provide. Fall also appeared to admire Pham Cong Tac's diplomatic ability to avoid conflict, since the Cao Dai also possessed a formidable militia to protect its followers and interests. According to historian Hue-Tam Ho Tai, by 1954, the Cao Dai had a far larger militia than the State of Vietnamese government had agreed to.[53] Fall might not have spelled it out in his *Pacific Affairs* article, but the Diem administration was fortunate that, at least in the political realm of existence, Pham Cong Tac embodied wisdom, restraint, and clear-eyed understanding of the Cao Dai's interests. And Pham Cong Tac's gravitas in the spiritual realm—at least as Cao Dai followers understood it—gave him a considerable amount of tangible power which he could quickly deploy if the Cao Dai's interests were provoked or endangered. Fall also acknowledged that, in addition to the Cao Dai based in Tay Ninh Province, other religious groups held sway. Among them, the Hoa Hao had a legacy of intense problems with Vietnamese Communists that paralleled the group's issues with the different state governments in South Vietnam.

In the spring of 1955, ongoing turbulence between the Ngo Dinh Diem administration and the Hoa Hao took an ominous turn. Since the mid-nineteenth century, the Hoa Hao had been anchored in the western Mekong Delta, observing a tradition based on a millenarian prophesy and a rural, communitarian way of life as represented in the phrase "Buu Son Ky Houng" ("Way of the Strange Fragrance from the Precious Mountain").[54] The Hoa Hao built upon this tradition by helping the poor and maintaining simple, non-costly demonstrations of religious observation. In 1939, the tradition evolved into a more well-formed group under the leadership of a young mystic named Huynh Phu So, whose followers became known as Hoa Hao, named after Huynh Phu So's village in An Giang Province.[55] The Hoa Hao had been politicized during the Japanese occupation of Vietnam, and their numbers swelled after the French Vichy administration detained Huynh Phu So as a political threat. To increase their appeal among Hoa Hao adherents, the Japanese released Huynh Phu So, took him under their protection, and helped promote Hoa Hao doctrine and organization.

In part because of antagonism between the Viet Minh and the Japanese, conflict between the Viet Minh and the Japanese-supported Hoa Hao was magnified during Japan's occupation and especially after the war. Fall described this, pointing out "In the words of a French observer, 'the Hoa-Hao had the habit of tying Viet-Minh sympathizers together with ropes and of throwing them into the rivers to drown in bundles ... One could see those bundles of bodies floating down the rivers like so many trains of junks, at the mercy of the currents and tides.'"[56] These actions were at considerable odds with the goodwill the Hoa Hao provided Vietnamese peasants and the humanitarian simplicity with which they promoted their Maitreya approach to Buddhism. The Hoa Hao's persecution of the Viet Minh further demonstrated to Fall the intense violence which Buddhist groups were capable of inflicting to achieve their political goals during the earthbound leg of their journey toward nirvana.

In 1945, Huynh Phu So, also known as the "Mad Bonze", began to call for greater Hoa Hao autonomy, and he spoke "privately against what he called

'Japanese imperialism' and 'pseudo independence.'"⁵⁷ Even though he was increasingly agitated with Japanese control, Huynh Phu So remained a target in the closing stages of World War II. Animosity between the Hoa Hao and Viet Minh continued to grow until 1947, when the Viet Minh assassinated Huynh Phu So. In Fall's words: "On April 16, 1947, the Mad Bonze was invited by southern Viet-Minh leaders to a 'reconciliation meeting.' He was waylaid on his way, executed and his body hacked to pieces. His remains were never found." This event, and the Viet Minh's generally antagonistic treatment of the Hoa Hao, created such an atmosphere of anger that it provided French Union forces an opportunity to exploit:

> The Viet-Minh's unwillingness to compromise and its outright stupidity in dealing harshly with the sects at a time when it needed every ally it could get, threw the sects (the Cao Dai and Hoa Hao) into the arms of the French and gave the latter control over wide area of South Viet-Nam which they could never have hoped to conquer militarily. Following the pattern which they had initiated with the Cao-Dai, the French signed a military convention with the Hoa-Hao on May 18, 1947, less than a month after the killing of the Mad Bonze.⁵⁸

According to historian Hue-Tam Ho Tai, after the murder of their leader, the Hoa Hao "pursued fiercely anti-Communist policies, for which they became well known during the Vietnam War."⁵⁹ By 1955, then, Fall was observing an organization whose numbers had grown exponentially since 1947. In his assessment, "the Hoa-Hao sect claims nearly 1,500,000 adherents, mostly concentrated in the highly fertile rice bowl of the Mekong Delta, particularly in the *Mien-Tay*, the 'new West' area of the Trans-Bassac [the western Mekong Delta region]."⁶⁰ The Hoa Hao, like the Cao Dai and Binh Xuyen crime syndicate based in Saigon, were therefore groups with considerable political and military strength by the time the First Indochina War concluded. France's departure, however, immensely complicated these groups' positions and access to resources, even though they were virulently anti-communist.

A significant reason why the Hoa Hao and Cao Dai became a threat to the South Vietnamese government was because French subsidies, which the religious groups had previously received, were cut off and controlled by the Diem administration as of 1 January 1955.⁶¹ According to Fall, "this (control) applied to all logistical support of the armed groups of the sects: the flow of arms and other equipment was reduced to a trickle, if not stopped altogether."⁶² The decision to constrict and even eliminate subsidies and other support, he explained, came about at a September 1954 French–American meeting in which "American economic aid was henceforth to be channeled directly to the Associated States, and American military missions in Indochina were to be transformed into training missions for the national forces in replacement of similar French teams," as they departed.[63] Moreover, Fall observed: "After the Washington conversations between France and the United States in September 1954, this policy of gradual elimination of France and direct relations between the United States and the Associated States was extended to the economic and military fields," with aid directed exclusively to the successor to the State of Vietnam which became the Republic of Vietnam, led by Diem, in 1955.[64] When in March 1955 Diem constrained and then eliminated subsidies for the Cao Dai and Hoa Hao, subsidies the French had previously used to ensure these groups' support, "The sects became an economic and social, as well as a political problem."[65] The Cao Dai and Hoa Hao militias, with their large numbers of devoted followers who operated with accurate and locally sourced intelligence, thus presented Diem with a serious military challenge.[66]

Fall viewed Diem's Cao Dai and Hoa Hao-related policies as a problem because "the loyalty of the sects to the cause of the West has been thus far based entirely on a type of self-interest that can hardly be called 'enlightened.'" Instead, "This situation now seems to have given way to a system of subventions, in effect bribes, paid to the sect leaders in a return for their nominal support for the Diem regime."[67] Diem, in reality, did provide payments to the groups through at least mid-March 1955, but even then the Cao Dai and Hoa Hao's compliance with Diem's policies remained suspect. In a 16 March 1955 memorandum from Edward Lansdale, the American advisor to Diem, to J. Lawton Collins, the US special representative in Vietnam, Lansdale wrote:

> At President Diem's request, I saw him early this morning. He said he needed $15,000,000 urgently to provide funds for Cao Dai troops, whose support he needed to retain in the present situation. This money would be used as an advance to pay the troops of General Phuong and General Thé [author's note, Generals Nguyen Thanh Phuong and Trinh Minh Thé were prominent Cao Dai military leaders] while they were awaiting full integration; he therefore needed the money only as a loan for a short time. The President has exhausted all his own funds except for $200,000. When asked whether he had previously mentioned requesting this money, the President said that he had mentioned it to Mr. Fishel, but that it had not been the subject of an official request.[68]

Lansdale was only relaying information to Collins through the memo, but he likely later argued against providing funds to maintain Phuong and Thé's support. It was perhaps unsurprising, to both Fall and Lansdale, that when financial support dried up the potential for conflict quickly grew. When

Diem's government moved against the Binh Xuyen in Saigon, this added to a volatile mix, and open conflict eventually broke out in May 1955.[69] Lansdale later confirmed his strong opposition to the Cao Dai and Hoa Hao in his memoir, *In the Midst of Wars*, where he expressed concern that the Cao Dai and Hoa Hao leaders' efforts "smelled of a naked power grab, with the sect armies to be used as blackmail, a threat to coerce Diem into turning over the government to a handful of warlords."[70] He added that "Collins suggested that I curb my emotions a bit but told me to keep after Thé and Phuong about resigning from the (Cao Dai/Hoa Hao) front."

Whether the funds in question were bribes, as Fall regarded them, or "an advance," as Lansdale stated, it was certain the Cao Dai and the Hoa Hao relied upon them as a key source of revenue.[71] Fall and Lansdale would later enter into a long-simmering debate (exacerbated by a host of other spats) over the extent of support that the United States should provide to Diem, and the wisdom of doing so at all. Fall's concerns centered on his contention that Diem only maintained a tenuous hold on power through bribes and coercion; genuine popular support was not yet forthcoming, and his scandalous electoral victory over Bao Dai only further supported this view. Fall's allegation that Diem had to pay the Cao Dai—a detail Lansdale likely preferred to remain unknown—eventually led Lansdale to question Fall's motivations. The debate over support for Diem, and Fall's other early and consistent critiques of RVN policy, even led to insinuations that Fall was a French agent.[72] Despite disagreements between Fall and Lansdale, which would ebb and flow in coming years, Diem was determined, "with the help of the American authorities, to reduce the influence of the sects to a point where they became politically and militarily manageable, and drying up their sources of income" was a means to achieve control.[73]

Diem's failure to provide the Cao Dai and Hoa Hao anything other than token representation in his government was another source of anger that sparked conflict. Such political exclusivity was counterproductive and further inflamed resentment because Diem's administration "consisted overwhelmingly of Catholics and his own friends and family, many of whom lacked the requisite experience to perform their jobs effectively."[74] As Jessica Chapman noted, "dissatisfaction with Ngo Dinh Diem's political favoritism ... drove them [the Cao Dai and Hoa Hao] to increase their pressure on the prime minister to broaden his government."[75] Yet attempts to include other religious leaders in Diem's cabinet mostly failed because they were perceived as superficial concessions. Even such compromises as when Hoa Hao leader Tran Van

Soai was appointed Minister of State were not enough, and they merely plastered over deeper political divisions. According to Fall, therefore, "in March 1955, Pham Cong Tac and Tran Van Soai and another Hoa Hao leader, Ba Cut, among other Binh Xuyen and sect leaders, sent an ultimatum to Diem, giving him five days to broaden the government."[76] When these efforts failed and were added to the aforementioned financial stresses involving subsidies, a decisive break occurred and contributed to an open struggle between the groups and the government.

Internal conflict involving large, angry, and well-armed political-religious groups in South Vietnam posed a serious risk to the young government, but this was one among many other sets of problems it faced. Not only was the Republic of Vietnam economically insolvent and almost entirely dependent on American assistance, but infiltration by Viet Minh cadres advanced another level of threat and portended significant instability. As early as spring 1955, Fall noted this, writing, "French intelligence and press reports show that in many cases, the Viet-Minh did not remove its most important personnel" from South Vietnam, as mandated in the Geneva Accords in 1954. Instead, the Viet Minh "shipped out its inexperienced levies for political indoctrination and military training in the north, while the hardcore of *chu-luc* (army regulars) and *can-bo* (party cadre) have remained behind with their weapons stored in well-hidden caches."[77] This insight was powerful. It provided a warning to readers who understood how a subversive vanguard operated and how it had effectively undermined French Union Forces and the State of Vietnam prior to large-scale military operations in late 1953 and early 1954.

Fall's statement—which appeared in his article "Indochina Since Geneva" and was published in the March 1955 issue of *Pacific Affairs*—was probably written as early as January, well before the crisis with the Cao Dai and Hoa Hao erupted. Based on this evidence, Fall was among the earliest analysts to see an emerging communist infiltration underway in South Vietnam, and he was possibly the first to recognize how the Viet Minh were recycling subversive practices they had used earlier during the First Indochina War. If Charles Lacheroy or Roger Trinquier had not been busy searching for FLN networks in Algeria, and if they had had the time to read Fall's article instead, they would have undeniably understood why there was a reason for continued alarm in Vietnam. Fall, for his part, was making an effort to point out why such alarm was well-founded. Ultimately, if anyone was the first to see and understand what formed the groundswell that eventually became the National Liberation Front (NLF) in 1959 and 1960, it was Bernard Fall.[78] There would be many differences between the Viet Minh and NLF, to be sure. Yet, new versions of subversive units within the NLF—that were based on and used Trinh Sat, Cong An, and Dich Van's tactics—would eventually begin chiseling away against the Republic of Vietnam's moorings and other authority. Moreover, they would do so much the same way as their predecessors did against French forces and Vietnamese competitors in the DRV during the First Indochina War.

There was yet another consequential political current that lay under the surface between March and May 1955.[79] According to the Pentagon Papers, US Representative to Vietnam General Lawton Collins "felt that Premier Diem was unequal to the task [of presidential leadership] and urged that he be removed," and Collins "flew back to Washington in late April to press his case personally with the Secretary of State" John Foster Dulles.[80] Based on Collins' advice, Dulles "reluctantly agreed to the replacing of Premier Diem and he cabled the embassy in Saigon to find an alternative."[81] Edward Lansdale played a pivotal role in preventing this by encouraging Diem's successful counterattack against the Cao Dai, Hoa Hao, and Binh Xuyen. The result was pivotal: "Washington responded with alacrity to Diem's success, superficial though it was ... Saigon was told to forget Secretary Dulles' order to drop Diem. The embassy then burned the April 27 message. Thereafter Mr. Diem had full American backing, and moved with more confidence."[82]

Diem's victory was critical because, in addition to reassuring American leaders' faith in him at this juncture in 1955, it would result in the United States consolidating its support of Diem's administration until it lost its faith in him again for good in 1963.[83] Fall undoubtedly did not know the specifics of US policy that almost entirely pulled support from Diem in the early stages leading to the Battle of Saigon. However, he remained convinced that Diem's success was not the result of authentic allegiance among most of the South Vietnamese population. Eventually, he would later recognize that the restoration of US faith in Diem—provided by Lansdale but also through the US Catholic lobby and other connections—had been fundamental to Diem's survival in 1955.[84] In subsequent years, Fall would often revisit this period in the early Republic of Vietnam's history and, most notably, he would do so again in mid-1963. By that time, much had changed in the Republic of Vietnam and for the United States. After that point in mid-1963, so much more would change for both.[85]

In 1955, therefore, Diem's victory over the Cao Dai, Hoa Hao, and Binh Xuyen in the Battle of Saigon was exceedingly significant. According to Fall, "the armed remnants of the sects are still able to carry on extensive harassing operations, just as the Viet-Minh did after the French reoccupied South Vietnam in force in 1945, but it is unlikely that they will ever regain even part of their erstwhile political strength."[86] Yet, well before the outbreak of open war between these groups and the Republic of Vietnam, a much different US position had been encapsulated by Collins, who was sent to Vietnam in November 1954, representing President Eisenhower as ambassador. Collins wrote that US policy had "to bring every possible aid to the government of Ngo Dinh Diem and to his government only," making, Fall argued, "it is clear that as before and no matter what his obvious shortcomings, that Diem was 'America's man.'"[87] Moreover, as a way of accepting shortcomings in "America's man and his government," Collins acknowledged: "We may disagree with their broad philosophy of how they ought to run the country and that sort of thing; but in order to have some kind of stable government we pretty nearly have to support this regime, whose political philosophy we may not agree with, we support it for other reasons."[88] While Collins possessed this view before traveling to Vietnam in November, his perspective on Diem began to drastically change soon after arrival. It is important to describe in greater detail why his views changed, because it closely reflects concerns Fall had expressed in late 1954, before Diem's victory at the May 1955 Battle of Saigon re-established American support which had almost entirely dried up.

Within weeks of arriving, Collins' negative impressions of Diem evolved quickly. The animosity between the Cao Dai and Hoa Hao was one factor, but Collins also knew of difficulties between Nguyen Van Hinh and Diem before Hinh—after attempting a coup to replace Diem—had emigrated to Paris in late November, where he continued to agitate against Diem in safety. Another key development changing Collins' view on Diem was Diem's refusal to assign Dr. Phan Huy Quat as either the Minister of Defense or the Minister of Interior. After the presidency, these were the two most important positions in the Republic of Vietnam, and Collins considered "each a full-time job."[89] Instead of filling these positions with competent leaders like Phan Huy Quat, Diem held on to the power of both offices, while also remaining the chief executive.

By 13 December 1955, Collins had seen enough. He cabled Dulles to inform him that he believed Diem was unwilling and unable to unite the numerous and diverse factions in South Vietnam. In writing to Dulles, Collins explained: "I said we should begin to consider alternatives to Diem, even including the possible return of Bao Dai or the gradual withdrawal of support from Vietnam."[90] Dulles, according to Collins, "objected strongly" but suggested that Collins "consider alternatives if the situation had not improved by mid-January."[91] Collins provided a step-by-step recounting of these developments in his 1979 autobiography. Undoubtedly, his account was aided by the clarity of hindsight, and perhaps also understandably propelled by a drive to ensure his positive legacy. Yet, Collins had nothing to hide. It is important to point out that his reflections almost directly align with contemporary accounts of his recommendations to Dulles as recorded in the Pentagon Papers. After three more months of evaluation and working with Diem, Collins offered his concluding assessment on Diem in April:

> I had wrestled with this decision for weeks, torn by our commitment to Diem—along with my personal agreement with his objectives—and my growing conviction that despite Diem's many admirable attributes, he did not have the leadership and political know-how to unite the divisive forces of Vietnam in the face of the unity and tough efficiency of the communists under Ho Chi Minh. That was the judgment I transmitted, with deep regret, to Secretary Dulles on April 7, 1955.[92]

Collins followed this assessment with more details about Diem. He pointed out positives, such as his incorruptibility and patriotism, but also noted how these joined with a stubborn narrowness that also worked against him. Collins added:

> his lack of political sense, his inability to compromise, and his distrust of anyone who disagreed with him, convinced me he would never make the grade as the leader of his country. I felt Diem was not indispensable, and that it would be better to support a change in the presidency before we became wedded to him.[93]

The Battle of Saigon, as both Fall and Collins quickly realized, was the event that not so much wedded but welded the United States to the Republic of Vietnam. As a key figure in these developments, Collins articulated a hard-nosed realist view that Fall could only assemble at the time through inference and previous research. However, Collins' position almost directly mirrored concerns Fall pointed out in his 1955 article on the Cao Dai and Hoa Hao which described Diem's inabilities to unite South Vietnam. In an excerpt from a long and detailed estimate of the situation from May 1955, after Diem's victory, Collins explained his concluding view:

> His [Diem's] present success may even make it harder for us to persuade Diem to take competent men into the government, to decentralize authority to his ministers, and to establish sound procedures for the implementation of reform programs. I am still convinced that Diem does not have the knack of handling men nor the executive capacity truly to unify the country and establish an effec-

tive government. If this should become evident, we should either withdraw from Vietnam, before our money will be wasted, or we should take such steps as can be legitimately taken to secure an effective new premier.[94]

Time would prove that Collins was correct, and Diem would become even more intractable and exclusive in holding on to power. In a key respect, Collins would have been greatly forewarned of the problems he encountered in South Vietnam had he read Bernard Fall's August 1954 assessment of Diem prior to his arrival in Vietnam. Instead of showing up with preconceptions that Diem was "America's Man," Collins might have seen the intensely divisive environment set before Diem as an insurmountable task. In his article "Representative Government in the State of Viet-Nam, 1949–54," published in *Far Eastern Survey*, Fall provided a succinct view:

> The recent replacement of the short-lived Buu-Loc regime by a new Vietnamese government under the anti-French, American-backed Catholic leader, Ngo Dinh Diem, in the hope that he may be able to inspire a wider Vietnamese popular participation, cannot be considered an adequate solution so long as the basic problem of eventually creating a solid basis for constitutional government has not been solved to the satisfaction of a sizable section of the Vietnamese population.[95]

The problem, therefore, was that it would take an exceptionally competent, openminded, humble, and popular leader to confront and fix the problems facing the new government of the Republic of Vietnam. As his August 1954 article indicated, Fall realized that Ngo Dinh Diem was not that leader.

In another *Far Eastern Survey* article published in September 1954, "The Cease-Fire in Indochina—An Appraisal," Fall established that Diem's exclusive approach to power was already counterproductive and did not address the serious problems facing his government. In describing how Diem formed his administration, Fall noted:

> Some observers remarked the predominance of the Ngo and Tran families in the cabinet and called it a "family affair"; others pointed to the unique fact that the government had no South Vietnamese members, despite the fact that it must depend more and more upon southern support for any sort of popular basis.[96]

Including the "Tran family" in his statement was accurate because Fall referenced Tran Van Chuong, the father of Tran Le Xuan (who was later known as Madame Nhu). At the time Fall described this "family affair," Tran Le Xuan was married to Ngo Dinh Diem's brother, Ngo Dinh Nhu. Providing even more evidence to support claims that his government was "a family affair," Diem appointed Tran Van Chuong to serve as the Republic of Vietnam's

Ambassador to the United States, and he held this position from 1954 to 1963.[97] In pointing this out at the time of the appointment in September 1954, Fall demonstrated how the Ngo-Tran family worked to entrench itself among American supporters. Calling attention to these problems also served as even more evidence that Fall was the earliest of analysts to see issues that seriously metastasized in coming years.

* * *

Once the dust and cordite from the Battle of Saigon had settled, Diem set about consolidating his family's grip over the Republic of Vietnam, now with greater assurance that the United States was also increasingly committed. To be sure, Diem did attempt to make progress in several areas, particularly in stimulating South Vietnam's economy. He called for measures to restrict overseas Chinese influence in numerous business sectors, to streamline and modernize agricultural practices, and he pushed for the development of light industries.[98] Diem's demands for agrarian reform in October 1956 were particularly important because he sought to raise critical rice yields, which had been subject to steep variations in production for over a decade. During the Japanese occupation, available rice had also been subject to severe expropriation with the requisitioning of the food staple for delivery to Japan. War with France also had not helped farmers in growing and delivering their crops. Before World War II, rice-producing regions in South Vietnam exported over 1.5 million tons of rice annually, but after the First Indochina War, this amount dropped to approximately 300,000 tons annually by 1951.[99] Increased rice production and potentially reinvigorating a more robust export market, would therefore provide both an essential commodity for local use and one that South Vietnam could exploit for economic growth. In another development, affecting refugees from the north who streamed south after the 1954 Geneva Settlement, the Cai San resettlement center was a positive indicator in an economic and social environment where many serious challenges existed.[100]

According to mandates established in Geneva, in December 1955 the Cai San project claimed land formerly controlled by the Hoa Hao and distributed it to North Vietnamese refugees who left the DRV-controlled region. New tenants would rent eight to ten acres with a progressive rent rate over four years, beginning with no rent the first calendar year.[101] Fall would eventually visit the Cai San project in August 1957, commenting, "No appraisal of the Vietnamese refugee problem would be complete without at least a passing reference to the vast Cai San project ... it is certainly one of the most ambitious undertakings of its kind anywhere."[102] However, he added:

upon questioning by the writer, the engineers there stated that they doubted that any other area in Free Viet-Nam could meet all the conditions found at Cai San ... it is useful per se, in view of its production capabilities and because it absorbs 90,000 refugees, but it cannot be considered as a pilot project for other major resettlement centers.[103]

Undoubtedly, a Potemkin-village effect further undermined the Cai San project's future as a model worth replicating in other areas of South Vietnam. The Cai San project revealed an unfavorable cost-benefit ratio in Diem's vision for Vietnam's future. Moreover, as Fall acknowledged, other constraints on the project's practical implementation elsewhere also limited its extension as a model. The settlement center's support may have been welcome by North Vietnamese moving south, but Hoa Hao adherents, whose land was taken away, became refugees to accommodate other refugees. Cai San was thus symptomatic of broader potential for the Republic of Vietnam, but it was founded in a way that disadvantaged others to benefit refugees who were predominantly Catholic. In all, the Cai San model was beset by challenges that were difficult to overcome. Fall wanted the Republic of Vietnam to succeed, yet he soon found fault with Diem's repressive measures, promulgated in breach of the 1954 Geneva Accords. Fall pointed out that these violations included subverting agreements in matters ranging from "graves registration" (Article 23 of the Accords) to Diem's expulsion of the Joint Commission of the International Control Commission, an organization created to resolve disputes between the north and south (Article 33).[104] These violations were further accentuated when Diem, according to Fall, "unilaterally abrogated the promise to hold reunification elections in 1956."[105]

Ngo Dinh Diem's refusal to hold elections not only contributed to later war between Vietnamese in the north and south, but the decision also alienated influential non-Vietnamese leaders who might have potentially helped resolve the war once it began. In particular, Zhou Enlai, the Chinese delegate to the Geneva Accords and the People's Republic of China Premier, felt frustration with Diem's failure to hold elections, and it was a resentment that would stick with him for years. According to historian Qiang Zhai:

> Zhou Enlai was very upset with this development ... later in August 1971, when James Reston of *The New York Times* asked Zhou if he was willing to mediate in the conflict between the United States and North Vietnam, the Chinese premier answered: "We don't want to be a mediator in any way. We were very badly taken in during the first Geneva Conference.[106]

Zhou Enlai's distrust of the Republic of Vietnam was one thing, but China's lingering unease with American leaders had not yet been overcome through reconciliation between China and the United States either. Additionally, it is possible that political disagreements with the North Vietnamese were an additional deterrent for China from stepping in for any potential negotiations. Zhou Enlai's reticence had a basis in a core problem: the refusal on the parts of the United States and Republic of Vietnam to decide Vietnam's future through a vote, which they believed would put Ho Chi Minh in command of a reunified Vietnam at some point in 1956 or 1957.

Fall was, therefore, not alone in voicing concerns over Diem's repudiation of elections. Nor was he alone in criticizing what he viewed as an increasingly harsh implementation of vigorous domestic policies. Abrogating key articles in the Geneva Accords was a problem, but so was losing the South Vietnamese popular support Diem needed at a critical point in time. In addition to Fall, C.J. Sulzberger of the *New York Times* and Saville R. Davis, the chief editor of the *Christian Science Monitor*, were even more prominent critics who argued that Diem's autocracy was counterproductive. In January 1956, Davis quoted a Diem opposition leader who claimed:

> The most serious mistake of President Diem is to crack down so hard on those nationalist groups which are not Communist, and which are frustrated by his dictatorship. His strategy is pushing them over into the other camp. If we continue with a tight dictatorship like this, the word will get around the country that things under Diem are not much better than things under the French, and then Ho Chi Minh and his fifth column will have another real wave of popular discontent to exploit.[107]

Amry Vandenbosch and Richard Butwell seconded this view in 1957, commenting:

> The achievements of the Diem regime in consolidating itself resulted from totalitarian tactics not much different from those used by the Viet Minh in the north. Diem's very successes seemed to underscore his primary weakness—his was an authoritarian, not a popular government ... President Diem may be digging his own political grave with his policy of opposition to nationwide elections.[108]

As these comments suggested, there was no shortage of critics of Diem's increasingly autocratic methods early after the founding of the Republic. Fall was certainly among the earliest of them, but unfortunately they had zero influence in getting Diem to change. Moreover, they had zero influence in getting anyone else with influence on Diem to heed their complaints.

Other misguided decisions further narrowed Diem's options for achieving legitimacy. Fall showed that Diem's policies, especially the 11 January 1956 decree, Ordinance 6, layered additional problems onto an underlying economic malaise.[109] Ordinance 6 stipulated "by decision of the President of the Republic upon proposal by the Minister of the Interior, may be sent to concentration camps ... all persons considered dangerous to national defense or collective security."[110] This undoubtedly set off a series of alarms for Fall. Such authoritarianism was worsened by the pretense that the Republic of Vietnam was somehow still a democracy worthy of massive American financial support. Rather than preventing dissent, Ordinance 6 inevitably created more of it. And as bad as it was, the damage created by Ordinance 6 was exacerbated by Diem's June 1956 decision to abolish elected village chiefs and councils and replace them with government appointees.[111]

According to Fall, the decision to remove village chiefs was the South Vietnamese government's "most fateful decision, made in defiance of one of the most hallowed Vietnamese traditions, according to which the power of the central authorities stops at the bamboo hedge of the village." He added, "In doing this, Diem outdid anything that either the North Vietnamese Communist regime or the French colonial administration ever did."[112] This self-inflicted calamity opened the door to Viet Minh infiltration. It sparked the growth, implementation, and network connectivity that enabled parallel hierarchies to form into shadow communist administrations across rural Vietnam. Fall was perhaps one of the first to see how Diem's momentous decision in June 1956 initiated a wave of dissent, but others eventually saw it, too. In discussing this topic, John McAlister and Paul Mus concluded that "the struggle over who is to govern in the villages of Viet Nam has been one of the most tragic examples of political violence since the end of World War II."[113] After Diem's removal of the village chiefs, recovering political legitimacy among many rural Vietnamese villagers in the south would be difficult, if not impossible in many places.

In 1956, therefore, Fall had serious reasons for concern. Only three years earlier, he had documented how Viet Minh assassinations of locally elected village leaders increased Viet Minh control over rural areas. The fact that the Viet Minh felt no compunction over murdering leaders whom villagers supported in 1953 demonstrated the Viet Minh's commitment to gaining control, even at the cost of angering villagers. In 1956, it was the South Vietnamese government who antagonized local villagers by getting rid of their leaders, thus doing half of the Viet Minh's work for them. Why would the Viet Minh not repeat an assassination campaign in 1956, especially since the local population would likely welcome it? Antagonizing villagers was unwise.

Replacing their leaders with appointed Republic of Vietnam officials would prove to be disastrous. In only a couple of years, by 1958, "the South Vietnamese were losing something like three (government appointed) village chiefs a day."[114] By 1960 and 1961, he reported, "The Communists were killing eleven village officials a day."[115]

These assassinations subverted the Republic of Vietnam's control but, more consequentially, did so in a manner that was not obvious as a military operation. In the government's eyes, "appointed village chiefs were not considered a military target. They were not considered part of our calculations with regard to what makes a war."[116] In other words, changes in local governance—embodied in the decision to remove village chiefs and replace them—were not military considerations, so their assassinations were not regarded as an act of war. Instead, their assassinations were regarded as a type of banditry. Yet, these assassinations indicated control at the local level more than officials in Saigon likely understood because of the crucial political function of village chiefs. In Fall's summary assessment:

> In South Viet-Nam, elected village chiefs were replaced by centrally appointed individuals who, in many cases, were not even native to the village and who, as insecurity grew, preferred to live in the nearby district town. This broke all normal feedback between the 80 per cent of the population which lives in village units of about 2000 people, and the South Vietnamese government. Once the traditional and homegrown village administrative structure had been destroyed by the South Vietnamese regime, the North Vietnamese and their sympathizers had found the chink in South Viet-Nam's armor. In a well-organized terror campaign involving massive assassination and kidnapping of local officials, they began to dismantle the South Vietnamese local administration and began to replace it gradually with their own men.[117]

This kind of infiltration, below the surface of more observable phenomena, created a serious undertow that flowed in the Vietnamese Communists' favor. In deciding to remove elected village officials, the Republic of Vietnam's leaders did much of this work for communist cadres, whose only remaining task centered on assassinating despised and vulnerable government officials.

Paul Mus, a fellow scholar of rural Vietnamese politics and culture, shared Fall's disbelief regarding the Republic of Vietnam's policy on the matter.[118] The government's removal of potential allies against the Viet Minh, who were locals elected by their communities, was incomprehensible. As a result, neither Mus nor Fall were surprised when local villagers displayed neither anger nor frustration in response to government appointees being assassinated. After having their elected officials removed, villagers' grievances against the government were difficult, if not impossible, to resolve. Diem had effectively shot himself in the foot, and now all the Viet Minh had to do was watch and further exploit the villagers' grievances. Undoubtedly, Viet Minh leaders saw Diem's June 1956 decision as a gift.

Communist leaders from South Vietnam, such as Le Duan, who was taking on an ever more critical role in the Democratic Republic of Vietnam Politburo, almost certainly understood the opportunity provided by Diem's decisions. The removal of village elders likely even improved Le Duan, Le Duc Tho, and other "South First" leaders' political leverage in the DRV because of the opportunities provided by Ordinance 6 and other decisions of the Diem administration. By 1959, according to Lien-Hang T. Nguyen, Le Duan:

> began to draft a more militant resolution [that would become Resolution 15], one that would bind the Party to supporting the armed conflict in the South ... it was a gamble that Le Duan and Le Duc Tho were ready to take not only because they had dedicated their careers up to that point to the southern revolution but also because the promotion of war below the seventeenth parallel was the key to their eventual seizure of power within the Politburo.[119]

Fall was also aware of these communist leaders' strategic vision, at least as it related to prioritizing revolution in the South: "Finally on September 5, 1960, at the Hanoi party congress, Le Duan, the Lao-Dong's party secretary and a former southern guerrilla leader himself, took official cognizance in his report of the 'southern People's revolutionary struggle' and advocated the creation of a 'broad national united front against the U.S.–Diem clique.'"[120] As a step in the comprehensive struggle for competitive control over the Vietnamese people in the south, the formation of the National Liberation Front was one critical half of the equation. The Republic of Vietnam's unwise decisions formed the other half. Ordinance 6 and the removal of village leaders contributed to conditions for the NLF's Resolution 15, and with this the Republic of Vietnam was in the process of losing as much as the Vietnamese Communists were in the process of winning.

In terms of potential open war between north and south, Fall knew that the Republic of Vietnam's forces were not prepared to confront the Viet Minh's military in a conventional conflict. The Viet Minh, after all, had not only demolished French Union Forces through numerous battles in late 1953 and 1954, it had recently destroyed most of France's best troops in the *Groupement Mobile 100*. Fall regarded this regimental combat team-sized group as "one of the best and heaviest units of its type."[121] The Viet Minh's ability to destroy it through intermittent fighting that continued after the Geneva Accords left no doubt about their sophisticated planning and capability to deliver considerable firepower.[122] Writing in 1956, Fall further described the DRV's status as a well-organized and determined adversary:

> The type of war the DRV has chosen to fight thus far is largely invulnerable to airpower, even if armed with "unconventional" weapons. Communist subversion from within, infantry divisions progressing single-file on jungle paths, and peasant-guerrillas striking suddenly and disappearing just as suddenly in the maze of teeming villages, can be fought successfully only at a price which the West might be unwilling to pay for what is, after all, but a secondary theater in the worldwide "Cold War."[123]

In a concluding thought, he added, "even optimistic Vietnamese military circles view their military mission as a 'holding' mission until Western forces arrive to the rescue. Western forces, under such circumstances, would have to be primarily American forces, faced with a tactically far more precarious situation than in 1954."[124] France's recent experiences, to be sure, provided no formulas for anything other than defeat. Yet, despite the DRV's strong organization and commitment, it also had problems. And, in a demonstration of academic objectivity, Fall pointed out failures in the DRV with as much alacrity as he pointed out problems in the Republic of Vietnam.

* * *

More than any other subject, issues related to land in North Vietnam formed internal challenges that divided and threatened Lao Dong authority. According to Benedict J. Tria Kerkvliet, "From the outset, collectivization exposed tensions between what Vietnam's national leaders wanted and what a large proportion of villagers in the Red River delta preferred."[125] Fall had written about problems stemming from land reform in 1953, but, after subsequent land-related initiatives in 1955, he returned to the subject with even more critical analysis in a January 1957 article for *Far Eastern Survey* called "Crisis in North Viet-Nam."[126] Even though he had respected the Viet Minh's drive for independence in prior years, he despised zealous ideology and implementation of policies that needlessly inflicted harm on civilians. He recognized that land reform contributed to mass mobilization against the French at a pivotal point in 1953. However, harsh reforms also created problems, including "The indiscriminate lumping together of practically all land-owning groups down to the middle-class farmers into the category of 'exploiters' [which] brought about a dangerous condition in which the regime risked alienating more farmers than it could afford to in time of war."[127]

The bigger problem was that the Viet Minh did not release their grip over farmers with the end of the First Indochina War. If anything, villagers faced even greater persecution as a series of farmers' revolts in Nghe An Province indicated in November 1956.[128] Also writing in an article in the Washington, DC *Sunday Star*, Fall noted, "A land reform program, designed to take away all land from 'capitalist landlords' was pushed through ruthlessly, until even the small farmers, driven to the wall by Communist cadres, rebelled against the government."[129] His broader purpose was to point out how "at the very same time as the city of Budapest rose against the Russians in November 1956, at the other end of the world Vietnamese farmers of Nghe An Province rose against their own brand of Communist oppressors—and suffered the same fate as the Hungarians, with the difference that their heroic stand never received any of the publicity which surrounded the plight of the Hungarians." The resistance of the North Vietnamese farmers "had been so fierce that, for a time at least, Ho Chi Minh's government had to stop its peasant purges. More than 50,000 innocently imprisoned farmers were released from jails and labor gangs ... and for a brief time some literary magazines critical of the regime were allowed to appear. But not for long."[130]

The revolts in Nghe An were especially surprising because "the territory was considered so thoroughly permeated by Communist ideas that the DRV had begun to establish Soviet-type collective farms in 1954. That open revolt against the regime should nevertheless take place in this area suggests the depth of popular resentment against the Hanoi government."[131] This was a unique and challenging view to present accurately and objectively in a US publication at the time. It was one thing to access information in South Vietnam or see the Diem administration's repression in action, but learning of dissent in the north was rare in the late 1950s. Fall illuminated this, writing, "Another type of unrest which may prove even more dangerous to the regime has arisen in the meantime—that of a press which refuses to be gagged." The press that was critical of the Lao Dong Party to which Fall referenced was *Nhan Van*, a periodical published by the Minh Duch publishing house.[132] In one article from *Nhan Van*, which Fall cited, an anonymous journalist described "an actual news item of people driven to suicide by continual persecutions," and a second example included "a story of Tran Dan, a member of the People's Army whose life was described in such a way to make the reader see that a talented and clear life is being trampled upon."[133] These kinds of remarks about the DRV's soul-crushing policies were not unique to *Nhan Van*. Citing another Hanoi-based paper, Fall called his readers' attention to an individual, Xuan Truong, who was the editor for the Communist party paper, *Nhan Dan*.[134] One of Truong's articles, "Opposing Slander and Distortion," was published in December 1956, stating:

> a group of pupils of the Chu An High School in Hanoi who, after reading the [*Nhan Van*] articles said: "Inside us we sensed a feeling of doubt and hatred for the *Lao-Dong* Party and the regime which had trampled on a man and stifled literature … We felt that everything we had previously thought about the troops and Communist fighters were wrong."[135]

Unsurprisingly, the Lao Dong leadership's action against *Nhan Dan* came swiftly, and "its next issue, though ready for publication, was never printed."[136] Fall's "Crisis in North Viet-Nam" was significant because, while it indicated his access to North Vietnamese sources, it also demonstrated levels of widespread local dissent against the DRV. To be sure, collectivization eventually succeeded. As Benedict Kerkvliet explained, "according to official figures, the intense campaign to collectivize agriculture in northern Vietnam was extremely successful."[137] Yet, "official" figures were unlikely to describe government programs as anything other than a success. Kerkvliet was also careful to note that coercion was one of several reasons why villagers in the north complied. However, other factors, including trust and a belief that things would get better, also added to villagers' compliance with the DRV's push for collectivization. All the same, revolts in Nghe An Province were a powerful reminder that people in North Vietnam were often as angry with Lao Dong leaders and their policies as Southerners were with Ngo Dinh Diem. Pushing unwelcomed policies on an unwilling populace did not go well anywhere in Vietnam.

Undeniably, Fall had far greater access to information regarding developments in the south than in North Vietnam. The DRV's poor decisions and severe repression of its people were deplorable, but so were developments below the 17th parallel. After Diem canceled elections meant to unify the country in 1956, the Cold War reinforced the continued division of Vietnam, a separation which would not be easily reversed. Fall pointed out the tragedy in this, explaining "that North Vietnam, with its raw materials and industrial base, and South Vietnam, with its food surplus, need each other like Siamese twins attached by vital organs. Attempts to separate them may end in the death of one—or both."[138] This was an ominous prediction to make in the revised 1956 edition of *The Viet-Minh Regime*. It was becoming clear to Fall that much was changing which required firsthand study to understand, so he returned to Southeast Asia in 1957. Determined to see how the country had

THE WIND AND THE WATER

changed, he turned to examine the financial and advisory assistance the United States offered to the Republic of Vietnam.

II—"Will South Viet-Nam Be Next?": May 1958

William Holland, the director of the Institute of Pacific Relations, approached Bernard Fall in early 1957 to request that Fall complete a study on developments in Vietnam.[139] Fall had co-published *The Viet-Minh Regime* with the Institute, and he had characterized that study as focusing on "special problems of administration" up to 1956.[140] His return to Vietnam in 1957 enabled him to explore how these and other problems had evolved, and his research resulted in three significant pieces of scholarship. The most extensive was Holland's requested study, *The International Position of South Vietnam, 1954–1958*, a comprehensive 240-page analysis divided into five volumes.[141] A second ninety-page analysis, entitled *Spring Is Triumphant, but Winter Will Surely Return: Three Years of Viet-Minh Rule in North Vietnam, 1954–1958*, was published in mimeograph form by the United States Information Agency.[142] The third, shortest, and most consequential of Fall's writings was his five-page article "Will South Viet-Nam Be Next?" published in *The Nation* in May 1958. As part of his overall effort, he presented his findings on South Vietnamese foreign policy since 1954 to the thirteenth International Conference of Pacific Relations in Lahore, Pakistan between 5 and 14 February 1958.[143] He would also present his findings at the April 1958 Association for Asian Studies conference held in New York City.[144]

Fall did not have the personal means to finance his return to Vietnam, and the Institute of Pacific Relations could not provide funds because of its limited resources. However, Fall "had developed a close relationship with the Vietnamese Embassy and with Ambassador Tran Van Chuong," and so "in February 1957 Bernard wrote to the ambassador" and asked for his support.[145] In his letter, Fall explained:

> During the course of our [past] conversations you had the kindness to express to me the interest of your government in all research having the objective and destined to make better known to the world the problems and successes of the new Viet-Nam. The Viet-Nam that I know thus, ravaged by war, is no longer the Viet-Nam of today. It would be an injustice to the work accomplished by Viet-Nam since 1954 if I permitted myself to write about it based on second-hand reports and my own recollections during the time of war.[146]

Fall added that he was "an independent researcher whose reputation is established in France as well as in the United States" and, "as for my sentiments towards free Viet-Nam, you, Excellence, know that better than anyone."[147]

In early 1957, Fall's support for the Republic of Vietnam was sincere, and he had made his anti-communist views known through numerous publications since first traveling to Vietnam in 1953. The criticism and concerns Fall expressed in 1956 regarding Diem's governance were because he wanted to see the Republic of Vietnam govern its population more effectively and generate greater legitimacy in the eyes of its citizens. Besides, his criticisms of governance in both North and South Vietnam were a matter of public record because the Institute of Pacific Relations had co-published *The Viet Minh Regime in 1954* and reissued it in 1956. Whether or not Ambassador Tran Van Chuong or anyone else had read his work was another question.

With Ambassador Chuong's backing, Fall received assistance from the South Vietnamese government, which enabled him to spend three months conducting on-site research during the summer of 1957. Ironically, these same individuals who provided him this vital support would subsequently resent Fall's interpretation of facts in his article "Will South Viet-Nam Be Next?"[148] Notably, Chuong was a key connection who was literally wedded to key decision-makers in South Vietnam because Chuong was Ngo Dinh Diem's in-law.[149] During his trip in 1957 and through his connection with Ambassador Chuong, Fall met with and personally thanked Ngo Dinh Nhu for the South Vietnamese government's support for his research. Fall also acknowledged Nhu, along with Chuong and others, in the author's preface to his study produced for the Institute of Pacific Relations. Among the many he recognized, Fall added:

> I would like to take this opportunity to acknowledge my deep thanks to the following persons: H.E. [author's note: His Excellency] Tran Van Chuong, without whose personal interest the trip could not have been made and H.E. Ngo Dinh Nhu, who was kind enough to explain to me some of his thoughts on Vietnamese foreign policy.[150]

In addition to other prominent Vietnamese and French individuals, Fall thanked an American advisory organization working in the country. He added, "Last, but not least, I wish to thank Dr. Wesley R. Fishel, of the Michigan State University Group, for his and his staff's kind hospitality and for his generosity in providing me with an extensive set of administrative studies completed by his staff."[151] This research assistance was especially significant because it enabled Fall to describe US and South Vietnamese policies with accuracy since he was using official government sources. In addition to Fishel and other Americans, Fall also interacted with French officials ranging from Marcel Ehret, inspector general of the *Terres Rouges* rubber plantation, Pierre-Bernard Lafont of the *École Français d'Extrême Orient*, and René de Berval, director and editor of the influential journal *France-Asie*.[152]

There was only one problem with all the support Vietnamese and US personnel provided: they assumed Fall would report solely on information he was given, and they underestimated his ability to dig into problems he identified. Instead, Fall meticulously scrutinized data, confirmed or denied it through field study, and framed his assessments with historical context. In addition to employing his technical and analytical skills, he approached his research with the tenacity of an investigative reporter, the realism of a war veteran, and the perspicacity of a well-seasoned intelligence analyst. These qualities enabled him to report on vital developments at work with regard to US and Republic of Vietnam trade policies and the financial assistance that was the critical lifeblood for South Vietnam. The reality of US-delivered assistance was not, unfortunately, as ideal as it was portrayed.

On 11 April 1957, Ambassador Tran Van Chuong delivered an address titled, "The Role to be Played by American Enterprise in the Strengthening of the Free World" to the Far East–American Council of Commerce and Industry at India House, the Indian Ambassador's residence in Washington, DC.[153] In the address, Chuong appealed to his audience with a core message:

> You, American leaders and businessmen, can stop Communism, help your country, your human brothers and yourselves by merely realizing that you can make greater profits in producing in Asia, for instance, more bicycles for Asians than in producing in the United States a second car or a second TV set for each American family.[154]

Chuong's descriptions of US–Republic of Vietnam relations generally filled much of the speech, but his central point focused on building US support for industry development in his country. Therefore, increasing Vietnamese-led and controlled production capability was likely the primary substantive issue Fall and Chuong agreed upon as necessary for the Republic's growth and stability. Fall's primary reason for soliciting Chuong's support, as he explained to him in a letter, was to chart developments in the country through direct observation. Given that Chuong agreed, it was apparent they shared the view that taking stock of the current development-assistance environment would be beneficial. In addition to gauging current production efforts, learning how assistance might be improved and locating specific investment opportunities which US business leaders might find appealing were reasons motivating Chuong to support Fall's research. However, the plans for commercial production that Chuong described in his address to the Far East–American Council were creating, as Fall found when he began his research in 1957, unintended outcomes that were more counterproductive than expected. Instead of benefiting from an import program of the kind already underway, Vietnam was receiving US-based products it did not need, which was undermining Vietnamese-produced output. Instead of getting better, Vietnamese industries were weakening, and the primary reason for this was excessive importation of American commercial goods. Making profits in Asia by producing "more bicycles," as Chuong suggested, was not what South Vietnam needed. Other issues unrelated to business were also growing.

Domestic security was significantly worse than Fall expected, and the outcry over Ordinance 6 and the replacement of village leaders had contributed to a worsening environment. He was, therefore, increasingly alarmed after reading accounts reporting an ever-growing number of attacks on government officials. In one case, he noted, "On September 14, 1957, the district chief of My Tho and his whole family were stopped in broad daylight on a main highway and killed in cold blood."[155] Fall described this and several other cases of violence, writing:

> These are items culled from hundreds of similar incidents reported over the past six months in the South Vietnamese press. They clearly express a trend which has been developing over the past year and one which is hidden from the casual foreign observer behind a screen of immaculate refugee camps, model nurseries and schools, and store displays in Saigon overflowing with Western consumer goods, from nylon shirts to tape-recorders, hi-fi sets and shiny automobiles.[156]

Model schools and stereo systems might distract others from underlying problems. However, Fall had seen this type of assassination campaign before, so he was able to obtain greater significance from news articles that reported on acts of violence across South Vietnam. Fall did not come to South Vietnam in 1957 hoping to find such problems. However, they were simply too consequential to ignore, in his view, and there were far too many incidents of political violence for them to be considered random. He began to recognize a pattern to the attacks, and, far from being isolated acts of banditry, they would become more clearly understood with time and as historians gathered concrete evidence of concerted planning. Writing in 2003, David Elliott confirmed that Vietnamese communists' targeting of government officials formed a larger strategic goal bent on undermining the Republic of Vietnam's administrative power. According to Elliott: "What seemed at the time to have been a nearly complete pacification of My Tho Province by 1958 looks in retrospect to have been the point at which the essential groundwork for a revolutionary revival was laid."[157]

It is critical to emphasize the divergence between the this perception that the government had achieved "complete pacification" and the reality that, instead, 1958 was a "point at which the essential groundwork for revolutionary revival was laid." This specific "point" was certainly not clear to Fall at the time, but he could see that there was a problem. Explaining this discrepancy would become one of his primary tasks in 1957 and 1958. He already had a sense of the reality gap between government pronouncements and events on the ground, but in "Will South Viet-Nam Be Next?" his primary concern was the vulnerability of South Vietnam's economy. As he had realized, economic dilemmas, security threats, and Ngo Dinh Diem's authoritarian measures acted in concert to make matters worse because it tangled all the problems together, so that causes and effects were difficult to distinguish. As events added other troubles, or as time changed the configuration of previous issues, it would become almost impossible to create practical solutions in what was such an integrated and complex environment. Fall's numerous publications in 1958, therefore, were an attempt to untangle the relationships between these factors, but he would address economic issues first in his article for *The Nation*.

With its establishment on 30 June 1955, the International Cooperation Administration (ICA), the precursor to USAID, coordinated US economic aid to the Republic of Vietnam.[158] Fall explained how US assistance through the ICA worked:

> About 80 per cent [of aid] consists of merchandise exported directly to South Vietnam. This merchandise, sold through normal commercial channels, "generates local currency." This currency, minus normal commercial profits, is deposited in a "Counterpart Fund." Out of which the receiver government covers the expenses for various projects approved jointly by the local United States Overseas Operations Mission (USOM) and the government.[159]

Counterpart funds were used as a mechanism to deliver foreign aid, in other words, through the selling of free US-supplied material goods, such as tractors, commodities, or other items which were purchased in the recipient country. As a result of this system of counterpart funding, the proceeds from these sales transactions could be converted into accessible reserves, as Fall pointed out, in the domestic currency. Counterpart funding was not new and had already been successfully employed in Europe after World War II, so it is helpful to describe the thinking behind implementing this system in Vietnam.

The system was initially developed to benefit American companies and countries receiving aid mutually. Through counterpart funding, the US government subsidized American manufacturing by purchasing large amounts of commodities and goods that were then shipped to Vietnam by shipping companies who also benefitted from having their invoices paid by the US government. Vietnamese companies and retailers then marketed these goods, which Vietnamese consumers purchased with their own—and, no doubt, hard-earned—currency. What was critical about this system was that the proceeds from these purchases entered the Vietnamese economy without direct import purchasing but, instead, through transactions among Vietnamese companies, retailers, and consumers. In effect, Vietnamese consumers purchased US imports that the US government had already purchased from US suppliers. At that point, the commodities and goods delivered from the United States—as if through transfiguration—helped the South Vietnamese government generate economic activity in Vietnam. Another key to counterpart funding was that there was no "cost" factor for Vietnamese businesses selling US-supplied goods. After completing transactions with consumers, sellers deducted a previously agreed percentage of net profit for their business. They then deposited the remaining proceeds into the counterpart funds for use by the South Vietnamese government. One definite downside was the enormous potential for unscrupulous activity, by which skimming proceeds and backchannel payoffs easily ended up in other places than the ICA planners in Washington, DC had envisioned.

The counterpart funding system was initially developed for the Marshall Plan and was effectively used in post-World War II Europe. The basic idea was that consumers in countries who joined the European Recovery Act would be able to purchase American goods while supporting local merchants. Consumers would benefit, but so especially would the government of the countries taking part, which accessed the funds in their counterpart accounts to rebuild their war-torn economies. This type of aid delivery, therefore, had a historical legacy, and even the phrase "counterpart funds" originated in the Marshall Plan days. When the United States provided assistance to Europe in the form of diesel engines, as an example, those engines were sold to European citizens, who paid in local currencies, such as French francs, Italian lire, or British pounds. American companies who sold the engines received payment in dollars directly from the US government through specific Marshall Plan funds appropriated by Congress.

Writing in 1964, Senate Foreign Relations Committee Chief of Staff Carl Marcy explained this system, noting: "The foreign currencies, which were not convertible to dollars, were deposited in the countries where they were received and became known as 'counterpart funds.'"[160] The system was specifically designed, as Marcy noted, to help reduce potential inflation.[161] In many respects, the United States created an indirect economy to resuscitate democracies in war-ravaged Europe. With the great success achieved by the Marshall Plan, it is perhaps unsurprising that the US government would seek to use this assistance approach elsewhere.

In addition to counterpart funding, the United States provided materiel and financial aid directly to the Vietnamese military. Fall described this assistance in 1958:

> More than $200 million out of an approximate $250 million a year of U.S. aid goes into the support and maintenance of the ten-division Vietnamese army and other security forces. The remaining 20 percent of the total aid is given [to] Vietnam in 'hard currency' granted for outright purchases in the United States and other countries.[162]

This "hard currency" could be distributed to purchase goods, resulting in additional proceeds deposited into counterpart funds. Regarding all RVN expenditures during the 1957 fiscal year, American aid "supported the whole cost of the Vietnamese armed forces, nearly 80 per cent of all other government expenditures, and almost 90 percent of all imports."[163] In other words, the United States, as it had during the First Indochina War, subsidized almost everything in South Vietnam.

Along with counterpart funding and direct US assistance, other financial inflows contributed to build the Republic of Vietnam. The Michigan State University advisory program, for example, provided training for administrators and the police that the ICA underwrote. As Fall publicly acknowledged in 1958, he relied on the program's director, Dr. Wesley Fishel, for research material, but the RVN also relied on the Michigan State University program.[164] As yet another source funded by the US government, the ICA underwrote the United States Military Advisory Assistance Group (MAAG), which was responsible for training the South Vietnamese military's Civil Guard.[165] Despite all this aid, remarkably, Fall determined, "the hard fact is that Vietnam's economy today is steadily deteriorating."[166] After describing US assistance programs for South Vietnam, he explained why these failures were occurring, and how they negatively affected Ngo Dinh Diem's ability to govern.

While a good deal of US aid was genuinely helpful, other supplies and consumer goods were not needed. Perishable products, such as milk, were relentlessly delivered to Vietnam, even if adequate cold-storage facilities did not exist and even when transportation was unavailable to distribute goods beyond the vicinity of ports. Fall observed that problems of these sorts, leading to a deteriorating economy, generally occurred "because the market is saturated with consumer goods of all kinds which the Vietnamese are no longer able to buy. Merchandise is left to rot on the docks by importers who haven't the money to pay for it."[167] A black-market cog undeniably placed another obstacle into the assistance machine that ICA leaders were attempting to establish. Another serious problem stood out to Fall as emblematic of cultural incomprehension:

> Last summer, the ICA (International Cooperation Agency) imported U.S. agricultural surpluses of milk, wheat, flour, and corn. Like all Asians, the Vietnamese are not fond of milk, prefer rice to wheat and detest corn. Yet, at the same time, American charitable agencies imported vast quantities of these same surpluses for free distribution to the refugees, who immediately resold them for whatever the market would bear.[168]

Vietnamese consumers were not being sent what they needed. They were being sent what the ICA believed they should want. Fall's explanation for South Vietnam's economic problems could be divided into three components. First, in 1958, the country was unable to generate enough surplus rice for export. In 1957, it exported only 195,000 tons, and in 1956 it had barely exported any rice.[169] This was a fundamental problem because rice was South Vietnam's most critical commodity, and insufficient export revenue of rice resulted in increased Vietnamese reliance on US support. Second, "South Vietnam has none of the basic requisites of an industrial nation: coal, iron, power, skilled labor, and markets."[170] Aside from importing natural resources—which North Vietnam had in abundance—US assistance failed to provide sufficient industrial resources, and it also failed to provide the resources needed to increase rice production. Instead of prioritizing equipment to aid irrigation, for example, or sending new plows to replace old or broken ones, the United States prioritized consumer goods South Vietnamese did not require or even have the ability to use.

The third problem was broader and institutional in nature. The ICA was an administration within and controlled by the US State Department, but the ICA was not designed to coordinate a long-term development program like its larger and more comprehensive predecessor, the Economic Cooperation

Administration (ECA), which was established in April 1948 to administer the Marshall Plan. In 1955, moreover, the ICA was new. It did not possess the type of institutional knowledge about Vietnam necessary to generate a satisfactory assistance program. Even though resources like the Human Relations Area Files (HRAF) existed, it is possible that the US State Department did not tap into HRAF in the same way the US Department of Defense did through its subcontracted partner at American University.

Europe, in addition, was more vital to the United States in 1948 than the Republic of Vietnam was after 1954. Ironically, the United States provided France with an amount of funds to fight the First Indochina War that came close to exceeding American support for the rehabilitation of metropolitan France through the Marshall Plan between 1948 and 1952.[171] The counterpart funding and import–export system that succeeded through the European Recovery Program's Marshall Plan, therefore, had several critical differences with the problematic ICA. When US President Harry S. Truman signed the Economic Cooperation Act on 3 April 1948 to establish the ECA, leaders in European counterpart countries established a coordinating agency to manage the implementation of aid in their respective countries. The broader coordinating agency for this was initially called the Organization for European Economic Cooperation, and this name was later changed to the Organization for Economic Cooperation and Development.[172] With its various unwieldy names, this agency was critical in ensuring that aid was assigned based on a specific recipient country's needs and implemented effectively. According to Jacob Kaplan, a US government official specializing in US foreign assistance between 1943 and 1954, the ECA and its European counterparts created a mutual review system that adjusted US assistance within each country according to the recipient's needs.[173] When disagreements emerged, US administrators acceded to recipient countries' requests and did not force US demands upon them or threaten to cut off funds if they did not comply with US wishes. In the case of the Marshall Plan, Kaplan explained thus:

> While we wanted them to free up their economies, to reestablish free markets, to remove many controls, every country was allowed to do so at its own pace. In fact, of course, they wanted the same thing as we did, but they wanted it in ways that were both politically acceptable and consistent with their judgment about economic possibility, as they did.[174]

Kaplan added in his retrospective interview:

> The ECA had missions in every one of the countries, headed by a political figure of a stature that made it possible to discuss policies with governments at the

highest levels. However, we never threatened to cut off aid if they didn't do as we urged. There was a lack of arrogance, I believe, in our behavior. People talk about American hegemony at that time. That is valid in the sense that we were the dominant economic power. But we didn't behave like the classic hegemon. We were interested in creating stable societies in western Europe, not in selling an ideology.[175]

When juxtaposed with this system of establishing well-staffed agencies in each country receiving assistance, the United States Operations Mission to Vietnam (USOM) paled in comparison.[176] According to Robert Scigliano, who was affiliated with Michigan State University:

> Like the Vietnamese government, USOM has lacked any real economic plan, and at the same time it has not encouraged planless capital formation on a scale large enough to achieve substantial results. Indeed, the mission *did not have a professional economist on its staff from 1954 through 1961* [emphasis not in original], though it has in the past intermittently drawn up the services of trained economists attached to the Michigan State University government-contract group in Saigon.[177]

By 1961, events in South Vietnam had changed for the worse. Time, more than money, is a critical resource that cannot be recovered, so by 1961 resuscitating the South Vietnamese economy to stabilize an already challenging political environment was beyond difficult. Rather than a program of mutual responsibility and shared design and control, US assistance to the Republic of Vietnam was handled in a one-sided fashion. The ECA was a separate government agency, even though it reported to the US Department of Commerce and the US State Department.[178] The ICA, in contrast, was not a separate agency but operated under the State Department. Fall did not address all these precise points of failure in his article for *The Nation*. Instead, he was interested primarily in the effects of what he perceived to be a poorly planned and implemented assistance program, and why it was counterproductive. In 1958, he certainly did not know how the South Vietnamese economy would evolve, but a robust, independent, mutual, and well-organized administration like the ECA would have been preferable to the ICA. Regrettably, the ECA had been disbanded and replaced by the Mutual Security Agency in 1951, which preceded the formation of the ICA in 1955. In one of many counterfactual hypotheticals that the numerous wars in Vietnam elicit, if the ECA had never been disbanded and had instead been mutually reconfigured with Vietnamese input to develop aid for the country, Bernard Fall might have found a more vital economy in 1957 instead of the weakening one that he did. However, this would have also depended on a stable and inclusive South Vietnamese government, and that, as Fall knew well, was also a missing part of the equation.[179]

Fall's analysis of South Vietnam's economy and US aid in 1957–8 revealed, therefore, that US foreign assistance programs were a failure. Unfortunately, insufficient aid—and the wrong type of aid—had been delivered to the Republic of Vietnam since its founding in 1955. The United States provided what it thought Vietnam needed instead of focusing on improving, for example, rice production, the most important economic sector in South Vietnam. Notably, these were not entirely new problems Fall discovered in 1957 and then wrote about in 1958. In late 1956, while he worked as an Associate for the Systems Analysis Corporation—a research organization supporting US policy development—Fall edited a 124-page study for the US Senate Foreign Relations Committee called: "Military Assistance Program of the United States: Two Studies and a Report by a Special Civilian–Military Review Panel."[180] It is likely that Fall already had a good idea of the economic turbulence in South Vietnam, and he undertook his 1957 research trip to confirm what was happening in greater detail. What he found was regrettably disappointing but also profoundly consequential for the country's future.

Fall was not the only one interested in the relationships between security, economics, and governance. William Lederer and Eugene Burdick also explored these subjects in their 1958 book *The Ugly American*, pointing out that "We spend billions on the wrong aid projects while overlooking the almost costless and far more helpful ones."[181] The even bigger problem was that the US State Department could not, or would not, adapt its policies to improve its assistance programs. The ICA's dismantling and its replacement by USAID in 1961 indicated that US foreign assistance had long required an overhaul. Waiting until 1961 to fix such problems, however, and wasting over three years in the process, meant the South Vietnamese economy continued to fester. Worse, its economic problems became further entangled with increasing security threats posed by Vietnamese Communists and the growth of contentious politics stewing in Saigon. The US State Department, however, did not even budge on issues related to its assistance policies until Fall's article was on the verge of reaching *The Nation*'s readership in May 1958. After Fall publicly presented his views in New York in April and then published them in *The Nation* in May, the US State Department would act on Fall's article with speed. However, it did not take action to improve its assistance programs to South Vietnam; instead, the US State Department's leadership moved to take action against Fall.

In "Will South Viet-Nam Be Next?" Fall described the more significant social implications of deficiencies related to agricultural production: "rice planting is more than an economic activity: It is a way of life, a whole *Weltanschauung* in itself ... And this rural population which represents ninety per cent of all the people in the area ... is the object of the various 'hot' and 'cold' wars fought today throughout southern Asia."[182] In a revealing line, he also adapted French statesman Georges Clemenceau's quip, "A drop of oil is worth a drop of blood," and changed it to "'A grain of rice is worth a drop of blood,'" adding, "and perhaps Red China and North Vietnam are willing to pay the price."[183] Rice production was undoubtedly an economic engine, but, as he noted, it functioned as the social center around which rural Vietnamese communal life and governance revolved.[184] The United States' failure to provide correct assistance in the later 1950s, the kind that might have resuscitated rice production to pre-World War II levels, was among the most serious of dilemmas facing Vietnam. While hypothetical, it is worth considering the potential diplomatic leverage that higher rice yields and an overall stronger agricultural sector might have provided in negotiations between North and South Vietnam, let alone in improving the South Vietnamese economy. Unfortunately, insufficient rice production was only made more noticeable with the importation of non-essential goods.

Fall explained:

> The process of "generating local currency" as a source of funds for various projects puts both the Vietnamese and American governments at the mercy of what the public is willing to spend its money on ... Compared to $800,000 allocated for tractors and industrial vehicles, $7 million were spent on private cars and $5.5 million on tires and tubes for them. This agricultural country imported $2 million worth of fertilizer, but imported $6.5 million worth of cigarettes and tobacco.[185]

With American support:

> the industries launched were exactly those it needed least: a watch-assembly plant which, after one year of operation, recently closed its doors; a scooter assembly plant, a sewing-machine assembly shop, etc. ... On January 30, 1958, Vietnam had a stock of typewriters and calculators to cover its needs for eight years. Neither of these items can be successfully stocked in the tropics for so long a time.[186]

Most bluntly, Fall claimed at the Association of Asian Studies conference in New York City in April 1958 that "South Vietnam needed a scooter assembly plant like it needed a hole in the head."[187]

THE WIND AND THE WATER

The United States, not surprisingly, looked to past successes for guiding its assistance policies, and the Marshall Plan, with its mechanisms that included counterpart funding and commercial import programs, had worked for Europe. In contrast, according to Fall, "they are definitely not a solution for an underdeveloped area such as Vietnam. On the contrary, they channel whatever little capital is available into goods that at best are useless, and are sometimes actually injurious, to a weak economy." Moreover, aid delivery was sloppy and counterproductive. In a letter to his spouse, Dorothy, he called attention to other problems:

> Yesterday I did the Saigon docks from wharf No. 14, under a blazing sun, and it was damn well worth it. My feelings as a U.S. taxpayer are more raw. Nearly all the merchandise I saw bore the two clasped hands on a U.S. shield of the Mutual Security Program (official figures have U.S. aid at 90% of total trade!!!) and the stuff so imported is in incredible condition thanks to local stupidity and mismanagement. I personally saw six brand new Ford trucks (1957–2 ton) crushed because somebody had unloaded on top of them a cargo of cement bags.[188]

Fall was appalled by this kind of waste, and it added obvious frustration and fuel for his article. He concluded "Will South Viet-Nam Be Next?" by writing:

> These are the hard facts, and they are not very pretty. But they must be revealed now, while it is not yet too late to change course. The change cannot be undertaken in Saigon, but must be carried out in Washington in the face of probable opposition by the well-established "Vietnamese lobby."[189]

He added:

> Perhaps the time has come to reappraise the impact of the vast commercial import programs to the economies of underdeveloped areas—in Latin America and the Middle East, as well as in Asia. It may be that despite their temporary usefulness as pump-primers, these programs, which have become the favored American form of foreign aid, in the long run create more problems than they solve.[190]

His suggestion that the United States should completely revamp its aid programs for much of the world was unfortunately ignored until 1961. Fall knew that US assistance was critical to these countries. However, it had to be carefully and intelligently planned in terms of cultural awareness and delivered far more effectively to be of help. He emphatically explained why this mattered in other areas, such as security, writing:

> the United States can't afford to take a "devil take the hindmost" attitude in this corner of Southeast Asia. For in this case the hindmost are the landless farmer

and the jobless worker. And they made up the Communist shock troops who defeated the French at Dien Bien Phu.[191]

This was a warning based on historical fact. Vietnamese Communists had already proved they were sophisticated and capable enough to defeat the French Empire in Indochina, even with all the materiel assistance provided to France by the United States. Communism, as it was developed and implemented in Vietnam, required more than blunt military instruments to defeat it. In contrast, well-designed aid that focused on generating massive increases in rice yields would improve the South Vietnamese economy and social environment in ways that were far more effective than military assistance. Fall appeared to know that cultural awareness and well-founded political analysis complemented an administration's ability to adapt and innovate. Together, these provided a more effective framework to combat the type of political-oriented warfare conducted by Vietnamese Communists. He believed that identifying and diagnosing problems, wherever they existed, was the first correct step toward making improvements. US assistance in 1957 and 1958 needed this kind of attention, and it needed fixing. Not everyone else reading his work felt the same way.

III—"An Extremely Independent and Audacious Man"

The preview of his *Nation* article, which Fall provided at the Association for Asian Studies conference on 9 April 1958, along with the article itself, provoked a reaction he did not anticipate.[192] Both generated more interest in his research than anything he had published previously, but this interest was primarily negative. His compulsion to relate the facts as he saw them would exact a professional price, even though President John F. Kennedy would later make similar criticisms of US assistance programs in Southeast Asia, and he would disband the ICA and completely re-organize foreign assistance planning and delivery.[193] Three years after Fall's article, the Foreign Assistance Act of 1961 created USAID as a separate government agency, and this marked a return to the more successful model demonstrated by the European Cooperation Administration in 1948. By 1961, Kennedy's critiques of foreign assistance mistakes, therefore, echoed those Fall had made in 1958 at the Association for Asian Studies conference and in his article for *The Nation*. In an address to Congress on 22 March 1961, Kennedy explained the need for reorganization of US foreign assistance so that it was more efficient than programs administered by the ICA:

No objective supporter of foreign aid can be satisfied with the existing program—actually a multiplicity of programs. Bureaucratically fragmented, awkward and slow, its administration is diffused over a haphazard and irrational structure covering at least four departments and several other agencies. The program is based on a series of legislative measures and administrative procedures conceived at different times and for different purposes, many of them now obsolete, inconsistent and unduly rigid and thus unsuited for our present needs and purposes. Its weaknesses have begun to undermine confidence in our efforts both here and abroad.[194]

While Fall was developing his article and conference presentation, an important backstory was in motion, and it would soon change the course of subsequent events and affect his career path. In the months before his article appeared, Fall had pursued a unique opportunity to take a leave of absence from Howard University to teach at the Royal Institute of Administration in Phnom Penh, Cambodia. During and soon after returning from his second research trip in 1957, he had established contact with two officials in the ICA, the very organization whose policies for aid delivery in Southeast Asia he found so counterproductive.[195] The first official he contacted was Alvin Roseman, whom Fall met in Cambodia in 1957 and who was the US Operations Mission (USOM) director in Phnom Penh, and the second official was named Thomas L. Eliot.[196] In his initial meetings with these officials, and in a subsequent meeting with another ICA official, Thomas Corcoran, Fall brought up numerous problems he saw with US assistance to Vietnam. He did so, as described in a memorandum between Corcoran and Fall, in the hope that the US and South Vietnam might improve their coordination and build up the South Vietnamese economy.[197]

Fall contacted these ICA officials because he had learned about the opportunity to teach at the Royal Institute from Wesley Fishel, who had provided much-needed research support at an early stage during Fall's 1957 research trip. As a result of Fishel's encouragement, Fall pursued this opportunity. In a letter to Thomas Eliot from November 1957, Fall explained, "Dr. Wesley Fishel of the MSUG in Saigon also expressed to me the hope that, should I be appointed to Phnom Penh, I could also teach a weekly course at the MSUG center in Saigon, by commuting. This is perfectly feasible and I would enjoy doing it."[198] This exchange between Fall and Eliot then initiated subsequent discussions, with the goal that Fall would receive a two-year appointment to the Royal Institute in Phnom Penh, scheduled to begin in July 1958.

The steps to gain the appointment began in November 1957, and Fall believed that teaching in Phnom Penh would be a positive experience in several ways. First, he would have the opportunity to apply knowledge gained through years of study with the intent of helping to improve US planned and coordinated assistance for Cambodia. Second, he could assist students at the Royal Institute in Phnom Penh in their preparation to support the Cambodian government develop and administer its policies more effectively. Third, living in Cambodia would deepen Fall's understanding of Indochina, giving him additional firsthand experience with the Royal Khmer government, along with a clear vantage of broader and dynamic political developments changing the region. In Fall's eyes, and among key ICA officials, his potential appointment was a win-win situation. Therefore, in late November 1957, the ICA submitted a proposal to the Cambodian government to gain their approval for Fall's appointment and his planned work supporting the Royal Institute. As Fall was a faculty member at Howard University, this appointment process would take time, and Fall wanted to make sure that he could return to Howard after his two-year appointment concluded in Cambodia. At the latest, he would need to know that the contract was confirmed by the spring of 1958 so that he could request a leave of absence from Howard administrators.

In late March 1958, the Cambodian government reached a decision. According to his application, located in US Foreign Assistance files held in the National Archives and Records Administration, the confirmation stated: "The Royal Khmer Government has advised USOM that it wishes to establish [a] chair of international relations [at the] Royal School of Administration and is definitely interested [in] Bernard Fall."[199] USOM subsequently notified Fall with the good news, and a formal application process within the US government's channels began. He applied for a USOM-mandated security clearance, submitted his application for federal employment, and completed other related bureaucratic steps over the next several months.[200] In addition to these administrative details, Fall refined the course curriculums he planned to teach at the Royal Institute. This provided insight into the training and "scope of service" he would provide the Cambodian government and its students at the school.

Other expected responsibilities he would incur included teaching courses in Public Administration, Comparative Government, International Relations, and a "Special Courses and Surveys" seminar, as requested by the Cambodian government. In addition, the Cambodian government requested that Fall help establish an "administrative documentation service for the use of all Cambodian Government Agencies."[201] In a memo simply called "Scope of

Service," this comprehensive set of tasks for an administrative documentation service included "finding factual information on problems of a political, economic, legislative or administrative nature."[202] Events were therefore in motion. As a positive sign, Fall's security clearance was granted on 4 April 1958, and notification that the Royal Khmer government formally approved his candidacy followed later on 25 April.[203]

The US State Department, because it controlled the ICA, had the final say in approving the contract. However, this decision was still pending as of late April while the application process was in its final stages. Months earlier, Fall had written to Dorothy, who was expecting their first child in September 1957, to express his outlook:

> Looks fascinating. Phnom Penh was lovely after the other places. At least it looks alive. Job would be for 1958–60 so that we finally have time to get the boy(!) growing before we leave and transplant him (her). I'm really enthused for the first time in 3 months. The next year will be a good one for all three of us. Yes, you're going on a trip next year, 95% certain—Cambodia ... Salary $12–14,000 plus house and trip for all of us. Two-year contract renewable.[204]

By later May 1958, however, Fall still had not received confirmation from USOM or ICA regarding his contract. Fall and other ICA officials did not know the reason for the delay. His security clearance had already been granted, his application with the Royal Cambodian government had been accepted in March and then formally confirmed in April. In a 24 April telegram, unspecified ICA officials discussed Fall's obligations to Howard University as a professor on leave:

> Fall now under pressure from his faculty head [at Howard University] to declare plans next academic year, needs affirmative word from USOM or ICA. Fall says he cannot afford [to] jeopardize his relationships [with] Howard University since he intends to return there on career basis. Advise priority.[205]

In the last week of April, numerous memorandums circulated among officials concerning administrative issues and other day-to-day arrangements for Fall's contract. A break in communication then occurred for most of May. Three weeks later, communication was reestablished on 25 May through a priority telegram from the "U.S. Department of State to the Ambassador Saigon and Phnom Penh." It read in full:

> Bernard Fall being considered for assignment under ICA contract to Royal School Administration as Professor Public Administration and International Relations. Fall has been consistent and vocal critic of U.S. policy, and in recent months has made public statements extremely critical U.S. aid program

Vietnam. Also has criticized vocally Diem and his Government to point where certain members Vietnamese Embassy and American Friends Vietnam are actively looking for means to offset his influence as one of self-styled experts on Vietnam in U.S. View these facts and fact Phnom Penh already has several French citizens both critical of and actively working against Diem government. Question whether Fall should be employed in above capacity by U.S. government at present time. Desire your comments. Reply priority. DULLES[206]

The next day, based on a memorandum he wrote on 26 May ICA official Thomas Eliot appeared unaware of Secretary of State John Foster Dulles' telegram to the Ambassadors in Vietnam and Cambodia. Eliot, demonstrating integrity on Fall's behalf, showed his support for Fall being employed in Phnom Penh by submitting additional documentation for Fall's contract that day:

> Efforts to obtain public administration advisors for Cambodia have not been generally successful. It is our good fortune to be able to obtain the service of Professor Fall, in response to the definite invitation to furnish a professor of American style public administration, as Advisor and Professor of Public Administration and International Relations at the Royal School of Administration, the principal institution education for future civil servants which has heretofore been exclusively a French institution. Dr. Fall, in addition to teaching and advising the school on the development of public administration curriculum and teaching materials and curriculum, will assist in establishing a political, economic, legislative and public administration documentation service in the school for the use of government agencies and the faculty and students of the school.[207]

In subsequent days, in late May and early June, a flurry of memorandums and telegrams followed Secretary of State Dulles' inquiry. Howard Elting, an official at the American Embassy in Vietnam, replied to Dulles' telegram, writing:

> Have not seen Fall's public criticisms [of] Diem regime and US aid program, but on the strength [of the] unpublished article by Fall ["Will South Viet-Nam Be Next?"] which came into possession USOM Saigon, strongly feel that Fall should not be employed under US sponsorship in Cambodia or elsewhere [in] Southeast Asia. Fall's views as set forth in proposed article parallel, but are more extreme than those of David Hotham in THE NEW REPUBLIC article November 25, 1957, and do not exhibit very high professional standards.[208]

Elting did not specify what constituted "very high professional standards" in his view. In any case, this was a questionable claim, especially in light of the value the Cambodian government and the ICA initially saw in Fall's potential contributions to their organizations. Elting's response to Dulles' inquiry, nonetheless, marked the beginning of the end of Fall's appointment. From that moment on, Fall would remain excluded from further contracts with the US government. Ironically, and in the following years, Fall would become a much sought-after lecturer in Department of Defense institutions, and the information he would provide to military personnel became increasingly relevant as the US military grappled with escalating problems in Vietnam.

In the days after Fall's contract was terminated, a State Department official for the Far Eastern Division named Ed Hough conducted a confidential telephone call with ICA official Tom Eliot. Hough informed Eliot that the State Department Division Chief for the Far East and Hough had "discussed Fall ... and agreed to let Fall 'fall.'"[209] Hough provided advice to Eliot regarding how to "handle [the] Fall approach and, as a personal friend, tell him [he] cooked his own goose by 'shooting off' or ... go further by saying Vietnamese complained to State and [that] certain countries in Southeast Asia will be closed to him."[210] Both approaches had downsides. First, criticizing Fall for "shooting off" was to argue with his facts because his assessments were based on firsthand reporting, which was often corroborated by government documents provided by Wesley Fishel and his staff. As demonstrated later in 1961, President Kennedy's willingness to scrap the ICA and form USAID as a separate agency outside of the State Department further indicated that Fall's critiques were justified. The second approach Hough recommended to Eliot was to tell Fall that Vietnamese leadership complained. The upshot of it all was that, a little over a week later, ICA staff informed Fall that his contract to teach in Cambodia had been dropped and his candidacy was "unacceptable due to Department of State concerns."[211]

Fall's reaction was professionally diplomatic but this, no doubt, masked personal frustration. Fall told Thomas Corcoran, the State Department official in charge of Laos affairs, that he "understood that Nguyen Phu Duc, First Secretary of the Vietnamese Embassy, attended the New York City meeting of the Association of Asian Studies in April 1958 and that he had persuaded the Ambassador of Vietnam to write to the State Department to protest Fall's employment in Cambodia."[212] Apparently, Fall did not know that a copy of his article for *The Nation* had come to the attention of Howard Elting at the American Embassy before its publication. Fall's public remarks were made in New York City on 9 April, so close to two months had elapsed before Elting or John Foster Dulles raised the matter on 25 May. According to Corcoran's account, "he (Fall) had made certain critical comments based on his honest opinion, but that he was not in fact anti-Vietnamese and that he clearly favored the Ngo Dinh Diem Government over the Communist regime. He intended, however, to tell the Cambodians why his contract had been dropped."[213]

Prior to this overall dispute, there was little indication that others perceived Fall's public statements as inappropriate. In a *Voice of America Vietnamese Service* report on the Asian Studies conference, not only was there no uproar over Fall's statements, but both the Asian Studies Association President, Hugh Borton of Haverford College, and Bernard Fall were selected to provide information about the conference proceedings.[214] Instead of questions concerning the content of his speech, Fall was asked about the growing interest in the study of politics and cultures of Southeast Asia among American university students. Innocuously, Fall replied that in his courses, the "Topics which we discuss are quite far reaching and wide ranging. They go from Chinese history to the economic problems of Southeast Asia."[215]

Another individual interviewed was Warren Huntsberger, a professor of International Economics at the University of Rochester, who was the chairman of the panel to which Fall had presented his work. Far from having anything critical to say concerning Fall, Huntsberger acknowledged that "I would say that the goals and aspirations of the peoples of Southeast Asia are not much different from the goals and aspirations that we have here in the United States."[216] It is possible that the substance of Fall's presentation was too detailed to cover in a brief interview, but it is difficult to believe that he would have been selected for the conference, along with the association's president and for a *Voice of America* broadcast, to represent a scholars view if he had been perceived as antagonistic.

Meanwhile, the State Department distributed internal memorandums describing Fall's New York speech in more detail. Selig Taubenblatt, a State Department official who heard Fall speak in April, was asked to provide his notes regarding Fall's actual remarks. Taubenblatt notes claimed that Fall mostly offered comments that were later published in his *Nation* article with only a few variations:

> He [Fall] stated that a candid appraisal would show that recent developments do not jibe with the "cook's tour" version purveyed to U.S. reporters. He blamed the U.S. for pumping in more consumer goods than the economy could absorb and criticized the mechanism of counterpart funds as inhibiting domestic industry ... The "high flying propaganda" about industrialization has resulted in a concentration on prestige items, such as a watch assembly plant and a scooter assembly plant which Vietnam needs "like a hole in the head." In addition, blame should also be assigned to the Vietnamese Government which has been exempt from criticism too long ... the situation is crucial and South Vietnam's

economic problems can be solved only by a basic policy change ... in the conclusion that followed, Fall stated that military costs in South Vietnam should be reduced and assistance for sound development projects expanded.[217]

Not long after the submission of Taubenblatt's memo in early June, Fredrick Bunting, the ICA director of the Far Eastern Affairs division in Washington, expressed apprehension about the decision to drop Fall's contract. Bunting wrote, "State feels that it would not be in the interest of the U.S. in the area to sponsor Fall ... I concur in this view, although I am not happy about it because of Fall's considerable knowledge and abilities."[218] The same day, Bunting met with Fall in Washington to explain why the ICA would no longer sponsor his contract. In a memorandum to Joseph Mendenhall and Thomas Corcoran, Bunting wrote, "Fall was aware that his talk in New York was indiscreet and that the Vietnamese Ambassador had called him to account for the talk on April 12." Bunting added:

> [Fall] feels aggrieved and I suspect he also feels that the U.S. has not a sufficient reason for refusing to conclude the contract. He showed me various publications of his, including one for USIA and another for ICA and the Department of Labor, saying that the U.S. had not hesitated to use his services in the past. Before he left my office, I made it clear that contract negotiations were at an end.[219]

After this meeting, Fall did not pursue the matter further. Several memorandums circulated among ICA staff to coordinate messages over how to handle the event, should it be brought up again later. One memorandum recorded a meeting between Eric Kocher, Officer of Southeast Asia Affairs; Pierre Landy, a counselor to the French Embassy; and Thomas Corcoran. According to the State Department memo:

> There was not a question of Dr. Fall's freedom to speak and write as he wished but some of his published charges against the U.S. aid program were inaccurate as well as highly emotional. It also seems that no useful purpose would be served by sending this man who had antagonized the friendly government of Viet-Nam to adjacent Cambodia in view of the delicate nature of Vietnamese-Cambodian relations. However, the Vietnamese government had made no request to us concerning Dr. Fall's proposed assignment to Phnom Penh. The Department had become aware of Dr. Fall's public comments on the aid program on its own.[220]

Pierre Landy added, in conclusion, that "Dr. Fall was an extremely independent and audacious man and that these characteristics were the cause of his recent difficulty."

7

AN UNASSAILABLE POSITION OF TOTAL WEAKNESS

Fall's article "South Viet-Nam's Internal Problems," published in September 1958, built upon his analysis from "Will South Viet-Nam Be Next?"[1] In "South Viet-Nam's Internal Problems," however, he examined economic issues and worsening security in the south in even greater detail. Instead of the United States sending the Vietnam unneeded commercial goods, Fall called for more significant US assistance in rice production, and he criticized the United States for excessive military expenditures, expensive transportation development, and other economic problems resulting from poor foreign aid coordination. Together, these two articles described how the International Cooperation Administration (ICA) and the Republic of Vietnam's (RVN) aid policies often worked at cross-purposes to weaken the RVN economy, which, in turn, contributed to growing discontent among communities in the South Vietnamese countryside. Other decisions by the Diem administration, such as removing villagers' elected leaders and replacing them with government officials and Ordinance 6, which permitted the incarceration of anyone deemed a threat to the state, also contributed to growing dissent among the rural population. The RVN's economic problems, therefore, often played into the hands of Vietnamese Communists, who diligently worked to exacerbate grievances whenever and wherever possible. Eventually, they would escalate and integrate physical attacks on installations and people in the south to widen existing divisions.

Increases in US-supplied military aid and an ever-growing assortment of civilian-oriented assistance programs, however, masked problems that were often agriculturally related and local, and this made them difficult for some US observers to notice. Instead of providing internal-oriented political and economic solutions to fix problems that would take time to address but whose solutions would eventually generate popular support, the attention of US policymakers was drawn to issues that might be readily addressed. Despite concerns regarding the RVN's political legitimacy, extensive US assistance for the Army of the Republic of Vietnam and a growing American advisory presence expanded the government's military strength. Coordinated through the US Military Advisory Assistance Group (MAAG), "the American aid program," George Herring noted, "accorded top priority to building the South Vietnamese Army," and "between 1955 and 1961, military assistance constituted 78 percent of the total American foreign aid program."[2] What was questionable was whether such rapidly growing military-related assistance could garner popular support for the RVN. In a US frame of reference, it was a matter of guns over butter. Instead, in Fall's view, this should have been approached from a Vietnamese frame of reference that prioritized rice over guns.

Increasing military programs to support Diem's government troubled Fall because in 1957 underlying political and economic weaknesses in the RVN were still insufficiently addressed. Large amounts of military aid sent to improve the Republic's arsenal obscured these problems of governance and provided the illusion that such robust capabilities would buy time and space to fix political issues. From 1955 onwards, the United States prioritized security over sound governance and, as George Herring noted, "(Secretary of State) Dulles had insisted from the outset that the development of a strong, modern army was an essential first step in promoting a stable government."[3]

Despite the United States' success in rebuilding Europe through the Marshall Plan, the section of American foreign policy referred to as "nation-building" would become a misnomer. In Vietnam and subsequent post-conflict regions, over the next seven decades the United States would adopt an approach that prioritized military-building that rarely, if ever, addressed more fundamental problems of governance. In the case of Vietnam, the disparity Herring pointed out between 78 percent of all aid consisting of military assistance versus 22 percent for economic and political development indicated a mismatch that would establish a precedent replicated in the future.[4] In "Will South Viet-Nam be Next?" and "South Viet-Nam's Internal Problems," Fall

AN UNASSAILABLE POSITION OF TOTAL WEAKNESS

pointed to deteriorating governance that more artillery or a more significant number of troops could not fix. Moreover, increasing materiel capacity would become counterproductive in the RVN's competition with Vietnamese communists for political legitimacy and popular support. In the face of its growing political instability, a paradox was in development: the RVN was militarily strong but politically weak. In Fall's description, the RVN was in "an unassailable position of total weakness."[5] This central problem mirrored France's and the Associated State of Vietnam's strategic and operational position that had disintegrated only a few years earlier. To be sure, Fall knew things were different in the RVN, given its stream of American support, but there were too many echoes of the First Indochina War—at least as Fall perceived the situation—to be ignored.

The first part of this chapter examines how Fall assessed insecurity in South Vietnam and how the Diem administration continued to address problems through inadequate and often counterproductive means. The second section of the chapter focuses on Fall's use and development of the term "revolutionary warfare." He acquired this term from French officers who developed a doctrine called *la guerre révolutionnaire* after France's defeat by the Viet Minh in May 1954. This group of officers relied upon lessons learned in conflicts ranging from Indochina to counterrevolution in Algeria after war broke out there in September 1954. As with his study of parallel hierarchies, Fall studied these officers' experiences from Indochina but kept them focused upon subsequent developments in South Vietnam and Laos. Moreover, he integrated their thoughts on warfare to knowledge he accumulated over the years as he continued to analyze growing instability in Southeast Asia. The lessons the French officers learned from the Viet Minh between 1946 and 1954 were, Fall quickly recognized, still relevant for assessing the security challenges emerging in South Vietnam and Laos in the late 1950s. In many cases, Vietnamese Communists relied upon and adapted similar tactical and political approaches to warfare in the south which the Viet Minh had used to dominate rural areas in the north before 1954.

The third and final section of the chapter describes how Fall believed an incipient Second Indochina War was emerging, bled over from the previous one. It was complicated by growing discord in South Vietnam which merged into the broader Cold War. Economic problems, government repression of dissent, anger with insufficient land reform, and other troubles contributed to a complex and contested political environment for the South Vietnamese government. Fall continued to describe how the United States worsened this situation through misguided foreign assistance and how the RVN's legitimacy continued to weaken. Instead of turning to Fall for his expertise, however, the United States government prevented him from teaching in Southeast Asia, so Fall focused on producing articles, such as "South Viet-Nam's Internal Problems." In it and others, he described how an increasingly capable Vietnamese Communist resistance movement in the south capitalized on mistakes and exacerbated the grievances of rural Vietnamese. It was these factors, as much as any, that positioned the RVN into a position of weakness. A growing US military presence and a militarily stronger RVN might not be defeated, but they could not correct what needed to be fixed.

I—"South Viet-Nam's Internal Problems"

After setbacks resulting from his article for *The Nation*, Fall's career rebounded. At Howard University, he was appointed the Ralph Bunche Chair in International Relations in late 1958, and he produced even more articles on developments in South Vietnam.[6] Fall met with Bunche on at least two occasions when Fall brought Howard University students to the United Nations' headquarters to meet with Bunche, who was then serving as undersecretary for Special Political Affairs and on the New York City Board of Education.[7] Fall had another connection with Bunche through his former teacher at SAIS, Amry Vandenbosch. Vandenbosch possibly knew Bunche as a colleague from the OSS or through their mutual participation at the 1945 San Francisco Conference. At the time of the conference, Bunche was in charge of the Department of Trusteeship of the UN while Vandenbosch served on the same department's subcommittee for territorial affairs.[8] Vandenbosch and Bunche shared, therefore, similar tasks at the founding of the United Nations, and both served in a mentorship role for Fall. Professionally and personally, Fall was therefore eager to perpetuate Bunche's legacy at Howard University and beyond.[9] Despite his promotion to the Ralph Bunche Chair in International Relations at Howard and a general and growing recognition of his expertise, Fall still had to contend with occasional backlash generated by his *Nation* article, "Will South Viet-Nam be Next?"

After receiving what he referred to as an "avalanche" of critical letters, including many from the US-based "American Friends of Viet-Nam" of which he was a member, Fall wrote *The Nation*'s editor to clarify points made in the article and to refute misinterpretations.[10] In the first of his letters, Fall explained: "I don't think my article was critical of [US] policies. It was critical of methods, which is fundamentally different."[11] His letter attempted to explain these differences in more detail, and he acknowledged how others appeared to interpret his criticism as anti-American. In another letter to the editor, Fall provided five detailed rebuttals to criticism from Christopher Emmet, a member of the Council on Foreign Relations. Fall explained:

> It is obvious that there are certain areas of disagreement between the United States and South Vietnam. I would say, and my observation is based upon solid evidence, that the feelings Vietnamese give vent to when it comes to American action in Viet-Nam is mostly DISAPPOINTMENT. The Vietnamese are not ungrateful. They know that U.S. aid and political support has saved them from disaster—but they're still disappointed, and that is their privilege. Perhaps a little more personal contact and human kindness would do the trick, who knows?[12]

In this remark and in the letter generally, Fall pointed out that US generosity was not at fault. Instead, the missing piece was greater Vietnamese participation in the early stages of assistance development and planning. On the job front, it is certain that Howard University administrators and department colleagues were aware that Fall's ICA contract had been canceled, since his anticipated leave of absence was now a moot point. In a show of support, Howard University authorities re-published "Will South Viet-Nam Be Next?" in the 8 November 1958 edition of *Howard Magazine*.[13] In a subsequent issue, *Howard Magazine*'s editors commented on Fall's forthright views in the article that had angered Dulles and others across town in Foggy Bottom: "Fall revealed many facts about the impending political situation in Vietnam which were generally unknown to Americans. The article brought about vigorous denials by Vietnamese officials, but what Dr. Fall wrote at that time has since been substantiated."[14]

Fall reflected further about the article's overall reception, writing:

> the roof literally caved in on me after that article. The editor of *The Nation* was swamped by an avalanche of letters originating from Diem's propaganda organizations in the United States, the gist of which was that (a) I was an unreconstructed French "colonialist"; (b) "hated" the Vietnamese; and (c) did not know what I was talking about.[15]

He added in hindsight, "The next reaction came from Saigon itself: apprised of the fact that neighboring Cambodia wanted to appoint me as professor to the Royal Institute of Administration, the Diem regime, via the U.S. Embassy in Saigon, had my appointment rescinded at the last moment."[16] His criticisms of US assistance programs, however, were later vindicated.

The Kennedy administration's decision to dismantle the ICA, and replace it with USAID through the US Foreign Assistance Act of 1961, indicated that Fall was paying a professional price only because he had been honest about what he saw and had published those findings. He had dialed accurately into the relationship between insecurity and the RVN's economic deterioration, but some had interpreted this as being critical of US policy. David Elliot later agreed with Fall's observations on the insecurity-economy nexus in the late 1950s before open war began a few years later, arguing that:

> the explosive situation existed even before the armed struggle began, and that the main cause of this was the actions of the Diem government ... it was the actions of the Diem government during the six years of peace as much as or more than the legacy of the Viet Minh that fueled the opposition to the Republic of Vietnam.[17]

It was this "situation that existed even before the armed struggle began," that had been a basis for Fall's article for *The Nation* as the Second Indochina War began to swell. In a September 1958 issue of the journal *Pacific Affairs*, Fall was emboldened enough to publish another article analyzing the RVN, entitled "South Viet-Nam's Internal Problems."[18] The article emphasized critical points from "Will South Viet-Nam Be Next?" but did so with far more evidence, at greater length, but also more temperately in several respects. To be sure, it had been frustrating to lose a confirmed contract to teach in Cambodia, but the professional safety net provided by Fall's position at Howard University braced his willingness to criticize policy. "South Viet-Nam's Internal Problems," based on numerous US government documents and RVN press reports, demonstrated how he relied upon these organizations for facts, which he used to argue for more effective governance as the RVN gained more substance as a sovereign state.[19] Fall may have moderated the delivery his criticisms after the repercussions from his *Nation* article, but the content of his critiques became more forceful as he accumulated evidence to support his assessments.

"South Viet-Nam's Internal Problems" revealed Fall's willingness to double down when he had extensive and undeniable evidence to support his claims. The article was also a turning point in his analysis because, after the dust from losing his teaching contract finally settled, he would unrelentingly call out problems as he saw them. In his new article, he first described the economic vacuum created in South Vietnam after French troops left.

> These French forces, spread throughout the countryside and relying far more on local goods and services than was usually imagined, constituted an economic

stabilization factor of no small importance. The expenditures of these troops, who ate much local food and used thousands of local clerks, mechanics, servants, or communication operators, contributed greatly to the wartime prosperity which, financially at least, was less artificial than is generally believed.[20]

One of the problems was the speed of their departure because "with the disappearance of this 'built-in' purchasing power ... the local market found itself facing a huge wave of imported products which had to be absorbed by a local economy suddenly deprived of any chance of increasing its resources."[21] After French consumption of locally produced goods, services, and support for local troops concluded in 1954, Fall noted that "The ICA must provide the necessary economic underpinning to the country to help it meet its force goals [for the Vietnamese military], with purely economic long-range undertakings necessarily assuming a role of secondary importance."[22] Fall's assessment actually turned out to be overly optimistic. Long-range development planning was not even of secondary importance because no US development plan even existed by the end of 1955. Dennis Duncanson, who served on British officer Robert Thompson's advisory mission to Vietnam from 1961 to 1965, and then as the Counsellor for Aid in the British Embassy in Saigon until 1966, noted this deficiency. According to Duncanson: "A twenty-man U.N. Technical Assistance Board team spent three months at the end of 1955 surveying almost every aspect of the South Vietnamese economy ... it produced no development plan."[23]

A lack of planning for a new RVN economy led to a host of problems. After France departed in 1954, the economic landscape and currency policies in Vietnam, which had previously undergirded trade and production, shifted in destabilizing ways that the excessive importation of US commercial goods made worse. Fall had developed a baseline of knowledge on this matter from 1953, and he had discussed fiscal and customs services and the DRV's economy in *The Viet-Minh Regime*.[24] Unlike the more difficult economic situation between the United States and the Republic of Vietnam after 1955, France had been able to bolster the Associated State of Vietnam because the Vietnamese currency (which was the piaster at the time) was pegged to the French franc. In difficult times, Fall explained, "the shock of all inflationary pressures eventually had to be absorbed by the French treasury at home," but this had been reinforced by US support between 1948 and 1954.[25]

As noted earlier, after World War II, economic turbulence in France's protectorates and colonies abroad was magnified because of economic malaise in metropolitan France. Even though the DRV introduced the *dong-viet* currency in 1946, and the Associated State of Vietnam introduced its currency in *dong* in 1953, these currencies were introduced while the Vietnamese piaster—which the French treasury backed with US support behind it—remained in place as a traded currency.[26] The piaster (formerly the *piastre de commerce* before 1952) was pegged to the French franc at rates that varied depending on zones of control between the DRV and the French-supported Associated State of Vietnam until 1954. Fall pointed out that territories under Franco-Nationalist control used Vietnamese piasters while the DRV standardized its use of the *dong-viet* in 1951, five years after it had been introduced.[27] In the broader economic picture, therefore, when French troops and administrators finally sailed away in 1954, a functioning economy and currency sailed with them.

National currency symbolized sovereignty, legitimacy, and the viability of state governance on a daily and transaction-by-transaction basis. In one of the most succinct descriptions of the importance of currency as a symbol in the DRV, David Marr emphasized that "For Vietnamese patriots, national independence and possession of a national currency went hand in hand."[28] French colonial administrators likely had a similar perspective on the symbolism of currency, but they organized regulation of local currency to maintain oversight of colonial possessions. In the French colonial context, in other words, currency control was instrumentalized and inextricably embedded within self-interested imperialist policies benefiting France. Controlling currency was a means of dominating Indochina, but these mechanisms extended to other places and persisted far beyond the Cold War era.

In Africa, for example, the *Colonies Françaises d'Afrique* (CFA) franc was created in December 1945 and was backed by the French franc with a fixed exchange rate with the US dollar after the Bretton Woods Agreement.[29] Even after independence was granted for former French colonies in the early 1960s, the *Communatué Financière d'Afrique* (Financial Community of Africa) directed the CFA franc in western and central Africa, which the French government guaranteed for decades.[30] According to Ndongo Samba Sylla, a researcher at the Rosa Luxemborg Foundation, the CFA franc has long been a colonial-era anachronism that was still in place through 2017. The use of the CFA franc, therefore, indicates a lack of complete sovereignty, and it reveals why at least thirteen countries in central and western Africa will remain under a state of French neocolonial control until the CFA franc is eliminated.[31]

Through most of the First Indochina War, France's economy had the United States-led Marshall Plan as a backstop for both metropolitan France

AN UNASSAILABLE POSITION OF TOTAL WEAKNESS

and France's overseas colonies. In a move that paralleled Africa's CFA Franc as early as 1945, and as David Marr noted, "France continued to crank out new currency to help finance its operations in Indochina."[32] Having a wealthy American ally, one who needed France to support the European Defense Community against a growing Soviet threat, also helped. France could therefore leverage their critical position to keep the colonial currency production presses in motion thanks to the financial backing provided by the United States through the European Recovery Act. In turn, the French-sponsored State of Vietnam functioned as a result, but through an economic system that was, even if indirectly, mainly under French control.

In terms of Fall's analysis related to economic policy in Vietnam, the demise of the system upheld by the State of Vietnam and France created problems. As Duncanson noted, the ICA and the Republic of Vietnam failed to develop adequate economic planning in the crucial year in which the RVN was founded in 1955. Timing mattered: a lost year where little if any development planning occurred led to the kinds of problems Fall found when he traveled to Vietnam in 1957 with the support of the RVN. Unsurprisingly, North Vietnam also had plenty of economic problems. According to Alec Holcombe, DRV party leaders early on "were beginning to see how the problem of production in particular and of the economy, in general, could imperil the DRV's war effort and the regime's viability."[33] Of foremost priority was achieving self-sufficiency in agricultural production, establishing industry, and collecting revenue to fund itself in ways that would not alienate its citizens or risk losing all of its material wealth to French-controlled zones. Funding in the DRV, just as in the RVN, carried over into governance and security in profound ways. The DRV's wartime leaders would be, as Truong Chinh explained, "collecting a little and spending a lot" through the entire First Indochina War and well into the Second Indochina War, as well.[34]

Another key difference, Fall explained to his readers, centered on France's reliance on Vietnamese-produced goods and services instead of imports the ICA later imposed on the South Vietnamese economy in and after 1955. Although imperialism was extractive in principle and practice, French support and encouragement of localized economic activity was a positive feature. But even with an emphasis upon purchasing locally produced products, there were downsides. In John McAlister's view, "economic growth in Viet Nam was so limited by the mercantilist policies of the colonial regime that its advantages could not be widely distributed without being dissipated altogether."[35] The system of counterpart funding was supposed to fix these kinds of problems.

289

When the United States implemented counterpart funding, Fall believed it did so because:

> The system has worked satisfactorily in the developed economies of Western Europe, whose relatively high per capita income permits the absorption of considerable amounts of consumer goods. In Vietnam, however, where the estimated per capita income lies in the vicinity of U.S. $130 per year ... economic development could not in the long run depend merely upon what the individual Vietnamese is willing to absorb for his personal consumption.[36]

In terms of military aid, it is not always clear in "South Viet-Nam's Internal Problems" why the United States' direct support for the Vietnamese military created different or more severe problems after 1955 than it did during the First Indochina War. The most straightforward reason Fall gave centered on the preponderance of aid for military-related expenditures, whereas previous assistance had been spread more evenly through the economy. He explained:

> It must be remembered, lest one assign blame where blame is not due, that in countries where the military aspect of the aid program is extremely heavy (as it is in South Vietnam and South Korea), the size of the over-all program often has little relation to the economic capabilities of the country. Thus far, the only practical way to find the necessary local currency for both the military and the economic projects has been the method of 'counterpart fund financing.'[37]

Problems Fall saw in 1957, to be sure, were partly structural. While French colonialism was undeniably deleterious and set Vietnam at a disadvantage, it was a system and framework that functioned. The United States, after 1955, imposed vast amounts of aid, but it did not provide an overall framework that worked as well.

Fall made it clear to readers of "South Viet-Nam's Internal Problems" that counterpart funding was not delivering results as expected. While readers might wonder why South Vietnamese troops paid by the United States were unable to prime the economy as French troops had previously, Fall pointed out that US aid was even more counterproductive than he had claimed in his previous article for *The Nation* in May. In September 1958, therefore, he assessed that:

> both sides (The U.S. and RVN) have tended to ignore the extremely serious and baffling economic decline from which South Viet-Nam now suffers in spite of generous aid from the United States which in the past four years has heaped close to a billion dollars-worth of funds and goods upon the twelve million inhabitants of this Missouri-sized country. Yet it is in the field of economics that the fate of a free Vietnam may well be decided in the long run.[38]

AN UNASSAILABLE POSITION OF TOTAL WEAKNESS

This would prove to be a prescient view. While Fall did not explain why the United States was so insistent on dumping unneeded consumer goods onto the Vietnamese economy, this was undoubtedly a contributing factor in undermining counterpart funding as a mechanism. Average Vietnamese citizens in the south simply did not need most of the goods the United States delivered, and they did not possess enough local currency to purchase the imports: successful use of counterpart funding relied on these two factors to function. Was this a case of blatant incomprehension of Vietnam's culture, greed subsidized by the US government, or a matter of good intentions that created unintended consequences? After all, the ICA's use of the Marshall Plan as a model, which relied on counterpart funding to help war-torn Europe, had been remarkably successful between 1948 and 1952. In the case of post-World War II Europe, and according to Benn Steil's authoritative assessment of the Marshall Plan's success, counterpart funding was "the single greatest tool we have for recovery."[39] Unfortunately, this system could not be easily transplanted from one place to another, and it could not fulfill the needs of a developing country without sufficient reorientation and planning. Intended as a type of "economy in a box" the United States could ship across the Pacific, it failed to deliver anything but problems.

Ultimately, the issue with counterpart funding in Vietnam was one of design as much as it was one of implementation. Fall specifically cited counterpart funding as the primary means of delivering foreign assistance to the South Vietnamese economy. However, he also regarded it as deluging South Vietnam with US products that caused economic problems. In one revealing quote, he pointed out that "the Federation of Vietnamese Industrialists (the local equivalent of the National Association of Manufacturers) stated that the 'invasion of the Vietnamese market by foreign products has almost paralyzed local production,' and asked that the amount of foreign imports be reduced by 80 percent." Fall, through his lengthy assessment in his *Pacific Affairs* article, conclusively viewed counterpart funding as a "crisis" that "created an even graver crisis in the Vietnamese economy itself."[40] To be sure, this was as far from Steil's assessment of successful counterpart funding in Europe as one could get.

Counterpart funding could not be applied in a generalized way, but this was what occurred when the United States introduced it as a funding mechanism for assistance in Vietnam. In a critical respect, counterpart funding was a complex system that depended on numerous sets of factors in both recipient and donor planning. As a subject, the failure of counterpart funding in

Vietnam deserves far more research and analysis, but a few crucial points may explain why this approach failed. According to Henry J. Bruton and Catherine B. Hill in "The Role of Counterpart Funds in Economic Development," successful use of counterpart funding depends almost entirely on detailed mutual planning and cooperation between recipients and donors throughout the period of assistance delivery. High-level organization existed, as discussed earlier in the case of the United States sending aid to European countries via the Marshall Plan, but this was simply lacking in the donor-recipient relationship between the United States and the Republic of Vietnam. One problem was the immediate need and fast pace of development after the formation of the RVN. The pressure to act quickly might have led the US State Department to dust off what had worked elsewhere and apply it to Vietnam. Also, as noted, the overall focus on military-related assistance proved to be a severe problem. In Bruton and Hill's assessment:

> Such an exploitation of counterpart funds requires, not only knowledge of the state of the economy, but flexibility and responsiveness on the part of the donor. Of equal importance is that their effective use requires a great deal of conversation with the relevant authorities in the developing countries—not leverage or conditionality—because it does not recognize that the institutions, traditions, practices, ideas peculiar to the country are highly relevant in determining what can be done, and what, indeed, should be done. Hence general principles cannot be the full story.[41]

Many conditions for success which Bruton and Hill pointed to were missing in the US–RVN relationship. Economic problems Fall wrote about in his articles in 1958, therefore, were not a matter of cultural incomprehension only, but a combination of cultural incomprehension as well as insufficient economic planning and lack of patience. As it pertains to this point, Bruton and Hill added:

> in a situation where broad general principles cannot be applied directly and universally, and where consideration must be given to the content of the specific economic, social, and political environment, then knowledge of that environment is crucial, and nationals, of course, know more about such matters than donors can ever know.[42]

In the US–RVN relationship, the time and give and take required to create a viable and constructive development plan anywhere near the level of the Marshall Plan did not exist. Instead, a fractured approach and an overreliance on military assistance was pursued, which proved to be counterproductive and contributed to a weakening economy that intersected with growing security concerns. Unlike perhaps any other analyst who was writing on the development of the South Vietnamese government and security problems before 1959, Fall was the only one to draw attention in any level of detail to problems associated with counterpart funding in US assistance to the Republic of Vietnam.[43] While future research may provide greater clarity on this subject, a signal contribution of his scholarship to this period in the US–RVN relationship centers on pointing out that it was not simply a matter of governance or communist threat, but that insufficient economic planning significantly contributed to the weakening state of the RVN.

Fall was also concerned with slowing rice and rubber production and exports after 1955 because they were Vietnam's most valuable commodities.[44] Rubber, which accounted for 62.5 percent of all exports in 1957, was a problem because, due to strikes calling for higher wages, France turned to Malayan and synthetic rubber as source material for its industries.[45] Prices for the commodity fell 35 percent, leading to deficits in the South Vietnamese economy, all of which American assistance had to address.

Fall did not rely on his reporting alone for this information. He cited the Vietnamese journal *Phong Thuong Mai Saigon* and fellow scholar Ellen Hammer for evidence. Using information these sources published, he pointed out how total deficits in 1956 and 1957 fell to $175 and $275 million respectively and how "in dealing with these deficits, South Vietnam has been entirely dependent on American aid."[46] Fall's search for a solution to these problems was also becoming more apparent to other specialists, and the subsequent reorganization of US assistance reflected this.[47] As noted earlier, his research and evidence were based on reports the US government had produced. However, the government failed to reassess their policy even when problems became apparent. Fall's pointing out these problems had only led to his marginalization. Even so, reports he cited included the United States Operations Mission (USOM) "activity reports" in Vietnam between 1954–6 and US Senate studies of assistance in 1957.[48] In other words, his articles in 1958 demonstrated not only government officials' inability to interpret and apply information that their own offices had generated, but also how they failed to incorporate better ways to address South Vietnam's problems.

Fall's solutions for correcting issues were threefold.[49] First, he recommended that overly ambitious projects be replaced by "more modest and concrete achievements." Second, far more effective use of military aid for the South Vietnamese Army was necessary. In 1958, he pointed out how "maintaining the Vietnamese National Army controls the magnitude of the budget ... [its] reduction to a lower level would free considerable funds for economic development while decreasing the demand for imported civilian goods."[50] This was a clear indication that he believed that prioritizing the "military aspect" was counterproductive. Last, he recommended that "A greater effort should be made to place good civil servants in field positions instead of keeping them in staff positions in Saigon, so as to provide the central government authorities with the necessary feedback to enable them to make sound decisions based upon real situations." In a closing point, Fall suggested that "less effort, on the other hand, go into prestige projects, such as the creation of lawns and miniature golf courses in the already beautiful city of Saigon."[51] As he would learn over the subsequent months and years, such recommendations were ignored.

A more considerable issue Fall could not have foreseen in 1958 was how dramatically US assistance focused on the Vietnamese army would grow over the next three years. In 1961, as George Herring noted, "Persuaded as Truman and Eisenhower before him that Vietnam was vital to America's global interests, Kennedy routinely approved an additional $42 million in aid to support an expansion of the South Vietnamese Army," and "the number of American advisors increased from 3,205 in December 1961 to over 9,000 by the end of 1962."[52] Such misaligned economic assistance was problematic, but sending more and more military aid further complicated governance in South Vietnam and delayed potential reforms. In Herring's view, "The Military Advisory Assistance Group's (MAAG) major concern was to develop an effective military response to the (communist) insurgency, and it felt that insistence upon 'democratic' reform would distract attention from the war and undercut Diem during a critical period."[53] In Fall's perspective, the exact reverse of this was what was required. Political reform and increased legitimacy mattered far more than increasing Diem's government's military capacity, and committing more US personnel and resources would create an untenable obligation. According to Fredrik Logevall, "What Kennedy perhaps did not understand ... was that even a relatively modest increase in the U.S. commitment to South Vietnam would make any future contraction of that commitment more difficult."[54] It was not impossible to choose another path at this point. As Logevall is careful to note, decisions that increased US commitment and escalated the advisory mission and active American air combat—as described in National Security Action Memorandum (NSAM) 111 issued in November 1961—did not mark a point of no return. It did, however, mark a point where turning course was "significantly more difficult."[55]

AN UNASSAILABLE POSITION OF TOTAL WEAKNESS

That US assistance failed to improve conditions after 1958 undoubtedly contributed to Kennedy's later decisions related to NSAM 111 in 1961, but there were other factors. As noted earlier, military-related expenditures formed almost 80 percent of all US assistance, while the remaining percentage of aid was allocated to economic and technical assistance. Of that remaining 20 percent, funds for police and other security services related to public administration formed approximately 7 percent, while another 7–8 percent was allocated for transportation development in the form of roads.[56] Scigliano and Fall were not the only ones to notice these problems. Authors William Lederer and Eugene Burdick saw similar troubles in 1958 and wrote: "We pay for huge highways through jungles in Asian lands where there is no transport except bicycle and foot."[57] This situation steadily worsened in subsequent years. Writing in 1963, Robert Scigliano commented on US assistance related to roads:

> Nearly all of the transportation projects entailed road construction, and while road-building served economic ends it was carried out in accordance with military strategy. A 20-mile stretch of highway [between Saigon and Bien Hoa] cost more money than the United States provided for all labor, community development, social welfare, housing, health, and education projects in Vietnam combined during the entire period 1954–1961.[58]

In critical ways, then, the structural problems of counterpart funding were only made worse by directing funds to projects that neither helped the Vietnamese population in meaningful ways nor assisted in building the South Vietnamese government's political legitimacy. Scigliano was charting a trajectory of US aid that would continue to create more problems than they solved for rural Vietnamese, and his research often corroborated Fall's assessments published in 1958. Despite the accuracy of Fall's claims, the US government continued to consider his work suspect, but while the State Department successfully blocked Fall's employment in Phnom Penh, it could not prevent the publication of his articles. However, it could complain to other departments of the US government about his criticisms. As early as 1959, the FBI began to monitor Fall and his communications, and the CIA would open a file on Fall as early as 1962, although he would not learn of this surveillance until later.[59]

In "South Viet-Nam's Internal Problems," Fall included a modicum of praise for the Republic of Vietnam, drawing brief positive attention to the Cai-San refugee camp in Kien Giang Province.[60] However, after describing its qualities, he concluded that "Diem's larger land reform had become bogged down in its early stages," so Cai-San, as Fall saw it, was merely a preview of

295

problems that would plague later settlement projects, such as the Agroville program in 1959 and the Strategic Hamlet program which began in late 1961.[61] In writing about Cai-San, he noted:

> In January 1958, the provincial governor [of Kien Giang] appeared at the settlement with an escort of Civil Guards to explain to the farmers that the word "distributed" used in their land grants was not be confused with "definitely granted," and that they owed rent or purchase payments to the "rightful owners" of the land. Needless to say, the situation became explosive.[62]

This was only yet another case in which the Diem administration antagonized Vietnamese farmers in ways that undermined any chance for it to achieve political legitimacy.[63] Altogether, these were internal problems and issues created by leaders in the United States and the Republic of Vietnam. These were not isolated from both internal and external security threats, but it was a more significant issue that government authorities failed to acknowledge these problems, just as they failed to acknowledge the counterproductive foreign assistance delivered through counterpart funding. Instead of a stable environment, Fall was increasingly identifying indicators of insurgency. Writing in 1958, he noted, "To the Vietnamese on the spot, the resurgence, rather than the continuance, of rebel activities has become a fact of life with which he has to cope on an increasing scale over the past twelve months. The extent and rise of this insecurity need not be explained in subjective terms which may be biased according to the particular viewpoint of the observer. It can be simply plotted for which daily newspapers or non-secret reports provide the basic raw material."[64] Just as he had plotted out Vietnamese Communist control in the Red River Delta in 1953, Fall took a similar approach in mapping openly available information that depicted a more severe problem. In noting divergences between the "official" government line that peace existed in rural Vietnam and the reality of a growing assassination campaign, he added, "There is a certain contradiction in the simultaneous assertions that there is peace and normal activity in the countryside of South Viet-Nam and in the justification of police-state measures because of the threat of internal subversion by still-existing Communist and sect guerrillas."[65] The first challenge in confronting this kind of threat was to acknowledge that one existed.

After publishing "South Viet-Nam's Internal Problems," a long and insightful work, Fall intensified his effort to diagnose challenges facing the Republic of Vietnam and the United States. In what would become another signal contribution to describing warfare in Southeast Asia, he began to use the term

AN UNASSAILABLE POSITION OF TOTAL WEAKNESS

"Vietnamese revolutionary warfare." More than referring to it as an insurgency, rebellion, or any other term, he preferred this description and believed it most accurately portrayed the integration of political, economic, social, and security threats that were deployed through a combination of old and newly established organizational frameworks of parallel hierarchies. He rarely used the term "revolutionary warfare" before 1958. Subsequently, however, he frequently used it to describe political processes that the Viet Minh used to control Vietnamese villages and the political violence involved in targeting government officials. Other than the French officers who had survived Indochina and wrote about the Viet Minh's methods, these were not political-military actions that Western authors often wrote about before 1958.[66] As Fall noted in "South Viet-Nam's Internal Problems":

> The new terrorists seek out the local police chiefs, security guards, village treasurers, and youth leaders and kill them in as spectacular a manner as possible. It would be pointless to describe here the hundreds of cases reported in detail in the Saigon press [in 1957 and 1958], but in general they document the fact that the objective of the rebels—gradual "insulation'"—of the central authorities from direct contact with the grass roots—was achieved.[67]

Fall found this approach more compelling and persuasive than direct military operations, and, at the time, he was unique in pointing out how Vietnamese communists used this "insulating" effort so effectively. "Insulation," in fact, was the same term he used to explain how during World War II the Maquis had separated French civilians from Nazi control by killing collaborators. Targeting collaborators in Haute-Savoie, Fall wrote, "was the kind of deterrent effect we were actually looking for, the kind that would isolate the German troops from the population, in fact insulate them. There would be complete loss of contact with the population without creating any kind of adverse reaction toward us [the Maquis]."[68] From personal experience, he recognized how violence could selectively achieve social and political control among Vietnamese villagers. This was significant because few, if any, were writing in English about the application of revolutionary warfare in 1958 while there was potential and time to change course. Years of thought, research, experience, and knowledge gained with the Maquis in the French Alps, at Nuremberg, and through an open mind shaped Fall's ability to see what was happening. To be sure, it would be difficult to describe also in a way that would enable others to recognize Vietnamese revolutionary warfare. It would be even more challenging for the Republic of Vietnam and the United States to counter it effectively.

297

II—*Vietnamese Revolutionary Warfare*

A dead Special Forces sergeant is not spontaneously replaced by his own social environment. A dead revolutionary usually is.[69]

– Bernard Fall

In 1958, Fall finally found the words he needed to describe the Viet Minh approach to conflict: revolutionary warfare. This term more concisely described the aggregate of social, political, and military ideas than previous designations he had used that varied slightly from one published article to another. The short phrase also undoubtedly improved his ability to communicate the complex and qualitative nature of war the Viet Minh used, but in a more efficient and comprehensive way. Before Fall adopted this term, succinctly describing intersections of guerrilla warfare, mass mobilization, land reform, communist organization, and the Viet Minh's subversion of French Union forces was a challenge. In an October 1956 article in *Military Review*, Fall's description of the Viet Minh's actions required lengthy explanations of multiple and complex operations that formed an integrated whole, but that he could not yet describe efficiently. For example, he described Viet Minh operations in 1956 this way: "In Indochina prevalent types of terrain have brought about four major types of guerrilla warfare: urban terrorism; rice field and swamp warfare; hill and mountain warfare; and jungle warfare."[70] Added to this mix, he used other terms as well: "the type of political-military-guerrilla warfare fought by the Communists within the main French Union position, the Red River Delta, proved to be the operation that, more than Dien Bien Phu, finally broke the back of the French war effort in Indochina …"[71] Fall could see what the Viet Minh were doing and that their way of warfare was successful, but it was difficult to describe consistently and through accessible and easily understood terms.

Descriptions like "a type of political-military-guerrilla warfare" were accurate but not concise. And while Fall's strings of adjectives were relevant, the varying combinations he used made it difficult for readers to understand what he meant unless they were familiar with his previous writing. Additionally, the progression in his study of the Viet Minh's approach to warfare was uncharted terrain in English-language journals and books, so readers may have found his ideas challenging to assess. Finally, his analysis expanded significantly between his first and second trips to Vietnam in 1953 and 1957, so the decision to settle on "revolutionary warfare" helped him consolidate his thought in words. Finding and using the term was as vital as it was efficient, and he was not alone in his search for a descriptive label.

AN UNASSAILABLE POSITION OF TOTAL WEAKNESS

The Central Intelligence Agency (CIA) also had trouble landing on a specific name for warfare conducted by Vietnamese Communists. A memorandum assessing South Vietnam from the CIA's Saigon desk on 18 May 1964, for example, echoed a similar problem Fall had encountered years earlier. As revealed in the memo where the author used "guerrilla-subversive" as a descriptive term, communists used a variety of irregular approaches:

> Viewed from Hanoi, the guerrilla-subversive war to dislodge U.S. forces and influence and establish Communist control in Laos and South Vietnam is doubtless going well. The time-tested technique of using terror against the populace, guerrilla warfare against anti-Communist armed forces, and subversion against governments friendly to the U.S. is paying off for the Communists.[72]

In this example, listing terror, guerrilla warfare, and subversion may have been preferable to using the term "insurgency," but insurgency was also inadequate. It lacked a comprehensiveness that included the immense social changes occurring in Vietnamese society, and it did not incorporate the full scope of political transformation communists sought. An insurgency might want only a change in government, and they could accomplish this goal without reordering society. Vietnamese Communism sought, over the course of decades of struggle, something entirely new for Vietnam. Using the term "revolutionary warfare" solved this problem for Fall in 1958 and described the war's socio-political nature more accurately. In the United States, however, the words "revolutionary war" undeniably evoked the spirit of 1776 in ways that complicated American readers' understanding, so providing context for its use in describing the situation in Vietnam mattered.

As he did with parallel hierarchies, Fall adopted the term "revolutionary warfare" from French officers fighting the Viet Minh in Indochina between 1946 and 1954. This group—again consisting of Charles Lacheroy, Jean Hogard, Roger Trinquier, and others—identified Viet Minh warfare through a framework known as *la guerre révolutionnaire*, which translated as "revolutionary warfare."[73] At the time Fall took up this term, these French officers were preoccupied with crushing the Algerian revolution after it broke out in September 1954. Fall's writing between 1955 and 1960, therefore, provides a crucial link between what French thinkers understood and described as revolutionary warfare in Vietnam during the late First Indochina War, how they adapted counterrevolutionary methods from Indochina for conflict in Algeria, and the ways in which their work influenced or differed from American formulations of counterinsurgency against the National Liberation Front (NLF) in South Vietnam after 1961. The Viet Minh Front, moreover, had dissolved into the NLF by 1958, but Vietnamese Communist forces adapted guerrilla tactics and renewed their socio-political doctrine of revolutionary warfare as the Second Indochina War continued to emerge. Perhaps more than anything, the Vietnamese Communists embodied the ability to adapt as they confronted a growing American presence and increasingly capable Army of the Republic of Vietnam (ARVN) after 1958.

As a flexible approach to undermining French control during the First Indochina War, successfully adapting or modifying revolutionary warfare depended on careful integration with local conditions and historical and social context. The most central and critical assessment to determine whether this was achieved was whether revolutionary warfare was perceived as politically legitimate among practitioners and, most critically, among the population which they sought to control. Popular support, as the Viet Minh knew, could be gained through coercion and terror, but also through genuine patriotic and nationalist appeal. This was a functional feature of revolutionary warfare that French officers recognized and which they sought to manipulate by studying Viet Minh approaches and applying them to warfare in Algeria.

However, revolutionary warfare could not be transferred as a strict and formulaic doctrine imposed on a conflict without careful consideration of differences in history and context. Likewise, in a manner very similar to counterpart funding, a systematic approach to countering revolutionary warfare could not be implemented without intense and careful study of the context in which it was to be used. Just because counterpart funding had been successfully used in Europe did not mean it would be successful in South Vietnam without serious recalibration to make it appropriate for South Vietnam's society and economy. Just as the United States could not simply flood South Vietnam with large amounts of consumer goods, it would be unproductive to flood it with US military supplies and personnel. Instead of a careful recalibration, the system of counterpart funding was transferred to South Vietnam (as noted earlier) as a type of "economy in a box," which turned out to be counterproductive and even weakened the South Vietnamese economy. Had counterpart funding been more carefully designed for South Vietnam's developing economy and implemented specifically for the RVN, this type of development mechanism for delivering assistance might have succeeded. Much the same might have been said of attempts to counter Vietnamese revolutionary warfare between 1956 and 1961. At the very core of Bernard Fall's writing, this was the central message he sought to convey to his readers.

While Vietnamese Communists possessed a historical and social advantage in adapting a general anti-colonial framework leading to revolutionary warfare

AN UNASSAILABLE POSITION OF TOTAL WEAKNESS

against the RVN and the growing American presence, US and ARVN forces, in contrast, were disadvantaged. The reasons behind the United States and RVN's difficulties in countering Vietnamese revolutionary warfare echoed many of the problems associated with US counterpart funding in South Vietnam. In addition, political legitimacy was not a principle that could be codified directly in words or assessed in a quantified way. Instead, it required qualitative analysis of cases where revolutionary warfare appeared to work and how it differed from cases where it appeared to fail. In a sense, French officers could see how revolutionary warfare functioned, but they could neither directly codify it as pure doctrine because of its qualitative nature, nor could they wield it because of who they were. As French officers, they could not force a revamped revolutionary warfare to meet their goals either, because they could not achieve political legitimacy among the Vietnamese population whose support they needed. A century of exploitation through colonialism was not going to be washed away, and they could not counter the message and efforts of Vietnamese communists who portrayed themselves as liberators. Military capacity could not change this outcome. This is how Fall thought of revolutionary warfare and why his work contrasted with that of French officers using lessons from Indochina for war against nationalists in Algeria.

Nonetheless, these French officers' frameworks retained a degree of flexibility. While they all shared an overall conceptual understanding of revolutionary warfare, individual officers' writing varied in the value accorded to psychological indoctrination or in the emphasis given to other social and political factors. However, what these officers had in common were the opponents from which they learned, the Viet Minh. Like other French officers, Fall also learned from the Viet Minh's methods while refining his knowledge from French theoretical development and building on the terminology that French officers such as Lacheroy, Trinquier, and others used during and shortly after the First Indochina War. The combination of Viet Minh operations Fall knew of personally and those he had read about and studied through others' experience formed a wellspring of thought from which he synthesized as much new knowledge as possible.[74]

Charles Lacheroy, Jacques Hogard, Jean Nemo, and Gabriel Bonnet were foremost among the officers who contributed to the concept of *la guerre révolutionnaire*.[75] Fall singled out Gabriel Bonnet's work as a central influence, writing "Colonel Bonnet, a former professor at the French Higher War College, wrote a book which was to become the 'bible' of the new school of thought [of *la guerre révolutionnaire*.]"[76] Bonnet's *Les Guerres Insurrectionnelles et Révolutionnaires*, published in 1958, "was simply a history of insurrections and revolutionary wars from 3000 B.C. to Algeria." However, Bonnet's analysis of collective characteristics among materiel-weak powers in conflict with stronger opponents impressed Fall.[77] While he noted that the term originated with Mao Tse-tung, he believed that Bonnet advanced descriptions and understanding of the concept of revolutionary warfare in an important way. In Fall's view:

> the French adopted the same term and Bonnet, in a book that is totally ignored in the United States, is likely to influence wars for decades to come because [in Bonnet's book] it was for the first time recognized that guerrilla warfare and revolutionary warfare are not interchangeable and that the major danger the West is faced with today is not one of being unable to cope with the armed forces of a revolution but with its spirit. [emphasis in original].[78]

In the sense Fall intended it, "spirit" is almost entirely to be equated with the social and political legitimacy of a revolution that includes the mass mobilization of the civilian population. The concept of warfare that Bonnet and others described formed an important step toward a new understanding of modern warfare. It was not an easy concept to grasp. According to French General Henri Navarre, the commander of French Union forces in Indochina in 1954 and author of the disastrous Navarre Plan that led to Dien Bien Phu, this type of political-subversive warfare was "enigmatic."[79] Navarre described the Viet Minh's way of war "as one never seriously studied, to my knowledge, in any military school!"[80] What is remarkable about Fall's scholarship is that he identified the nature of the Viet Minh's efforts as Vietnamese Communists adapted them prior to the outbreak of the Second Indochina War. The "school" contributing to his awareness was an aggregate of experience from his time in the Maquis and French army, at Nuremberg, through formal study with Amry Vandenbosch, and through interactions with Ralph Bunche and others.[81] Fall relied upon his ability to form a collective knowledge through study and experience instead of, as Navarre insinuated, through a program of instruction that did not yet exist in any army's system of professional military education. It was through building on Bonnet and others' work, in addition to his cumulative experience, that enabled Fall to bridge the First and Second Indochina Wars intellectually.

This phenomenon of warfare, which Fall and others recognized, was not just guerrilla or jungle warfare. Moreover, it was difficult to account for warfare that went "beyond the twin deadlocks of conventional war and nuclear war."[82] This is perhaps one reason why French General Henri Navarre had dif-

AN UNASSAILABLE POSITION OF TOTAL WEAKNESS

ficulty accounting for it during the First Indochina War. As Navarre learned with regret, revolutionary warfare was highly effective, and Fall quoted a French officer who added with notable emphasis: "Not even an atom bomb could have helped us; assuming that it would have hit one of their coolie trails, they would merely have bypassed 'ground zero' and hacked themselves a new path through the jungle.'"[83] In another officer's description, Fall quoted, by the time of Dien Bien Phu, the French were "like '*des grumeaux dans la soupe*' ('bread crumbs in the soup')."[84] Unsurprisingly, therefore, French officers made a concerted effort to devise improved tactics and operations against a type of political warfare that reduced their military power to crumbs.

Even the potential deployment of three tactical atomic bombs through a contingency US aerial support plan called Operation Vulture in the jungles of Northwest Tonkin failed to contain the Viet Minh's strategy to destroy France's garrison at Dien Bien Phu.[85] In subsequent years, French officers remained astounded by Viet Minh General Vo Nguyen Giap's operational planning, through which tens of thousands of porters were ordered to haul critical supplies and artillery to destroy the French position. Fall was also clearly struck by the operational success at Dien Bien Phu but recognized, quite critically, that the years of revolutionary warfare leading to the battle were critical contributions to the Viet Minh's victory in the spring of 1954. More than the battle itself, the political preparation of the battlefield— achieved through mass mobilization and political warfare in villages across North and Central Vietnam—was the decisive effort that effectively reduced the French position to "bread crumbs in the soup" once the battle was engaged.[86]

Vietnamese revolutionary warfare was, to be sure, a diverse phenomenon of socio-political processes mobilized to achieve strategic results, yet Fall sought to describe it even as he may have seen it evolving in the late 1950s and early 1960s. He relied on Bonnet's work describing revolutionary warfare as "a quasi-mathematical equation: partisan war plus psychological war equals revolutionary warfare." Fall refined the idea further: "Revolutionary Warfare occurs when guerilla methods are used to further an ideology."[87] He eventually broke this down into a formula: "RW=G+P where Revolutionary Warfare equals Guerrilla Warfare plus Political Action."[88] In perhaps his most illustrative description, he explained: "the formulation for Revolutionary Warfare is the result of the application of guerrilla methods to the furtherance of an ideology or a political system. This is the *real* difference between partisan warfare, guerrilla warfare and everything else" (emphasis in original).[89]

"Revolutionary" was used by French theorists and Fall because that was the term Mao Tse-tung used in 1936.[90] In the context of Indochina, the Viet Minh's communist ideology was not uncontested, but it was different from that which had existed before in Vietnamese history. This included not only replacing an entire colonial empire but also challenging a Confucianist social order already in decline when compared to previous centuries. This made it revolutionary.

In addition to Gabriel Bonnet's work, Fall read the work of many others. He regarded Jacques Hogard's "*Guerre Révolutionnaire et Pacification*" as another foundational text published in the March–April 1957 issue of *Revue Militaire d'Information*.[91] Fall regarded this entire issue of this journal as "A key study of the whole revolutionary problem."[92] More broadly, French theorists of *la guerre révolutionnaire* regarded revolutionary warfare as part of a larger historical arc of warfare in which communism served as a vanguard. According to historian Michael P.M. Finch, the "total war that the revolutionary war theorists described rested on a belief about the scale of a global subversive war which they contended had been underway since 1917, and for which France's post-1945 colonial wars were the most tangible evidence."[93] Moreover, in Finch's view, these theorists "relied upon the belief that the processes which led to the loss of control in Indochina could be applied anywhere: the global enemy who had built 'bases' in the colonies … could do the same in the metropole."[94] As a result, this group of French officers spearheaded counterrevolutionary approaches that were stringent and expansive. Moreover, "these theorists were beholden to an escalatory logic which suggested that only greater levels of popular support and mobilization and more ruthless methods of pursuing the fight would guarantee the security not just of the empire, but of France herself."[95] In the case of Indochina, however, the key to this was gaining more significant levels of popular support and mass mobilization of Vietnamese society. To be sure, this had long been the Viet Minh's goal as well.

During and after World War II, gaining mass support was the foundation on which the Viet Minh built their revolution. Despite severe problems in the way they conducted land reform in 1953, enforcing draconian collectivization in 1956 created even worse issues and resulted in the farmers' revolts and subsequent repression in Nghe An Province. Nonetheless, and aided by extensive Chinese and Soviet support, the Viet Minh and DRV endured. In contrast, the French military could not build competitive systems of control in Indochina to overcome the Viet Minh's use of revolutionary warfare. As an exploitative imperialist project, the French-led system failed because its supported government, the State of Vietnam, could not, unsurprisingly, gain sufficient legitimacy or popular support among the Vietnamese. Even after attempts were made to reform French authority and increase Vietnamese agency, France's failure to do so explained why anti-communist leaders, such as former Prime Minister of the Associated State of Vietnam, Nguyen Van Tam, left Vietnam for the United States.

French theorists' vision of total war also demanded a national security-state system, something Fall did not agree with and in fact feared. The type of "escalatory logic" guiding this conception of countering revolutionary warfare encompassed a subsequent mobilization using more ruthless methods of pursuing war. Such an overall pursuit and the autocracy needed to prosecute it too closely paralleled Nazi Germany's methods and demands for *Lebensraum* in the Sudetenland, Poland, Ukraine, Belarus, and other regions early in World War II. It was certainly not a system, Fall held, that French officers should pursue to regain lost colonies in the name of protecting France.

The reason he did not share this vision of a national-security state had apparent connections with his life during and after World War II. Subjectively, it was anchored in his own experience of how a state could manipulate "pursuing its security" and direct a victimized sense of sovereignty through autocratic rule to ignite a catastrophe leading to global war and genocide. It was terrifying to contemplate total war occurring again, mostly since civilians were invariably the ones who suffered the most. This acumen for sensing ominous rises in authoritarianism was something that Fall never lost. It originated with losing his parents, and it was accentuated by his recognition of how French theorists sought to apply their idea of "total war" to other contexts after losing their war in Indochina. Numerous administrations in autocratic Latin American governments used French systems to crush insurgent networks and repress dissent, and this vindicated Fall's serious concerns.[96] US support for such tactics and US military assistance and training for repressive regimes in Guatemala, Chile, and elsewhere would have further outraged him had he known the extent of the atrocities the United States supported in those countries.[97] In profound contrast to US and French warfighting and repression, Fall possessed a humanist perspective that would soon critically shape how he saw warfare in Vietnam as it developed into the Second Indochina War. American anti-authoritarian principles, as spelled out in the US Constitution's Bill of Rights, formed a preferable foundation for government authority related to the individual. Systems calling for total war to protect elite interests were anathema to these principles—and to Fall's humanism—as were policies supporting potential "total war" in countries from which existential threats to the US did not emanate.

According to François Sully, France's soldiers, particularly French officers who developed ideas of *la guerre révolutionnaire*, "were obsessed with the idea of proving that they could defeat an insurgency using guerrilla tactics they had learned from their defeat in Indochina."[98] Providing a model for Jean Larteguy's *The Centurions*, "many of these men, like the paratroopers of Colonel Bigeard, were not satisfied by a twenty-six-month tour of duty in Vietnam. As soon as their six-month leave in France was over, they re-volunteered for Vietnam, Laos, or Cambodia. They were anxious to learn the secrets of guerrilla warfare."[99] Fall was similar to these officers, but only in the sense that he was committed to studying these "secrets in Indochina" and to understanding how the Viet Minh adapted them for a continuation of war in Southeast Asia. Undoubtedly, Fall was repulsed by the idea of using the Viet Minh's system for total war in other contexts, such as in Algeria, or in the case of American intervention in Guatemala to topple President Jacobo Árbenz and the United States' support for the subsequent repressive regime of Carlos Armas.[100]

Other vital differences existed between Fall and French officers developing la guerre révolutionnaire. As historian Peter Paret explained, theorists of *la guerre révolutionnaire* were not interested in "understanding the complex origins of the Indochinese War," but instead "developed their theories to gain insights that could be turned to operational use in other contexts."[101] In contrast, Fall was extremely interested in understanding the complex origins of war in Indochina. Additionally, in stark contrast to Fall's belief that the Vietnamese people were the core principle over which revolutionary warfare was fought, French proponents of *la guerre révolutionnaire* believed, in Finch's perspective, that the "crowd was not influential, but rather existed to be influenced." As Finch described it, the "sociological, economic, and political study of a host population was secondary to the attention given to techniques and methods advocated in French conceptions of modern warfare."[102] Finch's point echoes Fall's belief that military aspects of war with the Viet Minh were overemphasized. Additionally, Fall prioritized Vietnamese agency and emphasized the importance of the support of Vietnamese civilians in creating and consolidating political legitimacy in governing systems leading them. Just as he pointed this out in his analysis of counterpart funding, the same ideas applied to how war was fought.

AN UNASSAILABLE POSITION OF TOTAL WEAKNESS

The importance of the Vietnamese "crowd" was not only influential to Fall, but it collectively formed a critical and active base for revolutionary warfare. In his descriptions of parallel hierarchies, Fall had already explained how political support among Vietnamese civilians—ranging from flower girls to merchants and beggars—was critical to the legitimacy Vietnamese revolutionary warfare sought to bring about, and did much to keep the movement alive. The central importance of the Vietnamese people explains why Fall was so critical of the United States' foreign assistance policy in "Will South Viet Nam be Next?" US assistance did not account for, and even willfully disregarded, what the Vietnamese needed. This indicated a lack of sufficient attention to, or maybe even interest in, the needs of the Vietnamese people. In contrast, Fall described how Vietnamese Communists fully understood the importance of the Vietnamese population:

> The Communists have correctly identified as the central objective of a revolutionary war the human beings that make up a nation; while on our side, the securing of communication lines, the control of crops and industrial installations, and the protection of one small power group to the exclusion of all others seems to be overriding considerations. Thus, the population as such can only become an "object"—something that gets shoved out of the way because it "impedes" military operations; whereas the Communists build the civilian population right into their battle plan and make the utmost use of it, from the simple 10-year old who becomes a messenger to the hapless villagers who are rounded up to serve as bullet shields in an attack on an ARVN outpost.[103]

This description demonstrated the importance of Vietnamese civilians, but also indicated how Vietnamese communists were willing to exploit them as machine-gun fodder. Fall was familiar with how Vietnamese Communists mistreated large sectors of their fellow Vietnamese as a matter of policy. For example, land reform in 1953 and collectivization in 1956 came with serious problems, including fanaticism, mismanagement, and poor decision-making in numerous cases. And Fall never failed to criticize idiocy and brutality, regardless of its ideological orientation; he pointed out collapses in communist policy with as much severity as he called attention to American and South Vietnamese failures.

In his view, revolutionary warfare had emerged as a broader strategic phenomenon that changed the economic, social, and political fabric of Vietnamese societies. Moreover, the Viet Minh uniquely adapted it to the postwar era of decolonization, and Fall was not the only one to see revolutionary warfare this way. According to historians John Shy and Thomas Collier, the end of European empire "under colonial and even domestic assault, and the rapid appearance amidst the imperial ruins of new successor states, often weak, are the main reasons why we see this new dimension of military theory [of revolutionary warfare] where none was apparent in 1941."[104] Thus, the era of postwar decolonization helps explain the context of Bernard Fall's analysis of revolutionary warfare, yet the following must also be emphasized. While Mao Tse-tung articulated revolution in the People's Republic of China, the ways in which Ho Chi Minh, Truong Chinh, Le Duan, and others appropriated revolutionary warfare for Vietnam were still in progress when Fall came to Indochina in 1953. It is certain, therefore, that Fall was among the first of Western analysts writing in English to see this progression. It is also certain that he was among the first to chart the ongoing evolution of revolutionary warfare that Vietnamese Communist leaders implemented and adapted to fit their goals within the unique historical and political context in which they lived.

In describing revolutionary warfare, Fall frequently adapted and refined his terminology because the phenomenon of revolutionary warfare he was analyzing was also evolving. His terminology, like revolutionary warfare itself, required a dynamic and flexible approach because this characterized the nature of the warfare he witnessed. Notably, he differentiated guerrilla and revolutionary warfare, writing, "guerrilla warfare is nothing but a tactical appendage of a far vaster political contest and that, no matter how expertly competent and dedicated professionals fight it, it cannot possibly make up for the absence of a political rationale."[105] He gained this awareness from his knowledge of the formidable tactical skill of French paratroopers and Legionnaires, and the commitment of commando units like GCMA (*Groupement de Commandos Mixte Aéroportés*), which he admired and recounted in detail.[106] Fall held GCMA corporal René Riesen, an individual who organized "H're tribesmen on the southern mountain plateau," in very high regard, believing him to be a model of courage, innovation, independence, and skill on which special operation forces should be based.[107] Riesen's mission with Highlanders in Central Vietnam in 1950 and 1951, Fall seemed to suggest, offered the single best approach to countering Vietnamese revolutionary warfare and undoubtedly provided a model for subsequent US Special Forces operations in the region. Moreover, Riesen was the epitome of an advisor "going native," learning several native highland dialects, marrying a H're woman, joining her tribe's community, and organizing that community against Viet Minh operations in their region.[108] Riesen's case, however, was exceptional.

AN UNASSAILABLE POSITION OF TOTAL WEAKNESS

As Fall explained, French forces were unable to provide an adequate political rationale that the Vietnamese would willingly support, and their military-oriented operations and solutions were poor substitutes. Western governments could not rely on such approaches, at least not with anything approaching wisdom. Rhetorically, Fall wondered:

> Why is it that we must use top-notch elite forces ... armed with the very best that advanced technology can provide to defeat the Viet Minh? The answer is very simple: It takes all the technical proficiency our system can provide to make up for the woeful lack of popular support and political savvy of most of the regimes that the West has thus far sought to prop up.[109]

Fall believed that emulating the independence, flexibility, and relevance with which René Riesen approached his mission—not to mention his ability to integrate himself into Vietnam's diverse cultures—was a better way to counter Vietnamese revolutionary warfare. Conventional military approaches, in contrast, were doomed to fail. After all, Indochina's ethnic populations were diverse. Vietnamese revolutionary warfare, because of its dependence on mass support, functioned in different ways throughout the region. In the south of Vietnam, social variance was exceptionally vast and had consistently frustrated centralized control over centuries. This remained a historical and endemic feature of the region prior to, during, and after World War II. Historian Shawn McHale noted this: "whereas in the north and center of the country, the Empire of Vietnam actually tried to shape events by taking over parts of the French colonial state and encouraging mass mobilization, in the south it had little impact."[110] McHale added, "It is no surprise that the struggle for the Mekong Delta was characterized by shifting tactical alliances, ethnic, political, and religious conflict, and the most extreme range of beliefs of any part of Vietnam."[111] Similarly, historian Keith Taylor observed that the geographical aspect "of Nam Bo [South Vietnam] is one of openness, vulnerability, possibility," while for individuals "Nam Bo was a place of cultural and ethnolinguistic encounter ... Nam Bo was the place with greatest prospect for incorporating new perspectives into a formation of Vietnameseness."[112] In a similar respect, it was a place where revolutionary warfare remained contested by Cao Dai, Hoa Hao, and other religious groups, which even the National Liberation Front after 1961 struggled to dominate, while having internal, but often atypical, conflicts of its own.[113] In addition, The Khmer Krom Cambodian minority in the western Mekong Delta region, Nung Chinese, and approximately 1.5 million Highlanders also contested Vietnamese Communist efforts to seize control in south and central Vietnam.[114]

309

The diverse environment, identities, and communities of Vietnam's southern region converged with a frontier mentality that eluded domination by Vietnamese Communists. Such frontiers—in both a geographical and social sense—along with the ethnic and religious diversity of the region made it extremely difficult for the Vietnamese Communists to consolidate Vietnamese identity into a uniform mold that suited their goals to control Vietnam. A sense of shared "Vietnamese-ness" could not originate exclusively through communism. In its many variations, Marxist–Leninist thought was not easily transferable to Vietnam and, for many, was likely as foreign a concept as French imperialism. However, political identity could be manipulated by Vietnamese Communists because kernels of communist ideology relied on idealized conceptions of communalism and cooperative society, and both these factors existed in Vietnam. Competition with these ideas, however, still existed in the south. For these reasons, among others, "the Viet Minh faced legions of local competitors," including powerful adversaries like the Hoa Hao and nationalist Vietnamese during the First Indochina War.[115] These kinds of competitors would continue to make life hard for Vietnamese Communists during the Second Indochina War, as well.

Fall's work before 1957 generally focused on the development of Vietnamese revolutionary warfare in the north. In contrast, his later work increasingly centered on the development of Vietnamese revolutionary warfare in the south.[116] After 1958, due to a worsening security environment that included assassination campaigns against government-appointed village officials and isolated attacks which were growing in frequency, Fall perceived a dangerous emerging threat to the Republic of Vietnam. However, this was more than an insurgency consisting of guerrilla attacks. It consisted of dynamic parallel hierarchies which Vietnamese Communists used to perpetrate revolutionary warfare against Ngo Dinh Diem's government. Fall was also becoming increasingly concerned that, in the south, Diem's authoritarian responses to dissent, local farmers' grievances stemming from problems with land reform, the weakened Vietnamese economy resulting from poorly conceived US foreign assistance planning, and communist infiltration all pointed toward a path of revolutionary warfare in development. There were fundamental differences in how this was transpiring in the south, to be sure, but there were also many similarities to communists' earlier transformation of Vietnamese society in the north. In 1958, Fall recognized that these differences were contributing to the development of a potential Second Indochina War. Among American policymakers, North Vietnamese forces would pose a different kind of threat than those emanating from within South and Central Vietnam that emerged as the National Liberation Front and known pejoratively as the Viet-Cong.

III—"Discontent with Existing Conditions"

> It is axiomatic in the field of Revolutionary Warfare that the potential insurgent takes his source of power from a population which has become discontented with existing conditions which cannot be changed by peaceful and legal means. That is close to a perfect definition of what was to happen in South Viet-Nam not—contrary to some later appraisals—after 1960 or 1961, but starting in 1956.
>
> – Bernard Fall[117]

After Fall settled on the term "revolutionary warfare," literally the words he was looking for since 1953, he possessed a verbal framework to describe what the Republic of Vietnam and the United States confronted in the years after France's defeat in 1954. In late 1958, he concluded his article "South Viet-Nam's Internal Problems," writing:

> South Viet-Nam thus finds itself at a crossroad. It is now an independent state, and, given the limitations imposed upon it by its precarious economic and military position, it is a free agent ... As *Time* magazine, once Ngo Dinh Diem's staunchest supporter, remarked caustically, "put simply, Diem is still taking U.S. money by the millions, but less and less U.S. advice." This relative independence from outside pressure is both a political asset and a dangerous liability for South Viet-Nam.[118]

He added, "[The government] must also consider the development of the economy and of the country's political life in line with the needs of the majority of the population—and that population, for a long time to come, will be devoted to rice farming to an overwhelming extent." He concluded "there are disturbing signs of loss of contact with the people in certain areas of the countryside, and there—as the Nationalist Chinese found out—is where wars may be lost in Asia."[119]

In "South Viet-Nam's Internal Problems," Fall had documented numerous obstacles which insulated the Republic from its people. These issues also included a weak National Assembly and a Supreme Court that, because it was still not confirmed as of late 1958, gave credence to the belief that it had been used only as a tool for implementing the Republic's constitution in 1956.[120] Poor US assistance planning also contributed to economic problems while militarizing South Vietnam. While the US Military Advisory Assistance Group (MAAG) began coordinating support for France's operations as early as 1950, by 1957, according to George Herring, the most severe problem was "the continued task of assuring the Vietnamese that the United States is not a colonial power—an assurance that must be renewed on an individual basis by each new advisor."[121] Fall similarly viewed these problems as a cycle of factors that fed upon each other as Diem's questionable political legitimacy, a degrading security environment, a widespread perception of neocolonialism, and an ever-worsening economy plodded forward. Fall's overall emphasis in 1958 was to call attention to these problems, which earned him few friends in positions of power when it came to making decisions.

The problem of a growing insurgency in South Vietnam was real, whether government authorities believed Fall or not. During his trip in 1957, Fall used similar methods to those he had employed in 1953, when he had examined tax records to document the lack of security in French-held territory, to illustrate the worsening situation. He described this, writing:

> I brought to the [South Vietnamese Government's] chief of economic aid's desk for the Indochina area a large-scale map of village chief killings in Viet-Nam which I had made in 1957–58 and which clearly pointed to the fact that the United States was in for an even worse Communist guerrilla threat than the French had been four years earlier.[122]

The Vietnamese official's response to Fall's map of assassinations was noncommittal. Even as he showed his research to government authorities, Fall noted, "Unbounded enthusiasm prevailed then. Diem had officially declared in July 1957 that 'the guerrilla threat in South Viet-Nam had ceased to exist,' and no one was going to challenge that assertion even as the grim statistics began to stare one in the face."[123] This, more than anything else, was the beginning of what David Halberstam would describe as the "reality gap."[124]

The problem, Fall found, was that decision-makers were unwilling to change the direction of US policy, despite evidence demonstrating growing political danger in Vietnam. Moreover, leaders such as John Foster Dulles had already demonstrated that they would block Fall's access to Indochina and downplay his scholarship because of his criticism. Following the reception of Fall's articles in 1958, it was clear that high-level officials in diplomatic channels in Vietnam and Washington, DC were aware of Fall's work but, more importantly, that they were troubled by it as well. High-level officials demonstrated this awareness in an illuminating case, mainly related to Fall's criticism of US aid and Ngo Dinh Diem's political standing.

AN UNASSAILABLE POSITION OF TOTAL WEAKNESS

Among the many prominent advisors to the South Vietnamese President, "one of Diem's earliest and staunchest backers was Wesley R. Fishel, professor of political science at Michigan State University where Diem had lectured once while visiting the United States in the 1930s."[125] Fishel was a key member of the Michigan State University Advisory Group, an organization financially underwritten by the International Cooperation Administration (ICA). The advisory group conducted important work that included assisting the Republic of Vietnam's administration and training its police and civil guards.[126] Due to his long-standing relationship with them, Fishel and Edward Lansdale were among the few prominent American advisors Diem heeded in the late 1950s. However, Fishel and Diem's relationship soured, and the Michigan State University group's mission eventually concluded in 1962.[127] Amid the growing tension between them, due in part to a worsening security environment in South Vietnam, Fishel wrote to Diem on 30 April 1960, to describe problems the United States government observed in South Vietnam.

Fishel outlined four critical issues in the Diem–US relationship: weak leadership, slowing democratic development, the security situation, and administrative reform and organization.[128] Although they had been colleagues for years, Fishel criticized Diem at length. Demonstrating honorable candor, he explained that the security situation in South Vietnam was a grave concern, writing:

> I have been carefully questioned by my friends in Washington concerning the "deterioration" in internal security in Vietnam. Among other things which I have been asked are the following: Is the security crisis genuine? Or is it faked because you want more American aid, much as the French were accustomed to stage a "crisis" just as the U.S. Congress was about to pass on Mutual Security aid to France/Indochina between 1950/1954?[129]

Fishel's point was significant because in 1953 US policy had increasingly bound the United States to France because of France's importance to European defense. President Eisenhower believed that France had leveraged their much-needed support for NATO to obtain more significant financial assistance for anti-communist operations in Indochina.[130] Fishel argued that if Diem staged "crises" to gain US support "between 1950/1954," then these manipulative efforts carried with them dire consequences, which would result in the United States increasing its involvement in Vietnam. Moreover, Fishel's concern to obtain the truth of the security situation involved Fall. In a letter to Diem, Fishel wrote:

> In this connection, Mr. Bernard Fall is preparing a sharply critical article on Vietnam. In New York the other day he boasted publicly that when he wrote

about the deterioration of security in *The Nation* magazine some two years ago ["Will South Viet-Nam Be Next?"]—and I had contradicted his interpretations and his facts at the time—he had been right and I had been wrong! Now he intends to prove that your government is about to fall; that the people oppose you; that corruption is rife in your regime; that your "government en famille" is destroying all possibility of democratic growth in Vietnam; that his map of terrorist activity in Vietnam which he published in *Pacific Affairs* in 1957 was correct; and that, furthermore, *he has once more secured from confidential French files* similar evidence of terrorist activity in Vietnam today, which he now plans to publish. It is a matter of some pain to us who are your *friends* that your *enemies* are better able to secure detailed information about what is happening in your country than we are!¹³¹

Fishel's admonitions verified Fall's claims in "Will South Viet-Nam Be Next?" and "South Viet-Nam's Internal Problems." Fishel had other problems with Diem. In the subject area of "Administrative reform and organization," Fishel added:

> There is also considerable criticism in the State Department, for instance, of the continuing failure of provincial chiefs, district chiefs, and so on, to get close to the population; there is also much criticism of your seeming reliance on "repression" in trying to solve the problems of government in the field. (In particular, the reputedly "brutal" activities of the Vietnamese marines have been severely criticized.)¹³²

The "insulation" between government officials and the population, which Fall had warned of, was clearly in effect. Fishel concluded by reminding Diem to send answers to multiple questions associated with these four troubled sectors discussed in his letter. "Otherwise," Fishel warned:

> you must continue to expect articles such as that which appeared in the New York *World Telegram* (by Mr. Colegrove) the other day, and those which *Time* magazine published in recent weeks. You may also be interested to know that Mr. Fall is in contact with Joseph Alsop, with whose writings you are quite familiar.¹³³

Fishel hoped these were suggestions that Diem would take on board to change his administration's approach to governance. Fishel's comments are revealing because he and Fall had previously worked together. During Fall's 1957 research trip, as noted, Fishel provided Fall with significant resources to complete his study for the Institute of Pacific Affairs and his many critical articles published in 1958.¹³⁴ The support Fall gained from Fishel suggested previous goodwill between them. While it is possible that Fall's outspoken criticism of US assistance and Diem's policies in 1958 angered Fishel, he did not criticize Fall in his letter to Diem, except to say that Fall "had publicly boasted" about his facts in New York. Fall was adamant that Diem's decision-making was a critical problem. This criticism applied to many areas but noticeably began—in Fall's view—with Diem's removing Vietnamese villagers' elected officials in 1956. This and other poor choices contributed to conditions through which the National Liberation Front (NLF) would form.

Subsequent authoritarian decrees, including Ordinance 6 and the Denunciation of Communist policy represented in Decree 10/59, brutally and effectively persecuted Vietnamese Communists, but they also antagonized non-committed and often innocent Vietnamese. While these policies drove the NLF underground, they also insulated the South Vietnamese population from the government in Saigon. International justice scholar Richard Falk, in an article evaluating the role of the United States in Vietnam in the context of international law, added: "Bernard Fall, among others, points out that the uprising of peasants against Saigon arose as a consequence of Diem's policies that preexisted the formation of the Vietcong (NLF) and was accomplished without any interference on the part of Hanoi."[135] This was a point David Elliott, one of the foremost contemporary scholars of the National Liberation Front, also reinforced in 2003. Yet, Fall was also concerned about changes to the Republic of Vietnam's constitution, particularly Article 98, which claimed: the "right to decree a temporary suspension of virtually all civil rights to meet the legitimate demands of public security and order and national defense."[136]

Article 98 was a decree that troubled Fall considerably, but not as much as Diem's apparent lack of sympathy for rural Vietnamese farmers. On this point, Fall claimed, the "Diem regime misunderstood its people to the last."[137] Diem's minority status as a Catholic, and his antipathy toward the majority Buddhist population in Vietnam in general and the Hoa Hao and the syncretic Cao Dai in particular, undermined his legitimacy with non-Catholic parts of the population. His decision to get rid of village leaders, who had been selected by Vietnamese farmers and their families, only further degraded his legitimacy among villagers "in the countryside," where, far more than in the cities, "wars may be lost in Asia."[138] As a result of these decisions, Fall concluded, the Republic of Vietnam in Saigon "slowly but surely created an unassailable position of total weakness."[139] Moreover, Vietnamese Communists were not going away, regardless of the severity of Diem's repressive policies. Fall provided a clear warning of this, writing:

> International Vandalism in the form of Revolutionary War is going to be with us for a long time to come. We might as well reconcile ourselves to its existence

and settle down to study its rules, so that we might be in a better position the next time when we have to face its grim realities.[140]

After years of study, Bernard Fall would work even harder to understand Vietnamese revolutionary warfare. In late 1958, it was evolving into a series of grim realities that the Republic of Vietnam and the United States would have to confront. In the years to come, it would also evolve into a grim reality that the people of Laos, Cambodia, and Vietnam would be forced to endure.

8

1961–1967

I—"Revolutionary Warfare in Laos"

On 24 March 1961, President John F. Kennedy spoke before a television audience from the State Department in Washington, DC about developments in Laos. He explained:

> It is important for all Americans to understand this difficult and potentially dangerous problem. In my last conversation with General Eisenhower, the day before the inauguration on January 19, we spent more time on this hard matter than on any other thing. And since then it has been steadily before the administration as the most immediate of the problems that we found upon taking office.[1]

As Eisenhower conceded in his memoir, published in 1965, his administration had "left a legacy of strife and confusion in Laos. This I regretted deeply."[2] The small Southeast Asian nation was therefore under close watch, and the question was whether to intervene or not to intervene because events in Vietnam had changed the regional security environment. Only two years earlier in 1959, as acting Secretary of State Douglas Dillon noted in a memorandum, "We had thought it best not to intervene but rather to stand aside and let the Lao work out their own relationships."[3] Eisenhower's administration contributed to division in Laos, but not nearly as much as the numerous coups, countercoups, rebellions, and the litany of endless strife among multiple Laotian factions which emerged after World War II.[4] Two months into office, Kennedy concluded:

The security of all Southeast Asia will be endangered if Laos loses its neutral independence. Its own safety runs with the safety of us all—in neutrality observed by us all. I want to make it clear to the American people and to all the world that all we want in Laos is peace, not war; a truly neutral government, not a cold war pawn; a settlement concluded at the conference table and not on the battlefield.[5]

In Laos, these hopes were beyond Kennedy's reach, much as they had been for Eisenhower's administration. Factional division in Laos and external pressures intensified after the former protectorate gained independence from France in 1953. According to Bernard Fall, this political turmoil grew to the point that "patriotism in Laos is at best a furious regionalism."[6] Vietnamese influence was especially a problem, and Sisouk na Champassak, an official in the Royal Laotian Government, expressed this frustration: "The history of Laos after Geneva in 1954 is essentially a history of the slow and patient sabotage, by the Viet Minh and the Pathet Lao allies, of the Geneva agreements concerning Laos."[7] As a Viet Minh sanctuary, Laos was geographically critical, and its importance escalated with spreading communist networks in South Vietnam in 1959. Fall explained that, by 1961, "the situation in Laos is a hopeless quagmire as rival factions supported by contending outside power blocs seek to resolve an essential socio-political problem by military means."[8] The making of a quagmire in Laos preceded, in many important ways, the making of a quagmire in Vietnam. A brief and limited delineation of the crisis in Laos, and some of its key points which Fall observed, demonstrates these connections.

Fall spent considerable time in Laos in 1953 and during his second and third visits to Indochina in 1957 and 1959, when he accompanied the Royal Laotian Army on multiple field operations.[9] His 1959 research trip was conducted with support from the Rockefeller Foundation and a SEATO grant to "study the effects of Communist subversion on the local administration of South Viet-Nam, Laos, northeastern Thailand, and northern Malaya."[10] When President Kennedy was just beginning to grapple with an expanding geopolitical calamity in Southeast Asia, Fall had already conducted more research and written more assessments on Laos than possibly any other Western scholar. As early as September 1956, he wrote the editors of *The New York Times* to correct inaccurate reporting on neutrality in Laos, since he had tracked developments in the country since 1953. The paper had erroneously claimed that the 1954 Geneva Convention ending the First Indochina War prevented "the existence of any foreign bases on its soil, including any from the free world."[11] Fall offered the correction that "Laos' statesmen extracted from Communist

1961–1967

Laos, Political Map, from Bernard B. Fall, *Anatomy of a Crisis*

China a formal pledge of non-aggression without abandoning a single one of Lao's many traditional ties with the free world."[12] Due to its geographical position, Laos was virtually unable to achieve political neutrality, and, as external forces violated its borders, contested internal politics added numerous obstacles to the state regaining even a semblance of neutrality. The combination of these factors made politics in Laos and relations with its neighbors an utter mess.

In numerous articles, Fall evaluated the intricate factional division that characterized conflict in Laos after World War II.[13] One of his earliest commercial monographs was provisionally titled *Crisis in Laos*, and Fall planned to publish it with Public Affairs Press, either in 1961 or possibly in 1962.[14] The work eventually appeared in 1968 under the title *Anatomy of a Crisis: The Laotian Crisis of 1960–1961*.[15] Two primary concerns provided an overall framework for the book. The first was documenting and critiquing political, diplomatic, and military developments that contributed to the conflict. A second goal focused on correcting inaccurate and sensationalist reporting that channeled a confusing and avoidable local conflict into the broader Cold War. With regard to Laos, Fall emphasized that the United States should have provided more significant financial and material assistance to the T'ai ethnic tribes and others on the Vietnam/Laos border to enable their defense of Laos's midland areas. Instead, the United States deployed a preponderance of its support to Meo (Hmong) highlanders defending against Vietnamese Communist incursions in less populated and accessible areas.[16] One resulting problem was that it aggravated ethnic divisions when one group believed that they received less assistance than others, and grievances ensued. This enabled North Vietnamese leaders, who had developed a sophisticated series of policies related to diverse populations in Laos and Vietnam's border areas as early as May 1955, to manipulate ethnic divisions.[17]

It was important for Fall to describe the history of Laos and its differences from Vietnam. After World War II, France regained control of Laos and granted it autonomy within the French Union as an independent sovereign state in 1953.[18] In the years preceding the conclusion of the First Indochina War in 1954, three factions based in the Royal Laotian family—consisting of the neutralist Souvanna Phouma, the right-wing Phetsarath Rattanavongsa, and the communist-oriented Souphanouvong—formed the Lao Issara, a nationalist movement, in 1945. Out of the Lao Issara, Souphanouvong later joined with Viet Minh forces in North Vietnam to establish the communist Pathet Lao ("Land of the Lao") in August 1950.[19] Like the Viet Minh, a political front called the Neo Lao Issara was formed in November 1950, to be renamed the Neo Lao Hak Sat ("Lao Patriotic Front") in 1956.[20] Within this front, a Vietnamese-controlled Lao political party, known as Dang Lao Doc Lap ("Lao Independence Party"), controlled Laos after 1951, and sponsoring this party was one of the Viet Minh's fundamental tasks.[21]

Laos was neutral, in accordance with the 1954 Geneva Accords. However, as directed by the Pathet Lao and Vietnamese Communists in the Lao Dong Party, the Neo Lao Hak Sat gained control of provinces Phong Saly and Sam Nuea, which bordered North Vietnam. Fall pointed out that, as early as 1951, "the Viet-Minh treated Pathet Lao territory merely as an extension of its own; Laos was divided into three territorial zones and each was subordinate to its neighboring Viet Minh Inter-Zone (Lien Khu), ensuring full coordination of all operations between the two countries."[22] The primary goal of the Pathet Lao and the Neo Lao Hak Sat front was to delay government-leaning front factions from potentially integrating with the Royal Laotian Government, because achieving a more unified government for Laos was one of many goals established in the Geneva Accords. Instead, the Neo Lao Hak Sat worked to buy time and space for more significant infiltration by Viet Minh forces who were consolidating control of provinces along the Vietnamese border.[23]

The practice of extending control through territorialization was one of several key aspects of state formation in Vietnam, and, to a degree, this also applied to Laos. According to Tuong Vu, the importance of coordination between communists in Laos, Cambodia, and Vietnam was "based on a general disregard for the principle of exclusivity embedded in the concept of national territory," and this "contributed to the success of Vietnamese communist state-building."[24] In Laos's case, Vietnamese revolutionaries did not recognize with the border between Vietnam and Laos and practically spilled over into Laotian territory. The creation of sanctuary and the Ho Chi Minh trail through Laos and Cambodia were the central motivating factors for this territorial enlargement. In 1954, Fall described this, writing:

> From what is known through the evaluation of captured documents, one arrives at the following overall conclusion regarding future relations between the DRV and its two "younger brother" states, Laos and Cambodia: "satellization" of the two states and outright annexation of certain provinces already given Vietnamese provincial administration, as is the case of the "Inter-Provinces" of Phong Saly and Sam Neua, occupied by the Pathet Lao; and perhaps of the Southwestern Zone in Cambodia.[25]

The following years, until 1959, marked a subversive period as the Viet Minh and Pathet Lao consolidated their hold over these areas. Fall's 1954 assessment that parts of Laos and Cambodia were added to the DRV as satellites was another signal piece of analysis related to the DRV's goals. Provinces in Laos adjacent to the DRV were important, not as potential dominoes as they were from a Western perspective, but as insulation and sanctuary for future operations designed to unify Vietnam under communist control.

After a series of political struggles escalated, open warfare broke out between the Pathet Lao and the Laotian Royal Government in 1959. This fracture was aggravated by the Soviet Union's support for the Pathet Lao while the United States backed the Royal Government through 1960 and 1961. When President Kennedy entered office in January 1961, this was the volatile geopolitical situation he inherited from Eisenhower, and Laos would remain in crisis until Kennedy and Soviet Party Chairman Nikita Khrushchev issued a joint statement supporting Laos's neutrality later that June.[26] Laos's neutrality, at least in spirit, was finally declared at the July 1962 Geneva Convention. In Fall's perspective, this step merely delayed communist goals, although it did ensure that the Royal Laotian Government remained in control of at least Laos's largest population areas.[27] After 1962, communist subversion continued in Laos, mainly as it concerned the logistic corridor forming the Ho Chi Minh trail.

In *Anatomy of a Crisis*, Fall provided a step-by-step account of conflict through the 1962 Geneva conference. He described the factional strife and numerous coups that took place prior to Laos receiving geopolitical attention from the United States and the Soviet Union. However, he also dedicated significant study to numerous ethnic groups throughout Laos. He was particularly interested in the T'ai and Meo (Hmong) and their role in conflict between the Pathet Lao/Viet Minh and the US-supported Lao government. At the time of the 1962 Geneva Conference, Fall determined that the only effective counterforce left to confront the Viet Minh was "the creation of the Meo maquis (Hmong tribesmen), and that was a U.S. Special Operations mission."[28] The crisis in Laos, as it escalated, contributed significantly to new requirements that called for the development of US Special Forces and capabilities in foreign internal defense and unconventional warfare, and support for such initiatives was due primarily to Kennedy's leadership.

As the crisis unfolded through 1961, Kennedy's interest in anti-guerrilla warfare and counterinsurgency took on greater urgency, but the US army required presidential-level pressure to adapt its warfighting skillsets. According to Arthur Schlesinger, "the Army had fallen into the hands of 'organizational generals' … who looked on the counterinsurgency business as a faddish distraction from the main responsibility of training for conventional assault."[29] Conflict in Laos thus became an early case in which counterinsurgency served as a diversion from the type of big-unit war the US military preferred to fight, as it had in Korea and during World War II. President Kennedy's vision of the utility of counterinsurgency was different. In turn, he ordered the army to increase its research and development into counterinsurgency and for the Special Warfare Center at Fort Bragg to expand its training and mission capacity. Major General William P. Yarborough, then serving as the Special Warfare Center and School commandant, was the central link in executing Kennedy's orders and making, in Schlesinger's words, "the Special Warfare Center into a vigorous and ingenious seminary in the new methods of counterinsurgency."[30] Increased funding and other resources for the elite training center, therefore, supported an organizational advancement sorely needed to confront the type of war Kennedy saw occurring in Laos and Vietnam.

Fall's research on Southeast Asia helped fill a need that Kennedy and Yarborough saw in 1961. The detailed analysis of tribal warfare in Laos Fall crafted in a 1962 Special Operations Research Office (SORO) report appealed to leaders such as William Yarborough. Fall was finally becoming recognized, and the new "elite command" within the growing Special Operations community began to seek him out. On the one hand, key leaders' interest in pursuing options that used irregular methods and smaller and more specialized military forces was a much-needed improvement. Instead of the blunt, heavy-instrument, conventional forces deployed in war, the conflict in Laos and Vietnam required more significant attention to these regions' political and historical context. Relying on specialists who studied local languages and history increased the likelihood that the United States might better support its allies in gaining political legitimacy. On the other hand, as it concerned Fall's research, his gaining respect among the Department of Defense's special warfare community—as demonstrated in General Yarborough's interest in Fall's scholarship on revolutionary warfare—was a stark reversal from the State Department demanding the cancellation of his contract to teach in Cambodia only a few short years earlier. After 1962, Fall would become a sought-after speaker at the Special Warfare Center and School at Fort Bragg, North Carolina.[31]

His attention to detail and descriptions of Viet Minh and Pathet Lao political organization stood out in the SORO report. In Fall's view, the Lao Dong Party's development and control of sanctuary in Laos and Cambodia remained central to supporting the DRV's warfighting capacity and its efforts to undermine the Republic of Vietnam's control over South Vietnam. This was a topic he had studied and written about since the publication of *The Viet-Minh Regime* in 1954.[32] The overall political and territorial tug-of-war among communist and anti-communist factions in Laos also contributed to instability. Worse, and as he described at length in *Anatomy of a Crisis*, it erupted into a considerable geopolitical struggle when superpower competition was layered on top of competing proxy forces.

As in Vietnam, the Viet Minh and Pathet Lao relied on revolutionary warfare and parallel hierarchies as a means of administering these border regions. A key to achieving this control was to increase the perceived local legitimacy of the Pathet Lao and minimize its actual role as a proxy for the DRV. Through such affiliates, controlling Laos was critical to supporting Vietnamese communists, who during the late 1950s and into 1960 were coalescing into the National Liberation Front. In terms of Laos, Fall described the Viet Minh's control over rural populations, despite the Royal Laotian being almost entirely supported by US financial and materiel assistance.

> Once the allegiance of the people has switched to the revolutionary side, the fact that the local government still possesses its regular army and is in control of the government's administrative apparatus in the capital becomes totally unimportant. They are nothing but "a cattle-on-the-hoof," ready to be overthrown when political conditions are ripe.[33]

Fall's analysis of administrative control and political legitimacy in Laos in the early 1960s relied on analytical approaches he had used during the First Indochina War. In addition to taxation, educational systems, and others, he focused on how belligerents competed politically and how they used parallel hierarchies, the "hidden administrative structures which parallels the legal structure and eventually supersedes it," to control contested areas.[34] In Laos, the same "process of established parallel hierarchies dogs the steps of the Royal Laotian government in Vientiane." Fall continued to expand upon the ideas of Gabriel Bonnet and Charles Lacheroy which he had adopted in 1957 and 1958, and he applied this knowledge to his analysis of Viet Minh-Pathet Lao control over Laos. In *Anatomy of a Crisis*, he explored how the implementation of parallel hierarchies was crucial for control over Laotian villages.

With the penetration of the Pathet Lao into northern Laos in 1953 began the establishment of a full-fledged "parallel hierarchy" of Pathet Lao administrators and cadres throughout the country, which reached down through most of the small villages. Like similar movements in other communist countries, the Pathet Lao practiced the rule-by-committee system, ranging from the central level down to the individual villages.[35]

He described the hierarchical organizational structure of an integrated Pathet Lao-Viet Minh shadow government that formed a network of parallel hierarchies through eastern Laos, particularly in Phong Saly and Sam Nuea, which extended into North Vietnam.[36] It is notable that subsequent scholarship on the relationship between the Pathet Lao and North Vietnamese also identified similar patterns but failed to credit Fall for his analysis completed in 1961. In their 1970 study, *North Vietnam and the Pathet Lao: Partners in the Struggle for Laos*, Paul F. Langer and Joseph J. Zasloff described the concept of "parallel hierarchies" with language derived from *Anatomy of a Crisis*, published in 1969. Langer and Zasloff reached a similar conclusion as Fall, writing:

> The Neo Lao Hak Sat reaches down to the village, where it commands a variety of constituent organizations, including those for farmers, young men, and young women. On the administrative level, the Pathet Lao have modified the traditional system, which operates through the provincial, district, and canton level down to the villages by adding a parallel chain of command whose function it is to provide the political supervision. At each level in the chain of command this political component adds the label "Neo" to the administrative designation.[37]

Instead of a citation, the only mention of Fall's work were references to several of his books in Langer and Zasloff's bibliography. The lack of acknowledgment is notable, particularly considering RAND analysts' general esteem for Fall's scholarship.[38] In 1961, Fall confirmed phenomena he had identified as early as 1953 and published in *The Viet-Minh Regime* in 1954. The administrative system of parallel hierarchies was possibly more complicated to achieve in Laos because of the requirements to gain support through Laotian proxies in the Pathet Lao. Still, Vietnamese Communists dominated the Phak Pasasson Lao (Lao People's Party), which controlled the Neo Lao Hak Sat (Lao Patriotic Front, founded in 1956). This dominance ensured communist control that was further consolidated by the Pathet Lao front, which had been founded in August 1950. Certainly, the numerous fronts and changes in organizations over time added a great deal of complexity to an already difficult conflict unfolding in Laos.[39] Ultimately, and earlier in 1951, Fall viewed the political party Dang Lao Doc Lap (Lao Independence Party) as central. However, he later revisited the organizational title of the group and identified it as "Phak Khon Ngan Lao," which was a Lao translation of "Lao Workers' Party."[40] Paul Langer later suggested in 1968 that the correct term for the party cadre operating the Pathet Lao was "Phak Pasasson Lao" (Lao People's Party).[41] Even if there were problems with terminology, the substance of Fall's work mattered since this core Lao group was an adjunct to the Vietnamese Lao Dong and possessed overall control of the Neo Lao Hak Sat front.[42]

The parallel hierarchy this core party created and the lack of attention given to it during much of the 1950s was troubling. Fall described the group, writing:

> Thus far, no Western source (outside some intelligence agencies) has thought it useful to study the Pathet Lao in any great detail. This is particularly regrettable in view of the fact that the Pathet Lao is precisely what its official name of Neo Lao Hak Sat indicates—a front for a hard-core Communist cadre party. The latter, known as the *Phak Khon Ngan Lao* or Laotian Workers' Party, is an extremely small elite organization of which practically nothing is known and which has a total estimated membership of less than one hundred ... the main job of this group is "political preparation."[43]

In a blunt assessment from 1961, he confirmed that "the local administration in Laos is often completely entwined with the Communist underground organization. Thus, had developed a system of 'parallel hierarchy' which is harder to bring under control than the usual situation where the legal administration is under open attack."[44]

This view was an updated version of an even earlier assessment of parallel hierarchies at work in 1959. There, he explained that this was "the old dreaded disease, so well-known from the Indochina War: 'pourissement'—the 'rotting away under your feet'—so hard to stop with conventional means of warfare."[45] Fall added that, to enforce the mechanics of parallel administration, the Pathet Lao system itself was under constant surveillance by a secret organization called the *Kene sane*, which consisted of "roving inspectors who constantly report on how the regular communist administrative echelon performs."[46] Sisouk na Champassak also recognized the infiltration of administrative control through parallel hierarchies, observing in 1961 that "the United States feels that a coalition with the Communists is a dangerous line of conduct, for the history of similar coalitions elsewhere in the world reveals that they end tragically in penetration and seizure of the country by the Communists" and by 1961 "the Pathet Lao had established a parallel underground administration."[47] Champassak, along with Fall, saw the methodology of parallel hierarchies at work, but few scholars articulated how this process functioned.

Parallel hierarchies were even more significant because of the terrain communist forces secured in Laos. Once control over such areas was consolidated, "the situation becomes entirely hopeless if the revolutionary warfare force is in possession of an 'active sanctuary.' Hard-core fighters can maintain themselves in the field almost indefinitely and will disappear only if the active sanctuary ceases to play its role."⁴⁸ This, as Fall explained consistently over the coming years, was a fact on the ground that successive American administrations could not alter once *pourissement* set in. He observed in 1959 how a paltry 1,500 Pathet Lao soldiers forming two Pathet Lao battalions "wreaked havoc throughout northern Laos."⁴⁹ He concluded, "The kind of war about to be fought was not 'modern warfare' but a far more insidious kind of war that, for want of a better term, is best described as 'Revolutionary War.'"⁵⁰ This was a phenomenon he saw in North Vietnam before 1954, and now it was in Laos. Fall knew that it was also emplaced in South Vietnam as well:

> Those are the facts of life of Revolutionary Warfare, and to have attempted for years to gloss over the steadily deteriorating security situation in both Laos and South Viet-Nam in the face of clear storm signs and of French and British warnings must now be paid with crash programs and a political situation which, from one day to the next, may erupt into a full-fledged war.⁵¹

In 1961, this full-fledged war was coming.

* * *

The United States moved toward greater involvement in Vietnam on 26 January 1961. Relying upon a report developed by General Edward Lansdale, Deputy National Security Advisor Walt Rostow, who brought Lansdale's report to President Kennedy, reflected that it provided "an extremely vivid and well-written account of a place that was going to hell in a hack."⁵² According to historian David Milne, Lansdale's bleak memorandum marked "a critical juncture in the history of the Vietnam conflict," which "from that moment, the president's work on Vietnam, guerrilla warfare and all the rest can be dated."⁵³ In Fall's perspective, the Vietnamese communists' groundwork was already well-entrenched and almost impossible to dislodge without serious social, economic, and political reform in the Republic of Vietnam.

In addition to Vietnamese Communists' pinpointed attacks targeting government installations and their extensive assassination campaign against RVN officials, communist agitation and propaganda focused on exploiting grievances caused by Ngo Dinh Diem's divisive decisions. A compendium of repressive policies unleashed by the Republic of Vietnam, along with other aggravating programs, had intensified since the 1955 Battle of Saigon. Key examples included the 1956 removal of South Vietnamese village elders, who were replaced by government-appointed officials. Other policies included Ordinance 6, Edict 10/59, and the failed Agroville Program that forced villagers to relocate to government-controlled camps against their will, and which eventually failed as a program in 1959. Collectively, these policies antagonized local populations and significantly contributed to dissent against Diem's administration. The Strategic Hamlet Program in 1962 added yet another layer to deep-seated unrest among non-communist South Vietnamese. Edward Lansdale, General J. Lawton Collins, and Walt Rostow were among the most prominent authorities who saw an accumulation of problems brewing between 1955 and 1961.[54]

In the coming years, Fall and Lansdale would maintain an uneasy relationship, as Lansdale did not welcome Fall's public criticism of Diem's policies. Nevertheless, they shared an appreciation for the critical importance of political reform in the Diem administration, which was currently an insurmountable challenge confronting Lansdale. Fall argued that political changes were critical but that the Ngo Dinh Diem regime "resisted reform unceasingly."[55] On a personal level, Fall expressed his admiration for Lansdale directly and cited Lansdale's efforts publicly.[56] As for Walt Rostow, Fall believed that his understanding of the political nature of problems in Vietnam was "muddled," and he criticized Rostow for not acknowledging the Diem administration's failures in building political support among the Vietnamese population.[57] In another problematic area, allegations of corruption in Diem's administration antagonized many who were already anti-communist. The critique of an anti-Diem faction, issued through the Caravelle Manifesto in April 1960, along with multiple coup attempts, prominently indicated frustration with Diem's policies and leadership.[58]

In between 1961 and 1963, Fall produced a cascade of publications that not only included a prodigious number of articles but books, such as *Anatomy of a Crisis* and *Street Without Joy*, consolidating his reputation as the foremost expert on Indochina at the time. In a letter to his senior editor for Stackpole publishers, J.B. Sweet, Fall acknowledged the completion of *Street Without Joy* on 8 February 1960, with a simple "Well—this is the 'great moment,' I suppose at least for me."[59] It would become, along with *Hell in a Very Small Place: The Siege of Dien Bien Phu*, the most widely known and influential of the many books Fall produced. According to Fredrik Logevall, *Street Without Joy* also positioned Fall as "the greatest writer on the struggle" that evolved into the Second Indochina War.[60] As Logevall explained, the book influenced an entire generation of military personnel preparing to deploy to Southeast Asia. Fall also produced numerous and extensive studies on Laos, Vietnam, and revolutionary warfare for the Special Operations Research Office (SORO), located at American University in 1962. Among these projects, a 45-page report summarized his findings on factionalism and conflict in Laos.[61] Another SORO publication was the "Casebook on Insurgency and Revolutionary Warfare Volume 1: 1933–1962." This collection, which remains in print, relied upon regional experts, and Fall was responsible for verifying and editing case studies on conflicts in Vietnam, Indonesia, and Malaya.[62] The casebook was significant because it was a primary source of information for US Special Forces deploying to Southeast Asia after 1962.[63] In 1964, he again served as an area specialist for an even more extensive, 150-page analysis on revolutionary warfare in Vietnam, which was a key document supporting SORO's mission to educate military personnel.[64]

1962 to 1963 was a critical juncture in Fall's career because increasing deployments of Special Operations Forces and American Advisors to Southeast Asia boosted demand for more information on the region. Fall's timing, experience, and education enabled him to provide what the developing Special Operations community needed. This made him a much sought-after speaker on Indochina at military institutions and for advisory roles for publications, such as those produced by SORO. In one case, on 18 January 1963, he presented a detailed lecture entitled "Counterinsurgency: The French Experience" at the Industrial College of the Armed Forces, and he used the presentation to explain how French forces confronted the Viet-Minh and lost.[65] Except for readers already familiar with *Street Without Joy*, this was new information for many Americans at the time. It is not surprising, then, that military personnel in the audience had an existential stake in learning about the type of warfare Fall described, especially as the conflict in Southeast Asia continued to grow.

Major General William P. Yarborough at the Special Warfare Center was among the most influential leaders impressed with Fall's scholarship. During World War II, Yarborough established himself as an authority on airborne operations and doctrine, designed US paratrooper boots, and created the distinctive Jump Wings insignia that earth-dwellers looked up to as the Parachutist Badge.[66] By the time World War II was over, Yarborough had made a combined total of forty-nine parachute jumps, foremost among these during the airborne insertion into southern France through Operation

Dragoon (initially called Operation Anvil) in August 1944.[67] Previously, Yarborough had participated in Operation Torch in North Africa, Operation Husky in Sicily, and helped spearhead the Anzio-Nettuno landing, later earning the Silver Star during the spring 1945 offensive in Italy.[68] Yarborough, credited as the "father" of American Special Forces, found in Bernard Fall the type of expert he and his soldiers needed as they prepared to fight in Vietnam. Fall's experience as a member of the French underground and FFI undoubtedly burnished Yarborough's respect for him, as did the fact that Fall had already studied the socio-political elements of warfare in Vietnam for years by the time he came to Yarborough's attention. And, conversely, Yarborough's competency and authority as a leader was not lost on Fall either, whose survival as a member of the French Maquis had depended in part on the successful invasion of Europe, of which Yarborough was a part.

In 1963 and 1964, the US Army's Special Warfare Center used *Street Without Joy* as a text for several classes.[69] In class A-700, "Problems of Development and Internal Defense," not only did *Street Without Joy* figure prominently, but Fall's monograph *Laos: Background of a Conflict* was also included in the course reading list.[70] In another class, "3610A/3: Counterinsurgency in Indo-China," *Street Without Joy* was the single text for the course. According to the syllabus, the course assignments included analysis of seven case studies drawn from Fall's book that examined varying subjects and events during the First Indochina War. These cases ranged from discussion of French *Dinassaut* riverine forces to Fall's analysis of the destruction of Mobile Group 100, the regimental task force in the French Far East Expeditionary Corps that had been destroyed at the Battle of Mang Yang Pass, also known as the Battle of Dak Po or An Khe, between 24–29 June 1954. Fall's detailed chapter on this event, "End of a Task Force," provided compelling lessons regarding the Viet Minh's operational strategy. *Street Without Joy*, it turned out, epitomized a type of applied history because it provided critical and practical information for military personnel preparing to deploy to Vietnam.[71]

Not only were Fall's books used, but Yarborough also repeatedly invited him to visit and give lectures for soldiers at Fort Bragg. In a letter from 1964, Yarborough indicated the value of Fall's visits for his soldiers:

> Dear Bernie, I would like to thank you for the Viet Cong document which you translated and were kind enough to leave here at the school during your last visit. We are always extremely interested in this type of information pertaining to the Montagnard tribes and will put it to good use here at the school. I was very sorry

to have missed seeing you on 5 Nov. I heard many fine comments about your presentation on communist revolutionary warfare and know you did your usual splendid job of putting this subject across to our students. I look forward to seeing you on 8 Dec. Best Regards, William P. Yarborough, MG, USA.[72]

At the US Special Warfare Center at Fort Bragg, then, an invitation from Yarborough validated Fall's scholarship and demonstrated how it possessed utility among soldiers studying revolutionary warfare in Southeast Asia. Among materials found in Yarborough's papers, a quote from Fall's "Revolutionary Warfare in Southeast Asia" was highlighted, suggesting that it stood out to Yarborough. Fall's quote read:

> Of the most essential requirement of winning a revolutionary war is the courage to face the truth that the problem exists at all. This is harder than one thinks. There is always a tendency to camouflage the problem as "banditry" or "mob-action" until one awakens one morning to find that the "chief bandit" now sits in the President's chair in the capital and that the "mob" is defeating one's finest regular troops in a battlefield not exactly suited to their heavy equipment. To lie to others (and be found out) may simply be embarrassing. To lie to oneself about the terrifying possibilities of Revolutionary Warfare may well be fatal.[73]

Fall's numerous presentations at Fort Bragg added to an already busy schedule centered around his role as a professor. In the years between 1961 and 1964, not only was he engaged across multiple professional fronts for the Department of Defense, he still held his position as Ralph Bunche Chair in International Relations at Howard University. This was an intensely dynamic period in Fall's career, in addition to which Fall had also become a father several years earlier. In 1957, Dorothy and Bernard had their first daughter, Nicole, and their second daughter Elisabeth was born in 1960. As a scholar and public intellectual, Fall was in the public eye, and he backed his credibility with years of experience studying Indochina. In turn, his publication track record and unique background opened up opportunities to him that others did not have access to. One such occasion included Fall's opportunity to interview DRV Prime Minister Pham Van Dong and the DRV President, Ho Chi Minh.

After obtaining permission to travel to North Vietnam, Fall met with Pham Van Dong at the Presidential Palace in Hanoi in July 1962. A complete account of this meeting and interview, published in the *Saturday Evening Post* in November 1962, demonstrated how Fall pressed Pham Van Dong on the subject of North Vietnamese materiel assistance to southern revolutionaries and infiltration of North Vietnamese troops to central and South Vietnam.[74] Fall asked: "Would it not be conceivable that some of the almost 100,000

South Vietnamese who went north after 1954 would attempt to slip across your border?" Pham Van Dong replied that, "Sir, in our country, one does not cross borders without permission." Sensing that the North Vietnamese leader wanted Fall's readers to regard conflict in South Vietnam as unassisted and purely internal to the South, Fall pursued the matter, asking, "Would not a spreading of the guerrilla war entail a real risk of American reaction against North Vietnamese territory? You have been to North Korea last year, Mr. Prime Minister; you saw what American bombers can do."[75] Pham Van Dong responded, "We shall offer them no pretext that would give rise to an American military intervention against North Viet-Nam." After this reply, they were joined by Ho Chi Minh. Two years earlier, Fall had written an extensive biographical essay on Ho Chi Minh, so it may have come as a surprise for the 33-year-old scholar to meet the Vietnamese leader.[76]

Their discussion quickly turned to South Vietnam and Ngo Dinh Diem, with Fall asking Ho Chi Minh: "How do you evaluate the situation in South Vietnam?" Ho replied: "Ngo Dinh Diem is in a very difficult position right now and it is not likely to improve in the future. He has no popular support." Fall: "But would you negotiate with South Viet-Nam?" Pham Van Dong: "The situation is not yet ripe for a real negotiation. The South Vietnamese don't really want to negotiate." Ho: "That is absolutely true. They are showing no intention to negotiate." Fall: "But are you not afraid that the situation might degenerate into a protracted war?" Ho:

> Sir, you have studied us for ten years, you have written about the Indochina War. It took us eight years of bitter fighting to defeat you French in Indochina. Now the Diem regime is well armed and helped by many Americans. The Americans are stronger than the French. It might perhaps take ten years, but our heroic counterparts in the South will defeat them in the end … I think the Americans greatly underestimate the determination of the Vietnamese people.[77]

Pham Van Dong then spoke of Ngo Dinh Diem at greater length after Fall asked: "Mr. Prime Minister, what do you think of Ngo Dinh Diem's personal position right now?" Pham Van Dong replied, "It is quite difficult. He is unpopular and the more unpopular he is, the more American aid he will need to remain in power. And the more American aid he gets, the more of an American puppet he'll look and the less likely he is to regain popularity." Fall: "That sounds pretty much like a vicious cycle, doesn't it?" Pham Van Dong: "No, sir. It is a descending spiral."[78] In this interview, recorded as conflict escalated in South Vietnam and a year before Ngo Dinh Diem's death in November 1963, Pham Van Dong's statement was prescient.

The interview also indicated that these leaders were potentially open to negotiations if South Vietnamese leaders would consider them before conflict spiraled out of control. Even if the statements were a propaganda stunt, it recorded at least a willingness to meet. Less known, at the time, were US fears that Ngo Dinh Diem and Ngo Dinh Nhu might consider discussions with the North Vietnamese. George Herring described how Ngo Dinh Diem was acutely aware of his dilemma that Pham Van Dong recognized and pointed out to Bernard Fall:

> Trapped in the dilemma he had feared from the start, he (Diem) recognized that the American presence, although necessary to hold the line against the Vietcong, had introduced another—perhaps pivotal—element into the already unstable Vietnamese political situation, and he became more and more sensitive to American criticism. His growing uneasiness was clearly revealed in May 1963 when Nhu publicly questioned whether the United States knew what it was doing in Vietnam and opposed the further expansion of American advisers. Sometime in the early summer of 1963, Diem and Nhu began to explore the possibility of a settlement with Hanoi which would result in an American withdrawal from Vietnam.[79]

Whether American leaders viewed Pham Van Dong's willingness to negotiate—if South Vietnamese leaders would—as a ploy or not would later factor into the US relationship with Diem in the months leading up to his and Ngo Dinh Nhu's deaths. The year before, in the issue of the *Saturday Evening Post* containing his interview with Pham Van Dong and Ho Chi Minh, Fall advocated a negotiated settlement in Vietnam, writing:

> If we took into account North Vietnamese fears of outside intervention, I believe we could press more effectively for some kind of truce settlement on terms that definitely would not be a "surrender." We could demand the immediate end of guerrilla fighting in the South and a far more effective international inspection system to police the truce. We may not achieve such a settlement, but I feel very strongly that we have no reason to fear it. And we must clearly realize that the alternative means the bloodshed and misery of a long and probably inconclusive guerrilla war—a war that Ho Chi Minh is well prepared to fight.[80]

Fall's interactions with these critical leaders were unique, and rarely were Western scholars provided with the type of opportunity Fall possessed in meeting Pham Van Dong and Ho Chi Minh. In the early and mid-1960s, however, Fall and essentially all others studying the political organization of Vietnamese Communism had limitations that are worth bearing in mind. It is also important to point out that Fall's interviews with Ho Chi Minh and Pham Van Dong might have given Western readers a strong impression, or reinforced already entrenched views, that the North Vietnamese leaders entirely controlled southern communists in the National Liberation Front. In their works published decades after the Vietnam War, David W.P. Elliott and Lien-Hang Nguyen conducted extensive archival research to demonstrate that the National Liberation Front possessed far greater autonomy than Fall could document. Nevertheless, Fall's ability to engage with leaders of such historical importance as Pham Van Dong and Ho Chi Minh was significant. Along with Edgar Snow and few others, Fall was among a small group of Western journalists who met, let alone interviewed, the highest levels of communist leadership in Asia.

In addition to meeting with Pham Van Dong and Ho Chi Minh, Fall introduced the writings of Vo Nguyen Giap and Truong Chinh to American and other Western audiences. Fall profiled Giap, the Minister of Defense and Commander in Chief of the North Vietnamese Army, in an October 1962 printing of Giap's work *People's War, People's Army*. In a detailed description of Giap's life, along with analysis of his strategic, operational, and tactical vision for communist forces in South Vietnam in the early 1960s, Fall concluded: "Giap may well be among the new breed of revolutionary warfare generals for whom the West may find it difficult to produce a worthy match in the foreseeable future," adding, "it is almost impossible within our military system to develop men with both brilliant tactical abilities and wide-ranging political training."[81]

The following year, in 1963, Fall wrote the introduction to *Primer for Revolt: The Communist Takeover in Viet-Nam*, by former Secretary-General of the Lao Dong Party, Truong Chinh.[82] *Primer for Revolt* consisted of two books: *The August Revolution*, first published in serialized form in the newspaper *Su-That (The Truth)* in 1946, and *The Resistance Will Win* published in 1947.[83] Fall provided extensive annotations and historical contextualization for critical events in the 1940s involving Truong Chinh and his party associates. While Fall was undeniably a vital resource for Department of Defense personnel, his academic teaching at Howard University and his outreach through commercial publications made him a public intellectual at an important inflection point in US policy related to Vietnam before large-scale intervention occurred.

As Fall explained in his introduction, Truong Chinh, originally named Dang Xuan Khu before adopting Truong Chinh as a pseudonym, was imprisoned by French forces in Hanoi and at the Son-La labor camp for almost six years between 1930 and 1936.[84] This experience, Fall explained, categorized

Truong Chinh as "a new category of Vietnamese Communist—not the 'parlor pinks' who argued Marx in Paris' Latin Quarter, but a group of prison-hardened Party fanatics who had scores to settle and who harbored no illusions about peaceful co-existence with the colonial administration."[85] Through his sixteen-page assessment, Fall provided readers with the first introduction to the leader who had helped defeat France and who had faced the United States as American forces began to deploy to Vietnam. In the early 1960s, if any Americans were reading about Vo Nguyen Giap or Truong Chinh's ideas, they did so with the notes and introductory lens which Fall provided.

He did not limit his editorial authority to texts by Vietnamese communist leaders. In 1960 and 1961, Fall produced various analyses on subversion and propaganda in Vietnam for government agencies, such as the Special Operations Research Office. However, he also commented on the development of warfare among Western practitioners.[86] In 1963, he wrote the introduction to French counterrevolutionary officer Roger Trinquier's *Modern Warfare: A French View of Counterinsurgency*, initially published in 1961 as *La Guerre Moderne*. Fall had much to say about Trinquier's prodigious skill as an officer leading GCMA (*Groupements de Commandos Mixtes Aéroportés*) units to infiltrate Viet Minh-held territory. Trinquier's position was even more remarkable considering that, as a major, he had almost 20,000 men under his command by 1953.[87]

However, Fall tempered his admiration because Trinquier had previously served as a captain in the Vichy government in Asia during the early stages of World War II, and had later refused to serve in Charles de Gaulle's Free French forces during the liberation of Europe. During most of World War II, Trinquier had acted as a deputy battalion commander of French forces at the International Concession in Shanghai, and then with forces protecting the French embassy in Peking. In December 1941, prior to the attack at Pearl Harbor, Trinquier had avoided Japanese capture in Shanghai because of his Vichy affiliation.[88] Had Trinquier served with Vichy forces in Europe during the war, he would have been the kind of collaborator, one complicit with Nazi Germany's occupation of France, whom Fall and other members of the French Maquis would have targeted.

Trinquier's career in Indochina was remarkable in terms of warfighting, managerial skill, and his capacity for conducting operations independent of supervision from higher levels of command. Operating primarily without much government support, Trinquier's forces were left to their own devices. Funding for GCMA operations was raised through monopolization of the opium trade conducted by Meo (Hmong) villagers during the First Indochina War.[89] Trinquier's connection to the *Service de Documentation Extérieure et du Contre-Espionage* (SDECE), France's external intelligence agency, facilitated access to Vang Pao, a Meo lieutenant supporting French forces from his network of bases in Laos.[90] To fund operations in 1951–3, Trinquier routinely purchased Meo-cultivated opium and sent it to Cap St. Jacques (currently Vũng Tàu), where it was subsequently trucked to a Binh Xuyen faction in Saigon.[91] After selling the opium, this Binh Xuyen faction split profits with Trinquier, who used the proceeds to fund GCMA operations against the Viet Minh.

After war in Indochina, Trinquier remained affiliated with General Raoul Salan, a founder of the anti-Gaullist *Organisation Armée Secrète* (OAS) and a former commander in Indochina. In April 1961, Trinquier, as an OAS supporter, narrowly avoided arrest during the General's Putsch in Algeria.[92] The cumulative effect of these experiences, along with his previous role as a mercenary in the Congo suppressing the Katangan rebellion in January 1961, positioned Trinquier as both a prototype and successor of the soldiers Jean Lartéguy described in his 1960 novel, *The Centurions*. Fall may have had deep moral reservations about Trinquier, but he also appeared to admire his diverse life experiences and qualities as a tactician and operator in Indochina. On the one hand, Fall appreciated how Trinquier understood the dynamic networked qualities of revolutionary warfare and harnessed street-smarts and political savvy to his formal military training to achieve considerable tactical and operational effects. On the other hand, Trinquier's use of torture against members of the FLN in Algeria Fall considered morally bankrupt, and this seriously tempered his respect for Trinquier's field expertise. In contrast, Fall's admiration for Trinquier as a counterrevolutionary officer was exceeded by Fall's respect for Lartéguy, who vividly described French soldiers fighting the Viet Minh against insurmountable odds in 1953 and 1954.

In 1963, there was another reason why Fall composed his introduction to Trinquier's work. He wanted Americans to recognize French mistakes in Indochina and understand how the French, despite their far more extensive experience with revolutionary warfare—especially when compared to those in the US military—still lost to the Viet Minh. He wanted American readers to recognize that technological innovations were not as useful as they may seem. Instead, they mostly created "mere rehashes of old tactics which add a new dimension of speed and bloodiness without basically changing the character of the struggle—nor its outcome."[93] This was especially true "if the same political errors that the French have made are repeated." Fall wanted

Americans to learn the depth of the political problems within Vietnam, which, he believed, "is only dimly perceived in America so far." Written in October 1963, Fall's introduction to Trinquier's work included numerous other warnings, which he began to deploy with greater force.

The same year Trinquier's work and Fall's introduction appeared in English, Fall published *The Two Viet-Nams: A Political and Military Analysis*.[94] The book comprehensively analyzed the United States' escalating intervention in Vietnam, the problem of corruption in the Diem administration, the growing and pervasive role of the National Liberation Front in South Vietnam, and, especially, the progress of revolutionary warfare across South Vietnam and into Laos. At almost 450 pages, the new book consolidated ongoing research Fall gathered since the publication of *Street Without Joy* in 1961. New scholarship provided readers with an updated perspective on economics, Vietnam's colonial history, the Viet Minh's formation, the First Indochina War, and early events leading to the Second Indochina War. Among scholars and other critics apprehensive of US policy in Southeast Asia, Fall's views were also making their presence known in a prodigious number of other accessible publications.[95] As a shorter example, an article called "Vietnam: The Unpleasant Truth" was published in *Newsweek* in August 1962. It was under François Sully's byline and consisted of an interview with Fall in which Fall previewed analysis of many of the themes explored in *The Two Vietnams*.[96] The article became controversial because of a critical caption and photo of a female RVN militia led by Madame Nhu and would lead to Sully's deportation in November 1962.[97] As to the article's content, it mainly consisted of Fall's views.

Among the many answers Fall provided to Sully's questions, two brief distillations stand out. In his assessment of the US effort, he explained, "We must not forget that this is a revolutionary war, that is, a military operation with heavy political overtones. To win the military battle but lose the political war could well become the U.S. fate in Vietnam."[98] In a related question concerning the chance of success in Vietnam, Fall replied, "To win this war we must have inspired leadership capable of developing popular enthusiasm. A U.S. Marine can fly a helicopter better than anyone else, but he simply cannot indoctrinate peasants with an ideology worth fighting for."[99] Variations of this statement peppered almost every study Fall completed over the next several years.

However, if revolutionary warfare was the means through which the National Liberation Front planned to achieve their goals in South Vietnam, parallel hierarchies formed an important organizational framework for facilitating those means. While Fall had learned of the term from French officers, as noted, the concept of alternative administrative systems was a phenomenon he first encountered during World War II. He explained this, writing, "In Nazi-occupied France, the first step involved placing anti-Vichy Resistance members in key posts of the pro-German administration. With the establishment of the CNR (*Conseil National de la Résistance*) in 1942, began the creation of a full-fledged nationwide parallel network of underground administrative organs."[100] Parallel hierarchies, therefore, were the linchpin needed to establish administrative and political control, and this made them the most central factor in determining the efficacy of Vietnamese revolutionary warfare. Fall described this in 1963:

> The DRV's major success lay not in the creation on paper of a central government, but in the effective control of much of the countryside—despite its occupation by a larger Western army—through the establishment of small but efficient administrative units that duplicated the existing Franco-Vietnamese administration. The French call this administrative network hiérachies parallèles. These, rather than the existence of guerrilla battalions, were the source of France's defeat and have also been the source of South Viet-Nam's difficulties from 1957 to the present.[101]

His review of parallel hierarchies revisited the most important primary sources used in his work: the February 1957 and the March/April 1957 issues of *Revue Militaire d'Information*.[102] In 1963, after years of studying parallel hierarchies and the work of French officers who had transplanted these ideas to their war against the FLN in Algeria, Fall remained focused on how these ideas remained so prominent in the National Liberation Front's attempt to gain administrative control over South Vietnam. Writing in *The Two Viet-Nams*, he added, "As far as this writer could ascertain, the Viet-Minh simply took over existing structures. This has an undeniable psychological importance for it leaves the bulk of the population in an administrative environment to which it has been inured—even though the system has been entirely changed from within."[103] Fall added that the National Liberation Front's internal security system enforced compliance whenever resistance to parallel hierarchies surfaced.

The Cong-An, Trinh-Sat, and Dich-Van, groups Fall had discussed at length in earlier writing from 1954, were assessed anew in his analysis of parallel hierarchies in *The Two Viet-Nams*.[104] Fall explored how, as this overall security service evolved in South Vietnam under the control of the National

Liberation Front, it broadened to include three other organizations that focused on turning intellectuals, military units, and "the peasant masses" away from the control of the South Vietnamese government. These groups included, respectively, the Tri-Van, Binh-Van, and Dan-Van.[105] The parallel hierarchies created by Vietnamese Communists had expanded since 1954, and internal surveillance organizations became even more draconian than they had been during the First Indochina War.

Fall focused on the renewed effectiveness of the Dich-Van in particular. "It is the Dich-Van operations which create havoc in South Viet-Nam and which, for obvious reasons, neither American helicopters nor U.S. Special Forces can cope with; the Dich-Van make themselves felt at a specifically 'Vietnamese' level of fighting upon which the foreigner simply has no effect."[106] He added:

> It will be a Dich-Van unit that will burst into a village meeting, call out the names of five boys who recently joined the South Vietnamese Government's youth movement, and gun them down after the reading of a death sentence. It is *that* type of operation—*the violent act for psychological rather than military reasons*—which was the source of the success of the Viet-Minh against the French-Vietnamese forces of the 1940s and 1950s and against the American-Vietnamese forces of the 1960s.[107]

Fall concluded that the Dich-Van would simply "go on murdering village chiefs, youth leaders, teachers, and antimalaria teams—thus isolating the Saigon government from the countryside. In a revolutionary war, that is precisely what separates victory from defeat: the control of the rural population."[108] Such writing expressed not only Fall's reading of other French officers' assessments, but it was also a transmission of his knowledge and experience of a certain type of war, amassed during and since World War II. Fall's adoption of an irregular approach to warfare and his emphasis on civilian populations suggest was likely a key factor to why leaders, such as William Yarborough at Fort Bragg, recognized the importance of his scholarship.

Others also looked to *The Two Viet-Nams* for potential political solutions. In the 28 October 1963 issue of I.F. Stone's *Weekly*, Stone pointed out the relevance of information Fall gained from his 1962 interview with Pham Van Dong and Ho Chi Minh, which he related in *The Two Viet-Nams*. Stone explained:

> The most important revelation in Bernard B. Fall's forthcoming book *The Two Viet-Nams* is that the North Vietnamese leaders in three interviews given Westerners last year made it obvious to all three that North Vietnam had backed away from outright conquest of South Vietnam and was veering toward a nego-

tiated solution embodying the existence of a neutral South Vietnamese state that would not be reunited for the North for a long time to come.[109]

There was a chance for peace in 1963 that Fall, Stone, and others believed could be achieved. At the time, as they understood it, negotiations offered a potential solution, and this was an outlook even Ngo Dinh Diem and Ngo Dinh Nhu, as George Herring noted, saw as an alternative to war. Whether it would become a lost chance for peace was still to be determined.

II—A New Father of the New Left

As the potential for negotiations lingered into October 1963, Americans seeking to prevent further intervention in Vietnam created the Vietnam Information Center in Washington, DC. Five months later, in March 1964, members of the group heard Bernard Fall speak about conflict in Vietnam and used his analysis to support the center's "Write to the President Drive."[110] This initiative signaled an important move in generating more considerable public interest in a diverse and quickly evolving anti-war movement. It also marked another point in Fall's career through which he contributed a realistic and moderate outlook to the New Left that became pronounced with the publication of *The Viet-Nam Reader*, which he co-edited with Marcus Raskin in 1965.

The Viet-Nam Reader was the earliest and most critical information source used in the emerging anti-war movement. It included material on the role of the US in the world, but it focused primarily upon policy related to intervention in Vietnam. Its goal was simple: to enable "the reader to guard against the ideological or rhetorical in analyzing the Viet-Nam crisis, since it is only in the comprehension of the political, that is, the highly particular, that the problem of Viet-Nam is capable of solution."[111] Collected documents ranged from John Quincy Adams' "Principles of Foreign Policy" to others written by George Kennan, Dean Acheson, and many other leaders. The book was hardly a liberal partisan manifesto, and it also included policy perspectives from Walt Rostow, McGeorge Bundy, Robert McNamara, and Dean Rusk, along with international perspectives offered by Charles de Gaulle and U Thant.

Fall's and Raskin's selections were comprehensive and provided a spectrum of views from which readers could formulate their own opinions. They intended that this would also increase its appeal among a large and politically mixed reading audience. By May 1965, *The Viet-Nam Reader* became especially popular among politically active students during nationwide teach-ins in 1965 and the following years. In Charles DeBenedetti's view, *The Viet-Nam Reader* filled a "vacuum of understanding" created by the 1965 teach-ins, which had "created a market for information."[112] In more ideological terms, the teach-ins "legitimized dissent at the outset of the war." If the teach-ins "legitimized dissent," *The Viet-Nam Reader* substantiated discourse on the subject by providing access to primary sources used to argue for or against further American intervention.

Fall had traveled a long road to this point. In addition to lecturing soldiers at Fort Bragg preparing to deploy to Vietnam, he was also receiving requests to speak at events from organizations in the early anti-war movement. Undoubtedly, this was an uneasy political balance to navigate, especially as debates over war in Vietnam grew divisive. However, he mostly avoided the extreme ends of liberal and conservative fundamentalism. He maintained a balanced perspective, in that he supported American personnel deploying to Vietnam even as he argued against US policy as the war escalated in and after 1965. Early that year, the side he had chosen to support was that of the civilian Vietnamese population, and of the soldiers volunteering and serving out of patriotism for a war that would be difficult to win. Early on, Fall remained anti-communist and believed that the war could be won, but this belief quickly dissipated as intervention grew in 1965. Not long after war escalated with Operation Rolling Thunder—the aerial bombardment of North and South Vietnam—Fall concluded that he could not support the war as it was being fought. The overmilitarized policy of the Lyndon Johnson administration was counterproductive, and operations such as Rolling Thunder drove the potential for political negotiations—of the kind Fall had envisioned as possible in October 1963—to an early grave.

As a result of *The Reader*, Fall's scholarship began reaching larger audiences. On the weekend of 15–16 May 1965, the Inter-University Committee for a Public Hearing on Vietnam organized a radio program to over 122 college campuses that reached "an incalculable number of home listeners" in addition to the thousands of students who dialed into the simulcast.[113] In the transmission from Washington, DC, Bernard Fall, Seymour Melman, and Hans Morgenthau participated as speakers opposing US policies in Vietnam, while Arthur Schlesinger, Jr., Zbigniew Brzezinksi, and Walt Rostow spoke in defense of the Johnson administration's policy positions.[114] The teach-ins were important, not just because they informed the American public but because they represented an impressive organizational movement that, in the view of Charles DeBenedetti, mattered more than "their novelty or the extent of student protest."[115] As an indication of the book's appeal, *The Viet-Nam Reader* sold through three printings by early 1965 and appeared in paperback later that year.

Reviewers for military journals also saw the book's value. In a 1966 *Naval War College Review*, *The Reader* was regarded as an "obvious textbook for dissension." Nevertheless, the review also explained that "the wealth of bibliographical material alone is highly recommended and that *The Reader* will provide considerable depth and insight to the student of international relations, be he supporter or dissenter."[116] As 1965 unfolded, Fall and Raskin both faced the fact that US intervention was not becoming more restrained, but was instead escalating dramatically. The book's conclusion revealed Fall's and Raskin's political position while offering comprehensive political solutions for ending the war in 1965.

Fall and Raskin held that, with its government seat in Saigon, the continued independence of a reformed and viable Republic of Vietnam was critical. Positing a potential political model that had succeeded in Europe, they described how the Austrian State Treaty of 15 May 1955 contributed to Austria's neutrality and helped support European political stability amid the Cold War.[117] Their recommendations explored the potential for a similar political reconciliation in Southeast Asia. If South Vietnam could maintain independence and achieve political neutrality, such as that achieved by Austria's Declaration of Neutrality, it might gain a similar form of international backing from Russia, France, the United States, and the United Kingdom.[118] If this kind of political neutrality could function in Austria—which was a fulcrum in two world wars—why could it not become a model to emulate in the case of South Vietnam as well?

Fall's interactions with Marcus Raskin also marked a turning point in his career. Raskin and Richard Barnet, a State Department lawyer, founded the Institute for Policy Studies (IPS) in 1963, a liberal Washington think tank which positioned itself almost immediately at the forefront of the anti-Vietnam War movement. Raskin had previously served as a staff member in the Kennedy administration but, along with Barnet, left in frustration over the lack of systematic transformation they believed could only be accomplished through policy research, advocacy, and grassroots activism.[119] Fall became an early associate fellow at the Institute for Policy Studies, and collaboration in 1965 on *The Viet-Nam Reader* pulled him and Raskin closer together politically.[120]

The IPS's anti-war position grew immensely, and by 1968 it had offshoots in the draft-resistance movement. In early 1968, Raskin was indicted with an anti-draft group known as the "Boston Five," composed of Dr. Benjamin Spock, Michael Ferber, William Sloan Coffin, and Mitchell Goodman.[121] However, it is unlikely that Fall would have taken part in this sort of political activism due primarily to his dedication to military service and his support for military personnel who volunteered out of a sense of duty and patriotism for the United States. Fall often scorched political policies without remorse, but his frustration did not extend to criticizing individuals willing to serve, or to preventing draft procedures. In contrast, partisan bickering often failed to acknowledge the differences between policy and the people ordered to execute policy.

Telford Taylor led the legal defense for the Boston Five. Taylor, a Columbia law professor at the time, had served as the chief of prosecution during the Nuremberg Military Tribunal. In 1948 and 1949, Taylor was Fall's supervisor while he worked as a research analyst during the Krupp Corporation's trial.[122] Taylor's prestige and intelligence, his reservations about using war as a policy instrument, and his growing and outspoken views against the war in Vietnam undoubtedly influenced his decision to defend Raskin and the Boston Five, who were later acquitted in the case.[123] Fall did not embrace an anti-draft position, yet his outspoken views had created a furor since the late 1950s. As noted, government officials' concern extended to the point where the FBI were surveilling Fall through wiretapping, trailing, and other invasions of his and his family's privacy.[124] FBI surveillance began as early as 1959, likely after Fall's critical remarks concerning American Foreign Assistance programs for South Vietnam, and it lasted until late 1964. The CIA also had a file on Fall that CIA Director John McCone distributed to President Kennedy to consult in 1962.[125] Characteristically undeterred by FBI pressure, Fall remained outspoken and focused his critical views on US intervention in Vietnam in a manner that also aligned with Telford Taylor's anti-war perspective.[126]

There was another intersection among Fall, Raskin, and the Institute for Policy Studies. In 1964, the IPS' platform converged with the Civil Rights Movement, including the Student Non-Violent Coordinating Committee (SNCC).[127] Stokely Carmichael, a key leader of SNCC, had been a student of Fall's at Howard University. Fall, as his wife Dorothy recalled, "had strong feelings about wars of liberation, and he was glad to impart them to young people who were often part of the American Civil Rights revolution."[128] While on a Southeast Asia Treaty Organization (SEATO) Research Fellowship, Fall met with French Colonel Jean Deuve, most likely in 1959, in Laos. When the colonel asked him what he taught at Howard University, Fall quipped: "*Nous fabriquons de futurs révolutionnaires!*"[129] The extent to which Fall meant for the remark to be taken seriously is debatable, but he had great affection for his students at Howard and sincerely wished for them to gain the social justice and equality they sought. Before Carmichael graduated from Howard with a BA in Philosophy in 1964, it is possible that Carmichael's and SNCC's affiliation with IPS facilitated Fall's awareness or even potential interaction with Marcus Raskin. His work at Howard and later with Raskin certainly further stirred in Fall a deep-seated sense of humanitarianism and morality, providing an outlet for voicing these concerns. The injustices he saw in Vietnam, which he also saw around him in Washington, DC, and in the United States more broadly, undeniably outraged him.[130]

This personal drive for justice shaped his scholarship, but he was also haunted by what he had lived through as a young man during World War II. Above all, these memories centered on the murder of his parents and his experiences of the rise and brutality of Nazi Germany. As he knew firsthand, the Nazis' depravity had reached unthinkable depths. He was determined to ensure that his students never lost sight of the atrocities authoritarianism could inflict. This was a point he drove home when he was interviewed for Howard University's magazine. Fall served as a faculty advisor for the "World Affairs" club on campus between 1959 and 1961, and according to the interviewing journalist, Percy Johnston:

> Prof. Bernard Fall stated recently, prior to the club's presentation of a documentary film on the War Crimes trial in Germany, that the club is intended for everyone who is interested in the external world. Dr. Fall emphasized that the club is not a club in which Government majors and minors sit around and toss their newly acquired knowledge of surface information back and forth.[131]

The viewing of the film of the Nuremberg trials, which included evidence filmed at Nazi camps, demonstrated Fall's goal to teach his students how it was possible to manipulate the democratic process with totalitarian ends in mind, to the ultimate destruction of democracy itself. Johnston added:

> For those who saw the film documentation of the Nazi brutality, and for those who did not see the film, but are aware of even the most infinitesimal amount of facts concerning the rise of Hitler and his Nazi gangsters, there exists a striking parallel to the rise of Hitler in the 1930s in contemporary America …Your reporter would like to point out that in the past 3 years there have been some sixty odd bombings, the majority of which were inflicted against property owned by or used by Negroes. Until the misguided bombers turned their attention to Jewish synagogues and Churches attended by whites, the Federal Government, the State governments and American college students did noth-

ing—just as the German Federal and State governments, and German college students did nothing when Adolf Hitler and his cut-throats (prior to his ascendency to the Chancellorship) first began attacking Jews.[132]

Even though he endured surveillance by the FBI, Fall did not write a statement that paralleled Johnston's concerns about rising domestic authoritarianism in the United States. However, he certainly wanted his students to stand against the violence they endured as black students in America, and to recognize how political power and political violence were organized and functioned. This information and Fall's teaching on political power more broadly were points Stokely Carmichael undeniably heeded. For Carmichael, governance was "simply a question of who has the power to legalize violence."[133] In Vietnam, according to Carmichael, "our violence is legalized by white America. In Washington D.C., my violence is not legalized, because Africans living in Washington D.C. do not have the power to legalize violence." For this reason, systemic legalized violence, as Carmichael perceived it, originated with white male dominance over American governance. In a view influenced by Frantz Fanon, Carmichael perceived the monopoly and wielding of violence as implicit in a colonial state's operation.[134] While a student at Howard, Carmichael appeared to be impressed with Fall, writing:

> Among the European expatriate professors at Howard had been a Frenchman named Bernard Fall. Before most people in the States even knew where Vietnam was—back in the Kennedy administration—this Frenchman was writing about the Vietnamese' twenty-five-year struggle for independence from France. I'll never forget a lecture he gave on the battle of Dien Bien Phu. The arrogant French generals—trained at Saint-Cyr, the French equivalent of West Point—were contemptuous of the "primitive and backward peasant army."[135]

After describing Fall's analysis of Dien Bien Phu in more detail, Carmichael added, "Of course we can say the French were ignorant and arrogant. But one could almost excuse them, because what the Vietnamese People's Army (the Viet-Minh) did was humanly impossible. At least to the Western mind."[136] Carmichael's descriptions of racial paternalism leading to France's underestimation of the Viet Minh likely reflected previous discussions he'd had in Fall's class. The United States, in all cases, could do better. Its potential for forming an improved, if not perfect, union was, in Fall's view, likely America's greatest strength. In contrast, its legitimization of violence and racist laws, as inflicted on America's black and Native American citizens, displayed a degradation in the values supposedly promulgated in the US Constitution. As it applied to the United States, the belief that "injustice anywhere is a threat to justice everywhere" said as much.[137] In terms of US foreign policy related to Southeast Asia, how would it be possible to implement conceptions of justice in Vietnam, or anywhere beyond America's shores, when equal justice before the law and equal rights as guaranteed by law remained unfulfilled in the United States?

III—The Fulbright Program Makes a Full Circle: Fall and Fulbright, Washington, DC, 1965

In addition to Carmichael and those reading *The Viet-Nam Reader*, a few leaders in the US government were also waking up to what Bernard Fall was writing. Chairman of the US Senate Foreign Relations Committee, J. William Fulbright, read *Street Without Joy* in 1965 and requested a meeting with its 38-year-old author that November. The results of this meeting were illuminating for Fulbright. According to historian Randall B. Woods: "The lunch meeting with Fall marked the beginning of Fulbright's efforts to educate himself on every aspect of the war in Southeast Asia."[138] Earlier in August 1964, Fulbright had shepherded the Gulf of Tonkin Resolution through Congress, which endeared him to Lyndon Johnson. Fulbright had, as Fredrik Logevall explained, "worked hard on doubters such as Mike Mansfield, George McGovern, and Frank Church, assuring them that the president would consult fully with Congress before embarking on any escalation of the conflict."[139] Logevall added that Wayne Morse, in contrast to Fulbright, "predicted that his colleagues would live to regret their votes, and many of them did."

Fulbright later affirmed Morse's prediction, writing in 1966 that "my role in the adoption of the resolution of August 7, 1964, is a source of neither pleasure nor pride to me today."[140] He continued: "the resolution was adopted during an election campaign in which the President was telling the American people that it would be a mistake for the United States to become involved in a major war in Asia while criticizing his opponent for proposing just that." Granting President Johnson such sweeping authority as was provided by the Tonkin Gulf Resolution, Fulbright conceded, "was a mistake which I trust will not soon be repeated."[141] In this context of growing misgivings within Congress, Fulbright sought Fall's expertise on Southeast Asia and his views on the potential consequences stemming from the escalation of US involvement as 1965 progressed.

Fulbright previously served as a member of the House of Representatives from January 1943 to January 1945 and represented Arkansas in the Senate from 1945 to 31 December 1974.[142] He was the Senate Committee on Foreign

Relations Chairman from 3 January 1959, until his retirement. Born in Sumner, Missouri in 1905, Fulbright excelled in academics, attended the University of Arkansas, was elected president of the student body, and was a four-year starting running back for the University of Arkansas Razorbacks football team between 1921 and 1924. After graduating with a degree in history, he became a Rhodes Scholar at Pembroke College at Oxford, graduating in 1928. He later earned a law degree at George Washington University in 1934.

Bernard Fall's initial introduction to Fulbright began in 1950, and it was entirely indirect. As a young researcher during the Nuremberg Trials, Fall had applied for one of the earliest rounds of the new Fulbright Exchange Program a few years after it was signed into law in August 1946.[143] In December 1950, Fall's Fulbright Scholarship application was accepted, and he traveled to the United States to begin graduate studies at the Maxwell School at Syracuse University in the autumn of 1951.[144] Thus, the Fulbright Scholarship provided an initial step in Fall's journey studying warfare in Southeast Asia. While it is impossible to know whether Fall would have found another scholarship of some sort to pursue graduate education, other than the Fulbright Scholar Program, few other opportunities existed when he applied for the scholarship in 1950. In the fifteen years after becoming a Fulbright Scholar, Fall's invitation to meet with J. William Fulbright to discuss the conflict in Vietnam brought the Fulbright exchange program full circle. After all, Fall was among the earliest cohorts to study through the program, and by 1965 his scholarship was beginning to shape Fulbright's views.

Fall's face-to-face meeting with Fulbright had simple origins. In November 1965, Fulbright met with Carl Marcy, the Senate Foreign Relations Committee's Chief of Staff; Pat Holt, a Latin American expert; and James Lowenstein, a Southeast Asia expert, to discuss the growing war in Vietnam. Fulbright remarked that he had recently read *Street Without Joy*, and he asked if anyone knew Fall, then teaching nearby at Howard University. Since Lowenstein knew Fall, he invited Fall to meet with Fulbright the following Monday.[145] Fulbright's perspective on the US role in Vietnam changed as a result of his meeting with Fall, and they continued to meet on several occasions in 1966. Carl Marcy later described how "Fall used to stop by the Committee every time he came back from Indochina," adding, "Fulbright developed an admiration for him."[146] The senator's reliance on Fall's expertise was a remarkable outcome and a concrete realization of the goals of the exchange program bearing Fulbright's name.

The Senator's renewed perspective on Vietnam quickly put him at odds with his old friend and fellow southern senator, Lyndon B. Johnson from

Johnson City, Texas. According to Randall Woods, "the break with Johnson over the Dominican intervention created in the (senator) alienation sufficient to prepare him emotionally for open conflict with the administration over Vietnam."[147] Historian William Berman shared this perspective concerning Fall's contributions to Fulbright's understanding of Vietnam, adding:

> Thanks to his conversations with the noted scholar Bernard Fall, Fulbright was able to see the conflict in Vietnam in a new and different light ... with Fall serving as a catalyst, Fulbright was led to a growing literature on the subject. The writings of Philippe Devillers and Jean Lacouture, I.F. Stone's *Weekly*, along with Fall's already distinguished work, provided him with a framework for understanding events in the region which was diametrically opposed to the one held by the administration.[148]

Due to his growing awareness of the realities of the Vietnam War, Fulbright perceived that his critique of American foreign policy demanded a transition from that of ardent Cold Warrior to a position where limited national commitment and greater international cooperation were increasingly important.

These changes in Fulbright's perception pertained both to Vietnam as well as American relations with the People's Republic of China. In 1965, divergent attitudes toward China existed. However, Secretary of Defense Robert McNamara expressed a prevailing view when he wrote to Johnson that "China ... looms as a major power threatening to undercut our importance and effectiveness in the world, and, more remotely but more menacingly, to organize all of Asia against us."[149] McNamara added: "Our ends cannot be achieved and our leadership role cannot be played if some powerful and virulent nation—whether Germany, Japan, Russia, or China—is allowed to organize their part of the world according to a philosophy contrary to ours."[150] In contrast, Fulbright's thoughts on China offered a different perspective, and his discussions with Fall about Vietnamese history had much to do with his changing views.

According to Fulbright, America's contentious outlook toward China created more problems than needed. In 1966, he explained that "The more pertinent questions for America are whether, by being so hostile, we are not helping to perpetuate the extremist phase of the Chinese Revolution and whether ... we could not encourage her progress toward moderation."[151] Fulbright recognized that a particularly horrendous war in Korea had understandably created a deeply pejorative image of America for Chinese leaders, and likewise of China for those in the United States. However, he noted, "my own hope is that one day soon we will moderate our hostility and offer China the hand of friendship, knowing full well that it is almost certain to be rejected but knowing as well that honest and repeated offers of friendship may weaken the Chinese image of a hostile America."[152] Even as early as 1966, McNamara and Fulbright differed widely in their perspective concerning the potential implications of the United States taking steps to initiate an improved relationship with the Chinese.

The opportunity for a potential resolution to the Vietnam War—by creating an opening to China and improving Sino-American relations—was not lost on Fulbright. Yet there was admittedly little concrete evidence, let alone intelligence, for US authorities to consult that might indicate the Politburo's position on the Sino-Soviet split within the Lao Dong Party, which controlled North Vietnam. Similarly, there was little evidence for knowing Chinese views with any clarity. Intelligence collection and reporting, however, was not necessarily the only way to make sense of relations among these communist states. Fall realized that there were other ways to assess the North Vietnamese state's potential political position concerning its relations with the Soviet Union and China. Centuries of conflict between Vietnam and China provided historical context for American leaders to gain insights from, but so did the cooperation between Vietnamese and Chinese communists which began in 1949. The idea of building a diplomatic bridge between Washington, DC and Beijing to potentially contribute to resolving war in Vietnam originated in Fall's meetings with Fulbright. This was a perspective Fall advocated that Senator Fulbright consider, and the potential for improved American-Sino relations having further positive effects in Vietnam was a matter Fulbright meditated on at length in 1966. He published these and other assessments in his book, *The Arrogance of Power*.[153]

The senator recognized in late 1965 after meeting with Fall that an Asian communist monolith did not exist. Vietnamese Communism followed a path that was not entirely locked in step with Maoist ideology or entirely under the PRC's control. Fall, it is likely, explained to Fulbright that land reform and collectivization in North Vietnam were disasters. Backlash leading to riots against DRV policy erupted even in Ho Chi Minh's home province, Nghe An. The horrible outcomes of collectivization had originated out of blindly following Chinese policy and attempting to force it to work in Vietnam. Truong Chinh, the former Lao Dong Party Secretary-General, was demoted in 1955 because of the massive failure that came from following Chinese directions too closely.

As Fulbright might have known, Truong Chinh's career and history was an area in which Fall had significant expertise when they met in 1965. And as for

Ho Chi Minh, he was a communist, but he was Vietnamese first. As Fulbright explained, "This means, as Bernard Fall wrote, that Ho is probably equipped with an instinctive fear of Chinese domination (no matter what its color) just as most observers agree that to Khrushchev any Germany might be slightly suspect."[154] Much later, evidence suggested that Fall and Fulbright were correct in their view regarding Vietnamese Communist leaders striking their own path toward the future, because in 1963 the Lao Dong Party sought to achieve an independent strategic course that took neither the Soviet nor the Chinese side in the Sino-Soviet split. In the Vietnamese Communist Party (Lao Dong) Central Committee's Twelfth Plenum in December 1965, Party General Secretary Le Duan reemphasized his party's independence—both political and intellectual—as had been proclaimed at the Ninth Plenum in late 1963. Instead of taking either the Soviet or Chinese side, Le Duan asserted that "the strategic policy of our party differs from the policies of the Soviet Communist Party and the Chinese Communist Party."[155]

The reality that China and Vietnam possessed a turbulent historical relationship, one marked by invasion but also through integration in many respects, was a central point Fall wanted Fulbright to recognize as he created more vigorous Congressional oversight of Vietnam War policy. Perhaps because they bordered each other, the historical divisions between China and North Vietnam endured, despite their cooperation against the French and then against the United States. Impossible to know at the time, relations between the two communist states would soon break down completely.[156] As Fulbright began to question the national security importance of Vietnam to the United States, in addition to his ongoing concerns regarding the overbearing power of the executive branch, he initiated the Senate Foreign Relations Committee Hearings in 1966. In January and February, the initial hearings included testimony by Secretary of State Dean Rusk, LTG James Gavin, George Kennan, General Maxwell Taylor, and Agency for International Development administrator David Bell.[157] It also included, on 4 February 1966, testimony by Bernard Fall.[158]

In Fall's hearing, he called for the committee to reassess the idea that intervention in Vietnam was a necessity for American national security, as well as the immense financial and moral cost to the United States that it entailed. According to William Berman, "Fall saw the United States victimized by the same illusions of military power that had earlier defeated the French," and as regarded the financial cost, Fall left the committee to "ponder his calculation that for every Viet-Cong casualty, the 'United States pays $311 in a country whose per capita is $102 a year.'"[159] Fall stressed in the months to come that moral costs would grow in correlation with the massive expenditure of ammunition that eventually exceeded amounts fired in both the European and Pacific theaters of World War II combined. If bullets and bombs were equivalent to the depletion of America's credit and standing in the world, the Vietnam War was digging America into a serious hole of debt.

Fulbright also used the Senate Foreign Relations Committee hearings to restrain the power of the executive branch, which expanded with Johnson's election in 1964. On move to curtail executive overreach, Fulbright explained that he sought a "restoration of a proper constitutional balance between the Executive and the Legislature."[160] This imbalance resulted from a series of crises beginning in 1940, when the executive branch gained an ascendency which continued to grow through five subsequent administrations. However, several events in the 1960s alarmed Fulbright concerning the degree and expansiveness of executive overreach. These included the Bay of Pigs Invasion; the Cuban Missile Crisis; the Dominican Intervention in 1965; the Tonkin Gulf Resolution; and the development of President Johnson's Asian Doctrine, which stemmed from the Honolulu Declaration of 19 April 1966 between Johnson and the Republic of Vietnam's Prime Minister Nguyen Cao Ky.

Ultimately, the Fulbright-led hearings analyzed the Johnson administration's efforts to counter Vietnamese revolutionary warfare. However, they also prepared the United States for minimizing containment as détente evolved between the Soviet Union and the United States in 1969, and with the onset of rapprochement with the People's Republic of China. Fulbright's vision of opening relations with China in 1966 also demonstrated foresight, on which subsequent American leaders would capitalize. In Randall Wood's view, "long before Nixon or Kissinger sought to open the door to China, Fulbright had advocated a fresh approach to Mao's regime. His China hearings in 1966 had gone far to demythologize the entire subject."[161] His conversations with Fall had much to do with Fulbright undertaking the hearings and furthering his understanding of Sino-Viet relations. According to David Elliott, the significance of the United States opening relations with China created a geopolitical context in which "U.S.–China rapprochement divested Vietnam of most of its significance to the superpowers."[162] And this issue, as Charles DeBenedetti explained, was a subject that "the Senator had been studying assiduously under the tutelage of Bernard Fall."[163]

The discussions between Fall and Fulbright began with a late autumn meeting in 1965, but their exchanges had originated in 1946 with the establishment of the Fulbright Exchange Program. As Fulbright believed, education formed the beating heart of diplomacy, and well-informed diplomacy and reconciliation were something that the world needed in 1965 as much as it needed it in 1946. According to William Berman, an improved understanding of Vietnam on Fulbright's part "revealed the inner journey he himself had taken since late 1965, in no small measure because of Fall."[164] Bernard Fall assisted J. William Fulbright in formulating the right questions to ask concerning American intervention in Vietnam. Once the war began, he helped J. William Fulbright recognize that the most pertinent and vital questions consisted of determining how the war could and should end.[165]

IV—"Two Thousand Years of War in Viet-Nam"

> I have read every French parliamentary debate on Indochina since 1945, and they make instructive reading as bewildered but honest men were faced, on one hand, with glowing reports that the war was being won and, on the other, with new requests for more funds and troops. Even when the United States made available to the French in 1953–54 almost unlimited funds and in many fields, more equipment than they could usefully handle, the war was not being won on the battlefield.
>
> <div align="right">– Bernard Fall, <i>New York Times</i>, 3 November 1966[166]</div>

In April 1846, François Guizot, head of the French government under Louis-Philippe I, sent a letter to the Governor-General of Algeria, Thomas-Robert Bugeaud. Guizot wrote:

> In response to each crisis, we have too often proclaimed a final triumph, complete control, the accomplishment of a pacification mission. Let us get rid of those illusions, this will be the only way for us to continue to make the efforts needed to ensure those claims do become a reality.[167]

To achieve the reality of "pacification" sought by Guizot, "Père" Bugeaud, father of the *razzia* in *les territoire Français*, resorted to war without restraint. French generals believed this was necessary to eliminate Algerian resistance, and their reasons for total war were simple. According to General le Comte de Castellane:

> In Europe, once you are master of two or three large cities, the entire country is yours. But in Africa, how do you act against a population whose only link with the land is the pegs of their tents? The only way is to take the grain which feeds them, the flocks which clothe them.[168]

After two decades of living through and studying war by 1966, Fall was opposed to the type of "pacification" Guizot, Bugeaud, and Castellane had inflicted on Algeria over a century prior. Fall had seen total war in Europe, and he had been one of those "whose only link with the land was the pegs of their tents" among the Maquis and as an émigré. He was well aware that US military power could completely devastate Vietnam, but he held that this would entail a corruption of American values.

Besides writing and working to inform his students and leaders, such as Fulbright or Yarborough, there was little Fall could do to change US policy in Vietnam. His prodigious scholarship, consisting of over 200 reports, commentaries, articles, and several books by late 1966, indicated he had put substantial effort toward educating readers about Vietnam and the reality of warfare there.[169] He planned to return to Southeast Asia in December 1966 to study the National Liberation Front and complete an article commissioned by Robert Cowley, a features editor of *Horizon* magazine who had formerly worked for the journal *American Heritage*. Fall met with Cowley in New York City in September 1966 to discuss the framework for his article on the history of warfare in Vietnam.[170]

While being interviewed in 2017 to discuss his meeting with Fall back in 1966, Cowley recalled that Fall had asked him, "How far back in time do you want me to go?" to which Cowley had replied: "As far back as you need."[171] This editorial latitude resulted in the twenty-page article, "Two Thousand Years of War in Viet-Nam." Cowley and Fall planned for the article to appear the following spring in the April–May issue of *Horizon*, a hardcover journal with J.M.W. Turner's painting "The Fighting Temeraire Tugged to Her Last Berth" on the cover.[172] The author byline described Fall as "a Frenchman and Professor of International Relations at Howard University, currently in South Viet-Nam on a Guggenheim Grant. His latest book, *Hell in a Very Small Place*, is about the battle of Dien Bien Phu."[173] Over fifty years later in 2017, Cowley recalled that meeting the well-known 39-year-old expert had been initially intimidating, but that Fall's "friendly demeanor really stood out." Cowley remembered especially how, upon meeting Fall, "he put me at ease."[174]

The study for *Horizon* was unique because of its historical scope, which extended to ancient Vietnam.[175] The article also departed from Fall's more typical analysis on contemporary topics, such as parallel hierarchies or another aspect related to contemporary Vietnamese politics and war. For example, he wrote:

> Until recently archeologists felt that much of Viet-Nam's Bronze Age culture, particularly the beautiful finds at Dong-Son, was "imported" from the Han civilization about 500 B.C., but one of the most brilliant of the new generation of French researchers, anthropologist Bernard Groslier, suggests that part of the

Dongsonian culture may have been indigenous to Vietnam. With Dong-Son culture, Viet-Nam entered the civilized world as we know it. Beautiful bronze statuary and huge drums of clearly Dongsonian origin began to show up throughout Southeast Asia and as far away as the Indonesian archipelago and the western Pacific.[176]

Fall was also interested in imperialism in the article, but of a type that had existed in Southeast Asia centuries before Dutch, British, French, and American colonists arrived.

In the late 15th century, Vietnamese rulers turned their sights southward. There the Chams had let fertile agricultural land lie fallow in their preoccupation with trading, raiding, and building temples, while the already teeming Vietnamese had been constricted to their lowland deltas in the Red River region. What began now was a nasty episode of colonialism with overtones of genocide. The Vietnamese began to destroy the Cham state piecemeal, city by city and province by province.[177]

Fall wrote "Two Thousand Years of War in Viet-Nam" so his readers could better understand Vietnam's history and its long and contentious relations with neighbors in China, Cambodia, and Laos. Colonialism was not only a Western phenomenon imposed on the people of Southeast Asia. It was horrible but endemic in all human societies. Long before 1492, conquering other societies and profiteering at their expense was as indigenous to Southeast Asia as it was to other regions in the world. Concerning the scope of the article, Fall's methodological adoption of the *longue durée* approach to Vietnamese history was notable. Historians Marc Bloch and Lucien Febvre founded the *Annales* school of thought, which focused on the study of history through the lens of social and economic developments over long periods, and Bloch did much to advance this approach to historical inquiry.[178] Bloch, like Fall, was a military veteran and he had served in the French army during World War I and again as a reserve officer from 1939 to July 1940 before joining the French Resistance. In 1942, Bloch was captured and executed by the Gestapo, the same year that Fall's mother, Anna, was detained and sent to Auschwitz. Bloch, as a historian and Resistance fighter, epitomized the type of soldier-scholar Fall emulated. It is unclear whether he knew Bloch's work or life story, but they both shared the drive to act as much as to study.

Fall's *longue durée* approach to his article on Southeast Asia appeared to be inspired by Bloch's methods of studying social and political history. After all, Fall's study of Vietnamese colonization of the Chams demonstrated how he assessed empire in Southeast Asia before Western influence even appeared on the horizon. More broadly, it demonstrated his understanding that Vietnam and Southeast Asia were not just tragic places where war was fought between the French and Viet Minh, or among the National Liberation Front and the United States and its South Vietnamese allies. Instead, as he related in his article, it was a region characterized by over two millennia of strife, and transformed by waves of immigration and economic encounters. The article, when completed, embodied the type of extended historical analysis of Vietnamese history that *Horizon* editor Robert Cowley had hoped for when he commissioned Fall to write it in September 1966.

Several months before Cowley and Fall met, Fall had received a Guggenheim Fellowship to conduct research in Vietnam for a study provisionally titled "The Viet Cong: Rise and Development of a Peasant Guerrilla Movement."[179] He intended to expand upon work that was forthcoming in the revised, second edition of *The Two Viet-Nams: A Political and Military History*.[180] The most substantive revisions to the updated second edition of this book included an entirely new fifty-page chapter, "National Liberation." In it, he synthesized information from dozens of Department of Defense reports, news articles from Vietnam, and many other sources, including Sir Robert Thompson's study, *Defeating Communist Insurgency*, and Douglas Pike's book, *Viet-Cong*.[181] The new chapter added to *The Two Viet-Nams* significant material describing the National Liberation Front's tactics, political organization, and strategic plans, all of which were quickly evolving after large-scale US intervention in 1965.

Fall's Guggenheim application noted that he planned to make a "significant contribution to the understanding of the phenomenon of peasant guerrilla movements," adding that "Their rise and evolution may well turn out to be one of the most important socio-political events of the latter part of the century."[182] Spending several months researching this subject in late 1966 and 1967 would, therefore, contribute to a potentially monumental study on the NLF. In the meantime, the second, revised edition of *The Two Viet-Nams*, scheduled for publication in early 1967, would tide readers over until Fall could complete a new manuscript. However, he was troubled by the growing escalation of war in Vietnam, which he saw as increasingly futile and counterproductive.

Among his many research subjects, Fall was particularly keen to study in more detail the weakening political legitimacy of the South Vietnamese government and US efforts to support it. His planned research would also enable him to examine what he regarded as a type of competition for control over the

Vietnamese people by the National Liberation Front, the Republic of Vietnam, and American forces. In his work planned for late 1966 and into 1967, he wanted to know the following: what was the basis of the National Liberation Front's commitment and credibility among the Vietnamese as a political administration? What would the South Vietnamese government have to accomplish or reform to be able to compete with the National Liberation Front and the North Vietnamese state?[183]

In 1966, Fall shared his views on the National Liberation Front with François Sully, noting: "Thanks to the RAND Corporation field researchers, the U.S. has by now a fairly good idea of why twenty thousand Vietcong turn themselves in to the government every year. What interests me, is to discover why the 260,000 Vietcong who do not defect continue the fight against considerable odds."[184] The motivation to continue fighting was something Fall could relate to as a former member of the Maquis during World War II. In addition, commitment to the Vietnamese Communist cause was the only viable option. When he referred to the 20,000 Vietcong who rallied to the government of South Vietnam during the Second Indochina War, it is undeniable that he saw them as resembling Vietnamese who defected to the French side during the First Indochina War. During that conflict, Fall had written to his wife, Dorothy, that defectors "came because we have better food, medicine, and no French bombers to worry them. The Viet-Minh merely sheds its weak sisters on us."[185]

The RAND study, to which Fall referred in his exchange with Sully, was the "Viet Cong Motivation and Morale Project," which began in 1964 and expanded to become RAND's most extensive research program in Vietnam.[186] The extension of the program occurred, as Mai Elliott observed in her history on RAND in Southeast Asia, because the think tank's social scientists "were shocked to discover what really sustained the [National Liberation Front] insurgency: the grievances the peasants held against the Saigon government and the ardent aspirations they had for education, economic opportunity, equality, and justice for themselves and their descendants."[187] The people turning to the National Liberation Front were motivated to such degrees that food, medicine, and protection against American bombers were not enough incentive for them to rally to the South Vietnamese government, as planners in the Chieu Hoi program hoped. Operation Rolling Thunder was not pulling those Vietnamese who survived American aerial bombardment away from the NLF; it was instead driving people to join it.[188] In fact, waves of Army of Republic of Vietnam soldiers were deserting their positions, in massive numbers that "reached an all-time high in 1968," providing a counterpunch to those National Liberation Front soldiers coming to the government side.[189]

Fall's only recorded involvement with RAND occurred when David Mozingo, a China expert in RAND's Social Science Department, invited Fall to speak at their offices in Santa Monica, California.

Mozingo remembered that Fall gave a "magnificent performance," during which he expressed his conviction that the United States would not do any better than the French had in Vietnam and that it would find it impossible to win the war because the situation "had metastasized and was already going in the other direction," and there was nothing "short of destroying the whole country that was going to change it."[190]

Fall, for his part, would attempt to change this through the only means he had available to him: finding and providing the facts for all to see. By this point, his efforts were not conducted in a naïve belief that he could change US policy. Instead, while possibly holding onto such hope privately, he continued to research with the motive of creating a documentary record that might echo the importance of the Nuremberg Legacy. If he could not change policy, he could attempt to document why such US decision-making in Vietnam was wrong.

* * *

Fall left Washington, DC for Hong Kong on 8 December 1966 to arrange housing for his family there before continuing to Saigon later that month.[191] The months preparing for his seventh trip to Vietnam appeared to be remarkably productive as well. In addition to preparing for the upcoming publication of his article for *Horizon* and finishing the edits for the second revised edition of *The Two Viet-Nams*, Fall also completed several other essays and projects. On Christmas Day 1966, he finished "Ho Chi Minh—A Profile," and in January 1967 he wrote an introduction to Kuno Knoebl's *Victor Charlie: The Face of War in Vietnam*.[192] These essays were on top of the forthcoming collection, *Ho Chi Minh: On Revolution: Selected Writings, 1920–66*, which he edited, and which was scheduled for publication the following year.[193] In addition, in 1966 he finally completed yet another book, *Hell in a Very Small Place: The Siege of Dien Bien Phu*, which was published in early 1967.[194] With all this material, readers seeking to learn more about the First Indochina War and contemporary events in Vietnam had a significant amount of Fall's writing to consider.

V—"This Isn't Munich, It's Spain"—Vietnam, 1966

> *Tragically, few seem to appreciate that this sort of war is lost, not won, by killing people.*
>
> – Denis Warner[195]

> *The question that must of necessity arise is whether the ultimate result of what has in effect become a "liberation-by-obliteration" policy can be politically—let alone morally—justified and will, indeed, deter.*
>
> – Bernard Fall[196]

As he looked forward to the imminent publication of *Hell in A Very Small Place*, Fall finally arrived in Vietnam on 21 December 1966. According to François Sully, "Fall explained his return to Vietnam as 'pure love' for the country on which he wrote his thesis on the Vietminh in 1953."[197] "For three weeks," Sully continued, "Fall was my house guest. After that he rented a modest one room flat on Nguyen Van Sam Street, a predominantly Chinese commercial district behind the Saigon central market ... Fall was happy like a boy scout on a Sunday cookout."[198] As much as they enjoyed exploring Saigon, the two friends were of a like mind regarding studying Vietnam away from the bustle of the rapidly expanding city. As Sully noted, "to escape Saigon's pervasive influence Fall convinced me to spend every weekend in the field. We successively visited the 4th Infantry Division in Pleiku, and the new U.S. base in the Mekong Delta at Dong Tam."[199]

These field visits to meet with troops were important to Fall. While he criticized American policymakers, he generally identified with young Americans deployed to Vietnam. In his view, military service was still closely linked to the anti-authoritarian liberation of Europe he had experienced only twenty-two years earlier. On a personal level, he relished telling marines and soldiers about the history of the First Indochina War, especially when it had a tie-in with their current location or operation. Sully commented on this, writing: "In the Iron Triangle, baffled American commanders learned from him that in April 1948, a company of French Tunisian troops had been decimated by the Viet Minh at exactly the same place."[200] Likely, this type of comment was not always welcomed. However, it might also have created a sense of empathy since he shared their vulnerability.

Sully continued, "With amusement, Fall discovered that he had earned the nickname of 'STREET WITHOUT JOY' among American officers who used this transparent code name to signal his arrival by radio from unit to unit."[201] Based on numerous other documents, it is undeniable that soldiers and journalists respected him. In one case, journalist David Halberstam wrote:

> Charley Mohr, one of the great *New York Times* reporters who covered the war, liked to tell of the time that he had come back from an operation late at night only to find that the mess hall was closing down and they would not feed him. Just then Bernard Fall walked in, and dinner was immediately served to both of them. "But why did you feed him and not me?" Charley asked the mess sergeant. "Because he is Bernard Fall and you are not," was the response.[202]

Another interaction revealed Fall's profound respect for the US Marine Corps, which was based on several factors: it valued its history and used the lessons from its past to improve its current and future operations. Moreover, the Marine Corps was elite and expeditionary. In a *Marine Corps Gazette* interview published in 1967, Fall recounted the Corps' first deployment to Vietnam in 1845, 120 years before "returning" to Danang in May 1965 on Lyndon Johnson's orders.[203] In his interview with Sgt. Roy Johnson, the forty-year-old Fall, explained how:

> the old U.S.S. *Constitution*, commanded by John 'Mad Jack' Percival, put into Da Nang on May 10th, 1845, to take on water and fruit. After being informed that a Catholic bishop, Dominique Lefèbvre had been imprisoned and was sentenced to death in Hue, Percival ordered the Marines to capture the Governor and Vice-Governor of Da Nang and held them hostage until the bishop was at least assured of not being put to death in Hue, whereupon Capt. Percival released the governors and evacuated Da Nang 14 days later.

Fall concluded the *Gazette* interview, observing:

> The Marines got to Da Nang, not only as early as 122 years ago, but beat the French by about two years, since the French troops landed in Da Nang in 1847 ... so, interestingly enough, the American Marines have a rather long history in Da Nang, although very few people know about it.

He concluded, "It is doubtful that a single one of the Marines who waded ashore at Danang in 1965 had an inkling that his appearance was a return engagement."[204] The historian side of Fall was fascinated by these kinds of stories, and he enjoyed telling marines about the history of the Marine Corps that they might not have known.

In contrast to these lighter moments, Fall had endured serious health conditions over the past several years because of persistent kidney problems. In late 1961, he suffered uremic poisoning, which had developed into retroperitoneal fibrosis, a scarring of his kidneys.[205] The origins of the disease were unknown, although a later study suggested that damage to the aortic wall might be one cause of retroperitoneal fibrosis.[206] After multiple medical consultations, Fall underwent four surgeries between November 1961 and January 1962 to address the ailment. At the time of his 1966 trip to Vietnam, he possessed only one functioning kidney.[207] In an interview recorded in November 1966, the month before he departed for Vietnam, he described his illness, stating: "It's got a very long Latin name, of course, like all these things, and it cost me my left kidney three years ago ... and four months, five operations and eight-thousand five hundred dollars later I came out of the hospital and I felt pretty despondent about the whole thing." He then recalled his doctor's honesty, writing that the doctor told him, "you only got one brain and one heart—if they stop, you're dead! So, all right, you only have one kidney—if the kidney stops, obviously you're in trouble ... So quit talking about it and start living ... and, I did ... it's never stopped me from anything."[208]

François Sully also commented on Fall's condition in late 1966:

> Because of his kidney ailment, drinking large quantities of liquid was a necessity. He never went out without two water bottles on his belt and a vial of expensive king size pills prescribed by his Washington doctor. Struck a few years ago by a rare fibrosis of the kidneys, Fall had gone through a costly series of surgical operations in which one kidney was removed. Fall was philosophical about his ailment. "I live on borrowed time," Fall said, "when my last kidney will cease to function, that will be the end. It can happen anytime. But here I feel like Mister Wonderful. Vietnam must be good for my health despite the heat, the dust, the tropical bugs. I am only vulnerable to sophisticated germs. Nowhere else do I feel better."

Sully continued:

> Fall was not morbid about his health problems. He was so certain to die eventually in his bed from kidney trouble that the idea of physical danger in Vietnam, never, I suspect, bothered him. For two eventful months, luck was on his side. He had many plans about the future such as growing a beard to amuse his three infant daughters and building a summer house in the Bahamas.[209]

Despite these medical problems, Fall continued to accompany military operations and interact with soldiers and marines while conducting field research. David Hackworth, one of the most decorated soldiers in the United States Army after Audie Murphy, explained that Fall was risking his life going out on operations so often.[210] Hackworth explained:

> The great irony was saying to Bernard, where are you going next? He said, "I'm going with the Marines." I said, "Look, this is coming from an infantryman with eight Purple Hearts. You cannot just continue rolling the dice. You're going to

crap out. You just can't go with the squad and platoon again and again and again, because you're going to get killed." He just smiled that big cheery smile.[211]

In addition to accompanying military personnel on operations, Sully commented on his ability to interact with high-ranking officers:

> While in Saigon, he was invited by Westmoreland's chief intelligence officer, U.S. Army General Joseph McChristian, on the tactics used by Vo Nguyen Giap to wrest control of North Vietnam's high region from the French between 1951 and 1954. It was a success. The arch critic of U.S. policy in Vietnam was the most sought-after lecturer and guest speaker in U.S. officialdom in Vietnam. Even if they did not like what he said, they always could learn from him.[212]

Sully might have been correct about these interactions in Vietnam, but when it counted most, too many policymakers in Washington failed to heed what Fall wrote. Decision-making power resided with the National Security Council [NSC], led by McGeorge Bundy in the late Kennedy and early Johnson administrations, and "this concentration of power in the hands of Bundy and the NSC staff ... would largely determine American policy in Southeast Asia."[213] There were multiple problems with this, but such centralization among critical decision-makers who were unwilling to seek out advice from external analysts and scholars was a fundamental issue. Along with Johnson's decision to delay decision-making concerning US policy in Vietnam until after the 1964 presidential election—through what Fredrik Logevall described as the "Long 1964"—the roots for American failure in Vietnam were already becoming well established.[214]

According to Andrew Preston, among Johnson's key advisors Bundy and the NSC staff "had become policy experts over regions in which they had no genuine expertise. In confronting Vietnamese communism, they applied their European Cold War lessons axiomatically, only to produce disastrous results."[215] Second, an overreliance on military solutions had already been decided, and this was a position that indicated how serious the security situation had become. The potential need for debate over which should come first—security versus governance or governance versus security—had already passed. As Preston pointed out, "ultimately, Bundy did believe in the primacy of military power to solve international problems in which America's national security, broadly defined, was at stake."[216] Such beliefs paved the way for the escalation of war and the deployment of military forces to Vietnam that would number over half a million US personnel by early 1968.

The belief that Vietnamese Communism was a threat to America's national security and that the United States could eventually deploy enough military power to confront Vietnamese revolutionary warfare formed two central problems and perceptions which Fall sought to change. The idea that military power could fix a social and political revolution with roots in anti-colonialism was misguided. More armaments would never accomplish US goals, no matter that they were of the latest technology and continually improving. Based on the resources available to the United States, forces exponentially more powerful than those in the French military, Fall understood how the technological advantages that a massive and formidable military force provided could blind policymakers who were unwilling to make the effort to understand Vietnamese revolutionary warfare. There were positive signs that change was possible, but they were coming too late. In 1963, former ambassador to South Vietnam Henry Cabot Lodge had advocated the punitive bombing of the DRV, but by 1965 Lodge's views had changed. Moreover, Lodge's influence was making headway with McGeorge Bundy, who was then Lyndon Johnson's Special Assistant. However, campus protests and the Dominican Crisis in 1965 marked a period in which Bundy's influence with Johnson diminished.[217] Lodge's influence with Johnson, thus, began to fade as well.

Once Johnson had staked his political legitimacy as president upon his commitment to escalating US intervention in Vietnam, it was too late for an outside expert like Fall, or even others within the Johnson administration, aside from the President himself, to change the course of events in Southeast Asia.[218] Even those views Lodge fielded in 1965—and they were all points Fall had tried to impress upon readers earlier—would not make enough of a difference. In a memo to Bundy, Lodge wrote: "Communist subversion-terrorism is the great unsolved problem in South Vietnam … It is, in a sense, a bigger threat than the nuclear, where we have superiority and a well understood procedure."[219] Lodge hardly had all the answers, but he came to believe, as did Fall, that "Rural pacification, economic development, and political reform, rather than sustained bombing, were the keys to victory; these nonmilitary measures were also the strengths of the NLF and DRV, which is why they were winning the war."[220]

Andrew Preston noted that Lodge "argued for a 'Plan for the Development of Southeast Asia, comparable in scope to the Marshall Plan and in addition to what we are doing already.'"[221] This was a good idea, to be sure, but timing mattered. In 1958, when Fall drew attention to the problems of counterpart funding for South Vietnam's economy and other failures in the US assistance policy, making corrections at that point might have made a difference. This would have provided an opportunity, but not a guarantee, to positively affect the security situation. No amount of US assistance, however, could change deleterious governance decisions by South Vietnamese leaders who antagonized the South Vietnamese population. There were genuine limits to what the US could affect using its political power and military might. Yet, too many American policymakers believed that there were no limits to what they could accomplish.

Other National Security Council staff members, including Chester L. Cooper and James C. Thomson, developed perspectives along the lines Fall advocated regarding a political solution.[222] However, if Lodge, Bundy, and former friends of the President, such as Fulbright, could not get through to Johnson, Fall never would. It was difficult to impose limits on executive branch overreach once the Tonkin Gulf Resolution allocated sweeping powers to Johnson in 1964. Fulbright had many reasons to regret sponsoring legislation to allow this. If there was a lesson to be learned from the authorizations the Tonkin Resolution conferred, it was to ensure and maintain stronger Congressional oversight of the executive branch when it came to deploying troops and authorizing military force. The mistake of enabling such an imbalance between the legislative and executive branches would cost more over the next decade than Americans could have known in 1964. More critically, for millions of Vietnamese, Cambodians, Laotians, and tens of thousands of Americans, this mistake had a much greater cost.[223]

In his 1965 article for *Ramparts*, "This Isn't Munich, It's Spain," Fall relayed his belief that war in Vietnam was not only a mistake, but that it had become an immoral testing ground for advanced military technology. Comparing Vietnam to Munich, an analogy which was used as a rallying cry to support anti-communism operations, was misguided. After Operation Rolling Thunder commenced in its full force, Vietnam was less similar to Munich than to Franco-era Spain and the military operations conducted in Guernica.[224] Fall knew this was not an analogy that would find a receptive audience in the seats of power in Washington, DC. Fall admired the United States. However, he was concerned about its loss of a moral compass when it came to decision-making related to intervention in Vietnam. As he described it: "What I really fear most, if this sort of situation drags on indefinitely, is the creation of a new ethics to match a new warfare."[225] This fear quickly grew into outrage. After personally witnessing military operations in 1965, he vented: "Vietnam had become a test-bed for in-combat innovation and new technologies."[226] As he saw it, Franco-era Guernica was a more accurate comparison for US military operations in Vietnam.

There was evidence to justify Fall's anger over Vietnam's destruction, especially concerning indiscriminate aerial bombing after several attacks on American installations that eventually led to Operation Rolling Thunder. After a National Liberation Front attack at Camp Holloway near Pleiku on 6–8 February 1965, and another attack at Qui Nhon on 10 February the United States launched Operation Flaming Dart and Flaming Dart II in retaliation. Planning for what became Operation Rolling Thunder began as early as mid-February, and constant bombing began in early March 1965 and continued through November 1968.[227] The amount of ordinance dropped on Vietnam quadrupled from 33,000 tons in 1965 to 128,000 tons in 1966 and escalated even further in the subsequent years. Civilian deaths rose from 13,000 in 1965 to 24,000 in 1966. In this, the United States was spending $9.60 for every dollar of economic and military damage to North Vietnam the same year.[228] Not only were financial costs expanding, moral condemnation and anti-war sentiment also increased.

On the ground, Fall was quick to condemn atrocities committed by communists against American and anti-communist Vietnamese. Equally, he condemned the mistreatment of the National Liberation Front and North Vietnamese captives as well. In his words, he explained, "The answer to any attempt to raise the question of America's moral responsibility for such actions is the same excuse the Army officer gave me about a bleeding, unattended prisoner: the violations of rules are done by the Vietnamese." Fall continued:

> I spent 1946–48 at the Nuremberg trials as a young research analyst, and in a number of cases I heard the Germans attempt to excuse atrocities as acts committed by troops of their allies. This did not absolve the Germans of their responsibility. Both Viet-Nam and the United States have signed and ratified the 1949 Geneva Convention on War Victims.[229]

He added:

> The reality in Viet-Nam is that the international rules of war are not obeyed and, contrary to popular belief, the rules do apply to guerrilla wars as well ... there seems to be a predisposition on our side to no longer be able to see the Vietnamese as people against whom crimes can be committed. This is the ultimate impersonalization of war.[230]

Bernard Fall's most pressing fear, "the creation of a new ethics to match a new warfare," centered on an unwillingness among decision-makers to guarantee principles in the conduct of warfare. The lack of guarantees protecting such principles resonated in Fall's critique of US policy because the Hague and Geneva Conventions on land warfare and the treatment of prisoners of 1949 were signed by South Vietnam in 1953, the United States in 1955, and North Vietnam in 1957.²³¹ Fall's initial recognition of US problems with creating a "new ethics" originated in 1951 with his frustration over the release of Alfried Krupp to support German rearmament in the early Cold War. Fall knew how Krupp's associations with the Nazi Party's leadership, as an armaments supplier and financial supporter for the Third Reich, were dismissed by American High Commissioner for Germany John J. McCloy to expedite preparation for potential military confrontation with the Soviet Union. Krupp's release signaled American leaders' willingness to forget about Nazi corporatism, only to turn around and endorse the development of a military-industrial complex for use in places where non-vital threats against US national security existed. The willingness to disregard the justice imposed through the Nuremberg Principles marked America's beginning down a road leading to the indiscriminate destruction of Vietnam that equally unraveled American society.

Mistakes in decision-making leading to large-scale intervention formed one set of problems. Enabling the type of warfare taking place in Vietnam, such as indiscriminate bombing through unobserved fire missions, was another. Fall described this in response to a statement made by Secretary of State Dean Acheson in December 1965, in which Acheson remarked:

> The end sought by our foreign policy ... is, as I have said, to preserve and foster an environment in which free societies may exist and flourish. Our policies and actions must be decided by whether they contribute to or detract from the achievement of this end. They need no other justification or moral or ethical embellishment.²³²

Fall was troubled by what exactly constituted "free societies" in Acheson's opinion. "Free societies" was a contested subject in the United States, let alone in other countries. The hypocrisy of Acheson's views was problematic: why would the United States foster an environment in which free societies could flourish abroad when it could not ensure that free and equal societies existed at home? Legislation centered on the 1965 Voting Rights Act and others indicated the United States had plenty of problems protecting the constitutional rights of its own citizens. And as for Acheson's claim that US policy needed "no other justification or moral or ethical embellishment," this was a troubling statement. In response to Acheson, Fall quoted a French priest, Cardinal Feltin, who had written a letter to military chaplains accompanying French troops conducting operations in Algeria in October 1960.

> There cannot be a morality which justifies efficacy by all means, if those means are in formal contradiction with Natural Law and Divine Law. Efficacy, in that

case, goes against the very aim it seeks to achieve. There can be exceptional laws for exceptional situations ... there cannot exist an exceptional morality which somehow takes leave of Natural Law and Divine Law.[233]

Cardinal Feltin's quote spoke to Fall because of his experience surviving the Nazis' aggression and destruction of Natural Law which had formed the basis for World War II. The Nuremberg Trials, to which Fall had contributed research, had sought to reestablish Natural Law as a foundation for how future wars might be conducted according to internationally agreed-upon rules.[234] The actions Fall witnessed in Vietnam were violations of the Nuremberg Legacy, and they undermined American principles as he saw them. Others, such as General Telford Taylor, with whom Fall had worked in Nuremberg in 1947 and 1948, also believed that American actions in Vietnam were subverting the core principles and central values of the United States.[235] Marcus Raskin and Fall certainly both understood the importance of power in international politics. However, they also believed:

> that without the context of law and morality for the use of power, we are reduced to the law of the jungle. Power, where it is used without wisdom and only in the name of one nation, will result in the ultimate corruption of the good ends that that nation originally might have wished to achieve—and the corruption of that nation itself. In the world of nuclear weapons, irrational men, frightened nations, rampant technology, and permanent revolution, it is the foolish nation which attempts to arrogate to itself the role of world policeman or moral arbiter without recourse to what others think, do, want, or need.[236]

Fall was additionally concerned that the American people were being misled over Vietnam's geopolitical importance to the United States. Appearing in a January 1965 NBC *Meet the Press* interview, Fall claimed, "American interests are involved in Vietnam," but "whether vital or not, I don't think so." He added that "bombing North Vietnam would be militarily useless."[237] Fall's more significant point was discrediting the relevance of the domino theory to Vietnam, pointing out that it "was no longer taken as gospel by most regional experts, although it continued to creep into official justifications for escalating the Vietnam war."[238] Fall tied his criticism of domino-theory thinking together in his *Meet the Press* interview, stating:

> I don't think that we have to lose South Vietnam any more than we have to lose Europe because we lost Czechoslovakia. The domino theory could have been invoked for that matter when we lost China. I would say that the United States has the wherewithal in Southeast Asia to contain communism on a basis that's acceptable to the West and without the loss of effective strength.[239]

Fall was not the only one who recognized that the domino theory was invalid when applied to Southeast Asia. Sherman Kent, one of the fathers of modern intelligence in the United States, then serving as the Chairman of the Board of National Estimates in 1964, shared Fall's perspective. On 9 June 1964, Kent sent a memorandum to CIA director John A. McCone with the subject: "Would the Loss of South Vietnam and Laos Precipitate a 'Domino Effect' in the Far East." In the six-page memo's primary finding, Kent wrote.

> We do not believe that the loss of South Vietnam and Laos would be followed by the rapid, successive communization of the other states of the Far East. Instead of a shock wave passing from one nation to the next, there would be a simultaneous, direct effect on all Far Eastern countries. With the possible exception of Cambodia, it is likely that no nation in the area would quickly succumb to communism as a result of the fall of Laos and South Vietnam. Furthermore, a continuation of the spread of communism in the area would not be inexorable, and any spread which did occur would take time—time in which the total situation might change in any of a number of ways unfavorable to the Communist Cause.[240]

Ultimately, in terms of utilizing military might to achieve America's strategic goals, Fall explained: "I cannot say that I have found anyone who seems to have a clear idea of the end—of the war aims—and if the end is not clearly defined, are we justified to use any means to attain it?"[241] Moreover, he continued, "what changed the character of the Viet-Nam war was not the decision to bomb North Viet-Nam; not the decision to use American ground troops in South Viet-Nam; but the decision to wage unlimited aerial warfare inside the country at the price of literally pounding the place to bits."[242] In contrast, he stated:

> What America should want to prove in Viet-Nam is that the Free World is "better," not that it can kill people more efficiently. If we could induce 100,000 Viet Cong to surrender to our side because our offers of social reform are better than those of the other side's, that would be victory. Hence, even a total military or technological defeat of the Viet Cong is going to be a partial defeat of our own purposes—a defeat of ourselves, by ourselves, as it were.[243]

Fall knew that the United States had problems with negotiations. He pointed out in 1966 that "should President Johnson encounter increasing pressure to blast to rubble the North Vietnamese sanctuary, due to every mounting casualty list in South Vietnam, his options would only worsen with escalation."[244] If Johnson's decision to escalate further included bombing irrigation dikes, not only would it possibly "drown more than a million Vietnamese in low-lying areas," it would exacerbate moral responsibility for loss of life, ecological devastation, and make negotiations even more unrealistic. Fall added:

> The high-flying arguments of "containment" or "deterrence of foreign aggression" become largely meaningless as the realities of Revolutionary Warfare take over, with their nonmilitary criteria of population support and low-level socioeconomic performance; here, victory goes to the side that "out-administers" the other, not to the one that outfights or outguns the other.[245]

What were the alternatives? While Fall argued that a two-state solution in which North and South Vietnam might eventually coexist, getting to that point proved impossible, at least as of 1966. Was neutralization of Vietnam an option, and, if so, in what way? He provided his most straightforward and extensive discussion on international and regional neutralization in the revised edition of *The Two Viet-Nams*, which appeared in early 1967. In a comparison, he pointed out that a communist government that did not pose a threat to the United States, similar to Josef Broz Tito's Yugoslavia, was a possibility. He added that an entirely disintegrated South Vietnam was undesirable for North Vietnamese leadership because this would also create severe problems and "might be a bigger burden to carry than a prosperous, neutral neighbor which, like Finland or Austria, would be a 'window' to the outside world.[246] On a regional level, Fall envisioned a "neutral belt" comprising Burma, Laos, Cambodia, and South Vietnam which the "major powers involved" would guarantee, but he also conceded that this was unlikely due to regional divisions that appeared insurmountable.[247] To him, therefore, neutralization was not simply a five-syllable word uttered without concrete meaning. Instead, it was a consideration he pointed to as something discussed by leaders, but that never entered into a serious realm of real possibility. Without international backing, neutralization remained difficult, so other options were matters of some importance to him.

In late 1966, Fall criticized political and military leaders for their policies that marines, sailors, soldiers, and airmen were tasked to execute, but his writing was also filled with solutions should neutralization never get off the ground as an alternative. Some, such as more significant political reform in South Vietnam, were only potentially viable. Others, such as accepting the fact that conflict could be solved by the Vietnamese alone, were unacceptable to US authorities in the White House. Despite his shortfalls in creating effective solutions, Fall recognized that the United States still had to address a central problem: "The real permanent problem in South Viet-Nam—and one that cannot and will not be solved by the presence of even a million American troops—is the reconstruction of the non-Communist Vietnamese body politic."[248] The Vietnam War was a political problem that it was up to the Vietnamese to decide. Unfortunately, this meant that civil war was likely unavoidable. Fall was becoming more compassionate to the plight of the Vietnamese; he identified with them, perhaps due to his earlier experiences when his own family had been victims of war.

Fall was compelled to determine the strength of the National Liberation Front, so he kept working, and this was one underlying motive for completing further research in 1967. After his September 1966 meeting with editor Robert Cowley in New York, he finally completed and submitted "Two Thousand Years of War in Vietnam" for publication in the upcoming spring edition of *Horizon*. Then, to understand the National Liberation Front and continue his work finding a resolution to the war, he returned to Vietnam. If there was any solution to be found, one that facts might reinforce, he knew he had to keep looking. Bernard Fall believed that to find the truth in Vietnam, he had to find it firsthand. On 21 February 1967, he went with Marines from 1st Battalion, 9th Regiment for a patrol along the Street Without Joy to search.

EPILOGUE

Bernard B. Fall died on 21 February 1967 on the Street Without Joy. As a US Marine Corps Company Commander with him observed, it had been "apparent that he was a man who wanted to be up front."[1] In the years before his death, journalists and others similarly regarded him as a meticulous and uncompromising scholar driven to recount the facts as he saw them. In the years after his death, Fall's legacy continued to grow as others learned more about Vietnamese aspirations for independence and how US policy in Southeast Asia was increasingly ineffective and even counterproductive. He had sought to provide others with information about why there was an intensifying need for political reconciliation as the Vietnam War expanded. In one of his most strongly worded articles condemning the United States' overmilitarized effort, he cited Tacitus' *Life of Agricola*, noting, "They have made a desert, and have called it peace."[2] In "Vietnam Blitz: A Report on the Impersonal War," published in the *New Republic* in October 1965, Fall concluded, "It is now Washington's turn to show whether it can come up with more statesmanship than Hanoi or the V.C., or whether it will fall prey to the attractiveness of its own deployed firepower." Failure to reach a settlement would eventually lead to US defeat because of the Republic of Vietnam's inability to respond sufficiently to the North's use of revolutionary warfare: "in the latter case, a prostrate South Vietnam, plowed under by bombers and artillery and still in the hands of a politically irrelevant regime, may become the victim of aroused social and political forces for which no aircraft carrier and eight-jet bomber can provide a ready answer."[3]

The use of "Blitz" in the article title would undeniably have been an evocative one for the World War II veteran to make. The problem, as he saw it, was that the escalation of military force was not working. In an interview with Fall for *Meet the Press* on 31 January 1965, Robert Goralski of NBC asked: "You don't believe that escalating the war would be helpful at all at this stage?" To which Fall replied:

> This has already been proved. The United States' massive bombardment operation in North Korea called "Operation Strangle" was an utter failure against Communist communication lines. The French "Operation Vulture" in 1954, which was designed to knock out Communist communications against Dien Bien Phu was a failure. There is no such thing as bombing supply lines in the jungle.[4]

For these and other reasons, Fall believed that negotiations offered the only effective solution before larger-scale US intervention created an untenable commitment that would be difficult to minimize once undertaken. François Sully discussed Fall's beliefs concerning negotiations and the prospects of peace writing, "Fall was convinced that the (LBJ) administration had purposely ignored several signals from Hanoi, one of them was the withdrawal of one North Vietnamese Division, 325, from the south last year." Sully explained that Fall had "unsuccessfully tried to convince Vietnamese leaders that the ideal solution to the conflict would be the existence of two Vietnams which will learn to coexist, perhaps like the two Germanys, will trade and explore all avenues of mutual interest. This, Fall warned, can only come when a viable Saigon government has learned to live in harmony with its own people and achieve a true reconciliation of all Vietnamese, whatever their political background."[5]

Fall added that "Sooner or later, the Vietcong resistance movement will have to be integrated with the rest of the nation. To believe that 280,000 guerrillas and their five million supporters will accept, once again, to be regrouped north, is utterly unrealistic. Like the resistance fighters of occupied Europe, most of them will rather fight to the bitter end than submit."[6]

This might eventually lead to communist dominance, but, as Fall argued in *The Two Viet-Nams*, the United States had learned to live with a communist Yugoslavia led by Josef Broz Tito, whose long-running quarrel with Stalin was well known.[7] The solutions and suggestions Fall made, however, were conclusions American policymakers struggled to understand or simply decided to ignore. In the case of Americans learning from France's disastrous war against the Viet Minh, David Halberstam explained:

> The Americans, my friend Bernard Fall once said, are fighting in the same footsteps as the French, though they're dreaming different dreams. Challenging a nation's myths and dreams, then, is a difficult task. We understood the hopelessness of the French cause when they fought first. The French understood the

EPILOGUE

hopelessness of our cause when we fought the second time. Hanoi understood the hopelessness of both causes from the start.[8]

Among the many tasks Fall left for others, the largest was set before the United States as it pursued a divisive foreign policy agenda and confronted Vietnamese revolutionary warfare while simultaneously struggling to fulfill the values of equality set forth in the US Constitution at home. Fall's position at Howard University gave him a perspective on racial relations that informed his understanding of US foreign policy. Ineffective and unequal policies in the United States, in his view, provided a foundation made of sand for US policy overseas. International engagement was critical, but it demanded legitimacy at its core and through its formation to avoid hypocrisy. Engagement also needed stronger statecraft based on a more robust historical understanding of Vietnam's past. Undoubtedly, Fall believed America's strength resided more in fulfilling the values promulgated in the US Constitution than through demonstrating its military capabilities on Vietnam.

His reputation was flourishing in the years before he left for Vietnam one last time in December 1966. In 1965, he was recognized with the George Polk Memorial Award for Outstanding Interpretive Reporting and had received numerous prestigious fellowships. In addition, his most well-known book, *Street Without Joy*, was already in its fourth edition, second printing by November 1965.[9] When he died, he left numerous other books he had only recently completed. After three years of work, his masterpiece on Dien Bien Phu, *Hell in a Very Small Place*, was published in 1966. In 1967, the second revised edition of his book, *The Two Viet-Nams: A Political and Military Analysis* was published posthumously along with *Last Reflections on a War*, an edited collection whose publication Dorothy Fall supervised. As to collecting and providing access to Fall's papers for all scholars and interested individuals, Dorothy's efforts were, and remain, vital. Fall's personal papers were first held at Howard University and then transferred to the John F. Kennedy Presidential Library in several stages between 1985 and 1989.[10]

In the broader scholarship on Southeast Asia published during and after Fall's life, thousands of writers worldwide produced untold numbers of books and articles that recounted, analyzed, criticized, justified, and remembered America's war in Vietnam and the First and Third Indochina Wars. When the First Indochina War broke out in 1946, it metastasized into different but connected wars. Years after America left Vietnam, war eventually reignited between Vietnam and China in 1978 and only concluded with the normalization of relations later in 1991.[11] Lasting almost five decades, and at the cost of millions of lives, war in Indochina was immeasurably violent, complex, and consequential.

The ongoing publication of numerous books about Indochina and war there, of which this book is only one, indicates the unending effort to understand. As a scholar whose writing bridges a large portion of the wars in Indochina, it is understandable that Bernard Fall should figure prominently. Writing in 2017, Fredrik Logevall remarked of Fall's standing among scholars, "The literature on the Vietnam War is enormous and growing, but Fall's work still stands out for its insight and sagacity. He remains our greatest writer on the struggle, although he died before the period of heavy American involvement had reached its halfway point."[12] Journalists reporting on the war also saw value in his work.

In 1968, Catherine Leroy was foremost in acknowledging Fall's contributions. Leroy came to Vietnam from France in January 1966 to work as a photojournalist for the Associated Press and *Life* Magazine.[13] At twenty-four years old and 4 feet, 10 inches tall, she was one of the first Associated Press-accredited journalists to participate in an airborne combat jump, and she jumped with the 173rd Airborne Brigade during Operation Junction City. Later in the war, the young journalist sustained shrapnel injuries in the Demilitarized Zone while accompanying marines on a mission, and in early 1968, she was detained by North Vietnamese soldiers in Hue during the Tet Offensive. In an interview from October 1968, Leroy commented on her sources, stating:

> I would rather be with people who have been here a long time and from whom I can learn. That limits me to a very few French and Vietnamese people....As for coverage of the war, the best pictures have been taken and the best stories have been written. Bernard Fall told the whole story. There is not much more to say.[14]

Regarding Fall's drive to participate in missions, Sully commented: "Fall loved to be out with the troops" and that he "was full of admiration for the Marines fighting in the mud of Quang Tri Province" and in other places.[15] He was also pragmatic and down-to-earth: "While he was in Vietnam, Fall practically lived on herb-scented 'soupe chinoise' and on Army C rations ... he was one of the few correspondents who could wolf down a cold can of lima beans with chlorinated water and call it a good meal."[16] He also understood that Vietnamese civilians and Vietnamese and American soldiers, and not the elites of either country, were the ones whose lives were at stake. His empathy extended to and focused on soldiers from vulnerable and working-class parts of American society. He explained: "This is a war paid by the poor and fought by the poor. Nowhere in Vietnam have I seen the sons and scions of the U.S. establishment. At least French generals were sending their sons to die in Indochina for the flag, even if they did not believe in the cause."[17] Based on this, it is likely that Fall would condemn the drafting of Americans to do the dirty work of war while providing deferments to those with means but unwilling to serve. In broader terms, Fall never forgot the big picture steering his work. On one occasion, he told Sully:

> The tragedy of this war is that on our side there is absolutely no accumulation of knowledge. Every American officer sent to Vietnam rediscovers the country. French books and army manuals on Indochina which could be invaluable to the U.S. Army now, have never been translated in English. Do you know that American Intelligence specialists in Saigon never had a Vietnamese meal? On the other side, the Viet-Cong is merely perfecting and improving the tactics invented by the Viet-Minh. For them, it is the same war. They don't have to reinvent it every twelve months as we do.[18]

This inability and unwillingness to learn from others' experiences—through potential lessons found in the French books and manuals on Indochina he mentioned to Sully—undoubtedly mystified him. For his part, he sought to provide as much information as he could to help others understand; willfully turning down opportunities to learn was antithetical to the way he worked.

Fall's research was also useful because it ranged from tactical to strategic analysis. His most accessible writing, notably *Street Without Joy*, channeled social and cultural awareness through a narrative that transcended an outdated "drums and bugle" approach to military history. His reliance on credible evidence was not debatable, and he collected his information from studying and meeting individuals, such as State of Vietnam Prime Minister Nguyen Van Tam, and religious leaders, such as Pham Cong Tac, the Cao Dai Ho Phap (Pope) in 1953. He also learned from Pham Van Dong and Ho Chi Minh, whom he interviewed in 1962. However, he did not center his scholarship on elites only. Instead, he saw and understood how the war affected the people fighting and enduring it. The dedication to his book *The Two Viet-Nams* spoke volumes: "To the Valiant and Long-suffering Vietnamese—North and South." This indicated whom Fall had in mind when he worked to find solutions to war in Indochina, and it signaled that his humanitarian perspective outweighed political considerations.

Fall took Vietnamese, Laotian, and Cambodian agency seriously, and his studies centered on how power functioned in Indochina, whether communist, nationalist, religious, or from other ideologies. The most vital part of his legacy was his focus on the historical and cultural context in which Vietnamese revolutionary warfare unfolded and his descriptions of how it functioned. This matters today because the phenomenon of revolutionary warfare remains relevant to understanding irregular-oriented warfare in an era of reemerging great power competition. Over the last sixty years, irregular conflict—consisting of counterinsurgency, information operations, and other forms—predominated in most of the conflicts in which the US has engaged. However, the US government's historical emphasis on and preparation for high-end conflict— and the aging legacy platforms required to conduct it—is not cost-effective and is problematic in several ways.

It is important to point out that this mindset does not necessarily originate or persist among contemporary military leaders. US Air Force Chief of Staff General Charles Q. Brown Jr., for example, questioned the consistent reliance on legacy programs, explaining in 2020 that "we must reframe platform-centric debates to focus instead on capabilities to execute the mission relative to our adversaries. Programs that once held promise, but are no longer affordable or will not deliver needed capabilities on competition-relevant timelines, must be divested or terminated."[19] This kind of leadership provides a compelling vision and a much-needed change of perspective, but it is also in competition with other American economic interests. As Christian Brose has described, US taxpayers continue to fund the production of revamped legacy platforms, such as Ford-class aircraft carriers, or outdated ones, such as Chinook helicopters, because they tie political election-cycle concerns to economic interests within congressional districts.[20]

Instead of an uncompromising focus on capabilities required to execute missions effectively, platform-centric budgeting as emphasized by contemporary domestic politics is counterproductive. As General Brown pointed out, if legacy platforms no longer suffice to confront adversaries in contemporary or potential high-end conflict, continued production is unwise. If a $13 billion Ford-class aircraft carrier is a "floating mountain of gold," while, in contrast, an adversary's Anti-Access/Area Denial anti-ship missiles deters to stand-off distances or risks destruction at a comparatively minimal financial cost to the adversary, the disadvantages are obvious and many.[21] Similarly, if legacy platforms mostly fail to address the type of conflicts the United States will confront in the future, such as irregular and revolutionary warfare, then such investments also lack utility.

It is impossible to know with certainty, but with history as a guide, irregular warfare will remain the primary form of conflict in the future. If wars like the 1991 Gulf War are unlikely to recur, and if nuclear war with China is inconceivable because it is apocalyptic, US military intervention in conflicts, such as those in Syria, Libya, and Yemen, should be avoided. US intervention has, at least historically, often intensified suffering and increased the duration and scope of conflict. Instead, increased efforts should be made through multilateral political means to assist in reducing humanitarian crises. Similarly, so should US-induced regime change be avoided, such as that undertaken in Iraq in 2003. In contrast, and where American interests are authentic and convincingly shared, such as the counterterrorism and irregular warfare missions in the early stages of conflict in Afghanistan in 2001–3, far better political preparation must be conducted to recognize the limits of American influence. Minimizing operations and America's footprint is important to consider when a long-duration mission should be expected. Doing so may help decision-makers gain reasonable public support. In turn, more realistic expectations provide more substantial support to military commanders, and are less costly in terms of budgets and human life. In such conflicts, and despite the immense firepower an aircraft carrier may deploy, forward-deployed power projection rarely delivers political solutions in irregular conflicts, should any such solutions exist. In the case of war in Southeast Asia, Fall had these kinds of problems in mind which he indicated in a statement to Sully in 1962:

> But we must not forget that this is a revolutionary war, that is, a military operation with heavy political overtones. To win the military battle but lose the political war could well become the U.S. fate in Vietnam .... A U.S. Marine can fly a helicopter better than anyone else, but he simply cannot indoctrinate peasants with an ideology worth fighting for.[22]

In a security environment where few solutions exist, excessive militarization often gives the illusion that intractable problems can be solved. Instead of relying on this, the United States and its allies should prioritize developing political warfare capabilities to shape outcomes more effectively before deployment of military forces. To this end, the development of a Functional Center for Security Studies in Irregular Warfare, as described in Section 1299L of the 2021 National Defense Authorization Act (House Resolution 6395), should be explored further.[23] A July 2018 proposal published in the RAND Corporation's *Perspective* is a key point of origin for this idea, and it is the kind of approach to irregular warfare Bernard Fall likely would have emphasized.[24] The authors of the 2018 study suggest that the United States has "proven to be ill-equipped to address the use of nonconventional means by revisionist, revolutionary, and rogue powers."[25] Therefore, it is imperative to create a National Political Warfare Center in which the United States may improve its abilities to address such threats, and doing so would be a step toward more effective use of US power.

Currently, the overall lack of emphasis on irregular warfare must be addressed. The 2018 National Defense Strategy acknowledges but minimizes the importance of irregular-oriented warfare, and this is indicated by the brevity of the seven-page declassified Irregular Warfare Annex. David Ucko succinctly noted that "The I.W. Annex is therefore a step in the right direction, but it is also inadequate in the face of the challenge at hand."[26] The importance of legitimacy and influence, Ucko added, is critical. In terms of global leadership, "This competition for legitimacy and influence is fundamentally what irregular warfare is all about and, for this reason, the annex—while very welcome and important—is also insufficient for the reform and change that must now take place."[27] For starters, reexamining the use of legacy platforms, such as aircraft carriers and others, is a place to begin.

In Fiscal Year (FY) 2021, the US Department of Defense budget was $705.4 billion, and allocations for Special Operations Command's readiness consisted of $9.5 billion.[28] With this allocation breakdown described in the US Comptroller's 2021 Budget Proposal, readiness of Special Operations Command represents only 1.35% of the anticipated DoD budget for FY 21. In comparison, SOCOM's entire readiness budget is almost $4 billion less than the cost of one Ford-class Aircraft Carrier ($13 billion). To be sure, a Ford-class carrier is designed for long operational life, but there are more cost-effective platforms, such as Wasp-class Landing Helicopter Dock (LHD) amphibious ships, which also carry air support to include the MV-22 Osprey, F-35B Lightning II strike fighters and many others. Moreover, Wasp-class ships cost almost four times less than a Ford-class carrier.[29] It is equally important to keep in mind that the most significant capacity for addressing revolutionary or irregular warfare does not exist with legacy platforms, such as in another and updated carrier. Instead, it is located primarily among the people in organizations, such as Special Operations Command, and among other smaller and currently underfunded partners who focus on diplomatic solutions and creating more relevant assistance programs with the potential to effect positive changes.

AI, machine learning, "Big Data," and integrating all sensor-collected data through Joint All-Domain Command and Control (JADC2) is undoubtedly critical for potential, high-end conflict. However, these advancements will only be contextually effective in conflict when leveraged alongside increased investment in political warfare and diplomatic interaction to develop political solutions on a mutual basis and with multi-lateral support. It is perhaps easy to deride such notions as unrealistic or weak, but in what ways will JADC2 prepare civilian and military personnel, who will confront tribal networks and societies which organize, communicate, and conduct operations in ways sophisticated military sensors cannot detect? In what ways will JADC2 reconcile and adapt to a non-technological-oriented effort of social organization? How will military forces conduct operations against opponents living among civilian populations and in ways that are impervious or immune to effects directed through JADC2? Military capacities failed to effect change in Afghanistan because political solutions were not viable to sustain them. If a window of opportunity had ever existed in which political effects could be implemented in Afghanistan in a lasting way, that window closed before such changes could be implemented. Ultimately, a US Space Force officer can perhaps orchestrate a part of JADC2 better than anyone else. However, she or he simply cannot indoctrinate a villager anywhere with an ideology worth fighting for.

As history demonstrates, most conflicts worldwide since the Vietnam War have included a recurring cycle of civil wars, terrorism, and violence at the intrastate level. Increasing the study of history, both in military and civilian professional education, and carefully applying it to policy formulation is one way to improve preparation. As war in Iraq, Afghanistan, and Syria revealed in the years between 2001 and 2020, counterinsurgency and irregular warfare have been common occurrences the United States has had to engage with, and it will continue to do so in the years ahead. In the event that genuine national security threats warrant military action, it is critical to analyze potential conflicts holistically, to anticipate counterproductive outcomes intervention will inevitably create.

Operations in Iraq and Libya are only the most recent demonstrations of problems that follow intervention when conflict mutates in unforeseen ways. In Iraq's case, it is difficult to imagine Al-Qaeda in Iraq (AQI) forming, let alone spawning the Al-Nusra Front or the Islamic State, had the United States not invaded Iraq in 2003. When security threats from insurgencies, terrorism, and others interconnect with climate change and issues related to commodity and water scarcity, integrated problems will be severely magnified. As H.R. McMaster pointed out in 2020, "Efforts to address only one challenge can exacerbate others and perpetuate rather than ameliorate threats to security and prosperity ... We need a dose of strategic empathy to develop solutions that address the interrelated nature of this problem set."[30] Strategic empathy, as McMaster indicates, is "fundamental to improving strategic competence."[31] In many respects, McMaster's points echo ones Fall made at a time when climate change and other contemporary problems facing us were not yet recognized, even if they were already in motion.

In areas where changes are viable, albeit not on the magnitude of reversing global warming, US military and civilian leaders should take further stock of failures in Iraq and Afghanistan to learn from them, unlike past leaders who failed to learn from defeat in Vietnam. As John A. Nagl, an officer involved in developing the US Army's Field Manual for Counterinsurgency, FM 3–24, explained:

> The British historian Michael Howard noted that it is impossible to perfectly prepare military forces for the next war; what is important is to make sure that you have not gotten the preparations so wrong that the military cannot quickly adapt when it is next needed. The Department of Defense failed that test in both Iraq and Afghanistan. It ignored preparations for counterinsurgency operations and was all but criminally unprepared for the demands of occupying Iraq after the invasion caused its government to collapse and Saddam Hussein to disappear into hiding.[32]

In a manner that echoes Fall's work, Nagl's concerns deserve deliberation. In what other ways are the United States and its allies unprepared, should difficult and population-centric war break out in a place and time we neither want nor anticipate? It is unrealistic for the United States to disengage from the world, so what capabilities and knowledge are worth investing in to address great-power competition and potential proxy conflict in cost-effective ways that ensure preparedness and mitigate conflict? A center for studying political warfare and dynamic investment in foreign service and education are the means to improve preparation for future conflict when it inevitably occurs.

In terms of balancing between coercion and diplomacy, supporting and assisting governance that is legitimate and that authentically seeks to reduce conflict is the hardest of all work. In one summation, Stephen Walt explained: "Fighting and governing are very different activities, and being able to blow things up with great precision does not confer a similar capacity to administer conquered territory effectively."[33] Walt's view also contains echoes of Fall's writing. Gaining more profound strategic empathy contributes to preventing conflict, and a more cooperative outlook may help avoid many of the dire consequences associated with past wars in Vietnam and other places. According to Walt, the United States' attempts at remaking the world according to an American vision for it has had a dismal track record:

EPILOGUE

Pursuing liberal hegemony did not make the United States safer, stronger, more prosperous, or more popular. Nor did it make the rest of the world more tranquil and secure. On the contrary, America's ambitious attempts to reorder world politics undermined its own position, sowed chaos in several regions, and caused considerable misery in a number of other countries.[34]

This, in many respects, mirrors ideas Fall put forth in his *New Republic* article, "Blitz in Vietnam," in October 1965. There are alternatives to the type of US-led hegemony Walt wrote about in 2018. For one, Walt's vision of offshore balancing focuses on alliance-building, diplomatic solutions, and deploying "power abroad only when there are direct threats to vital U.S. interests."[35] Strengthening American society as a constructive global partner and using that power to achieve a more stable and secure global environment is a desirable goal. It certainly embodies a type of open-minded perspective Fall undoubtedly sought in the 1950s and 1960s but which, because of endless wars in Southeast Asia lasting almost the entire twentieth century, could not be achieved. His call for embracing opportunities to negotiate in early 1965 before war escalated to a point of no return indicated his position on this matter. In our contemporary era of remerging great-power competition, readers, policymakers, and military professionals—not only in China and the United States, but everywhere—would all benefit from considering Fall's search for political solutions and building diplomatic and assistance capacities. There are simply too many complex problems that affect all humans, and they invariably all require unilateral cooperation. In terms of addressing serious problems such as climate change, competition between great powers—as well as economic competition—should be welcomed if it facilitates innovation directed toward improving environmental qualities and living standards that are globally shared in a sustainable manner. Ultimately, any competition that contributes to the achievement of what should be a mutually shared goal of global prosperity should be embraced. In another sense, one more directed toward domestic policy in the United States, Americans should also focus on making effective change within their own civil and political society before attempting to fix similar problems they might believe they see elsewhere.

Even though cooperation is preferred and may be achieved, conflicts are inevitable. Fall's research on revolutionary warfare is useful to bear in mind when irregular and political warfare breaks out. Organizations, including ISIS, found Maoist-inspired revolutionary warfare compelling to turn to in early stages of conflict, before they took on the identity of a state with military forces that were susceptible to targeting. Their brutality aside, ISIS in

Iraq and Syria was initially successful because the group focused on achieving administrative control in large portions of western Iraq and eastern Syria. As Craig Whiteside has argued, ISIS proved to be a challenge because they integrated historical awareness, ideological purity, and a willingness to harness technological tools—including encrypted messaging apps—onto a keen appreciation for the power of information operations. Whiteside indicated the group's complexity, noting: "The idea of a Salafi jihadist group like the Islamic State using political-military doctrine spawned and honed by Marxists might seem fantastical. However, even a casual glance at movement pronouncements over more than a decade reveals strategic thought that is influenced by Mao's protracted war concept."[36] ISIS's predilection for administrative control proved, therefore, to be a severe challenge for an Iraqi army into which the United States had invested years and millions of US dollars. At the same time, ISIS, like other organizations, failed to see the limits to its own power, and this contributed to overreach and subsequent demise at the time.

When ISIS decided to adopt a more conventional military direction in 2017 and 2018, it opened itself to targeting, at which the United States and its allies excelled. Had ISIS remained a lower-level political and social threat, it might have retained more significant control over large portions of Iraq and possibly Syrian border enclaves. It is debatable that it might have consolidated into an organization prioritizing administrative capacity like the Lebanese Shia group Hezbollah. Yet, it is undeniable that ISIS developed a sophisticated approach and appreciation for administrative control. Whiteside's analysis indicates that, regardless of ISIS's degraded status as of 2018–20, they successfully integrated Maoist principles and Salafi-Jihadism to reintroduce revolutionary warfare after 2013.[37]

Political and military analysts should anticipate similar adaptations in the future among jihadi as well as state-sponsored groups. Additional integration of technological advancements in AI, encrypted communication applications, and new ways to recruit and operate through networks will continue to challenge military professionals and analysts. Yet, even with such innovations, humans and networks will remain at the center of conflict. While ISIS is among the most recent of organizations to manipulate the advantages revolutionary warfare provides, revisiting Fall's scholarship and incorporating key thinkers' analyses—such as those authored by Craig Whiteside, David Kilcullen, and others—are positive means through which to prepare for changes to warfare.

EPILOGUE

As it pertains to Bernard Fall, he was a humanitarian to the end, perhaps above all other considerations, and his sensitivity to the plight of civilians in times of war originated in empathy. It is impossible to know from what wellspring empathy emerged for him, and establishing its source within anyone, let alone in oneself, is elusive. However, in this author's view, a sense of strategic and personal empathy was the core factor in Fall's ability to identify Vietnamese revolutionary warfare and understand why it was effective. He was not alone in possessing this capacity, and on this point his life and work echo another individual, Victor Serge, who described living through a maelstrom of war during World War I and the Russian Revolution. As a committed libertarian communist who despised Joseph Stalin and fell out with Leon Trotsky, Serge described his overall ethic for living:

> Defense of man. Respect for man. Man must be given his rights, his security, his value. Without these, there is no Socialism. Without these, all is false, bankrupt, and spoiled. I mean: man, whoever he is, be he the meanest of men—"class enemy," son or grandson of a bourgeois, I do not care. It must never be forgotten that a human being is a human being.[38]

Fall might have written this. Like Serge, he was thorough in his demand for an honest appraisal of problems that obscured humans as both central to and the target of power. In a 1960 lecture given at Fort Bragg, North Carolina, he pointed out the importance of honesty as it related to identifying revolutionary warfare:

> The most essential requirement of winning a revolutionary war is the courage to face the truth that the problem exists at all. This is harder than one thinks. There is always a tendency to camouflage the problem as "banditry" or "mob-action"— until one awakens one morning to find that the "chief bandit" now sits in the President's chair in the capital and that the "Mob" is defeating one's finest regular troops on a battle-field not exactly suited to their heavy equipment. To lie to others (and be found out) may simply be embarrassing. To lie to oneself about the terrifying possibilities of Revolutionary Warfare may well be fatal.[39]

After Fall provided these comments in 1960, and by the time *The Viet-Nam Reader* appeared in 1965, he had worked to identify Vietnamese revolutionary warfare for over a decade. Many of the components he recognized in revolutionary warfare were ones he had experienced during World War II. Vietnamese revolutionary warfare grew in importance in his eyes because of its survivability. Despite the massive military power inflicted upon people in Southeast Asia, as ordered by French and later by American policymakers, the Vietnamese people wielding revolutionary warfare survived, much as Fall had after losing his family during World War II. In the years leading to his death in February 1967, he sought to help others understand Vietnamese revolutionary warfare. He did everything he could to resolve conflict in Vietnam and to show that finding a peaceful solution to war required far more strength, willpower, integrity, and skill than anything in the US military arsenal. It would take a kind of power found in Vietnamese revolutionary warfare. During the many years of war in Vietnam, that power would be difficult for Americans to find.

NOTES

ACKNOWLEDGMENTS

1. David A. Bell, *Shadows of Revolution: Reflections on France, Past and Present* (New York: Oxford University Press, 2016), 336.

PROLOGUE

1. "Obituary: Ansgar Sovik," Andy Langehough, *Northfield.org*, 20 January 2007. Hankow later merged with Hanyang and Wuchang as sister cities to form the modern city of Wuhan, Hubei Province. See Jonathan Fenby, *Chiang Kai-shek: China's Generalissimo and the Nation He Lost* (New York: Carroll & Graf Publishers, 2004), 30.
2. For more on the Northern Expedition, see Donald A. Jordan, *The Northern Expedition: China's National Revolution of 1926–1928* (Honolulu, HI: University of Hawai'i Press, 1976).
3. "Obituary: Ansgar Sovik," Andy Langehough, *Northfield.org*, 20 January 2007.
4. *Ibid*.
5. Jeff Sauve, "Chaplain Ansgar Sovik Writes Home," *Currents: The Newsletter of the Norwegian–American Historical Association*, Vol. 176, Summer 2020, 8.
6. The distance from Rabaul to Guadalcanal with return was 565 miles. For information on these aircraft, see Richard B. Frank, *Guadalcanal: The Definitive Account of the Landmark Battle* (New York: Penguin Books, 1990), 65–6.
7. *Ibid.*, 80. For details on the second landing day at Guadalcanal and the attack on the USS *George Elliott*, see *Ibid.*, 79–82.
8. For a concise overview of this battle, see *Ibid.*, 150–8.
9. Jeff Sauve, "Chaplain Ansgar Sovik Writes Home," *Currents: The Newsletter of the Norwegian–American Historical Association*, Vol. 176, Summer 2020, 8.
10. *Ibid.*, 8.
11. Operations on Guadalcanal continued until early February 1943. Details recount-

ing Sovik's service on Guadalcanal are available in Jeff Suave, "Chaplain Ansgar Sovik Writes Home," *Currents: The Newsletter of the Norwegian–American Historical Association*, Volume 176, Summer 2020, 9, available at: https://naha.stolaf.edu/wp-content/uploads/2020/11/2020_summer.pdf (accessed 15 January 2021); for a comprehensive overview of the Solomon Islands campaign and the battle on Guadalcanal, see Richard B. Frank, *Guadalcanal: The Definitive Account of the Landmark Battle* (New York: Penguin Books, 1990).
12. "In Memory of Ansgar Sovik, My Professor, My Mentor, My Longtime Friend," Jeff Johnson, *St. Olaf Magazine*, Spring 2007, 52.
13. "Obituary: Ansgar Sovik," Andy Langehough, *Northfield.org*, 20 January 2007.
14. Jeff Sauve, "Chaplain Ansgar Sovik Writes Home," *Currents: The Newsletter of the Norwegian–American Historical Association*, Vol. 176, Summer 2020, 10.
15. George Orwell, *Homage to Catalonia* (New York: Harcourt, Brace, Jovanovich, 1952), 180.

INTRODUCTION

1. Jean Lacouture quoted in Roger Lévy, *Politique Étrangèr*, Vol. 32, No. 3 (1967), 268.
2. Bernard B. Fall, Letter to the Editor, *Newsweek*, 11 October 1965, Series 1.1., Box F-1, Bernard B. Fall Papers (BBF), JFK Presidential Library (JFKL), Boston, Massachusetts.
3. Lao Tse, *Tao Te Ching*, translated by Gia-Fu Feng and Jane English (New York: Vintage Books, 1972). This excerpt is from saying seventy-eight.
4. Bernard B. Fall, "Transcript, Originals for Last Reflections on a War," Series 1.02, "Books by Dr. Fall," Box B-08, p. 1, BBF, JFKL.
5. "USG Memorandum," "Photographs; case of Dr. Bernard Fall," From Director of Information to Historical Branch, G-3 Division, 23 March 1967. 1st Battalion, 9th Marines Command Chronology for period 5 February to 28 February 1967, p. 6., USMC Heritage Division, Quantico, Virginia.
6. Bernard B. Fall, "Transcript, Originals for Last Reflections on a War," Series 1.02, Books by Dr. Fall, Box B-08, p. 2, BBF, JFKL.
7. "Sully comments on Bernard Fall," François Sully Papers and Photographs, *Newsweek* Files, Feb.–March 1967, UMass-Boston, Series II, Subject Files, Box 2, Folder 31, p. 1.
8. *Ibid.*
9. Sgt. Roy Johnson Interview with Dr. Bernard Fall, *Marine Corps Gazette*, April 1967, "Bernard Fall PhD Published Information," USMC Heritage Division, Quantico, Virginia. For a personal account of the USMC Combined Arms Platoon Concept, see Francis J. West, Jr., *The Village* (Madison, WI: University of Wisconsin Press, 1972).
10. David Marshall email correspondence with author, 9 January 2019.

11. Fredrik Logevall, Foreword to 2018 Edition of Bernard B. Fall, *Street Without Joy: The French Debacle in Indochina* (Guilford, CT: Stackpole Books, 2018).
12. "Sully comments on Bernard Fall," François Sully Papers and Photographs, *Newsweek* Files, February–March 1967, UMass-Boston, Series II, Subject Files, Box 2, Folder 31, p. 2.
13. "Fall's book was the first full-length study on the subject in English and quickly became the standard Western account ... it was not until the siege's fiftieth anniversary (that) all the information necessary to disprove Fall's conclusions became publicly available—though only in Vietnamese-language works." See Kevin Boylan and Luc Olivier, *Valley of the Shadow: The Siege of Dien Bien Phu* (New York: Osprey), 266.
14. Con Thien was two miles south of the Demilitarized Zone (DMZ), and "Leatherneck Square" was technically marked by Cam Lo, Gio Linh, Con Thien, and Dong Ha, but was viewed as extending along the Cua Viet River to points south in Thua Thien along Route 1. "COMUSMACV 1967 Command Chronology," Box 5, Folder 25, p. 5, USMC History Division, Quantico, Virginia.
15. 1/9th Marines earned the nickname "The Walking Dead" during the Vietnam War because of its high casualty rate. The unit was formed during World War I and deactivated 29 August 2014, "'Walking Dead' marine battalion to be deactivated," *Washington Times*, 29 August 2014.
16. Michael Herr, "Dispatches: A Correspondent's Memoir: 1967–1975" in *Reporting Vietnam: Part Two: American Journalism 1969–1975* (New York: The Library of America, Literary Classics of the United States, Inc., 1998), 651.
17. David Marshall letter to Dorothy Fall, 3 April 2014. Marshall provided a copy of this letter to the author.
18. *Ibid.*
19. "USG Memorandum," "Photographs; case of Dr. Bernard Fall," From Director of Information to Historical Branch, G-3 Division, 23 March 1967. 1st Battalion, 9th Marines Command Chronology for period 5–28 February 1967, p. 3, USMC Heritage Division, Quantico, Virginia.
20. *Ibid.*
21. Bernard B. Fall, "Transcript, Originals for Last Reflections on a War," Series 1.02, Books by Dr. Fall, Box B-08, p. 4–5, BBF, JFKL. In support of Fall's comments, the Marine Corps' chronology states, "During the period that the battalion was conducting Phase I of CHINOOK II rain and overcast conditions curtailed the use of helicopter transportation for troop lifts and resupply." "USG Memorandum," "Photographs; case of Dr. Bernard Fall," From Director of Information to Historical Branch, G-3 Division, March 23, 1967. 1st Battalion, 9th Marines Command Chronology for period 5–28 February 1967, USMC Heritage Division, Quantico, Virginia.

22. Bernard B. Fall, "Transcript, Originals for Last Reflections on a War," Series 1.02, Books by Dr. Fall, Box B-08, pp. 6–7, BBF, JFKL.
23. David Marshall letter to Dorothy Fall, 3 April 2014. Mr. Marshall provided this letter to author.
24. Bernard B. Fall, "Transcript, Originals for Last Reflections on a War," Series 1.02, Books by Dr. Fall, Box B-08, p. 8, BBF, JFKL.
25. David Marshall letter to Dorothy Fall, 3 April 2014.
26. The command narrative concluded, "It should be noted that Dr. Bernard Fall, Professor of International Relations at Howard University, and author of 'The Street Without Joy,' was killed on February 21 1967, by a V.C. explosive device while accompanying a rifle company on a routine search and destroy operation along 'The Street Without Joy.' The command narrative added that causalities during Phase I of Chinook II were 6 USMC KIA, 45 USMC WIA, 2 USMC DOW, 1 USN WIA, 1 U.S. Army WIA, 1 U.S. Civilian Killed." Fall was identified as the '1 U.S. Civilian Killed,' but Fall was not a US citizen at the time of his death (he was a French citizen). The narrative further explained that "Contact was made with an estimated company on February 21. Because of a river our elements could not cross, it was not possible to close with the enemy." pp. 4–6. "USG Memorandum," "Photographs; case of Dr. Bernard Fall," From Director of Information to Historical Branch, G-3 Division, 23 March 1967. 1st Battalion, 9th Marines Command Chronology for period 5 to 28 February 1967, 6, 7. USMC Heritage Division, Quantico, Virginia.
27. J. William Fulbright, "Bernard Fall Eulogy," J. William Fulbright Papers (JWFP), 1942–1990, Series 72, Box 28, Folder 6, Special Collections, University of Arkansas Libraries, Fayetteville, Arkansas.
28. *Ibid.*, 2–3.
29. "*Congressional Senate Record*—Statement," 24 February 1967, S 2609, JWFP, Series 71, Box 32.
30. Roger Lévy, "Bernard Fall devant le Congrès Américain," *Politique Étrangère*, Vol. 32, No. 3, Spring 1967, 268.
31. Representative González served in the 87th Congress (1961) to the 105th Congress (1999). See González, Henry B., US House of Representatives, History, Art & Archives, https://history.house.gov/People/Detail/13906
32. Bernard Fall, 2360308011. Vietnam Center and Archive. 02 March 1967, Box 03, Folder 08, Douglas Pike Collection: Unit 08—Biography, Vietnam Center and Sam Johnson Vietnam Archive, Texas Tech University.
33. Over twenty-four obituaries from Europe and the United States are available in the Bernard B. Fall Papers. Series 2.08, Box O-1, BBF, JFKL.
34. Guy Le Clec'h, "Bernard Fall, 'Mort au champ d'honneur des observateurs,'" *Le Figaro*, 2 March 1967. Series 2.8, Box, O-1, BBF, JFKL.
35. "Bernard Fall est tué par une mine près de Hué," *Le Monde*, 23 February 1967, Series 2.8, Box O-1, BBF, JFKL.

36. Hugh A. Mulligan, "V.C. Booby Trap Kills U.S. Journalist," *Nashville Tennessean*, 22 February 1967, Vann-Sheehan Vietnam War Collection, Research File, 1920–1991, Box 66, Folder 6, Individuals, Bernard Fall, 1973, Library of Congress Manuscripts Division, Washington, DC.
37. "Bernard B. Fall," no writer attributed, *Harvard Crimson*, 24 February 1967.
38. United Nations, Department of Public Information, *Agreements on a Comprehensive Political Settlement of the Cambodia Conflict: Paris, 23 October 1991*, January 1992, 1–6. For information on the conflict between China, Cambodia, and the State of Vietnam in what is known as the "Third Indochina War," see Nayan Chanda, *Brother Enemy, the War After the War: A History of Indochina Since the Fall of Saigon* (New York: Harcourt Brace Jovanovich, 1986).
39. "John McCain: By the Book," *New York Times*, 3 May 2018.
40. "Colin L. Powell: By the Book," *New York Times*, 28 June 2012.
41. Course syllabi for courses at Fort Bragg that included Fall's book, *Street Without Joy*, includes: "A-700 Course, Problems of Development and Internal Defense" and "3610A/3-Counter-Insurgency in Indo-China," United States Army Special Warfare School, Fort Bragg. These syllabi are located in the Alan F. Grant Papers, Box 10, Dwight D. Eisenhower Presidential Library, Abilene, Kansas.
42. General Ronald H. Griffith, USA (Ret.), in Admiral James Stavridis, USN (Ret.) and R. Manning Ancell, *The Leader's Bookshelf* (Annapolis, MD: Naval Institute Press, 2017), 100.
43. For details on Yarborough and his contributions to US Army airborne operations, see William Pelham Yarborough, *Bail Out Over North Africa: America's First Combat Parachute Missions 1942* (Williamstown, NJ: Philips Publications, 1979).
44. "Fall—Yarborough Correspondence, July—December 1964," William P. Yarborough Papers (WPYP), Box 6 and 94, Howard Gotlieb Archival Research Center (HGARC), Boston University (BU), Boston, Massachusetts; Bernard B. Fall, "Authority on Communism Lectures at S.W. School," *The Paraglide*, 21 May 1964, Page 6A, Series, 1.05, Box P-01, BBF, JFKL.
45. The author was unable to locate Yarborough's eulogy for Fall in Yarborough's papers. Yarborough's desk calendar entry for the event is located in his files, but not his comments. See "Fall—Yarborough Correspondence, July–December 1964," William P. Yarborough Papers (WPYP), Box 6 and 94, Howard Gotlieb Archival Research Center (HGARC), Boston University (BU), Boston, Massachusetts.
46. NBC's *Meet the Press*, p. 3, 31 January 1965, Series 1.1., Box F-1, BBF, JFKL.
47. *Ibid.*, 3.
48. In the 1950s, Fall's interest in anthropology and sociology of Indochina coincided with the development of operational anthropology. He did not refer to this discipline by name, but, substantively, his research adopted many of its approaches. Writing in 1951, anthropologist Laura Thompson described this field, writing, "it may be thought of as an emergent, integrative discipline which has not yet been

theoretically systematized, but which has demonstrated its usefulness to a marked degree … [as] applied to large scale human problems, especially those of community and regional administration, wherein the need for solutions has been urgent." For a foundational text, see Laura Thompson, "Operational Anthropology as an Emergent Discipline," *ETC: A Review of General Semantics*, Vol. 8, No. 2 (Winter 1951), 117–28.

49. For examples of these scholars work, see Pierre Gourou, *The Tropical World: Its Social and Economic Conditions and Its Future Status* (London: Longmans, Green and Company, 1953); Bernard Philippe Groslier, *Indochina: Art of the World*, translated by George Lawrence (London: Methuen, 1962); Paul Mus, *Le Viet Nam Chez Lui* (Paris: Centre d'Études de Politique Étrangère, 1946); Gerald Hickey, *The Village* (New Haven, CT: Yale University Press, 1964); and Charles Robequain, *L'Indochine Française* (Paris: A. Colin, 1948).

50. David W.P. Elliott, *The Vietnamese War: Revolution and Social Change in the Mekong Delta 1930–1975*, Concise Edition (Armonk, NY: M.E. Sharpe, 2007), 87.

51. Jeremy Black, *Rethinking Military History* (New York: Routledge, 2004), 19.

52. Bernard B. Fall, *Last Reflections on a War* (New York: Doubleday & Company, 1967).

53. *Ibid.*, 210.

54. For an example of the influence of these officers on Fall, see Bernard Fall, "Laos, Vietnam, and Revolutionary Warfare," Undated, p. 61, Series 1.09, Box T-1, BBF, JFKL.

55. Fall's collection of *Revue Militaire D'Information* is found in Series 2.06, Boxes J097 and J098, BBF, JFKL.

56. *Ibid.*

57. *Ibid.*, and Bernard B. Fall, *Street Without Joy: The French Debacle in Indochina* (Guilford, CT: Stackpole Books, 1961), 370.

58. Bernard B. Fall, *The Two Vietnams: A Political and Military Analysis* (New York: Praeger, 1963), 344.

59. For analysis on sanctuary, see Michael A. Innes, *Streets Without Joy: A Political History of Sanctuary and War, 1959–2009* (London, UK: Hurst Publishers, 2021).

60. Bernard B. Fall, *The Two Vietnams: A Political and Military Analysis* (New York: Praeger, 1963), 344–5.

61. *Ibid.*, 344–5.

62. Bernard B. Fall, "This Isn't Munich, It's Spain," in *Last Reflections on a War* (New York: Doubleday & Company, 1967), 234.

63. Nancy Zaroulis and Gerald Sullivan, *Who Spoke Up? American Protest Against the War in Vietnam 1963–1975* (New York: Doubleday and Company, 1984), 38.

64. Bernard B. Fall, "Two Thousand Years of War in Viet-Nam," *Horizon*, Vol. IX, No. 2, Spring 1967.

65. Bernard Fall, "The Theory and Practice of Insurgency and Counterinsurgency," *Last Reflections on a War* (New York: Doubleday & Company, 1967), 220.
66. *Ibid.*, 210.
67. "Bernard Fall Correspondence, January 1, 1965," Vann-Sheehan Vietnam War Collection, Research File, Circa 1920–1991, Box 27, Folder 10, Library of Congress Manuscripts Division, Washington, DC.
68. François Sully, "Vietnam: The Unpleasant Truth," *Newsweek*, 20 August 1962.
69. Douglas E. Pike, *PAVN: People's Army of Vietnam* (New York: Da Capo Press, 1983), 213.
70. Fredrik Logevall, *Embers of War: The Fall of an Empire and the Making of America's Vietnam* (New York: Random House, 2014), 713.
71. Craig Whiteside, "The Islamic State and the Return of Revolutionary Warfare," *Small Wars & Insurgencies*, Vol. 27, No. 5, August 2016, 744.
72. *Ibid.*, 744.
73. See Chapter 3, "The Theory of Competitive Control" in David Kilcullen, *Out of the Mountains: The Coming Age of the Urban Guerrilla* (New York: Oxford University Press, 2013).
74. *Ibid.*, 133.
75. Philippe Devillers, *France-Asie*, No. 188 (*Hiver* 1966–7), 146–60; Jean Lacouture quoted in Roger Lévy, *Politique Étrangère*, Vol. 32, No. 3 (1967).
76. Bernard B. Fall, *Le Viet-Minh: La Republique Democratique du Viet-Nam, 1945–1950*. With Preface by Paul Mus (Paris: Libraire Armand Colin, 1960), v–xii.
77. *Ibid.*, vii.
78. See François Sully Papers and Photographs, 1958–63, Joseph P. Healey Archives and Special Collections, University of Massachusetts Boston, Massachusetts. See especially "Sully comments on Bernard Fall," *Newsweek* Files, February–March 1967, Series II, Subject Files, Box 2, Folder 31.
79. Gerald Hickey, *Window on a War: An Anthropologist in the Vietnam Conflict* (Lubbock: Texas Tech University Press, 2002), 275.
80. Among the limited number of articles about Fall, see Christopher E. Goscha, "'Sorry About That ...' Bernard Fall, the Vietnam War and the Impact of a French Intellectual in the US," in *La Guerre du Vietnam et L'Europe 1963–1973*, Eds. Christopher Goscha and Marice Vaïsse (Bruxeles: Bruylant, 2003); Gary Hess and John McNay, "'The Expert': Bernard Fall and His Critique of America's Involvement in Vietnam," in *The Human Tradition in the Vietnam Era*, edited by David L. Anderson (Wilmington, DE: SR Books, 2000); Fredrik Logevall, "Bernard Fall: The Man Who Knew the War," *New York Times*, 21 February 2017; Frances FitzGerald, "The Reporter Who Warned Us Not to Invade Vietnam 10 Years before the Gulf of Tonkin," *The Nation*, 23 March 2015.
81. Quoted in Dorothy Fall, *Bernard Fall: Memories of a Soldier-Scholar* (Washington, DC; Potomac Books, 2007), 246–47.

82. David Halberstam, foreword to Dorothy Fall, *Bernard Fall: Memories of a Soldier-Scholar* (Washington, DC: Potomac Books, 2007), xiv–xv.
83. Bernard Fall interview with Walter Cronkite, 1965. https://www.youtube.com/watch?v=V76LDCW86I0
84. For a representative article, see "Lost Chances for Peace in Indochina," in I.F. Stone, *In a Time of Torment, 1961–1967* (Boston, MA: Little, Brown, and Company, 1967), 178–88.
85. Dorothy Fall, *Bernard Fall: Memories of a Soldier-Scholar* (Washington, DC; Potomac Books, 2007), 245–7. See especially David Halberstam, Foreword, xiii–xvi.
86. Sherman Kent, one of the fathers of modern intelligence in the United States, served as the Chairman of the Board of National Estimates in 1964 and contributed to a weakening view on the domino theory in official channels. According to Kent, "We do not believe that the loss of South Vietnam and Laos would be followed by the rapid, successive communization of the other states of the Far East … it is likely that no nation in the area would quickly succumb to communism as a result of the fall of Laos and South Vietnam. Furthermore, a continuation of the spread of communism in the area would not be inexorable, and any spread which did occur would take time—time in which the total situation might change in any of a number of ways unfavorable to the Communist cause." See "Sherman Kent Memorandum to the CIA Director," 9 June 1964, National Security File, Vietnam Country File: Box 54, LBJP, LBJL.
87. Bernard B. Fall, "This Isn't Munich, It's Spain," in *Last Reflections on a War* (New York: Doubleday & Company, 1967), 233.
88. *Ibid.*, 234.
89. Bernard B. Fall, "Will South Viet-Nam Be Next?" *The Nation*, 31 May 1958, BBF, JFKL, Series 1.06, Box A-2.
90. Bernard B. Fall, "South Viet-Nam's Internal Problems," *Pacific Affairs*, September 1958, Series 1.01, Box F-1, BBF, JFKL.

1. FIRST IMPRESSIONS OF A WAR

1. Bernard B. Fall, *Last Reflections on a War* (New York: Doubleday & Company, 1967), 16.
2. "Street Without Joy" was a term later used by French troops to describe an area in Vietnam, north of Hue. The film was released on 13 April 1938 and produced by Films André Hugon.
3. Philippe Devillers, *France-Asia*, No. 188 (Winter 1966–7), 148.
4. Dorothy Fall, *Bernard Fall: Memories of a Soldier-Scholar* (Washington, DC: Potomac Books, 2007), 13–14.
5. The Vichy government's seizure of Jews from both zones was determined in an agreement between Vichy authorities and the Nazis on 4 July 1942. See Michael

R. Marrus and Robert O. Paxton, *Vichy France and the Jews* (New York: Basic Books, 1981), 255–62.
6. *Ibid.*, 16; Philippe Devillers, *France-Asia*, No. 188, (Winter 1966–7), 148. This deportation through Vichy authorities mirrored those directly undertaken by German forces. For example, in the Netherlands, historian István Deák described how "Jews were duly registered, and beginning in 1941 they were ordered to proceed to assembly points. From there, they were gradually deported to German concentration and death camps." István Deák, *Europe on Trial: The Story of Collaboration, Resistance, and Retribution During World War II* (Boulder, CO: Westview Press, 2015), 126.
7. Dorothy Fall, *Bernard Fall: Memories of a Soldier-Scholar* (Washington, DC: Potomac Books, 2007), 16.
8. *Ibid.*, 18.
9. *Ibid.*, 24.
10. Adam Rayski, *The Choice of the Jews Under Vichy: Between Submission and Resistance* (South Bend, IN: Notre Dame University Press, 2005), 48.
11. *Ibid.*, 49.
12. Timothy Snyder, *Black Earth: The Holocaust as History and Warning* (New York: Tim Duggan Books), 248.
13. *Ibid.*, 248.
14. Stathis N. Kalyvas, *The Logic of Violence in Civil War* (Cambridge, UK: Cambridge University Press, 2006), 192.
15. *Ibid.*, 192.
16. Dorothy Fall, *Bernard Fall: Memories of a Soldier-Scholar* (Washington, DC: Potomac Books, 2007), 187.
17. *Ibid.*, 22.
18. *Ibid.*, 20–5.
19. Bernard B. Fall, *Last Reflections on a War* (New York: Doubleday & Company, 1967), 18.
20. For more on these social divides, see Michael R. Marrus and Robert O. Paxton, *Vichy France and the Jews* (New York: Basic Books, 1981) and Adam Rayski, *The Choice of the Jews Under Vichy: Between Submission and Resistance* (South Bend, IN: Notre Dame University Press, 2005).
21. Bernard Fall, "Letter to MAJ Nulsen," Series 1.01, Box F-01, BBF, JFKL.
22. Bernard B. Fall, *Last Reflections on a War* (New York: Doubleday & Company, 1967), 20.
23. Dorothy Fall, *Bernard Fall: Memories of a Soldier-Scholar* (Washington, DC: Potomac Books, 2007), 25.
24. Bernard B. Fall, *Last Reflections on a War* (New York: Doubleday & Company, 1967), 20.

25. Claude Chambard, *The Maquis: A History of the French Resistance Movement* (New York: The Bobbs-Merrill Company, Inc., 1976), 47.
26. Bernard Fall, "The Guerrilla Craze," Undated, Series 1.5, Box P-1, BBF, JFKL.
27. Bernard B. Fall, *Last Reflections on a War* (New York: Doubleday & Company, 1967), 20.
28. Bernard Fall, "The Guerrilla Craze," Undated, Series 1.5, Box P-1, BBF, JFKL.
29. Bernard B. Fall, *Last Reflections on a War* (New York: Doubleday & Company, 1967), 20.
30. Bernard Fall, "CV", Series 1.01, Box F-1; "Howard University Magazine, Vol. II, No. 3, April 1965," Series 1.10, Box AM-1, BBF, JFKL.
31. Bernard Fall, "Maquis Note," Series 2.03, Box W-2, Folder "April 1945—La Contre Attaque Allemande Au Mont-Froid," BBF, JFKL.
32. Stathis N. Kalyvas, *The Logic of Violence in Civil War* (Cambridge, UK: Cambridge University Press, 2006), 116.
33. Dorothy Fall, *Bernard Fall: Memories of a Soldier-Scholar* (Washington, DC: Potomac Books, 2007), 21.
34. Eugene Davidson, *The Trial of the Germans: An Account of the Twenty-Two Defendants Before the International Military Tribunal at Nuremberg* (New York: Macmillan Company, 1966), 520–1.
35. Bernard B. Fall, *Last Reflections on a War* (New York: Doubleday & Company, 1967), 20.
36. Claude Chambard, *The Maquis: A History of the French Resistance Movement* (New York: The Bobbs-Merrill Company, Inc., 1976), 57, 89.
37. Robert Gildea, *Fighters in the Shadows: A New History of the French Resistance* (Cambridge, MA: Belknap Press of Harvard University, 2015), 17.
38. For an account of Jewish persecution in these countries, see Vasily Grossman, *A Writer at War: Vasily Grossman With the Red Army, 1941–1945*, edited and translated by Antony Beevor and Luba Vinogradova (New York: Pantheon Books, 2005).
39. Philippe Devillers, *France-Asia*, No. 188 (Winter 1966–7), 148.
40. Bernard Fall, "CV," Series 1.1, Box F-1, BBF, JFKL.
41. Bernard Fall, "Biography," Series 1.1, Box F-1, BBF, JFKL.
42. Bernard B. Fall, *Last Reflections on a War* (New York: Doubleday & Company, 1967), 20.
43. Bernard Fall, "CV," Series 1.1, Box F-1, BBF, JFKL.
44. Claude Chambard, *The Maquis: A History of the French Resistance Movement* (New York: The Bobbs-Merrill Company, Inc., 1976), 102.
45. Bernard Fall, "Biography," Series 1.1, Box F-1, BBF, JFKL.
46. Philippe Devillers, *France-Asia*, No. 188 (Winter 1966–7). 148; Dorothy Fall, *Bernard Fall: Memories of a Soldier-Scholar* (Washington, DC: Potomac Books, 2007), 30.

47. Bernard Fall, "The Guerrilla Craze," Undated, Series 1.5, Box P-1, BBF, JFKL.
48. H.R. Kedward, *In Search of the Maquis: Rural Resistance in Southern France 1942–1944* (Oxford: Clarendon Press, 1994), 205–6.
49. See Benn Steil, *The Marshall Plan: Dawn of the Cold War* (New York: Oxford University Press, 2018), 16.
50. Bernard Fall, "CV," Series 1.01, Box F-1; "Howard University Magazine, Vol. II, No. 3, April 1965," Series 1.10, Box AM-1, BBF, JFKL.
51. As an example, Roger Trinquier, a soldier and author whose work Fall knew well, served as a captain in the Vichy Government. See Bernard Fall Introduction, p. xiv in Roger Trinquier, *Modern Warfare: A French View of Counterinsurgency* (Westport, CT: Praeger, 2006).
52. Charles de Gaulle, *The Call to Honour 1940–1942* (New York: The Viking Press, 1955), 271.
53. *Ibid.*, 272.
54. Fighting at Monte Cassino and during the Allied drive to Rome is one example. See Matthew Parker, *Monte Cassino: The Hardest-Fought Battle of World War II* (New York: Doubleday, 2004).
55. Bernard B. Fall, *Last Reflections on a War* (New York: Doubleday & Company, 1967), 20.
56. *Ibid.*, 21.
57. Bernard Fall, "Howard University Magazine," Vol. II, No. 3, April 1965, Series 1.10, Box AM-1, BBF, JFKL.
58. *Ibid.*, 21.
59. Bernard Fall, "CV," Series 1.1, Box F-1, BBF, JFKL.
60. Robert O. Paxton, "Vichy on Trial." *New York Times*, 16 October 1997, https://www.nytimes.com/1997/10/16/opinion/vichy-on-trial.html (accessed 15 September 2018).
61. István Deák, *Europe on Trial: The Story of Collaboration, Resistance, and Retribution During World War II* (Boulder, CO: Westview Press, 2015), 151.
62. Robert O. Paxton, "Vichy on Trial." *New York Times*, 16 October 1997, https://www.nytimes.com/1997/10/16/opinion/vichy-on-trial.html (accessed 15 September 2018).
63. H.R. Kedward, *In Search of the Maquis: Rural Resistance in Southern France 1942–1944* (Oxford: Clarendon Press, 1994), 65.
64. *Ibid.*, 65–6.
65. Extensive research on this subject is available. For further reference, see Richard Vinen, *The Unfree French: Life Under the Occupation* (New Haven, CT: Yale University Press, 2006); Robert Gildea, *Marianne in Chains: Everyday Life in the French Heartland Under the German Occupation* (New York: Metropolitan Books, 2002); Michael R. Marrus and Robert O. Paxton, *Vichy France and the Jews* (New York: Basic Books, 1981); Jean Guéhenno, *Diary of the Dark Years, 1940–1944*,

translated by David Ball (New York: Oxford University Press, 2014). Robert O. Paxton, "Vichy on Trial," *New York Times*, 16 October 1997, https://www.nytimes.com/1997/10/16/opinion/vichy-on-trial.html (accessed 15 September 2018).

66. See Eric Meyer, *Devil's Guard—The Real Story* (London: Swordwork Books, 2009).
67. René Riesen is an example of a soldier who served in the Vichy military but then served with distinction for the cause of France in Indochina and Algeria. See René Riesen, *Jungle Mission* (New York: Thomas Crowell, 1957).
68. Stathis N. Kalyvas, *The Logic of Violence in Civil War* (Cambridge, UK: Cambridge University Press, 2006), 192.
69. Mary L. Dudiak, *War-Time: An Idea, Its History, Its Consequences* (New York: Oxford University Press, 2012), 38.
70. Stephen Walt analyzes what Robert Jervis has called "the Spiral Model" in terms of geopolitical competition among revolutionary states and other state powers. See Stephen M. Walt, "Revolution and War," published in *Revolution: Critical Concepts in Political Science, Volume II*, Edited by Rosemary O'Kane (New York: Routledge, 2000), 427.
71. Bernard B. Fall, *Street Without Joy: The French Debacle in Indochina* (Guilford, CT: Stackpole Books, 1961), 386.
72. Fall's numbers of executed collaborators were reported in 1961 and Paxton's in 1997. See Robert O. Paxton, "Vichy on Trial." *New York Times*, 16 October 1997, https://www.nytimes.com/1997/10/16/opinion/vichy-on-trial.html (accessed 15 September 2018). Also, See Benn Steil, *The Marshall Plan: Dawn of the Cold War* (New York: Oxford University Press, 2018), 16.
73. David A. Bell, *Shadows of Revolution: Reflections on France, Past and Present* (New York: Oxford University Press, 2016), 326.
74. All quotes in this paragraph are from Fall's account, see pp. 286–90 in Bernard B. Fall, *Street Without Joy: The French Debacle in Indochina* (Guilford, CT: Stackpole Books, 1961).
75. Enzo Traverso, *Fire and Blood: The European Civil War 1914–1945*, translated by David Ferbach (New York: Verso, 2016), 81. Traverso's account of Dirlewanger is drawn from Christian Ingrao, *Les Chasseurs Noirs, La Brigade Dirlewanger* (Paris: Perrin, 2006).
76. *Ibid.*, 81.
77. Bernard Fall, "The Way It Is," Series 1.2, Books by Fall, Box B-08, BBF, JFKL.
78. Fall discussed this point at length, see "Blitz in Vietnam: Bernard B. Fall on the Impersonal War," *The New Republic*, 9 October 1965, in François Sully Papers, Box 6, Folder 28. For technical distinctions, also see Joint Publication 1–04, 17 August 2011, *Legal Support to Military Operations*.
79. Lt. Col. Dave Grossman, *On Killing: The Psychological Cost of Learning to Kill in War and Society* (New York: Little, Brown, and Company, 2009), 253–8.

80. *Ibid.*, 253–8.
81. Marcus Raskin and Bernard Fall (eds.), *The Viet-Nam Reader: Articles and Documents on American Foreign Policy and the Viet-Nam Crisis* (New York: Vintage Books, 1965), 367–9.
82. See Bernard Fall, "Blitz in Vietnam: Bernard B. Fall on the Impersonal War," *The New Republic*, 9 October 1965, p. 20 in François Sully Papers, Box 6, Folder 28, UMass-Boston.
83. *Ibid.*
84. Bernard B. Fall, "Liberation vs. Pacification" lecture, Yale University, 3 March 1966, quoted in Dorothy Fall, *Bernard Fall: Memories of a Soldier-Scholar* (Washington, DC: Potomac Books, 2007), 22–3.
85. *Ibid.*, 22–3; See also, Bernard Fall, "Subversive Warfare—A Structural Analysis," Undated, Series 1.5, Box P-3, BBF, JFKL; Bernard Fall, "Memorandum—Some Thoughts on the Problem of Subversion," Series 1.5, Box P-3, BBF, JFKL.
86. Bernard B. Fall, *Last Reflections on a War* (New York: Doubleday & Company, 1967), 210.
87. Bernard B. Fall, "CV," Box F-1, Series 1.1, BBF, JFKL.
88. Quoted in Enzo Traverso, *Fire and Blood: The European Civil War, 1914–1945*, translated by David Ferbach (New York: Verso, 2016), 133.
89. Bernard Fall, "CV," Series 1.01, Box F-1, BBF, JFKL.
90. Bernard Fall, "Correspondence," Series 2.3, Box W-01, BBF, JFKL. Fall's position id was ETO-AG-424. The original text reads: "Bernard FALL est un traducteur serieux et comptetent qui travaille avec application et assiduité. Sa connaissance parfait de l'Allemand, qu'il parle comme sa langue maternelle, font de lui un auxillaire precieux."
91. Telford Taylor, *The Anatomy of the Nuremberg Trials: A Personal Memoir* (New York: Alfred A. Knopf, 1992), xii.
92. Bernard Fall, "CV," Series 1.01, Box F-1, BBF, JFKL.
93. *Ibid.*, v–vii.
94. Jackson was appointed to the Supreme Court by Franklin D. Roosevelt and served from 11 July 1941 to 9 October 1954. He took a leave of absence from the Supreme Court to assume the position of US Chief of Counsel for the International Military Tribunal. For more on Jackson's appointments, see Peter Irons, *A People's History of the Supreme Court: The Men and Women Whose Cases and Decisions Have Shaped Our Constitution* (New York: Penguin Books 1999), 343.
95. *History of the United Nations War Crimes Commission and the Development of the Laws of War*, compiled by the United Nations War Crimes Commission (London: His Majesty's Stationary Office, 1948), v–viii.
96. *Ibid.*, v.
97. *Ibid.*, v.
98. *Ibid.*, vii.

99. Telford Taylor, *Nuremberg and Vietnam: An American Tragedy* (Chicago, IL: Quadrangle Books, 1970), 78–9.
100. Norbert Ehrenfreund, *The Nuremberg Legacy: How the Nazi War Crimes Trials Changed the Course of History* (New York: Palgrave Macmillan, 2007), 106, 123–4.
101. See Francine Hirsch, *Soviet Judgment at Nuremberg: A New History of the International Military Tribunal After World War II* (New York: Oxford University Press, 2020).
102. Telford Taylor, *Nuremberg and Vietnam: An American Tragedy* (Chicago, IL: Quadrangle Books, 1970), 90.
103. *Ibid.*, 90.
104. *Ibid.*, 89.
105. Telford Taylor, *The Anatomy of the Nuremberg Trials: A Personal Memoir* (New York: Alfred A. Knopf, 1992), 7.
106. Norbert Ehrenfreund, *The Nuremberg Legacy: How the Nazi War Crimes Trials Changed the Course of History* (New York: Palgrave Macmillan, 2007), 121.
107. Telford Taylor, *Nuremberg and Vietnam: An American Tragedy* (Chicago, IL: Quadrangle Books, 1970), 79.
108. Telford Taylor, *The Anatomy of the Nuremberg Trials: A Personal Memoir* (New York: Alfred A. Knopf, 1992), 11.
109. *Ibid.*, 11.
110. *Ibid.*, 13.
111. *Ibid.*, 15.
112. *Ibid.*, 15.
113. Bernard Fall, "*Trois Rapports sur l'Armement et la Cavalerie du IIIe Reich*," Series 2.3, Box W-03, BBF, JFKL. This report served almost as an early draft or foundation for Bernard Fall's master's degree thesis on German illegal rearmament between 1919 and 1936 which he completed at Syracuse University in 1952.
114. Telford Taylor, *The Anatomy of the Nuremberg Trials: A Personal Memoir* (New York: Alfred A. Knopf, 1992), 13–15.
115. Nuremberg Military Tribunal (NMT), XI. Judgment, A. Opinion and Judgment of Military Tribunal III, 1338. 1340; Bernard Fall, "*Trois Rapports sur l'Armement et la Cavalerie du IIIe Reich*," Series, 2.3, Box W-03, BBF, JFKL.
116. Viscount Maugham, *U.N.O. and War Crimes* (London: John Murray Publishers, 1951), 25–6.
117. Bernard Fall, "Blitz in Vietnam: Bernard B. Fall on the Impersonal War," *The New Republic*, 9 October 1965, p. 19 in François Sully Papers, Box 6, Folder 28, UMass-Boston.
118. *Ibid.*, 20.
119. *Ibid.*, 20.
120. Nuremberg Military Tribunal (NMT), XI. Judgment, A. Opinion and Judgment of Military Tribunal III, 1376.

121. Viscount Maugham, *U.N.O. and War Crimes* (London: John Murray Publishers, 1951), 30–7; Telford Taylor, *The Anatomy of the Nuremberg Trials: A Personal Memoir* (New York: Alfred A. Knopf, 1992), 20.
122. Sheldon Glueck, *War Criminals: Their Prosecution and Punishment* (New York: Alfred A. Knopf, 1944), 10, 12–17.
123. William Manchester, *The Arms of Krupp, 1587–1968* (Boston, MA: Little, Brown and Company, 1968), 631.
124. See Mark Mazower, "The Nomos of the Earth" in *Hitler's Empire: How the Nazis Ruled Europe* (New York: Penguin Press, 2008), 576–81.
125. Nazi efforts extended to build alliances with the Islamic world and other potential allies. See David Motadel, *Islam and Nazi Germany's War* (Cambridge, MA: Belknap Press, Harvard University Press, 2017).
126. See Adam Tooze, *The Wages of Destruction: The Making and Breaking of the Nazi Economy* (New York: Viking, 2006).
127. Philippe Devillers, *France-Asia*, No. 188 (Winter 1966–7), 148: "B. Fall, qui voulait participer à la recherche de la vérité, a alors demandé et obtenu d'entrer dans l'organisme de recherche de crimes de guerre auprès du Tribunal International et a participé de 1946 à 1948, à ces enquêtes qui font date dans l'histoire contemporaine et qui ont révélé, dans toute sa dimension, l'horreur de la guerre 'moderne'."
128. Telford Taylor, *Nuremberg and Vietnam: An American Tragedy* (Chicago, IL: Quadrangle Books, 1970), 80–1.
129. Markus Urban, translated by John Jenkins, *The Nuremberg Trials* (Geschichte Für Alle e.V.—Institut für Regionalgeschichte, 2012), 43–4, 70.
130. Telford Taylor, *Nuremberg and Vietnam: An American Tragedy* (Chicago, IL: Quadrangle Books, 1970), 81; Nuremberg Military Tribunal (NMT), XI. Judgment, A. Opinion and Judgment of Military Tribunal III, 1330.
131. Markus Urban, translated by John Jenkins, *The Nuremberg Trials* (Geschichte Für Alle e.V.—Institut für Regionalgeschichte, 2012), 43–4.
132. Nuremberg Military Tribunal (NMT), XI. Judgment, A. Opinion and Judgment of Military Tribunal III, 1327.
133. *Ibid.*, 1327.
134. Eugene Davidson, *The Trial of the Germans: An Account of the Twenty-Two Defendants Before the International Military Tribunal at Nuremberg* (New York: Macmillan Company, 1966), 506.
135. John C. Beyer and Stephen A. Schneider, *Forced Labor Under the Third Reich, Part One*, Nathan Associates, Arlington, Virginia, 1 January 1999, 3.
136. Eugene Davidson, *The Trial of the Germans: An Account of the Twenty-Two Defendants Before the International Military Tribunal at Nuremberg* (New York: Macmillan Company, 1966), 492. On the area of underground facilities, there

are 4046.8564 square meters in 1 acre, thus, 300,000 square meters is equivalent to 74.13 acres.
137. *Ibid.*, 492.
138. Speer was sentenced to twenty years in prison and Sauckel was hung on 16 October 1946. See Markus Urban, translated by John Jenkins, *The Nuremberg* Trials (Geschichte Für Alle e.V.—Institut für Regionalgeschichte, 2012), 45, 70.
139. Eugene Davidson, *The Trial of the Germans: An Account of the Twenty-Two Defendants Before the International Military Tribunal at Nuremberg* (New York: Macmillan Company, 1966), 491–4, 500–4.
140. Approximately $500,000 at the time. For information on Flick, see L.M. Stallbaumer, "Frederick Flick's Opportunism and Expediency," *Dimensions: A Journal of Holocaust Studies*, Vol. 13, No. 2.
141. Bernard Fall, *The Keystone of the Arch: A Study of German Illegal Rearmament 1919–1936*, MA Thesis, Maxwell School of Citizenship, Syracuse University, 1952, Series 1.5, Box P-2, BBF, JFKL.
142. Telford Taylor, *The Anatomy of the Nuremberg Trials: A Personal Memoir* (New York: Alfred A. Knopf, 1992), 91.
143. *Ibid.*, 90–1.
144. William Manchester, *The Arms of Krupp, 1587–1968* (Boston, MA: Little, Brown and Company, 1968), 3–5.
145. Telford Taylor, *The Anatomy of the Nuremberg Trials: A Personal Memoir* (New York: Alfred A. Knopf, 1992), 91.
146. Christopher Clark, *The Sleepwalkers: How Europe Went to War in 1914* (New York: Harper Perennial, 2012), 331. According to Clark, in 1913, the German "peacetime army grew by 136,000 to 890,000 officers and men."
147. William Manchester, *The Arms of Krupp, 1587–1968* (Boston, MA: Little, Brown and Company, 1968), 870 ("Big Bertha"), 305–6 (*Pariskanone*), 437–8 ("Big Gustav").
148. Dorothy Fall, *Bernard Fall: Memories of a Soldier-Scholar* (Washington, DC: Potomac Books, 2007), 10.
149. *Der Weltkrieg in Bildern und Dokumenten nebst einem Kriegstagebuch* (Leipzig, Germany: Johannes M. Meulenhoff Verlag, 1914 and 1915).
150. William Manchester, *The Arms of Krupp, 1587–1968* (Boston, MA: Little, Brown and Company, 1968), 35.
151. Eugene Davidson, *The Trial of the Germans: An Account of the Twenty-Two Defendants Before the International Military Tribunal at Nuremberg* (New York: Macmillan Company, 1966), 26.
152. *Ibid.*, 26.
153. Nuremberg Military Tribunal (NMT), XI. Judgment, A. Opinion and Judgment of Military Tribunal III, 1332, 1336, 1445–6; See also, William Manchester, *The

Arms of Krupp, 1587–1968 (Boston, MA: Little, Brown and Company, 1968), 459, 462, 464–5.
154. William Manchester, *The Arms of Krupp, 1587–1968* (Boston, MA: Little, Brown and Company, 1968), 664–5.
155. *Ibid.*, 364.
156. "NMT—Case No. 10, "Krupp Case" closing statement, 24 June 1948. Telford Taylor Papers, Butler Library, Columbia University, Series 5, Subseries 2, Box 39, Folder 2.
157. On the 1933 Reichstag Fire Act and the 1933 Enabling Act, see Benjamin Carter Hett, *The Death of Democracy: Hitler's Rise to Power and the Downfall of the Weimar Republic* (New York: Henry Hold and Company, 2018).
158. William Manchester, *The Arms of Krupp, 1587–1968* (Boston, MA: Little, Brown and Company, 1968), 368, 374–6; also, see Telford Taylor, *The Anatomy of the Nuremberg Trials: A Personal Memoir* (New York: Alfred A. Knopf, 1992), 91.
159. Adam Tooze, *The Wages of Destruction: The Making and Breaking of the Nazi Economy* (New York: Viking, 2006), 100–101.
160. Albert Speer, *Inside the Third Reich* (London: Weidenfeld & Nicholson, 1995), 137–8.
161. Harold James, *Krupp: A History of the Legendary Firm* (Princeton, NJ: Princeton University Press, 2012), 225. While James notes on p. 225 that the Krupp Corporation's use of slave labor was "vile," James' book is a revisionist account because the copyright for the book is held neither by James nor by the book's publisher, Princeton University Press. The copyright is held by the Krupp Foundation, meaning the Alfried Krupp von Bohlen und Halbach Foundation, which funded James's research. This foundation was established in 1967, when the financial holdings of the Krupp family were transferred to the foundation for philanthropic purposes after Alfried's death. Notably, James is forthright, and he acknowledged and thanked the Alfried Krupp von Bohlen und Halbach-Stiftung (foundation) for financial support for research used in producing his book. The Alfried Krupp von Bohlen und Halbach-Stitfung (website: https://www.krupp-stiftung.de/alfried-krupp/ [accessed 20 January 2021]) makes no reference to the Krupp Corporation's wartime exploitation of slave labor, stating only: "Shortly before the end of the Second World War, on April 11, 1945, Alfried Krupp von Bohlen und Halbach was arrested by American troops. Three years later, an American military court sentenced him to twelve years in prison and confiscated all of his property. After he was pardoned in 1951 and the confiscation of Krupp's assets were lifted, he returned to the helm of his company in 1953."
162. Telford Taylor, *The Anatomy of the Nuremberg Trials: A Personal Memoir* (New York: Alfred A. Knopf, 1992), 92–3.
163. *Ibid.*, 92–3.

164. Eugene Davidson, *The Trial of the Germans: An Account of the Twenty-Two Defendants Before the International Military Tribunal at Nuremberg* (New York: Macmillan Company, 1966), 27; Norbert Ehrenfreund, *The Nuremberg Legacy: How the Nazi War Crimes Trials Changed the Course of History* (New York: Palgrave Macmillan, 2007), 22.
165. Telford Taylor, *The Anatomy of the Nuremberg Trials: A Personal Memoir* (New York: Alfred A. Knopf, 1992), 93.
166. William Manchester, *The Arms of Krupp, 1587–1968* (Boston, MA: Little, Brown and Company, 1968), 450.
167. Fall's Nuremberg Sources used to investigate the Krupp Corporation are held at the John F. Kennedy Library, see Bernard Fall, "World War II/Nuremberg Trial Materials," Series 2.03, Boxes W-01, W-02, W-03, W-04, BBF, JFKL.
168. *History of the United Nations War Crimes Commission and the Development of the Laws of War*, compiled by the United Nations War Crimes Commission (London: His Majesty's Stationary Office, 1948). 220, 227–8.
169. *Ibid.*, 227. Also, see The International Committee of the Red Cross, "Practice Related to Rule 95. Forced Labour," ICRC, Customary IHL Database, https://ihl-databases.icrc.org/customary-ihl/eng/docs/v2_rul_rule95 (accessed 22 January 2021).
170. "Practice Related to Rule 95. Forced Labour," ICRC, Customary IHL Database, https://ihl-databases.icrc.org/customary-ihl/eng/docs/v2_rul_rule95 (accessed 22 January 2021).
171. Bernard Fall, "World War II/Nuremberg Trial Materials," Series 2.03, Box W-01, BBF, JFKL.
172. Bernard Fall, "World War II/Nuremberg Trial Materials," Series 2.03, Box W-02, BBF, JFKL; also, see Norbert Ehrenfreund, *The Nuremberg Legacy: How the Nazi War Crimes Trials Changed the Course of History* (New York: Palgrave Macmillan, 2007), 23.
173. *History of the United Nations War Crimes Commission and the Development of the Laws of War*, compiled by the United Nations War Crimes Commission (London: His Majesty's Stationery Office, 1948), 228.

2. GERMANY, 1946–1951

1. Fall's official title was "research analyst on the staff of the office of the chief of counsel for war crimes." His ID# was ETO-AG 424, Bernard Fall, "WWII/Nurnberg Trial Materials," Series, 2.3, Box W-01, BBF, JFKL.
2. Fall's papers at the John F. Kennedy Presidential Library contain dozens of his staff evidence analyses that he kept. See Series 2.03, Box W-01. Fall's additional research files and material related to Nuremberg are in boxes W-02, W-03 and W-04, BBF, JFKL.
3. *Ibid.*

NOTES

4. *Ibid.*
5. *Ibid.*
6. Bernard Fall, Series 2.03, Box W-02, BBF, JFKL.
7. Bernard Fall, Series 2.03, Box W-01, BBF, JFKL.
8. See Terry Gander and Peter Chamberlain, *Weapons of the Third Reich: An Encyclopedic Survey of All Small Arms, Artillery and Special Weapons of the German Land Forces 1939–1945* (New York: Doubleday, 1979).
9. Bernard Fall, Series 2.03, Box W-01, BBF, JFKL.
10. "NMT—Case No. 10, "Krupp Case" closing statement, 24 June 1948. Telford Taylor Papers, Butler Library, Columbia University, Series 5, Subseries 2, Box 39, Folder 2.
11. Bernard Fall, Series 2.03, Box W-02, Folder "Krupp Case," BBF, JFKL.
12. *Ibid.*
13. *Ibid.*
14. John C. Beyer and Stephen A. Schneider, *Forced Labor Under the Third Reich, Part One*, Nathan Associates, Arlington, Virginia, 1 January 1999, Table B-3, p. 22; see also, Eugene Davidson, *The Trial of the Germans: An Account of the Twenty-Two Defendants Before the International Military Tribunal at Nuremberg* (New York: Macmillan Company, 1966), 492.
15. *Women Under Nazi Persecution: A Primary Source Supplement Based on Documents From the International Tracing Service*, Elizabeth Anthony, Akim Jah, Christine Schmidt, Susanne Urban (Eds.), (United States Holocaust Memorial Museum, ITS, The Wiener Library, 2017), 7.
16. Bernard B. Fall, "The Case of Alfried Krupp," *Prevent World War III*, Summer 1951, ISSN/ISBN: 0032-7999, 39–40; Bernard Fall, Series 2.03, Box W-01, BBF, JFKL; Eugene Davidson, *The Trial of the Germans: An Account of the Twenty-Two Defendants Before the International Military Tribunal at Nuremberg* (New York: Macmillan Company, 1966), 516; Nuremberg Military Tribunal (NMT), XI. Judgment, A. Opinion and Judgment of Military Tribunal III, 1408, 1447–1448.
17. William Manchester, *The Arms of Krupp, 1587–1968* (Boston, MA: Little, Brown and Company, 1968), see pp. 562–70 for detailed description of the atrocity at Buschmannshof.
18. *Ibid.*, 568.
19. *Ibid.*, 568–9.
20. *Ibid.*, 568–9; Nuremberg Military Tribunal (NMT), XI. Judgment, A. Opinion and Judgment of Military Tribunal III, 1408.
21. The city of Voerde website describing this memorial is available at: https://www.voerde.de/de/inhalt/buschmannshof/ (accessed 20 January 2021). The city's memorial specifically states that these children were offspring of forced laborers in Krupp's factories.
22. Bernard B. Fall, "Fall Memorandum to Thayer," Series 2.03, Box W-02, BBF, JFKL.

23. *Ibid.*
24. Harold James, *Krupp: A History of the Legendary German Firm* (Princeton, NJ: Princeton University Press, 2012), 224.
25. Document NIK 12356, Nuremberg Military Tribunal (NMT), XI. Judgment, A. Opinion and Judgment of Military Tribunal III, 1385. The full report of proceedings against Krupp and other defendants during the Nuremberg Military Tribunal is available through the Library of Congress at: https://www.loc.gov/rr/frd/Military_Law/pdf/NT_Vol-XXXV.pdf (accessed 23 January 2021).
26. Bernard B. Fall, "The Case of Alfried Krupp," *Prevent World War III*, Summer 1951, ISSN/ISBN: 0032–7999, 40.
27. Document NIK 12356, Nuremberg Military Tribunal (NMT), XI. Judgment, A. Opinion and Judgment of Military Tribunal III, 1385.
28. NMT—Case No. 10, "Krupp Case" closing statement, 24 June 1948. Telford Taylor Papers, Butler Library, Columbia University, Series 5, Subseries 2, Box 39, Folder 2.
29. Claude Chambard, *The Maquis: A History of the French Resistance Movement* (New York: The Bobbs-Merrill Company, Inc., 1976), 47.
30. Bernard Fall, "CV," Series 1.01, Box F-1, BBF, JFKL.
31. NMT—Case No. 10, "Krupp Case" closing statement, 24 June 1948. Telford Taylor Papers, Butler Library, Columbia University, Series 5, Subseries 2, Box 39, Folder 2, 1401. 240 grams of bread is equivalent in weight to seven to eight slices of 2,018 commercially produced bread loaves in the United States but receipt of bread at the camps was inconsistent. For additional sources on this subject, see Eugene Davidson, *The Trial of the Germans: An account of the twenty-two defendants before the International Military Tribunal at Nuremberg* (New York: Macmillan Company, 1966), 509.
32. NMT—Case No. 10, "Krupp Case" closing statement, 24 June 1948. Telford Taylor Papers, Butler Library, Columbia University, Series 5, Subseries 2, Box 39, Folder 2, pp. 14–18.
33. Telford Taylor, *Nuremberg and Vietnam: An American Tragedy* (Chicago, IL: Quadrangle Books, 1970), 83.
34. Eugene Davidson, *The Trial of the Germans: An Account of the Twenty-Two Defendants Before the International Military Tribunal at Nuremberg* (New York: Macmillan Company, 1966), 521.
35. *Ibid.*, 508.
36. Bernard Fall, Series 2.3, W-01, BBF, JFKL.
37. "Defense Testimony and Affidavit, Translation of Von Buelow Document 642, Defense Exhibit 1362," Nuremberg Military Tribunal, Vol. IX, p. 1078. https://phdn.org/archives/www.mazal.org/archive/nmt/09/NMT09-T1078.htm, accessed 24 July 2018.

38. William Manchester, *The Arms of Krupp, 1587–1968* (Boston, MA: Little, Brown and Company, 1968), 498–9.
39. Bernard Fall, "The Guerrilla Craze," Undated, Series 1.5, Box P-1, BBF, JFKL.
40. Bernard Fall, Series 2.3, Box W-01, BBF, JFKL.
41. Uzhhorod is located along the border between Slovakia and Ukraine.
42. Bernard Fall, "Document, No. NIK-13428," Series, 2.3, Box W-01, BBF, JFKL.
43. Nuremberg Military Tribunal (NMT), XI. Judgment, A. Opinion and Judgment of Military Tribunal III, 1428.
44. Bernard B. Fall, "The Case of Alfried Krupp," Prevent World War III, Summer 1951, ISSN/ISBN: 0032-7999.
45. *Ibid.*
46. Nuremberg Military Tribunal (NMT), XI. Judgment, A. Opinion and Judgment of Military Tribunal III., 1428–29; William Manchester, *The Arms of Krupp, 1587–1968* (Boston, MA: Little, Brown and Company, 1968), 548.
47. Nuremberg Military Tribunal (NMT), XI. Judgment, A. Opinion and Judgment of Military Tribunal III, 1426–9.
48. NMT—Case No. 10, "Krupp Case" closing statement, 24 June 1948. Telford Taylor Papers, Butler Library, Columbia University, Series 5, Subseries 2, Box 39, Folder 2, 17–18.
49. *Ibid.*, 18.
50. William Manchester, *The Arms of Krupp, 1587–1968* (Boston, MA: Little, Brown and Company, 1968), 556.
51. *Ibid.*, 555.
52. *Ibid.*, 554–5.
53. Bernard Fall, Series 2.3, Box W-01, BBF, JFKL.
54. Kaltenbrunner succeeded Reinhard Heydrich as Director of the Reich Main Security Office, RSHA. Markus Urban, translated by John Jenkins, *The Nuremberg Trials* (Geschichte Für Alle e.V.—Institut für Regionalgeschichte, 2012), 70; Also, see NMT—Case No. 10, "Krupp Case" closing statement, 24 June 1948. Telford Taylor Papers, Butler Library, Columbia University, Series 5, Subseries 2, Box 39, Folder 2, pp. 1–12. The closing statement rebutted Krupp's attorney's defense point by point. For Krupp's defense, see NMT—Case No. 10, "Krupp Case" opening statement, 22 March 1948 by Otto Kanzbuehler, Attorney for Alfried Krupp," Telford Taylor Papers, Butler Library, Columbia University, Series 5, Subseries 2, Box 39, Folder 1.
55. Nuremberg Military Tribunal (NMT), XI. Judgment, A. Opinion and Judgment of Military Tribunal III, 31 July 1948, p. 1426.
56. *Ibid*, 1426.
57. William Manchester, *The Arms of Krupp, 1587–1968* (Boston, MA: Little, Brown and Company, 1968), 560.
58. *Ibid.*, 585–6.

59. Bernard Fall, Series 2.03, Box W-01, BBF, JFKL.
60. William Manchester, *The Arms of Krupp, 1587–1968* (Boston, MA: Little, Brown and Company, 1968), 585.
61. Bernard Fall, "Document No. NIK 13428," Series 2.03, Box W-01, BBF, JFKL.
62. *Ibid.* See also, NMT—Case No. 10, "Krupp Case" closing statement, 24 June 1948. Telford Taylor Papers, Butler Library, Columbia University, Series 5, Subseries 2, Box 39, Folder 2, pp. 17–18.
63. Dorothy Fall, *Bernard Fall: Memories of a Soldier-Scholar* (Washington, DC: Potomac Books, 2007), 40.
64. NMT—Case No. 10, "Krupp Verdicts." Telford Taylor Papers, Butler Library, Columbia University, Series 5, Subseries 2, Box 45, Folder 1; William Manchester, *The Arms of Krupp, 1587–1968* (Boston, MA: Little, Brown and Company, 1968), 634.
65. *Ibid.*, 656–7.
66. Telford Taylor, *Nuremberg and Vietnam: An American Tragedy* (Chicago, IL: Quadrangle Books, 1970), 88.
67. William Manchester, *The Arms of Krupp, 1587–1968* (Boston, MA: Little, Brown and Company, 1968), 649–50.
68. *Ibid.*, 631, 657–8; Telford Taylor, *The Anatomy of the Nuremberg Trials: A Personal Memoir* (New York: Alfred A. Knopf, 1992), 94.
69. William Manchester, *The Arms of Krupp, 1587–1968* (Boston, MA: Little, Brown and Company, 1968), 647.
70. *History of the United Nations War Crimes Commission and the Development of the Laws of War*, compiled by the United Nations War Crimes Commission (London: His Majesty's Stationery Office, 1948), 8.
71. *Ibid.*, 8.
72. A central debate over international jurisdiction concerns the subject of sovereignty for citizens of member states as signatories to international law-related mandates. *Erga Omnes* is linked to international jurisdiction and suggests that norms such as war crimes, torture, genocide, and others apply to the international community, while *jus cogens* are international law commitments required by states. See Lyal S. Sunga, "Individual Responsibility," in *International Law for Serious Human Rights Violations* (Leiden, Netherlands: Martinus Nijhof Publishers, 1992), 252.
73. Michael Geyer, "German Strategy in the Age of Machine Warfare, 1914–1945," in Peter Paret (Ed.), *Makers of Modern Strategy: From Machiavelli to the Nuclear Age* (Princeton, NJ: Princeton University Press, 1986), 566.
74. John P. Kenny, *Moral Aspects of Nuremberg* (Washington, DC: Pontifical Faculty of Theology Dominican House of Studies, 1949), 80.
75. Enzo Traverso has argued that the dialectic between fascism/communism and enlightenment/romantic reaction as it applies to conflict in Europe in the twentieth century is a result of dialectical tension between Thomas Hobbes' Leviathan

and Behemoth. See pp. 196–203 in Enzo Traverso, *Fire and Blood: The European Civil War 1914–1945*, edited by David Ferbach (New York: Verso, 2016).

76. The Tokyo Tribunals significantly complicated the Allies' legal and moral position vis-à-vis the use of fire-bombing against civilians in Tokyo and the deployment of atomic weapons against civilians in Hiroshima and Nagasaki; see Norbert Ehrenfreund, *The Nuremberg Legacy: How the Nazi War Crimes Trials Changed the Course of History* (New York: Palgrave Macmillan, 2007), 113–21.

77. Michael Geyer, "German Strategy in the Age of Machine Warfare, 1914–1945," in *Makers of Modern Strategy: From Machiavelli to the Nuclear Age*, Peter Paret (Ed.) (Princeton, NJ: Princeton University Press, 1986), 573–4.

78. Mark Mazower, *Hitler's Empire: How the Nazis Ruled Europe* (New York: Penguin Press, 2008), 587.

79. Eugene Davidson, *The Trial of the Germans: An Account of the Twenty-Two Defendants Before the International Military Tribunal at Nuremberg* (New York: MacMillan, 1966), 583. Davidson writes, "Pogroms, racial murders, lynchings have usually been spontaneous local reactions toward people believed to be inferior. In the Third Reich they were the result of a well-considered, duly codified and paragraphed, public policy."

80. An important example of such an institutionally backed agreement is the Convention on the Prevention and Punishment of the Crime of Genocide adopted by the United Nations General Assembly on 9 December 1948 as advocated by Rafael Lemkin. See Office of the High Commissioner, United Nations Human Rights. https://www.ohchr.org/en/professionalinterest/pages/crimeofgenocide.aspx (accessed on 19 September 2018).

81. See Lawrence Freedman, *The Future of War: A History* (New York: Public Affairs, 2017), 135–7, 201. Notably, these documents, the UN Declaration, and others did not fully account for the Holocaust to the degree that Jewish lobbyists in 1948 believed they should. See Nathan A. Kurz (2020), "'Hide a Fact Rather Than State it': The Holocaust, the 1940s Human Rights Surge, and the Cosmopolitan Imperative of International Law," *Journal of Genocide Research*, DOI: 10.1080/14623528:2020.1807833.

82. William Shakespeare, *Richard III*, Act 1, Scene 2.

83. Bernard Fall, "CV," Series 1.01, Box F-1, BBF, JFKL.

84. *Ibid.*

85. *Ibid.*

86. Bernard Fall, Series 2.03, Box W-02, BBF, JFKL.

87. Bernard Fall, Series, 2.03, Box W-01, BBF, JFKL. The International Commission took over responsibility for the International Tracing Service in 1955 with financial support from the Federal Republic of Germany. It maintains an archive and serves as a center for documenting Nationalist Socialist persecution. For more on ITS, see https://www.its-arolsen.org/en/about-its/

88. Bernard Fall, "CV," Series 1.01, Box F-1, BBF, JFKL.
89. Bernard Fall, Series 1.10, Box AM-01, BBF, JFKL. Fall's papers include original pamphlets on the Overseas European Program.
90. Bernard Fall, Series 2.03, Box W-01, BBF, JFKL.
91. Bernard Fall, "CV," Series 1.01, Box F-1, BBF, JFKL. In interviews he potentially might have had, he could also point to his attention to detail during his military service. While transitioning between the Maquis and FFI, for example, Fall transcribed French BBC transcripts for the radio section of an element from the Régiment de Marche de la Légion Etrangère (RMLE,) which had been created out of the 4th Demi-Brigade of the Foreign Legion (1ere 4me Demi Brigade).
92. Bernard Fall, Series 2.03, Box W-01, BBF, JFKL.
93. On the origins of Fulbright Program funding, see "an amendment to the Surplus Property Act of 1944" in "Senate Floor—The Fulbright Program: A History," JWF Papers, Series 71, Box 32, Folder 3.
94. Fulbright Student Program, United States Department of State, Bureau of Educational and Cultural Affairs. https://us.fulbrightonline.org/about/history (accessed 1 May 2018).
95. J. William Fulbright, *The Arrogance of Power* (New York: Vintage Books, 1966), 207.
96. *Ibid.*, 207.
97. Dorothy Fall, *Bernard Fall: Memories of a Soldier-Scholar* (Washington, DC: Potomac Books, 2007), 43.
98. Bernard Fall, Series 1.05, Box P-02, BBF, JFKL.
99. William Manchester, *The Arms of Krupp, 1587–1968* (Boston, MA: Little, Brown and Company, 1968), 668.
100. Bernard B. Fall, "The Case of Alfried Krupp," *Prevent World War III*, Summer 1951, ISSN/ISBN: 0032–7999, 39–40.
101. *Ibid.*, 39.
102. *Ibid.*, 39.
103. *Ibid.*
104. Walter Isaacson and Evan Thomas, *The Wise Men: Six Friends and the World They Made* (New York: Touchstone Books, 1986), 515–17; see also, Norbert Ehrenfreund, *The Nuremberg Legacy: How the Nazi War Crimes Trials Changed the Course of History* (New York: Palgrave Macmillan, 2007), 25.
105. Bernard B. Fall, "The Case of Alfried Krupp," *Prevent World War III*, Summer 1951, ISSN/ISBN: 0032–7999, 39–40.
106. Steven Casey, "The Campaign to Sell a Harsh Peace for Germany to the American Public, 1944–1948," London: LSE Research Online, 24. http://eprints.lse.ac.uk/736/ (accessed, 10 May 2018).
107. Benn Steil, *The Marshall Plan: Dawn of the Cold War* (New York: Oxford University Press, 2018), 105.

108. *Ibid.*, 106.
109. Charles Van Devander, "Taylor Report on Nazi Crimes Buried by Army Without Honor," *New York Post*, 22 November 1949, Telford Taylor Papers, Butler Library, Columbia University, Series 5, Subseries 2, Box 46, Folder 17.
110. Thomas L. Stokes, "War Aim Diluted: Despite Plan to Raze Reich Arms Plants Nazi Masters Back in Control of Cartels," *Washington Evening Star*, 18 November 1949. Telford Taylor Papers, Butler Library, Columbia University, Series 5, Subseries 2, Box 46, Folder 17.
111. 18 percent of the Polish population and 10 percent of Yugoslavia's population were either killed or wounded. See Enzo Traverso, *Fire and Blood: The European Civil War, 1914–1945*, translated by David Ferbach (New York: Verso Books, 2016), 127.
112. Walter Isaacson and Evan Thomas, *The Wise Men: Six Friends and the World They Made* (New York: Touchstone Books, 1986), 515.
113. *Ibid.*, 516–17.
114. Ingo Trauschweizer, *Maxwell Taylor's Cold War: From Berlin to Vietnam* (Lexington, KY: University of Kentucky Press, 2019), 40.
115. *Ibid.*, 40.
116. An important case that undermined the legitimacy of Tribunal trial (#1) against Nazi medical doctors concerned US postwar action in the Pacific theater. During the war, Japanese scientists conducted biological warfare experiments on human beings, and after the war US officials granted these scientists immunity against prosecution for war crimes in exchange for the results of their experiments. See Sheldon H. Harris, *Factories of Death: Japanese Biological Warfare, 1932–1945 and the American Cover-Up* (New York: Routledge, 1994).
117. William Manchester, *The Arms of Krupp, 1587–1968* (Boston, MA: Little, Brown and Company, 1968), 660.
118. Telford Taylor, *The Anatomy of the Nuremberg Trials: A Personal Memoir* (New York: Alfred A. Knopf, 1992), 238–9.
119. "Taylor letter to Judge Samuel Rosen, May 18, 1949." Telford Taylor Papers, Butler Library, Columbia University, Series 5, Subseries 2, Box 46, Folder 13.
120. Walter Isaacson and Evan Thomas, *The Wise Men: Six Friends and the World They Made* (New York: Touchstone Books, 1986), 515.
121. William Manchester, *The Arms of Krupp, 1587–1968* (Boston, MA: Little, Brown and Company, 1968), 671.
122. *Ibid.*, 517.
123. Adam Tooze, *The Wages of Destruction: The Making and Breaking of the Nazi Economy* (New York: Viking, 2006), 672.
124. World War II did not technically end until July 1951. According to Mary Dudziak, "[President Harry S.] Truman didn't call for an end to this state of war until July 1951, but also stressed that this would not affect the occupation of

Germany." See Mary L. Dudziak, *War-Time: An Idea, Its History, and Its Consequences* (New York: Oxford University Press, 2012), 38.
125. "Office of the U.S. High Commission for Germany Statement, January 31, 1951." Telford Taylor Papers, Butler Library, Columbia University, Series 5, Subseries 2, Box 46, Folder 11, p. 11.
126. *Ibid.*, 12.
127. *Ibid.*, 12–13.
128. Nuremberg Military Tribunal (NMT), XI. Judgment, A. Opinion and Judgment of Military Tribunal III, 1385.
129. *Ibid.*, 1385, Document NIK 12356.
130. "Office of the U.S. High Commission for Germany Statement, January 31, 1951." Telford Taylor Papers, Butler Library, Columbia University, Series 5, Subseries 2, Box 46, Folder 11, p. 13.
131. *Ibid.*, 14.
132. *Ibid.*, 14.
133. Walter Isaacson and Evan Thomas, *The Wise Men: Six Friends and the World They Made* (New York: Touchstone Books, 1986), 517.
134. NMT—Case No. 10, "Krupp Case" closing statement, 24 June 1948. Telford Taylor Papers, Butler Library, Columbia University, Series 5, Subseries 2, Box 39, Folder 2.
135. Bernard B. Fall, "The Case of Alfried Krupp," *Prevent World War III*, Summer 1951, ISSN/ISBN: 0032–7999, 39.
136. For a detailed account of the complex political history of the European Defense Community, NATO, and US-French relations pertaining to German rearmament and origins of US support for French operations in Indochina, see Frank Costigliola, *France and the United States: The Cold War Alliance Since World War II* (New York: Twayne Publishers, 1992), 90–117.
137. Bernard B. Fall, "The Case of Alfried Krupp," *Prevent World War III*, Summer 1951, ISSN/ISBN: 0032–7999, 40.
138. Frank Costigliola, *France and the United States: The Cold War Alliance Since World War II* (New York: Twayne Publishers, 1992), 91.
139. *Ibid.*, 91.
140. Bernard B. Fall, "The Case of Alfried Krupp," *Prevent World War III*, Summer 1951, ISSN/ISBN: 0032–7999, 40.
141. NMT—Case No. 10, "Krupp Case" closing statement, 24 June 1948. Telford Taylor Papers, Butler Library, Columbia University, Series 5, Subseries 2, Box 39, Folder 2.
142. Bernard B. Fall, "The Case of Alfried Krupp," *Prevent World War III*, Summer 1951, ISSN/ISBN: 0032–7999, 40.
143. William Manchester, *The Arms of Krupp, 1587–1968* (Boston, MA: Little, Brown and Company, 1968), 680–1.

144. *Ibid.*, 682.
145. Steven Casey, "The Campaign to Sell a Harsh Peace for Germany to the American Public, 1944–1948," 32. London: LSE Research Online, http://eprints.lse.ac.uk/736/ (accessed 10 May 2018).
146. *Ibid.*, 40
147. J. William Fulbright, "'What About Russia?', NBC address, Friday, November 23, 1945," J. William Fulbright Papers, University of Arkansas Special Collections, Fayetteville, Arkansas, Series 72, Box 4, Folder 1, 6.
148. Samuel Moyn, "From Aggression to Atrocity: Rethinking the History of International Criminal Law," (7 July 2016), *Oxford Handbook of International Criminal Law* (Forthcoming), 26.
149. The idea of a "passing moment," during which the prosecution of law during war differed from "times of peace," is inspired by Samuel Moyn and also by Mary Dudziak's concept of "war-time." See "The Idea of War-time" in Mary L. Dudziak, *War-Time: An Idea, Its History, and Its Consequences* (New York: Oxford University Press, 2012), 21–6.
150. J. William Fulbright, "'What About Russia?', NBC address, Friday, November 23, 1945," J. William Fulbright Papers, University of Arkansas Special Collections, Fayetteville, Arkansas, Series 72, Box 4, Folder 1, 6.
151. Mary L. Dudziak, *War-Time: An Idea, Its History, and Its Consequences* (New York: Oxford University Press, 2012), 26.
152. In addition to Indochina, examples of these countries range from Guatemala (1954), Iran (1955), the Congo (1960–1), Chile (1973), and Iraq (2003).
153. Robert H. Jackson, "Opening Statement Before the International Military Tribunal," "Second Day, Wednesday, 11/21/1945, Part 04", in *Trial of the Major War Criminals before the International Military Tribunal*. Volume II. Proceedings: 14/11/1945–30/11/1945. Nuremberg: IMT, 1947, 98–102. Jackson cited William Shakespeare, *Richard III*, Act 1, Scene 2. Jackson's references are a slight adaptation taken from lines 88–9 in *The Oxford Shakespeare*, Stanley Wells and Gary Taylor (Eds.), 1988.
154. Bernard Fall, "The Keystone of the Arch: A Study of German Illegal Rearmament, 1919–1936," MA Thesis, Maxwell School of Citizenship, Syracuse University, 1952, Series 1.5, Box P-2, BBF, JFKL.
155. Bernard Fall, "The Anglo-Egyptian Controversy," Summer Session 1952, "Papers and Reports by Dr. Fall," Series 1.05, Box P-01, BBF, JFKL.
156. Bernard Fall, "The Keystone of the Arch: A Study of German Illegal Rearmament 1919–1936, Vol. 1–2," MA Thesis, Syracuse University, 1952, "Papers and Reports by Dr. Fall," Series 1.05, Box P-02, 1, BBF, JFKL.
157. A large number of scholars have studied the Treaty of Versailles, its construction, and its failures. As a recent example, see Michael S. Neiberg, *The Treaty of Versailles: A Concise History* (New York: Oxford University Press, 2017).

158. Bernard Fall, "The Keystone of the Arch: A Study of German Illegal Rearmament 1919–1936, Vol. 1–2," MA Thesis, Syracuse University, 1952, "Papers and Reports by Dr. Fall," Series 1.05, Box P-02, 1, BBF, JFKL.
159. *Ibid.*, 2.
160. *Ibid.*, 2.
161. For more on the interactions between the SA and SS, see Timothy Snyder, *Black Earth: The Holocaust as History and Warning* (New York: Tim Duggan Books, 2015), 40.
162. Bernard Fall, "The Keystone of the Arch: A Study of German Illegal Rearmament 1919–1936, Vol. 1–2,", p. 111. MA Thesis, Syracuse University, 1952, "Papers and Reports by Dr. Fall," Series 1.05, Box P-02, 1, BBF, JFKL.
163. *Ibid.*, 111.
164. Bernard Fall, "The Guerrilla Craze," Undated, Series 1.5, Box P-1, BBF, JFKL.
165. Bernard Fall, "The Keystone of the Arch: A Study of German Illegal Rearmament 1919–1936, Vol. 1–2,"134. MA Thesis, Syracuse University, 1952, "Papers and Reports by Dr. Fall," Series 1.05, Box P-02, 1, BBF, JFKL.
166. *Ibid.*, 131.
167. The arson of the Reichstag was contested because German factions blamed each other for the event. Benjamin Carter Hett argues that, due to his role as President of the Reichstag, Göring's home was connected to the Reichstag by a tunnel through which *Sturmabteilung* arsonists maneuvered to burn the Reichstag. See Benjamin Carter Hett, *The Death of Democracy: Hitler's Rise to Power and the Downfall of the Weimar Republic* (New York: Henry Holt and Company, 2018).
168. Bernard Fall, "The Keystone of the Arch: A Study of German Illegal Rearmament 1919–1936, Vol. 1–2." MA Thesis, Syracuse University, 1952, "Papers and Reports by Dr. Fall," Series 1.05, Box P-02, BBF, JFKL. Also, see William Manchester, *The Arms of Krupp, 1587–1968* (Boston, MA: Little, Brown and Company, 1968), 363.
169. William Manchester, *The Arms of Krupp, 1587–1968* (Boston, MA: Little, Brown and Company, 1968), 363.
170. Nuremberg Military Tribunal (NMT), XI. Judgment, A. Opinion and Judgment of Military Tribunal III, 1327–1484. On the decree and act, see also Benjamin Carter Hett, *The Death of Democracy: Hitler's Rise to Power and the Downfall of the Weimar Republic* (New York: Henry Holt and Company, 2018), 83–4, 187.
171. *Ibid.*, 83–4, 187.
172. Mark Mazower, *Hitler's Empire: How the Nazis Ruled Europe* (New York: Penguin Press, 2008), 43.
173. Michael Geyer, "German Strategy in the Age of Machine Warfare, 1914–1945," in Peter Paret (Ed.), *Makers of Modern Strategy: From Machiavelli to the Nuclear Age* (Princeton, NJ: Princeton University Press, 1986), 596–7.
174. Bernard B. Fall, *Last Reflections on a War* (New York: Doubleday & Company, 1967), 20.

175. Bernard Fall, "The Keystone of the Arch: A Study of German Illegal Rearmament 1919–1936, Vol. 1–2," MA Thesis, Syracuse University, 1952, "Papers and Reports by Dr. Fall," Series 1.05, Box P-02), 253, BBF, JFKL.
176. *Ibid.*, 253.
177. Hal Brands and Charles Edel, "How Woodrow Wilson Lost the Peace," *The American Interest*, 30 January 2019. https://www.the-american-interest.com/2019/01/30/how-woodrow-wilson-lost-the-peace/
178. *Ibid.*, 254.
179. In John Keegan's view, the Holocaust and other criminal atrocities would have not been possible without World War II. See "The Fate of the Jews," in John Keegan, *The Second World War* (New York: Viking Press, 1989), 288–9.

3. FIRST REFLECTIONS ON A WAR

1. Bernard Fall, "CV," Series 1.01, Box F-1, BBF, JFKL.
2. Bernard B. Fall, *Last Reflections on a War* (New York: Doubleday & Company, 1967), 22–3.
3. David K. Wyatt, *Thailand: A Short History* (New Haven, CT: Yale University Press, 1984), 202–5.
4. John T. McAlister, Jr. and Paul Mus, *The Vietnamese and Their Revolution* (New York: Harper Torchbooks, 1970), 161.
5. Jonathan Fenby, *Chiang Kai Shek: China's Generalissimo and the Nation He Lost* (New York: Carroll & Graf Publishers, 2004), 495.
6. Bernard B. Fall, *Last Reflections on a War* (New York: Doubleday & Company, 1967), 214.
7. Philippe Devillers, *France-Asia*, No. 188 (Winter 1966–7), 149. "Le problème du Vietnam apparaissait à Fall, déjà, comme le plus important et le plus lourd de dangers de l'époque."
8. "Obituary for Dr. Amry Vandenbosch," *The Advocate-Messenger*, Danville, Kentucky, Tuesday, 23 October 1990.
9. Bernard Fall, "Academic Materials," Series 1.10, Box AM-1, 56, BBF, JFKL; see also Dorothy Fall, *Bernard Fall: Memories of a Soldier-Scholar* (Washington, DC: Potomac Books, 2007), 56.
10. "Amry Vandenbosch Obituary," *Political Science and Politics*, Vol. 24, Issue 2 (June 1991), 256. https://www.cambridge.org/core/journals/ps-political-science-and-politics/article/amry-vandenbosch/71D0496E5FA4E77A2C3176DE1485095A (accessed 20 September 2018).
11. *Ibid.*
12. "Obituary for Dr. Amry Vandenbosch," *The Advocate-Messenger*, Danville, Kentucky, Tuesday, 23 October 1990.
13. Gabriel A. Almond, "Harold Dwight Lasswell, A Biographical Memoir," National Academy of Sciences, 1987, http://www.nasonline.org/publications/biographi-

cal-memoirs/memoir-pdfs/lasswell-harold.pdf (accessed 21 November 2018). This influential study was Harold D. Lasswell, "The Garrison State," *American Journal of Sociology*, Vol. 46, No. 4 (January 1941). JSTOR, www.jstor.org/stable/2769918 (accessed 31 July 2017).

14. Gabriel A. Almond, "Harold Dwight Lasswell, A Biographical Memoir," National Academy of Sciences, 1987, http://www.nasonline.org/publications/biographical-memoirs/memoir-pdfs/lasswell-harold.pdf (accessed 21 November 2018), 252.
15. Harold D. Lasswell, "The Garrison State," *American Journal of Sociology*, Vol. 46, No. 4, (January 1941), 455, 459. JSTOR, www.jstor.org/stable/2769918, (accessed 31 July 2017); also, see "Garrison State," 130–68, in Bernard B. Fall, *The Two Vietnams: A Political and Military Analysis* (New York: Praeger, 1963).
16. Gabriel A. Almond, "Harold Dwight Lasswell, A Biographical Memoir," National Academy of Sciences, 1987, http://www.nasonline.org/publications/biographical-memoirs/memoir-pdfs/lasswell-harold.pdf (accessed 21 November 2018).
17. Harold D. Lasswell, "The Garrison State," *American Journal of Sociology*, Vol. 46, No. 4 (January 1941).
18. *Ibid.*, 455.
19. "Obituary for Dr. Amry Vandenbosch," *The Advocate-Messenger*, Danville, Kentucky, Tuesday, 23 October 1990.
20. Not to be confused with the International Criminal Court, which was established in 1998, the International Court of Justice was created in 1945. For the history of the International Court of Justice, see https://www.icj-cij.org/en/history (accessed 25 October 2018).
21. Formally, the Charter was referred to as "Agreement for the prosecution and punishment of the major war criminals of the European Axis. Signed at London, on 8 August 1945." Charter of the International Military Tribunal, Article 1, p. 284. http://www.un.org/en/genocideprevention/documents/atrocity-crimes/Doc.2_Charter%20of%20IMT%201945.pdf, accessed on 25 October 2018.
22. Mark Philip Bradley, *Imagining Vietnam and America: The Making of Postcolonial Vietnam, 1919–1950* (Chapel Hill, NC: University of North Carolina Press, 2000), 84. See Chapter 3 in Bradley's study, "Trusteeship and the American Vision of Postcolonial Vietnam," and Dixee R. Bartholomew-Feis, *The O.S.S. and Ho Chi Minh: Unexpected Allies in the War Against Japan* (Lawrence, KS: University of Kansas Press, 2006), 41–8.
23. On Point Five of the Fourteen Points, see especially Erez Manela, *The Wilsonian Moment: Self-Determination and the International Origins of Anticolonial Nationalism* (New York: Oxford University Press, 2007), 40–1. Point Five reads: "A free, open-minded and absolutely impartial adjustment of all colonial claims based upon a strict observance of the principle that in determining all such questions of sovereignty the interests of the populations concerned must have equal

weight with the equitable claims of the government whose title is to be determined."

24. Point Three of the Atlantic Charter affirmed "the right of all peoples to choose the form of government under which they will live." See William E. Leuchtenburg, *The American President: From Teddy Roosevelt to Bill Clinton* (New York: Oxford University Press, 2015), 201; Office of the Historian, Department of State, "The Atlantic Conference and Charter, 1941," https://history.state.gov/milestones/1937–1945/atlantic-conf (accessed 22 November 2018).

25. "Memorandum, November 22, 1944, FDR to Stettinius, Jr.," Indochina Folder, 1–44, p. 27/57, Indochina File, Box 39, President's Secretary File (PSF), 1933–1945, Franklin D. Roosevelt Library, Hyde Park, New York.

26. Michitake Aso, *Rubber and the Making of Vietnam: An Ecological History, 1897–1975* (Chapel Hill, NC: University of North Carolina Press, 2018), 6–7.

27. For a detailed analysis of how the development of rubber altered the political-environmental landscape of Indochina, see Michitake Aso, "The Scientist, the Governor, and the Planter: The Political Economy of Agricultural Knowledge in Indochina During the Creation of a 'Science of Rubber,' 1900–1940," *East Asian Science, Technology and Society: An International Journal*, DOI 10.1007/s12280-009-9092-7.

28. For these developments in the Mekong Delta, see David Biggs, *Quagmire: Nation-Building and Nature in the Mekong Delta* (Seattle, WA: University of Washington Press, 2010).

29. On the importance of Michelin as an importer of Fordism and Taylorism to France and exporter of tires to the US automotive industry, see Stephen L. Harp, *Marketing Michelin: Advertising and Cultural Identity in Twentieth-Century France* (Baltimore, MD: Johns Hopkins University Press, 2001). On the plantation economy of rubber, see Christopher E. Goscha, *Vietnam: A New History* (New York: Basic Books, 2016), 156–8; Donald Lancaster, *The Emancipation of French Indochina* (New York: Oxford University Press, 1961), 63–4. On the matter of "war tires" made out of reclaimed rubber, the subsequent development of synthetic rubber stemmed from necessity as access to rubber diminished 90 percent during World War II. In competition with Michelin, Goodyear and Firestone both promoted themselves as "pioneers of reclaimed rubber tires." See https://www.moderntiredealer.com/article/311239/unsung-heroes-in-ww-ii-tire-dealers-manufacturers-kept-war-effort-rolling (accessed 1 December 2018).

30. See Tran Tu Binh, *The Red Earth: A Vietnamese Memoir of Life on a Colonial Rubber Plantation*, translated by John Spragens, Jr. and edited by David G. Marr, (Athens, OH: Ohio University Center for International Studies, 1985). Notably, Tran Tu Binh later became a top leader in the North Vietnamese army, and his memory of French brutality, as one of his many motivations for lending his support to Vietnamese independence, is a key component of his memoir.

31. Dixee R. Bartholomew-Feis, *The O.S.S. and Ho Chi Minh: Unexpected Allies in the War Against Japan* (Lawrence, KS: University of Kansas Press, 2006), 41–8.
32. Mark Mazower, *Hitler's Empire: How the Nazis Ruled Europe* (New York: Penguin Press, 2008), 592.
33. Octavian Manea, "Reflections on the French School of Counter-Rebellion: An Interview With Étienne de Durand," *Small Wars Journal*, 3 March 2011, 2.
34. *Ibid.*, 2.
35. Quoted in Cordell Hull, *The Memoirs of Cordell Hull*, Vol. 2 (New York: MacMillan, 1948), 1597.
36. Bernard B. Fall, *Last Reflections on a War* (New York: Doubleday & Company, 1967), 23.
37. Bernard Fall, "Academic Materials," Series 1.10 Academic Material, Box AM-1, BBF, JFKL.
38. Dorothy Fall, *Bernard Fall: Memories of a Soldier-Scholar* (Washington, DC: Potomac Books, 2007), 57.
39. Bernard Fall, "Academic Materials," Series 1.10 Academic Material, Box AM-1, BBF, JFKL.
40. *Ibid.*
41. *Ibid.*
42. "Southeast Asia Treaty Organization (SEATO), 1954." Office of the Historian, https://history.state.gov/milestones/1953–1960/seato (accessed 1 December 2018).
43. Bernard B. Fall, *Last Reflections on a War* (New York: Doubleday & Company, 1967), 23.
44. *Ibid.*, 23.
45. *Ibid.*, 23.
46. Ben L. Martin, "The New 'Old China Hands': Shaping a Specialty," *Asian Affairs*, Vol. 3, No. 2, November–December 1975, 123–4.
47. *Ibid.*, 116. For scholarship on US–China relations prior to World War II, see Barbara W. Tuchman, *Stilwell and the American Experience in China, 1911–1945* (New York: Grove Press, 1985). For Tuchman's analysis on this period of US–Chinese interactions, see especially 83–9. Regarding the "Washington Conference," this conference was an "Anglo-American effort to stabilize a safe balance of naval power in the Pacific without the expenditure of a naval race." Chinese delegates sought changes in trade and tariff autonomy and treaty revisions of what were known as the Treaty Ports between China and Great Britain going back to the Opium Wars from 1839–42 and 1856–60. For history of the Treaty Ports, see Tuchman, 28–9.
48. Bernard B. Fall, *Last Reflections on a War* (New York: Doubleday & Company, 1967), 22–3.
49. *Ibid.* See "Celebrity's Choice: November 21, 1966," 15–29.

50. Dorothy Fall, *Bernard Fall: Memories of a Soldier-Scholar* (Washington, DC: Potomac Books, 2007), 58.
51. *Ibid.*, 76.
52. *Ibid.*, 61; For Fall's detailed description of French fortifications in Indochina, see Bernard B. Fall, *Street Without Joy: The French Debacle in Indochina* (Guilford, CT: Stackpole Books, 1961), 175–9.
53. *Ibid.*, 175; See also, Henry Ainley, *In Order to Die* (London: Burke Publishing Company, 1955), 27.
54. Jacques Frémeaux and Bruno C. Reis, "French Counterinsurgency in the Era of the Algerian Wars, 1830–1962," in Beatrice Heuser and Eitan Shamir (Eds.), *Insurgencies and Counterinsurgencies: National Styles and Strategic Cultures* (Cambridge, UK: Cambridge University Press, 2016), 59. "Vietnamization" would be introduced again in the Second Indochina War during President Richard Nixon's administration.
55. Bernard B. Fall, *Street Without Joy: The French Debacle in Indochina* (Guilford, CT: Stackpole Books, 1961), 176.
56. Bernard B. Fall, "Indochina—The Seven Year Dilemma," *Military Review*, Vol. 32, No. 7 (30 October 1953), "Articles by Fall," Series 1.06, Box A-1, BBF, JFKL.
57. Bernard B. Fall, *Street Without Joy: The French Debacle in Indochina* (Guilford, CT: Stackpole Books, 1961), 176.
58. Quoted in Dorothy Fall, *Bernard Fall: Memories of a Soldier-Scholar* (Washington, DC: Potomac Books, 2007), 64.
59. François Sully, *Age of the Guerrilla* (New York: Avon Books, 1968), 132.
60. *Ibid.*, 136.
61. See Bernard B. Fall, *Hell in a Very Small Place: The Siege of Dien Bien Phu* (New York: Da Capo Press, 1966).
62. Quoted in Dorothy Fall, *Bernard Fall: Memories of a Soldier-Scholar* (Washington, DC: Potomac Books, 2007), 56.
63. Bernard B. Fall, "Indochina—The Seven Year Dilemma," *Military Review*, Vol. 32, No. 7 (October 1953), 35, "Articles by Fall," Series 1.06, Box A-1, BBF, JFKL.
64. On African soldiers, see especially Ruth Ginio, *The French Army and Its African Soldiers: The Years of Decolonization* (Lincoln, NE: University of Nebraska Press, 2017), 77–104.
65. Bernard B. Fall, "Indochina—The Seven Year Dilemma," *Military Review*, Vol. 32, No. 7 (October 1953), 35, "Articles by Fall," Series 1.06, Box A-1, BBF, JFKL.
66. Bernard B. Fall, *The Viet-Minh Regime: Government and Administration in the Democratic Republic of Vietnam*, 2nd edition (New York: Institute of Pacific Relations, 1956), reprinted by Greenwood Press, Westport, CT, 1975. This work was first published in 1954 as a joint publication with the Institute of Pacific Relations and the Southeast Asia Program, Department of Far Eastern Studies, Cornell University.
67. For more on Pham Cong Tac, see Tran My-Van, "Vietnam's Caodaism,

Independence, and Peace: The Life and Work of Pham Cong Tac (1890–1959)," Program for Southeast Asian Area Studies, Research Paper No. 38, September 2000. On the Cao Dai Army, see p. 21.
68. Bernard B. Fall, *The Viet-Minh Regime: Government and Administration in the Democratic Republic of Vietnam* (New York: Institute of Pacific Relations, 1956), reprinted by Greenwood Press, Westport, CT, 1975, v.
69. Quoted in Dorothy Fall, *Bernard Fall: Memories of a Soldier-Scholar* (Washington, DC: Potomac Books, 2007), 76–77.
70. For context regarding Nguyen Van Tam's operations in My Tho, see David W.P. Elliott, *The Vietnamese War: Revolution and Social Change in the Mekong Delta 1930–1975* (Armonk, NY: M.E. Sharpe, 2003). On Tam, see Elliott, 31, 147, 151, and 275.
71. Associated Press, "Nguyen Van Tam, Vietnamese Stateman, 97," *New York Times*, 11 November 1990. https://www.nytimes.com/1990/11/28/obituaries/nguyen-van-tam-vietnamese-statesman-97.html (accessed 9 October 2018).
72. "La Guerre D'Indochine," Université du Québec à Montréal, "Nguyen Van Tam (1895–1990)." http://indochine.uqam.ca/fr/component/content/article/1/1061-nguyen-vn-tam-18951990.html (accessed 9 October 2018).
73. *Ibid.*
74. *Ibid.*
75. *Ibid.*
76. Roger Lévy, "Bernard Fall devant le Congrès Américain," *Politique étrangère*, Vol. 32, No. 3 (1967), 263.
77. Bernard B. Fall, "Indochina: The Seven-Year Dilemma," *Military Review*, Vol. 32, No. 7 (October 1953), "Articles by Fall," Series 1.06, Box A-1, BBF, JFKL.
78. Bernard B. Fall, *The Viet-Minh Regime: Government and Administration in the Democratic Republic of Vietnam*, First Edition (New York: Institute of Pacific Relations, 1954), reprinted by Greenwood Press, Westport, CT, 1975, viii.
79. *Ibid.*, viii.
80. *Ibid.*, viii.
81. David G. Marr, *Vietnam: State, War, and Revolution (1945–1946)* (Berkeley, CA: University of California Press, 2013).
82. See Lauriston Sharp "Forward to the First Edition," in Bernard B. Fall, *The Viet-Minh Regime: Government and Administration in the Democratic Republic of Vietnam*, First Edition (New York: Institute of Pacific Relations, 1954), reprinted by Greenwood Press, Westport, CT, 1975, viii.
83. Joseph Buttinger, *Vietnam: A Dragon Embattled, Volume II, Vietnam at War* (New York: Frederick A. Praeger, Publishers, 1967), 1266.
84. "Fall Ph.D. Dissertation Abstract," Series 1.05, Box P-2, BBF, JFKL.
85. See Lauriston Sharp "Forward to The First Edition" in Bernard B. Fall, *The Viet-Minh Regime: Government and Administration in the Democratic Republic of*

Vietnam (New York: Institute of Pacific Relations, 1956), reprinted by Greenwood Press, Westport, CT, 1975, viii.
86. Ibid., vii.
87. See Ellen J. Hammer, *The Struggle for Indochina* (Palo Alto, CA: Stanford University Press, 1954). In a critical review of Hammer's work in September 1954, Fall commented, "This reviewer seriously missed a more comprehensive documentation of the Indo-China problem as seen from a larger point of view than mere Franco-Viet relations," "Book Reviews by Fall," *Asian Student*, 21 September 1954, Series 1.08, Box BR-1, BBF, JFKL.
88. Bernard B. Fall, *Last Reflections on a War* (New York: Doubleday & Company, 1967), 23.
89. J. Lawton Collins Papers, 1896–1975, "Summary of Events in Indochina Since 1940," 2. Subseries A, Briefing Book, Box 24, Dwight D. Eisenhower Presidential Library, Abilene, Kansas.
90. Bernard B. Fall, "Indochina: The Seven-Year Dilemma," *Military Review*, Vol. 32, No. 7 (October 1953), 26–7, "Articles by Fall," Series 1.06, Box A-1, BBF, JFKL.
91. Fredrik Logevall, *Embers of War: The Fall of an Empire and the Making of America's Vietnam* (New York: Random House, 2014), 133.
92. Bernard B. Fall, "Indochina: The Seven-Year Dilemma," *Military Review*, Vol. 32, No. 7 (October 1953), 26–7, "Articles by Fall," Series 1.06, Box A-1, BBF, JFKL.
93. Ibid., 26.
94. Bernard B. Fall, "Representative Government in the State of Vietnam," August 1954, *Far Eastern Survey*, American Institute of Pacific Relations, 122. In Bernard Fall, "Articles by Fall," Series 1.06, Box A-1, BBF, JFKL.
95. Ibid.
96. Bernard B. Fall, *Last Reflections on a War* (New York: Doubleday & Company, 1967), 217.
97. Ibid., 217.
98. Ibid., 218.

4. SEVEN YEARS OF WAR IN INDOCHINA

1. Mark Atwood Lawrence, *Assuming the Burden: Europe and the American Commitment to War in Vietnam* (Berkeley: University of California Press, 2005). For the postwar history of Indochina, see especially Chapter 4, "Crisis Renewed," 147–89.
2. Ibid., 148.
3. Hue-Tam Ho Tai, *Radicalism and the Origins of the Vietnamese Revolution* (Cambridge, MA: Harvard University Press, 1992), 2.
4. See Bernard Fall, "The French Communists and Indochina," *Foreign Affairs*, Vol. 33, No. 5 (April 1955), in Bernard Fall, *Viet-Nam Witness, 1953–1966* (New York: Praeger, 1966).
5. Allan B. Cole, (Ed.), *Conflict in Indo-China and International Repercussion: A*

Documentary History, 1945–1955 (Ithaca, NY: The Fletcher School of Law and Diplomacy, Tufts University and the Southeast Asia Program, Cornell University Press, 1956), Appendix II, 259–61.

6. Leclerc was made commander of *Les Corps Expéditionnaire Français en Extrême-Orient*, in May 1945 and represented France at the surrender of Japan on the USS *Missouri* in Tokyo Bay on 2 September 1945. The source for this quote is David Halberstam, "Vietnam: Reporting and the War," 2000. David Halberstam Papers, Box 55, Folder 48, Howard Gotlieb Archival Research Center, Boston University. Halberstam's exact reference in describing Leclerc was: "Jacques Phillipe Leclerc, one of Charles DeGaulle's favorite Generals, to Paul Mus a French scholar of Indochina, 1945, just before the start of the French Indo-china war."
7. On divisions between the military and civilian population of France, see Douglas Porch, *The French Secret Services: From the Dreyfus Affair to the Gulf War* (New York: Farrar, Strauss and Giroux, 1995), 294.
8. Bernard B. Fall, "The Anatomy of Insurgency in Indochina, 1946–54," Lecture presented at National War College, Washington, DC, 22 April 1965, Series 1.05, Box P-01, BBF, JFKL; see also, Bernard B. Fall, *Street Without Joy: The French Debacle in Indochina* (Guilford, CT: Stackpole Books, 1961), 16.
9. Bernard B. Fall, *The Viet-Minh Regime: Government and Administration in the Democratic Republic of Vietnam* (New York: Institute of Pacific Relations, 1956), reprinted by Greenwood Press, Westport, CT, 1975.
10. *Ibid.*, 1.
11. Bernard Fall, "The Anatomy of Insurgency in Indochina, 1946–54," Lecture presented at National War College, Washington, DC, 22 April 1965, Series 1.05, Box P-01, BBF, JFKL.
12. Bernard B. Fall, *Last Reflections on a War* (New York: Doubleday & Company, 1967), 122–5.
13. *Ibid.*, 122; also, see Bernard B. Fall, *Street Without Joy: The French Debacle in Indochina* (Guilford, CT: Stackpole Books, 1961), 24.
14. *Ibid.*, 23.
15. See Dixee R. Bartholomew-Feis, *The O.S.S. and Ho Chi Minh: Unexpected Allies in the War Against Japan* (Lawrence, KS: University of Kansas Press, 2006) and Charles Fenn, *At the Dragon's Gate: With the OSS in the Far East* (Annapolis, MD: Naval Institute Press, 2004).
16. Bernard B. Fall, "Indochina—The Seven Year Dilemma," *Military Review*, Vol. 32, No. 7 (October 1953), 24, "Articles by Fall," Series 1.06, Box A-1, BBF, JFKL.
17. Vo Nguyen Giap, *People's War, People's Army: The Viet Cong Insurrection Manual for Undeveloped Countries* (New York: Bantam Books, 1968), 13.
18. David G. Marr, *Vietnam: State, War, and Revolution (1945–1946)* (Berkeley, CA: University of California Press, 2013), 415. Marr provides the most detailed account and analysis for this complex period in Vietnamese history. For more, see Chapter

7. "Dealing with Domestic Opposition," in *Vietnam: State, War, and Revolution (1945–1946)*.
19. For a detailed account of domestic rivalry between the Viet Minh, Nationalists, and other Vietnamese political factions, see William J. Duiker, *The Communist Road to Power in Vietnam* (Boulder, CO: Westview Press, 1996). On internal conflict in 1945–6, see especially Chapter 6: "The Uneasy Peace (September 1945– December 1946)."
20. Vo Nguyen Giap, *People's War, People's Army: The Viet Cong Insurrection Manual for Undeveloped Countries* (New York: Bantam Books, 1968), 14.
21. David G. Marr, *Vietnam: State, War, and Revolution (1945–1946)* (Berkeley, CA: University of California Press, 2013), 427.
22. Bernard B. Fall, *The Viet-Minh Regime: Government and Administration in the Democratic Republic of Vietnam* (New York: Institute of Pacific Relations, 1956), reprinted by Greenwood Press, Westport, CT, 1975, 1.
23. *Ibid.*, 1.
24. *Ibid.*, 1–2.
25. *Ibid.*, 2.
26. *Ibid.*, 2.
27. *Ibid.*, 2.
28. *Ibid.*, 24.
29. Bernard B. Fall, "Indochina—The Seven Year Dilemma," *Military Review*, Vol. 32, No. 7 (October 1953), 24, "Articles by Fall," Series 1.06, Box A-1, BBF, JFKL.
30. *Ibid.*, 24.
31. Bernard B. Fall, *The Viet-Minh Regime: Government and Administration in the Democratic Republic of Vietnam* (New York: Institute of Pacific Relations, 1956), reprinted by Greenwood Press, Westport, CT, 1975, 3.
32. *Ibid.*, 5.
33. Bernard B. Fall, "Indochina—The Seven Year Dilemma," *Military Review*, Vol. 32, No. 7 (October 1953), 27, "Articles by Fall," Series 1.06, Box A-1, BBF, JFKL.
34. Bernard B. Fall, *The Viet-Minh Regime: Government and Administration in the Democratic Republic of Vietnam* (New York: Institute of Pacific Relations, 1956), reprinted by Greenwood Press, Westport, CT, 1975, 5.
35. *Ibid.*, 6.
36. *Ibid.*, 6.
37. *Ibid.*, 6. The ICP was eventually reestablished and renamed the Worker's Party of Vietnam in February 1951 (Lao Dong—đảng lao động Việt Nam).
38. *Ibid.*, 6. For Fall's comments on the formation of the Worker's Party of Vietnam (Lao Dong), see also "The Republic at War," 24–38.
39. Amry Vandenbosch and Richard A. Butwell, *Southeast Asia Among the World Powers* (Lexington, KY: University of Kentucky Press, 1957), 113–14.

40. Zhai, Qiang, "China and the Geneva Conference of 1954," *The China Quarterly*, No. 129, March 1992, 103–5.
41. J. Lawton Collins Papers, 1896–1975, "Indochina Phase—Background Paper: Chronological History of Events in Indochina Since 1940," 1 April 1954. "Part I, Summary of Events in Indochina Since 1940," 2, Subseries A. Briefing Book, Box 24, Dwight D. Eisenhower Presidential Library, Abilene, Kansas.
42. See Bernard Fall, "U.S. Policies in Indochina 1940–1960," in Bernard B. Fall, *Last Reflections on a War* (New York: Doubleday & Company, 1967), 135–6.
43. For a comprehensive account of the First Indochina War, see Fredrik Logevall, *Embers of War: The Fall of an Empire and the Making of America's Vietnam* (New York: Random House, 2014).
44. Shawn McHale, "Understanding the Fanatic Mind? The Viet Minh and Race Hatred in the First Indochina War (1945–954)," *Journal of Vietnamese Studies*, Vol. 4, Issue 3 (2009), 106.
45. The Navarre Plan was named after General Henri Navarre, who became the supreme commander of French Forces in Indochina. For more on the Navarre Plan, see Philippe Devillers and Jean Lacouture, *End of a War: Indochina 1954* (New York: Praeger, 1969), 65 and 72.
46. For Bernard Fall's comprehensive historical account, see *Hell In a Very Small Place: The Siege of Dien Bien Phu* (New York: DaCapo Press, 1967).
47. See Bernard Fall, "The French Communists and Indochina," *Foreign Affairs*, Vol. 33, No. 5 (April 1955), in Bernard Fall, *Viet-Nam Witness, 1953–1966* (New York: Praeger, 1966).
48. William P. Bundy, "*Foreign Affairs*, History," https://www.foreignaffairs.com/history (accessed 12 December 2018).
49. *Foreign Affairs*, Vol. 33, No. 3, April 1955, https://www.foreignaffairs.com/issues/1955/33/3 (accessed 12 December 2018).
50. Jonathan Fenby, *The History of Modern France: From the Revolution to the Present Day* (New York: Simon & Schuster, 2015), 325–31.
51. Herriot was prime minister three times between June 1924 and December 1932. See Bernard Fall, "The French Communists and Indochina," *Foreign Affairs*, Vol. 33, No. 3 (April 1955), in Bernard Fall, *Viet-Nam Witness, 1953–1966* (New York: Praeger, 1966), 23.
52. *Ibid.*, 23.
53. *Ibid.*, 23.
54. Paul Mus, *Viet-Nam, Sociologie d'une Guerre* [Sociology of a War] (Paris: Editions du Seuil, 1952), 342.
55. The debate over the extent Vietnamese Communists included nationalist agendas is a perennial source of discussion. For a remarkable and detailed analysis of ideology in Vietnam during a large portion of the twentieth century, see Tuong Vu, *Vietnam's Communist Revolution: The Power and Limits of Ideology* (Cambridge, UK: Cambridge University Press, 2017).

56. On these divisions, also see Bernard B. Fall, *Last Reflections on a War* (New York: Doubleday & Company, 1967), 47.
57. Benn Steil, *The Marshall Plan: Dawn of the Cold War* (New York: Oxford University Press, 2018), 341.
58. Bernard Fall, "The French Communists and Indochina," *Foreign Affairs*, Vol. 33, No. 3 (April 1955), in Bernard Fall, *Viet-Nam Witness, 1953–1966* (New York: Praeger, 1966), 28.
59. *Ibid.*, 28.
60. Benn Steil, *The Marshall Plan: Dawn of the Cold War* (New York: Oxford University Press, 2018). For a detailed analysis of the loss of Czechoslovakia in 1948, see pp. 235–45.
61. Bernard Fall, "The French Communists and Indochina," *Foreign Affairs*, Vol. 33, No. 5 (April 1955), in Bernard Fall, *Viet-Nam Witness, 1953–1966* (New York: Praeger, 1966), 28–9.
62. Bernard B. Fall, "Solution in Indo-China: Cease-Fire, Negotiate," *The Nation*, 6 March 1954, 193, "Articles by Fall," Series 1.06, Box A-1, BBF, JFKL.
63. For detailed accounting of financial assistance to France and French allocations in support of operations in Indochina, see Allan B. Cole (Ed.), *Conflict in Indo-China and International Repercussion: A Documentary History, 1945–1955* (Ithaca, NY: The Fletcher School of Law and Diplomacy, Tufts University and the Southeast Asia Program, Cornell University Press, 1956), 259.
64. Irwin Wall, "The Marshall Plan and French Politics," in Martin A. Schain (Ed.), *The Marshall Plan Fifty Years Later* (London: Palgrave MacMillan, 2001), 175.
65. Frank Costigliola, *France and the United States: The Cold War Alliance Since World War II* (New York: Twayne Publishers, 1992), 104.
66. Richard A. Hunt, "Avoiding Lessons from the Past? The U.S. in the Vietnam War," in *La Guerre du Vietnam et L'Europe 1963–1973*, Christopher Goscha and Maurice Vaisse (Eds.), (Brussels: Bruylant; Paris: LGDJ, 2003), 18, 20.
67. George C. Herring, *The American Century & Beyond: U.S. Foreign Relations, 1893–2014* (New York: Oxford University Press), 337.
68. Bernard B. Fall, "Solution in Indo-China: Cease-Fire, Negotiate," *The Nation* (6 March 1954), 195, "Articles by Fall," Series 1.06, Box A-1, BBF, JFKL.
69. *Ibid.*, 195.
70. "J.A. Dennis Letter to Senator Lyndon B. Johnson, May 28, 1954," Case and Project Files, Box 1195, Papers of Lyndon Baines Johnson (LBJP), Lyndon Baines Johnson Presidential Library, Austin, Texas (LBJL).
71. Bernard B. Fall, Editor and Introduction, *Ho Chi Minh: On Revolution, Selected Writings, 1920–66* (New York: Frederick A. Praeger, 1967), ix–x.
72. The ideological content of the Vietnamese Independence Movement remains a matter of debate. Whether Ho and other senior leaders in his circle might have been persuaded to adopt other ideological means to achieve independence remains

a lively counterfactual question among some historians. For historical analysis on Ho Chi Minh's complexity and experiences, see Sophie Quinn-Judge, *Ho Chi Minh: The Missing Years (1919–1941)* (Berkeley, CA: University of California Press, 2002); David Marr, *Vietnamese Tradition on Trial, 1920–1945* (Berkeley, CA: University of California Press, 1981); Dixee R. Bartholomew-Feis, *The O.S.S. and Ho Chi Minh: Unexpected Allies in the War Against Japan* (Lawrence, KS: University of Kansas Press, 2006); Charles Fenn, *At the Dragon's Gate: With the OSS in the Far East* (Annapolis, MD: Naval Institute Press, 2004); William J. Duiker, *Ho Chi Minh: A Life* (New York: Hatchette Books, 2000). Most recently, see Tuong Vu, *Vietnam's Communist Revolution: The Power and Limits of Ideology* (New York: Cambridge University Press, 2017).

73. David Marr, *Vietnamese Tradition on Trial, 1920–1945* (Berkeley, CA: University of California Press, 1981), 317.
74. Bernard B. Fall, Editor and Introduction, *Ho Chi Minh: On Revolution, Selected Writings, 1920–66* (New York: Frederick A. Praeger, 1967), vii.
75. *Ibid.*, ix.
76. See Christoph Giebel, *Imagined Ancestries of Vietnamese Communism: Ton Duc Thang and the Politics of History and Memory* (Seattle, WA: University of Washington Press, 2006).
77. Bernard B. Fall, *The Two Viet-Nams: A Political and Military Analysis* (New York: Praeger, 1963), 91.
78. *Ibid.*, 91.
79. *Ibid.*, 91.
80. Nikita Khrushchev, *Khrushchev Remembers*, Translated by Strobe Talbott (Boston, MA: Little, Brown and Company, 1970), 480–1.
81. Bernard B. Fall, *The Viet-Minh Regime: Government and Administration in the Democratic Republic of Vietnam* (New York: Institute of Pacific Relations, 1956), reprinted by Greenwood Press, Westport, CT, 1975, 18.
82. Paul Staniland, *Networks of Rebellion: Explaining Insurgent Cohesion and Collapse* (Ithaca, NY: Cornell University Press, 2014), 211.
83. Edwin E. Moïse, *Land Reform in China and North Vietnam: Consolidating the Revolution at the Village Level* (Chapel Hill, NC: University of North Carolina Press, 1983). Moïse's book is one of the few publications that cite Bernard Fall's 1954 study, *The Viet-Minh Regime*, in its bibliography. Moïse's book may be regarded as the definitive study on land reform in English, particularly because of his reliance on primary sources, especially *Nhan Dan*. Moïse also corrects errors found in Fall's 1954 study, see Moïse, 152.
84. Bernard B. Fall, *The Viet-Minh Regime: Government and Administration in the Democratic Republic of Vietnam* (New York: Institute of Pacific Relations, 1956), reprinted by Greenwood Press, Westport, CT, 1975, 118.
85. Qiang Zhai, *China and the Vietnam War, 1950–1975* (Chapel Hill, NC: University of North Carolina Press, 2000), 38, 39.

86. Bernard B. Fall, *The Viet-Minh Regime: Government and Administration in the Democratic Republic of Vietnam* (New York: Institute of Pacific Relations, 1956), reprinted by Greenwood Press, Westport, CT, 1975, 131.
87. *Ibid.*, 131.
88. *Ibid.*, 132. For Fall's comments on 1953 Land Reform more broadly, see pp. 125–35.
89. Bernard B. Fall, *The Two Vietnams: A Political and Military Analysis* (New York: Praeger, 1963), 154.
90. *Ibid.*, 155–6.
91. *Ibid.*, 155.
92. *Ibid.*, 156.
93. *Ibid.*, 157. Fall used the term "VPA" to stand for the Vietnamese People's Army. Contemporary conventions use the term PAVN, People's Army of Vietnam.
94. *Ibid.*, 157. Amry Vandenbosch and Richard Butwell also cited problems these revolts created. See Amry Vandenbosch and Richard A. Butwell, *Southeast Asia Among the World Powers* (Lexington, KY: University of Kentucky Press, 1957), 135.
95. Bernard B. Fall, *The Viet-Minh Regime: Government and Administration in the Democratic Republic of Vietnam* (New York: Institute of Pacific Relations, 1956), reprinted by Greenwood Press, Westport, CT, 1975, 132.
96. Bernard Fall, "Commentary: Bernard Fall on Bui Van Luong," in Richard W. Lindholm, Editor, *Viet-Nam—The First Five Years: An International Symposium* (Lansing, MI: Michigan State University Press, 1959), 55.
97. Fall relied on the DRV decree number 149 that was announced via Radio on Voice of Vietnam on 20 May 1953. See fn. 26 on p. 137 in Bernard B. Fall, *The Viet-Minh Regime: Government and Administration in the Democratic Republic of Vietnam* (New York: Institute of Pacific Relations, 1956), reprinted by Greenwood Press, Westport, CT, 1975. For Fall's detailed analysis of Agrarian Reform articles noted in the text, see Part Six, in Viet-Minh Regime, pp. 118–38.
98. *Ibid.*, 126.
99. Bernard B. Fall, *The Two Vietnams: A Political and Military Analysis* (New York: Praeger, 1963), 156–7.
100. Bernard B. Fall, *The Viet-Minh Regime: Government and Administration in the Democratic Republic of Vietnam* (New York: Institute of Pacific Relations, 1956), reprinted by Greenwood Press, Westport, CT, 1975, 133.
101. *Ibid.*, 133.
102. *Ibid.*, 133.
103. *Ibid.*, 118.
104. *Ibid.*, 118.
105. According to Christopher Goscha, "The rice trade constitutes one of the most

important components of the Vietnamese economy to this day. While the colonial infrastructure improvements mentioned above certainly helped make Vietnam the third most important rice exporter in the world after Thailand and Burma before 1940 (and second only to Thailand today), the Chinese and Vietnamese operated this sector of the economy." See Christopher Goscha, *Vietnam: A New History* (New York: Basic Books, 2016), 154–5.

106. The diversity of South Vietnam's society and the Viet Minh's conflicts with the Hoa Hao also contributed. See Bernard B. Fall, "The Political-Religious Sects of Viet-Nam." *Pacific Affairs*, Vol. 28, No. 3 (September 1955).
107. Bernard B. Fall, *The Viet-Minh Regime: Government and Administration in the Democratic Republic of Vietnam* (New York: Institute of Pacific Relations, 1956), reprinted by Greenwood Press, Westport, CT, 1975), 119–20.
108. *Ibid.*, 118.
109. *Ibid.*, 118.
110. *Ibid.*, 118. Fall quoted data from *The Agriculture of Indochina*, US Department of Agriculture, Washington, DC, 1950, 5–6.
111. *Ibid.*, 118.
112. *Ibid.*, 118.
113. *Ibid.*, 121.
114. *Ibid.*, 121.
115. "Part Six: Agrarian Reforms" includes Fall's account of land-related debate in Indochina since the 1920s, and his article-by-article analysis of different DRV land reform edicts and decrees is found between pp. 118–38. Also, see "Part Seven: Labor Organization and Legislation," pp. 139–51. Fall provides detailed analysis of the Viet-Nam Tong Lien Doan Lao Dong (TLD). Fall writes, "This organization was modeled on the French, Communist-dominated General Confederation of Labor (CGT) and oversaw four major labor federations: The Armaments Workers' Union; the Postal Workers' Union; the Teachers' Union; and that of the 'Medical Workers.'" See pp. 139–40.
116. For an analysis of land reform that updated and corrected information in Fall's scholarship, see Edwin E. Moïse, *Land Reform in China and North Vietnam: Consolidating the Revolution at the Village Level* (Chapel Hill, NC: University of North Carolina Press, 1983).
117. Marilyn B. Young, *The Vietnam Wars, 1945–1990* (New York: Harper Perennial, 1991), 10, 29.
118. Bernard B. Fall, "Representative Government in the State of Vietnam," August 1954, *Far Eastern Survey*, American Institute of Pacific Relations, 122. In Bernard Fall, "Articles by Fall," Series 1.06, Box A-1, BBF, JFKL.
119. *Ibid.*, 122–3.
120. *Ibid.*, 125.
121. Bernard B. Fall, "Representative Government in the State of Vietnam," August

1954, *Far Eastern Survey*, American Institute of Pacific Relations, 122. In Bernard Fall, "Articles by Fall," Series 1.06, Box A-1, BBF, JFKL.

122. Mark Atwood Lawrence, *Assuming the Burden: Europe and the American Commitment to War in Vietnam* (Berkeley, CA: University of California Press, 2005), 255–6.
123. Qiang Zhai, *China and the Vietnam War, 1950–1975* (Chapel Hill, NC: University of North Carolina Press, 2000), 20.
124. *Ibid.*, 15, 23. North Korea also established ties with the DRV in 1950 and provided troops, pilots, and materiel support. See Ha Hoang Hop and Lye Liang Fook, "Trump-Kim Summit: Why Vietnam?" Yusof Ishak Institute, 13 February 2019. See also, Zhai, Qiang, "China and the Geneva Conference of 1954," *The China Quarterly*, No. 129 (March 1992), 104.
125. David Halberstam, *The Coldest Winter: America and the Korean War* (New York: Hyperion, 2007), 52.
126. Dwight D. Eisenhower, *Mandate for Change* (New York: Doubleday & Company, 1963), 336.
127. Bernard B. Fall, "Representative Government in the State of Vietnam," August 1954, *Far Eastern Survey*, American Institute of Pacific Relations, 123–4. In Bernard Fall, "Articles by Fall," Series 1.06, Box A-1, BBF, JFKL.
128. *Ibid.*, 123.
129. *Ibid.*, 123.
130. Shawn McHale *Print and Power: Confucianism, Communism, and Buddhism in the Making of Modern Vietnam* (Honolulu, HI: University of Hawai'i Press, 2004).
131. Bernard B. Fall, "Representative Government in the State of Vietnam," August 1954, *Far Eastern Survey*, American Institute of Pacific Relations, 123–4. In Bernard Fall, "Articles by Fall," Series 1.06, Box A-1, 123, BBF, JFKL.
132. *Ibid.*, 124. This was a barely veiled swipe at Bao Dai, who often stayed in the mountain resort town of Dalat.
133. Bernard B. Fall, "Solution in Indo-China: Cease-Fire, Negotiate," *The Nation* (6 March 1954), 195, Series 1.06 "Articles by Fall," Box A-1, BBF, JFKL.
134. "Mrs. William R. Chappell to Senator Lyndon B. Johnson, April 10, 1954," Papers of Lyndon B. Johnson, US Senate, 1949–61, Case and Project Files, Box 1194, LBJP, LBJL.
135. "Maury Maverick Letter to Senator Lyndon Johnson, April 7, 1954," Case and Project Files, Box 1194, LBJP, LBJL.
136. "Thomas Hudson McKee Letter to Senator Lyndon Johnson, April 7, 1954," Case and Project Files, Box 1194, LBJP, LBJL.
137. "Mrs. and Mr. R. G. Nabors Letter to Senator Lyndon Johnson, April 7, 1954," Case and Project Files, Box 1194, LBJP, LBJL.
138. For analysis of Lyndon Johnson's perspective toward Indochina and US policy

related to later intervention, see Fredrik Logevall, *Choosing War: The Lost Chance for Peace and the Escalation of War in Vietnam* (Berkeley, CA: University of California Press, 1999).
139. Ted Morgan, *Valley of Death: The Tragedy at Dien Bien Phu That Led America into the Vietnam War* (New York: Random House), 495–6.
140. François Sully, *Age of the Guerrilla* (New York: Avon Books, 1968), 137.
141. Bernard B. Fall, *The Viet-Minh Regime: Government and Administration in the Democratic Republic of Vietnam* (New York: Institute of Pacific Relations, 1956), reprinted by Greenwood Press, Westport, CT, 1975, 18.
142. Le Duan, *The Vietnamese Revolution: Fundamental Problems and Essential Tasks* (New York: International Publishers, 1971). 139. On changes in leadership, see especially 125–9.
143. Bernard B. Fall, *The Viet-Minh Regime: Government and Administration in the Democratic Republic of Vietnam* (New York: Institute of Pacific Relations, 1956), reprinted by Greenwood Press, Westport, CT, 1975, 42–3.
144. See Bernard B. Fall "Truong Chinh: Portrait of a Party Thinker," in Truong Chinh, *Primer for Revolt: The Communist Takeover in Viet-Nam, with an Introduction and Notes by Bernard B. Fall* (New York: Praeger, 1963), xix–ix.
145. See "Part Nine: Conclusion: The D.R.V. in Perspective," in Bernard B. Fall, *The Viet-Minh Regime: Government and Administration in the Democratic Republic of Vietnam* (New York: Institute of Pacific Relations, 1956), reprinted by Greenwood Press, Westport, CT, 1975, 152–5.
146. See Bernard B. Fall "Truong Chinh: Portrait of a Party Thinker," in Truong Chinh, *Primer for Revolt: The Communist Takeover in Viet-Nam, With an Introduction and Notes by Bernard B. Fall* (New York: Praeger, 1963), xix. Truong Chinh was demoted for his support of land collectivization in 1956 and, Fall believed, was a scapegoat for disastrous land reform policies.
147. Bernard B. Fall, *The Viet-Minh Regime: Government and Administration in the Democratic Republic of Vietnam* (New York: Institute of Pacific Relations, 1956), reprinted by Greenwood Press, Westport, CT, 1975, 35–6.
148. *Ibid.*, 35.
149. Bernard Fall, "Local Administration Under the Viet-Minh," *Pacific Affairs*, March 1954, reprinted as "The Grass-Roots Rebellion," in *Viet-Nam Witness, 1953–66* (New York: Frederick A. Praeger, 1966), 87.
150. See Fall's footnotes, for Part One, on pp. 37–8. Bernard B. Fall, *The Viet-Minh Regime: Government and Administration in the Democratic Republic of Vietnam* (New York: Institute of Pacific Relations, 1956), reprinted by Greenwood Press, Westport, CT, 1975.
151. *Ibid.*, 35.
152. *Ibid.*, 35.
153. Bernard B. Fall, *Last Reflections on a War* (New York: Doubleday & Company, 1967), 210.

154. François Sully, *Age of the Guerrilla* (New York: Avon Books, 1968), 136–7.
155. François Sully Papers and Photographs, 1958–83, "Sully Comments on Bernard Fall," *Newsweek* Files, February–March 1967, Box 2, Folder 31, Joseph P. Healey Archives and Special Collections, University of Massachusetts Boston.

5. THE ENDING IS A BEGINNING

1. The only other contemporary book in English that addressed the First Indochina War was Ellen J. Hammer, *The Struggle for Indochina, 1940–1955* (Palo Alto, CA: Stanford University Press, 1955).
2. See John Shy's chapter "Jomini," in *Makers of Modern Strategy: From Machiavelli to the Nuclear Age* (Princeton, NJ: Princeton University Press, 1986).
3. Bernard B. Fall, "Solution in Indo-China: Cease-Fire, Negotiate," *The Nation* (6 March 1954), 193, "Articles by Fall," Series 1.06, Box A-1, BBF, JFKL.
4. Bernard B. Fall, *The Viet-Minh Regime: Government and Administration in the Democratic Republic of Vietnam* (New York: Institute of Pacific Relations, 1956), reprinted by Greenwood Press, Westport, CT, 1975, iv.
5. Ben L. Martin, "The New 'Old China Hands': Shaping a Specialty," *Asian Affairs*, Vol. 3, No. 2 (November–December 1975), 124.
6. *Ibid.*, 124. See also, Zhai, Qiang, "China and the Geneva Conference of 1954," *The China Quarterly*, No. 129 (March 1992), 119.
7. Mary L. Dudziak, *War-Time: An Idea, Its History, and Its Consequences* (New York: Oxford University Press, 2012), 89–91.
8. George C. Herring, *America's Longest War: The United States and Vietnam, 1950–1975* (New York: Alfred A. Knopf, 1979), 9.
9. On the problem of "losing" China, and McCarthy, see Fredrik Logevall, *Embers of War: The Fall of an Empire and the Making of America's Vietnam* (New York: Random House, 2014), 234–5. On McCarthy's censure, see Arthur M. Schlesinger, Jr., *A Thousand Days: John F. Kennedy in the White House* (Cambridge, MA: Houghton Mifflin Company, 1965), 13.
10. Another early example of research published the next year in 1955 is Ellen J. Hammer, *The Struggle for Indochina 1940–1955: Viet Nam and the French Experience* (Palo Alto, CA: Stanford University Press, 1955). In contrast to Fall, Hammer based her research on French documentation, whereas Fall utilized far more comprehensive research. See Fall's review of Hammer's book in *Asian Student* (21 September 1954), "Book Reviews by Fall," Series 1.08, Box BR-1, BBF, JFKL.
11. See Bernard Fall, "The French Communists and Indochina," *Foreign Affairs*, Vol. 33, No. 3 (April 1955), in Bernard Fall, *Viet-Nam Witness, 1953–1966* (New York: Praeger, 1966).
12. Dorothy Fall, *Bernard Fall: Memories of a Soldier-Scholar* (Washington, DC: Potomac Books, 2007), 70.
13. Fall referred to this army as the Vietnamese People's Army (VPA) but, in accor-

dance with modern convention, People's Army of Vietnam (PAVN) is used in this text to refer to the Viet Minh's army, except when used in direct quotations by Fall.
14. David G. Marr, *Vietnam: State, War, and Revolution (1945–1946)* (Berkeley, CA: University of California Press, 2013), 384.
15. See "Part Four: Fighting a Total War," in Bernard B. Fall, *The Viet-Minh Regime: Government and Administration in the Democratic Republic of Vietnam* (New York: Institute of Pacific Relations, 1956), reprinted by Greenwood Press, Westport, CT, 1975, 87.
16. *Ibid.*, 87–8.
17. *Ibid.*, for references on which Fall relied pertaining to the judiciary and internal security of the DRV, see pp. 37–8. *Viet Nam Dan Quoc Cong Bao* decrees Fall analyzed included 59, 60, 63–6, 70, 77b, 77c, 85. See also Fall's comments on the DRV's penal code in "The New Code of Justice," *Viet-Minh Regime*, pp. 33–5.
18. The "New Directive on Mass Mobilization and Its New Relations With the Rich Farmers" and the "Rectification of Errors Campaign" are examples. See Bernard B. Fall, *The Viet-Minh Regime: Government and Administration in the Democratic Republic of Vietnam* (New York: Institute of Pacific Relations, 1956), reprinted by Greenwood Press, Westport, CT, 1975), 132; and Bernard B. Fall, *The Two Vietnams: A Political and Military Analysis* (New York: Praeger, 1963), 156–7.
19. *Ibid.*, 88.
20. Marie-Monique Robin, *Escadrons de la Mort, l'école Française* (Paris: Le Decouverte/Poche, 2004), 246. As an example of their continued interactions, Fall later wrote the introduction for Trinquier's 1964 study on modern warfare. See "Introduction: A Portrait of the 'Centurion,'" by Bernard Fall in Roger Trinquier, *Modern Warfare: A French View of Counterinsurgency* (New York, Praeger, 2006).
21. For Fall's collection of issues of *Revue Militaire d'Information*, Publication Mensuelle du Ministère de la Défense National et des Forces Armèes (Paris: Les Èditions Haussmann), see "Journals and Serials," Series 2.06, Box J-97, BBF, JFKL. Issues from January and February–March 1957 stand out in Fall's collection as critical in his research.
22. The literature on the Algerian War is vast. For a book on the subject that Fall read, see Jules Roy, *The War in Algeria* (New York: Grove Press, Inc, 1961). For a comprehensive list of material Fall read and suggested on the subject of modern warfare in the early 1960s, see Appendix IV: A Military Bibliography of Indochina, in Bernard Fall, *Street Without Joy* (New York: Da Capo Press, 1961).
23. Peter Paret, *French Revolutionary Warfare From Indochina to Algeria: The Analysis of a Political and Military Doctrine* (New York: Praeger, 1964), 6–7.
24. Jean Hogard, "Guerre Révoutionnaire et Pacification," *Revue Militaire d'Information*, Janvier, 1957, 8. Publication Mensuelle du Ministère de la Défense National et Paris: Les Èditions Haussmann), see "Journals and Serials," Series 2.06, Box J-97, BBF, JFKL.

25. Authored by "Un Groupe d'Officiers," Article titled, "Le Guerre du Viet-Minh," in *Revue Militarie d'Information*, Fevrier–Mars, 1957, 30. For Fall's copy, see Series 2.06, Box J-97, BBF, JFKL.
26. Bernard B. Fall, *The Two Vietnams: A Political and Military Analysis* (New York: Praeger, 1963), 134.
27. *Ibid.*, 134.
28. *Ibid.*, 134.
29. Boaz Ganor's perspective on terrorism and insurgent goals is notable in the case of the Viet Minh. See Ganor, "Defining Terrorism: Is One Man's Terrorist Another Man's Freedom Fighter?" in *Police Practice and Research*, Vol. 3, No. 4 (2002).
30. Paul Staniland, *Networks of Rebellion: Explaining Insurgent Cohesion and Collapse* (Ithaca, NY: Cornell University Press, 2014), 215.
31. Ton Duc Thang, the DRV second-in-command after Ho Chi Minh, provided an allegedly direct link to the Russian Revolution. See Christoph Giebel, *Imagined Ancestries of Vietnamese Communism: Ton Duc Thang and the Politics of History and Memory* (Seattle, WA: University of Washington Press, 2006).
32. Bernard Fall, *Last Reflections on a War: Bernard Fall's Last Comments on Viet-Nam* (New York: Doubleday & Company), 210.
33. *Ibid.*, 217.
34. *Ibid.*, 217.
35. See George C. Herring and Richard H. Immerman, "Eisenhower, Dulles, and Dienbienphu: 'The Day We Didn't Go to War,' Revisited," *Journal of American History*, Vol. 71, No. 2 (September 1984), 343–63. For Herring and Immerman's discussion regarding the potential use of "atomic bombs," see p. 357.
36. Bernard Fall, *Last Reflections on a War: Bernard Fall's Last Comments on Viet-Nam* (New York: Doubleday & Company), 217.
37. *Ibid.*, 216–17.
38. *Ibid.*, 217.
39. *Ibid.*, 217–18.
40. Dorothy Fall, *Bernard Fall: Memories of a Soldier-Scholar* (Washington, DC: Potomac Books, 2007), 75.
41. Michael P.M. Finch, *A Progressive Occupation: The Gallieni–Lyautey Method and Colonial Pacification in Tonkin and Madagascar, 1885–1900* (New York: Oxford University Press, 2013). For analysis on Gallieni and Lyautey's methods, see 60–3.
42. Jacques Frémeaux and Bruno C. Reis, "French Counterinsurgency in the Era of the Algerian Wars, 1830–1962," in Beatrice Heuser and Eitan Shamir (Eds.), *Insurgencies and Counterinsurgencies: National Styles and Strategic Cultures* (Cambridge, UK: Cambridge University Press, 2016), 60.
43. Bernard B. Fall, *Last Reflections on a War* (New York: Doubleday & Company, 1967), 220.
44. Bernard Fall, "Indochina: The Last Year of the War: Communist Organization

and Tactics," *Military Review*, Vol. 36, No. 7 (October 1956), 11, Series 1.06, Box A-1, BBF, JFKL.
45. Bernard B. Fall, *The Two Vietnams: A Political and Military Analysis* (New York: Praeger, 1963), 133–8.
46. Shawn McHale, "Understanding the Fanatic Mind? The Viet Minh and Race Hatred in the First Indochina War (1945–1954)," *Journal of Vietnamese Studies*, Vol. 4, Issue 3, 102.
47. *Ibid.*, 102.
48. *Ibid.*, 102.
49. Patricia M. Pelley, *Postcolonial Vietnam: New Histories of the National Past* (Durham, NC: Duke University Press, 2002), 236–7.
50. Frances FitzGerald, *Fire in The Lake: The Vietnamese and the Americans in Vietnam* (Boston, MA: Little, Brown and Company, 1972), 64.
51. David W.P. Elliott, *The Vietnamese War: Revolution and Social Change in the Mekong Delta 1930–1975* (Armonk, NY: M.E. Sharpe, 2003), 14. For Elliott's discussion of social change in Vietnam, see especially Chapter 3 "Prelude," pp. 16–40 and Chapter 4, "Revolution," 41–61.
52. Alexander B. Woodside, *Community and Revolution in Modern Vietnam* (Boston, MA: Houghton Mifflin Company, 1976), 37; Hue Tam Ho Tai, *Radicalism and the Origins of the Vietnamese Revolution* (Cambridge, MA: Harvard University Press, 1992), 170. The transformation of Vietnamese society is an extensively studied subject in environmental and Vietnamese histories, which also account for technological and communication advancements as features of modernity. The scholarship of Michitake Aso, David Biggs, Kim Ngoc Bao, Shawn McHale, and Edwin Martini provide accounts of transformative changes in Vietnamese society through rubber production, water management, print media, and chemical warfare using Agent Orange, respectively.
53. David Hunt, *Vietnam's Southern Revolution: From Peasant Insurrection to Total War* (Amherst, MA: University of Massachusetts Press, 2008),136.
54. Dan Van Sung, "A Historical View of the Vietnamese Nationalist Cause," in *We the Vietnamese: Voices from Vietnam*, François Sully (Ed.), (New York: Praeger, 1971), 136.
55. See "2000 Years of War in Vietnam," in Bernard B. Fall, *Last Reflections on a War* (New York: Doubleday & Company, 1967).
56. Hue Tam Ho Tai, *Radicalism and the Origins of the Vietnamese Revolution* (Cambridge, MA: Harvard University Press, 1992), 22.
57. *Ibid*. On Phan Boi Chau and Phan Chu Trinh, see 22–6; on Nguyen An Ninh, see 72–87. On Bui Quang Chieu, see 39–46.
58. Shawn McHale, "Understanding the Fanatic Mind? The Viet Minh and Race Hatred in the First Indochina War (1945–1954)," *Journal of Vietnamese Studies*, Vol. 4, Issue 3, 110.

59. Information about Tran Van Giau in these paragraphs is gathered from *The Indochina War: 1945–1956, An Interdisciplinary Tool*, University of Québec at Montréal. http://indochine.uqam.ca/en/historical-dictionary/1464-trn-vn-giau-h-nam-hoang-trn-vn-19112010.html (accessed 20 January 2021).
60. Lien-Hang T. Nguyen, *Hanoi's War: An International History of the War for Peace in Vietnam* (Chapel Hill, NC: University of North Carolina Press, 2012), 24.
61. Ellen J. Hammer, *The Struggle for Indochina 1940–1955* (Palo Alto, CA: Stanford University Press, 1955), 158.
62. *Ibid.*, 158.
63. Bernard B. Fall, *Last Reflections on a War* (New York: Doubleday & Company, 1967), 46. On Fall's views on secret societies in Vietnam, see "2000 Years of War in Viet-Nam," 45–7.
64. *Ibid.*, 214.
65. Henry Ainley, *In Order to Die* (London: Burke Publishing Company, 1955).
66. *Ibid.*
67. Fall later built upon his early analysis of these groups by examining their evolution and pervasiveness in South Vietnam after 1958 "as the Central Research Agency (CRA) (Cuc Nghien Cuu Trung Uong) under the National Defense Committee of the North Vietnamese Government." In addition to the Cong An, Trinh Sat, and Dich Van analyzed in this chapter, Fall also expanded his scope of analysis on these groups to include Tri Van, who "worked with professionals, students and intellectuals and were concentrated in cities" and Binh Van who "directed its attention to Government soldiers and Government paramilitary organizations." See Bernard Fall, "South Viet-Nam (1956 up to November 1963)," Special Operations Research Office, Series 1.05, Box P-3, BBF, JFKL.
68. Bernard Fall, *The Two Vietnams: A Political and Military Analysis* (New York: Praeger, 1963), 136.
69. *Ibid.*, 137.
70. David Marr's work on this subject also supports Fall's conclusion and clarifies the dates of this merger. Marr states, "In late February 1946, the DRV government merged the Security Service and various police units to become the Vietnam Public Security Department (*Viet Nam Cong An Vu*), which we will call the Cong An." David G. Marr, *Vietnam: State, War, and Revolution (1945–1946)* (Berkeley, CA: University of California Press, 2013), 402.
71. Bernard Fall, *The Two Vietnams: A Political and Military Analysis* (New York: Praeger, 1963), 136.
72. Bernard Fall, *The Viet-Minh Regime: Government and Administration in the Democratic Republic of Vietnam* (New York: Institute of Pacific Relations, 1956), reprinted by Greenwood Press, Westport, CT, 1975, 35.
73. Christopher E. Goscha, "Intelligence in a Time of Decolonialization: The Case of the Democratic Republic of Vietnam at War (1945–50)," *Intelligence and National Security*, Vol. 22, No. 1 (February 2007), 119.

74. Bernard Fall, *The Viet-Minh Regime: Government and Administration in the Democratic Republic of Vietnam* (New York: Institute of Pacific Relations, 1956), reprinted by Greenwood Press, Westport, CT, 1975, 36.
75. Douglas Porch, *The French Secret Services: From the Dreyfus Affair to the Gulf War* (New York: Farrar, Strauss and Giroux, 1995), 308.
76. On the extensive military and advisory aid provided by China and other communist countries in and after 1950 see Bernard Fall, *The Viet-Minh Regime: Government and Administration in the Democratic Republic of Vietnam* (New York: Institute of Pacific Relations, 1956), reprinted by Greenwood Press, Westport, CT, 1975, 81–3, 87–8. See also, Zhai, Qiang, "China and the Geneva Conference of 1954," *The China Quarterly*, No. 129 (March 1992), 103–22. Zhai writes, "between 1950 and 1954 China provided the Vietminh with 116,000 guns and 4,630 cannons, equipping five infantry divisions, one engineering and artillery division, one anti-aircraft regiment, and one guard regiment" (Zhai, 106).
77. One exception was Fall's article "… Und den Krieg führen die Dummen," Series in *Münchner Illustrierte*, September–Oktober 1953. (Fall translated this as "… It's the Imbeciles Who Fight the War.") It was one of numerous articles Fall wrote and published in German but the only known article that openly criticized French commanders before 1954. See Bernard Fall, *The Viet-Minh Regime: Government and Administration in the Democratic Republic of Vietnam* (New York: Institute of Pacific Relations, 1956), reprinted by Greenwood Press, Westport, CT, 1975, 194.
78. Bernard Fall, *The Viet-Minh Regime: Government and Administration in the Democratic Republic of Vietnam* (New York: Institute of Pacific Relations, 1956), reprinted by Greenwood Press, Westport, CT, 1975, 91–92.
79. Bernard Fall, *The Two Vietnams: A Political and Military Analysis* (New York: Praeger, 1963), 137.
80. Henry Ainley, *In Order to Die* (London: Burke Publishing Company, 1955), 106.
81. Bernard Fall, *The Two Vietnams: A Political and Military Analysis* (New York: Praeger, 1963), 137.
82. *Ibid.*, 134.
83. *Ibid.*, 134.
84. *Ibid.*, 133–4.
85. Christopher Andrew and Vasili Mitrokhin, *The Sword and The Shield: The Mitrokhin Archive and the Secret History of the KGB* (New York: Basic Books, 1999), 23–9. According to Andrew, p. 23, "During the late 1930s the KGB (then known as the NKVD) had been the chief instrument of Stalin's Great Terror, the greatest peacetime persecution in European History."
86. Bernard B. Fall, "The Guerrilla Craze," Undated, Series 1.5, Box P-1, BBF, JFKL. Note, the John Birch Society was founded in 1958.
87. Bernard Fall, *The Two Vietnams: A Political and Military Analysis* (New York: Praeger, 1963), 137.

88. Christopher E. Goscha, "Intelligence in a Time of Decolonization: The Case of the Democratic Republic at War (1945–1950), *Intelligence and National Security*, Vol. 22., No. 1 (February 2007), 131.
89. *Ibid.*, 132.
90. *Ibid.*, 132.
91. Eric Hoffer, *The True Believer: Thoughts on the Nature of Mass Movements* (New York: Harper Perennial, 1951). For Hoffer's thoughts on persuasion and coercion, see 105–11.
92. Bernard Fall, *The Two Vietnams: A Political and Military Analysis* (New York: Praeger, 1963), 137.
93. Henry Ainley, *In Order to Die* (London: Burke Publishing Company, 1955), 107.
94. *Ibid.*, 107. See also, Bernard B. Fall, *Street Without Joy: The French Debacle in Indochina* (Guilford, CT: Stackpole Books, 1961), 141.
95. Bernard B. Fall, *Street Without Joy: The French Debacle in Indochina* (Guilford, CT: Stackpole Books, 1961), 132–4.
96. Ruth Ginio, *The French Army and Its African Soldiers: The Years of Decolonization* (Lincoln, NE: University of Nebraska Press, 2017), 98.
97. Douglas Porch, *The French Secret Services: From the Dreyfus Affair to the Gulf War* (New York: Farrar, Strauss and Giroux, 1995), 308–9.
98. Bernard Fall, *The Viet-Minh Regime: Government and Administration in the Democratic Republic of Vietnam* (New York: Institute of Pacific Relations, 1956), reprinted by Greenwood Press, Westport, CT, 1975, 54.
99. Michel Goya, *Innovations en Indochine: Les Transformations du Corps Expéditionnaire Français en Extrême-Orient (1945–1954)* (Amazon Kindle Edition, 2017).
100. Bernard Fall, *The Viet-Minh Regime: Government and Administration in the Democratic Republic of Vietnam* (New York: Institute of Pacific Relations, 1956), reprinted by Greenwood Press, Westport, CT, 1975, 54.
101. *Ibid.*, 54.
102. See especially, Shawn McHale, "Understanding the Fanatic Mind? The Viet Minh and Race Hatred in the First Indochina War (1945–1954)," *Journal of Vietnamese Studies*, Vol. 4, Issue 3 (1990).
103. See John W. Dower, *War Without Mercy: Race & Power in the Pacific War* (New York: Pantheon Books, 1986).
104. Christopher Capozzola, *Bound by War: How the United States and the Philippines Built America's First Pacific Century* (New York: Basic Books, 2020), 30.
105. Ruth Ginio, *The French Army and Its African Soldiers: The Years of Decolonization* (Lincoln, NE: University of Nebraska Press, 2017), 78.
106. Bernard Fall, *The Viet-Minh Regime: Government and Administration in the*

Democratic Republic of Vietnam (New York: Institute of Pacific Relations, 1956), reprinted by Greenwood Press, Westport, CT, 1975, 54.
107. J. Lawton Collins Papers, 1896–1975, "Indochina Phase—Background Paper: Chronological History of Events in Indochina Since 1940," 1 April 1954, 27. "Part I, Summary of Events in Indochina Since 1940," Subseries A. Briefing Book, Box 24, Dwight D. Eisenhower Presidential Library, Abilene, Kansas.
108. William J. Duiker, *The Communist Road to Power in Vietnam* (Boulder, CO: Westview Press, 1996), 111.
109. Jeremy M. Weinstein, "Resources and the Information Problem in Rebel Recruitment," *The Journal of Conflict Resolution*, Vol. 49, No. 4, "Paradigm in Distress? Primary Commodities and Civil War," August 2005, 622.
110. In addition to equipment captured in Korea, the Viet Minh could rely "upon U.S. parts captured from Franco-Nationalist forces to repair and maintain its American material." In Bernard Fall, *The Viet-Minh Regime: Government and Administration in the Democratic Republic of Vietnam* (New York: Institute of Pacific Relations, 1956), reprinted by Greenwood Press, Westport, CT, 1975, 81, 87.
111. A valuable contemporary analysis of changes in the Viet Minh security apparatus is Christopher E. Goscha, David G. Marr, and Merle Pribbenow, "The Creation of a Vietnamese Intelligence Service, 1945–1950," in *Exploring Intelligence Archives: Enquires into the Secret State*, R. Gerald Hughes, Peter Jackson, and Len Scott (Eds.), (New York: Routledge, 2008). For Pribbenow's analysis, see 119.
112. Merle L. Pribbenow (Trans.), The Military History Institute of Vietnam, *Victory in Vietnam: The Official History of the People's Army of Vietnam, 1954–1975* (Lawrence, KS: University Press of Kansas, 2002), 5.
113. *Ibid.*, 14.
114. Henry Ainley, *In Order to Die* (London: Burke Publishing Company, 1955), see especially pp. 30–5, 42–3, 96–104. In the brutal violence they inflicted, *Bande Noire* units foreshadowed Provincial Reconnaissance Units active especially in the CIA's Phoenix Program during the later stages of the Second Indochina War.
115. Stathis N. Kalyvas, *The Logic of Violence in Civil War* (Cambridge, UK: Cambridge University Press, 2006), 143.
116. Henry Ainley, *In Order to Die* (London: Burke Publishing Company, 1955), 33.
117. See Appendix IV in Bernard B. Fall, *Street Without Joy* (New York: Da Capo Press, 1963), 399. Fall's annotated bibliography appears in Appendix III in versions prior to the 4th edition of *Street Without Joy*.
118. Douglas Porch, *The French Secret Services: From the Dreyfus Affair to the Gulf War* (New York: Farrar, Strauss and Giroux, 1995), 305.
119. Henry Ainley, *In Order to Die* (London: Burke Publishing Company, 1955), 106.

120. *Ibid.*, 106–7.
121. Neil Sheehan, *A Bright Shining Lie: John Paul Vann and America in Vietnam* (New York: Vintage Books, 1988), 101–3. A Cambodian soldier, Thuong, who Sheehan describes committing atrocities, "had been taught how to soldier in the French colonial paratroops long before the Americans had persuaded Diem to form Ranger companies to fight the guerrillas, and he was proud of his antecedents." (102). Methods like Thuong's are almost identical to those in Ainley's descriptions. In addition to rape, murder, and looting, the extremity of actions against the Vietnamese population suspected of Viet Minh support were severe. Some of these included setting attack dogs upon bound prisoners, kidney and liver targeting, and electrocution of genitalia. See Henry Ainley, *In Order to Die* (London: Burke Publishing Company, 1955), 31–5, 42–3, 96–100.
122. *Ibid.*, 109.
123. Bernard B. Fall, *Street Without Joy: The French Debacle in Indochina* (Guilford, CT: Stackpole Books, 1961), 292–3.
124. *Ibid.*, 294.
125. *Ibid.*, 294.
126. Frantz Fanon, *The Wretched of the Earth* (New York: An Evergreen Book published by Grove Weidenfeld, 1963), 53. Paul Mus also criticized colonialism. See Paul Mus, *Le Destin de l'Union Française: de l'Indochine à l'Afrique* (1954).
127. Frantz Fanon, *The Wretched of the Earth* (New York: An Evergreen Book published by Grove Weidenfeld, 1963), 61.
128. Stathis N. Kalyvas, *The Logic of Violence in Civil War* (Cambridge, UK: Cambridge University Press, 2006), 389.
129. Christopher E. Goscha, *Vietnam: A New History* (New York: Basic Books, 2016), 33.
130. Bernard Fall, *The Viet-Minh Regime: Government and Administration in the Democratic Republic of Vietnam* (New York: Institute of Pacific Relations, 1956), reprinted by Greenwood Press, Westport, CT, 1975, 83.
131. *Ibid.*, 84.
132. Christopher E. Goscha, "A 'Total War' of Decolonization? Social Mobilization and State-Building in Communist Vietnam (1949–54)," *War and Society*, Vol. 31, No. 2 (August 2012), 155.
133. Bernard Fall, "Indochina: The Last Year of the War: Communist Organization and Tactics," *Military Review*, Vol. 36, No. 7 (October 1956), 7, Series 1.06, Box A-1, BBF, JFKL.
134. Bernard Fall, *The Viet-Minh Regime: Government and Administration in the Democratic Republic of Vietnam* (New York: Institute of Pacific Relations, 1956), reprinted by Greenwood Press, Westport, CT, 1975, 85.
135. *Ibid.*, 85.
136. Christopher E. Goscha, "A 'Total War' of Decolonization? Social Mobilization

and State-Building in Communist Vietnam (1949–54)," *War and Society*, Vol. 31, No. 2 (August 2012), 138.
137. Bernard Fall, *The Viet-Minh Regime: Government and Administration in the Democratic Republic of Vietnam* (New York: Institute of Pacific Relations, 1956), reprinted by Greenwood Press, Westport, CT, 1975, 86.
138. *Ibid.*, 86.
139. *Ibid.*, 86.
140. *Ibid.*, 86. Fall did not provide a name for this operation but only referred to it as part of a "Viet-Minh Retreat." It was likely an early effort involved with the campaign that eventually concluded at Dien Bien Phu.
141. Christopher E. Goscha, "A 'Total War' of Decolonization? Social Mobilization and State-Building in Communist Vietnam (1949–54)," *War and Society*, Vol. 31, No. 2 (August 2012), 156.
142. Bernard Fall, *The Viet-Minh Regime: Government and Administration in the Democratic Republic of Vietnam* (New York: Institute of Pacific Relations, 1956), reprinted by Greenwood Press, Westport, CT, 1975, 84.
143. Michael Kaponya, *The French Foreign Legion and Indochina: In Retrospect* (Mustang, OK: Tate Publishing, 2013), 111.
144. Bernard Fall, *The Viet-Minh Regime: Government and Administration in the Democratic Republic of Vietnam* (New York: Institute of Pacific Relations, 1956), reprinted by Greenwood Press, Westport, CT, 1975, 58.
145. *Ibid.*, 58–9.
146. For assessment of Thai-Indochinese networks, see Christopher E. Gosha, *Thailand and the Southeast Asian Networks of the Vietnamese Revolution, 1885–1954* (Richmond, Surrey, UK: Curzon Press, 1999), Nordic Institute of Asian Studies Monograph Series, 79.
147. Jeremy M. Weinstein, "Resources and the Information Problem in Rebel Recruitment," *The Journal of Conflict Resolution*, Vol. 49, No. 4, "Paradigm in Distress? Primary Commodities and Civil War," August 2005, 619.
148. Paul Staniland, *Networks of Rebellion: Explaining Insurgent Cohesion and Collapse* (Ithaca, NY: Cornell University Press, 2014). For Staniland's analysis of communist networks in Southeast Asia, see especially Chapter 7, "Peasants and Commissars," 181–216.
149. Bernard Fall, *The Viet-Minh Regime: Government and Administration in the Democratic Republic of Vietnam* (New York: Institute of Pacific Relations, 1956), reprinted by Greenwood Press, Westport, CT, 1975, 61. For more about the formation of the Pathet Lao, see Sisouk Na Champassak, *Storm Over Laos: A Contemporary History* (New York Praeger, 1961).
150. Fall, *The Viet-Minh Regime, Ibid.*, 61.
151. *Ibid.*, 61.
152. Shawn McHale, "Understanding the Fanatic Mind? The Viet Minh and Race

Hatred in the First Indochina War (1945–1954)," *Journal of Vietnamese Studies*, Vol. 4, Issue 3 (1990), 112.

153. See "2000 Years of War in Viet-Nam," in Bernard B. Fall, *Last Reflections on a War* (New York: Doubleday & Company, 1967), 33–48.

154. See Christopher E. Gosha, *Thailand and the Southeast Asian Networks of the Vietnamese Revolution, 1885–1954* (Richmond, Surrey, UK: Curzon Press, 1999), Nordic Institute of Asian Studies Monograph Series. For further analysis on pre-war networks in Southeast Asia, see Paul Staniland, *Networks of Rebellion: Explaining Insurgent Cohesion and Collapse* (Ithaca, NY: Cornell University Press, 2014), 206–12.

155. Bernard Fall, *The Viet-Minh Regime: Government and Administration in the Democratic Republic of Vietnam* (New York: Institute of Pacific Relations, 1956), reprinted by Greenwood Press, Westport, CT, 1975, 64.

156. In a 1970 study, Paul Langer and Joseph Zasloff offered evidence supporting Fall's earlier analysis on the development of relations between Lao and Vietnamese Communists. According to Langer and Zasloff: "Before 1954, the Viet Minh helped recruit and train the 'seed' cadres—that is, the older generation of Lao Communist movement, who are now in the important civil and military posts—and the Vietnamese style of the Lao Communist organization and operations reveals the significant impact of that training." See Paul F. Langer and Joseph J. Zasloff, *North Vietnam and the Pathet Lao: Partners in the Struggle for Laos* (Cambridge, MA: Harvard University Press, 1970), 116.

157. Cambodia was particularly important during the American era of the Second Indochina/Vietnam War. Kenneth Conboy and John Prados reported that approximately 70 percent of all logistical supplies allocated to the National Liberation Front were channeled through Sihanoukville instead of along the Ho Chi Minh Trail in Laos. The Cambodian port of Sihanoukville eventually funneled, according to Kenneth Conboy, "70 percent of communist arms to the lower provinces of South Vietnam" during the Second Indochina War and would become a "prolonged misreading" of Cambodia's importance. By 1970, the "revelation turned on its head the common wisdom about the role played by the Ho Chi Minh Trail corridor, and obviously it called into question U.S. military strategy that centered on disrupting the logistical flow down the Laotian panhandle." See Kenneth Conboy, *The Cambodian War: Clashing Armies and CIA Covert Operations* (Lawrence, KS: University Press of Kansas, 2013), 33; also, John Prados, *The Blood Road: The Ho Chi Minh Trail and the Vietnam War* (New York: Wiley & Sons, 1999), 296.

158. Dwight D. Eisenhower, *Mandate for Change* (New York: Doubleday & Company, 1963), 336, 352. For Eisenhower's comprehensive analysis of US-French relations pertaining to Indochina, see Chapter 14, "Chaos in Indochina," 332–75.

159. *Ibid.*, 360.

160. *Ibid.*, 373.

161. Bernard B. Fall, *Street Without Joy: The French Debacle in Indochina* (Guilford, CT: Stackpole Books, 1961), 64.
162. Group Mobile units were regimental task forces. Bernard Fall provides a comprehensive account and analysis of Operation Lorraine, a complex four-stage operation in "Set-Piece Battle-II." See pp. 61–106 in *Street Without Joy: The French Debacle in Indochina* (Guilford, CT: Stackpole Books, 1961); see also, Donald Lancaster, *The Emancipation of French Indo-China* (New York: Oxford University Press, 1961), 254–8.
163. Fredrik Logevall, *Embers of War: The Fall of an Empire and the Making of America's Vietnam* (New York: Random House, 2014), 324.
164. On French force strength and organization, see Bernard B. Fall, *Street Without Joy: The French Debacle in Indochina* (Guilford, CT: Stackpole Books, 1961), 78, 96–7.
165. See Fall's footnote on p. 78 of Bernard B. Fall, *Street Without Joy: The French Debacle in Indochina* (Guilford, CT: Stackpole Books, 1961). Also, see Martin Windrow, *The Last Valley: Dien Bien Phu and the French Defeat in Vietnam* (New York: Da Capo Press, 2004), 122–6.
166. Bernard B. Fall, *Street Without Joy: The French Debacle in Indochina* (Guilford, CT: Stackpole Books, 1961), 105.
167. *Ibid.*, 105.
168. *Ibid.*, 105. See especially, "Set-Piece Battle-II", 61–106.
169. *Ibid.*, 106.
170. *Ibid.*, 104–5.
171. *Ibid.*, 63.
172. *Ibid.*, 268.
173. *Ibid.*, 275.
174. For an example of such operations, see Pierre Schoendoerffer, *La 317e Section* (Paris: Gallimard, 1963).
175. Bernard B. Fall, *Street Without Joy: The French Debacle in Indochina* (Guilford, CT: Stackpole Books, 1961), 44.
176. Joint, as used here, means the integration of military service components, air force, army, and navy in the execution of a unified single military operation at tactical, operational, or strategic levels.
177. John Darrell Sherwood, *War in the Shallows: U.S. Navy Coastal and Riverine Warfare in Vietnam 1965–1968* (Washington, DC: Naval History and Heritage Command, 2015), 6.
178. Bernard Fall, "Indochina: The Last Year of the War: Communist Organization and Tactics," *Military Review*, Vol. 36, No. 7 (October 1956), 7, Series 1.06, Box A-1, BBF, JFKL. Qiang Zhai, writing in 1992, reinforced Fall's point by noting, "Under the direction of Chinese advisers, the Vietminh liberated the north-western region in late 1952, which in turn served as a convenient staging area for the

later siege of Dien Bien Phu." See, Zhai, Qiang, "China and the Geneva Conference of 1954," *The China Quarterly*, No. 129 (March 1992), 105.

179. See Fall's references to sources used in *Hell in a Very Small Place* in Bernard B. Fall, *Last Reflections on a War* (New York: Doubleday & Company, 1967), 23–4. Fall's comments on his research trip and experiences gathered in 1953 are cited in *Street Without Joy*, 19–20. The "upshot of my personal experiences and interviews which I could not use for my research went into a diary in the form of letters to the American girl who is now my wife." See Bernard B. Fall, *Street Without Joy: The French Debacle in Indochina* (Guilford, CT: Stackpole Books, 1961), 19–20.

180. Dorothy Fall, *Bernard Fall: Memories of a Soldier-Scholar*, (Washington, DC: Potomac Books, 2007), 75–6. Salicylic acid in merthiolate was a similar concoction used in the South Pacific during World War II. See James A. Michener, *Tales of the South Pacific* (New York: Macmillan Publishing Company, 1947), 132–3.

181. Bernard B. Fall, *Last Reflections on a War* (New York: Doubleday & Company, 1967), 23.

182. Bernard B. Fall, *Street Without Joy: The French Debacle in Indochina* (Guilford, CT: Stackpole Books, 1961), 19.

183. Dorothy Fall, *Bernard Fall: Memories of a Soldier-Scholar*, (Washington, DC: Potomac Books, 2007), 80.

184. *Ibid.*, 80.

185. "Sully comments on Bernard Fall," François Sully Papers and Photographs, *Newsweek* Files, February–March 1967, UMass-Boston, Series II, Subject Files, Box 2, Folder 31, 5.

186. Bernard B. Fall, *Street Without Joy: The French Debacle in Indochina* (Guilford, CT: Stackpole Books, 1961), 21.

187. *Ibid.*, 257.

6. THE WIND AND THE WATER

1. Fall's resume lists over fourteen articles published in 1955 and 1956. See "CV," Box F-1, Series 1.1, BBF, JFKL.
2. Bernard Fall, "Indochina Since Geneva," *Pacific Affairs*, Vol. 28, No. 1 (March 1955); "La Politique Americaine au Viet-Nam," *Politique Étrangère*, July 1955; "The Political-Religious Sects of Viet-Nam," *Pacific Affairs*, Vol. 28, No. 3 (September 1955).
3. Dorothy Fall, *Bernard Fall: Memories of a Soldier-Scholar* (Washington, DC: Potomac Books, 2007), 87.
4. *Ibid.*, 87.
5. HRAF, established in 1949 and headquartered at Yale University, provides cultural information for education and research. See: www.hraf.yale.edu. For Fall's work at HRAF see Bernard Fall, "CV," Series 1.01, Box F-1, BBF, JFKL. At HRAF at American University, Fall completed a wide range of scholarship, contributing to

chapters on a book on Iran (1956), Cambodia (1959), Laos (1960), and others. At SAIS, he edited a handbook on Iraq in 1957 and numerous other studies on Southeast Asia for the US Department of Labor, The Office of Naval Research, the Foreign Policy Institute at the University of Pennsylvania, and Special Studies on Military Aid Programs for the U.S. Senate Foreign Relations Committee. This is only a partial list of studies and projects listed in Fall's CV for the years between 1956 and 1958.
6. See Paul Mus interview, *In the Year of the Pig*, documentary (1968), minute 39:10–41:10. https://www.dailymotion.com/video/x2zpgbw
7. Robert Vitalis, *White World Order, Black Power Politics: The Birth of American International Relations* (Ithaca, NY: Cornell University Press, 2005), 12.
8. Dorothy Fall provides a detailed overview of Bernard Fall's contributions to the intellectual life at Howard University in *Bernard Fall: Memories of a Soldier-Scholar* (Washington, DC: Potomac Books, 2007), 139–47. See Carmichael's reflections on Fall as his teacher in Stokely Carmichael, *Ready for Revolution: The Life and Struggles of Stokely Carmichael* (Kwame Ture) (New York: Scribner, 2005), 596–7.
9. *Ibid.*, 102.
10. Bernard Fall, "CV," Series 1.01, Box F-1, BBF, JFKL.
11. *Ibid.*
12. *Ibid.*
13. Bernard Fall, "Indochina Since Geneva," *Pacific Affairs*, Vol. 28, No. 1 (March 1955), 3.
14. *Ibid.*, 3.
15. Edward Miller, *Misalliance: Ngo Dinh Diem, the United States, and the Fate of South Vietnam* (Cambridge, MA: Harvard University Press, 2013), 124, 140.
16. Bernard Fall, "Indochina Since Geneva," *Pacific Affairs*, Vol. 28, No. 1 (March 1955), 5.
17. Quoted in *Ibid.*, 5.
18. Seth Jacobs, *America's Miracle Man in Vietnam: Ngo Dinh Diem, Religion, Race, and U.S. Intervention in Southeast Asia, 1950–1957* (Durham, NC: Duke University Press, 2004), 5.
19. *Ibid.* 57.
20. Bao Dai, as quoted in Jacobs, *Ibid.*, 57.
21. *Ibid.*, 57.
22. Bernard B. Fall, *The Two Vietnams: A Political and Military Analysis* (New York: Praeger, 1963), 254.
23. On these elections/referendums, see Edward Miller, *Misalliance: Ngo Dinh Diem, the United States, and the Fate of South Vietnam* (Cambridge, MA: Harvard University Press, 2013), 136–48.

24. Bernard B. Fall, *The Two Vietnams: A Political and Military Analysis* (New York: Praeger, 1963), 257.
25. *Ibid.*, 140–2.
26. Amry Vandenbosch and Richard A. Butwell, *Southeast Asia Among the World Powers* (Lexington, KY: University of Kentucky Press, 1957), 129.
27. Robert D. Schulzinger, *A Time for War: The United States and Vietnam, 1941–1975* (New York: Oxford University Press, 1997), 86–7.
28. Zhai, Qiang, "China and the Geneva Conference of 1954," *The China Quarterly*, No. 129, March 1992, 112.
29. Amry Vandenbosch and Richard A. Butwell, *Southeast Asia Among the World Powers* (Lexington, KY: University of Kentucky Press, 1957), 129.
30. George C. Herring, *America's Longest War: The United States and Vietnam, 1950–1975* (New York: Alfred A. Knopf, 1979), 41.
31. Bernard B. Fall, "Indo-China's Precarious Four Years," *The Sunday Star*, 13 July 1958, Washington, DC, Series 1.06, Box A-2, BBF, JFKL. On the failure to hold elections, see also A.J. Langguth, *Our Vietnam: The War 1954–1975* (New York: Simon and Schuster, 2000), 180.
32. Bernard B. Fall, *Viet-Nam Witness, 1953–1966* (New York: Frederick A. Praeger, 1966), 78.
33. One of the earliest and most extensive analysis of Diem was Fall's "Ngo Dinh Diem: Man and Myth" in Bernard B. Fall, *The Two Vietnams: A Political and Military Analysis* (New York: Praeger, 1963). See pp. 234–54.
34. Bernard Fall, "Indochina Since Geneva," *Pacific Affairs*, Vol. 28, No. 1 (March 1955).
35. *Ibid.*, 7.
36. The 1954 conflict between forces allied to Chief of Staff of the Vietnamese National Army, Nguyen Van Hinh, and Ngo Dinh Diem's faction foreshadowed internal threats to Diem's administration later in April 1960, when eighteen members of a dissenting political party, the "Bloc for Liberty and Progress," issued the Caravelle Manifesto (named after the Saigon hotel where the statement was signed). According to historian Ronald Bruce Frankum, Jr. the 1960 manifesto, "represented a legitimate threat to the Saigon government and raised questions [concerning Diem's political legitimacy] that [Ambassador Elbridge] Durbrow had long believed to be valid." See Ronald Bruce Frankum, Jr., *Vietnam's Year of the Rat: Elbridge Durbrow, Ngo Dinh Diem and the Turn in U.S. Relations, 1959–1961* (Jefferson, NC: McFarland and Company, 2014), 50.
37. For a comprehensive study of the "Hinh" crisis, see "Sink or Swim with Ngo Dinh Diem," in Jessica Chapman, *Cauldron of Resistance: Ngo Dinh Diem, The United States, and 1950s Southern Vietnam* (Ithaca, NY: Cornell University Press, 2013).
38. Donald Lancaster, *The Emancipation of French Indochina* (New York: Oxford University Press, 1961), 283. Tam was compelled to resign, according to Lancaster,

because of disagreements with "the imperial cabinet at Dalat, and also with the French authorities." Lancaster notes that Tam was also under a political and social cloud after his daughter received wedding gifts from the Chinese community in Cholon.

39. Bernard Fall, "Indochina Since Geneva," *Pacific Affairs*, Vol. 28, No. 1 (March 1955), 6.
40. *Ibid.*, 22.
41. George C. Herring also described political disputes between France and the United States concerning support for Diem. See George Herring, *America's Longest War: The United States and Vietnam, 1950–1975* (New York: Alfred A. Knopf, 1979), 53–4.
42. Bernard Fall, "Indochina Since Geneva," *Pacific Affairs*, Vol. 28, No. 1 (March 1955), 21–2.
43. Jayne Susan Warner, *Peasant Politics and Religious Sectarianism: Peasant and Priest in the Cao Dai in Viet Nam* (New Haven, CT: Monograph Series 23/Yale University Southeast Asia Studies, 1981), 45.
44. Dorothy Fall, *Bernard Fall: Memories of a Soldier-Scholar* (Washington, DC: Potomac Books, 2007), 77–8.
45. Bernard B. Fall, "The Political-Religious Sects of Viet-Nam." *Pacific Affairs*, Vol. 28, No. 3 (September 1955).
46. Clellan S. Ford, *Human Relations Area Files: 1949–1969, A Twenty-Year Report* (New Haven, CT: Human Relations Area Files Incorporated, 1970).
47. *Ibid.*, 15.
48. *Ibid.*, see Appendix for reference to Fall as a HRAF contributor/author on p. 30 and the corresponding publications to which he contributed on p. 29.
49. *Ibid.*, see p. 54 in Appendix F: *HRAF Publications—1949–1969*.
50. Bernard B. Fall, "The Political-Religious Sects of Viet-Nam." *Pacific Affairs*, Vol. 28, No. 3 (September 1955), 236. For more on the Buu Son Ky Huong tradition, on which Hoa Hao belief is based, see Hue-Tam Ho Tai, *Millenarianism and Peasant Politics in Vietnam* (Cambridge, MA: Harvard University Press, 1983). For more on the Cao Dai, see Jayne Susan Warner, *Peasant Politics and Religious Sectarianism: Peasant and Priest in the Cao Dai in Viet Nam* (New Haven, CT: Monograph Series 23/Yale University Southeast Asia Studies, 1981).
51. Bernard B. Fall, "The Political-Religious Sects of Viet-Nam." *Pacific Affairs*, Vol. 28, No. 3 (September 1955), 241.
52. *Ibid.*, 243.
53. Hue-Tam Ho Tai, *Millenarianism and Peasant Politics in Vietnam* (Cambridge, MA: Harvard University Press, 1983), 164.
54. *Ibid.* 3.
55. *Ibid.*, 19.

56. Bernard B. Fall, "The Political-Religious Sects of Viet-Nam." *Pacific Affairs*, Vol. 28, No. 3 (September 1955), 246.
57. Ellen J. Hammer, *The Struggle for Indochina 1940–1955: Viet Nam and the French Experience* (Palo Alto, CA: Stanford University Press, 1955), 52.
58. Bernard B. Fall, "The Political-Religious Sects of Viet-Nam." *Pacific Affairs*, Vol. 28, No. 3 (September 1955), 247.
59. Hue-Tam Ho Tai, *Millenarianism and Peasant Politics in Vietnam* (Cambridge, MA: Harvard University Press, 1983), vii.
60. Bernard B. Fall, "The Political-Religious Sects of Viet-Nam." *Pacific Affairs*, Vol. 28, No. 3 (September 1955), 243.
61. *Ibid.*, 251.
62. *Ibid.*, 251.
63. Bernard Fall, "Indochina Since Geneva," *Pacific Affairs*, Vol. 28, No. 1 (March 1955), 20.
64. *Ibid.*, 22.
65. Bernard B. Fall, "The Political-Religious Sects of Viet-Nam." *Pacific Affairs*, Vol. 28, No. 3 (September 1955), 251.
66. Fall's views on the Cao Dai and Hoa Hao were well respected by other contemporary scholars. Joseph Buttinger, for example, commented on Fall's 1955 article, "The Political Religious Sects of Viet-Nam," stating: "it is probably the best short report on, and discussion of, the origins of leadership, and the political role of the Cao Dai, Hoa Hao, and Binh Xuyen, and their destructive effect on the political life in South Vietnam." See Joseph Buttinger, *Vietnam: A Dragon Embattled, Vol. 2, Vietnam at War* (New York: Praeger, 1967), 1265–6. This view contrasts strongly with Jérémy Jammes' criticism that Fall's perspectives on the Cao Dai were "cynical." See Jammes, *Les Oracles du Cao Dai: Étude d'un Mouvement Religieux Vietnamien et de ses Reseaux* (Paris: Les Indes Savants, 2014), 24–5.
67. Bernard Fall, "Indochina Since Geneva," *Pacific Affairs*, Vol. 28, No. 1 (March 1955), 8.
68. "Memorandum from Edward Lansdale to J. Lawton Collins," 16 March 1955, J. Lawton Collins Papers, 1896–1975, Subseries D, Box 28, Folder 1, Eisenhower Presidential Library.
69. The conflict is known as the Battle of Saigon. See Jessica Chapman, *Cauldron of Resistance: Ngo Dinh Diem, The United States, and 1950s Southern Vietnam* (Ithaca, NY: Cornell University Press, 2013), 110–13.
70. Edward Geary Lansdale, *In the Midst of Wars: An American's Mission to Southeast Asia* (New York: Fordham University Press, 1991), 248.
71. A.J. Langguth, *Our Vietnam: The War 1954–1975* (New York: Simon and Schuster, 2000), 93.
72. Carl M. Marcy, Foreign Relations Committee, Chief of Staff, "Interview #5 Fulbright Breaks with Johnson," 19 October 1984, interviewed by Donald A. Ritchie, *United States Senate Historical Office—Oral History Project*, p. 156.

73. Bernard Fall, "Indochina Since Geneva," *Pacific Affairs*, Vol. 28, No. 1 (March 1955), 8.
74. Jessica Chapman, *Cauldron of Resistance: Ngo Dinh Diem, The United States, and 1950s Southern Vietnam* (Ithaca, NY: Cornell University Press, 2013), 88.
75. Ibid., 88.
76. Bernard B. Fall, "The Political-Religious Sects of Viet-Nam." *Pacific Affairs*, Vol. 28, No. 3 (September 1955), 251.
77. Bernard Fall, "Indochina Since Geneva," *Pacific Affairs*, Vol. 28, No. 1 (March 1955), 15.
78. According to Nguyen Thi Dinh, "The 'National Front for the Liberation of South Vietnam'—the sole organization leading the resistance by the entire population of the South—was timely created and presented to the people on December 20, 1960." See Nguyen Thi Dinh, *No Other Road to Take: Memoir of Nguyen Thi Dinh*, translated by Mai V. Elliott (Ithaca, NY: Southeast Asia Program Publications, Cornell University, 2000).
79. For a detailed account of the Battle of Saigon, see Seth Jacobs, *America's Miracle Man in Vietnam: Ngo Dinh Diem, Religion, Race, and U.S. Intervention in Southeast Asia, 1950–1957* (Durham, NC: Duke University Press, 2004). See especially Chapter 5, "The Sects and the Gangs Mean to Get Rid of the Saint: 'Lightning Joe' Collins and the Battle for Saigon."
80. *The Pentagon Papers, as Published by the New York Times* (New York: Quadrangle Books, 1971), 20–1. See Fox Butterfield, "Lansdale in the Breach,"
81. Ibid., 21.
82. Ibid., 21–2.
83. For a comprehensive study of the Battle of Saigon, see Jessica Chapman, *Cauldron of Resistance: Ngo Dinh Diem, The United States, and 1950s Southern Vietnam* (Ithaca, NY: Cornell University Press, 2013).
84. For detailed analysis on Diem's Catholic supporters in the United States, see Seth Jacobs, *America's Miracle Man in Vietnam: Ngo Dinh Diem, Religion, Race, and U.S. Intervention in Southeast Asia, 1950–1957* (Durham, NC: Duke University Press, 2004). On Ngo Dinh Diem, also see Edward Miller, *Misalliance: Ngo Dinh Diem, the United States, and the Fate of South Vietnam* (Cambridge, MA: Harvard University Press, 2013).
85. See Chapter 12, "Ngo Dinh Diem—Man and Myth," and Chapter 13, "Ngo's Republic" in Bernard B. Fall, *The Two Viet-Nams: A Political and Military History* (New York: Praeger, 1963, 1st edition).
86. Bernard B. Fall, "The Political-Religious Sects of Viet-Nam." *Pacific Affairs*, Vol. 28, No. 3 (September 1955), 253.
87. Bernard Fall, "Indochina Since Geneva," *Pacific Affairs*, Vol. 28, No. 1 (March 1955), 23.

88. J. Lawton Collins Papers, United States Army War College, Heritage and Education Center, Carlisle, Pennsylvania, Box 1, Folder 3, Interview, 418.
89. General J. Lawton Collins, *Lightning Joe: An Autobiography* (Baton Rouge, LA: Louisiana State University Press, 1979), 390. For Collins' account of his time as special representative to Vietnam, see Chapter 19, "Mission to Vietnam, 1954–1955."
90. *Ibid.*, 391.
91. *Ibid.*, 391.
92. *Ibid.*, 404.
93. *Ibid.*, 404.
94. *Ibid.*, 408.
95. Bernard B. Fall, "Representative Government in the State of Vietnam, 1949–54," *Far Eastern Survey*, American Institute of Pacific Relations, August 1954, 122–6, Series 1.06, Box A-01, BBF, JFKL.
96. Bernard B. Fall, "The Cease-Fire in Indochina—An Appraisal," *Far Eastern Survey*, Vol. 23, No. 9 (September 1954), 135–93, Series 1.06, Box A-01, BBF, JFKL. Fall wrote another short companion piece in the subsequent October 1954 edition of *Far Eastern Survey*. See Series 1.06, Box A-01, BBF, JFKL.
97. "Former Saigon Envoy and Wife Found Dead," AP, 25 July 1986, *New York Times*, Section B, 4.
98. Amry Vandenbosch and Richard A. Butwell, *Southeast Asia Among the World Powers* (Lexington, KY: University of Kentucky Press, 1957), 151.
99. *Ibid.*, 149.
100. For more on the Cai San Project, see Edward Miller, *Misalliance: Ngo Dinh Diem, the United States, and the Fate of South Vietnam* (Cambridge, MA: Harvard University Press, 2013), 165–70.
101. *Ibid.*, 152.
102. Richard W. Lindholm, (Ed.), *Viet-Nam—The First Five Years: An International Symposium* (Lansing, MI: Michigan State University Press, 1959), 94.
103. *Ibid.*, 94.
104. Bernard B. Fall, *Last Reflections on a War* (New York: Doubleday & Company, 1967), 196.
105. *Ibid.*, 196.
106. Zhai, Qiang, "China and the Geneva Conference of 1954," *The China Quarterly*, No. 129 (March 1992), 113.
107. Saville R. Davis, *Christian Science Monitor*, 10 January 1956. Quoted in Amry Vandenbosch and Richard A. Butwell, *Southeast Asia Among the World Powers* (Lexington, KY: University of Kentucky Press, 1957), 127.
108. *Ibid.*, 127.
109. Bernard B. Fall, *Last Reflections on a War* (New York: Doubleday & Company, 1967), 184.

110. *Ibid.*, 198.
111. David W.P. Elliott, *The Vietnamese War: Revolution and Social Change in the Mekong Delta 1930–1975* (Armonk, NY: M.E. Sharpe, 2003), 86–7. Ordinance 6 and similar decrees in 1956 were followed by other excessive laws and, according to Elliott, included "Diem's repression of the revolutionary forces via the Communist Denunciation campaign as well as the even more draconian Decree 10/59 (National Security Law)." See pages 86–7. Fall addressed the Communist Denunciation campaign and Decree 10/59 (National Security Law) in his later scholarship.
112. Bernard B. Fall, *Last Reflections on a War* (New York: Doubleday & Company, 1967), 198–9.
113. John T. McAlister, Jr. and Paul Mus, *The Vietnamese and Their Revolution* (New York: Harper Torchbooks, 1970), 161. For additional commentary on the importance of the village, see McAlister and Mus "The Village Foundation of Vietnamese Society," in *Ibid.*, 50–4.
114. Bernard B. Fall, *Last Reflections on a War* (New York: Doubleday & Company, 1967), 215.
115. *Ibid.*, 218.
116. *Ibid.*, 215.
117. Bernard B. Fall, *Last Reflections on a War* (New York: Doubleday & Company, 1967), 199.
118. See Paul Mus' interview, *In the Year of the Pig*, documentary (1968), minute 39:10–41:10. https://www.dailymotion.com/video/x2zpgbw
119. Lien-Hang T. Nguyen, *Hanoi's War: An International History of the War for Peace in Vietnam* (Chapel Hill, NC: University of North Carolina Press, 2012), 43. According to Lien-Hang T. Nguyen, Resolution 15, adopted on 22 January 1959, "sanctioned armed force to support the political struggle in the South, it constituted the first stage in Le Duan and Le Duc Tho's campaign for total war." See p. 47.
120. Bernard B. Fall, *Last Reflections on a War* (New York: Doubleday & Company, 1967), 203, 241.
121. See "End of a Task Force," in Bernard B. Fall, *Street Without Joy* (New York: Shocken Paperback, 1972), 185.
122. *Groupement Mobile 100* was officially dissolved by French officials on 1 September 1954 after their defeat in July of that year. The French army also had armored groups, known as *Groupement Blindés* (GB). See *Ibid.*, 384.
123. Bernard B. Fall, *The Viet-Minh Regime: Government and Administration in the Democratic Republic of Vietnam* (New York: Institute of Pacific Relations, 1956), reprinted by Greenwood Press, Westport, CT, 1975, 152.
124. *Ibid.*, 152.
125. Benedict J. Tria Kerkvliet, *The Power of Everyday Politics: How Vietnamese*

Peasants Transformed National Policy (Ithaca, NY: Cornell University Press, 2005), 8.

126. Bernard B. Fall, "Crisis in North Viet-Nam," *Far Eastern Survey*, January 1957, Series 1.06, Box A-1, BBF, JFKL.
127. Bernard B. Fall, *The Viet-Minh Regime: Government and Administration in the Democratic Republic of Vietnam* (New York: Institute of Pacific Relations, 1956), reprinted by Greenwood Press, Westport, CT, 1975, 132.
128. Fall also described these revolts in a 1958 report for the US Information Agency, see Bernard B. Fall, "Three Years of Viet-Minh Rule in North Vietnam, 1954–1957," USIA Washington, DC, 1958, Series 1.05, Box P-03, BBF, JFKL. This report is also available at the US Army War College, Ridgway Hall, DS558.153. F34.1958.
129. Bernard B. Fall, "Indo-China's Precarious Four Years," *The Sunday Star*, 13 July 1958, Series 1. 06, Box A-2, BBF, JFKL.
130. *Ibid.*
131. Bernard B. Fall, "Crisis in North Viet-Nam," *Far Eastern Survey*, January 1957, 14., Series 1.06, Box A-1, BBF, JFKL.
132. *Ibid.*, 15.
133. *Ibid.*, 15.
134. *Ibid.*, 15.
135. *Ibid.*, 15.
136. *Ibid.*, 15.
137. Benedict J. Tria Kerkvliet, *The Power of Everyday Politics: How Vietnamese Peasants Transformed National Policy* (Ithaca, NY: Cornell University Press, 2005), 78.
138. *Ibid.*, 155.
139. Dorothy Fall, *Bernard Fall: Memories of a Soldier-Scholar* (Washington, DC: Potomac Books, 2007), 107.
140. Bernard Fall, "CV," Series 1.01, Box F-1, BBF, JFKL. The Southeast Asia Studies Department at Cornell University also sponsored and co-published this study.
141. Bernard Fall, *The International Position of South Vietnam, 1954–1958*, Series, 1.05, Boxes P-01 and P-02, BBF, JFKL.
142. This title is available in Bernard Fall Papers, Series, 1.05, Box P-03, BBF, JFKL and also in mimeograph form at the US Army War College, Heritage and Education Center, Carlisle, PA, Call Number: DS 558.153.F4 1958/OCLC Number: 22149988.
143. Bernard Fall, "CV," Series 1.01, Box F-1, 7, BBF, JFKL. Fall obtained an American Council of Learned Societies (ACLS) travel grant to finance his trip to Pakistan in February 1958. See also, Dorothy Fall, *Bernard Fall: Memories of a Soldier-Scholar* (Washington, DC: Potomac Books, 2007), 107.
144. Bernard Fall, "CV," Series 1.01, Box F-1, 7, BBF, JFKL.

145. Dorothy Fall, *Bernard Fall: Memories of a Soldier-Scholar* (Washington, DC: Potomac Books, 2007), 108.
146. *Ibid.*, 108–9.
147. *Ibid.*, 109.
148. Bernard Fall, "Will South Viet-Nam Be Next?" *The Nation*, 31 May 1958, Series 1.06, Box A-2, 489, BBF, JFKL.
149. Discussed earlier, Tran Van Chuong's daughter was Tran Le Xuan (also known as Madame Nhu). Tran Le Xuan was married to Ngo Dinh Nhu, a key senior leader of the Can Lao political party, and Ngo Dinh Diem's brother.
150. Bernard Fall, *The International Position of South Vietnam, 1954–1958*, "Author's Preface," page i. Series 1.05, Boxes P-01 and P-02, BBF, JFKL.
151. *Ibid.*, iii.
152. *Ibid.*, iii.
153. See "Speeches not by Fall, Tran Van Chuong, 11 April 1957," Series 1.4, Box SC-1A, BBF, JFKL.
154. *Ibid.*, transcript p. 5.
155. Bernard Fall, "Will South Viet-Nam Be Next?" *The Nation* (31 May 1958), Series 1.06, Box A-2, 489, BBF, JFKL.
156. *Ibid.*, 489.
157. David W.P. Elliott, *The Vietnamese War: Revolution and Social Change in the Mekong Delta 1930–1975* (Armonk, NY: M.E. Sharpe, 2003), 87.
158. The ICA operated from 30 June 1955 to 4 September 1961 and was responsible for foreign assistance and coordinating non-military security programs. USAID was not established until the Foreign Assistance Act of 4 September 1961 and signed into law in November 1961. See USAID.gov, "USAID History," at https://www.usaid.gov/who-we-are/usaid-history; also, see James S. Olson, *Dictionary of the Vietnam War* (New York: Greenwood Press, 1988), 464–5.
159. Bernard Fall, "Will South Viet-Nam Be Next?" *The Nation* (31 May 1958), Series 1.06, Box A-2, 490, BBF, JFKL.
160. "Carl Marcy letter to Richard Nolte," 22 February 1964, 1. Institute of Current World Affairs, http://www.icwa.org/wp-content/uploads/2015/09/CMM-8.pdf (accessed 15 February 2019). Carl Marcy was Chief of Staff for the Senate Foreign Relations Committee, and Richard Nolte was the Director of the Institute of Current World Affairs in 1965. The Institute of Current World Affairs was established in 1925. For more on the Institute, go to www.icwa.org. Marcy described the use of these funds abroad after a yearlong trip around the world studying the effects of United States foreign policy. See "Carl M. Marcy, 77, Long Chief of Staff of Key Senate Panel," Obituary, *New York Times*, 21 September 1990, available at: https://www.nytimes.com/1990/09/21/obituaries/carl-m-marcy-77-long-chief-of-staff-of-key-senate-panel.html
161. See "Carl Marcy letter to Richard Nolte," 22 February 1964, 1. Institute of

Current World Affairs, http://www.icwa.org/wp-content/uploads/2015/09/CMM-8.pdf (accessed 15 February 2019).
162. Bernard Fall, "Will South Viet-Nam Be Next?" *The Nation* (31 May 1958), Series 1.06, Box A-2, 490, BBF, JFKL.
163. *Ibid.*, 490.
164. Fall acknowledged Wesley Fishel in Bernard B. Fall, "The International Position of South Viet-Nam, 1954–1958," iii. Available at Box P-01, Series 1.5. BBF, JFKL.
165. According to Brigadier General James Lawton Collins, Jr., (Lawton Collins' son), MAAG also assumed responsibility for training the Civil Guard, "with the cost to be borne by the International Cooperation Administration." See Brigadier General James Lawton Collins, Jr., *The Development and Training of the South Vietnamese Army, 1950–1972* (Washington, DC: Department of the Army, 1975), 19.
166. Bernard Fall, "Will South Viet-Nam Be Next?" *The Nation* (31 May 1958), Series 1.06, Box A-2, 491.
167. *Ibid.*, 491.
168. *Ibid.*, 491–2.
169. *Ibid.*, 491–2.
170. *Ibid.*, 492.
171. According to Mark Atwood Lawrence, "By 1954, the United States had sent as much aid to Indochina as it had to France itself under the Marshall Plan." 285 in Mark Atwood Lawrence, *Assuming the Burden: Europe and the American Commitment to War in Vietnam* (Berkeley: University of California Press, 2005); also, see "Military Expenditures by France and Associated States in Indo-China, 1946–1954," 259–61 in Allan B. Cole (Ed.), *Conflict in Indo-China and International Repercussion: A Documentary History, 1945–1955* (Ithaca, NY: The Fletcher School of Law and Diplomacy, Tufts University and the Southeast Asia Program, Cornell University Press, 1956).
172. Charles L. Mee, Jr., *The Marshall Plan* (New York: Touchstone, 1984), 243. See Chapter 24, "The Marshall Plan in Action."
173. Jacob J. Kaplan, Interviewed by W. Haven North, 22 March 1999, the Association for Diplomatic Studies and Training, Foreign Affairs Oral History Project, Foreign Assistance Series.
174. *Ibid.*, 5.
175. *Ibid.*, 5.
176. US records on US Foreign Assistance to Vietnam are located in Record Group (RG) 469, with USOM records on Civilian Assistance, Community Development, Land Reform, and Migration and Resettlement located in Entries UD-1442, 1446, 1447, 1438, 1437, 1452, 1453, 1454, The National Archives Records and Administration (NARA), College Park, Maryland.

177. Robert Scigliano, *South Vietnam: Nation Under Stress* (Boston, MA: Houghton Mifflin Company, 1963), 127.
178. Michael J. Hogan, *The Marshall Plan: America, Britain, and the reconstruction of Western Europe, 1947–1952* (New York: Cambridge University Press, 1987), 106, 149.
179. For more on limitations to the ICA, see http://www.usaid.gov/about_usaid/usaidhist.html, pp. 1–2.
180. The full report was titled "Military Assistance Program of the United States: Two Studies and a Report by a Special Civilian-Military Review Panel, The Institute of War and Peace Studies at Columbia University, and the Systems Analysis Corporation." *Legislative History of the Committee on Foreign Relations, United States Senate, 85th Congress*, Document 128, US Printing Office, Washington, DC, 1959, Bernard Fall, "CV," p. 4. Series 1.01, Box F-1, BBF, JFKL.
181. See "A Factual Epilogue," pp. 271–85 in William J. Lederer and Eugene Burdick, *The Ugly American* (New York: W.W. Norton & Company, 1958), 281. See especially the stories of Tom Knox and Homer Atkins in Chapters 14 and 17, respectively.
182. Bernard B. Fall, *Last Reflections on a War* (New York: Doubleday & Company, 1967), 54.
183. *Ibid.*, 49.
184. Bernard Fall, "Will South Viet-Nam Be Next?" *The Nation* (31 May 1958), Series 1.06, Box A-2, 491, BBF, JFKL.
185. *Ibid.*, 491.
186. *Ibid.*, 492.
187. "Cambodia-Contracts-Bernard Fall," Records of U.S. Foreign Assistance Agencies, 1948–1961, "Taubenblatt Memo," 6 June 1958, Record Group [RG] 469, Entry P85, Box 9, National Archives and Records Administration, [NARA], College Park, Maryland.
188. Dorothy Fall, *Bernard Fall: Memories of a Soldier-Scholar* (Washington, DC: Potomac Books, 2007), 115.
189. Bernard Fall, "Will South Viet-Nam Be Next?" *The Nation* (31 May 1958), Series 1.06, Box A-2, 493, BBF, JFKL.
190. *Ibid.* Institutional problems in aid delivery were connected to political legitimacy in multiple ways and were targeted by communist organizations through careful selection. See "The Need for Situational Thinking" in Philip Selznick, *The Organizational Weapon: A Study in Bolshevik Strategy and Tactics* (Glencoe, IL: The Free Press of Glencoe, 1960), 317–21. Selznick's study was first published by the RAND Corporation in 1952.
191. *Ibid.*, 493.
192. Bernard Fall, "Abstract of AAS Paper," Series, 1.04, Box SC-01, BBF, JFKL.
193. US Foreign Assistance problems that Fall pointed out in 1957 and 1958 were

later described and reappraised before the U.S. Congress in 1961. See "President Kennedy's Message on U.S. Foreign Aid Programs," In *CQ Almanac 1961*, 17th ed., 888–91 (Washington, DC: *Congressional Quarterly*, 1961). http://library.cqpress.com/cqalmanac/cqal61-879-29200-1371311 The Foreign Assistance Act of 1961 consolidated Kennedy's vision to fix these problems.
194. *Ibid.*
195. The author acknowledges Dr. Robert Fahs' scholarship on this subject. Fahs, an archivist for the National Archives and Records Administration, was the first to write about the NARA files discussed in this section after they were declassified and available at the NARA facility in College Park, Maryland. See Fahs, "Back to a Forgotten Street: Bernard B. Fall and the Limits of Armed Intervention," in *Prologue*, The US National Archives and Records Administration, Spring 2011, Vol. 43, No. 1.
196. The primary sources referenced are "Cambodia-Contracts-Bernard Fall," Records of US Foreign Assistance Agencies, 1948–1961, Record Group [RG] 469, Entry P85, Box 9, National Archives and Records Administration, [NARA], College Park, Maryland. Hereafter, references to this file/source in subsequent notes will be cited NARA RG469/EntryP85/Box 9 as in: "source title," NARA RG469/P85/9. USOM were the local missions of the International Coordination Administration (ICA) which administered U.S. foreign assistance programs.
197. "Memorandum of Conversation between Thomas Corcoran and Bernard Fall," 3 June 1958, NARA RG469/P85/9.
198. "Fall letter to Eliot, ICA," 1 November 1957, NARA RG469/P85/9.
199. "Fall Application," 25 March 1958, NARA RG469/P85/9.
200. *Ibid.*
201. "Scope of Service," undated, NARA RG469/P85/9.
202. *Ibid.*
203. "Security Clearance Cablegram," 8 April 1958, NARA RG469/P85/9.
204. Dorothy Fall, *Bernard Fall: Memories of a Soldier-Scholar* (Washington, DC: Potomac Books, 2007), 121, 124.
205. "Telegram," 24 April 1958, NARA RG469/P85/9.
206. "Department of State Telegram," 25 May 1958, NARA RG469/P85/9.
207. "Eliot ICA Memorandum," 26 May 1958, NARA RG469/P85/9.
208. "Elting Telegram to Secretary of State Dulles," 28 May 1958, NARA RG469/P85/9.
209. "Record of Confidential Telephone Call, Hough to Eliot," 29 May 1958, NARA RG469/P85/9.
210. *Ibid.*
211. "ICA Cablegram," 9 June 1958, NARA RG469/P85/9.
212. "Memorandum of Conversation between Thomas Corcoran and Bernard Fall," 3 June 1958, NARA RG469/P85/9.

213. *Ibid.*
214. This news outlet was established in 1947. For more information, see https://www.voatiengviet.com/
215. "Interviews: Vietnam Service, Association for Asian Studies, April 9, 1958," Series 1.1, Box F-01, BBF, JFKL.
216. *Ibid.*
217. Taubenblatt Memo," 6 June 1958, NARA RG469/P85/9.
218. "Bunting Memo," 7 June 1958, NARA RG 469/P85/9.
219. "Bunting Memo—II," 7 June 1958, NARA, RG469/P85/9.
220. "State Department Memo," 12 June 1958, NARA RG469/P85/9.

7. AN UNASSAILABLE POSITION OF TOTAL WEAKNESS

1. Bernard B. Fall, "South Viet-Nam's Internal Problems," *Pacific Affairs*, Vol. 31, No. 3 (September 1958), Series 1.06, Box A-02, BBF, JFKL.
2. The Army of the Republic of Vietnam was founded in December 1955 and MAAG was originally created in 1950 to coordinate assistance to France for its operations in Indochina. See George Herring *America's Longest War: The United States and Vietnam, 1950–1975* (New York: Alfred A. Knopf, 1979), 57.
3. *Ibid.*, 57.
4. In Iraq, according to Anthony Cordesman, "The Department of Defense has reported that it spent over $765 billion on the Iraq conflict and the fight against ISIS as of March 31, 2019—and this is only a fraction of the direct cost. There is not clear stream of reporting on State of USAID spending, but it seems to have reached another $100 billion." The difference between Defense of State/USAID spending echoes George Herring's research of 78 percent Defense vs. 22 percent all other aid in Vietnam between 1955–61. For Herring's analysis, see *Ibid.*, 56–8. For Cordesman's analysis, see Anthony H. Cordesman, "America's Failed Strategy in the Middle East: Losing Iraq and the Gulf," Center for Strategic and International Studies, 2 January 2020.
5. Bernard B. Fall, *The Two Vietnams: A Political and Military Analysis* (New York: Praeger, 1963), 399.
6. Bernard Fall, "CV," Series 1.01, Box F-1, BBF, JFKL.
7. Dorothy Fall, *Bernard Fall: Memories of a Soldier-Scholar* (Washington, DC: Potomac Books, 2007), 142; Ralph Bunche Biography, nobelprize.org, https://nobelprize.org/prizes/peace/1950/bunche/biographical/
8. Ralph Bunche Biography, nobelprize.org, https://nobelprize.org/prizes/peace/1950/bunche/biographical/
9. Dorothy Fall, *Bernard Fall: Memories of a Soldier-Scholar* (Washington, DC: Potomac Books, 2007), 141.
10. Bernard Fall "Letter to the Editor," *The Nation*, 9 July 1958, Series 1.01, Box F-01, BBF, JFKL. The multiple letters referred to are located in the same folder.

11. *Ibid.*
12. *Ibid.*
13. Bernard Fall "Will South Viet-Nam Be Next? reprint, *Howard Magazine*, November 1958, Vol. 1, No. 1, Series 1.06, Box A-2, BBF, JFKL.
14. "Howard University Biography," Series 1.10, Box AM-1, BBF, JFKL.
15. Bernard Fall, "Book Reviews by Fall," Series 1.08, Box BR-1, BBF, JFKL.
16. *Ibid.*
17. David W.P. Elliott, *The Vietnamese War: Revolution and Social Change in the Mekong Delta 1930–1975* (Armonk, NY: M.E. Sharpe, 2003), 110.
18. Fall's article for *Pacific Affairs*, "South Viet-Nam's Internal Problems," is available in the Bernard Fall Papers, Series 1.1, Box F-1, BBF, JFKL. It was commercially reprinted as "The Birth of an Insurgency," in Chapter 13 of Bernard B. Fall, *Viet-Nam Witness, 1953–1966* (New York: Praeger 1966). Due to its greater accessibility, page number references to this article are taken from *Viet-Nam Witness, 1953–1966*.
19. Historian Robert Buzzanco argued that the Republic of Vietnam was "fictive." Buzzanco's and historian Keith Taylor's positions on the Vietnam War included debates over the South Vietnamese state's authenticity. See Edward Miller, "War-Stories: The Taylor–Buzzanco Debate and How We Think About the Vietnam War," *Journal of Vietnamese Studies*, Vol 1. No. 1–2 (February–August 2006), 466–7. Fall's 1958 article for *Pacific Affairs* began with a citation expressing that "the Republic of Viet-Nam has taken on substance as a state." See Bernard B. Fall, *Viet-Nam Witness, 1953–1966* (New York: Frederick A. Praeger, 1966), 169.
20. Bernard B. Fall, *Viet-Nam Witness, 1953–1966* (New York: Frederick A. Praeger, 1966), 173.
21. *Ibid.*, 173.
22. *Ibid.*, 174. Fall describes "force goals" as: "the number of military units planned to be activated and maintained on a basis of varying readiness by virtue of U.S. aid."
23. Dennis J. Duncanson, *Government and Revolution in Vietnam* (New York: Oxford University Press, 1968), 240.
24. See "Fiscal and Customs Services" in the DRV, pp. 107–9 in Bernard B. Fall, *The Viet-Minh Regime: Government and Administration in the Democratic Republic of Vietnam* (New York: Institute of Pacific Relations, 1956), reprinted by Greenwood Press, Westport, CT, 1975.
25. Bernard B. Fall, *Viet-Nam Witness, 1953–1966* (New York: Frederick A. Praeger, 1966), 173.
26. See "Fiscal and Customs Services" in the DRV, pp. 107–9 in Bernard B. Fall, *The Viet-Minh Regime: Government and Administration in the Democratic Republic of Vietnam* (New York: Institute of Pacific Relations, 1956), reprinted by Greenwood Press, Westport, CT, 1975.
27. Bernard B. Fall, *The Viet-Minh Regime: Government and Administration in the*

28. David G. Marr, *Vietnam: State, War, and Revolution (1945–1946)* (Berkeley: University of California Press, 2013), 365. For Marr's study of currency in the DRV, see 365–72.
29. Landry Signé, "How the France-Backed African CFA Franc Works as an Enabler and Barrier to Development," Brookings Institute, 7 December 2019.
30. Ndongo Samba Sylla, "The CFA Franc: French Monetary Imperialism in Africa," LSE Blog, https://blogs.lse.ac.uk/africaatlse/2017/07/12/the-cfa-franc-french-monetary-imperialism-in-africa/ (accessed 20 November 2020). According to researcher Ndongo Samba Sylla, the CFA Franc was and remains a colonial relic. As of 2017, thirteen central and western African countries continue to use the CFA, which "was born of France's need to foster economic integration among the colonies under its administration, and thus control their resources, economic structures and political systems."
31. Ibid.
32. David G. Marr, *Vietnam: State, War, and Revolution (1945–1946)* (Berkeley, CA: University of California Press, 2013), 371.
33. Alec Holcombe, *Mass Mobilization in the Democratic Republic of Vietnam, 1945–1960* (Honolulu, HI: University of Hawai'i Press, 2020), 68.
34. Ibid., 70.
35. John T. McAlister, *Viet Nam: The Origins of Revolution* (New York: Knopf, 1969), 324.
36. Bernard B. Fall, *Viet-Nam Witness, 1953–1966* (New York: Frederick A. Praeger, 1966), 174.
37. Ibid., 174.
38. Bernard B. Fall, "South Viet-Nam's Internal Problems," *Pacific Affairs*, Vol. 31, No. 3 (September 1958), 243. Series 1.06, Box A-02, BBF, JFKL. Note: This quote was edited out of the version of the article that appeared in *Viet-Nam Witness*.
39. Benn Steil, *The Marshall Plan: Dawn of the Cold War* (New York: Oxford University Press, 2018), 347–8.
40. Bernard B. Fall, "South Viet-Nam's Internal Problems," *Pacific Affairs*, 246, Series 1.1, Box F-1, BBF, JFKL.
41. Henry J. Bruton and Catherine B. Hill, "The Role of Counterpart Funds in Economic Development," *IDS Bulletin*, 1984, 32, ISSN: 0265–5012.
42. Ibid., 32.
43. Five years after Fall analyzed counterpart funding in Vietnam, Robert Scigliano discussed this system funding in 1963. See "The Pattern of Development," pp. 102–10 in Chapter 5, "Economic and Social Development" in Robert Scigliano, *South Vietnam: Nation Under Stress* (Boston, MA: Houghton Mifflin Company, 1963).

By 1963, however, the security and governance situation in the RVN was much worse than it was in 1958.

44. Bernard B. Fall, *Viet-Nam Witness, 1953–1966* (New York: Frederick A. Praeger, 1966), 176.
45. These figures for rubber export percentage and the commodity prices are located in *Ibid.*, 176.
46. *Ibid.*, 176.
47. Robert Scigliano exemplifies a specialist supporting Fall's evidence. See Robert Scigliano, *South Vietnam: Nation Under Stress* (Boston, MA: Houghton Mifflin Company, 1963).
48. Fall cited, for example, "USOM-Vietnam," *Activity Report*, 30 June 1954–30 June 1956 and *The Military Assistance Program to the United States*, US Senate Special Committee to Study the Foreign Aid Program (Washington, DC: Government Printing Office, 1957) in Bernard B. Fall, *Viet-Nam Witness, 1953–1966* (New York: Frederick A. Praeger, 1966), 173–4.
49. *Ibid.*, 188.
50. *Ibid.*, 188.
51. Ibid., 188.
52. George C. Herring, *America's Longest War: The United States and Vietnam, 1950–1975* (New York: Alfred A. Knopf, 1979), 76, 86.
53. *Ibid.*, 70.
54. Fredrik Logevall, *Choosing War: The Lost Chance for Peace and the Escalation of War in Vietnam* (Berkeley, CA: University of California Press, 1999), 33.
55. *Ibid.*, 33. For NSAM 111, see Papers of John F. Kennedy. Presidential Papers. National Security Files, Meeting and Memoranda. National Security Action Memoranda (NSAM): NSAM 111, First Phase of Vietnam Program. JFKNSF-332-013, JFKL.
56. Robert Scigliano, *South Vietnam: Nation Under Stress* (Boston, MA: Houghton Mifflin Company, 1963), 114–15.
57. William J. Lederer and Eugene Burdick, *The Ugly American* (New York: W.W. Norton & Company, 1958), 282. *The Ugly American* is well known but, in relation to Fall's work, also provides a narrative-fictional equivalent to Fall's analysis of problems associated with aid, security, politics, and cultural interaction in Southeast Asia.
58. See "Dominant Characteristics of Development," in Robert Scigliano, *South Vietnam: Nation Under Stress* (Boston, MA: Houghton Mifflin Company, 1963), 110–15.
59. Dorothy Fall, *Bernard Fall: Memories of a Soldier-Scholar* (Washington, DC: Potomac Books, 2007). For documentation and Dorothy Fall's account on this matter, see "Surveillance," Chapter 14, pp. 189–204. For an early entry in the file the CIA developed on Fall, see "Memo From The Central Intelligence Agency

Concerning Dr. Bernard B. Fall," 1070221002. Vietnam Center and Archive. 1962, Box 02, Folder 21, Glenn Helm Collection, Vietnam Center and Sam Johnson Vietnam Archive, Texas Tech University.

60. Bernard B. Fall, *Viet-Nam Witness, 1953–1966* (New York: Frederick A. Praeger, 1966), 179–80.
61. On the formation of Agrovilles, see Joseph J. Zasloff, "Rural Resettlement in South Viet Nam: The Agroville Program," *Pacific Affairs*, Vol. 35, No. 4, Winter, 1962–3. On the formation of the Strategic Hamlet Program, see, *Foreign Relations of the United States (FRUS)*, 1961–3, Vol. IIII, Vietnam, January–August 1963, Department of State, S/P Files: Lot 70 D 199, Vietnam 1963.
62. Bernard B. Fall, *Viet-Nam Witness, 1953–1966* (New York: Frederick A. Praeger, 1966), 180.
63. *Ibid.*, 180–1. Fall pointed out how hundreds of farmers rioted against Diem's policies at Cai-San.
64. *Ibid.*, 184.
65. *Ibid.*, 184.
66. Philip Selznick's study of Bolshevik strategy and tactics is an exception but it is not contextualized in the setting of Vietnam. See Philip Selznick, *The Organizational Weapon: A Study in Bolshevik Strategy and Tactics* (Glencoe, Illinois: The Free Press of Glencoe, 1960). This work was published by RAND in 1952. Another early example is George K. Tanham, *Communist Revolutionary Warfare: From the Vietminh to the Viet Cong* (Westport, CT: Praeger Security International, 2006), originally published in 1961.
67. Bernard B. Fall, *Viet-Nam Witness, 1953–1966* (New York: Frederick A. Praeger, 1966), 185.
68. Bernard Fall, "Subversive Warfare—A Structural Analysis," Undated, Series 1.5, Box P-3, BBF, JFKL; Bernard Fall, "Memorandum—Some Thoughts on the Problem of Subversion," Series 1.5, Box P-3, BBF, JFKL, see also, Bernard B. Fall, "Liberation vs. Pacification" lecture, Yale University, 3 March 1966, quoted in Dorothy Fall, *Bernard Fall: Memories of a Soldier-Scholar* (Washington, DC: Potomac Books, 2007), 22–3.
69. Bernard B. Fall, *Street Without Joy: The French Debacle in Indochina* (Guilford, CT: Stackpole Books, 1961), 375.
70. Bernard Fall, "Indochina: The Last Year of the War," *Military Review*, Vol. 36, No. 7 (October 1956), 7, BBF, JFKL.
71. *Ibid.*, 9.
72. See "CIA Memorandum: The Situation in Southeast Asia," 18 May 1964, National Security File, Country File: Vietnam, Box 53, Folder: Southeast Asia Memos, LBJP, LBJL.
73. George K. Tanham, *Communist Revolutionary Warfare: From the Vietminh to the Viet Cong* (Westport, CT: Praeger Security International, 2006).

74. See Peter Paret, *French Revolutionary Warfare From Indochina to Algeria: The Analysis of a Political and Military Doctrine* (New York: Praeger, 1964).
75. See Marie-Monique Robin, *Escadrons de la Mort, L'école Française* (Paris: Le Decouverte/Poche, 2004). As a representative example, see Jean Nemo, *Enseignements: A—L'Infanterie, La Guerre en Surface au Tonkin de 1946 à 1954* (Quang Yet, 1955), 36, 10 2509 Service Historique de l'Armée de Terre, Vincennes, Paris. The overwhelming majority of French writing on this subject is found in this archive.
76. Colonel Gabriel Bonnet, *Les Guerres Insurrectionnelles et Révolutionnaires* (Paris: Plon, 1958); For Fall's reference to Bonnet, see Bernard Fall, "Laos, Viet-Nam, and Revolutionary Warfare," 1–2, Series 1.09, Box T-1, page 2, undated, BBF, JFKL.
77. *Ibid.*
78. The book to which Fall referred was Colonel Gabriel Bonnet, *Les Guerres Insurrectionnelles et Révolutionnaires* (Paris: Plon, 1958); Bernard Fall, "Laos, Viet-Nam, and Revolutionary Warfare," 1–2, Series 1.09, Box T-1, 2, undated, BBF, JFKL. Fall slightly varied this description in 1962. See his article from November 1962 in Bernard B. Fall, *Viet-Nam Witness, 1953–1966* (New York: Frederick A. Praeger, 1966), 265.
79. Henri Navarre, *Agonie d'Indochina 1953–1954* (Paris: Plon, 1956), 38.
80. *Ibid.* 38.
81. Bunche served in the OSS' Research and Analysis Bureau, see Ralph Bunche Personnel File, *NARA*, RG 226, Records of the Office of Strategic Services, Entry 224: OSS Personal Files, Box 92.
82. Bernard B. Fall, *Viet-Nam Witness, 1953–1966* (New York: Frederick A. Praeger, 1966), 257.
83. Bernard Fall, "Indochina: The Last Year of the War," *Military Review*, Vol. 36, No. 7 (October 1956), 9, BBF, JFKL.
84. *Ibid.*, 11.
85. Operation Vulture was the aerial support plan to aid the French garrison at Dien Bien Phu. According to Fredrik Logevall, Operation Vulture "always, from its inception, had an atomic dimension. In early April, a study group in the Pentagon examined the possibility of using atomic weapons at Dien Bien Phu and concluded that three tactical A-bombs, properly employed, would be sufficient to obliterate the Viet Minh effort there." See Fredrik Logevall, *Embers of War: The Fall of an Empire and the Making of America's Vietnam* (New York: Random House, 2014), 499.
86. Bernard Fall, "Indochina: The Last Year of the War," *Military Review*, Vol. 36, No. 7 (October 1956), 9, BBF, JFKL; Fall's account of the battle stands as the standard in English after more than sixty years. See Kevin Boylan and Luc Olivier, *Valley of the Shadow: The Siege of Dien Bien Phu* (New York: Osprey, 2018), 266.

Readers familiar with Mao Tse-tung's theory of protracted war may recognize the revolutionary phase to which Fall gave so much attention within a parameter of "equilibrium" found in Mao's second stage. Fall did not directly frame his writing in terms of Mao's three stages even though it is likely that he knew Mao Tse-tung's writings through Samuel B. Griffith's translations, originally produced in 1940. Griffith's updated translated version of Mao's writings appeared in 1961. See Samuel B. Griffith, *Mao Tse-tung on Guerrilla Warfare* (New York: Praeger, 1961). It is undeniable that Fall was well-versed in Mao's writing, especially as it was interpreted by Vietnamese, such as Truong Chinh. See Bernard B. Fall, *Street Without Joy: The French Debacle in Indochina* (Guilford, CT: Stackpole Books, 1961), 400.

87. Bernard Fall, "Laos, Viet-Nam, and Revolutionary Warfare," 2, Series 1.09, Box T-1, page 2, undated, BBF, JFKL.
88. Bernard B. Fall, *Viet-Nam Witness, 1953–1966* (New York: Frederick A. Praeger, 1966), 265.
89. Bernard B. Fall, *Last Reflections on a War* (New York: Doubleday & Company, 1967), 210.
90. Bernard B. Fall, *Viet-Nam Witness, 1953–1966* (New York: Frederick A. Praeger, 1966), 265.
91. Fall referred to Hogard as Jean Hogard in his notes. For a short assessment of Hogard and others, see fn. 3, p. 459 in Bernard B. Fall, *The Two Vietnams: A Political and Military Analysis* (New York: Praeger, 1963), 459.
92. See Bernard B. Fall, *Street Without Joy: The French Debacle in Indochina* (Guilford, CT: Stackpole Books, 1961), 400. The special issue of *Revue Militaire d'Information* was entitled "*La Guerre Révolutionnaire,*" edited by Col. Charles Lacheroy. Fall's collection of this journal includes almost every issue published between 1957 and 1963. It is located in BBF, JFKL, Series 2.06, Boxes J-097 and J-098.
93. Michael P.M. Finch, "A Total War of the Mind: The French Theory of *La Guerre Révolutionnaire*, 1954–1958," *War in History*, Vol. 23, Issue 3 (2018), 412.
94. *Ibid.*, 412.
95. *Ibid.*, 412.
96. See Marie-Monique Robin, *Éscadrons de la mort, l'école Française* (Paris: Le Decouverte/Poche, 2004).
97. See Lesley Gill, *The School of the Americas: Military Training and Political Violence in the Americas* (Durham, NC: Duke University Press, 2004).
98. François Sully, *Age of the Guerrilla* (New York: Avon Books, 1968), 40.
99. *Ibid.*, 124.
100. For Fall's thoughts on French operations in Algeria, see his Introduction to Roger Trinquier, *Modern Warfare: A French View of Counterinsurgency* (New York, Praeger, 2006). For information on Guatemala, see Nick Cullather, *Secret History:*

The CIA's Classified Account of Its Operations in Guatemala, 1952–1953 (Palo Alto, CA: Stanford University Press, 2006).

101. Peter Paret, *French Revolutionary Warfare From Indochina to Algeria: The Analysis of a Political and Military Doctrine* (New York: Praeger, 1964), 7.
102. Michael P.M. Finch, "A Total War of the Mind: The French Theory of *La Guerre Révolutionnaire*, 1954–1958," *War in History*, Vol. 23, Issue 3 (2018), 14.
103. Bernard Fall, "Books by Fall," *Street Without Joy*, 309, Series 1.2, Box B-3, BBF, JFKL.
104. John Shy and Thomas W. Collier, "Revolutionary War" in Peter Paret (Ed.), *Makers of Modern Strategy: From Machiavelli to the Nuclear Age* (Princeton, NJ: Princeton University Press, 1986), 816.
105. Bernard Fall, "Books by Fall," *Street Without Joy*, 299, Series 1.2, Box B-3, BBF, JFKL.
106. Fall provided perhaps the most extensive recounting of GCMA operations available in commercial publications prior to 1967. For his comments on GCMAs and the Foreign Legion's effectiveness, see Bernard B. Fall, *Street Without Joy: The French Debacle in Indochina* (Guilford, CT: Stackpole Books, 1961), 267–86.
107. For Fall's comments on Riesen, see *Ibid.*, 269 and 400. It is highly likely that Fall viewed the type of skill and approaches that René Riesen exemplified as the most effective method to counter Vietnamese revolutionary warfare. Fall referred to Riesen numerous times throughout his scholarship and Riesen's extraordinary personal narrative can be found in René Riesen, *Jungle Mission*, translated by James Oliver (London: Hutchinson, 1957). Fall would later lecture at the US Army Special Warfare Center and School on numerous occasions, forming a close relationship with Special Operations Center Commandant General William P. Yarborough in the early 1960s.
108. Riesen's example preceded memorable accounts written by American advisors, in some cases, by over a decade. A representative example of a similar American account is David Donovan, *Once a Warrior King: Memoirs of an Officer in Vietnam* (New York: Ballantine Books, 1985).
109. Bernard B. Fall, *Street Without Joy: The French Debacle in Indochina* (Guilford, CT: Stackpole Books, 1961), 373.
110. Shawn McHale, "Understanding the Fanatic Mind? The Viet Minh and Race Hatred in the First Indochina War (1945–1954)," *Journal of Vietnamese Studies*, Vol. 4, Issue 3 (2009), 106.
111. *Ibid.*, 102.
112. Keith W. Taylor, "Surface Orientations in Vietnam: Beyond Histories of Nation and Region," *Journal of Asian Studies*, Vol. 57, No. 4 (November 1998), 966.
113. As an example, see David W.P. Elliott, *The Vietnamese War: Revolution and Social Change in the Mekong Delta 1930–1975* (Armonk, NY: M.E. Sharpe, 2003), 266–8.

114. Kuno Knoebl, *Victor Charlie: The Face of War in Vietnam* (New York: Praeger, 1967), 181.
115. Shawn McHale, "Understanding the Fanatic Mind? The Viet Minh and Race Hatred in the First Indochina War (1945–1954)," *Journal of Vietnamese Studies*, Vol. 4, Issue 3 (2009), 106.
116. Exceptions to this exist, especially Fall's article, "The Political-Religious Sects of Viet-Nam," *Pacific Affairs*, Vol. 28, No. 3 (September 1955).
117. Bernard B. Fall, *Last Reflections on a War* (New York: Doubleday & Company, 1967), 197.
118. Bernard B. Fall, *Viet-Nam Witness, 1953–1966* (New York: Frederick A. Praeger, 1966), 187.
119. *Ibid.*, 188–9.
120. *Ibid.*, 182.
121. George C. Herring, *America's Longest War: The United States and Vietnam, 1950–1975* (New York: Alfred A. Knopf, 1979), 57.
122. Bernard Fall, "Book Reviews by Fall," 2, Series 1.08, Box BR-1, BBF, JFKL.
123. *Ibid.*, 3.
124. David Halberstam Papers, Howard Gotlieb Archival Research Center, Boston University, Box 54, Folder 9.
125. General J. Lawton Collins, *Lightning Joe, An Autobiography* (Novato, CA: Presidio Press, 1994), 394.
126. Robert D. Schulzinger, *A Time for War: The United States and Vietnam, 1941–1975* (New York: Oxford University Press, 1997), 89.
127. Ronald Bruce Frankum, Jr., *Vietnam's Year of the Rat: Elbridge Durbrow, Ngo Dinh Diem and the Turn in U.S. Relations, 1959–1961* (Jefferson, NC: McFarland and Company, 2014), 207.
128. *Foreign Relations of the United States* (FRUS): "149. Letter from Professor Wesley R. Fishel of Michigan State University to the President of the Republic of Vietnam (Diem)," 30 April 1960, *FRUS*, 1958–1960, Vietnam, Vol. 1.
129. *Ibid.*
130. Dwight D. Eisenhower, *Mandate for Change* (New York: Doubleday & Company, 1963), 362.
131. *Foreign Relations of the United States* (FRUS): "149. Letter from Professor Wesley R. Fishel of Michigan State University to the President of the Republic of Vietnam (Diem)," 30 April 1960, *FRUS*, 1958–1960, Vietnam, Vol. 1.
132. *Ibid.*
133. *Ibid.*
134. Bernard Fall, *The International Position of South Viet-Nam 1954–58*, iii, Series 1.05, "Papers and Reports by Dr. Fall," Box P-01, BBF, JFKL. See Fall's acknowledgments expressing his gratitude to Fishel and his staff for providing documentation and their assistance.

135. Richard Falk, *Revisiting the Vietnam War and International Law: Views and Interpretations of Richard Falk*, edited by Stefan Andersson (New York: Cambridge University Press, 2018), 108.
136. Bernard B. Fall, *The Two Viet-Nams: A Political and Military Analysis* (New York: Praeger, 1963), 245.
137. Bernard Fall "Vietnam's Twelve Elections," *Last Reflections on a War* (New York: Doubleday & Company, 1967), 168.
138. *Ibid.*, 188–9.
139. Bernard B. Fall, *The Two Vietnams: A Political and Military Analysis* (New York: Praeger, 1963), 399.
140. Bernard B. Fall, *Street Without Joy: The French Debacle in Indochina* (Guilford, CT: Stackpole Books, 1961), 380.

8. 1961–1967

1. "Transcript of the President's News Conference on World and Domestic Affairs," *New York Times*, 24 March 1961. https://timesmachine.nytimes.com/timesmachine/1961/03/24/issue.html
2. Dwight D. Eisenhower, *Waging Peace, 1956–1961* (New York: Doubleday & Company, 1965), 612.
3. "Memorandum of Conversation, Subject: Laos: Government Crisis," 23 December 1959. D.D. Eisenhower Papers as President, 1953–1961 (Ann Whitman File), International Series, Box 37, Laos Folder 1. Eisenhower Presidential Library.
4. The intense factionalism of Laotian politics, leading to civil war, began in 1945 when the Lao Issara (Laos Independence Movement) broke into three factions: those led by Phetsarath, Souvanna Phouma, and Souphanovoung. In 1948, Souphannovoung joined with communist factions, forming the Pathet Lao in 1950 and cooperating with the Viet Minh, whereas Souvanna Phouma and Phetsarath formed a Royal Laotian Government led, after 1949, by Prince Boun Oum. For a text on this history, one which Fall consulted, see Sisouk Na Champassak, *Storm Over Laos: A Contemporary History* (New York: Frederick A. Praeger, 1961), especially Chapter 2, "Laos in 1945." Concern over the loss of Laos was sincere and real. Champassak added, "Americans and Asians interested in the stability of Laos believed that the collapse of Laos, whether caused by internal subversion, indirect aggression, or direct invasion, would touch off a series of wars, and perhaps the third world war" (Champassak, 102).
5. Quoted in Roger Warner, *Shooting at the Moon: The Story of America's Clandestine War in Laos* (South Royalton, VT: Steer Forth Press, 1996), 48.
6. Bernard B. Fall, *Anatomy of a Crisis: The Laotian Crisis of 1960–1961* (New York: Doubleday and Company, 1969), 23.
7. Sisouk Na Champassak, *Storm Over Laos: A Contemporary History* (New York: Frederick A. Praeger, 1961), 33.

8. See Fall's study of the Viet Minh in Laos and Cambodia, in "Cambodia's International Position," *Current History*, March 1961, Series 1.06, Box A-01, BBF, JFKL.
9. Bernard B. Fall, "Diary of a 'Quiet' Weekend in Laos," *Sunday Star*, 27 September 1959, Series 1.6, Box A-2, BBF, JFKL.
10. Bernard B. Fall, "Review of the Situation," Series 1.8, Box BR-1, BBF, JFKL.
11. Bernard B. Fall, "Situation in Laos," Letter to the Editor of *New York Times*, 9 September 1956, Series 1.06, Box A-1, BBF, JFKL.
12. *Ibid.*
13. A representative sample of Fall's publications include "The International Relations of Laos," *Pacific Affairs*, Vol. 30, No. 1, March 1957; "Reappraisal in Laos," *Current History*, Vol., 42, No. 245 (January 1965); and "Laos: Who Broke the Ceasefire?" *The New Republic*, 18 June 1962. These are located in Series 1.06, Box A-02, BBF, JFKL. For other studies on Laos after World War II, see Martin Stuart-Fox, *A History of Laos* (Cambridge, UK: Cambridge University Press, 1997) and Norman G. Owen (Ed.), *The Emergence of Modern Southeast Asia: A New History* (Honolulu, HI: University of Hawai'i Press, 2005).
14. See Fall's biography in "Reappraisal in Laos," *Current History*, Vol. 42, No. 245 (January 1962) in Series 1.06, Box A-02, BBF, JFKL. In February 1968, the book was published as *Anatomy of a Crisis: The Laos Crisis of 1960–1961*, by Doubleday. See Kirkus Reviews, 1 February 1968, available at: https://www.kirkusreviews.com/book-reviews/a/bernard-b-fall/anatomy-of-a-crisis-the-laos-crisis-of-1960–196/ (accessed 10 April 2020). A critical peer review of Fall's manuscript for a potential publication with the firm, Public Affairs, provided extensive suggestions for revisions. The document did not provide recommendations for Public Affairs to publish the book, nor did it suggest that Fall's manuscript should be rejected. For the peer-reviewed comments for the potential Public Affairs published work, see "Laos—Critique," Series 1.2, Box. B 07, BBF, JFKL.
15. Fall's depiction of Laos, as recorded in *Street Without Joy* (1961), included two chapters that appeared in a modified form in the published draft of *Anatomy of a Crisis*. In *Street Without Joy*, Fall's chapter "Laos Outpost" recounts events in 1953 during the First Indochina War. These events are also recounted in the first chapter of *Anatomy of a Crisis* in "Prelude at Sop Nao."
16. Bernard Fall, *Street Without Joy: The French Debacle in Indochina* (Guilford, CT: Stackpole Books, 1961), 340–1.
17. See "Letter to the Compatriots in the Thai-Meo Autonomous Region," 7 May 1955. In Ho Chi Minh, *On Revolution: Selected Writings, 1920–66*, edited by Bernard B. Fall (New York: Praeger, 1967), 287–9. In this letter, Ho was focused on the upland border areas of North Vietnam/Laos.
18. Sisouk Na Champassak, *Storm Over Laos: A Contemporary History* (New York: Frederick A. Praeger, 1961), 8. Independence was gained through a series of steps

before 1953 that included the formation of a Laotian constitution in 1947. Laos's independence was supported by a Franco-Laotian Convention signed in Paris on 19 July 1949. See Champassak's full account of Laos's progression toward independence in *Storm Over Laos: A Contemporary History*, 11–29. Fall made extensive use of Champassak's chronology in *Anatomy of a Crisis*.

19. Bernard B. Fall, "The Pathet Lao: A 'Liberation' Party," in *The Communist Revolution in Asia: Tactics, Goals, and Achievements*, edited by Robert A. Scalapino, (Englewood, NJ: Prentice-Hall, Inc., 1965), 178; see also Bernard B. Fall, *Anatomy of a Crisis: The Laotian Crisis of 1960–1961* (New York: Doubleday and Company, 1969), 43.

20. Bernard B. Fall, *Laos (1959–1962)*, Special Operations Research Office, 18, available in Series 1.05, Box P-02, BBF, JFKL.

21. *Ibid.*, 64.

22. Bernard B. Fall, *Anatomy of a Crisis: The Laotian Crisis of 1960–1961* (New York: Doubleday and Company, 1969), 45.

23. For Fall's comments, see Bernard B. Fall, *Laos (1959–1962)*, Special Operations Research Office, available in Series 1.05, Box P-02, BBF, JFKL.

24. See Tuong Vu, "The Revolutionary Path to State Formation in Vietnam: Opportunities, Conundrums, and Legacies," *Journal of Vietnamese Studies*, Vol. 11, Issue 3–4, 267–97, 2016. Tuong Vu argues that five key aspects of state formation were key for Vietnamese Communists: legitimization, establishing sovereignty, territoriality, creating a centralized bureaucracy, and monopolizing violence. For more on Tuong Vu's perspective on territorialization, see pp. 277–80.

25. Bernard Fall, *The Viet-Minh Regime: Government and Administration in the Democratic Republic of Vietnam* (New York: Institute of Pacific Relations, 1956), reprinted by Greenwood Press, Westport, CT, 1975, 64.

26. Bernard B. Fall, *Anatomy of a Crisis: The Laotian Crisis of 1960–1961* (New York: Doubleday and Company, 1969), 226.

27. Bernard B. Fall, *Laos (1959–1962)*, Special Operations Research Office, available in Series 1.05, Box P-02, BBF, JFKL.

28. *Ibid.*

29. Arthur M. Schlesinger, Jr., *A Thousand Days: John F. Kennedy in the White House* (Boston, MA: Houghton Mifflin Company, 1965), 340.

30. *Ibid.*, 341.

31. This mission supporting Vang Pao and Hmong forces expanded to include covert support from the CIA through Operation Momentum in January 1961 and Operation Millpond. See Roger Warner, *Shooting at the Moon: The Story of America's Clandestine War in Laos* (South Royalton, VT: Steer Forth Press, 1996), 34 and 43.

32. Bernard Fall, *The Viet-Minh Regime: Government and Administration in the*

Democratic Republic of Vietnam (New York: Institute of Pacific Relations, 1956), reprinted by Greenwood Press, Westport, CT, 1975, 62–4.
33. Bernard Fall, "Laos, Vietnam, and Revolutionary Warfare," Series 1.9 "Typescripts," Box T-1, BBF, JFKL.
34. *Ibid.*
35. Bernard B. Fall, *Anatomy of a Crisis: The Laotian Crisis of 1960–1961* (New York: Doubleday and Company, 1969), 113.
36. *Ibid.*, 114.
37. Paul F. Langer and Joseph J. Zasloff, *North Vietnam and the Pathet Lao: Partners in the Struggle for Laos* (Cambridge, MA: Harvard University Press, 1970), 97.
38. Mai Elliott, *RAND in Southeast Asia: A History of the Vietnam War Era* (Santa Monica, CA: RAND Corporation, 2010), 139.
39. The Neo Lao Hak Sat also included the Santiphab party, led by Quinim Pholsina. See Sisouk Na Champassak, *Storm Over Laos: A Contemporary History* (New York: Frederick A. Praeger, 1961), 158. A detailed description of the Phak Pasasson Lao is available in Paul F. Langer and Joseph J. Zasloff, *North Vietnam and the Pathet Lao: Partners in the Struggle for Laos* (Cambridge, MA: Harvard University Press, 1970), 92.
40. Bernard B. Fall, "The Pathet Lao: A 'Liberation' Party," in *The Communist Revolution in Asia: Tactics, Goals, and Achievements*, edited by Robert A. Scalapino, (Englewood, NJ: Prentice-Hall, Inc., 1965), 180, fn 13, and 195.
41. Paul F. Langer, "Comments on Bernard Fall's "The Pathet Lao: A 'Liberation' Party" (Santa Monica, CA: RAND Corporation, 1968, P-3751), 3–4.
42. Bernard B. Fall, "The Pathet Lao: A 'Liberation' Party," in *The Communist Revolution in Asia: Tactics, Goals, and Achievements*, edited by Robert A. Scalapino, (Englewood, NJ: Prentice-Hall, Inc., 1965), 180.
43. Bernard B. Fall, *Anatomy of a Crisis: The Laotian Crisis of 1960–1961* (New York: Doubleday and Company, 1969), 112–13. In 1968, RAND Corporation analyst Paul Langer claimed that Fall misidentified the core communist cadre which directed the Neo Lao Hak Sat, the Pathet Lao's front organization. Langer also claimed that Fall exaggerated the significance of communist policies designed to appeal to minorities to gain their support. Langer overlooked, or was unaware of, Fall's comments on the importance of North Vietnam's policies toward ethnic minorities in the T'ai-Meo and Viet-Bac autonomous zones, and Hanoi's sponsorships of tribal schools for administrators and teachers for these zones. Fall's account of the importance of minorities to leaders in Hanoi is recorded in "Problems of Minority Administration in Laos, Cambodia, and Viet-Nam," prepared for the 5th World Congress of the International Association of Political Science, 26–30 September 1961, Paris France, Series 1.5, Box P-2, BBF, JFK. It is possible that Langer was unfamiliar with Fall's speech or this text since it was not commercially published.

44. Bernard B. Fall, *Anatomy of a Crisis: The Laotian Crisis of 1960–1961* (New York: Doubleday and Company, 1969), 114.
45. Bernard B. Fall, "Diary of a 'Quiet' Weekend in Laos," *Sunday Star*, 27 September 1959, Series 1.6, Box A-2, BBF, JFKL.
46. Bernard B. Fall, "The Pathet Lao: A 'Liberation' Party," in *The Communist Revolution in Asia: Tactics, Goals, and Achievements*, edited by Robert A. Scalapino, (Englewood, NJ: Prentice-Hall, Inc., 1965), 182.
47. Sisouk Na Champassak, *Storm Over Laos: A Contemporary History* (New York: Frederick A. Praeger, 1961), 60 and 64.
48. Bernard Fall, "Laos, Vietnam, and Revolutionary Warfare," Series 1.9 "Typescripts," Box T-1, BBF, JFKL.
49. Bernard B. Fall, "The Pathet Lao: A 'Liberation' Party," in *The Communist Revolution in Asia: Tactics, Goals, and Achievements*, edited by Robert A. Scalapino, (Englewood, NJ: Prentice-Hall, Inc., 1965), 187.
50. Bernard B. Fall, *Anatomy of a Crisis: The Laotian Crisis of 1960–1961* (New York: Doubleday and Company, 1969), 109. Fall also discusses core principles of Revolutionary War on p. 110.
51. Bernard Fall, "Laos, Vietnam, and Revolutionary Warfare," Series 1.9 "Typescripts," Box T-1, BBF, JFKL.
52. David Milne, *America's Rasputin: Walt Rostow and the Vietnam War* (New York: Hill and Wang, 2008), 85.
53. *Ibid.*, 86.
54. Lansdale described problems in US operations in Indochina in a 1955 memo to J. Lawton Collins, then in Vietnam on the orders of the Eisenhower administration to coordinate efforts while holding the rank of Ambassador. See "Memo from Lansdale to Collins," 3 January 1955, "J. Lawton Collins Papers, 1896–1976, Subseries D. Box 28, D.D. Eisenhower Library.
55. Bernard Fall, *The Two Vietnams: A Political and Military Analysis* (New York: Praeger, 1963), 342.
56. "Fall to Lansdale," 22 May 1965, Edward G. Lansdale Correspondence, Box 37, Folder 916, Lansdale Papers, Hoover Institute.
57. Bernard Fall, *The Two Vietnams: A Political and Military Analysis* (New York: Praeger, 1963), 343–5.
58. For analysis of problems in the Diem administration and on the Caravelle Manifesto, see Ronald Bruce Frankum, Jr., *Vietnam's Year of the Rat: Elbridge Durbrow, Ngo Dinh Diem and the Turn in U.S. Relations, 1959–1961* (Jefferson, NC: McFarland and Company, 2014).
59. "Fall to Sweet Letter," 8 February 1960, Series 1.1., Box F-1, BBF, JFKL.
60. Fredrik Logevall "Foreword" to the 2018 edition of Bernard B. Fall, *Street Without Joy: The French Debacle in Indochina* (Guilford, CT: Stackpole Books, 2018), vii.

61. "Laos (1959–1962)," Special Operations Research Office, available in Series 1.05, Box P-02, BBF, JFKL.
62. *Casebook on Insurgency and Revolutionary Warfare: Volume I: 1933–1962*, Assessing Revolutionary and Insurgent Strategies. US Special Operations Command, December 1962. For access to the pdf of this study, readers are directed to ARIS products located at www.soc.mil (accessed 20 January 2021).
63. This study was republished for military personnel in 2013 and remains an important historical source used to assess revolutions across the globe through its analyses of twenty-three revolutions.
64. *Case Studies in Insurgency and Revolutionary Warfare: Vietnam 1941–1954*, Special Operations Research Office, Washington, DC, 1964. For reference to Fall's role, see p. vii. Access to a pdf of this text is available at: https://apps.dtic.mil/dtic/tr/fulltext/u2/436429.pdf (accessed 2 April 2020).
65. Bernard B. Fall, "Counterinsurgency: The French Experience," 18 January 1963, Industrial College of the Armed Forces, Washington, DC, Transcript, Series 1.05, Box P-1, BBF, JFKL.
66. William P. Yarborough, "Autobiographical Sketch of Yarborough," William P. Yarborough Papers, Box 1, Folder 2, Department of Special Collections, Howard Gotlieb Archival Research Center, Boston University.
67. For an overview of Yarborough's career, see William Pelham Yarborough, *Bail Out Over North Africa: America's First Combat Parachute Missions 1942* (Williamstown, NJ: Phillips Publications, 1979).
68. William P. Yarborough, "Autobiographical Sketch of Yarborough," William P. Yarborough Papers, Box 1, Folder 2, Department of Special Collections, Howard Gotlieb Archival Research Center, Boston University.
69. The syllabi for these courses are located in the Alan Grant Jr. Papers, Courses and Seminars, US Army Special Warfare School, Box 10, D.D. Eisenhower Library. The course's purpose, for which Fall's book was the central text, explained: "In 1946 the French embarked on operations designed at the 'pacification of bandit groups' in Indo-China. Seven years later, and after a final set-piece battle between regular forces, France ceased to exist as a colonial power in southeast Asia. The discussion of this course will evaluate the resistance movement of the Viet-Minh, and the counter-insurgency principles as interpreted and applied by the French."
70. A large amount of *Laos: Background of a Conflict* eventually appeared in *Anatomy of A Crisis: The Laotian Crisis of 1961–1962*.
71. For information on the utility of Applied History, see Graham Allison and Niall Ferguson, "Why the U.S. President Needs a Council of Historians," *The Atlantic*, September 2016.
72. "William P. Yarborough Letter to Bernard Fall, 30 November 1964," Yarborough Papers, Correspondence, Box 6, Department of Special Collections, Howard Gotlieb Archival Research Center, Boston University.

73. Yarborough Papers, Subject Files, Box 128, Office Files Folder B, 9. Department of Special Collections, Howard Gotlieb Archival Research Center, Boston University.
74. "Master of the Red Jab," *Saturday Evening Post*, 24 November 1962, in Bernard B. Fall, *Viet-Nam Witness: 1953–1966* (New York: Praeger), 105–14.
75. Ho Chi Minh, *On Revolution: Selected Writings, 1920–1966*, edited and with an introduction by Bernard B. Fall (New York: Praeger, 1967), 354.
76. *Le Viet-Minh: La Republique Democratique du Viet-Nam, 1945–1950*. With preface by Paul Mus (Paris: Libraire Armand Colin, 1960), See "Ho Chi Minh: l'homme et son mythe," 20–38.
77. Ho Chi Minh, *On Revolution: Selected Writings, 1920–1966*, edited and with an introduction by Bernard B. Fall (New York: Praeger, 1967), 355.
78. *Ibid.*, 356.
79. George C. Herring, *America's Longest War: The United States and Vietnam 1950–1975*, 2nd Edition (New York: Knopf, 1986), 94.
80. "Master of the Red Jab," *Saturday Evening Post*, 24 November 1962, in Bernard B. Fall, *Viet-Nam Witness: 1953–1966* (New York: Praeger), 114.
81. Vo Nguyen Giap, *People's War People's Army: The Viet Cong Insurrection Manual for Undeveloped Countries*, foreword by Roger Hilsman, profile of Giap by Bernard Fall (New York: Bantam Books, 1968). First printed by Praeger in 1962.
82. Truong Chinh, *Primer for Revolt: The Communist Takeover in Viet-Nam*, with an introduction by Bernard Fall (New York: Praeger 1963).
83. These books were printed in English in Hanoi by the Foreign Language Publishing House in 1960 (*The Resistance Will Win*) and 1962 (*The August Revolution*).
84. To demonstrate the detail in Fall's account, he described how, as Party Secretary-General, Truong Chinh was preceded by first Secretary-General Tran Phu who died in prison in 1931, second Secretary-General Le Hong Phong who was captured and executed by the Sûreté in 1940, and by third Secretary-General Nguyen Van Cu who was also captured and executed in 1940 before party leadership retreated to south China. Fall also points out Le Duan's rise to power as Secretary-General in 1960. *Ibid.* See pages xiii–xv. Fall's comments on Le Duan's political ascent precedes the importance contemporary historians (as of 2019) have given to Le Duan by decades.
85. *Ibid.*, xiii.
86. Fall's papers include numerous analyses and commentaries on subversive and irregular warfare. As examples, see "Informal Communications in Southeast Asia," August 1960, Series 1.5, Box P-1, and "Some Thoughts on Subversion," 1963, Series 1.5. Box P-3, BBF, JFKL.
87. See Bernard B. Fall "Introduction: A Portrait of the 'Centurion,'" in Roger Trinquier, *Modern Warfare: A French View of Counterinsurgency* (Westport, CT: Praeger Security International, 2006), xv.

88. See *Ibid.*, xiii.
89. For information on Trinquier's role in this operation, see Roger Warner, *Shooting at the Moon: The Story of America's Clandestine War in Laos* (South Royalton, VT: Steerforth Press, 1996), 28–9. Fall also discussed the French opium monopoly on p. 7 of *Laos (1959–1962)*, Special Operations Research Office, available in Series 1.05, Box P-02, BBF, JFKL.
90. Fall, *Ibid.*, All data in the paragraph referenced is gathered from these two sources listed in fn. 89 and 91.
91. The Binh Xuyen also had factions which cooperated with the Viet Minh. See Gerald Hickey, *Village in Vietnam* (New Haven, CT: Yale University Press, 1964), 294.
92. For these details, see Bernard B. Fall "Introduction: A Portrait of the 'Centurion,'" in Roger Trinquier, *Modern Warfare: A French View of Counterinsurgency* (Westport, CT: Praeger Security International, 2006),
93. Bernard B. Fall "Introduction: A Portrait of the 'Centurion,'" in Roger Trinquier, *Modern Warfare: A French View of Counterinsurgency* (Westport, CT: Praeger Security International, 2006), xviii.
94. Bernard Fall, *The Two Vietnams: A Political and Military Analysis* (New York: Praeger, 1963).
95. In one assessment, Joseph Buttinger, the founder of American Friends of Vietnam and former supporter of Ngo Dinh Diem, described *The Two Viet-Nams*: "It is an account and analysis of both South and North Vietnam almost up to the fall of Diem. The book abounds in statistics. It contains a comparison of institutions and achievements of both regimes and an up-to-date biography of Ho Chi Minh. Highly critical of the Diem regime and of U.S. policy in Vietnam." See Joseph Buttinger, *Vietnam: A Political History* (New York: Praeger, 1968), 529.
96. "Vietnam: The Unpleasant Truth," *Newsweek*, 20 August 1962, Series 1.1, Box F-1, BBF, JFKL.
97. This article became controversial because of a critical caption to a photo of Madame Nhu's female militia, which Sully claimed did not possess motivation comparable to female militias in the NLF. For more about this incident, see Nathaniel L. Moir, "To Each His Turn, Tomorrow Yours, Tomorrow Mine: François Sully's Turn in History," forthcoming article.
98. Vietnam: The Unpleasant Truth," *Newsweek*, 20 August 1962, Series 1.1, Box F-1, BBF, JFKL.
99. *Ibid.*, also available in Bernard B. Fall, *Street Without Joy* (Guilford, CT: Stackpole Books, 2018), quoted in Foreword by Fredrik Logevell, ix.
100. Bernard Fall, *The Two Vietnams: A Political and Military Analysis* (New York: Praeger, 1963), 134.
101. *Ibid.*, 133.
102. Fall regarded these sources as "one of the best over-all studies of the problem."

See *Ibid.*, 459, fn. 3. Fall collected issues of this journal between 1957 and December 1963. These issues are located in Series 2.06, Boxes J-97 and J-98, BBF, JFKL.
103. Bernard Fall, *The Two Vietnams: A Political and Military Analysis* (New York: Praeger, 1963), 134.
104. Bernard Fall, *The Viet-Minh Regime: Government and Administration in the Democratic Republic of Vietnam* (New York: Institute of Pacific Relations, 1956), reprinted by Greenwood Press, Westport, CT, 1975, 51.
105. Bernard B. Fall, "South Viet-Nam (1956 to November 1963)," SORO working paper, Series 1.5, Box P-3, BBF, JFKL.
106. Bernard Fall, *The Two Vietnams: A Political and Military Analysis* (New York: Praeger, 1963), 137.
107. *Ibid.*, 137.
108. *Ibid.*, 137.
109. I.F. Stone, *In a Time of Torment, 1961–1967* (Boston, MA: Little, Brown, and Company, 1967), 179.
110. Nancy Zaroulis and Gerald Sullivan, *Who Spoke Up? American Protest Against the War in Vietnam 1963–1975* (New York: Doubleday and Company, 1984), 19.
111. Bernard Fall and Marcus Raskin (Eds.), *The Viet-Nam Reader: Articles and Documents on American Foreign Policy and the Viet-Nam Crisis* (New York: Vintage Press, 1965), xiv.
112. Charles DeBenedetti, *An American Ordeal: The Antiwar Movement of the Vietnam Era (Syracuse Studies on Peace and Conflict Resolution* (Syracuse, NY: University of Syracuse, 1990), 109.
113. Nancy Zaroulis and Gerald Sullivan, *Who Spoke Up? American Protest Against the War in Vietnam 1963–1975* (New York: Doubleday and Company, 1984), 38.
114. *Ibid.*, 38.
115. Charles DeBenedetti, *An American Ordeal: The Antiwar Movement of the Vietnam Era*, Syracuse Studies on Peace and Conflict Resolution (Syracuse, NY: University of Syracuse, 1990), 109.
116. C.O. Wakeman, USN, *Naval War College Review*, Vol. 19, No. 6 (October 1966).
117. Bernard Fall and Marcus Raskin (Eds.), *The Viet-Nam Reader: Articles and Documents on American Foreign Policy and the Viet-Nam Crisis* (New York: Vintage Press, 1965), 373.
118. US Department of State Archive, "Austrian State Treaty, 1955." https://2001-2009.state.gov/r/pa/ho/time/lw/107185.htm
119. For further analysis on Raskin and the role of the Institute for Policy Studies, see Brian S. Mueller, "Confronting America's National Security State: The Institute for Policy Studies and the Vietnam War," *Diplomatic History*, Vol. 41, No. 4 (September 2018).

120. Institute for Policy Studies, "Our History," https://ips-dc.org/about/history/
121. Nancy Zaroulis and Gerald Sullivan, *Who Spoke Up? American Protest Against the War in Vietnam 1963–1975* (New York: Doubleday and Company, 1984), 149.
122. Richard Severo, "Telford Taylor, Who Prosecuted Top Nazis at the Nuremberg War Trials, Is Dead at 90." *New York Times*, 24 May 1998.
123. Nancy Zaroulis and Gerald Sullivan, *Who Spoke Up? American Protest Against the War in Vietnam 1963–1975* (New York: Doubleday and Company, 1984), 149.
124. For a full account of the FBI's surveillance of Fall, see Dorothy Fall, *Bernard Fall: Memories of a Soldier-Scholar* (Washington, DC: Potomac Books, 2007), 189–205.
125. "John McCone Memo to President Kennedy," in *CIA Research Reports. Vietnam and Southeast Asia*, edited by Robert E. Lester (Frederick, MD: University Publications of America, 1983).
126. See Telford Taylor, *Nuremberg and Vietnam: An American Tragedy* (Chicago, IL: Quadrangle Books, 1970).
127. Institute for Policy Studies, "Our History," https://ips-dc.org/about/history/
128. Dorothy Fall, *Bernard Fall: Memories of a Soldier-Scholar* (Washington, DC: Potomac Books, 2007), 141.
129. *Ibid.*, 141. Translated as "We are making future revolutionaries!"
130. Examples of this controlled anger abound in Fall's writing, and his book reviews were often sharply worded. For a collection of Fall's reviews, see Series 1.8, Box BR-1, BBF, JFKL.
131. Percy Johnston, "World Affairs Club Open to All," *Howard University Magazine*, undated, Series 2.3, Box W-01, BBF, JFKL.
132. *Ibid.*
133. Stokely Carmichael (Kwame Ture), *Stokely Speaks: From Black Power to Pan-Africanism* (Chicago, IL: Lawrence Hill Books, 2007).
134. Fanon is recognized for his views on the relationship between colonialism and violence. He argued that "colonialism is violence in its natural state, and it will only yield when confronted with greater violence." See Frantz Fanon, *The Wretched of the Earth* (New York: Grove Weidenfeld, 1963), 61.
135. Stokely Carmichael (Kwame Ture), *Ready for Revolution: The Life and Struggles of Stokely Carmichael* with Ekwueme Michael Thelwell (New York: Scribner, 2003), 596–8. In addition to Fall, numerous scholars and writers, such as Toni Morrison, who taught Carmichael's freshman English course, found a home at Howard University and were among Carmichael's teachers. See Peniel E. Joseph, *Stokely: A Life* (New York: Basic Civitas, 2014), 26.
136. *Ibid.*, 26.

137. Martin Luther King, Jr., "Letter from Birmingham Jail," 16 April 1963, Estate of Martin Luther King, Jr.
138. Randall Bennett Woods, *J. William Fulbright, Vietnam, and the Search for a Cold War Foreign Policy* (New York: Cambridge University Press, 1998), 105.
139. Fredrik Logevall, *Choosing War: The Lost Chance for Peace and the Escalation of War in Vietnam* (Berkeley, CA: University of California Press, 1999), 203–4.
140. J. William Fulbright, *The Arrogance of Power* (New York: Vintage Books, 1966), 52.
141. *Ibid.*, 52.
142. For this biographical information on Fulbright, see *Ibid.*, 1–15.
143. Fulbright Program History, https://foreign.fulbrightonline.org/about/history
144. Dorothy Fall, *Bernard Fall: Memories of a Soldier-Scholar* (Washington, DC: Potomac Books, 2007), 43–4.
145. Randall Woods, *J. William Fulbright, Vietnam, and the Search for a Cold War Foreign Policy* (New York: Cambridge University Press, 1998), 104–5.
146. Carl Marcy, "Interview #5," 156. Interviewed by Donald A. Richie, United States Senate Historical Office, Oral History Project.
147. Randall Woods, *J. William Fulbright, Vietnam, and the Search for a Cold War Foreign Policy* (New York: Cambridge University Press, 1998), 105.
148. William C. Berman, *William Fulbright and the Vietnam War: The Dissent of a Political Realist* (Kent, OH: Kent University Press, 1988), 51.
149. Draft memorandum from Secretary of Defense McNamara to President Johnson, 3 November 1965, *Foreign Relations of the United States, 1964–1968* (Washington, DC), III: 514–15.
150. *Ibid.* 515.
151. J. William Fulbright, *The Arrogance of Power* (New York: Vintage, 1966), 155.
152. *Ibid.*, 155.
153. See J. William Fulbright, *The Arrogance of Power* (New York: Vintage, 1966).
154. *Ibid.*, 112.
155. See Merle E. Pribbenow II, "General Vo Nguyen Giap and the Mysterious Evolution of the Plan for the 1968 Tet Offensive," *Journal of Vietnamese Studies*, Vol. 3, Issue 2, 21.
156. According to Nayan Chanda, there was mutual hostility between the Chinese and the Vietnamese, and it boiled over thirteen years after the publication of Fulbright's *Arrogance of Power* in 1966. With the eventual loss of the Republic of Vietnam, one year after Fulbright retired from the Senate in 1974, "Peking had decided to 'teach Vietnam a lesson' and had intensified its effort to establish full diplomatic relations with the United States" (Chanda, 6). The long-term mutual assistance between Vietnam and China during the Second Indochina War was replaced by a much longer-held mutual antagonism after the DRV's victory over the United States and the Republic of Vietnam in April 1975. Ironically,

only three years after the Third Indochina War began in 1975, the United States normalized relations with China on 15 December 1978. In effect, by 1979, "three decades after going to war in Vietnam to fight 'Chinese expansionism,' the United States became a silent partner in Peking's war against Vietnam." See Nayan Chanda, *Brother Enemy, The War After the War: A History of Indochina Since the Fall of Saigon* (New York: Free Press, 1988), 6–7.
157. *The Vietnam Hearings*, Introduction by J. William Fulbright (New York, Vintage Press, 1966).
158. JWF Papers, Series 72, Box 4, Folder 1. Also, see William C. Berman, *William Fulbright and the Vietnam War: The Dissent of a Political Realist* (Kent, OH: Kent University Press, 1988), 56.
159. William C. Berman, *William Fulbright and the Vietnam War: The Dissent of a Political Realist* (Kent, OH: Kent University Press, 1988), 56.
160. J. William Fulbright, *The Arrogance of Power* (New York: Vintage, 1966), 46–7.
161. Randall Woods, *J. William Fulbright, Vietnam, and the Search for a Cold War Foreign Policy* (New York: Cambridge University Press, 1998), 254.
162. David Elliott, *The Vietnamese War: Revolution and Social Change in the Mekong Delta, 1930–1975* (Pacific Basin Institute Book), (New York: Routledge, 2006), 62.
163. Charles DeBenedetti, *An American Ordeal: The Antiwar Movement of the Vietnam Era*, Syracuse Studies on Peace and Conflict Resolution (Syracuse, NY: University of Syracuse, 1990), 143.
164. William C. Berman, *William Fulbright and the Vietnam War: The Dissent of a Political Realist* (Kent, OH: Kent University Press, 1988), 81.
165. J. William Fulbright, *The Arrogance of Power* (New York: Vintage, 1966), 142, 149.
166. Bernard B. Fall, "Letter to the Editor," *New York Times*, 3 November 1966, Series 1.01, Box F-1, BBF, JFKL.
167. Quoted in Jacques Frémeaux and Bruno C. Reis, "French Counterinsurgency in the Era of the Algerian Wars, 1830–1962," in Beatrice Heuser and Eitan Shamir (Eds.), *Insurgencies and Counterinsurgencies: National Styles and Strategic Cultures* (Cambridge, UK: Cambridge University Press, 2016), 70.
168. Douglas Porch, "Bugeaud, Galléni, Lyautey: The Development of French Colonial Warfare" in Peter Paret (Ed.), *Makers of Modern Strategy: From Machiavelli to the Nuclear Age* (Princeton, NJ: Princeton University Press, 1986), 380.
169. Bernard B. Fall, "CV," Series, 1.01, Box F-1, BBF, JFKL.
170. Author interview with Robert Cowley, Newport, Rhode Island, 9 May 2017. Cowley worked with *American Heritage* from 1956 to 1963 before editing *Horizon*. He would later edit and publish numerous works of history, including *What If? The World's Foremost Historians Imagine What Might Have Been* (New York: Berkley, 2000) and *The Great War: Perspectives on the First World War* (New

York: Random House, 2004). He was the founding editor of *MHQ: The Quarterly Journal of Military History* and continues to publish with a current focus on the Battle of Ypres during World War I.
171. Author interview with Robert Cowley, Newport, Rhode Island, 9 May 2017.
172. Bernard B. Fall, "Two Thousand Years of War in Viet-Nam," *Horizon*, Volume IX, Number 2, Spring 1967.
173. *Ibid.*, 22.
174. Author interview with Robert Cowley, Newport, Rhode Island, 9 May 2017.
175. Fall cited the scholarship of Bernard Philippe Groslier, *Indochina: Art of the World*, translated by George Lawrence (London: Methuen, 1962) and Bernard Philippe Groslier, *Indochina*, Translated by James Hogarth (New York: The World Publishing Company, 1966).
176. Bernard B. Fall, "Two Thousand Years of War in Viet-Nam," *Horizon*, Volume IX, Number 2, Spring 1967. This article is also published in Bernard B. Fall, *Last Reflections on a War* (New York: Doubleday & Company, 1967). Fall's quote is located on pp. 34–5 in *Last Reflections*.
177. Bernard B. Fall, *Last Reflections on a War* (New York: Doubleday & Company, 1967), 39.
178. See Marc Bloch, *The Historian's Craft* (New York: Vintage Books, 1953).
179. Dorothy Fall, *Bernard Fall: Memories of a Soldier-Scholar* (Washington, DC: Potomac Books, 2007), 231.
180. Bernard B. Fall, *The Two Viet-Nams: A Political and Military Analysis*, Second Revised Edition (New York: Praeger, 1967).
181. For Fall's references to Pike, see *Ibid.*, 357 and 362. Fall praised Pike's study and especially Pike's claim that "The NLF was not simply an indigenous organization in which the Communists played a part. Neither was it simply a robot-like instrument of the DRV. Fall appreciated the nuances in command and control that existed between the NLF and DRV, a subject that remains contested by historians. For Pike's study see, Douglas Pike, *Viet Cong: The Organization and Techniques of the National Liberation Front of South Vietnam* (Cambridge, MA: The MIT Press, 1966).
182. Dorothy Fall, *Bernard Fall: Memories of a Soldier-Scholar* (Washington, DC: Potomac Books, 2007), 231–2.
183. *Ibid.*, 231.
184. François Sully Papers, "Sully Comments on Bernard Fall," *Newsweek* Files, February–March 1967, Series II, Subject Files, Box 2, Folder 31, 5.
185. Dorothy Fall, *Bernard Fall: Memories of a Soldier-Scholar* (Washington, DC: Potomac Books, 2007), 75.
186. Mai Elliott, *RAND in Southeast Asia: A History of the Vietnam War Era* (Santa Monica, CA: RAND Corporation, 2010), 53.
187. *Ibid.*, 53, 59. Elliott's work is the most comprehensive study of this program cur-

rently available. See especially, Chapter 2, "What Makes the Viet Cong Tick," 45–90. The "Viet Cong Motivation and Morale" research program was modeled on Lucian Pye's study of insurgency in Malaya and was intended to answer a Robert McNamara question, "Who are the Viet Cong and what makes them tick?" (Elliott, 51, 53) A member of the Department of State Policy Planning Council, Robert H. Johnson, suggested that the study be considered, and it was developed and led by Guy Pauker, a Southeast Asia Specialist in the RAND Social Science Department, John Donnell, and Joseph Zasloff. It began in 1964 but was taken in a different direction by Lou Goure late that year to support Air Force requests to better understand the effects of its air operations. This focus centered on psychological effects of operations upon Vietnamese as a result of operations conducted by air-based platforms such as AC-47 gunships and B-52s. On this early program planning, see pp. 45–53.

188. For a brief description of the Chieu Hoi Program, see George C. Herring, *America's Longest War: The United States and Vietnam, 1950–1975* (New York: Alfred A. Knopf, 1979), 210.
189. *Ibid.*, 210.
190. Mai Elliott, *RAND in Southeast Asia: A History of the Vietnam War Era* (Santa Monica, CA: RAND Corporation, 2010), 139.
191. Dorothy Fall, *Bernard Fall: Memories of a Soldier-Scholar* (Washington, DC: Potomac Books, 2007), 238.
192. Kuno Kneobl, *Victor Charlie: The Face of War in Vietnam* (New York: Praeger, 1967).
193. Bernard B. Fall (Ed.), *Ho Chi Minh: On Revolution, Selected Writings, 1920–66* (New York: Frederick A. Praeger, 1967), v–xiii.
194. *Hell in a Very Small Place*, according to historians Kevin Boylan and Luc Olivier, was "the first-full length study on the subject in English and quickly became the standard Western account of Dien Bien Phu. See Kevin Boylan and Luc Olivier, *Valley of the Shadow: The Siege of Dien Bien Phu* (New York: Osprey, 2018), 266.
195. Denis Warner, *The Last Confucian: Vietnam, South-East Asia, and the West* (Middlesex, UK: Penguin Books, 1964), 151.
196. Bernard Fall, *The Two Viet-Nams: A Political and Military Analysis* (New York: Praeger, 1967), 386–7.
197. François Sully Papers, "Sully comments on Bernard Fall," *Newsweek* Files, February–March 1967, Series II, Subject Files, Box 2, Folder 31, 1.
198. *Ibid.*, 1.
199. *Ibid.*, 3.
200. *Ibid.*, 6.
201. *Ibid.*, 4.
202. David Halberstam, "Foreword," in Dorothy Fall, *Bernard Fall: Memories of a Soldier-Scholar* (Washington, DC: Potomac Books, 2007), xvi.

203. "Then and Now: An Interview with Bernard Fall," Interview with SGT Roy Johnson, 12 February 1967, Combat Info Bureau Danang, *Marine Corps Gazette*, April 1967, reprinted in *Marine Corps Gazette* in November 2002. "Bernard Fall PhD Published Information, USMC Heritage Division, Quantico, Virginia.
204. Bernard B. Fall, "Two Thousand Years of War in Viet-Nam," *Last Reflections on a War* (New York: Doubleday & Company, 1967), 45.
205. Dorothy Fall, *Bernard Fall: Memories of a Soldier-Scholar* (Washington, DC: Potomac Books, 2007), 184.
206. M.J. Mitchinson, "The Pathology of Idiopathic Retroperitoneal Fibrosis," *Journal of Clinical Pathology*, Spring 1970, 23, 681–9.
207. Dorothy Fall, *Bernard Fall: Memories of a Soldier-Scholar* (Washington, DC: Potomac Books, 2007), 185.
208. Bernard B. Fall, *Last Reflections on a War* (New York: Doubleday & Company, 1967), 25.
209. François Sully Papers, "Sully Comments on Bernard Fall," *Newsweek* Files, February–March 1967, Series II, Subject Files, Box 2, Folder 31, 2–3. The Falls purchased a plot of land in the Abaco islands in Northern Bahamas. See Dorothy Fall, *Bernard Fall: Memories of a Soldier-Scholar* (Washington, DC: Potomac Books, 2007), 231.
210. See David H. Hackworth, *About Face: The Odyssey of an American Warrior* (New York: Touchstone, 1989).
211. Dorothy Fall, *Bernard Fall: Memories of a Soldier-Scholar* (Washington, DC: Potomac Books, 2007), 249–50.
212. François Sully Papers, "Sully Comments on Bernard Fall," *Newsweek* Files, February–March 1967, Series II, Subject Files, Box 2, Folder 31, 7.
213. Andrew Preston, *The War Council: McGeorge Bundy, the NSC, and Vietnam* (Cambridge, MA: Harvard University Press, 2010), 53.
214. The idea of the "Long 1964" is a guiding theme in Fredrik Logevall, *Choosing War: The Lost Chance for Peace and the Escalation of War in Vietnam* (Berkeley, CA: University of California Press, 1999).
215. *Ibid.*, 3.
216. *Ibid.*, 30.
217. *Ibid.*, 201.
218. For a comprehensive study on this matter, see Fredrik Logevall, *Choosing War: The Lost Chance for Peace and the Escalation of War in Vietnam* (Berkeley, CA: University of California Press, 1999).
219. Andrew Preston, *The War Council: McGeorge Bundy, the NSC, and Vietnam* (Cambridge, MA: Harvard University Press, 2010), 193.
220. *Ibid.*, 193.
221. *Ibid.*, 193.
222. Ibid., 192–3.

223. See "The Senator and the Senate," 44–65 in J. William Fulbright, *The Arrogance of Power* (New York: Vintage Books, 1966).
224. Bernard B. Fall, "This Isn't Munich, It's Spain," in *Last Reflections on a War* (New York: Doubleday & Company, 1967), 224–36.
225. *Ibid.*, 236.
226. See David E. Johnson, "You Go to COIN With the Military You Have: The United States and 250 Years of Irregular War," in Jacques Frémeaux and Bruno C. Reis, "French Counterinsurgency in the Era of the Algerian Wars, 1830–1962," in Beatrice Heuser and Eitan Shamir (Eds.), *Insurgencies and Counterinsurgencies: National Styles and Strategic Cultures* (Cambridge, UK: Cambridge University Press, 2016), 132–3.
227. For an overview on this early escalation and data quoted in this paragraph, see Robert D. Schulzinger, *A Time for War: The United States and Vietnam, 1941–1975* (New York: Oxford University Press, 1997), 170–4.
228. *Ibid.*, 213.
229. *Ibid.*, 232–3.
230. *Ibid.*, 234.
231. Bernard Fall and Marcus Raskin (Eds.), *The Viet-Nam Reader: Articles and Documents on American Foreign Policy and the Viet-Nam Crisis* (New York: Vintage Book 1965), 368.
232. Bernard B. Fall, "This Isn't Munich, It's Spain," in *Last Reflections on a War* (New York: Doubleday & Company, 1967), 233.
233. *Ibid.*, 236.
234. See "Say I Slew Them Not" in Chapter II of this book.
235. See Telford Taylor, *Nuremberg and Vietnam: An American Tragedy* (Chicago, IL: Quadrangle Books, 1970).
236. Bernard Fall and Marcus Raskin (Eds.), *The Viet-Nam Reader: Articles and Documents on American Foreign Policy and the Viet-Nam Crisis* (New York: Vintage Book 1965), xv.
237. The National Broadcasting Company, "Meet the Press," produced by Lawrence E. Spivak, Guest: Bernard Fall, Vol. 9, 31 January 1965, 3, Series 1.01, Box F-1, BBF, JFKL.
238. George C. Herring, *The American Century and Beyond: U.S. Foreign Relations, 1893–2014* (New York: Oxford University Press, 2008), 439.
239. "NBC's 'Meet the Press,'" 31 January 1965, Series 1.01, Box F-1, 3, BBF, JFKL.
240. "Sherman Kent Memorandum to the CIA Director," 9 June 1964, National Security File, Vietnam Country File: Box 54, LBJP, LBJL.
241. Bernard B. Fall, "This isn't Munich, It's Spain," *Ramparts*, 1965, quoted in Fall, *Last Reflections on a War* (New York: Doubleday & Company, 1967), 236.
242. Bernard B. Fall, *Viet-Nam Witness, 1953–1966* (New York: Frederick A. Praeger, 1966), 299.

243. Bernard B. Fall, "This Isn't Munich, It's Spain," *Ramparts*, 1965, quoted in Fall, *Last Reflections on a War*, (New York: Doubleday & Company, 1967), 234.
244. Bernard B. Fall, *Viet-Nam Witness, 1953–1966* (New York: Frederick A. Praeger, 1966), 326.
245. *Ibid.*, 343–4.
246. Bernard B. Fall, *The Two Viet-Nams: A Political and Military History*, Second Revised Edition (New York: Praeger, 1967). Fall's discussion of neutralization is located on pp. 409–11 in this revised edition.
247. *Ibid.*, 411.
248. Bernard B. Fall, *Viet-Nam Witness, 1953–1966* (New York: Frederick A. Praeger, 1966), 344.

EPILOGUE

1. "USG Memorandum," "Photographs; case of Dr. Bernard Fall," From Director of Information to Historical Branch, G-3 Division, 23 March 1967. 1st Battalion, 9th Marines Command Chronology for period 5 to 28 February 1967, USMC Heritage Division, Quantico, Virginia.
2. Bernard B. Fall, "Vietnam Blitz: A Report on the Impersonal War," *New Republic*, 9 October 1965. The author was unable to locate this article in Fall's archived papers. It was located in François Sully's Papers and Photographs, *Newsweek* Files, February–March 1967, UMass-Boston, Series II, Subject Files, Box 6, Folder 208.
3. *Ibid.*, 21.
4. The National Broadcasting Company, "Meet the Press," produced by Lawrence E. Spivak, Guest: Bernard Fall, Vol. 9, 31 January 1965, 6–7, Series 1.01, Box F-1, BBF, JFKL.
5. "Sully comments on Bernard Fall," François Sully Papers and Photographs, *Newsweek* Files, February–March 1967, UMass-Boston, Series II, Subject Files, Box 2, Folder 31, 23.
6. *Ibid.*, 23.
7. Bernard B. Fall, *The Two Viet-Nams: A Political and Military History*, Second Revised Edition (New York: Praeger, 1967), 196.
8. "Requiem for the Cold War" in *Playboy*, January 1994, David Halberstam Papers, Box 54, Folder 9, Howard Gotlieb Archival Research Center, Boston University.
9. The George Polk Awards, 1965, Long Island University; https://www.liu.edu/polk-awards/past-winners#1965 (accessed 10 January 2021).
10. Bernard B. Fall Personal Papers Finding Aid, JFKL: https://www.jfklibrary.org/asset-viewer/archives/BBFPP (accessed 10 January 2021).
11. On the Third Indochina War, see Odd Arne Westad, Sophie Quinn-Judge (Eds.), *The Third Indochina War: Conflict Between China, Vietnam, and Cambodia, 1972–1979* (London, UK: Routledge, 2006). On normalization, see Kathy Wilhelm, "China and Vietnam Normalize Relations," *Washington Post*, 6 November 1991.

12. Fredrik Logevall, "Bernard Fall: The Man Who Knew the War," *New York Times*, 21 February 2017, https://nyti.ms/2m39aiT (accessed 10 January 2021).
13. For information about Catherine Leroy, see the non-profit Catherine Leroy Fund (DCL) at: https://dotationcatherineleroy.org/en/biography/ (accessed 2 January 2021).
14. Catherine Leroy, J.W. Cohn, *Women's Wear Daily*, 9 October 1968 (Penske Business Corporation, New York).
15. "Sully comments on Bernard Fall," François Sully Papers and Photographs, *Newsweek* Files, February–March 1967, UMass-Boston, Series II, Subject Files, Box 2, Folder 31, 2.
16. *Ibid.*, 8, 10.
17. *Ibid.*, 11.
18. *Ibid.*, 6.
19. General Charles Q. Brown, Jr., Air Force Chief of Staff, "Accelerate Change or Lose," August 2020, https://www.af.mil/Portals/1/documents/csaf/CSAF_Action_Orders_Letter_to_the_Force.pdf (accessed 20 January 2021).
20. Christian Brose, *The Kill Chain: Defending America in the Future of High-Tech Warfare* (New York: Hatchette Books, 2020). For discussion of defense spending and current and anticipated threats, see pp. 184–205.
21. Since production began, CVN-78, Gerald R. Ford has cost $13.3 billion. See "Report to Congress on Gerald R. Ford Carrier Program," *USNI News*, 18 August 2020. https://news.usni.org/2020/08/18/report-to-congress-on-gerald-r-ford-carrier-program-3 (accessed 15 January 2021).
22. Bernard B. Fall, *Street Without Joy: The French Debacle in Indochina*, Foreword by Fredrik Logevall, (Guildford, CT: Stackpole Books, 2018), ix.
23. H.R.6395, National Defense Authorization Act for Fiscal Year 2021, sponsored by Rep. Adam Smith (D-WA-9), Introduced 26 March 2020. Available at: https://www.congress.gov/bill/116th-congress/house-bill/6395/text (accessed 20 February 2021).
24. Charles T. Cleveland, Ryan Crocker, Daniel Egel, Andre M. Liepman, David Maxwell, "An American Way of Political Warfare," *Perspective*, RAND, PE-304, July 2018.
25. *Ibid.*, 2.
26. David H. Ucko, "Nobody Puts IW in an Annex: It's Time to Embrace Irregular Warfare as a Strategic Priority," 14 October 2020, *Modern War Institute*.
27. *Ibid.*
28. US Department of Defense, "DOD releases Fiscal Year 2021 Budget Proposal," 10 February 2020. https://comptroller.defense.gov/Budget-Materials/ (accessed 12 January 2021.).
29. For cost comparison on Wasp-class decks, replacing the USS *Bonhomme Richard*, which underwent a complex and costly refit, was estimated to cost of $3–4 bil-

lion. See Craig Hooper, "A Burnt *Bonhomme Richard* Is No Longer a Headache for the New Navy Boss," *Forbes*, 1 December 2020. For more on the LHD, see "Fact Files" at www.navy.mil/Resources/Fact-Files (accessed 22 January 2021).
30. H.R. McMaster, *Battlegrounds: The Fight to Defend the Free* World (New York: Harper Collins, 2020), 419.
31. *Ibid.*, 432.
32. LTC John A. Nagl (RET), *Knife Fights: A Memoir of Modern War in Theory and Practice* (New York: Penguin 2014), 213–14.
33. Stephen M. Walt, *The Hell of Good Intentions: America's Foreign Policy Elite and the Decline of U.S. Primary* (New York: Farrar, Straus and Giroux, 2018), 76.
34. *Ibid.*, 23.
35. *Ibid.*, see Walt's description in "An Alternative: Offshore Balancing," 260–78.
36. Craig Whiteside, "New Masters of Revolutionary Warfare: The Islamic State Movement (2002–2016)," *Perspectives on Terrorism*, Vol. 10, No. 4., August 2016, 4–5.
37. Craig Whiteside, "The Islamic State and the Return to Revolutionary Warfare," *Small Wars & Insurgencies*, Vol. 27, No. 5 (2016), 743–76.
38. Victor Serge, *Memoirs of a Revolutionary* (New York: NYRB Classics, 2012), 327.
39. Bernard B. Fall, "Revolutionary Warfare in Southeast Asia," In *Readings in Guerrilla Warfare*, U.S. Army Special Warfare Center, Fort Bragg, NC, Special Text 31–180, December 1960, p. 160. William P. Yarborough Papers, Box 128, Howard Gotlieb Archival Research Center, Boston University, Boston, Massachusetts.

BIBLIOGRAPHY

Notes on Archives

Bernard B. Fall's papers contain unpublished essays, book reviews, professional correspondence, notes, and drafts of published papers and are held at the John F. Kennedy Presidential Library, Boston, Massachusetts. This collection also contains Bernard Fall's extensive research materials related to German Interwar Rearmament; the Nuremberg Trials; numerous maps of Europe and Southeast Asia; and French, US, Republic of Vietnam, State of Vietnam, and limited Democratic Republic of Vietnam government publications and journals. Fall's papers include numerous Vietnamese posters from World War II to the early Second Indochina War era, extensive news clippings from 1950–66, and other materials.

Archives and Collections Consulted

Dwight D. Eisenhower Presidential Library, Abilene, Kansas.
    J. Lawton Collins Papers.
    John Foster Dulles Papers, 1951–9.
    National Security Council Staff Papers.
    Alan Grant Jr. Papers.
Franklin D. Roosevelt Presidential Library, Hyde Park, New York.
    Franklin D. Roosevelt Papers, Indochina Files, President's Secretary File, 1933–45.
John F. Kennedy Presidential Library, Columbia Point, Boston, Massachusetts.
    Bernard B. Fall Papers.
Joseph P. Healey Archives and Special Collections, University of Massachusetts Boston, Massachusetts.
    François Sully Papers and Photographs, 1958–63.
Hoover Institute, Stanford University, Palo Alto, California.

BIBLIOGRAPHY

Edward Lansdale Papers.
Howard Gotlieb Archival Research Center, Boston University, Boston, Massachusetts.
William P. Yarborough Papers.
David Halberstam Papers.
Lyndon B. Johnson Presidential Library, Austin, Texas.
Papers of Lyndon Baines Johnson.
Manuscript Division, Library of Congress, Washington, DC.
Neil Sheehan-John Paul Vann Papers.
National Archive and Records Administration (NARA), College Park, Maryland.
Record Group 469 (Records of US Foreign Assistance Agencies, 1948–61).
Butler Library, Columbia University, Rare Book and Manuscript Library Collections, Columbia University, New York City, New York.
Telford Taylor Papers.
United States Army War College, Heritage and Education Center, Carlisle, Pennsylvania.
J. Lawton Collins Papers.
Matthew B. Ridgway Papers.
United States Marine Corps, Archives Branch, Marine Corps History Division, Quantico, Virginia.
Vietnam War Collection.
University of Arkansas Special Collections, Fayetteville, Arkansas.
J. William Fulbright Papers.

Interviews

Robert Cowley, interview with author, Newport, Rhode Island, 9 May 2017.
David Marshall, interview with author, Machias, Maine, 22 August 2017.
Karl Purnell, interview with author, Lewisburg, Pennsylvania, 26 October 2017.

Non-Archival Sources

Henry Ainley, *In Order to Die* (London: Burke Publishing Company, 1955).
Christopher Andrew and Vasili Mitrokhin, *The Sword and the Shield: The Mitrokhin Archive and the Secret History of the KGB* (New York: Basic Books, 1999).
Elizabeth Anthony, Akim Jah, Christine Schmidt, Susanne Urban (Eds.), *Women Under Nazi Persecution: A Primary Source Supplement Based on Documents From the International Tracing Service*, United States Holocaust Memorial Museum, ITS, The Wiener Library, 2017.
Michitake Aso, *Rubber and the Making of Vietnam: An Ecological History, 1897–1975* (Chapel Hill, NC: University of North Carolina Press, 2018).
 – "The Scientist, the Governor, and the Planter: The Political Economy of

BIBLIOGRAPHY

Agricultural Knowledge in Indochina During the Creation of a 'Science of Rubber,' 1900–1940, *East Asian Science, Technology and Society: An International Journal*, DOI 10.1007/s12280-009-9092-7.

Robert Asprey, *War in the Shadows: The Guerrilla in History* (New York: William Morrow and Company, Inc., 1994).

Dixee R. Bartholomew-Feis, *The O.S.S. and Ho Chi Minh: Unexpected Allies in the War Against Japan* (Lawrence, KS: University of Kansas Press, 2006).

David A. Bell, *Shadows of Revolution: Reflections on France, Past and Present* (New York: Oxford University Press, 2016).

William C. Berman, *William Fulbright and the Vietnam War: The Dissent of a Political Realist* (Kent, OH: Kent State University Press, 1988).

John C. Beyer and Stephen A. Schneider, *Forced Labor Under the Third Reich, Part One*, Nathan Associates, Arlington, Virginia, 1 January 1999.

David Biggs, *Quagmire: Nation-Building and Nature in the Mekong Delta* (Seattle, WA: University of Washington Press, 2010).

Jeremy Black, *Rethinking Military History* (New York: Routledge, 2004).

Dennis J. Blasko, "Ten Reasons China Will Have Trouble Fighting a Modern War," *War on the Rocks*, https://warontherocks.com/2015/02/ten-reasons-why-china-will-have-trouble-fighting-a-modern-war/ (accessed 28 December 2015).

Pierre Boddard, *The Quicksand War: Prelude to Vietnam* (London: Faber and Faber, 1967).

Kevin Boylan and Luc Olivier, *Valley of the Shadow: The Siege of Dien Bien Phu* (New York: Osprey, 2018).

Mark Philip Bradley, *Imagining Vietnam and America: The Making of Postcolonial Vietnam, 1919–1950* (Chapel Hill, NC: University of North Carolina Press, 2000).

Ron Briley, "Bernard Fall," *The Scribner Encyclopedia of American Lives: The 1960s*, Edited by William L. O'Neill (New York: Charles Scribner's Sons, 2003).

Christopher R. Browning, *Ordinary Men: Reserve Police Battalion 101 and the Final Solution in Poland* (New York: Harper Collins, 1998).

Henry, J. Bruton, "The Role of Counterpart Funds in Economic Development," *IDS Bulletin*, January 1992, ISSN: 0265–5012.

Joseph Buttinger, *Vietnam: A Dragon Embattled, Volume II, Vietnam at War* (New York: Frederick A. Praeger, Publishers, 1967).

Joseph Buttinger, *Vietnam: A Political History* (New York: Praeger, 1968).

Rukmini Callimachi, "Described as Defeated, Islamic State Punches Back with Guerrilla Tactics, *New York Times*, 21 January 2019.

Christopher Capozzola, *Bound By War: How the United States and the Philippines Built America's First Pacific Century* (New York: Basic Books, 2020).

Stokely Carmichael, *Ready for Revolution: The Life and Struggles of Stokely Carmichael* (Kwame Ture) (New York: Scribner, 2005).

BIBLIOGRAPHY

Steven Casey, "The Campaign to Sell a Harsh Peace for Germany to the American Public, 1944–1948," London: LSE Research Online, http://eprints.lse.ac.uk/736/ (accessed 10 May 2018).

Robert Cassidy and Jacqueline Tame, "The Wages of War Without Strategy, Part I: Clausewitz, Vietnam, and the Roots of Strategic Confusion," 5 January 2017, *War on the Rocks*, https://warontherocks.com/2017/01/the-wages-of-war-without-strategy-part-i-clausewitz-vietnam-and-the-roots-of-strategic-confusion/ (accessed on 5 January 2017).

Claude Chambard, *The Maquis: A History of the French Resistance Movement* (New York: The Bobbs-Merrill Company, Inc., 1976).

Sisouk Na Champassak, *Storm Over Laos: A Contemporary History* (New York: Frederick A. Praeger, 1961).

Nayan Chanda, *Brother Enemy, the War After the War: A History of Indochina Since the Fall of Saigon* (New York: Harcourt, Brace, Jovanovich, 1986).

David Chandler, "Paul Mus (1902–1969): A Biographical Sketch," *Journal of Vietnamese Studies*, Vol. 4, No. 1 (Winter 2009), 149–191.

David Chanoff, "A Casualty of War and Then of Love." *Washington Post*, 3 October 2006 http://www.pressreader.com/usa/the-washington-post/20061003/282278135819950 (accessed 15 June 2017).

Jessica Chapman, *Cauldron of Resistance: Ngo Dinh Diem, The United States, and 1950s Southern Vietnam* (Ithaca, NY: Cornell University Press, 2013).

Jean Chesneaux, *Contribution a l'Histoire de la Nation Vietnamienne* (Paris: Editions Sociales, 1955).

Truong Chinh, *Primer for Revolt: The Communist Takeover in Viet-Nam*, with an introduction by Bernard Fall (New York: Praeger 1963).

C.J. Chivers, *The Fighters: Americans in Combat in Afghanistan and Iraq* (New York: Simon & Schuster, 2018).

Noam Chomsky, *Class Warfare: Interviews With David Barsamian* (Monroe, ME: Common Courage Press, 1996).

Christopher Clark, *The Sleepwalkers: How Europe Went to War in 1914* (New York: Harper Perennial, 2012).

Allan B. Cole (Ed.), *Conflict in Indo-China and International Repercussion: A Documentary History, 1945–1955* (Ithaca, NY: The Fletcher School of Law and Diplomacy, Tufts University and the Southeast Asia Program, Cornell University Press, 1956).

General J. Lawton Collins, *Lightning Joe, An Autobiography* (Novato, CA: Presidio Press, 1994).

Brigadier General James Lawton Collins, Jr., *The Development and Training of the South Vietnamese Army, 1950–1972* (Washington, DC: Department of the Army, 1975).

Kenneth Conboy, *The Cambodian War: Clashing Armies and CIA Covert Operations* (Lawrence, KS: University Press of Kansas, 2013).

BIBLIOGRAPHY

Robert E. Conot, *Justice at Nuremberg* (New York: Basic Books, 1983).

Frank Costigliola, *France and the United States: The Cold War Alliance Since World War II* (New York: Twayne Publishers, 1992).

James Eliot Cross, *Conflict in the Shadows: The Nature and Politics of Guerrilla Warfare* (New York: Doubleday & Company, 1963).

Nick Cullather, *Secret History: The CIA's Classified Account of Its Operations in Guatemala, 1952–1953* (Palo Alto, CA: Stanford University Press, 2006).

Eugene Davidson, *The Trial of the Germans: An Account of the Twenty-Two Defendants Before the International Military Tribunal at Nuremberg* (New York: Macmillan Company, 1966).

Charles de Gaulle, *The Call to Honour 1940–1942* (New York: The Viking Press, 1955).

István Deák, *Europe on Trial: The Story of Collaboration, Resistance, and Retribution During World War II* (Boulder, CO: Westview Press, 2015).

Charles DeBenedetti, *An American Ordeal: The Antiwar Movement of the Vietnam War* (Syracuse, NY: Syracuse University Press, 1990).

Philippe Devillers, *Histoire du Viet-Nam* (Paris: Seuil, 1962).

– *France-Asie*, No. 188 (*Hiver* 1966–67), 146–60.

Philippe Devillers and Jean Lacouture, *End of a War, Indochina 1954* (New York: Praeger 1969).

David Donovan, *Once a Warrior King: Memoirs of an Officer in Vietnam* (New York: Ballantine Books, 1985).

John W. Dower, *War Without Mercy: Race & Power in the Pacific War* (New York: Pantheon Books, 1986).

Mary L. Dudziak, *War-Time: An Idea, Its History, and Its Consequences* (New York: Oxford University Press, 2012).

William J. Duiker, *The Communist Road to Power in Vietnam* (Boulder, CO: Westview Press, 1996).

– *Ho Chi Minh: A Life* (New York: Hatchette Books, 2000).

Dwight D. Eisenhower, *Mandate for Change: The White House Years, 1953–1956* (New York: Doubleday & Company, 1963).

– *Waging Peace: The White House Years, 1956–1961* (New York: Doubleday & Company, 1965).

Norbert Ehrenfreund, *The Nuremberg Legacy: How the Nazi War Crimes Trials Changed the Course of History* (New York: Palgrave Macmillan, 2007).

David W.P. Elliott, *The Vietnamese War: Revolution and Social Change in the Mekong Delta 1930–1975* (Armonk, NY: M.E. Sharpe, 2003).

Mai Elliott, *RAND in Southeast Asia: A History of the Vietnam War Era* (Santa Monica, CA: RAND Corporation, 2010).

Robert Fahs, "Back to a Forgotten Street: Bernard B. Fall and the Limits of Armed Intervention," *Prologue*, US National Archives and Records Administration,

Vol. 43, No. 1 (Spring 2011), http://www.archives.gov/publications/prologue/2011/spring/bernard-fall.html (accessed 6 December 2016).

Richard Falk, *Revisiting the Vietnam War and International Law: Views and Interpretations of Richard Falk*, edited by Stefan Andersson (New York: Cambridge University Press, 2018).

Bernard B. Fall, *Anatomy of a Crisis: The Laotian Crisis of 1960–1961* (New York: Doubleday & Company, 1969).

– "The Case of Alfred Krupp," *Prevent World War III*, Summer 1951, ISSN/ISBN: 0032–7999.

– Editor and Introduction, *Ho Chi Minh: On Revolution, Selected Writings, 1920–66* (New York: Frederick A. Praeger, 1967).

– *Hell in a Very Small Place: The Siege of Dien Bien Phu* (New York: Da Capo Press, 1967).

– "Indochina Since Geneva," *Pacific Affairs*, Vol. 28, No. 1 (March 1955).

– *Last Reflections on a War* (New York: Doubleday & Company, 1967).

– "The Pathet Lao: A 'Liberation' Party," in *The Communist Revolution in Asia: Tactics, Goals, and Achievements*, edited by Robert A. Scalapino, (Englewood, NJ: Prentice-Hall, Inc., 1965).

– "The Political-Religious Sects of Viet-Nam," *Pacific Affairs*, Vol. 28, No. 3 (September 1955).

– "South Viet-Nam's Internal Problems," *Pacific Affairs*, September 1958, Series 1.01, Box F-1, BBF, JFKL.

– *Street Without Joy: The French Debacle in Indochina* (Guilford, CT: Stackpole Books, 1961).

– "Two Thousand Years of War in Viet-Nam," *Horizon*, Vol. IX, No. 2 (Spring 1967).

– *The Two Viet-Nams: A Political and Military Analysis* (New York: Praeger, 1963).

– *The Two Viet-Nams: A Political and Military Analysis*, Second Revised Edition (New York: Praeger, 1967).

– *The Viet-Minh Regime: Government and Administration in the Democratic Republic of Vietnam* (New York: Institute of Pacific Relations, 1956), reprinted by Greenwood Press, Westport, CT, 1975.

– *Viet-Nam Witness, 1953–1966* (New York: Frederick A. Praeger, 1966).

– *Le Viet-Minh: La République Démocratique du Viêt-Nam, 1945–1950*. With Preface by Paul Mus (Paris: Libraire Armand Colin, 1960).

– "Will South Viet-Nam Be Next?" *The Nation*, 31 May 1958, BBF, JFKL, Series 1.06, Box A-2.

Bernard B. Fall and Marcus G. Raskin (Eds.), *The Viet-Nam Reader: Articles and Documents on American Foreign Policy and the Viet-Nam Crisis* (New York: Vintage Book 1965).

Dorothy Fall, *Bernard Fall: Memories of a Soldier-Scholar* (Washington, DC: Potomac Books, 2007).

BIBLIOGRAPHY

Frantz Fanon, *The Wretched of the Earth* (New York: An Evergreen Book published by Grove Weidenfeld, 1963).

Bardo Fassbender, "Compensation for Forced Labour in World War II: The German Compensation Law of 2 August 2000," *Journal of International Criminal Justice*, Vol. 3, Issue 1, 243–52, 2005. Available at SSRN: http://ssrn.com/abstract=915693

Jonathan Fenby, *Chiang Kai Shek: China's Generalissimo and the Nation He Lost* (New York: Carroll & Graf Publishers, 2004).

– *The History of Modern France: From the Revolution to the Present Day* (New York: Simon & Schuster, 2015).

Charles Fenn, *At the Dragon's Gate: With the OSS in the Far East* (Annapolis, MD: Naval Institute Press, 2004).

Michael P.M. Finch, "A Total War of the Mind: The French Theory of *La Guerre Révolutionnaire*, 1954–1958," *War in History*, 2018, Vol. 23, Issue 3.

Francis FitzGerald, *Fire in The Lake: The Vietnamese and the Americans in Vietnam* (Boston, MA: Little, Brown and Company, 1972).

– "The Reporter Who Warned Us Not to Invade Vietnam 10 Years Before the Gulf of Tonkin," *The Nation*, 23 March 2015.

Ronald Bruce Frankum, Jr., *Vietnam's Year of the Rat: Elbridge Durbrow, Ngo Dinh Diem and the Turn in U.S. Relations, 1959–1961* (Jefferson, NC: McFarland and Company, 2014).

Lawrence Freedman, *The Future of War: A History* (New York: Public Affairs, 2017).

Jacques Frémeaux and Bruno C. Reis, "French Counterinsurgency in the Era of the Algerian Wars, 1830–1962," in Beatrice Heuser and Eitan Shamir (Eds.), *Insurgencies and Counterinsurgencies: National Styles and Strategic Cultures* (Cambridge, UK: Cambridge University Press, 2016).

J. William Fulbright, *The Arrogance of Power* (New York: Vintage Books, 1966).

David Galula, *Contre-Insurrection: Théorie et Pratique* (Paris: Economica, 2008).

– *Counterinsurgency Warfare: Theory and Practice* (Westport, CT: Praeger, 2006).

Boaz Ganor, "Defining Terrorism: Is One Man's Terrorist Another Man's Freedom Fighter?" *Police Practice and Research*, Vol. 3, No. 4 (2002).

James George, "Rediscovering Bernard Fall," *News & Politics Examiner*, 19 August 2014.

James A. George and James A. Rodger, *Smart Data: Enterprise Performance Optimization Strategy* (New York: Wiley, 2010).

Emmanuel Gerard and Bruce Kuklick, *Death in the Congo: Murdering Patrice Lumumba* (Cambridge, MA: Harvard University Press, 2015).

Michael Geyer, "German Strategy in the Age of Machine Warfare, 1914–1945," in Peter Paret (Ed.), *Makers of Modern Strategy: From Machiavelli to the Nuclear Age* (Princeton, NJ: Princeton University Press, 1986).

Vo Nguyen Giap, *People's War People's Army: The Viet Cong Insurrection Manual for*

BIBLIOGRAPHY

Undeveloped Countries, Foreword by Roger Hilsman, Profile of Giap by Bernard Fall (New York: Bantam Books, 1968). First printed by Praeger in 1962.

Christoph Giebel, *Imagined Ancestries of Vietnamese Communism: Ton Duc Thang and the Politics of History and Memory* (Seattle, WA: University of Washington Press, 2006).

Robert Gildea, *Fighters in the Shadows: A New History of the French Resistance* (Cambridge, MA: Belknap Press of Harvard University, 2015).

Lesley Gill, *The School of the Americas: Military Training and Political Violence in the Americas* (Durham, NC: Duke University Press, 2004).

Ruth Ginio, *The French Army and Its African Soldiers: The Years of Decolonization* (Lincoln, NE: University of Nebraska Press, 2017).

Sheldon Glueck, *War Criminals: Their Prosecution and Punishment* (New York: Alfred A. Knopf, 1944).

Cecil E. Goins, "Bernard B. Fall: An Analysis of the Man and His Mission as Limited by His Biases on Vietnam," MA Thesis, Southern Oregon College, 1968. OCLC Number: 27114163.

Christopher E. Goscha, *Vietnam: A New History* (New York: Basic Books, 2016).

– "Intelligence in a Time of Decolonialization: The Case of the Democratic Republic of Vietnam at War (1945–50), *Intelligence and National Security*, Vol. 22, No. 1 (February 2007), 100–38.

– "'Sorry About That …' Bernard Fall, the Vietnam War and the Impact of a French Intellectual in the US," in *La Guerre Du Vietnam et L'Europe 1963–1973*, Christopher Goscha and Maurice Vaisse (Eds.) (Paris: LGDJ, 2003).

– *Thailand and the Southeast Asian Networks of the Vietnamese Revolution, 1885–1954* (Richmond, Surrey, UK: Curzon Press, 1999), Nordic Institute of Asian Studies Monograph Series, 79).

– "A 'Total War' of Decolonization? Social Mobilization and State-Building in Communist Vietnam (1949–54)," *War and Society*, Vol. 31, No. 2 (August 2012).

Christopher E. Goscha, David G. Marr, and Merle Pribbenow, "The Creation of a Vietnamese Intelligence Service, 1945–1950," *Exploring Intelligence Archives: Enquires into the Secret State*, R. Gerald Hughes, Peter Jackson, and Len Scott (Eds.), (New York: Routledge, 2008).

Samuel B. Griffith, translator, *Mao Tse-tung on Guerrilla Warfare* (New York: Praeger, 1961).

Bernard Philippe Groslier, *Indochina: Art of the World*, translated by George Lawrence (London: Methuen, 1962).

– *Indochina*, Translated by James Hogarth (New York: World Publishing Company, 1966).

Lt. Col. Dave Grossman, *On Killing: The Psychological Cost of Learning to Kill in War and Society* (New York: Little, Brown, and Company, 2009).

BIBLIOGRAPHY

Vasily Grossman, *A Writer at War: Vasily Grossman with the Red Army*, Edited and Translated by Antony Beevor and Luba Vinogradova (New York: Pantheon Books, 2005).

Jean Guéhenno, *Diary of the Dark Years, 1940–1944*, translated by David Ball (New York: Oxford University Press, 2014).

David H. Hackworth, *About Face: The Odyssey of an American Warrior* (New York: Touchstone, 1989).

Ellen J. Hammer, *The Struggle for Indochina 1940–1955: Viet Nam and the French Experience* (Palo Alto, CA: Stanford University Press, 1955).

Stephen L. Harp, *Marketing Michelin: Advertising and Cultural Identify in Twentieth-Century France* (Baltimore, MD: Johns Hopkins University Press, 2001).

Sheldon H. Harris, *Factories of Death: Japanese Biological Warfare, 1932–1945 and the American Cover Up* (New York: Routledge, 1994).

Michael Herr, *Dispatches: A Correspondent's Memoir: 1967–1975* in *Reporting Vietnam: Part Two: American Journalism 1969–1975* (New York: Library of America, Literary Classics of the United States, Inc., 1998).

– *Dispatches* (New York: Vintage Books, 1991).

George C. Herring, *America's Longest War: The United States and Vietnam, 1950–1975* (New York: Alfred A. Knopf, 1979).

– *The American Century & Beyond: U.S. Foreign Relations, 1893–2014* (New York: Oxford University Press).

Benjamin Carter Hett, *The Death of Democracy: Hitler's Rise to Power and the Downfall of the Weimar Republic* (New York: Henry Holt and Company, 2018).

Gerald Hickey, *Window on a War: An Anthropologist in the Vieinam Conflict* (Lubbock, TX: Texas Tech University Press, 2002).

– *Village in Vietnam* (New Haven, CT: Yale University Press, 1964).

LTC Rolfe L. Hillman, "Bernard Fall: Vietnam Was His Small Hell, and Remains Ours," Review of *Hell in a Very Small Place: The Siege of Dien Bien Phu*, in *Army*, April 1967.

Francine Hirsch, *Soviet Judgment at Nuremberg: A New History of the International Military Tribunal after World War II* (New York: Oxford University Press, 2020).

History of the United Nations War Crimes Commission and the Development of the Laws of War, Compiled by the United Nations War Crimes Commission (London: His Majesty's Stationery Office, 1948).

Ho Chi Minh, *On Revolution: Selected Writings, 1920–66*, Edited by Bernard B. Fall (New York: Praeger, 1967).

Adam Hochschild, *King Leopold's Ghost* (New York: Mariner Books, 1998).

Eric Hoffer, *The True Believer: Thoughts on the Nature of Mass Movements* (New York: Harper, 1951).

Hajo Holborn, "The Origins and Political Character of Nazi Ideology," *The Political Science Quarterly* (December 1964), in *Revolution: A Reader* (Cambridge, MA: Department of Humanities, MIT).

BIBLIOGRAPHY

Stephen Hosmer and Sibylle O. Crane, *Counterinsurgency: A Symposium, April 16–20, 1962* (Santa Monica, CA: RAND Corporation, 2006).

Hue Tam Ho Tai, *Millenarianism and Peasant Politics in Vietnam* (Cambridge, MA: Harvard University Press, 1983).

– *Radicalism and the Origins of the Vietnamese Revolution* (Cambridge, MA: Harvard University Press, 1992).

David Hunt, *Vietnam's Southern Revolution: From Peasant Insurrection to Total War* (Amherst, MA: University of Massachusetts Press, 2008).

Michael H. Hunt and Steven I. Levine, *Arc of Empire: America's Wars in Asia From the Philippines to Vietnam* (Chapel Hill, NC: University of North Carolina Press, 2012).

Richard A. Hunt, "Avoiding Lessons From the Past? The US in the Vietnam War," in *La Guerre Du Vietnam et L'Europe 1963–1973*, Christopher Goscha and Maurice Vaisse (Eds.), (Brussels: Bruylant; Paris: LGDJ, 2003).

In the Name of America, Clergy and Laymen Concerned About Vietnam, January 1968, Director of Research Seymour Melman (Annandale, VA: The Turnpike Press, Inc., 1968).

Michael A. Innes, *Streets Without Joy: Afghanistan, Iraq and the American Sanctuary Discourses of 2001–2008*, PhD dissertation, Department of Politics, School of Oriental and African Studies, University of London, 2019.

– *Streets Without Joy: A Political History of Sanctuary and War, 1959–2009* (London: Hurst Publishers, 2021).

International Military Tribunal (IMT), XI. Judgment, A. Opinion and Judgment of Military Tribunal III, 1327–1484.

Peter Irons, *A People's History of the Supreme Court: The Men and Women Whose Cases and Decisions Have Shaped Our Constitution* (New York: Penguin Books 1999).

Walter Isaacson and Evan Thomas, *The Wise Men: Six Friends and the World They Made* (New York: Touchstone Books, 1986).

Seth Jacobs, *America's Miracle Man in Vietnam: Ngo Dinh Diem, Religion, Race, and U.S. Intervention in Southeast Asia, 1950–1957* (Durham, NC: Duke University Press, 2004).

Harold James, *Krupp: A History of the Legendary German Firm* (Princeton, NJ: Princeton University Press, 2012).

Jérémy Jammes, *Les Oracles du Cao Dai, Étude d'un movement religieux vietnamien et de ses reseaux* (Paris: Les Indes Savantes, 2014).

Stathis N. Kalyvas, *The Logic of Violence in Civil War* (Cambridge, UK: Cambridge University Press, 2006).

Michael Kaponya, *The French Foreign Legion and Indochina: In Retrospect* (Mustang, OK: Tate Publishing, 2013).

Stanley Karnow, *Vietnam: A History* (New York: Penguin Books, 1997).

H.R. Kedward, *In Search of the Maquis: Rural Resistance in Southern France 1942–1944* (Oxford: Clarendon Press, 1994).

BIBLIOGRAPHY

John Keegan, *The Second World War* (New York: Viking Press, 1989).

Charles Keith, *Catholic Vietnam: A Church from Empire to Nation* (Berkeley, CA: University of California Press, 2012).

John P. Kenny, *Moral Aspects of Nuremberg* (Washington, DC: Pontifical Faculty of Theology Dominican House of Studies, 1949).

Benedict J. Tria Kerkvliet, *The Power of Everyday Politics: How Vietnamese Peasants Transformed National Policy* (Ithaca, NY: Cornell University Press, 2005).

Nikita Khrushchev, *Khrushchev Remembers*, Translated by Strobe Talbott (Boston, MA: Little, Brown and Company, 1970).

David Kilcullen, *The Accidental Guerrilla: Fighting Small Wars in the Midst of a Big One* (New York: Oxford University Press, 2009).

– *Counterinsurgency* (New York: Oxford University Press, 2010).

– *Out of the Mountains: The Coming Age of the Urban Guerrilla* (New York: Oxford University Press, 2013).

Kuno Knoebl, *Victor Charlie: The Face of War in Vietnam*, With an introduction by Bernard Fall (New York: Praeger, 1967).

Albin Krebs, "Raoul Salan Dies; Led Algerian Plot," *New York Times*, 4 July 1984, http://www.nytimes.com/1984/07/04/obituaries/raoul-salan-dies-led-algeria-plot.html (accessed October 22, 2016).

Bruce Kuklick, *Blind Oracles: Intellectuals and War From Kennan to Kissinger* (Princeton, NJ: Princeton University Press, 2006).

Franck Lambert, *Free French Saboteurs* (Paris: Histoire & Collections, 2015).

Donald Lancaster, *The Emancipation of French Indo-China* (New York: Oxford University Press, 1961).

Paul F. Langer, "Comments on Bernard Fall's The Pathet Lao: A 'Liberation' Party" (Santa Monica, CA: RAND Corporation, 1968, P-3751).

Paul F. Langer and Joseph J. Zasloff, *North Vietnam and the Pathet Lao: Partners in the Struggle for Laos* (Cambridge, MA: Harvard University Press, 1970).

A.J. Langguth, *Our Vietnam: The War 1954–1975* (New York: Simon and Schuster, 2000).

Edward Geary Lansdale, *In the Midst of Wars: An American's Mission to Southeast Asia* (New York: Fordham University Press, 1991).

Jean Lartéguy, *The Centurions*, Translated by Xan Fielding (New York: Penguin Books, 2015).

Harold D. Lasswell, "The Garrison State," *American Journal of Sociology*, Vol. 46, No. 4 (January 1941), 455, 459. JSTOR, www.jstor.org/stable/2769918 (accessed 31 July 2017).

Mark Atwood Lawrence, *Assuming the Burden: Europe and the American Commitment to War in Vietnam* (Berkeley, CA: University of California Press, 2005).

Le Duan, *The Vietnamese Revolution: Fundamental Problems and Essential Tasks* (New York: International Publishers, 1971).

William J. Lederer and Eugene Burdick, *The Ugly American* (New York: W.W. Norton & Company, 1958).

William E. Leuchtenburg, *The American President: From Teddy Roosevelt to Bill Clinton* (New York: Oxford University Press, 2015).

Marc Levinson, *The Box: How the Shipping Container Made the World Smaller and the World Economy Bigger* (Princeton, NJ: Princeton University Press, 2006).

Roger Lévy, "Bernard Fall devant le Congrès Américain," *Politique Étrangère*, Vol. 32, No. 3 (1967), 262–8.

Richard W. Lindholm (Ed.), *Viet-Nam—The First Five Years: An International Symposium* (Lansing, MI: Michigan State University Press, 1959).

Fredrik Logevall, *Choosing War: The Lost Chance for Peace and the Escalation of War in Vietnam* (Berkeley, CA: University of California Press, 1999).

– *Embers of War: The Fall of an Empire and the Making of America's Vietnam* (New York: Random House, 2014).

– "Bernard Fall: The Man Who Knew the War," *New York Times*, 21 February 2017, https://www.nytimes.com/2017/02/21/opinion/bernard-fall-the-man-who-knew-the-war.html

William Manchester, *The Arms of Krupp, 1587–1968* (Boston, MA: Little, Brown and Company, 1968).

Octavian Manea, "Reflections on the French School of Counter-Rebellion: An Interview with Étienne de Durand," *Small Wars Journal*, 3 March 2011.

Erez Manela, *The Wilsonian Moment: Self-Determination and the International Origins of Anticolonial Nationalism* (New York: Oxford University Press, 2007).

Carl M. Marcy, Foreign Relations Committee, Chief of Staff, "Interview #5 Fulbright Breaks with Johnson," 19 October 1984, interviewed by Donald A. Ritchie, *United States Senate Historical Office—Oral History Project*.

– Foreign Relations Committee, Chief of Staff, "Interview #4 Fulbright and Kennedy," 12 October 1984, interviewed by Donald A. Ritchie, *United States Senate Historical Office—Oral History Project*.

David G. Marr, *Vietnam: State, War, and Revolution (1945–1946)* (Berkeley, CA: University of California Press, 2013).

– *Vietnamese Tradition on Trial, 1920–1945* (Berkeley, CA: University of California Press, 1981).

Michael R. Marrus and Robert O. Paxton, *Vichy France and the Jews* (New York: Basic Books, 1981).

Ben L. Martin, "The New 'Old China Hands': Shaping a Specialty," *Asian Affairs*, Vol. 3, No. 2 (November–December 1975).

Nick M. Masellis, "Counterinsurgency Theoretical and Practical Principles," Unpublished Thesis, Naval Postgraduate School, September 2012.

Viscount Maugham, *U.N.O. and War Crimes* (London: John Murray Publishers, 1951).

BIBLIOGRAPHY

Mark Mazower, *Hitler's Empire: How the Nazis Ruled Europe* (New York: Penguin Press, 2008).

John T. McAlister, Jr. and Paul Mus, *The Vietnamese and Their Revolution* (New York: Harper Torchbooks, 1970).

John McCain, "John McCain: By the Book," *New York Times*, 3 May 2018. https://www.nytimes.com/2018/05/03/books/review/john-mccain-by-the-book.html

Stanley McChrystal, *Team of Teams: New Rules of Engagement for a Complex World* (New York: Penguin/Portfolio, 2015).

Shawn McHale, *Print and Power: Confucianism, Communism, and Buddhism in the Making of Modern Vietnam* (Honolulu, HI: University of Hawai'i Press, 2004).

– "Understanding the Fanatic Mind? The Viet Minh and Race Hatred in the First Indochina War (1945–1954)," *Journal of Vietnamese Studies*, Vol. 4, Issue 3 (2009), 98–138.

Eugene Methvin, "Ideology and Organization in Counterinsurgency," *Orbis*, Spring 1964, in *Revolution: A Reader* (Cambridge, MA: Department of Humanities, MIT).

James A. Michener, *Tales of the South Pacific* (New York: Macmillan Publishing Company, 1947).

Edward Miller, *Misalliance: Ngo Dinh Diem, the United States, and the Fate of South Vietnam* (Cambridge, MA: Harvard University Press, 2013).

– "War-Stories: The Taylor–Buzzanco Debate and How We Think About the Vietnam War," *Journal of Vietnamese Studies*, Vol. 1., No. 1–2 (February–August), 2006.

David Milne, *America's Rasputin: Walt Rostow and the Vietnam War* (New York: Hill and Wang, 2008).

– *Worldmaking: The Art and Science of American Diplomacy* (New York: Farrar, Strauss, and Giroux, 2015).

Ho Chi Minh, *On Revolution: Selected Writings, 1920–1966*, Edited and with an Introduction by Bernard B. Fall (New York: Praeger, 1967).

Nathaniel L. Moir, "Bernard Fall and Vietnamese Revolutionary Warfare in Indochina," *Small Wars & Insurgencies*, Vol. 28, No. 6 (30 October 2017), https://www.tandfonline.com/doi/full/10.1080/09592318.2017.1374594

Edwin E. Moïse, *Land Reform in China and North Vietnam: Consolidating the Revolution at the Village Level* (Chapel Hill, NC: University of North Carolina Press, 1983).

Samuel Moyn, "From Aggression to Atrocity: Rethinking the History of International Criminal Law," (7 July 2016), *Oxford Handbook of International Criminal Law* (Forthcoming), Available at SSRN: https://ssrn.com/abstract=2805952

Brian S. Mueller, "Confronting America's National Security State: The Institute for Policy Studies and the Vietnam War," *Diplomatic History*, Vol. 41, No. 4 (September 2018).

BIBLIOGRAPHY

Paul Mus, *Le Viet Nam Chez Lui* (Paris: Centre d'Études de Politique Étrangère, 1946).

Jonathan Nashel, *Edward Lansdale's Cold War* (Amherst and Boston, MA: University of Massachusetts Press, 2005).

Lien-Hang T. Nguyen, *Hanoi's War: An International History of the War for Peace in Vietnam* (Chapel Hill, NC: University of North Carolina Press, 2012).

Nguyen Thi Dinh, *No Other Road To Take: Memoir of Nguyen Thi Dinh*, translated by Mai V. Elliott (Ithaca, NY: Southeast Asia Program Publications, Cornell University, 2000).

Edgar O'Ballance, *The Indo-China War 1945–1954: A Study in Guerrilla Warfare* (London: Faber and Faber, 1964).

James S. Olson, *Dictionary of the Vietnam War* (New York: Greenwood Press, 1988).

George Orwell, *Homage to Catalonia* (New York: Harcourt, Brace, Jovanovich, 1952).

Norman G. Owen (Ed.), *The Emergence of Modern Southeast Asia: A New History* (Honolulu: University of Hawai'i Press, 2005).

Christian Parenti, "Empire Fall," *The Nation*, 27 February 2007. https://www.thenation.com/article/empire-fall/ (accessed 6 December 2016).

Peter Paret, *French Revolutionary Warfare from Indochina to Algeria: The Analysis of a Political and Military Doctrine* (New York: Praeger, 1964).

Robert O. Paxton, "Vichy on Trial," *New York Times*, 16 October 1997, https://www.nytimes.com/1997/10/16/opinion/vichy-on-trial.html (accessed 15 September 2018).

Patricia M. Pelley, *Postcolonial Vietnam: New Histories of the National Past* (Durham, NC: Duke University Press, 2002).

The Pentagon Papers, as Published by the New York Times (New York: Quadrangle Books, 1971).

Terence Peterson, "Myth-Busting French Counterinsurgency," *War On The Rocks*, 3 December 2015, https://warontherocks.com/2015/12/myth-busting-french-counterinsurgency/ (accessed 20 May 2017).

David Lan Pham, *Two Hamlets in Nam Bo: Memoirs of Life in Vietnam* (Jefferson, NC: McFarland & Company, 2000).

Douglas Pike, *Viet-Cong: The Organization and Techniques of the National Liberation Front of South Vietnam* (Cambridge, MA: MIT Press, 1966).

- *PAVN: People's Army of Vietnam* (New York: Da Capo Press, 1983).

Douglas Porch, *The French Secret Services: From the Dreyfus Affair to the Gulf War* (New York: Farrar, Strauss and Giroux, 1995).

- "Bugeaud, Galléni, Lyautey: The Development of French Colonial Warfare" in Peter Paret (Ed.), *Makers of Modern Strategy: From Machiavelli to the Nuclear Age* (Princeton, NJ: Princeton University Press, 1986).

Patrick Porter, *Military Orientalism: Eastern War Through Western Eyes* (New York: Oxford University Press, 2014).

BIBLIOGRAPHY

Colin L. Powell, "Colin L. Powell: By the Book," *New York Times*, 28 June 2012. https://www.nytimes.com/2012/07/01/books/review/colin-l-powell-by-the-book.html

John Prados, *The Blood Road: The Ho Chi Minh Trail and the Vietnam War* (New York: Wiley & Sons, 1999).

Andrew Preston, *The War Council: McGeorge Bundy, the NSC, and Vietnam* (Cambridge, MA: Harvard University Press, 2010).

Merle L. Pribbenow (Translator), The Military History Institute of Vietnam, *Victory in Vietnam: The Official History of the People's Army of Vietnam, 1954–1975* (Lawrence, KS: University Press of Kansas, 2002).

Sophie Quinn-Judge, *Ho Chi Minh: The Missing Years* (Berkeley, CA: University of California Press, 2002).

Jeffrey Race, *War Comes to Long An*: *Revolutionary Conflict in a Vietnamese Province* (Berkeley, CA: University of California Press, 1972).

Adam Rayski, *The Choice of the Jews Under Vichy: Between Submission and Resistance* (South Bend, IN: Notre Dame University Press, 2005).

René Riesen, *Jungle Mission*, translated by James Oliver, (London: Hutchinson, 1957).

Marie-Monique Robin, Escadrons de la Mort: L'école Française (Paris: Le Decouverte/Poche, 2004).

William Roseberry, "Hegemony and the Language of Contention," *Everyday Forms of State Formation: Revolution and the Negotiation of Rule in Modern Mexico*, Gilbert M. Joseph and Daniel Nugent (Eds.) (Durham, NC: Duke University Press, 1994).

Michael E. Ruane, "Bernard Fall: A Portrait," 3 December 2007, *Los Angeles Times*.

Jean Sainteny, *Histoire d'une Paix Manquée* (Paris: Seuil, 1953).

Oscar Salemink, *The Ethnography of Vietnam's Central Highlanders: A Historical Contextualization, 1850–1900* (Honolulu, HI: University of Hawai'i Press, 2003).

Arthur M. Schlesinger, Jr., *A Thousand Days: John F. Kennedy in the White House* (Cambridge, MA: Houghton Mifflin Company, 1965).

Pierre Schoendoerffer, *La 317e Section* (Paris: Gallimard, 1963).

Robert D. Schulzinger, *A Time for War: The United States and Vietnam, 1941–1975* (New York: Oxford University Press, 1997).

Frederick J. Schwarz, "Doctrines of Defeat: La Guerre Revolutionnaire and Counterinsurgency Warfare," December 1992, unpublished thesis, Indiana University, Bloomington, Indiana.

Robert Scigliano, *South Vietnam: Nation Under Stress* (Boston, MA: Houghton Mifflin Company, 1963).

Philip Selznick, *The Organizational Weapon: A Study in Bolshevik Strategy and Tactics* (Glencoe, IL: Free Press of Glencoe, 1960).

Neil Sheehan, *A Bright Shining Lie: John Paul Vann and America in Vietnam* (New York: Vintage Books, 1988).

– *A Fiery Peace in a Cold War: Bernard Schriever and the Ultimate Weapon* (New York: Random House, 2009).

BIBLIOGRAPHY

John Darrell Sherwood, *War in the Shallows: U.S. Navy Coastal and Riverine Warfare in Vietnam 1965–1968* (Washington, DC: Naval History and Heritage Command, 2015).

Landon Shroder, "What if the Islamic State Won?" *VICE News*, 16 September 2015, http://news.vice.com/article/what-if-the-islamic-stat-won?utm_source=vicenewsemail (accessed 4 November 2016).

John Shy and Thomas W. Collier, "Revolutionary War" in Peter Paret (Ed.), *Makers of Modern Strategy: From Machiavelli to the Nuclear Age* (Princeton, NJ: Princeton University Press, 1986).

Paul Staniland, *Networks of Rebellion: Explaining Insurgent Cohesion and Collapse* (Ithaca, NY: Cornell University Press, 2014).

Benn Steil, *The Marshall Plan: Dawn of the Cold War* (New York: Oxford University Press, 2018).

I.F. Stone, *In a Time of Torment, 1961–1967* (Boston, MA: Little, Brown, and Company, 1967).

François Sully, *Age of the Guerrilla* (New York: Avon Books, 1968).

– (Ed.), *We the Vietnamese: Voices From Vietnam* (New York: Praeger, 1971).

Robert Taber, *War of the Flea* (New York: L. Stuart, 1965).

George K. Tanham, *Communist Revolutionary Warfare: From the Vietminh to the Viet Cong* (Westport, CT: Praeger Security International, 2006).

Telford Taylor, *The Anatomy of the Nuremberg Trials: A Personal Memoir* (New York: Alfred A. Knopf, 1992).

– *Nuremberg and Vietnam: An American Tragedy* (Chicago, IL: Quadrangle Books, 1970).

Laura Thompson, "Operational Anthropology as an Emergent Discipline," *ETC: A Review of General Semantics*, Vol. 8, No. 2 (Winter 1951), 117–28.

Robert R. Tomes, *Apocalypse Then: American Intellectuals and the Vietnam War, 1954–1975* (New York: New York University Press, 1998).

Adam Tooze, *The Wages of Destruction: The Making and Breaking of the Nazi Economy* (New York: Viking, 2006).

Tran Tu Binh, *The Red Earth: A Vietnamese Memoir of Life on a Colonial Plantation*, Translated by John Spragens, Jr., Edited by David G. Marr, (Athens, OH: Ohio University Press, 1985).

Enzo Traverso, *Fire and Blood: The European Civil War 1914–1945*, Translated by David Fernbach (New York: Verso, 2016).

Roger Trinquier, *Modern Warfare: A French View of Counterinsurgency* (New York, Praeger, 2006).

Barbara W. Tuchman, *Stilwell and the American Experience in China, 1911–1945* (New York: Grove Press, 1985).

Tuong Vu, "The Revolutionary Path to State Formation in Vietnam: Opportunities, Conundrums, and Legacies," *Journal of Vietnamese Studies*, Vol. 11, Issue 3–4 (2016), 1–33.

BIBLIOGRAPHY

– *Vietnam's Communist Revolution: The Power and Limits of Ideology* (New York: Cambridge University Press, 2017).

Markus Urban, translated by John Jenkins, *The Nuremberg Trials* (Nurnberg, Germany: Geschichte Für Alle e.V.—Institut für Regionalgeschichte, 2012).

Amry Vandenbosch and Richard A. Butwell, *Southeast Asia Among the World Powers* (Lexington, KY: University of Kentucky Press, 1957).

Irwin Wall, "The Marshall Plan and French Politics," in Martin A. Schain (Ed.), *The Marshall Plan Fifty Years Later* (London: Palgrave MacMillan, 2001).

Denis Warner, *The Last Confucian: Vietnam, Southeast Asia, and the West* (New York: Penguin 1964).

Jayne Susan Warner, *Peasant Politics and Religious Sectarianism: Peasant and Priest in the Cao Dai in Viet Nam* (New Haven, CT: Monograph Series 23/Yale University Southeast Asia Studies, 1981).

Roger Warner, *Shooting at the Moon: The Story of America's Clandestine War in Laos* (South Royalton, VT: Steer Forth Press, 1996).

Jeremy M. Weinstein, "Resources and the Information Problem in Rebel Recruitment," *Journal of Conflict Resolution*, Vol. 49, No. 4 (August 2005).

Francis J. West, Jr., *The Village* (Madison, WI: University of Wisconsin Press, 1972).

Craig Whiteside, "The Islamic State and the Return of Revolutionary Warfare," *Small Wars & Insurgencies*, Vol. 27, No. 5 (August 2016).

– "Lighting the Path: the Evolution of the Islamic State Media Enterprise (2003–2016), ICCT Research Paper, November 16, DOI: 10.19165/2016.1.14, ISSN: 2468-0656

– "New Masters of Revolutionary Warfare: The Islamic State Movement (2002–2016)," *Perspectives on Terrorism*, August 2016, available at, http://www.terrorismanalysts.com/pt/index.php/pot/article/view/523/1036

Martin Windrow, *The Last Valley: Dien Bien Phu and the French Defeat in Vietnam* (New York: Da Capo Press, 2004).

Randall Bennet Woods, *J. William Fulbright, Vietnam, and the Search for a Cold War Foreign Policy* (Cambridge, UK: Cambridge University Press, 1998).

Alexander B. Woodside, *Community and Revolution in Modern Vietnam* (Boston, MA: Houghton Mifflin Company, 1976).

David K. Wyatt, *Thailand: A Short History* (New Haven, NC: Yale University Press, 1984).

William Pelham Yarborough, *Bail Out Over North Africa: America's First Combat Parachute Missions 1942* (Williamstown, NJ: Phillips Publications, 1979).

Nancy Zaroulis and Gerald Sullivan, *Who Spoke Up? American Protest Against the War in Vietnam 1963–1975* (New York: Doubleday and Company, 1984).

Qiang Zhai, *China and the Vietnam War, 1950–1975* (Chapel Hill, NC: University of North Carolina Press, 2000).

– "China and the Geneva Conference of 1954," *China Quarterly*, No. 129 (March 1992), 103–22.

BIBLIOGRAPHY

Peter Zinoman, *The Colonial Bastille: A History of Imprisonment in Vietnam, 1892–1940* (Berkeley, CA: University of California Press, 2001).

Obituaries Cited:

"Carl M. Marcy, 77, Long Chief of Staff of Key Senate Panel," Obituary, *New York Times*, 21 September 1990, available at: https://www.nytimes.com/1990/09/21/obituaries/carl-m-marcy-77-long-chief-of-staff-of-key-senate-panel.html

"Howard Elting, 93; Relayed News of Holocaust," 8 August 2001, *New York Times*.

"In Memory of Ansgar Sovik, My Professor, My Mentor, My Longtime Friend," Jeff Johnson, *St. Olaf Magazine*, Spring 2007, 52.

"Obituary: Ansgar Sovik," Andy Langehough, *Northfield.org*, 20 January 2007.

"Obituary for Bernard B. Fall," *The Harvard Crimson*, 24 February 1967.

"Obituary for Dr. Amry Vandenbosch," *The Advocate-Messenger*, Danville, Kentucky, Tuesday, October 23, 1990.

"Postscript: First Thoughts on the Announcement of the Death of Bernard Fall," Murray N. Rothbard, Leonard P. Liggio, H. George Resch (editors), *Left and Right: A Journal of Libertarian Thought*, Autumn 1968, Volume IV, 68–9.

Tran Van Chuong Obituary, "Former Saigon Envoy and Wife Found Dead," Associated Press, 25 July 1986, *New York Times*, https://www.nytimes.com/1986/07/25/world/former-saigon-envoy-and-wife-found-dead.html

INDEX

Note: Page numbers followed by "*n*" refer to notes, "*f*" refer to figures.

Acheson, Dean, 29, 340, 365
Adams, John Quincy, 340
Adenauer, Konrad, 92, 97
Agrarian Reform Committee in Hanoi, 161
Agroville program, 296
Ainley, Henry, 200, 211–12
Al-Qaeda in Iraq (AQI), 379
Alderman, Sydney, 71
Allgemeine SS, 84
Almond, Gabriel, 114
American Council of Learned Societies (ACLS), 449*n*143
American Foreign Assistance programs, 343
American Heritage journal, 353
American Office of Strategic Services (OSS), 46
Anatomy of a Crisis: The Laotian Crisis of 1960–1961(Fall), 320, 322, 324–5, 328
Andrew Rankin Memorial Chapel, Washington, DC on 6 Mar 1967, 8–10
Annales school of thought, 354
Anschluss of Austria, 34–5
anti-colonial agendas, 183

anti-communism, 138, 183
anti-Diem Vietnamese, 234
anti-Nazi resistance in Oyonnax, 49
anti-Semitism in Austria, 35
Anzio-Nettuno landing, 330
Arbeitzeinsatz, 80
Árbenz, Jacobo (President), 306
Armée Juive, 38
Army of the Republic of Vietnam (ARVN), 300
Arnett, Peter, 27
Arrogance of Power, The, 349
Aso, Michitake, 117
Associated State of Vietnam (SVN), 127, 165–73
Atlantic Charter, 116
August Revolution, The, 145, 198, 334
Austria's Declaration of Neutrality, 342
Austrian State Treaty, 342
Bande Noire, 211
Barnet, Richard, 342
Battle of Dak Po or An Khe. *See* Battle of Mang Yang Pass
Battle of Mang Yang Pass, 330
Battle of Saigon, 248, 250, 445*n*69
802nd Battalion, 2
Bay of Pigs Invasion, 351

INDEX

Bell, David (Agency for International Development administrator), 350
Berman, William (Historian), 348, 350, 352
Berthawerks, 76
béton armé (reinforced concrete), 125
Big Berthas, 69
Binh, Tran Tu, 118
Binh Xuyen in Saigon, 244, 246
Black, Jeremy, 15
Black Sea Mutiny, 156–7
Blitz, 371
"Blitz in Vietnam" (article), 381
"Bloc for Liberty and Progress", 443n36
Bloch, Marc, 354
Bolsheviks, 143
Bonnet, Gabriel, 16, 18, 301, 324
Bordel Mobile de Campagne (BMC), 206
Bormann, Martin, 70
Boston Five, 343
Boston University (BU), 389n44, 389n45
Bright Shining Lie, A (Sheehan), 9
British Red Cross, 90
British Special Operatives Executive (SOE), 46
Brown, Charles Q. Jr., 376
Bruton, Henry J., 292
Brzezinksi, Zbigniew Jr., 341
Bugeaud, Thomas-Robert (Governor-General of Algeria), 352
Bunche, Ralph, 232, 284
Bundy, McGeorge, 340, 361–2
Bunting, Fredrick (ICA director), 279
Burdick, Eugene, 269, 295
Buschmannshof, 78
Buttinger, Joseph, 132
Butwell, Richard, 252
Buu Son Ky Houng, 241

Cai San project, 250–1, 447n100
Cai-San refugee camp, 295–6
Cambodia: Its People, Its Society, Its Culture (HRAF book), 240
Cao Dai, 148, 236, 239–41, 309
 faith, 127
 leaders' efforts, 244
 militias, 243
Capozzola, Christopher, 208
Caravelle Manifesto, 328
Carmichael, Stokely (leader of SNCC), 343, 345
Carroll, Camp J. J., 2
Cartesian coordinate system analogy, 188
Caserne d'Auvare, 36
Cavell, Edith, 62
Central Intelligence Agency (CIA), 299, 343
Central Research Agency (CRA), 433n67
Centurions, The (Larteguy), 306, 336
Champassak, Sisouk na, 326
Chappell, William R., 172
Charlie Company, 5, 7
Chatelain, Verne, E., 90
Chau, Pham Boi, 156, 197
Chieu, Bui Quang, 197, 199
Chinese Communist Party (CCP), 169
Chinese Communists, 112
Chinese Military Advisory Group (CMAG), 169
Chinese-supplied arms, 210
Chinh, Truong, 174, 289, 308, 334–5
 career and history, 349–50
 directives, 186
Chinh Luan, 197
Christian Science Monitor (Davis), 252
Chu Teh, also Zhu De, 147
Chuong, Tran Van (father of Tran Le Xuan), 249, 259–62
Church, Frank, 346

INDEX

Churchill, Winston, 101
Cimetière du Monastère, 39
Civil Rights Movement, 343
Civilian collaboration, 48
civilizing mission, 118
Clay, Lucius, 92, 96–7, 99
Clemenceau, Georges, 270
Cochinchina, 162
Coffin, William Sloan, 343
Cold War, 155
collaboration, 48
  problem of, 50–8
Collier, Thomas, 307
Collins, Lawton J., 243, 246–9, 328
Colonel Bigeard, paratroopers of, 306
Colonel Breyer, 80, 98
colonialism, 118–19, 354, 472n134
Colonies Françaises d'Afrique (CFA), 288
Combined Action Company (CAC), 2
Communist Denunciation campaign, 14
Communist-dominated General Confederation of Labor (CGT), 426n115
Compagnons, 38
"competitive control" process, 56
Compulsory Labor Service, 80–1
Con Thien, 3, 5
Condor Legion, 53
Cong An, 31, 180, 199–215, 338
Conseil National de la Resistance (CNR), 203, 338
"Control Council Law No. 10", 67
Convention on the Prevention and Punishment of the Crime of Genocide, 407n80
Cooper, Chester L., 363
Corcoran, Thomas, 277, 279
Costigliola, Frank, 100
counter-terror pacification programs, 129

counterpart funding, 291–2
counterpart funds, 263–5
Covenant of the League of Nations, 64
Cowley, Robert, 353, 369
crime of crimes, 58
criminal liability, 81
Crimson, Harvard, 9
"Crisis in North Viet-Nam", 256
Cronkite, Walter, 27–8
"Crusade in Europe", 22
Cu'u Quoc (Viet Minh newspaper), 131, 165
Cuban Missile Crisis, 351

D-Day, 46
Dai, Bao (Vietnamese Emperor), 30, 129, 133, 166, 168, 234–5
Dang Lao Doc Lap ("Lao Independence Party"), 321, 325
Davis, Saville R., 252
Davis, Vincent, 113–14
DC *Sunday Star*, 257
de Berval, René, 261
de Durand, Étienne, 119
de Gaulle, Charles, 44, 46, 62, 119, 335
de Hauteclocque, Philippe Leclerc (Commander of French Expeditionary Force), 139
de Lattre Line, 125, 202, 216
de Pellepoix, Louis Darquier, 39
de Tassigny, de Lattre, 124–25
Deák, Istvan, 36, 48
DeBenedetti, Charles, 341–2, 351
Defeating Communist Insurgency (Thompson), 355
dehumanizing process, 54
Demilitarized Zone (DMZ), 387n14
Democratic Republic of Vietnam (DRV), 112, 121, 130, 138, 140, 157–65, 180, 475n181
  communist leadership's integration, 121

503

INDEX

declaration of independence, 146
doctrine, 185
  at end of the war, 173–7
  failures, 159
  familiarity with, 230
  leaders, 167
  leadership, 142
  one-party rule in, 161
  policies, 229
  repression, 160
Dennis, J. A., 154
Der Weltkrieg in Bildern (*The World War in Pictures*), 69
Deutschland über alles, 88
Deuve, Jean (French Colonel), 343
"Devil's Brigade" of Canada's 1st Special Service Force, 46
Devillers, Philippe, 27, 66, 113
Dich Van, 31, 180, 199–215, 338–9
Diem, Ngo Dinh, 14, 21, 31–32, 228, 230–1, 233–4, 237, 251, 263, 314–15, 332–3
Dien Bien Phu, 2–3, 19, 100, 126, 131, 148, 170, 175, 177, 181–2, 220, 223
  battle, 353
  France's defeat at, 3
  time of, 303
Dillon, Douglas, 100
Dinassaut naval forces, 223
Dirlewanger, Oskar, 53–4
"dirty war" (*la guerre sale*), 131
Displaced Person (DP), 85
distinction, 54
Doctors' Trial, 67
Dominican Intervention, 351
Dong, Lao, 121, 163
Dong, Pham Van (DRV Prime Minister), 28, 174, 235, 331–4
dong-viet currency, 287–8
Draconian National Security Law, 14
Duan, Le (Party General Secretary), 174, 198, 255, 308, 350

Dudiak, Mary L., 50–1
Dulles, John Foster, 246
Duncanson, Dennis, 287

École Français d'Extrême Orient (Lafont), 261
Economic Cooperation Administration (ECA), 266–8
Ehret, Marcel, 261
Einstein, Alfred, 94
Eisenhower, Dwight, 169, 220, 313, 317
Eliot, Tom, 277
Elliott, David W. P., 14, 196–7, 262–3, 286, 334
Embers of War, 25
Enabling Act of 1933, 70, 109
Enlai, Zhou, 251
Erga Omnes, 406n72
escalatory logic, 305
Essen, evidence in, 75–89
European Defense Community (EDC), 100, 220
European Recovery Act, 289
ex post facto claims, 63–4
"*Extremely Independent and Audacious Man*", *An*, 272–9

Fa-kwei, Chang, 144
Falk, Richard (International justice scholar), 315
Fall, Bernard, B. (journalist-historian), 2–3, 5, 7–10, 33, 38, 47, 49, 58, 66, 92, 111, 120, 123–4, 201, 245, 341, 347, 350, 352, 358, 364, 371, 374, 383
  analysis, 35
  family, 36–7
  history and relevance, 10–32
  military experience, 45
  participation in warfare, 42

INDEX

scholarship, 41
Fall, Dorothy (Fall's spouse), 38, 42, 92, 233
Fall, Leo, 35, 38–9
family affair, 249
Fanon, Frantz, 214
Far Eastern Survey, 249, 256
fatalism, 41
FBI surveillance, 343
Febvre, Lucien, 354
Feltin, Cardinal (French priest), 365–6
Ferber, Michael, 343
Le Figaro, 9
Finch, Michael P. M., 304
Fire Decree, 108
First Indochina War, 139–57, 172
Fishel, Wesley R. (professor of political science), 31, 260, 273, 313–14
Flick, Friedrich, 68
Flick KG, 67, 99
force goals, 455n22
Forces Françaises de l'Intérieur (FFI), 40–1, 44
Foreign Affairs, 138–9, 149, 151–3, 184
Foreign Assistance Act of 1961, 272
Foreign Relations of the United States (*FRUS*), 458n61, 462n131
Forward Air Controller (FAC), 3
France-Asie (de Berval), 261
Frankiel, Henry, 35
Free French forces (de Gaulle), 335
French army, 41, 44
French collaborators, 50
French colonialism, 117–18, 290
French Colonialism on Trial (Ho), 155–6
French colonies in Indochina, 152
French Communist Party (PCF), 138, 149
French Communists, 150–2

French Communists and Indochina, The, 149
French Far East Expeditionary Corps, 330
French Jewish councils, 37
French officials in Indochina, 117
French Resistance, 34
French subsidies, 242
Fulbright, William, J., 8, 22, 32, 91, 103, 346, 351
Fulbright Exchange Program, 346–52

Gallieni, Joseph, 194
Garrison State, The, 114
Gavin, James LTG, 350
"generating local currency" process, 270
Geneva Conference (1962), 322
Geneva Convention (1954), 318
Geneva Convention of 1929, 72
Geng, Chen, 147
Genocide Convention, 89
German armed forces, 34
German Army High Command, 67, 98
German Communist Party (KPD), 108
German occupation forces, 56
German soldiers, 56, 61
Germany
  evidence in Essen, 75–89
  Keystone of Arch, 105–10
Geyer, Michael, 87–8
Gian-sang in Hanoi, 171
Giap, Vo Nguyen, 141–2, 144, 148, 170, 174, 181–2, 334
Giau, Tran Van, 198
Gildea, Robert, 42–3
González, Henry B., 8–9
Goodman, Mitchell, 343
Goralski, Robert, 372
Göring, Herman, 66, 72, 86
Goscha, Christopher, 201, 215–17
Gourou, Pierre, 14

505

INDEX

"Government and Politics 105: Course in American Foreign Relations" (Moser), 90
Goya, Michel, 207
Gracey, Douglas, 132
graves registration, 251
"Gray Zone" conflict, 32
"Greater East-Asian Co-Prosperity Sphere", 118
Griffith, Ronald H., 10
Groslier, Philippe, 14
Groupement de Commandos Mixtes Aéroportés (GCMA), 222, 308, 335, 461n106
Groupement Mixte d'Intervention (GMI), 222
Groupement Mobile 100, 255
Groupes Administratif Mobile Opérationnel (GAMO), 194–5
"*Guerre Révolutionnaire et Pacification*" (Hogard), 304
guerrilla bands, 46
guerrilla fighters, 19, 46
guerrilla warfare, 308
  tactics, 13
"guilt by membership" principle, 97–8
Guizot, François (head of French government), 352
Gulf of Tonkin Incident, 21
Guoqing, Wei, 147
Gusstalhfabrik, 76
Gustav, Schwerer, 69
Gutersohn, Peter, 83, 85

Ha, Dong, 3
Hackworth, David, 360
Hague Convention of 1907, 62, 72, 81
Hague Conventions of 1899 and 1907, 64
Halbach, Gustav Krupp von Bohlen und, 69
Halberstam, David (journalist), 27, 169, 312, 359, 372
Hammer, Ellen, 199, 293
Hao, Hoa, 148, 195–6
hard-core fighters, 327
Harriman, Averell, 94
Heavy Gustav, 69
Hell in a Very Small Place: The Siege of Dien Bien Phu, 2–3, 9, 224, 328
Herr, Michael, 3
Herring, George, 183, 235, 282, 294, 312
Herriot, Édouard, 150
Hess, Rudolf, 66, 71
Hickey, Gerald, 14, 219
Hill, Catherine B., 292
Himmler, Heinrich, 68
Himmler Circle of Friends, 68
Hinh, Nguyen Van, 237
Hirsch, Francine, 60
History of American Civilization (Chatelain), 90
Hitler, Adolf, 70–71
Spende, 70
Ho Phap (Pope) of the Cao Dai, 238
Ho-Sainteny Agreement. *See* March Accords
Hoa Hao, 236, 239–41, 309
  leaders' efforts, 244
  militias, 243
Hoach, Le Van, 127
Hogard, Jacques, (1918–1999), 16, 187–8, 301, 304
Holland, William, 259
Holocaust, 37
Holt, Pat (Latin American expert), 347
Honolulu Declaration, 351
"Honor Squads to Eliminate Traitors" (*doi Danh du tru gian*), 197
Hôpital Pasteur, 38
Horizon magazine (Cowley), 353, 355

INDEX

Horst-Wessel-Lied, 88
Hough, Ed, 277
Howard Gotlieb Archival Research Center (HGARC), 389n44, 389n45
Howard Magazine, 285
Hugon, André, 33
Hull, Cordell, 120
Hum, Phan Van, 197
Human Relations Area Files (HRAF), 228, 239, 267, 441–2n5
humanitarianism (Fall), 55
Hungarian Jewesses, 82
Hunt, Richard, 153
Huntsberger, Warren (professor of International Economics), 278
Huynh Phu So, 241

IG Farben Corporation, 67, 99
"impersonalization" of war, 30
In the Midst of Wars, 244
"In the Mood" music, 47
Indo-China problem, 419n87
Indochina, 11f, 12, 14, 100, 138, 141
 conflict in, 111
 exploitation of local populations in, 120
 French colonies in, 152
 French control, 118
 international trusteeship for, 115–16
 Japan's occupation, 145
 political economy, 117
 political legitimacy in, 130
Indochina Since Geneva, 233, 236, 442n13, 445n67, 446n87
Indochinese Communist Party (ICP), 121, 142, 190–1, 201, 218, 421n37
Inside the Third Reich (Speer), 70
Institute for Policy Studies (IPS), 342
 anti-war position, 342
Institute of Pacific Relations, 183
insurgency, 299

Inter-University Committee, 341
internal security, 176
International Cooperation Administration (ICA), 231, 263, 266, 268, 281, 287, 313, 450n158, 453n196
International Court of Justice, 115, 414n20
International Criminal Court, 414n20
international duties, 87
international justice, 58
International Military Tribunal (IMT), 59–60, 66
International Position of South Vietnam, The, 259
International Tracing Service (ITS), 90
Irregular Warfare Annex, 378
Isaacson, Walter, 99
ISIS, 382
Islamic State and the Return of Revolutionary Warfare, The (paper), 25
Jackson, Robert H. (Associate US Supreme Court Justice), 58–9, 66, 72, 88, 104
Jacob, Seth, 234
Jaeger, Oberlagerarzt, 79
James, Harold, 71, 79
Japanese imperialism, 242
Jewish councils, 36
Jewish resistance, 43
Jodl, Alfred, 66
John Birch Society, 204
Johnson, Lyndon Baines (LBJP), 3, 154, 172–3, 347–8, 362, 423n70
Johnson's Asian Doctrine, 351
Joint All-Domain Command and Control (JADC2), 378–9
Joint Chiefs of Staff (JCS), 94
 JCS 1067, 94
 JCS 1779, 94
Jomini, Antoine-Henri, 181

INDEX

Judges' Trial, 67
Jus cogens, 406n72

Kai-shek, Chiang, 183
Kaltenbrunner, Ernst, 84
Kalyvas, Stathis, 37, 41, 50, 211, 214
Kaplan, Jacob, 267
Katangan rebellion, 336
Kellogg-Briand Pact, 63, 65
Kene sane (organization), 326
Kennan, George, 340, 350
Kennedy, John F., 10, 272, 343, 317–18, 322, 327, 373
Kent, Sherman, 29, 367
Kerkvliet, Benedict Tria, J., 256, 258
Keystone of Arch, 105–10
Khe Sanh, 3
Khmer Krom Cambodian minority, 309
Khrushchev, Nikita (Soviet Party Chairman), 157, 322
Khu, Dang Xuan. *See* Chinh, Truong
Kiem Thao sessions, 205
Kilcullen, David, 26, 382
Kissinger, Henry, 149
Kocher, Eric (Officer of Southeast Asia Affairs), 279
Konzentrationslager, 78
Korean War, 97, 169
Krupp, Alfried, 71–2, 76, 79, 84–6, 92, 96, 98, 102, 365
   corporation assets, 92
   factories, 83–4
   firm, 84
   fortune, 99
   Tribunal's judgment, 86
   workers, 82
Krupp, Bertha, 69–70
Krupp, Gustav, 109
Krupp Corporation, 59, 64–5, 67–8
   annual production charts, 76

   board of directors, 92
   development, 75
   factories, 180
   history, 69
   trial, 343
Krupp of Essen, 69
Kruppianer (Krupp's workers), 83
Kulski, W. W., 225
Kuomintang Party, 143

La Guerre Moderne, 335
La guerre révolutionnaire, 283, 299, 301, 304, 306
La Rue Sans Joie (André Hugon's 1938 film), 3, 33
Lacheroy, Charles, 16, 49, 187, 190, 245, 301, 324
Lacouture, Jean, 1, 27
Lafont, Pierre-Bernard, 261
Lagerfuhrer, 83
land reform and collectivization, 209
Landing Helicopter Dock (LHD), 378
Landy, Pierre (counselor to French Embassy), 279
Langer, Paul F., 325–6
Lansdale, Edward, 31, 327–8
Lao, Pathet (Land of the Lao), 219, 320, 322–4, 326
   Laotian proxies in, 325
   penetration, 324
Lao Dong party, 158, 350
Lao Issara nationalist movement (Souphanouvong), 320
Laos, revolutionary warfare in, 317–40
Laos: Background of a Conflict, 330
Laotian Crisis, 32
Laotian Royal Government, 322
Larteguy, Jean, 306, 336
Lasswell, Harold, 114
   academic approach, 114
   arguments, 115

INDEX

scholarship, 114
Lawrence, Mark Atwood, 137, 168
Le Viet-Minh, 130
Leatherneck Square, 3, 4f, 387n14
Lebensraum, 109, 305
Leclerc, Philippe, 132, 150–1
Lederer, William, 269, 295
Lemkin, Rafael, 89
Leroy, Catherine, 374
Les Anciens Combattants Français, 233
Les Compagnons de France (Vichy youth paramilitary organization), 36, 38–9
Les Eclaireurs Israélites de France (EIF), 38–9
Les Guerres Insurrectionnelles et Révolutionnaires (Bonnet), 301
Les Troupes Coloniales, 212
Lex Krupp, 70–1
Lieu, Tran Huy, 196
Life Magazine, 374
Life of Agricola, 371
Linh, Gio, 3
Lissette (Bernard's sister), 35
Lo, Cam, 3
Lo, Nghia, 175
Loc, Buu, 166, 234
local administration in Laos, 326
Lodge, Henry Cabot, 362
Logevall, Fredrik, 2, 25, 294, 329, 346, 361, 374
London Charter, 64, 115
London conference, 62
Long, Deo Van, 128
"Long 1964" (Logevall), 361
longue durée approach, 354
Lowenstein, James (Southeast Asia expert), 347
Lucet, Charles (French Ambassador to United States), 8, 10
Lyautey, Hubert, 194

Lyndon Baines Johnson Presidential Library, Austin, Texas (LBJL), 423n70

Mad Bonze. *See* Huynh Phu So
Malagasy Uprising, 102, 158
Maloney, W. J. G., 76
Malot, Remy, 126
Manchester, William, 72, 78, 86, 97–8
Mansfield, Mike, 346
manufactured contempt, 54–5
Maquis, 39, 42–50
  actions, 49
  efforts, 62
  in Haute-Savoie, 40
March Accords, 147
Marcy, Carl (Senate Foreign Relations Committee Chief of Staff), 265, 347
Marine Corps, 2, 5, 7, 359
1/9th Marines, 3, 5, 387n15
Marr, David, 142–3, 155, 288–9
Marshall, David, 3, 5, 7
Marshall Plan, 94, 103, 151, 267, 271, 282, 288–9
martial-infiltration techniques, 210
Martin, Ben, 183
Marxist–Leninist ideological orientation, 121
Marxist–Leninist thought, 310
mass mobilization, 215
Maverick, Maury, 172
Mazower, Mark, 88–9, 119
McAlister, John T., 112, 289
McCain, John (Navy pilot), 9
McCarthy, Joe, 183
McCloy, John J., 92–3, 95, 97–9, 154, 365
McCone, John, 343
McGovern, George, 346
McHale, Shawn, 148, 195, 309
McKee, Thomas Hudson, 172–3

509

McMaster, H. R., 379
McNamara, Robert (Secretary of Defense), 340, 348–9
Médaille de la France Libérée, 47
Meet the Press interview, 12, 366, 372
Mekong Delta region, 195
Melman, Seymour, 341
Mendenhall, Joseph, 279
Mendès-France, Pierre, 238
Mengele, Josef, 67
Meo maquis, 322
Merrill, Frank D., 222
Michigan State University Advisory Group, 313
militarists, 67
Military Review, 130, 298
Miller, Glenn, 47
Minh, Ho Chi (DRV President), 9, 23, 28, 30, 133, 144, 155, 161, 235, 308, 331–4
   guerrillas, 145
   nationalist aims, 146
   political flexibility, 156
   trail, 321
Mobile Field Bordellos. *See Bordel Mobile de Campagne* (BMC)
Modern Warfare: A French View of Counterinsurgency (Trinquier), 335
Mohr, Charley, 359
Le Monde, 9
Morgenthau, Hans, 341
Morgenthau, Henry, 94
Morgenthau Plan, 94
Moroccan soldiers, 207
Morrison, Toni, 232
Moser, Martin, 90
Mouvement de la Jeunesse Sioniste, 38
Moyn, Samuel, 103–4
Mozingo, David, 357
Müller, Erich, 84
Mumford, Lewis, 94

Murphy, Audie, 360
Mus, Paul, 14, 27, 112, 150–1, 162, 228–9, 254
My Tho province, 14–15, 129

Nabrit, James, Jr. (Howard University President), 8, 10
Nacht der langen Messer (Night of the Long Knives), 107
Nagl, John A., 380
Nation, The, 31, 154, 184, 231, 259, 263, 268, 272, 284, 286
National Archives Records and Administration (NARA), 451*n*176
National Defense Authorization Act, 377
National Defense Strategy (2018), 378
National Liberation Front (NLF), 187, 245, 299, 315, 356, 364, 475*n*181
   capacity, 21
   formation, 14–15, 24, 198
   mistreatment, 364
   strength, 369
National Security Action Memorandum (NSAM), 294, 457*n*55
National Security Council (NSC), 361
National Socialist German Workers' Party (NSDAP), 107, 109
"national vs. communist" debate, 155
Nationalist Party label, 143
Natural Law, 366
Naval War College Review, The Reader (1966), 342
Navarre, Henri (French General), 131, 302–3
Navarre Plan, 148, 182, 221–2, 422*n*45
Nazi imperialism, 29
Nazi planning, 89
Nazi SS connections, 102
Nazism, 89, 107
Nehru, Jawaharlal, 172

INDEX

Nemo, Jean, 187, 301
Neo Lao Hak Sat (Lao Patriotic Front), 321, 325, 466*n*39
Neo Lao Issara, 321
New Left, 340–6
New Republic, 371
New York, 223–6
New York Times (Sulzberger), 252, 318
Newsweek, 2
Nghe An province, 349
Nguyen, Lien-Hang T., 255, 334
Nhan Dan (newspaper), 165, 174–5
Nhan Van, 257–8
Nhu, Madame. *See* Chuong, Tran Van (father of Tran Le Xuan)
Nhu, Ngo Dinh (Diem brother), 228, 333
Nice, France, 33–42
Nice Refugee Committee, 35
nihilism, 214
Ninh, Nguyen An, 156, 197
Nohles, Peter, 81–2
Non-commissioned officers (NCOs), 202
North Vietnam and the Pathet Lao: Partners in the Struggle for Laos (Langer and Zasloff), 325
North Vietnamese, 130
 forces, 310–11
 troops, 331
Number One Realist, 1, 10–32
Nung Chinese, 209
Nuremberg and Vietnam: An American Tragedy, 61
Nuremberg Charter, 60, 64, 67, 74, 87, 115
Nuremberg Legacy, 87, 95
Nuremberg Military Tribunal (NMT), 58–67, 343, 398*n*115, 398*n*120, 399*n*132, 400*n*153, 404*n*25, 405*n*43, 405*n*46, 405*n*47, 405*n*55, 410*n*128, 412*n*170

Nuremberg Principles, 59–60, 89, 94
Nuremberg Trials, 21, 34, 55, 58–60, 95, 366
Nuremberg Tribunals, 57

O'Hara, James Grant, 130
Office of Strategic Services (OSS), 115, 141
Officier de la Légion d'honneur, 129
one-party rule in DRV, 161
Operation Chinook II, 3, 5
Operation Flaming Dart, 21
Operation Flaming Dart II, 364
Operation Hummingbird, 107
Operation Husky in Sicily, 330
Operation Lorraine, 31, 148, 181–2, 215–23, 440*n*162
Operation Rolling Thunder, 21, 89, 364
Operation Torch in North Africa, 330
Operation Vulture, 303, 459*n*85
operational anthropology, 389–90*n*48
Operations in Iraq and Libya, 379
Organisation Armée Secrète (OAS), 336
Organization for European Economic Cooperation, 267
organizational configuration, 209
organizational dynamics, 218
Out of the Mountains (Kilcullen), 26
Overseas European Program, 90–1
Oyonnax, 49–50

Pacific Affairs, 31, 227, 236, 245, 286, 291
pacification, 352–3
Pao, Vang, 336
Paraglide, The (newspaper), 10
parallel hierarchies, 16–17, 187–90, 324–7, 338
Paret, Peter, 187
Paris conference (1919), 63

INDEX

Partisans, 19
Pathet Lao front, 325
Paxton, Robert, 48–9, 52
Penerf, La (French tanker), 39, 42
People's Army of Vietnam (PAVN), 165, 211, 430n13
People's Republic of China (PRC), 112–13, 123, 149, 168–9
People's War, People's Army (Giap), 334
"People's Workers" (*Dan Cong*), 216
Pétain, Marshall, 40, 42
Phak Khon Ngan Lao, 325
Phak Pasasson Lao (Lao People's Party), 325–6
Phong Saly, 325
Phong Thuong Mai Saigon (Vietnamese journal), 293
Phouma, Souvanna (neutralist), 320
Phu-Rieng, Michelin, 118
Pike, Douglas, 25, 355
planters, 117
Pleven, René, 221
Point Five in Woodrow Wilson's Fourteen Points, 116
"Political Development in Indo-China", 120
political legitimacy, 24
  in Indochina, 130
political turbulence in South Vietnam, 21
Political-Religious Sects of Viet-Nam, The (article), 239
politics, 114
Politique Etrangère, 227
Porch, Douglas, 206, 212
Potemkin-village effect, 251
Potsdam Conference, 132
Powell, Colin, 10
pragmatism, 41
Preston, Andrew, 361–2
"Prevent World War III", 94

Pribbenow, Merle, 210
Primer for Revolt: The Communist Takeover in Viet-Nam, 334
"Principles of Foreign Policy" (Adams), 340
"pro-communist" policies, 123
Provincial Reconnaissance Units (PRU), 212
Provisional National Council, 165
pseudo independence, 242
Punch, Max, 58

Quoc, Nguyen Ai, 143

Radical Party (PRV), 150
Radio Frankfurt, 92
Ramparts, 21–2
RAND study, 356
Raskin, Marcus, 340, 342
Rattanavongsa, Phetsarath, 320
Red River Delta, 134, 195
Régiment de Marche de la Légion Etrangère (RMLE), 408n91
Reichstag Fire Act, 70
Reichstag Fire Decree, 109
Republic of Vietnam (RVN), 20–1, 228, 233, 260, 281, 283, 289
  leadership, 229
  policies, 230
  Rangers, 212
Resistance Will Win, The, 334
revolutionary warfare, 15–17, 23–4, 31, 180, 283, 299, 303, 311
  fighters, 19
  Gabriel Bonnet's description of, 18
  in Laos, 317–40
Revue Militaire D'Information (French journal), 16–17, 187, 189–90, 194, 203, 237, 304, 338
Rieck, Oskar, 83
Riesen, René (GCMA corporal), 308–9

INDEX

Robequain, Charles, 14
Röhm, Ernst, 107
Role of Counterpart Funds in Economic Development, The (Bruton and Hill), 292
Roosevelt, Eleanor, 94
Roosevelt, Franklin, D., 59, 115–17
   trusteeship plan, 118
Rostow, Eugene, 94
Rostow, Walt (Deputy National Security Advisor), 327–8, 340–1
Roth, Elizabeth, 82–3, 85, 93
   testimony, 83
Roth, Ernestine, 83, 85, 93
Rouge, Khmer, 9
Royal Laotian Army, 318
"rubber stamp" national assembly, 237
Rusk, Dean (Secretary of State), 340, 350
Russia-France alliance, 101
Russian Civil War, 143

Salan, Raoul, 194–5, 336
Sam Nuea, 321, 325
Saturday Evening Post, 331
Sauckel, Fritz, 42, 66, 68, 81
Saur, Karl Otto, 86
"*Say I slew them not*", 90–105
Schell, Jonathan, 28
Schlesinger, Arthur, 322, 341
School of Advanced International Studies (SAIS), 30, 111, 113, 120
Schutzstaffel (SS), 65, 77
Scigliano, Robert, 268, 295
Second Indochina War, 283
Second Red Scare, 153
Second Sino-Japanese War, 123
Seligmann, Anna, 35
Service de Documentation Extérieure et du Contre-Espionage (SDECE), 336
"Service for Obligatory Labor", 39, 42

Sharpe, Lauriston, 131–2
Shawcross, Hartley, 71
Sheehan, Neil, 9, 212
Shirer, William, 94
Shy, John, 307
Sicherheitsdienst (SD), 84, 180
Silver Star, 330
"Sinews of Peace" speech, 101
Sino-American relations, 349
Slavern, 67
Snyder, Timothy, 37
Soai, Tran Van, 244–5
Social Democrats Party (SPD), 108
Souphanouvong, 320
"South Viet-Nam's Internal Problems", 31, 281–2, 284–97, 311
South Vietnamese government, 260
Southeast Asia League, 217
Southeast Asia Treaty Organization (SEATO), 122, 343, 416n42
Southeast Asian Federation, 122
Soviet involvement, 60
Soviet Red Army, 34
Special Operations Research Office (SORO), 323, 329
Special Warfare Center, 323
Speer, Albert, 66, 68, 70
Spende, 70
Spiral Model, 396n70
Spivak, Lawrence, 12
Spock, Benjamin, 343
spoliation, 86
Spring Is Triumphant, but Winter Will Surely Return: Three Years of Viet-Minh Rule in North Vietnam, 1954–1958, 255
SS *Obergruppenführer*, 84
staff evidence analyses, 75
Stalin, Joseph, 383
Staniland, Paul, 190
Stars and Stripes (US military's newspaper), 91

513

INDEX

State of Vietnam (SVN), 133–4, 139, 165, 170, 233
Stokes, Thomas, L., 94
Stone, I. F., 27–8
Strategic Hamlet program, 296, 328
"*Street Without Joy*", *The*, 2–10, 6*f*, 27, 33, 52, 138, 224, 328–30, 346
Student Non-Violent Coordinating Committee (SNCC), 343–4
Sturmabteilung (SA), 107, 180
   domestic terrorism, 236
Su-That (*The Truth*), 334
"Subcommittee on Territorial Problems", 115–16
Sud-Est Asiatique, 126
Sully, François (*Newsweek* correspondent and friend), 2–3, 24, 27, 125–6, 225, 356, 360
Sulzberger, C. J., 233–4, 252
"Summary of the Progress of the War of National Liberation" (Giap), 141
Sung, Dan Van, 196–7
Sweet, J. B., 328
Sylla, Ndongo Samba, 288
Systems Analysis Corporation, 233

Tac, Pham Cong, 127–8, 238–40, 245
tache d'huile (oil spot), 192
Tai, Hue-Tam Ho, 240, 242
Tam, Nguyen Van, 128–30, 148, 168, 234, 238, 305
targeting collaborators, 51, 54–5
Tate, Merze, 232
Taubenblatt, Selig, 278
Tay Ninh, 127
Taylor, Keith, 309
Taylor, Maxwell, 350
Taylor, Telford (US Army Brigadier General), 58–62, 69, 71, 79, 81, 86–8, 97, 343
Tennessean, Nashville, 9

Terres Rouges rubber plantation (Ehret), 261
Tet holiday, 3
Thai-Indochinese networks, 438*n*146
Than, Nguyen Hai, 143
Thang, Ton Duc, 156, 174
Thau, Ta Thu, 197
Thayer, Russell, H., 79, 83
Theory and Practice of Insurgency and Counterinsurgency, The, 16
theory-based analysis, 204
Third Reich, 66–67, 365
   massive war production effort, 66
   sovereignty, 89
   subjection, 35
"This Isn't Munich, It's Spain" (essay), 21, 358–69
Tho, Le Duc, 174
Thomas, Evan, 99
Thompson, Robert, 287, 355
Thomson, James C., 363
Thong, Vu Quoc, 128
Time-Life, 126, 177
Tito, Josef Broz, 372
Tokyo Tribunals, 407*n*76
Tong Lien Doan Lao Dong (TLD), 426*n*115
Tonkin Gulf Resolution, 351, 363
Tooze, Adam, 71, 97
Traverso, Enzo, 53–4
Treaty of Paris (1928), 63
Treaty of Versailles, 107, 110, 411*n*157
Tri, Nguyen Huu, 128
Trinh, Phan Chu, 156, 197
Trinh Sat, 31, 180, 199–215, 338
Trinquier, Roger, 16, 49, 187, 190, 245, 335–6
"*Trois Rapports sur l'Armement et la Cavalerie du IIIe Reich*", 63
Trotsky, Leon, 383
Truman, Harry S. (US President), 59, 92, 267

INDEX

Tse-tung, Mao, 18, 45, 147, 168, 179, 182–3, 302, 304, 308
Tsu, Lao, 1
"*Two Thousand Years of War in Viet-Nam*", 352–7
Two Viet-Nams: A Political and Military Analysis, The (Fall), 27, 114, 337–9, 355
U.N. agency, 90
U.S. fire-power, 1
U.S. frontline, 2
U.S. Marine Corps, 2
Ucko, David, 378
Ugly American, The, 269
UN Charter, 64
UN-mandated Nuremberg Charter, 74
United Nations Relief and Rehabilitation Administration (UNRRA), 90
United States Operations Mission (USOM), 263, 268, 273, 293
US Foreign Assistance Act (1961), 20
US Military Advisory Assistance Group (MAAG), 265, 282, 294, 312
US officials in Germany, 92
US-supplied assistance, 167
US–RVN relationship, 292
Uy Ban Hang Lien-Khu, 188

Van Devander, Charles, 94
Van Ribbentrop, Joachim, 66
Vandenbosch, Amry, 113–16, 120, 122, 124, 252, 284
  claim, 123
  class with, 122
Vann, John Paul, 9
Verlag, Johannes Meulenhoff, M., 69
Vichy
  forces, 49
  government's seizure of Jews, 392–3n5
  police, 35, 37

soldiers, 50
Victor's Justice, 65
"Viet Cong Motivation and Morale Project", 356, 476n187
Viet Minh, 15–19, 24, 30, 113, 137, 141, 219, 304
  approach to warfare, 12
  commitment, 253
  communist ideology, 304
  communist-driven land reform, 159
  efforts, 138
  goals, 141
  internal security apparatus, 31
  internal security system, 180
  land-reform policies, 161
  leaders, 255
  leadership, 195
  military failures, 20
  operations, 126
  socio-political-military doctrine, 179
  struggle, 23
  survivability, 174
  Tam's persecution, 129
  top leadership, 144
  urban offensive operations, 129
  victory, 19
Viet Minh Front, 299–300
Viet Nam Dan Quoc Cong Bao, 176, 185
Viet Nam Quoc Dan Dang (VN-QDD), 142
Viet-Cong (Pike), 355
Viet-gian (traitors), 171
Viet-Minh Regime, The, 30, 132, 138, 147, 140, 162, 164–5, 174, 179–80, 182–200, 258–9, 287, 324–5
  conflict within, 191–200
  Cong An, 199–215
  Dich Van, 199–215
  New York, 223–6
  Operation Lorraine, 215–23

INDEX

Trinh Sat, 199–215
Viet-Minh Regime: Government and Administration in the Democratic Republic of Vietnam, The, 131
Viet-Minh Retreat, 438*n*140
Viet-Nam Reader, The (Raskin), 340–2, 346
Vietcong resistance movement, 372
Vietnam, May 1953, 124–35
Vietnam Information Center, 340
Vietnam Liberation Army, 145
Vietnam National Gazette (*Viet Nam Dan Quoc Cong Bao*), 131
Vietnam National Government, 124
Vietnam People's Liberation Committee, 145
Vietnam Quoc Dan Dang (VNQDD), 137, 199
Vietnamese blocs, 170–1
Vietnamese Communism, 186, 349, 361–2
Vietnamese Communists, 25, 151, 272, 300–1, 307, 310, 422*n*55
Vietnamese independence, 155
Vietnamese Independence Movement, 423–4*n*72
Vietnamese Nguyen dynasty, 218
Vietnamese People's Army (VPA), 158, 202, 425*n*93, 429–30*n*13
Vietnamese revolutionary warfare, 10–32, 298–311
vietnamization, 125
"*Village Is the Spirit of a Place*", *The*, 232–59
Vitalis, Robert, 232
Voice of America Vietnamese Service, 278
von Buelow, Fritz, 80, 84

Walking Dead, The, 387*n*15
War Crimes Commission, 34, 55, 60, 76, 78, 90, 115
war criminals, 64
Warner, Denis, 358
Warner, Jayne Susan, 238
Washington, DC, 1952, 111–24
Washington Conference, 416*n*47
Washington Post, 122
Weapon Forge of the Reich, 67–74
Weekly (Stone), 28
Weimar Republic, 87, 108–9
Weinstein, Jeremy, 209, 218
Weltanschauung, 270
Werkschutz (Works Police), 77, 84
West Berlin, industrial production in, 96
Whiteside, Craig, 25–6, 382
"Will South Viet-Nam Be Next?" (article), 231, 259–72
William P. Yarborough Papers (WPYP), 389*n*44, 389*n*45
Wilson, Woodrow, 116
Winer, Dorothy, 124, 128, 227
Woods, Randall B., 346, 348, 351
Worker's Party, 121
Wright, Robert, 59

Xuan, Tran Le, 249

Yarborough, William P. (United States Army Major General), 8, 10, 323, 329–31

Zasloff, Joseph J., 325
Zhai, Qiang, 168, 251–2
Ztzkovitz, Eliahu, 52–5